FIFTH EDITION

AUTOMATIC TRANSMISSIONS AND TRANSAXLES

Tom Birch

Boston   Columbus   Indianapolis   New York   San Francisco   Upper Saddle River
Amsterdam   Cape Town   Dubai   London   Madrid   Milan   Munich   Paris   Montreal
TorontoDelhi   Mexico City   São Paulo   Sydney   Hong Kong   Seoul   Singapore   Taipei   Tokyo

Editorial Director: Vernon Anthony
Acquisitions Editor: Vernon Anthony
Editorial Assistant: Yvette Schlarman
Director of Marketing: David Gesell
Senior Marketing Manager:
Harper Coles
Senior Marketing Coordinator:
Alicia Wozniak
Marketing Assistant: Les Roberts
Senior Managing Editor: JoEllen Gohr
Project Manager: Jessica H. Sykes
Senior Operations Supervisor:
Pat Tonneman

Senior Art Director: Diane Ernsberger
Text and Cover Designer: Anne DeMarinis
Cover Art: Shutterstock
Media Editor: Michelle Churma
Lead Media Project Manager: Karen Bretz
Full-Service Project Management: Kelli Jauron
Composition: S4Carlisle Publishing Services
Printer/Binder: Edwards Brothers Malloy
Cover Printer: Lehigh-Phoenix Color/Hagerstown
Text Font: Helvetica Neue

Credits and acknowledgements borrowed from other sources and reproduced, with permission, in this textbook appear on the appropriate page within text.

Microsoft® and Windows® are registered trademarks of the Microsoft Corporation in the U.S.A. and other countries. Screen shots and icon reprinted with permission for the Microsoft Corporation. This book is not sponsored or endorsed by or affiliated with the Microsoft Corporation.

If you purchased this book within the United States or Canada, you should be aware that it has been imported without the approval of the Publisher or the Author.

Many of the designations by manufacturers and seller to distinguish their products are claimed as trademarks. Where those designations appear in this book, and the publisher was aware of a trademark claim, the designations have been printed in initial caps or all caps.

10 9 8 7 6 5 4

ISBN 10:   0-13-262227-0
ISBN 13: 978-0-13-262227-1

FIFTH EDITION

AUTOMATIC TRANSMISSIONS AND TRANSAXLES

Tom Birch

Boston   Columbus   Indianapolis   New York   San Francisco   Upper Saddle River
Amsterdam   Cape Town   Dubai   London   Madrid   Milan   Munich   Paris   Montreal
TorontoDelhi   Mexico City   São Paulo   Sydney   Hong Kong   Seoul   Singapore   Taipei   Tokyo

Editorial Director: Vernon Anthony
Acquisitions Editor: Vernon Anthony
Editorial Assistant: Yvette Schlarman
Director of Marketing: David Gesell
Senior Marketing Manager:
Harper Coles
Senior Marketing Coordinator:
Alicia Wozniak
Marketing Assistant: Les Roberts
Senior Managing Editor: JoEllen Gohr
Project Manager: Jessica H. Sykes
Senior Operations Supervisor:
Pat Tonneman

Senior Art Director: Diane Ernsberger
Text and Cover Designer: Anne DeMarinis
Cover Art: Shutterstock
Media Editor: Michelle Churma
Lead Media Project Manager: Karen Bretz
Full-Service Project Management: Kelli Jauron
Composition: S4Carlisle Publishing Services
Printer/Binder: Edwards Brothers Malloy
Cover Printer: Lehigh-Phoenix Color/Hagerstown
Text Font: Helvetica Neue

Credits and acknowledgements borrowed from other sources and reproduced, with permission, in this textbook appear on the appropriate page within text.

Microsoft® and Windows® are registered trademarks of the Microsoft Corporation in the U.S.A. and other countries. Screen shots and icon reprinted with permission for the Microsoft Corporation. This book is not sponsored or endorsed by or affiliated with the Microsoft Corporation.

If you purchased this book within the United States or Canada, you should be aware that it has been imported without the approval of the Publisher or the Author.

Many of the designations by manufacturers and seller to distinguish their products are claimed as trademarks. Where those designations appear in this book, and the publisher was aware of a trademark claim, the designations have been printed in initial caps or all caps.

10 9 8 7 6 5 4

ISBN 10: 0-13-262227-0
ISBN 13: 978-0-13-262227-1

PREFACE

PROFESSIONAL TECHNICIAN SERIES Part of Pearson Automotive's Professional Technician Series, the fifth edition of *Automatic Transmissions and Transaxles* represents the future of automotive textbooks. The series is a media-integrated solution for today's students and instructors. The series includes textbooks that cover all eight areas of ASE certification, plus additional titles covering common courses.

Current revisions are written by a team of very experienced writers and teachers. The series is also peer reviewed for technical accuracy.

UPDATES TO THE FIFTH EDITION

- All content is correlated to the latest ASE and NATEF tasks.
- A dramatic new design enhances the subject matter.
- New material describing the wet clutch, which replaces the torque converter, is included.
- New material describing the continuously variable transmission (CVT) is included.
- New and expanded description of electronic controls has been added.
- New and expanded description of ATF has been added.
- Photographs, charts, and line drawings have been added to help students understand the content material and bring the subject alive.
- The discussion of each technical topic is followed by a chapter that describes the diagnosis, testing, and repair of that system. Unlike other textbooks, this book is written so that theory, construction, diagnosis, and service of a particular component or system are presented in one location.

ASE AND NATEF CORRELATED

NATEF certified programs need to demonstrate that they use course material that covers NATEF and ASE tasks. All Professional Technician textbooks have been correlated to the appropriate ASE and NATEF task lists. These correlations can be found in an appendix to each book.

A COMPLETE INSTRUCTOR AND STUDENT SUPPLEMENTS PACKAGE

All Professional Technician textbooks are accompanied by a full set of instructor and student supplements. Please see page vi for a detailed list of supplements.

A FOCUS ON DIAGNOSIS AND PROBLEM SOLVING

The Professional Technician Series has been developed to satisfy the need for a greater emphasis on problem diagnosis. Automotive instructors and service managers agree that students and beginning technicians need more training in diagnostic procedures and skill development. To meet this need and demonstrate how real-world problems are solved, "Real World Fix" features included throughout the text highlight how real-life problems are diagnosed and repaired.

The following pages highlight the unique core features that set the Professional Technician Series books apart from other automotive textbooks.

chapter 1 — **SERVICE INFORMATION, TOOLS, AND SAFETY**

OBJECTIVES AND KEY TERMS appear at the beginning of each chapter to help students and instructors focus on the most important material. The chapter objectives are based on specific ASE and NATEF tasks.

TECH TIP

It Just Takes a Second

Whenever removing any automotive component, it is wise to screw the bolts back into the holes a couple of threads by hand. This ensures that the right bolt will be used in its original location when the component or part is put back on the vehicle.

TECH TIPS feature real-world advice and "tricks of the trade" from ASE-certified master technicians.

SAFETY TIP

Shop Cloth Disposal

Always dispose of oily shop cloths in a closed container to prevent a fire. ● **SEE FIGURE 1-69**. If oily cloths are thrown together on the floor or workbench, a chemical reaction might occur, which can ignite the cloth even without an open flame. This process of ignition is called spontaneous combustion.

SAFETY TIPS alert students to possible hazards on the job and how to avoid them.

REAL WORLD FIX

The 2002 Dodge Durango came in with a complaint of delayed engagement into reverse after sitting for awhile. A check in the pan showed metal, evidence of a converter failure, so the transmission was rebuilt. A new solenoid pack and pressure sensor were installed. A Quick Learn was done and the vehicle was driven 60 miles to relearn from harsh N–R and 2–3 shifts. The original problem of reverse shift delay is still there.

FIX A fellow technician told of a TSB (21-016-05) that describes filters with a faulty check valve. Replacement of the filter cured this problem.

REAL WORLD FIXES AND REAL WORLD PROBLEMS present students with actual automotive scenarios and show how these common (and sometimes uncommon) problems were diagnosed and repaired.

FREQUENTLY ASKED QUESTION

What Is Dingy or Flat Tow?

Some new transaxles incorporate a *dingy* or *flat tow* feature to lubricate the final drive gears while the vehicle is towed with the wheels on the road. This allows towing behind a motorhome using only a towbar.

FREQUENTLY ASKED QUESTIONS are based on the author's own experience and provide answers to many of the most common questions asked by students and beginning service technicians.

NOTE: Most of these "locking nuts" are grouped together and are commonly referred to as *prevailing torque nuts.* This means that the nut will hold its tightness or torque and not loosen with movement or vibration.

NOTES provide students with additional technical information to give them a greater understanding of a specific task or procedure.

CAUTION: *Never* use hardware store (nongraded) bolts, studs, or nuts on any vehicle steering, suspension, or brake component. Always use the exact size and grade of hardware that is specified and used by the vehicle manufacturer.

CAUTIONS alert students to potential damage to the vehicle that can occur during a specific task or service procedure.

☠ WARNING

Do not use incandescent trouble lights around gasoline or other flammable liquids. The liquids can cause the bulb to break and the hot filament can ignite the flammable liquid, which can cause personal injury or even death.

WARNINGS alert students to potential dangers to themselves during a specific task or service procedure.

STEP-BY-STEP photo sequence show and the How To Service Operations (Appendix G) tell in detail the steps involved in performing a specific task or service procedure.

THE SUMMARY, REVIEW QUESTIONS, AND QUIZZES at the end of each chapter help students review the material presented in the chapter and test themselves to see how much they've learned.

INSTRUCTOR SUPPLEMENTS

The comprehensive **Instructor's Manual** includes chapter outlines, answers to all questions in the book, teaching tips, and additional exercises. To access supplementary materials online, instructors need to request an instructor access code. Go to www.pearsonhighered.com/irc to register for an instructor access code. Within 48 hours of registering, you will receive a confirming e-mail including an instructor access code. Once you have received your code, go to the site and log on for full instructions on downloading the materials you wish to use.

Here you will find:

- PowerPoint presentations*
- Test Generator software and test bank*
- Chapter quizzes
- Chapter review questions
- English and Spanish glossary*
- NATEF Correlated Task Sheets* (also available as a printed supplement [ISBN: 0-13-260608-9])
- NATEF/ASE correlation charts

* All of these are available for download from

www.pearsonhighered.com.

MYAUTOMOTIVEKIT

An offshoot of the extremely popular MyAutomotiveLab, these online kits can be used with all Professional Technician Series textbooks for quizzing, testing, homework, and multimedia activities. All assignments are automatically graded and entered into a gradebook for the course. In addition to assessment materials, MyAutomotiveKit includes:

- **Interactive animations**
- Two- to 5-minute **video clips** showing procedures

- A **3-D virtual garage** that simulates the shop experience in the real world by focusing on customer complaints, conducting tests to determine the problem with the vehicle, and submitting a written work order to the instructor
- A guide to topics broken down by chapter for easy navigation and use

For instructor access to MyAutomotiveKit, please visit

www.myautomotivekit.com.

STUDENT SUPPLEMENTS NO MORE CDs!!

As a result of extensive student input, Pearson is no longer binding CDs into automotive students' textbooks. Today's student has more access to the Internet than ever, so all supplemental materials are downloadable at the following site for no additional charge: www.pearsoned.com/autostudent.

On the site, students will find:

- PowerPoint presentations
- Chapter review questions and quizzes
- English and Spanish glossary
- A full Spanish translation of the text
- Links to MyAutomotiveKit

MYAUTOMOTIVEKIT FOR THE STUDENT

For the student, **MyAutomotiveKit** is a one-stop shop for homework, quizzes, tests, and a new way of learning. Key concepts are reinforced through media. Students will find part identification activities, word search games, interactive animations, and a 3-D virtual garage for help with diagnosis.

ACKNOWLEDGMENTS

A large number of people and organizations have cooperated in providing the reference material and technical information used in this text. The author wishes to express sincere thanks to the following organizations for their special contributions:

A-1 Automatic Transmissions
Aceomatic Recon
AFM, Raytech Automotive Components Comp.
Alto Products Corp.
American Honda Motor Company
ATEC Trans-Tool and Cleaning Systems
Autotrans
AxiLine, Hicklin Engineering
BorgWarner, Morse TEC
Tom Broxholm, Skyline College
Chassis Ear, Steelman
Chrysler Corporation
Ethyl Corporation
Mark Ferner, Pennzoil-Quaker State
Fluid Rx
Fluke Corporation
Ford Motor Company
General Motors Corporation
Goodall Manufacturing Co.
Roger Griffen, Nissan North America, Inc.
G-Tec
James Halderman
HECAT Inc.
International Lubricants, Inc.
Tony Jewel, Reedley College
J. S. Products/Steelman
KD Tools
Kent-Moore, SPX Corporation
Life Automotive Products
Dennis Madden, ATRA
The Mighty Mover

Mooq Automotive Division, Federal-Moqul Corp.
NEAPCO Inc.
Nissan North America, Inc.
OTC, SPX Corporation
Pennzoil-Quaker State Comp.
Raybestos Aftermarket Products Co.
Ken Redick
Robinair, SPX Corporation
Rostra Precision Controls
Slauson Transmission Parts, Christopher Wilson
Snap-on Tools
Sonnax Industries
SPX Filtran
Superior Transmission Parts
T.C.R.S. Inc., Hicklin Engineering
Toyota Motor Sales, U.S.A., Inc.
Tribco, Inc.
Waekon Corporation
Williams Technology Inc., Division of Delco Remy Int.
Yank Converters
ZF Group North American Operations
Zoom Technology
"Portions of materials contained herein have been reprinted with permission of General Motors Corporation, Service Operations."

REVIEWER   Special thanks to instructional designer **Alexis I. Skriloff James.**

Tom Birch

ABOUT THE AUTHOR

TOM BIRCH Before entering the army, Tom was a Ford dealership mechanic. As a soldier, he attended Wheel Vehicle Mechanic school and performed as a mechanic in Europe. After completing his military duty, he graduated from college with BA and MA degrees and began teaching automotive technology in the California schools. He retired from Yuba College in Northern California after 30 years of teaching. He is a past president and board member of CAT (California Auto Teachers) and a past board member of NACAT (North American Council of Automotive Teachers). Tom is a long-time member of MACS (Mobile Air Conditioning Society), ASC-CA (Automotive Service Council-California), and SAE (Society of Automotive Engineers). He is also the author of several automotive textbooks.

BRIEF CONTENTS

CONTENTS

chapter 6
HYDRAULIC SYSTEM THEORY 132

chapter 7
HYDRAULIC SHIFT CONTROL 158

chapter 8
ELECTRONIC TRANSMISSION CONTROLS 182

chapter 13
ELECTRONIC TRANSMISSION PROBLEM SOLVING AND DIAGNOSIS   319

chapter 14
IN-VEHICLE TRANSMISSION REPAIR   356

chapter 15
TRANSMISSION/TRANSAXLE REMOVAL AND REPLACEMENT   380

chapter 16
TRANSMISSION OVERHAUL: DISASSEMBLY AND REASSEMBLY   396

chapter 17
TRANSMISSION OVERHAUL PROCEDURES   426

chapter 18
SUBASSEMBLY REPAIR   445

SERVICE INFORMATION, TOOLS, AND SAFETY

OBJECTIVES: After studying Chapter 1, the reader will be able to: • Understand the National Institute for Automotive Service Excellence (ASE) knowledge content for vehicle identification and the proper use of tools and shop equipment. • Retrieve vehicle service information. • Identify the strength ratings of threaded fasteners. • Describe how to safely hoist a vehicle. • Discuss how to safely use hand tools. • Identify the personal protective equipment (PPE) that all service technicians should wear. • Describe what tool is the best to use for each job. • Discuss how to safely use hand tools. • Explain the difference between the brand name (trade name) and the proper name for tools. • Explain how to maintain hand tools. • Identify the precautions that should be followed when working on hybrid-electric vehicles.

KEY TERMS: Bolts 4 • Breaker bar 9 • Bump cap 21 • Calibration codes 2 • Campaign 3 • Casting number 2 • Cheater bar 11 • Chisel 16 • Drive sizes 9 • Extensions 9 • Eye wash station 29 • Files 14 • Fire blankets 28 • Fire extinguisher classes 27 • Grade 5 • Gross axle weight rating (GAWR) 2 • Gross vehicle weight rating (GVWR) 2 • Hacksaws 16 • Hammers 12 • Hybrid electric vehicle (HEV) 29 • Light emitting diode (LED) 19 • Metric bolts 4 • Nuts 6 • Pinch weld seams 24 • Pitch 4 • Pliers 13 • Punches 15 • Ratchet 9 • Recall 3 • Screwdrivers 11 • Snips 15 • Socket 9 • Socket adapter 11 • Special service tools (SSTs) 20 • Spontaneous combustion 23 • Stud 4 • Technical service bulletin (TSB) 3 • Tensile strength 6 • Trouble light 18 • Unified National Coarse (UNC) 4 • Unified National Fine (UNF) 4 • Universal joint 9 • Vehicle emissions control information (VECI) 2 • Vehicle identification number (VIN) 1 • Washers 7 • Wrenches 7

1.1 SERVICE INFORMATION

1.1.1 VEHICLE IDENTIFICATION

MAKE, MODEL, AND YEAR. All service work requires that the vehicle and its components be properly identified. The most common identification is the make, model, and year of the vehicle.

> **Make:** for example, Chevrolet
>
> **Model:** for example, Impala
>
> **Year:** for example, 2008

VEHICLE IDENTIFICATION NUMBER. The year of the vehicle is often difficult to determine exactly. A model may be introduced as the next year's model as soon as January of the previous year. Typically, a new model year starts in September or October of the year prior to the actual new year, but not always. This is why the **vehicle identification number**, usually abbreviated **VIN**, is so important. ● **SEE FIGURE 1–1.**

Since 1981, all vehicle manufacturers have used a VIN that is 17 characters long. Although every vehicle manufacturer assigns various letters or numbers within these 17 characters, there are some constants, including:

- The first number or letter designates the country of origin. ● **SEE CHART 1–1.**

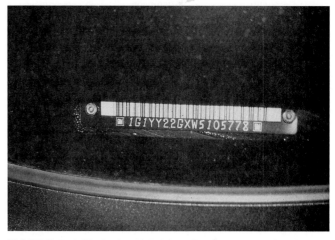

FIGURE 1–1 Typical vehicle identification number (VIN) as viewed through the windshield.

- The fourth or fifth character is the car line/series.
- The sixth character is the body style.
- The seventh character is the restraint system.
- The eighth character is often the engine code. (Some engines cannot be identified by the VIN number.)
- The tenth character represents the year on all vehicles. ● **SEE CHART 1–2.**

1 = United States	J = Japan	W = Germany
2 = Canada	K = Korea	X = Russia
3 = Mexico	L = China	Y = Sweden
4 = United States	R = Taiwan	Z = Italy
5 = United States	S = England	
6 = Australia	T = Czechoslovakia	
8 = Argentina	U = Romania	
9 = Brazil	V = France	

CHART 1–1

The first number or letter in the VIN identifies the country where the vehicle was made.

A = 1980/2010	L = 1990/2020	Y = 2000/2030
B = 1981/2011	M = 1991/2021	1 = 2001/2031
C = 1982/2012	N = 1992/2022	2 = 2002/2032
D = 1983/2013	P = 1993/2023	3 = 2003/2033
E = 1984/2014	R = 1994/2024	4 = 2004/2034
F = 1985/2015	S = 1995/2025	5 = 2005/2035
G = 1986/2016	T = 1996/2026	6 = 2006/2036
H = 1987/2017	V = 1997/2027	7 = 2007/2037
J = 1988/2018	W = 1998/2028	8 = 2008/2038
K = 1989/2019	X = 1999/2029	9 = 2009/2039

CHART 1–2

The pattern repeats every 30 years for the year of manufacture.

VEHICLE SAFETY CERTIFICATION LABEL. A vehicle safety certification label is attached to the left side pillar post on the rearward-facing section of the left front door. This label indicates the month and year of manufacture as well as the **gross vehicle weight rating (GVWR)**, the **gross axle weight rating (GAWR)**, and the vehicle identification number (VIN).

VECI LABEL. The **vehicle emissions control information (VECI)** label under the hood of the vehicle shows informative settings and emission hose routing information. ● **SEE FIGURE 1–2**.

The VECI label (sticker) can be located on the bottom side of the hood, the radiator fan shroud, the radiator core support, or on the strut towers. The VECI label usually includes the following information:

- Engine identification
- Emissions standard that the vehicle meets
- Vacuum hose routing diagram
- Base ignition timing (if adjustable)
- Spark plug type and gap

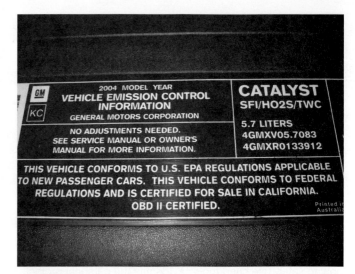

FIGURE 1–2 The vehicle emission control information (VECI) sticker is placed under the hood.

FIGURE 1–3 A typical calibration code sticker on the case of a controller. The information on the sticker is often needed when ordering parts or a replacement controller.

- Valve lash
- Emission calibration code

CALIBRATION CODES. **Calibration codes** are usually located on powertrain control modules (PCMs) or other controllers. Whenever diagnosing an engine operating fault, it is often necessary to use the calibration code to be sure that the vehicle is the subject of a technical service bulletin or other service procedure. ● **SEE FIGURE 1–3**.

CASTING NUMBERS. When an engine part such as a block is cast, a number is put into the mold to identify the casting. ● **SEE FIGURE 1–4**. These **casting numbers** can be used to identify the part, check dimensions such as the cubic inch displacement, and determine other information, such as the year of manufacture. Sometimes changes are made to the mold,

FIGURE 1–4 Casting numbers on major components can be either cast or stamped.

yet the casting number is not changed. Most often the casting number is the best piece of identifying information that the service technician can use for identifying an engine.

1.1.2 SERVICE INFORMATION

SERVICE MANUALS. Service information is used by the service technician to determine specifications and service procedures and any special tools needed. Factory and aftermarket service manuals contain specifications and service procedures. Factory service manuals cover just one year and one or more models of the same vehicle, but most aftermarket service manufacturers cover multiple years and/or models in one manual. Included in most service manuals are the following:

- Capacities and recommended specifications for all fluids
- Specifications, including engine and routine maintenance items
- Testing procedures
- Service procedures, including the use of special tools when needed
- Special tools that are required and their use

ELECTRONIC SERVICE INFORMATION. Electronic service information is available mostly by subscription and provides access to an Internet site where service manual–type information is available. ● **SEE FIGURE 1–5**. Most vehicle manufacturers also offer electronic service information to their dealers and to most schools and colleges that offer corporate training programs.

TECHNICAL SERVICE BULLETINS. **Technical service bulletins**, often abbreviated **TSBs**, sometimes called *technical service information bulletins (TSIB)*, are issued by the vehicle manufacturer to notify service technicians of a problem and include the necessary corrective action. Technical service bulletins are designed for dealership technicians but are republished by aftermarket companies and made available along with other service information to shops and vehicle repair facilities. ● **SEE FIGURE 1–6**.

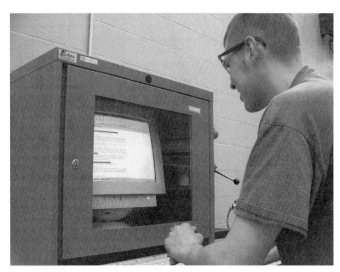

FIGURE 1–5 Electronic service information is available from aftermarket sources such as All-Data and Mitchell-on-Demand, as well as on websites hosted by vehicle manufacturers.

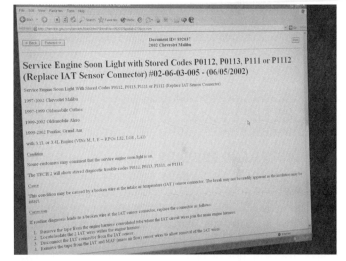

FIGURE 1–6 Technical service bulletins (TSBs) are issued by vehicle manufacturers when a fault occurs that affects many vehicles with the same problem. The TSB then provides the fix for the problem, including any parts needed and detailed instructions.

THE INTERNET. The Internet has made possible the open exchange of information and access to technical advice. One of the most useful websites is the International Automotive Technician's Network at www.iatn.net. This is a free site but service technicians must register to join. If a small monthly sponsor fee is paid, the shop or service technician can gain access to the archives, which include thousands of successful repairs in the searchable database.

RECALLS AND CAMPAIGNS. A **recall** or **campaign** is issued by a vehicle manufacturer and a notice is sent to all owners in the event of a safety-related fault or concern. Although these faults

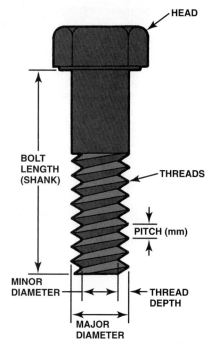

? FREQUENTLY ASKED QUESTION

What Should Be Included on a Work Order?

A work order is a legal document that should include the following information:

1. Customer information
2. Identification of the vehicle, including the VIN
3. Related service history information
4. The "three Cs":
   - Customer concern (complaint)
   - Cause of the concern
   - Correction or repairs required to return the vehicle to proper operation

may be repaired by shops, they are generally handled by a local dealer. Items that have created recalls in the past have included potential fuel system leakage problems, exhaust leakage, or electrical malfunctions that could cause a possible fire or engine stall. Unlike technical service bulletins whose cost is covered only when the vehicle is within the warranty period, a recall or campaign is always done at no cost to the vehicle owner.

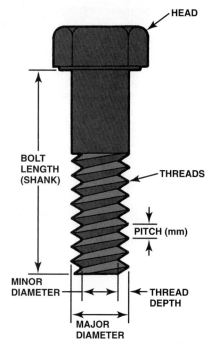

FIGURE 1–7 The dimensions of a typical bolt showing where sizes are measured.

FIGURE 1–8 Thread pitch gauge used to measure the pitch of the thread. This bolt has 13 threads to the inch.

1.2 THREADED FASTENERS

1.2.1 BOLTS AND THREADS Most of the threaded fasteners used on vehicles are **bolts**. Bolts are called *cap screws* when they are threaded into a casting. Automotive service technicians usually refer to these fasteners as bolts regardless of how they are used, and in this chapter they are called bolts. Sometimes, studs are used for threaded fasteners. A **stud** is a short rod with threads on both ends. Often, a stud will have coarse threads on one end and fine threads on the other end. The end of the stud with coarse threads is screwed into the casting. A nut is used on the opposite end to hold the parts together.

The fastener threads *must* match the threads in the casting or nut. The threads may be measured either in fractions of an inch (called fractional) or in metric units. The size is measured across the outside of the threads, called the *crest* of the thread. ● **SEE FIGURE 1–7.**

FRACTIONAL BOLTS. Fractional threads are either coarse or fine. The coarse threads are called **Unified National Coarse (UNC)**, and the fine threads are called **Unified National Fine (UNF)**. Standard combinations of sizes and number of threads per inch (called **pitch**) are used. Pitch can be measured with a thread pitch gauge as shown in ● **FIGURE 1–8.** Bolts are identified by their diameter and length as measured from below the head, not by the size of the head or the size of the wrench used to remove or install the bolt.

? FREQUENTLY ASKED QUESTION

How Many Types of Screw Heads Are Used in Automotive Applications?

Many types of screw heads are used, including Torx, hex (also called Allen), and others that are used in custom vans and motor homes. ● **SEE FIGURE 1–9.**

Fractional thread sizes are specified by the diameter in fractions of an inch and the number of threads per inch. Typical UNC thread sizes would be 5/16–18 and 1/2–13. Similar UNF thread sizes would be 5/16–24 and 1/2–20. ● **SEE CHART 1–3.**

METRIC BOLTS. The size of a **metric bolt** is specified by the letter *M* followed by the diameter in millimeters (mm) across the outside (crest) of the threads. Typical metric sizes would be M8 and M12. Fine metric threads are specified by the thread

ROUND HEAD SCREW FLATHEAD SCREW CAPSCREW HEX-HEAD BOLT

TORX® BOLT ALLEN BOLT CHEESE HEAD SCREW PAN HEAD SCREW

FIGURE 1–9 Bolts and screws have many different heads, which determine what tool is needed.

METRIC HEXAGON HEAD CAP SCREWS
ALL MEASUREMENTS IN MILLIMETERS

M = NOMINAL THREAD DIAMETER
P = PITCH
D = HEAD SIZE ACROSS FLATS

M	P	D	M	P	D	M	P	D
1.6	0.35	3.2	10	1.00	17	20	1.50	30
1.7	0.35	3.5	10	1.25	17	20	2.50	30
2	0.40	4	10	1.50	17	22	1.50	32
2.3	0.40	4.5	12	1.25	19	22	2.50	32
2.5	0.45	5	12	1.50	19	24	2.00	36
3	0.50	5.5	12	1.75	19	24	3.00	36
3.5	0.60	6	14	1.50	22	27	3.00	41
4	0.70	7	14	2.00	22	30	3.50	46
5	0.80	8	16	1.50	24	33	3.50	50
6	1.00	10	16	2.00	24	36	4.00	55
7	1.00	11	18	1.50	27	39	4.00	60
8	1.00	13	18	2.50	27	42	4.50	65
8	1.25	13				45	4.50	70

FIGURE 1–10 The metric system specifies fasteners by diameter, length, and pitch.

diameter followed by X and the distance between the threads measured in millimeters (M8 X 1.5). ● **SEE FIGURE 1–10**.

GRADES OF BOLTS. Bolts are made from many different types of steel, and for this reason some are stronger than others. The strength or classification of a bolt is called the **grade**. The bolt heads are marked to indicate their grade strength. The actual grade of bolts is two more than the number of lines on the bolt head. Metric bolts have a decimal number to indicate the grade. More lines or a higher grade number indicate a stronger bolt. In some cases, nuts and machine screws have similar grade markings.

Higher-grade bolts usually have threads that are rolled rather than cut, which also makes them stronger. ● **SEE FIGURE 1–11**.

	THREADS PER INCH		OUTSIDE DIAMETER INCHES
SIZE	NC UNC	NF UNF	
0	..	80	0.0600
1	64	..	0.0730
1	..	72	0.0730
2	56	..	0.0860
2	..	64	0.0860
3	48	..	0.0990
3	..	56	0.0990
4	40	..	0.1120
4	..	48	0.1120
5	40	..	0.1250
5	..	44	0.1250
6	32	..	0.1380
6	..	40	0.1380
8	32	..	0.1640
8	..	36	0.1640
10	24	..	0.1900
10	..	32	0.1900
12	24	..	0.2160
12	..	28	0.2160
1/4	20	..	0.2500
1/4	..	28	0.2500
5/16	18	..	0.3125
5/16	..	24	0.3125
3/8	16	..	0.3750
3/8	..	24	0.3750
7/16	14	..	0.4375
7/16	..	20	0.4375
1/2	13	..	0.5000
1/2	..	20	0.5000
9/16	12	..	0.5625
9/16	..	18	0.5625
5/8	11	..	0.6250
5/8	..	18	0.6250
3/4	10	..	0.7500
3/4	..	16	0.7500
7/8	9	..	0.8750
7/8	..	14	0.8750
1	8	..	1.0000
1	..	12	1.0000
1 1/8	7	..	1.1250
1 1/8	..	12	1.1250
1 1/4	7	..	1.2500
1 1/4	..	12	1.2500
1 3/8	6	..	1.3750
1 3/8	..	12	1.3750
1 1/2	6	..	1.5000
1 1/2	..	12	1.5000
1 3/4	5	..	1.7500
2	4 1/2	..	2.0000
2 1/4	4 1/2	..	2.2500
2 1/2	4	..	2.5000
2 3/4	4	..	2.7500
3	4	..	3.0000
3 1/4	4	..	3.2500
3 1/2	4	..	3.5000
3 3/4	4	..	3.7500
4	4	..	4.0000

CHART 1–3

American standard is one method of sizing fasteners.

SAE BOLT DESIGNATIONS				
SAE GRADE NO.	SIZE RANGE	TENSILE STRENGTH, PSI	MATERIAL	HEAD MARKING
1	1/4 through 1 1/2	60,000	Low or medium carbon steel	
2	1/4 through 3/4	74,000		
	7/8 through 1 1/2	60,000		
5	1/4 through 1	120,000	Medium carbon steel, quenched and tempered	
	1-1/8 through 1 1/2	105,000		
5.2	1/4 through 1	120,000	Low carbon martensite steel,* quenched and tempered	
7	1/4 through 1 1/2	133,000	Medium carbon alloy steel, quenched and tempered	
8	1/4 through 1 1/2	150,000	Medium carbon alloy steel, quenched and tempered	
8.2	1/4 through 1	150,000	Low carbon martensite steel,* quenched and tempered	

CHART 1–4

The tensile strength rating system as specified by the Society of Automotive Engineers (SAE).
*Martensite steel is steel that has been cooled rapidly, thereby increasing its hardness. It is named after a German metallurgist, Adolf Martens.

ROLLING THREADS

FIGURE 1–11 Stronger threads are created by cold-rolling a heat-treated bolt blank instead of cutting the threads, using a die.

CAUTION: *Never* use hardware store (nongraded) bolts, studs, or nuts on any vehicle steering, suspension, or brake component. Always use the exact size and grade of hardware that is specified and used by the vehicle manufacturer.

1.2.2 TENSILE STRENGTH OF FASTENERS
Graded fasteners have a higher tensile strength than nongraded fasteners. **Tensile strength** is the maximum stress used under tension (lengthwise force) without causing failure of the fastener. Tensile strength is specified in pounds per square inch (psi).

The strength and type of steel used in a bolt is supposed to be indicated by a raised mark on the head of the bolt. The type of mark depends on the standard to which the bolt was manufactured. Most often, bolts used in machinery are made to SAE standard J429. ● **CHART 1–4** shows the grade and specified tensile strength.

The tensile strength property class of metric bolts is shown on the head of the bolt as a number, such as 4.6, 8.8, 9.8, and 10.9; the higher the number, the stronger the bolt. ● **SEE FIGURE 1–12**.

1.2.3 NUTS
Nuts are the female part of a threaded fastener. Most nuts used on cap screws have the same hex size as the cap screw head. Some inexpensive nuts use a hex size larger than the cap screw head. Metric nuts are often marked with dimples to show their strength. More dimples indicate stronger nuts. Some nuts and cap screws use interference fit threads to keep them from accidentally loosening. This means that the shape of the nut is slightly distorted or that a section of the threads is deformed. Nuts can also be kept from loosening with a nylon washer fastened in the nut or with a nylon patch or strip on the threads. ● **SEE FIGURE 1–13**.

4.6	8.8	9.8	10.9	METRIC CLASS
60,000	120,000	130,000	150,000	APPROXIMATE MAXIMUM POUND FORCE PER SQUARE INCH

FIGURE 1–12 Metric bolt (cap screw) grade markings and approximate tensile strength.

| HEX NUT | JAM NUT | NYLON LOCK NUT | CASTLE NUT | ACORN NUT |

FIGURE 1–13 Nuts come in a variety of styles, including locking (prevailing torque) types, such as the distorted thread and nylon insert type.

| FLAT WASHER | LOCK WASHER | STAR WASHER | STAR WASHER |

FIGURE 1–14 Washers come in a variety of styles, including flat and serrated, used to help prevent a fastener from loosening.

FIGURE 1–15 A forged wrench after it has been forged but before the flashing (extra material around the wrench) has been removed.

 TECH TIP

A 1/2-Inch Wrench Does Not Fit a 1/2-Inch Bolt

A common mistake made by persons new to the automotive field is to think that the size of a bolt or nut is the size of the head. The size of the bolt or nut (outside diameter of the threads) is usually smaller than the size of the wrench or socket that fits the head of the bolt or nut. Examples are given in the following table:

Wrench Size	Thread Size
7/16 in.	1/4 in.
1/2 in.	5/16 in.
9/16 in.	3/8 in.
5/8 in.	7/16 in.
3/4 in.	1/2 in.
10 mm	6 mm
12 mm or 13 mm*	8 mm
14 mm or 17 mm*	10 mm

*European (Systeme International d'Unités–SI) metric.

NOTE: Most of these "locking nuts" are grouped together and are commonly referred to as *prevailing torque nuts*. This means that the nut will hold its tightness or torque and not loosen with movement or vibration. Most prevailing torque nuts should be replaced whenever removed to ensure that the nut will not loosen during service. Always follow the manufacturer's recommendations. Anaerobic sealers, such as Loctite, are used on the threads where the nut or cap screw must be both locked and sealed.

1.2.4 WASHERS **Washers** are often used under cap screw heads and under nuts. ● **SEE FIGURE 1–14.** Plain flat washers are used to provide an even clamping load around the fastener. Lock washers are added to prevent accidental loosening. In some accessories, the washers are locked onto the nut to provide easy assembly.

 TECH TIP

It Just Takes a Second

Whenever removing any automotive component, it is wise to screw the bolts back into the holes a couple of threads by hand. This ensures that the right bolt will be used in its original location when the component or part is put back on the vehicle. Often, the same diameter of fastener is used on a component, but the length of the bolt may vary. Spending just a couple of seconds to put the bolts and nuts back where they belong when the part is removed can save a lot of time when the part is being reinstalled. Besides making certain that the right fastener is being installed in the right place, this method helps prevent bolts and nuts from getting lost or kicked away. How much time have you wasted looking for that lost bolt or nut?

1.3 HAND TOOLS

1.3.1 WRENCHES Wrenches are the hand tool most used by service technicians. **Wrenches** are used to grasp and rotate threaded fasteners. Most wrenches are constructed of forged alloy steel, usually chrome-vanadium steel. ● **SEE FIGURE 1–15.**

FIGURE 1–16 A typical open-end wrench. The size is different on each end; notice that the head is angled 15 degrees at the end.

FIGURE 1–17 The end of a box-end wrench is angled 15 degrees to allow clearance for nearby objects or other fasteners.

FIGURE 1–18 A combination wrench has an open end at one end and a box end at the other.

FIGURE 1–19 An adjustable wrench. Adjustable wrenches are sized by the overall length of the wrench and not by how far the jaws open. Common sizes of adjustable wrenches include 8, 10, and 12 inch.

FIGURE 1–20 The end of a typical line wrench, which shows that it is capable of grasping most of the head of the fitting.

After the wrench is formed, the wrench is hardened, then tempered to reduce brittleness, and then chrome plated. There are several types of wrenches.

OPEN-END WRENCH. An open-end wrench is usually used to loosen or tighten bolts or nuts that do not require a lot of torque. Because of the *open* end, this type of wrench can be easily placed on a bolt or nut at an angle of 15 degrees, which allows the wrench to be flipped over and used again to continue to rotate the fastener. The major disadvantage of an open-end wrench is the lower torque that can be applied due to the fact that the open jaws of the wrench contact only two flat surfaces of the fastener. An open-end wrench has two different sizes; one at each end. ● **SEE FIGURE 1–16.**

BOX-END WRENCH. A *box-end wrench*, also called a *closed-end wrench*, is placed over the top and grips the points of the fastener. A box-end wrench is angled 15 degrees to allow it to clear nearby objects. Therefore, a box-end wrench should be used to loosen or to tighten fasteners because it grips around the entire head of the fastener. A box-end wrench has two different sizes; one at each end. ● **SEE FIGURE 1–17.**

Most service technicians purchase *combination wrenches*, which have the open end at one end and the same size box end on the other. ● **SEE FIGURE 1–18.**

A combination wrench allows the technician to loosen or tighten a fastener using the box end of the wrench and then turn

it around to use the open end to increase the speed of rotating the fastener.

ADJUSTABLE WRENCH. An *adjustable wrench* is often used where the exact size wrench is not available or when a large nut, such as a wheel spindle nut, needs to be rotated but not tightened. An adjustable wrench should not be used to loosen or tighten fasteners because the torque applied to the wrench can cause the moveable jaws to loosen their grip on the fastener, causing it to become rounded. ● **SEE FIGURE 1–19.**

LINE WRENCHES. Line wrenches are also called *flare-nut wrenches, fitting wrenches,* or *tube-nut wrenches* and are designed to grip almost all the way around a nut used to retain a fuel or refrigerant line and yet, be able to be installed over the line. ● **SEE FIGURE 1–20.**

SAFE USE OF WRENCHES. Wrenches should be inspected before use to be sure they are not cracked, bent, or damaged. All wrenches should be cleaned after use before being returned to the toolbox. Always use the correct size wrench for the fastener being loosened or tightened to help prevent the rounding of the flats of the fastener. When attempting to loosen a fastener, pull a wrench—do not push a wrench. If a wrench is pushed, you can hurt your knuckles if they are forced into another object

FIGURE 1–23 The most commonly used socket drive sizes include 1/4-inch, 3/8-inch, and 1/2-inch drives.

FIGURE 1–21 A typical ratchet used to rotate a socket. A ratchet makes a ratcheting noise when it is being rotated in the opposite direction from loosening or tightening. A knob or lever on the ratchet allows the user to switch directions.

FIGURE 1–22 A typical flex handle used to rotate a socket, also called a breaker bar because it usually has a longer handle than a ratchet and therefore can be used to apply more torque to a fastener than a ratchet.

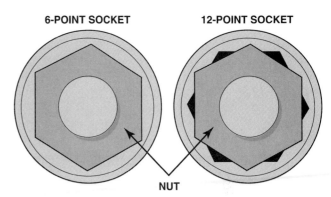

FIGURE 1–24 A 6-point socket fits the head of a bolt or nut on all sides. A 12-point socket can round off the head of a bolt or nut if a lot of force is applied.

 TECH TIP

Hide Those from the Boss

An apprentice technician started working for a dealership and put his top toolbox on a workbench. Another technician observed that, along with a complete set of good-quality tools, the box contained several adjustable wrenches. The more experienced technician said, "Hide those from the boss." The boss does not want any service technician to use adjustable wrenches. If any adjustable wrench is used on a bolt or nut, the movable jaw often moves or loosens and starts to round the head of the fastener. If the head of the bolt or nut becomes rounded, it becomes that much more difficult to remove.

FIGURE 1–25
Deep-well sockets allow access to nuts that have a stud plus other locations at great depth, such as spark plugs.

when the fastener breaks loose or the wrench slips. Always keep wrenches and all hand tools clean to help prevent rust and to allow for a better, firmer grip. Never expose any tool to excessive heat. High temperatures can reduce the strength ("draw the temper") of metal tools. Never use a hammer on any wrench unless you are using a special "staking face" wrench designed to be used with a hammer. Replace any tools that are damaged or worn.

1.3.2 RATCHETS, SOCKETS, AND EXTENSIONS A
socket fits over the fastener and grips the points and/or flats of the bolt or nut. The socket is rotated (driven) using either a long bar called a **breaker bar** (flex handle) or a ratchet. ● **SEE FIGURES 1–21 AND 1–22.**

A **ratchet** is a tool that turns the socket in only one direction and allows the rotating of the ratchet handle back and forth in a narrow space. Socket **extensions** and **universal joints** are also used with sockets to allow access to fasteners in restricted locations.

DRIVE SIZE. Sockets are available in various **drive sizes**, including 1/4-inch, 3/8-inch, and 1/2-inch sizes for most automotive use. ● **SEE FIGURES 1–23 AND 1–24.**

The drive size is the width of each side of the square drive. Many heavy-duty truck and/or industrial applications use 3/4-inch and 1-inch sizes. Sockets and ratchets of the same size are designed to work together.

REGULAR AND DEEP WELL. Sockets are available in regular length for use in most applications or in a deep-well design that allows access to a fastener that uses a long stud or other similar conditions. ● **SEE FIGURE 1–25.**

FIGURE 1–26 Using a clicker-type torque wrench to tighten connecting rod nuts on an engine.

TECH TIP

Right to Tighten

Which way to rotate a wrench or screwdriver is sometimes confusing, especially when the head of the fastener is pointing away from you. To help visualize, say, while looking at the fastener, "righty tighty, lefty loosey."

TORQUE WRENCHES. Torque wrenches are socket-turning handles that are designed to apply a known amount of force to the fastener. There are two basic types of torque wrenches:

1. **Clicker type.** This type of torque wrench is first set to the specified torque and then it "clicks" when the set torque value has been reached. When force is removed from the torque wrench handle, another click is heard. The setting on a clicker-type torque wrench should be returned to zero after use and checked for proper calibration regularly. ● **SEE FIGURE 1-26.**

2. **Beam-type.** This type of torque wrench is used to measure torque, but instead of presetting the value, the actual torque is displayed on the dial of the wrench as the fastener is being tightened. Beam-type torque wrenches are available in 1/4-inch, 3/8-inch, and 1/2-inch drives and in both English and metric units. ● **SEE FIGURE 1-27.**

SAFE USE OF SOCKETS AND RATCHETS. Always use the socket that correctly fits the bolt or nut. All sockets and ratchets should be cleaned before being returned to the toolbox. As stated in the description of wrenches, never expose any tool to excessive heat because high temperatures can reduce the strength ("draw the temper") of metal tools. Replace any tools that are damaged or worn.

FIGURE 1–27 A beam-type torque wrench that displays the torque reading on the face of the dial. The beam display is read as the beam deflects, which is in proportion to the amount of torque applied to the fastener.

FIGURE 1–28 Torque wrench calibration checker.

TECH TIP

Check Torque Wrench Calibration Regularly

Torque wrenches should be checked regularly. For example, Honda has a torque wrench calibration setup at each of its training centers. The expectation is that a torque wrench will be checked for accuracy before every use. Most experts recommend that torque wrenches be checked and adjusted as needed at least every year and more often if possible. ● **SEE FIGURE 1-28.**

Also select the appropriate drive size. For example, for small work, such as on the dash, select a 1/4-inch drive. For most general service work, use a 3/8-inch drive, and for suspension

BLADE WIDTH

FIGURE 1–29 A flat-tip (straight-blade) screwdriver. The width of the blade should match the width of the slot in the fastener being loosened or tightened.

FIGURE 1–30 Two stubby screwdrivers that are used to access screws that have limited space above. A straight blade is on top and a #2 Phillips screwdriver is on the bottom.

 TECH TIP

Use Socket Adapters with Caution

A **socket adapter** allows you to use sockets with ratchets or breaker bars of different sizes. Combinations include:

1/4 in.-drive – 3/8-in. sockets
3/8-in. drive – 1/4-in. sockets
3/8 in.-drive – 1/2-in. sockets
1/4-in. drive – 3/8-in. sockets

Using a larger-drive ratchet or breaker bar on a smaller-size socket can apply too much force to the socket, which could crack or shatter. Using a smaller drive tool on a larger socket will usually not cause any harm, but would greatly reduce the amount of torque that can be applied to the bolt or nut.

 TECH TIP

Avoid Using "Cheater Bars"

Whenever a fastener is difficult to remove, some technicians will insert the handle of a ratchet or a breaker bar into a length of steel pipe, sometimes called a **cheater bar**. The extra length of the pipe allows the technician to exert more torque than can be applied using the drive handle alone. However, the extra torque can easily overload the socket and ratchet, causing them to break or shatter, which could cause personal injury.

and steering and other large fasteners, select a 1/2-inch drive. When loosening a fastener, always pull the ratchet toward you rather than push it outward.

1.3.3 SCREWDRIVERS

STRAIGHT-BLADE SCREWDRIVER. Many smaller fasteners are removed and installed by using a **screwdriver**. Screwdrivers are available in many sizes and tip shapes; the one most commonly used is called a *straight blade* or *flat tip*. Flat-tip screwdrivers are sized by the width of the blade; this width should match the width of the slot in the screw. ● SEE FIGURE 1–29.

CAUTION: Do not use a screwdriver as a pry tool or as a chisel. Screwdrivers are hardened steel only at the tip and are not designed to be pounded on or used for prying because they could bend easily. Always use the proper tool for each application.

PHILLIPS SCREWDRIVER. Another type of commonly used screwdriver is called a Phillips screwdriver, named for Henry F. Phillips, who invented the crosshead screw in 1934. Due to the shape of the crosshead screw and screwdriver, a Phillips screw can be driven with more torque than can be achieved with a slotted screw. A Phillips head screwdriver is specified by the length of the handle and the size of the point at the tip. A #1 tip has a sharp point, a #2 tip is the most commonly used, and a #3 tip is blunt and is used only for larger sizes of Phillips head fasteners. For example, a #2 × 3-in. Phillips screwdriver would typically measure 6 in. from the tip of the blade to the end of the handle (3-in.-long handle and 3-in.-long blade) and have a #2 tip.

Both straight-blade and Phillips screwdrivers are available with a short blade and handle to access fasteners in tight spaces. ● SEE FIGURE 1–30.

OFFSET SCREWDRIVERS. Offset screwdrivers are used in places where a conventional screwdriver cannot fit. An offset screwdriver is bent at the ends and is used similarly to a wrench. Most offset screwdrivers have a straight blade at one end and a Phillips head at the opposite end. ● SEE FIGURE 1–31.

IMPACT SCREWDRIVER. An *impact screwdriver* is used to break loose or tighten a screw. A hammer is used to strike the end after the screwdriver holder is placed in the head of the screw

FIGURE 1–31 An offset screwdriver is used to install or remove fasteners in spaces that do not allow use of a conventional screwdriver.

FIGURE 1–32 An impact screwdriver used to remove slotted or Phillips head fasteners that cannot be broken loose using a standard screwdriver.

FIGURE 1–33 A typical ball-peen hammer.

FIGURE 1–34 A rubber mallet used to deliver a force to an object without harming the surface.

---

and rotated in the desired direction. The force from the hammer blow does two things: It applies a force downward, holding the tip of the screwdriver in the slot and then applies a twisting force to loosen (or tighten) the screw. ● **SEE FIGURE 1–32**.

SAFE USE OF SCREWDRIVERS. Always use the proper type and size screwdriver to match the fastener. Try to avoid pressing down on a screwdriver, because if it slips, the screwdriver tip could go into your hand, causing serious personal injury. All screwdrivers should be cleaned after use. Do not use a screwdriver as a pry bar; always use the correct tool for the job.

1.3.4 HAMMERS AND MALLETS
Hammers and mallets are used to force objects together or apart. The shape of the back part of the hammer head (called the *peen*) usually determines the name; for example, a ball-peen hammer has a rounded end like a ball. It is used to straighten oil pans and valve covers, using the hammer head, and for shaping metal, using the ball peen. ● **SEE FIGURE 1–33**.

NOTE: A claw hammer has a claw that is used to remove nails; it is not used for automotive service.

A hammer is usually sized by the weight of the head of the hammer and the length of the handle. For example, a commonly used ball-peen hammer has an 8-ounce head with an 11-in. handle.

MALLETS. *Mallets* are a type of hammer with a large striking surface, which allows the technician to exert force over a larger area than a hammer does, so as not to harm the part or component. Mallets are made from a variety of materials, including rubber, plastic, or wood. ● **SEE FIGURE 1–34**.

DEAD-BLOW HAMMER. A *dead-blow hammer* is a shot-filled plastic hammer. The small lead balls (shot) inside the plastic head prevent the hammer from bouncing off an object when struck. ● **SEE FIGURE 1–35**.

FIGURE 1–35 A dead-blow hammer that was left outside in freezing weather. The plastic covering was damaged, which destroyed this hammer. The lead shot is encased in the metal housing and then covered.

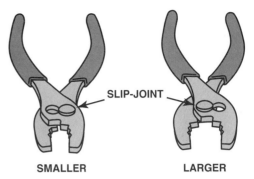

FIGURE 1–36 Typical slip-joint pliers are common household pliers. The slip joint allows the jaws to be opened to two different settings.

SAFE USE OF HAMMERS AND MALLETS. All mallets and hammers should be cleaned after use and not exposed to extreme temperatures. Never use a hammer or mallet that is damaged in any way and always use caution to avoid doing damage to the components and the surrounding area. Always follow the hammer manufacturer's recommended procedures and practices.

1.3.5 PLIERS

SLIP-JOINT PLIERS. Pliers are capable of holding, twisting, bending, and cutting objects and are extremely useful tools. The common household pliers are called *slip-joint pliers.* The handles meet at two different positions to make possible the gripping of objects in a wide range of sizes. ● SEE FIGURE 1–36.

MULTIGROOVE ADJUSTABLE PLIERS. For gripping larger objects, the tool of choice of many service technicians is a set of *multigroove adjustable pliers.* Because they were

FIGURE 1–37 Multigroove adjustable pliers are known by many names, including the trade name "Channel-Locks."

originally designed to remove the various size nuts holding rope seals used in water pumps, these pliers are also called *water pump pliers* or by their trade name, *Channel-Locks®.* ● SEE FIGURE 1–37.

LINESMAN'S PLIERS. *Linesman's pliers* are specifically designed for cutting, bending, and twisting wire. Commonly used by construction workers and electricians, linesman's pliers are a very useful tool as well for the service technician who deals with wiring. The center parts of the jaws are designed to grasp round objects such as pipe or tubing without slipping. ● SEE FIGURE 1–38.

DIAGONAL PLIERS. Constructed of hardened steel, *diagonal pliers* are designed only to cut. The cutting jaws are set at an angle to make it easier to cut wires. Diagonal pliers are also called *side cuts* or *dikes*. ● SEE FIGURE 1–39.

NEEDLE-NOSE PLIERS. *Needle-nose pliers* are designed to grip small objects or objects in tight locations. They have long, pointed jaws, which allow the tips to reach into narrow openings or groups of small objects. ● SEE FIGURE 1–40.

Most needle-nose pliers have a wire cutter located at the base of the jaws near the pivot. Several variations of needle-nose pliers include those with jaws at a right angle or slightly angled to allow access to certain cramped areas.

FLAT GRIP

PIPE GRIP

SIDE CUTTERS

JOINT CUTTERS

CUTS SOFT WIRE

GRIPS SMALL OBJECTS

FIGURE 1–38 Linesman's pliers are very useful because they can help perform many automotive service jobs.

CUTTING WIRES CLOSE TO TERMINALS

PULLING OUT AND SPREADING COTTER PIN

FIGURE 1–39 Another common tool that has many names is diagonal-cut pliers.

FIGURE 1–40 Needle-nose pliers are used where there is limited access to a wire or pin that needs to be installed or removed.

LOCKING PLIERS. *Locking pliers* are adjustable pliers that can be locked to prevent objects from moving. Most locking pliers also have wire cutters built into the jaws near the pivot point. Commonly referred to by the trade name *Vise-Grip®*, they come

RELEASE LEVER

FIGURE 1–41 Locking pliers are best known by their trade name, Vise-Grips.

INTERNAL SNAP RING

EXTERNAL SNAP RING

FIGURE 1–42 Snap-ring pliers are also called lock-ring pliers; most are designed to remove internal and external snap rings (lock rings).

in a variety of styles and sizes, the size indicating the length of the pliers, not how far the jaws open. ● **SEE FIGURE 1–41**.

SNAP-RING PLIERS. *Snap-ring pliers* are used to remove and install snap rings. Many snap-ring pliers are designed to be able to remove and install both inward—as well as outward—expanding snap rings. The pliers can be equipped with serrated-tip jaws for grasping the opening in the snap ring; others are equipped with points, which are inserted into the holes in the snap ring. ● **SEE FIGURE 1–42**.

SAFE USE OF PLIERS. Pliers should not be used to remove any bolt or other fastener. Pliers should be used only when specified by the vehicle manufacturer.

1.3.6 CUTTING TOOLS

FILES. **Files** are constructed of hardened steel and have diagonal rows of teeth used to smooth metal. Files are available with a single

FIGURE 1–43 Files come in many different shapes and sizes. Never use a file without a handle.

row of teeth, called a *single-cut file*, as well as two rows of teeth cut at an opposite angle, called a *double-cut file*. They are available in a variety of shapes and sizes, including small flat files, half-round files, and triangular files. ● **SEE FIGURE 1–43.**

SAFE USE OF FILES. Always use a file with a handle. Because files cut only when moved forward, a handle must be attached to prevent possible personal injury. After making a forward stroke, lift the file and return it to the starting position; avoid dragging the file backward.

SNIPS. Service technicians are often asked to fabricate sheet metal brackets or heat shields and need to use one or more types of cutters called **snips**. The simplest are called *tin snips*, designed to make straight cuts in a variety of materials, such as sheet steel, aluminum, or even fabric. A variation of the tin snips are *aviation tin snips*, which come in three designs: one designed to cut straight (called a *straight-cut aviation snip*), one designed to cut left (called an *offset-left aviation snip*), and one designed to cut right (called an *offset-right aviation snip*). ● **SEE FIGURE 1–44.**

UTILITY KNIFE. A *utility knife* uses a replaceable blade to cut a variety of materials—carpet, plastic, wood, and paper products, such as cardboard. ● **SEE FIGURE 1–45.**

STRAIGHT CUT TIN SNIP

OFFSET RIGHT-HAND AVIATION SNIP

FIGURE 1–44 Tin snips are used to cut thin sheets of metal or carpet.

FIGURE 1–45 A utility knife uses replaceable blades to cut carpet and other materials.

PIN

FIGURE 1–46 A punch used to drive pins from assembled components. This type of punch is also called a pin punch.

SAFE USE OF CUTTERS. Whenever using cutters, always wear eye protection or a face shield to guard against the possibility of metal pieces being ejected during the cut. Always follow recommended procedures.

PUNCHES AND CHISELS. A **punch** is a small-diameter steel rod with a smaller diameter machined at one end. It is used to drive out a pin used to retain two components. Punches come in a variety of sizes, which are measured across the diameter of the machined end. Sizes include 1/16 in. 1/8 in., 3/16 in., and 1/4 in. ● **SEE FIGURE 1–46.**

FIGURE 1–47 Warning stamped on the side of a punch stating that goggles should be worn when using this tool. Always follow safety warnings.

FIGURE 1–48 Use a grinder or a file to remove the mushroomed material on the end of a punch or chisel.

FIGURE 1–49 A typical hacksaw that is used to cut metal. If cutting sheet metal or thin objects, a blade with more teeth should be used.

A **chisel** has a straight, sharp, cutting end that is used for cutting off rivets or to separate two pieces of an assembly. The most common design of chisel used for automotive service work is called a *cold chisel*.

SAFE USE OF PUNCHES AND CHISELS. Always wear eye protection when using a punch or a chisel because the hardened steel is brittle and parts of the punch could fly off and cause serious personal injury. See the warning stamped on the side of this automotive punch in ● **FIGURE 1–47**.

The tops of punches and chisels can become rounded off from use, a condition called "mushroomed." This material must be ground off to help prevent the possibility that the overhanging material will come loose and become airborne during use. ● **SEE FIGURE 1–48**.

HACKSAWS. A **hacksaw** is used to cut metals, such as steel, aluminum, brass, or copper. The cutting blade of a hacksaw is replaceable and the sharpness and number of teeth can be varied to meet the needs of the job. Use a blade with 14 or 18 teeth per inch (TPI) for cutting plaster or soft metals, such as aluminum and copper. Use 24 or 32 teeth per inch for steel or pipe. Hacksaw blades should be installed with the teeth pointing away from the handle. This means that a hacksaw cuts only when the blade is pushed in the forward direction. ● **SEE FIGURE 1–49**.

SAFE USE OF HACKSAWS. Check that the hacksaw is equipped with the correct blade for the job and that the teeth are pointed away from the handle. When using a hacksaw, move the hacksaw slowly away from you, then lift slightly and return for another cut.

1.4 BASIC HAND TOOLS

The following is a list of hand tools every automotive technician should possess. Specialty tools are not included.

Safety glasses

Tool chest

1/4-in. drive socket set (1/4-in. to 9/16-in. standard and deep sockets; 6-mm to 15-mm standard and deep sockets)

1/4-in. drive ratchet

1/4-in. drive 2-in. extension

1/4-in. drive 6-in. extension

1/4-in. drive handle

3/8-in. drive socket set (3/8-in. to 7/8-in. standard and deep sockets; 10-mm to 19-mm standard and deep sockets)

3/8-in. drive Torx set (T40, T45, T50, and T55)

3/8-in. drive 13/16-in. plug socket

3/8-in. drive 5/8-in. plug socket

3/8-in. drive ratchet

3/8-in. drive 1½-in. extension

3/8-in. drive 3-in. extension

3/8-in. drive 6-in. extension

3/8-in. drive 18-in. extension

3/8-in. drive universal

1/2-in. drive socket set (1/2-in. to 1-in. standard and deep sockets)

1/2-in. drive ratchet

1/2-in. drive breaker bar

1/2-in. drive 5-in. extension

1/2-in. drive 10-in. extension

3/8-in. to 1/4-in. adapter

1/2-in. to 3/8-in. adapter

3/8-in. to 1/2-in. adapter

Crowfoot set (fractional in.)

Crowfoot set (metric)

3/8- through 1-in. combination wrench set

10-mm through 19-mm combination wrench set

1/16-in. through 1/4-in. hex wrench set

2-mm through 12-mm hex wrench set

3/8-in. hex socket

13-mm to 14-mm flare nut wrench

15-mm to 17-mm flare nut wrench

5/16-in. to 3/8-in. flare nut wrench

7/16-in. to 1/2-in. flare nut wrench

1/2-in. to 9/16-in. flare nut wrench

FIGURE 1–50 A typical beginning technician tool set that includes the basic tools to get started.

FIGURE 1–51 A typical large toolbox, showing just one of many drawers.

Diagonal pliers

Needle-nose pliers

Adjustable-jaw pliers

Locking pliers

Snap-ring pliers

Stripping or crimping pliers

Ball-peen hammer

Rubber hammer

Dead-blow hammer

Five-piece standard screwdriver set

Four-piece Phillips screwdriver set

#15 Torx screwdriver

#20 Torx screwdriver

Awl

Mill file

Center punch

Pin punches (assorted sizes)

Chisel

Utility knife

Valve core tool

Filter wrench (large filters)

Filter wrench (smaller filters)

Test light

Feeler gauge

Scraper

Pinch bar

Magnet

1.4.1 TOOL SETS AND ACCESSORIES

A beginning service technician may wish to start with a small set of tools before purchasing an expensive tool set. ● **SEE FIGURES 1–50 AND 1–51.**

FIGURE 1–52 A typical 12-volt test light.

TECH TIP

Need to Borrow a Tool More Than Twice? Buy It!

Most service technicians agree that it is okay for a beginning technician to borrow a tool occasionally. However, if a tool has to be borrowed more than twice, then be sure to purchase it as soon as possible. Also, whenever a tool is borrowed, be sure that you clean the tool and let the technician you borrowed the tool from know that you are returning the tool. These actions will help in any future dealings with other technicians.

1.4.2 ELECTRICAL TOOLS

TEST LIGHT. A test light is used to test for electricity. A typical automotive test light consists of a clear plastic screwdriver-like handle that contains a lightbulb. A wire is attached to one terminal of the bulb, which the technician connects to a clean metal part of the vehicle. The other end of the bulb is attached to a point that can be used to test for electricity at a connector or wire. When there is power at the point and a good connection at the other end, the lightbulb lights up. ● **SEE FIGURE 1–52.**

BUTANE-POWERED

ELECTRIC

FIGURE 1–53 An electric and a butane-powered soldering gun used to make electrical repairs. Soldering guns are sold by the wattage rating. The higher the wattage, the greater the amount of heat created. Most soldering guns used for automotive electrical work fall within the 60- to 160-watt range.

ELECTRIC SOLDERING GUN. This type of soldering gun is usually powered by 110-volt AC and often has two power settings, expressed in watts. A typical electric soldering gun will produce from 85 to 300 watts of heat at the tip, which is more than adequate for soldering.

ELECTRIC SOLDERING PENCIL. This type of soldering iron is less expensive and creates less heat than an electric soldering gun. A typical electric soldering pencil (iron) creates 30 to 60 watts of heat and is suitable for soldering smaller wires and connections.

BUTANE-POWERED SOLDERING IRON. A butane-powered soldering iron is portable and very useful for automotive service work because an electrical cord is not needed. Most butane-powered soldering irons produce about 60 watts of heat, which is enough for most automotive soldering. ● **SEE FIGURE 1–53.**

HAND TOOLS FOR ELECTRICAL WORK. In addition to a soldering iron, most service technicians who do electrical-related work should have the following:

- Wire cutters
- Wire strippers
- Wire crimpers
- Heat gun for heat-shrink tubing

DIGITAL METER. A digital meter is a necessary tool for any electrical diagnosis and troubleshooting. A digital multimeter, abbreviated DMM, is usually capable of measuring the following units of electricity:

- DC volts
- AC volts
- Ohms
- Amperes

1.4.3 HAND TOOL MAINTENANCE Most hand tools are constructed of rust-resistant metals but they can still rust or corrode if not properly maintained. For best results and long tool life, take the following steps:

- Clean each tool before placing it back in the toolbox.
- Keep tools separated. When moist, metal tools will rust more readily if the tools are in contact with another metal tool.
- Line the drawers of the toolbox with a material that will prevent the tools from moving as the drawers are opened and closed. This helps to quickly locate the proper tool and size.
- Release the tension on all "clicker-type" torque wrenches.
- Keep the toolbox secure.

INCANDESCENT TROUBLE LIGHTS. *Incandescent lights* use a bulb with a filament that produces light when electric current flows through the bulb. For many years, these were the standard **trouble light**, also called a *work light*, until safety issues caused most shops to switch to safer fluorescent or LED lights. If incandescent trouble lights are used, try to locate bulbs that are rated "rough service," which are designed to withstand more shock and vibration than conventional lightbulbs.

 WARNING

Do not use incandescent trouble lights around gasoline or other flammable liquids. The liquids can cause the bulb to break and the hot filament can ignite the flammable liquid, which can cause personal injury or even death.

FLUORESCENT TROUBLE LIGHTS. A trouble light is an essential piece of shop equipment, and, for safety, should be a fluorescent light rather than incandescent. Incandescent lightbulbs

FIGURE 1–54 A fluorescent trouble light operates cooler and is safer to use in the shop because it is protected against accidental breakage where gasoline or other flammable liquids might come in contact with the light.

FIGURE 1–55 A typical 1/2-in.-drive air impact wrench. The direction of rotation can be changed to loosen or tighten a fastener.

can shatter or break if gasoline were to be splashed onto the bulb, creating a serious fire hazard. Fluorescent light tubes are not as likely to be broken and are usually protected by a clear plastic enclosure. Trouble lights are usually attached to a retractor, which can hold 20 to 50 feet of electrical cord. ● **SEE FIGURE 1–54.**

LED TROUBLE LIGHT. **Light-emitting diode (LED)** trouble lights are excellent to use because they are shock resistant, long lasting, and do not represent a fire hazard. Some trouble lights are battery powered and therefore can be used in places where an attached electrical cord could present problems.

1.4.4 AIR AND ELECTRICALLY OPERATED TOOLS

IMPACT WRENCH. An impact wrench, either air or electrically powered, is a tool that is used to remove and install fasteners. The air-operated 1/2-in.-drive impact wrench is the one most commonly used. ● **SEE FIGURE 1–55.**

FIGURE 1–56 A typical battery-powered 3/8-in.-drive impact wrench.

FIGURE 1–57 A black impact socket. Always use an impact-type socket whenever using an impact wrench to avoid the possibility of shattering the socket, which could cause personal injury.

Electrically powered impact wrenches commonly include:

- Battery-powered units. ● **SEE FIGURE 1–56.**
- 110-volt AC-powered units. This type of impact wrench is very useful, especially if compressed air is not readily available.

 WARNING

Always use impact sockets with impact wrenches, and always wear eye protection in case the socket or fastener shatters. Input sockets are thicker-walled and constructed with premium alloy steel. They are hardened with a black oxide finish to help prevent corrosion and distinguish them from regular sockets. ● **SEE FIGURE 1–57.**

FIGURE 1–58 An air ratchet is a very useful tool that allows fast removal and installation of fasteners, especially in areas that are difficult to reach or where there is not room enough to move a hand ratchet or wrench.

FIGURE 1–59 This typical die grinder surface preparation kit includes the air-operated die grinder as well as a variety of sanding disks for smoothing surfaces or removing rust.

AIR RATCHET. An air ratchet is used to remove and install fasteners that would normally be removed or installed using a ratchet and a socket. ● **SEE FIGURE 1–58.**

DIE GRINDER. A die grinder, a commonly used air-powered tool, can also be used to sand or remove gaskets and rust. ● **SEE FIGURE 1–59.**

BENCH- OR PEDESTAL-MOUNTED GRINDER. These high-powered grinders can be equipped with a wire brush wheel and/or a stone wheel.

- **Wire brush wheel.** This is used to clean bolt threads as well as to remove gaskets from sheet metal engine parts.
- **Stone wheel.** This is used to grind metal or to remove the mushroom from the top of punches or chisels. ● **SEE FIGURE 1–60.**

Most *bench grinders* are equipped with a grinder wheel (stone) on one end or the other of a wire brush. A bench grinder is a very

FIGURE 1–60 A typical pedestal grinder with a wire wheel on the left side and a stone wheel on the right side. Even though this machine is equipped with guards, safety glasses or a face shield should always be worn whenever using a grinder or wire wheel.

 WARNING

Always wear a face shield when using a wire wheel or a grinder.

useful piece of shop equipment and the wire wheel end can be used for cleaning bolt threads and cleaning gaskets from sheet metal parts, such as steel valve covers.

CAUTION: Use a steel wire brush only on steel or iron components. If a steel wire brush is used on aluminum or copper-based metal parts, it can remove metal from the part.

The grinding stone end of the bench grinder can be used to sharpen blades and drill bits, grind off the heads of rivets or parts, and reshape sheet metal parts for custom fitting.

1.4.5 HEATING, VENTILATION AND AIR CONDITIONING, HVAC, SPECIAL SERVICE TOOLS Specialized tools are required to properly disassemble and assemble a automatic transmission. These **special service tools (SSTs)** are available from the vehicle or drivetrain manufacturers and/or their tool suppliers. However, many technicians do not have access to SSTs, so they use generic versions available from aftermarket sources (● **FIGURE 1–61**).

1.5 SAFETY PRECAUTIONS

1.5.1 PERSONAL PROTECTIVE EQUIPMENT Service technicians should wear protective devices to prevent personal injury. The personal protection devices include the following:

- **Safety glasses.** Be sure that they meet ANSI standard Z87.1. They should be worn at all times while servicing any vehicle. ● **SEE FIGURE 1–62.**

FIGURE 1–61 Special tools for automatic transmission service include snap-ring pliers that are available in various sizes (a), bushing drivers (b), specialized pullers (c), clutch spring compressor (d), slide hammers (e), servo cover compressor (f), electronic transmission tester (g), scan tool (h), and a set of pressure gauges (i).

(a)　　(b)　　(c)

(d)　　(e)　　(f)

(g)　　(h)　　(i)

FIGURE 1–62 Safety glasses should be worn at all times when working on or around any vehicle or servicing any components.

Steel-toed safety shoes. ● **SEE FIGURE 1–63**. If safety shoes are not available, then leather-topped shoes offer more protection than canvas or cloth.

Bump cap. Service technicians working under a vehicle should wear a **bump cap** to protect the head against under-vehicle objects and the pads of the lift. ● **SEE FIGURE 1–64**.

Hearing protection. Hearing protection should be worn if the sound around you requires that you raise your voice

FIGURE 1–63 Steel-toed shoes are a worthwhile investment to help prevent foot injury due to falling objects. Even these well-worn shoes can protect the feet of this service technician.

(sound level higher than 90 decibels). For example, a typical lawnmower produces noise at a level of about 110 dB. This means that everyone who uses a lawnmower or other lawn or garden equipment should wear ear protection.

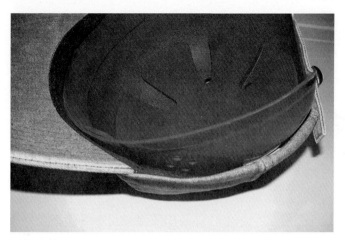

FIGURE 1–64 One version of a bump cap is a molded plastic insert that is worn inside a regular cloth cap.

FIGURE 1–65 Protective gloves are available in several sizes and materials.

- **Gloves.** Many technicians wear gloves not only to help keep their hands clean but also to help protect their skin from the effects of dirty engine oil and other possibly hazardous materials. There are several types of gloves:

  - **Latex surgical gloves.** These gloves are relatively inexpensive but tend to stretch, swell, and weaken when exposed to gas, oil, or solvents.

  - **Vinyl gloves.** These gloves are also inexpensive and are not affected by gas, oil, or solvents.

  - **Polyurethane gloves.** These gloves are more expensive, yet very strong. Even though they are also not affected by gas, oil, or solvents, they do tend to be slippery.

  - **Nitrile gloves.** These gloves are exactly like latex gloves but are not affected by gas, oil, or solvents, yet they tend to be expensive.

  - **Mechanic's gloves.** These gloves are usually made of synthetic leather and spandex and provide thermo protection, as well as protection from dirt and grime.
    ● **SEE FIGURE 1–65.**

In addition to wearing personal safety equipment, there are also many precautions that should be followed to keep safe in the shop. These precautions include:

- Remove jewelry that may get caught on something or act as a conductor to an exposed electrical circuit. ● **SEE FIGURE 1–66.**

- Take care of your hands. Keep your hands clean by washing with soap and hot water that is at least 110°F (43°C).

- Avoid loose or dangling clothing.

- When lifting any object, get a secure grip with solid footing. Keep the load close to your body to minimize the strain. Lift with your legs and arms, not your back.

- Do not twist your body when carrying a load. Instead, pivot your feet to help prevent strain on the spine.

FIGURE 1–66 Remove all jewelry before performing service work on any vehicle.

- Ask for help when moving or lifting heavy objects.

- Push a heavy object rather than pull it. (This is opposite to the way you should work with tools—never push a wrench! If you do and a bolt or nut loosens, your entire weight is used to propel your hand(s) forward. This usually results in cuts, bruises, or other painful injury.)

- Always connect an exhaust hose to the tailpipe of any running vehicle to help prevent the build-up of carbon monoxide inside a closed garage space. ● **SEE FIGURE 1–67.**

- When standing, keep objects, parts, and tools with which you are working between chest height and waist height. If seated, work at tasks that are at elbow height.

- Always make sure the hood of the vehicle is held securely open.

FIGURE 1–67 Always connect an exhaust hose to the tailpipe of a vehicle to be run inside a building.

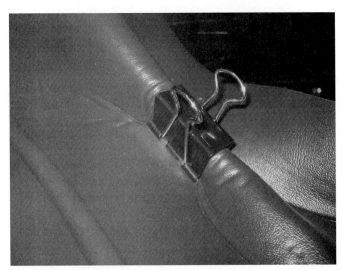

FIGURE 1–68 A binder clip being used to keep a fender cover from falling off.

1.6 WORKING SAFE

1.6.1 VEHICLE PROTECTION

FENDER COVERS. Whenever working under the hood of any vehicle, be sure to use fender covers. They not only help protect the vehicle from possible damage but also provide a clean surface on which to place parts and tools. The main problem with using fender covers is that they tend to move and often fall off the vehicle. To help prevent this, secure them to a lip of the fender using a *binder clip*, available at most office supply stores. ● **SEE FIGURE 1–68.**

INTERIOR PROTECTION. Always protect the interior of the vehicle from accidental damage or dirt and grease by covering the seat, steering wheel, and floor with a protective covering. ● **SEE FIGURE 1–69.**

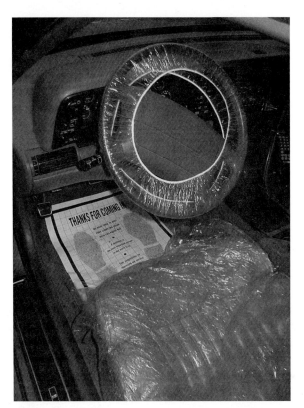

FIGURE 1–69 Covering the interior as soon as the vehicle comes in for service helps improve customer satisfaction.

 SAFETY TIP

Shop Cloth Disposal

Always dispose of oily shop cloths in an enclosed container to prevent a fire. ● **SEE FIGURE 1–70.** Whenever oily cloths are thrown together on the floor or workbench, a chemical reaction may occur, which can ignite the cloth even without an open flame, a process called **spontaneous combustion**.

1.6.2 LIFTING (HOISTING) A VEHICLE SAFELY   Many chassis and underbody service procedures require that the vehicle be hoisted or lifted off the ground. The simplest methods involve the use of drive-on ramps or a floor jack and safety (jack) stands, but in-ground or surface-mounted lifts provide greater access.

HOISTS. *Setting the pads is a critical part of the hoisting procedure.* All automobile and light-truck service manuals include recommended pad locations for hoisting (lifting) a vehicle. Newer vehicles have a triangle decal on the driver's door indicating the recommended lift points. The recommended standards for the lift points and lifting

FIGURE 1–70 All oily shop cloths should be stored in a metal container equipped with a lid to help prevent spontaneous combustion.

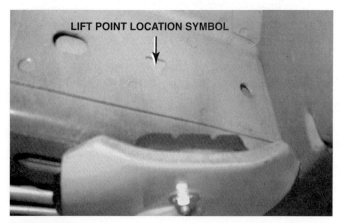

FIGURE 1–71 Most newer vehicles have a triangle symbol indicating the recommended hoisting lift location.

procedures are found in SAE Standard JRP-2184. ● **SEE FIGURE 1–71**.

These recommendations typically include the following points:

1. The vehicle should be centered on the lift or hoist so as not to overload one side or put too much force either forward or rearward. ● **SEE FIGURE 1–72.**

2. The pads of the lift should be spread as far apart as possible to provide a stable platform.

3. Each pad should be placed under a portion of the vehicle that is strong and capable of supporting the weight of the vehicle.
   a. Pinch welds at the bottom edge of the body are generally considered to be strong.

(a)

(b)

FIGURE 1–72 (a) Tall safety stands can be used to provide additional support for the vehicle while on the hoist.
(b) A block of wood should be used to avoid doing damage to components supported by the stand.

CAUTION: Even though pinch weld seams are the recommended location for hoisting many vehicles with unitized bodies (unit-body), care should be taken not to place the pad(s) too far forward or rearward. Incorrect placement of the vehicle on the lift could imbalance the vehicle and cause it to fall. This is exactly what happened to the vehicle in ● FIGURE 1–73.

b. Boxed areas of the body are the best places to position the pads for a vehicle without a frame. Be careful to note whether the arms of the lift could come into contact with other parts of the vehicle before the pad

FIGURE 1–73 This training vehicle fell from the hoist because the pads were not set correctly. No one was hurt but the vehicle was damaged.

touches the intended location. Commonly damaged areas include the following:

(1) Rocker panel moldings

(2) Exhaust system (including catalytic converter)

(3) Tires or body panels (● **SEE FIGURES 1–74 AND 1–75**.)

4. The vehicle should be raised about a foot (30 centimeters [cm]) off the floor, then stopped and shaken to check for stability. If the vehicle seems to be stable when checked at a short distance from the floor, continue raising the vehicle and continue to view the vehicle until it has reached the desired height. The hoist should be lowered onto the mechanical locks and then raised off of the locks before lowering.

CAUTION: Do not look away from the vehicle while it is being raised (or lowered) on a hoist. Often one side or one end of the hoist can stop or fail, resulting in the vehicle being slanted enough to slip or fall, creating physical damage not only to the vehicle and/or hoist but also to the technician or others who may be nearby.

HINT: Most hoists can be safely placed at any height. For ease while working, the area in which you are working should be at chest level. When working on brakes or suspension components, it is not necessary to work on them down near the floor or over your head. Raise the hoist so that the components are at chest level.

5. Before lowering the hoist, the safety latch(es) must be released and the direction of the controls reversed. The speed downward is often adjusted to be as slow as possible for additional safety.

(a)

(b)

FIGURE 1–74 (a) An assortment of hoist pad adapters that are often needed to safely hoist many pickup trucks, vans, and sport utility vehicles (SUVs). (b) A view from underneath a Chevrolet pickup truck showing how the pad extensions are used to attach the hoist lifting pad to contact the frame.

JACKS AND SAFETY STANDS. Floor jacks properly rated for the weight of the vehicle being raised are a common vehicle lifting tool. They are portable and relatively inexpensive, and they must be used with safety (jack) stands, which should be placed under the frame or reinforced areas under the vehicle body. The weight of the vehicle should never rest only on the hydraulic floor jack because a failure of the jack could cause the vehicle to fall. ● **SEE FIGURE 1–76**. The jack is then slowly released to allow the vehicle weight to be supported on the safety stands. If the front or rear of the vehicle is being raised, the opposite end of the vehicle must be blocked.

CAUTION: Safety stands should be rated higher than the weight they support.

(a)

(b)

FIGURE 1–75 (a) The pad arm is just contacting the rocker panel of the vehicle. (b) The pad arm has dented the rocker panel on this vehicle because the pad was set too far inward underneath the vehicle.

(a)

(b)

FIGURE 1–76 (a) A typical 3-ton (6,000-pound) capacity hydraulic jack. (b) Whenever a vehicle is raised off the ground, a safety stand should be placed under the frame, axle, or body to support the weight of the vehicle.

DRIVE-ON RAMPS. Ramps are an inexpensive way to raise the front or rear of a vehicle. ● **SEE FIGURE 1–77.** They are easy to store, but they can be dangerous because they can "kick out" when driving the vehicle onto the ramps.

CAUTION: Professional repair shops do not use ramps because they are dangerous. Use only with extreme care.

1.6.3 ELECTRICAL CORD SAFETY Use correctly grounded three-prong sockets and extension cords to operate power tools. Some tools use only two-prong plugs. Make sure these are double insulated, and repair or replace any electrical cords that are cut or damaged to prevent the possibility of an electrical shock. When not in use, keep electrical cords off the floor to prevent tripping over them. Tape the cords down if they are placed in high-foot-traffic areas.

1.6.4 JUMP-STARTING AND BATTERY SAFETY To jump-start another vehicle with a dead battery, connect good-quality copper jumper cables, as indicated in ● **FIGURE 1–78,**

FIGURE 1–77 Drive-on ramps can be dangerous to use. The wheels on the ground level must be chocked (blocked) to prevent accidental movement down the ramp.

FIGURE 1–78 Jumper cable usage guide. Follow the same connections if using a portable jump box.

SAFETY TIP

Air Hose Safety

Improper use of an air nozzle can cause blindness or deafness. Compressed air must be reduced to less than 30 psi (206 kPa). ● **SEE FIGURE 1–79.** If an air nozzle is used to dry and clean parts, make sure the airstream is directed away from anyone else in the immediate area. Coil and store air hoses when they are not in use.

FIGURE 1–79 The air pressure going to the nozzle should be reduced to 30 psi or less to help prevent personal injury.

or a jump box. The last connection made should always be to the engine block or an engine bracket as far from the battery as possible because it is normal for a spark to be created when the jumper cables finally complete the jumping circuit, and this spark could cause an explosion of the gases around the battery. Many newer vehicles have special ground connections built away from the battery just for the purpose of jump-starting. Check the owner's manual or service information for the exact location.

Batteries contain acid and should be handled with care to avoid tipping them at greater than a 45-degree angle. Always remove jewelry when working around a battery to avoid the possibility of electrical shock or burns, which can occur when the metal comes in contact with a 12-volt circuit and ground, such as the body of the vehicle.

1.6.5 FIRE EXTINGUISHERS There are four **fire extinguisher classes**. Each class is designed to be used on specific

types of fires, although many extinguishers can handle multiple types of fires. The class rating is clearly marked on the side of every fire extinguisher. ● **SEE FIGURE 1–80.**

- *Class A* is designed for use on general combustibles, such as cloth, paper, and wood.
- *Class B* is designed for use on flammable liquids and greases, including gasoline, oil, thinners, and solvents.
- *Class C* is used only on electrical fires.
- *Class D* is effective only on combustible metals such as powdered aluminum, sodium, or magnesium.

When using a fire extinguisher, remember the word "PASS."

P = Pull the safety pin.

A = Aim the nozzle of the extinguisher at the base of the fire.

FIGURE 1–80 A typical fire extinguisher designed to be used on type A, B, or C fires.

FIGURE 1–82 A treated wool blanket is kept in an easy-to-open wall-mounted holder and should be placed in a central location in the shop.

FIGURE 1–81 A CO_2 fire extinguisher being used on a fire set in an open drum during a demonstration at a fire training center.

S = Squeeze the lever to actuate the extinguisher.

S = Sweep the nozzle from side to side.

● **SEE FIGURE 1–81.**

TYPES OF FIRE EXTINGUISHERS. Types of fire extinguishers include the following:

- **Water.** A water fire extinguisher, usually in a pressurized container, is good to use on Class A fires by reducing the temperature to the point where a fire cannot be sustained.

- **Carbon Dioxide (CO_2).** A carbon dioxide fire extinguisher is good for almost any type of fire, especially Class B or Class C materials. A CO_2 fire extinguisher works by removing the oxygen from the fire, and the cold CO_2 also helps reduce the temperature of the fire.

FIGURE 1–83 A first aid box should be centrally located in the shop and kept stocked with the recommended supplies.

- **Dry Chemical (Yellow).** A dry chemical fire extinguisher is good for Class A, B, or C fires by coating the flammable materials, which eliminates the oxygen from the fire. A dry chemical fire extinguisher tends to be very corrosive and will cause damage to electronic devices.

1.6.6 FIRE BLANKETS
Fire blankets are required in shop areas. If a person is on fire, a fire blanket should be removed from its storage bag and thrown over and around the victim to smother the fire. ● **FIGURE 1–82** shows a typical fire blanket.

1.6.7 FIRST AID AND EYE WASH STATIONS
All shop areas must be equipped with a centrally located first aid kit kept stocked with emergency supplies and an eye wash station. ● **SEE FIGURE 1–83.**

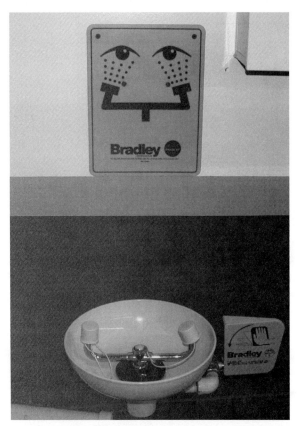

FIGURE 1–84 A typical eye wash station. A thorough flushing of the eyes with water is the first and often the best treatment in the event of eye contamination.

FIRST AID KIT. A first aid kit should include:

- Bandages (variety)
- Gauze pads
- Gauze roll
- Iodine swab sticks
- Antibiotic ointment
- Hydrocortisone cream
- Burn gel packets
- Eye wash solution
- Scissors
- Tweezers
- Gloves
- First aid guide

Every shop should have a person trained in first aid. If there is an accident, call for help immediately.

EYE WASH STATION. An **eye wash station** should be centrally located and used whenever any liquid or chemical gets into the eyes. If such an emergency does occur, keep eyes in a constant stream of water and call for professional assistance. ● **SEE FIGURE 1–84.**

1.6.8 HYBRID ELECTRIC VEHICLE SAFETY ISSUES

Hybrid electric vehicles (HEV) use a high-voltage battery pack

FIGURE 1–85 A warning label on a Honda hybrid warns that a person can be killed due to the high-voltage circuits under the cover.

 SAFETY TIP

Infection Control Precautions

Working on a vehicle can result in personal injury, including the possibility of being cut or hurt enough to cause bleeding. Some infections such as hepatitis B, HIV (which can cause acquired immunodeficiency syndrome, or AIDS), hepatitis C, and others are transmitted in the blood. These infections are commonly called blood-borne pathogens. Report any injury that involves blood to your supervisor and take the necessary precautions to avoid coming in contact with blood from another person.

and an electric motor(s) to help propel the vehicle. ● **SEE FIGURE 1–85** for an example of a typical warning label on a hybrid electric vehicle. The gasoline or diesel engine also is equipped with a generator or a combination starter and an integrated starter generator (ISG) or integrated starter alternator (ISA). To safely work around a hybrid electric vehicle, the high-voltage (HV) battery and circuits should be shut off following these steps:

STEP 1 Turn off the ignition key (if equipped) and remove the key from the ignition switch. (This will shut off all high-voltage circuits if the relay[s] is [are] working correctly.)

STEP 2 Disconnect the high-voltage circuits.

 WARNING

Some vehicle manufacturers specify that rubber insulated *lineman's gloves* be used whenever working around the high-voltage circuits to prevent the danger of electrical shock.

FIGURE 1–86 The high-voltage disconnect switch is in the trunk area of a Toyota Prius. High-voltage linemen's gloves should be worn when removing this plug. *(Courtesy of Tony Martin)*

FIGURE 1–87 The high-voltage shutoff switch on a Ford Escape hybrid. The switch is located under the carpet at the rear of the vehicle.

TOYOTA PRIUS. The Prius cutoff switch is located in the trunk. To gain access, remove three clips holding the upper left portion of the trunk side cover. To disconnect the high-voltage system, pull the orange-handled plug while wearing insulated rubber lineman's gloves. ● **SEE FIGURE 1–86**.

FORD ESCAPE/MERCURY MARINER. Ford and Mercury specify the following steps when working with the high-voltage (HV) systems of a hybrid vehicle:

- Four orange cones are to be placed at the four corners of the vehicle to create a buffer zone.
- High-voltage insulated gloves are to be worn with an outer leather glove to protect the inner rubber glove from possible damage.
- The service technician should also wear a face shield, and a fiberglass hook should be in the area and used to move a technician in the event of electrocution.

The high-voltage shutoff switch is located in the rear of the vehicle under the right-side carpet. ● **SEE FIGURE 1–87**. Rotate the handle to the "service shipping" position, lift it out to disable the high-voltage circuit, and wait 5 minutes before removing high-voltage cables.

HONDA CIVIC. To totally disable the high-voltage system on a Honda Civic, remove the main fuse (labeled number 1) from the driver's side underhood fuse panel. This should be all that is necessary to shut off the high-voltage circuit. If this is not possible, then remove the rear seat cushion and seat back. Remove the metal switch cover labeled "up" and remove the red locking cover. Move the "battery module switch" down to disable the high-voltage system.

FIGURE 1–88 The shutoff switch on a GM parallel hybrid truck is green because this system uses 42 volts instead of higher, possibly fatal, voltages used in other hybrid vehicles.

CHEVROLET SILVERADO/GMC SIERRA PICKUP TRUCK. The high-voltage shutoff switch is located under the rear passenger seat. Remove the cover marked "energy storage box" and turn the green service disconnect switch to the horizontal position to turn off the high-voltage circuits. ● **SEE FIGURE 1–88**.

 WARNING

Do not touch any orange wiring or component without following the vehicle manufacturer's procedures and wearing the specified personal protective equipment.

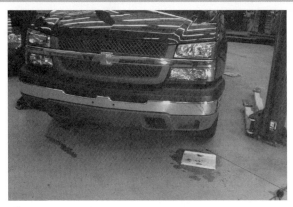

1 The first step in hoisting a vehicle is to properly align the vehicle in the center of the stall.

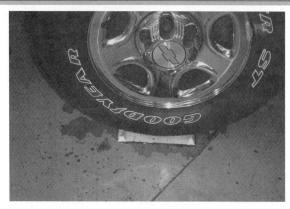

2 Most vehicles will be correctly positioned when the left front tire is centered on the tire pad.

3 The arms can be moved in and out and most pads can be rotated to allow for many different types of vehicle construction.

4 Most lifts are equipped with short pad extensions that are often necessary to allow the pad to contact the frame of a vehicle without causing the arm of the lift to hit and damage parts of the body.

5 Tall pad extensions can also be used to gain access to the frame of a vehicle. This position is needed to safely hoist many pickup trucks, vans, and sport utility vehicles.

6 An additional extension may be necessary to hoist a truck or van equipped with running boards to give the necessary clearance.

CONTINUED ▶

7 Position the pads under the vehicle under the recommended locations.

8 After making sure all pads are correctly positioned, use the electromechanical controls to raise the vehicle.

9 With the vehicle raised almost off the ground, push down on it to see if it is stable on the pads. If the vehicle rocks, lower the vehicle and reset the pads. The vehicle can be raised to any desired working level. Be sure the safety is engaged before working on or under the vehicle.

10 If raising a vehicle without a frame, place the flat pads under the pinch weld seam to spread the load. If additional clearance is necessary, the pads can be raised as shown.

11 When the service work is completed, the hoist should be raised slightly and the safety released before using the hydraulic lever to lower the vehicle.

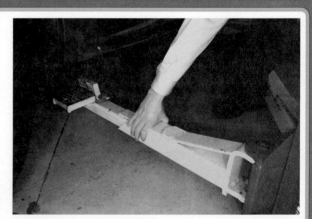

12 After lowering the vehicle, be sure all arms of the lift are moved out of the way before driving the vehicle out of the work stall.

1. Bolts, studs, and nuts are commonly used as fasteners in the chassis. The sizes for fractional and metric threads are different and are not interchangeable. The grade is the rating of the strength of a fastener.

2. Whenever a vehicle is raised above the ground, it must be supported at a substantial section of the body or frame.

3. Wrenches are available in open-end, box-end, and combination open- and box-end.

4. An adjustable wrench should be used only when the proper size is not available.

5. Line wrenches are also called flare-nut wrenches, fitting wrenches, or tube-nut wrenches and are used to remove fuel or refrigerant lines.

6. Sockets are rotated by a ratchet or breaker bar, also called a flex handle.

7. Torque wrenches measure the amount of torque applied to a fastener.

8. Screwdriver types include straight-blade (flat-tip) and Phillips.

9. Hammers and mallets come in a variety of sizes and weights.

10. Pliers are a useful tool and are available in many different types, including slip-joint, multigroove, lineman's, diagonal, needle-nose, and locking pliers.

11. Other common hand tools include snap-ring pliers, files, cutters, punches, chisels, and hacksaws.

12. Hybrid electric vehicles should be depowered if any of the high-voltage components are going to be serviced.

REVIEW QUESTIONS

1. List three precautions that must be taken whenever hoisting (lifting) a vehicle.

2. Describe how to determine the grade of a fastener, including how the markings differ between fractional and metric bolts.

3. List four items that are personal protective equipment (PPE).

4. List the types of fire extinguishers and their usage.

5. Why are wrenches offset 15 degrees?

6. What are the other names for a line wrench?

7. What are the standard automotive drive sizes for sockets?

8. Which type of screwdriver allows the use of a hammer or mallet?

9. What is inside a dead-blow hammer?

10. What type of cutter is available in left and right cutters?

CHAPTER QUIZ

1. The correct location for the pads when hoisting or jacking the vehicle can often be found in the _____.
   a. service manual
   b. shop manual
   c. owner's manual
   d. all of the above

2. For the best working position, the work should be _____.
   a. at neck or head level
   b. at knee or ankle level
   c. overhead by about 1 foot
   d. at chest or elbow level

3. A high-strength bolt is identified by _____.
   a. a UNC symbol
   b. lines on the head
   c. strength letter codes
   d. the coarse threads

4. A fastener that uses threads on both ends is called a _____.
   a. cap screw
   b. stud
   c. machine screw
   d. crest fastener

5. When working with hand tools, always _____.
   a. push the wrench—don't pull toward you
   b. pull a wrench—don't push a wrench away from you

6. The proper term for Channel-Locks is _____.
   a. Vise-Grips
   b. crescent wrench
   c. locking pliers
   d. multigroove adjustable pliers

7. The proper term for Vise-Grips is _____.
   a. locking pliers
   b. slip-joint pliers
   c. side cuts
   d. multigroove adjustable pliers

8. Two technicians are discussing torque wrenches. Technician A says that a torque wrench is capable of tightening a fastener with more torque than a conventional breaker bar or ratchet. Technician B says that a torque wrench should be calibrated regularly for the most accurate results. Which technician is correct?
   a. Technician A only
   b. Technician B only
   c. Both Technicians A and B
   d. Neither Technician A nor B

9. What type of screwdriver should be used if there is very limited space above the head of the fastener?
   a. Offset screwdriver
   b. Stubby screwdriver
   c. Impact screwdriver
   d. Robertson screwdriver

10. What type of hammer is plastic coated, has a metal casing inside, and is filled with small lead balls?
    a. Dead-blow hammer
    b. Soft-blow hammer
    c. Sledge hammer
    d. Plastic hammer

chapter 2

HAZARDOUS ENVIRONMENTAL MATERIALS

OBJECTIVES: **After studying Chapter 2, the reader will be able to:** • Fulfill the ASE requirements for all service technicians to adhere to environmentally appropriate actions and behavior. • Define the Occupational Safety and Health Act (OSHA). • Explain the Material Safety Data Sheet (MSDS). • Identify hazardous waste materials in accordance with state and federal regulations and follow proper safety precautions while handling hazardous waste materials. • Define the steps required to safely handle and store automotive chemicals and waste.

KEY TERMS: Aboveground storage tank (AGST) 38 • Asbestosis 37 • Battery Council International (BCI) 41 • Clean Air Act (CAA) 36 • Code of Federal Regulations (CFR) 35 • Environmental Protection Agency (EPA) 35 • Hazardous waste materials 35 • HEPA vacuum 37 • Material Safety Data Sheets (MSDS) 36 • Mercury 42 • Occupational Safety and Health Act (OSHA) 35 • Resource Conservation and Recovery Act (RCRA) 36 • Right-to-know laws 36 • Solvent 37 • Used oil 38 • Underground storage tank (UST) 38 • Workplace Hazardous Materials Information Systems (WHMIS) 36

2.1 HAZARDOUS WASTE

2.1.1 DEFINITION OF HAZARDOUS WASTE **Hazardous waste materials** are chemicals, or components, that the shop no longer needs that pose a danger to the environment and people if they are disposed of in ordinary garbage cans or sewers. However, no material is considered hazardous waste until the shop has finished using it and is ready to dispose of it.

2.1.2 PERSONAL PROTECTIVE EQUIPMENT (PPE)
When handling hazardous waste material, one must always wear the proper protective clothing and equipment detailed in the right-to-know laws. This includes respirator equipment. All recommended procedures must be followed accurately. Personal injury may result from improper clothing, equipment, and procedures when handling hazardous materials.

2.2 FEDERAL AND STATE LAWS

2.2.1 OCCUPATIONAL SAFETY AND HEALTH ACT
The United States Congress passed the **Occupational Safety and Health Act (OSHA)** in 1970. This legislation was designed to assist and encourage safe and healthful working conditions for the citizens of the United States:

- by providing research, information, education, and training in the field of occupational safety and health.
- by authorizing enforcement of the standards developed under the act.

Because about 25% of workers are exposed to health and safety hazards on the job, the OSHA standards are necessary for monitoring, controlling, and educating workers regarding health and safety in the workplace.

2.2.2 EPA The **Environmental Protection Agency (EPA)** publishes a list of hazardous materials, which is included in the **Code of Federal Regulations (CFR)**. The EPA considers waste hazardous if it has one or more of the following characteristics:

- **Reactive.** Any material that reacts violently with water or other chemicals is considered hazardous.
- **Corrosive.** If a material burns the skin, or dissolves metals and other materials, a technician should consider it hazardous. On the pH scale, where the number 7 indicates neutral (pure water has a pH of 7), lower numbers indicate an acidic solution and higher numbers indicate a caustic solution. If a material releases cyanide gas, hydrogen sulfide gas, or similar gases when exposed to low pH acid solutions, the material is considered hazardous.
- **Toxic.** Materials are hazardous if they leak one or more of eight different heavy metals in concentrations greater than 100 times the primary drinking water standard.

- **Ignitable.** A liquid is hazardous if it has a flash point below 140°F (60°C), and a solid is hazardous if it ignites spontaneously.
- **Radioactive.** Any substance that emits measurable levels of radiation is radioactive. When individuals bring containers of a highly radioactive substance into the shop environment, qualified personnel with the appropriate equipment must test them.

 WARNING

Hazardous waste disposal laws include serious penalties for anyone responsible for breaking these laws.

2.2.3 RIGHT-TO-KNOW LAWS

The **right-to-know laws** state that employees have a right to know when the materials they use at work are hazardous. The right-to-know laws are based on the Hazard Communication Standard published by the Occupational Safety and Health Administration (OSHA) in 1983. Originally, this document was intended for chemical companies and manufacturers that required employees to handle hazardous materials in their work situation, but the federal courts have decided to apply these laws to all companies, including automotive service shops. Under the right-to-know laws, employers have responsibilities regarding the handling of hazardous materials by their employees. All employees must be trained about the types of hazardous materials they will encounter in the workplace, and they must be informed about their legal rights regarding the handling of hazardous materials.

MATERIAL SAFETY DATA SHEETS (MSDS). All hazardous materials must be properly labeled, and information about each hazardous material must be posted on **Material Safety Data Sheets (MSDS)** available from the manufacturer. In Canada, MSDS sheets are called **Workplace Hazardous Materials Information Systems (WHMIS).** The employer is responsible for placing MSDS sheets where they are easily accessible to all employees. These sheets provide the following information about the hazardous material: chemical name, physical characteristics, protective handling equipment, explosion/fire hazards, incompatible materials, health hazards, medical conditions aggravated by exposure, emergency and first-aid procedures, safe handling, and spill/leak procedures.

The employer is also responsible for making sure that all hazardous materials are properly labeled. The label information must include health, fire, and reactivity hazards posed by the material, as well as the protective equipment necessary for handling the material. The manufacturer must supply all warning and precautionary information about hazardous materials, which must be read and understood by the employee before handling the material. ● **SEE FIGURE 2–1**.

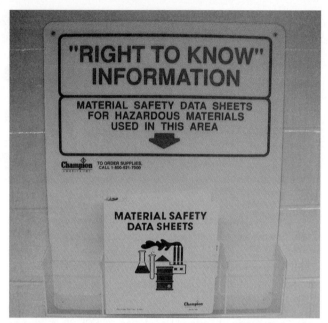

FIGURE 2–1 Material Safety Data Sheets (MSDS) should be readily available for use by anyone in the area who may come into contact with hazardous materials.

2.2.4 RESOURCE CONSERVATION AND RECOVERY ACT (RCRA)

Federal and state laws control the disposal of hazardous waste materials and every shop employee must be familiar with these laws. Hazardous waste disposal laws include the **Resource Conservation and Recovery Act (RCRA)**. This law states that hazardous material users are responsible for hazardous materials from the time they become a waste until the proper waste disposal is completed. Many shops hire an independent hazardous waste hauler to dispose of hazardous waste material. The shop owner, or manager, should have a written contract with the hazardous waste hauler. A shop may choose to recycle the material in the shop rather than have hazardous waste material hauled to an approved hazardous waste disposal site. Therefore, the user must store hazardous waste material properly and safely and be responsible for the transportation of this material until it arrives at an approved hazardous waste disposal site, where it can be processed according to the law. The RCRA controls the following types of automotive waste:

- Paint and body repair products waste
- Solvents for parts and equipment cleaning
- Batteries and battery acid
- Mild acids used for metal cleaning and preparation
- Waste oil and engine coolants or antifreeze
- Air-conditioning refrigerants and oils
- Engine oil filters

2.2.5 CLEAN AIR ACT

Air-conditioning (A/C) systems and refrigerants are regulated by the **Clean Air Act (CCA)**, Title VI, Section 609, which also regulates technician certification and service equipment. Any technician working on automotive A/C systems must be certified. A/C refrigerants must not be released or vented into the atmosphere, and used refrigerants must be recovered.

2.3 ASBESTOS HAZARDS

Friction materials such as brake and clutch linings often contain asbestos. While asbestos has been eliminated from most original equipment friction materials, the automotive service technician cannot know whether the vehicle being serviced is or is not equipped with friction materials containing asbestos. It is important that all friction materials be handled as if they do contain asbestos.

Asbestos exposure can cause scar tissue to form in the lungs, a condition called **asbestosis**. It gradually causes increasing shortness of breath, and the scarring to the lungs is permanent. Even low exposures to asbestos can cause *mesothelioma*, a type of fatal cancer of the lining of the chest or abdominal cavity. Asbestos exposure can also increase the risk of *lung cancer* as well as cancer of the voice box, stomach, and large intestine. It usually takes 15 to 30 years or more for cancer or asbestos lung scarring to show up after exposure. Scientists call this the *latency period*.

Government agencies recommend that asbestos exposure should be eliminated or controlled to the lowest level possible. These federal agencies—the National Institute for Occupational Safety and Health (NIOSH), Occupational Safety and Health Administration (OSHA), and Environmental Protection Agency (EPA)—have developed recommendations and standards that the automotive service technician and equipment manufacturer should follow.

2.3.1 OSHA ASBESTOS STANDARDS
The Occupational Safety and Health Administration (OSHA) has established three levels of asbestos exposure. Any vehicle service establishment that does either brake or clutch work must limit employee exposure to asbestos to less than 0.2 fibers per cubic centimeter (cc) as determined by an air sample. If the level of exposure to employees is greater than specified, corrective measures must be taken and a large fine may be imposed.

NOTE: **Research has found that worn asbestos fibers such as those from automotive brakes or clutches may not be as hazardous as first believed. Worn asbestos fibers do not have sharp, flared ends that can latch onto tissue, but rather are worn down to a dust form that resembles talc. Grinding or sawing operations on unworn brake shoes or clutch discs *will* contain *harmful* asbestos fibers. To limit health damage, always use proper handling procedures while working around any component that may contain asbestos.**

FIGURE 2–2 All brakes should be moistened with water or solvent to help prevent brake dust from becoming airborne.

2.3.2 EPA ASBESTOS REGULATIONS
The federal Environmental Protection Agency (EPA) has established procedures for the removal and disposal of asbestos. These procedures require that products containing asbestos be "wetted" to prevent the asbestos fibers from becoming airborne. According to the EPA, asbestos-containing materials can be disposed of as regular waste. Only when asbestos becomes airborne is it considered to be hazardous.

2.3.3 ASBESTOS HANDLING GUIDELINES
The air in the shop area can be tested by a testing laboratory, but this can be expensive. Tests have determined that asbestos levels can easily be kept below the recommended levels by using a liquid, like water, or a special vacuum.

NOTE: **Even though asbestos is being removed from brake and clutch lining materials, the service technician cannot tell whether the old brake pads, shoes, or clutch discs contain asbestos. Therefore, to be safe, the technician should assume that all brake pads, shoes, or clutch discs do contain asbestos.**

- **HEPA vacuum.** A special high-efficiency particulate air (HEPA) vacuum system has been proven effective in keeping asbestos exposure levels below 0.1 fibers per cubic centimeter.

- **Solvent spray.** Many technicians use an aerosol can of brake cleaning solvent to wet the brake dust and prevent it from becoming airborne. A **solvent** is a liquid that is used to dissolve dirt, grime, or solid particles. Commercial brake cleaners are available that use a concentrated cleaner that is mixed with water. ● **SEE FIGURE 2–2.**

The waste liquid is filtered, and when dry, the filter can be disposed of as solid waste.

DISPOSAL OF BRAKE DUST AND BRAKE SHOES. The hazard of asbestos occurs when asbestos fibers are airborne. Once the asbestos has been wetted down, it is then considered to be solid waste, rather than hazardous waste. Old brake shoes and pads should be enclosed, preferably in a plastic bag, to help prevent any of the brake material from becoming airborne. *Always follow current federal and local laws concerning disposal of all waste.*

2.4 USED BRAKE FLUID

Most brake fluid is made from polyglycol, is water soluble, and can be considered hazardous if it has absorbed metals from the brake system.

2.4.1 STORAGE AND DISPOSAL OF BRAKE FLUID

- Collect brake fluid in containers clearly marked to indicate that they are dedicated to that purpose.
- If the waste brake fluid is hazardous, be sure to manage it appropriately and use only an authorized waste receiver for its disposal.
- If the waste brake fluid is nonhazardous (such as old, but unused), determine from your local solid waste collection provider what should be done for its proper disposal.
- Do not mix brake fluid with used engine oil.
- Do not pour brake fluid down drains or onto the ground.
- Recycle brake fluid through a registered recycler.

2.5 USED OIL

During normal use, any petroleum-based or synthetic oil may take on impurities such as dirt, metal scrapings, water, or chemicals. Eventually, this **used oil** must be replaced with virgin or re-refined oil. The EPA's used oil management standards take a three-pronged approach to determining if a substance meets the definition of *used oil*. To meet this definition, a substance must satisfy each of the following three criteria:

- **Origin.** The first criterion for identifying used oil is based on the oil's origin. Used oil must have been refined from crude oil or made from synthetic materials. Animal and vegetable oils are excluded from the EPA's definition of used oil.

- **Use.** The second criterion is based on whether and how the oil is used. Oils used as lubricants, hydraulic fluids, heat transfer fluids, and for other similar purposes are considered used oil. The EPA's definition excludes products used as cleaning agents, as well as certain petroleum-derived products like antifreeze and kerosene.

- **Contaminants.** The third criterion is whether or not the oil is contaminated with either physical or chemical impurities. In other words, to meet the EPA's definition, used oil must become contaminated as a result of being used. This aspect of the EPA's definition includes residues and contaminants generated from handling, storing, and processing used oil.

NOTE: The release of only 1 gallon of used oil (a typical oil change) can make a million gallons of fresh water undrinkable.

If used oil is dumped down the drain and enters a sewage treatment plant, concentrations as small as 50 to 100 ppm (parts per million) in the wastewater can foul sewage treatment processes. Never mix a listed hazardous waste, gasoline, wastewater, halogenated solvent, antifreeze, or unknown waste material with used oil. Adding any of these substances will cause the used oil to become contaminated, which classifies it as hazardous waste.

2.5.1 STORAGE AND DISPOSAL OF USED OIL

Once oil has been used, it can be collected, recycled, and used over and over again. An estimated 380 million gallons of used oil are recycled each year. Sometimes recycled used oil can be used again for the same job or can take on a completely different task. For example, used engine oil can be re-refined and sold as engine oil or processed for furnace fuel oil. After collecting used oil in an appropriate container, such as a 55-gallon steel drum, the material must be disposed of in one of two ways:

1. Shipped offsite for recycling
2. Burned in an onsite or offsite EPA-approved heater for energy recovery

Used oil must be stored in compliance with existing **underground storage tank (UST)** or an **aboveground storage tank (AGST)** standards or kept in separate containers. ● SEE FIGURE 2–3. The containers are portable receptacles, such as a 55-gallon steel drum.

- **Keep used oil storage drums in good condition.** This means that they should be covered, secured from vandals, properly labeled, and maintained in compliance with local fire codes. Frequent inspections for leaks, corrosion, and spillage are an essential part of container maintenance.

- **Never store used oil in anything other than tanks and storage containers.** Used oil may also be stored in regulated hazardous waste storage units.

- **Used oil filter disposal regulations.** Used oil filters contain engine oil that may be hazardous. Before an oil filter is put in the trash or sent to recycling, it must be

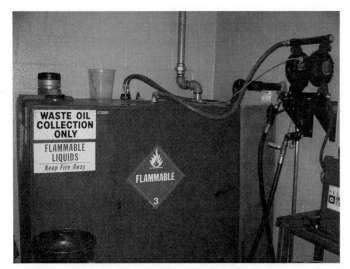

FIGURE 2–3 A typical aboveground oil storage tank.

FIGURE 2–4 Washing hands and removing jewelry are two important safety habits all service technicians should practice.

drained using one of the following hot draining methods approved by the EPA:

- Puncturing the filter anti-drainback valve or filter dome end and hot draining for at least 12 hours
- Hot draining and crushing
- Dismantling and hot draining
- Any other hot draining method, which will remove all the used oil from the filter

After the oil has been drained from the oil filter, the filter housing can be disposed of by recycling or pickup by a service contract or regular trash company.

2.6 SOLVENTS

The major sources of chemical danger are liquid and aerosol brake cleaning fluids that contain chlorinated hydrocarbon solvents. Other chemicals that do not deplete the ozone, such as heptane, hexane, and xylene, are now being used in nonchlorinated brake cleaning solvents. Some manufacturers are also producing solvents they describe as environmentally responsible, which are biodegradable and noncarcinogenic (non–cancer-causing). Although there is no specific standard for physical contact with chlorinated hydrocarbon solvents or the chemicals replacing them, all contact should be avoided whenever possible. The law requires an employer to provide appropriate protective equipment and ensure proper work practices by an employee handling these chemicals.

2.6.1 EFFECTS OF CHEMICAL POISONING
The effects of exposure to chlorinated hydrocarbon and other types of solvents can take many forms. Short-term exposure at low levels can cause one or more of the following symptoms:

- Headache
- Nausea
- Drowsiness

 SAFETY TIP

Hand Safety

Service technicians should wash their hands with soap and water after handling engine oil or differential or transmission fluids or wear protective rubber gloves. Also, the service technician should not wear watches, rings, or other jewelry that could come in contact with electrical or moving parts of a vehicle. ● **SEE FIGURE 2–4.**

- Dizziness
- Lack of coordination
- Unconsciousness

Exposure may also cause irritation of the eyes, nose, and throat and flushing of the face and neck. Short-term exposure to higher concentrations can cause liver damage with symptoms such as yellow jaundice or dark urine. Liver damage may not become evident until several weeks after the exposure.

2.6.2 REGULATORY STATUS OF HAZARDOUS SOLVENTS
Most solvents are classified as hazardous wastes. Other characteristics of solvents include the following:

- Solvents with flash points below 140°F are considered flammable and, like gasoline, are federally regulated by the Department of Transportation (DOT).
- Solvents and oils with flash points above 140°F are considered combustible and, like engine oil, are also regulated by the DOT. All flammable items must be stored in a fireproof container. ● **SEE FIGURE 2–5.**

It is the responsibility of the repair shop to determine if its spent solvent is hazardous waste. Solvent reclaimers are available that clean and restore the solvent so that it lasts indefinitely.

FIGURE 2–5 Typical fireproof flammable storage cabinet.

FIGURE 2–6 Using a water-based cleaning system helps reduce the hazards from using strong chemicals.

2.6.3 USED SOLVENTS
Used or spent solvents are liquid materials that have been generated as waste and may contain xylene, methanol, ethyl ether, and methyl isobutyl ketone (MIBK). These materials must be stored in OSHA-approved safety containers with tightly closed lids or caps. Additional requirements include the following:

- Containers should be clearly labeled "Hazardous Waste" and the date the material was first placed into the storage receptacle should be noted.
- Labeling is not required for solvents being used in a parts washer.
- Used solvents will not be counted toward a facility's monthly output of hazardous waste if a contracted vendor removes the material.
- Used solvents may be disposed of by recycling with a local vendor, such as SafetyKleen®, and they are removed according to specific terms in the vendor agreement.
- Aqueous-based (nonsolvent) cleaning systems can help avoid the problems associated with chemical solvents. ● SEE FIGURE 2–6.

2.7 COOLANT

Coolant is a mixture of antifreeze and water. New antifreeze is not considered hazardous even though it can cause death if ingested, but used antifreeze may be hazardous due to dissolved metals from the engine and other components of the cooling system. These metals can include iron, steel, aluminum, copper, brass, and lead (from older radiators and heater cores).

- Coolant should be recycled either onsite or offsite.
- Used coolant should be stored in a sealed and labeled container. ● SEE FIGURE 2–7.

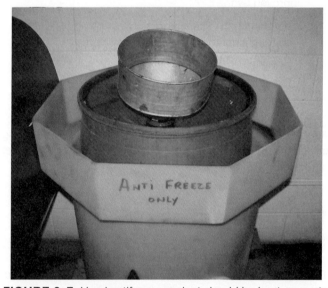

FIGURE 2–7 Used antifreeze coolant should be kept separate and stored in a leak-proof container until it can be recycled or disposed of according to federal, state, and local laws. Note that the storage barrel is placed inside another container to catch any coolant that may spill out of the inside barrel.

- Used coolant can often be disposed of in municipal sewers with a permit. Check with local authorities and obtain a permit before discharging used coolant into sanitary sewers.

2.8 LEAD-ACID BATTERY WASTE

About 70 million spent lead-acid batteries are generated each year in the United States alone. The lead in battery plates is classified as a toxic metal and is highly poisonous, and the acid used in lead-acid batteries is highly corrosive. Battery electrolyte contains sulfuric acid, which is a very corrosive substance capable of causing serious personal injury, such as skin burns and eye damage. For this reason, disposing of batteries improperly can cause environmental contamination and lead to severe health problems. The vast majority (95% to 98%) of batteries are recycled through lead reclamation operations and secondary lead smelters for use in the manufacture of new batteries.

2.8.1 BATTERY DISPOSAL

To be exempt from hazardous waste regulations, used lead-acid batteries must be reclaimed or recycled. Leaking batteries must be stored and transported as hazardous waste. Some states have stricter regulations that require special handling procedures and transportation of all batteries. According to the **Battery Council International (BCI)**, battery laws usually include the following rules:

1. Lead-acid battery disposal is prohibited in landfills or incinerators. Batteries are required to be delivered to a battery retailer, wholesaler, recycling center, or lead smelter.

2. All retailers of automotive batteries are required to post a sign that displays the universal recycling symbol and indicates the retailer's specific requirements for accepting used batteries.

2.8.2 BATTERY HANDLING AND STORAGE

Batteries, whether new or used, should be kept indoors if possible. The storage location should be an area specifically designated for battery storage and must be well ventilated (to the outside). If outdoor storage is the only alternative, a sheltered and secured area with acid-resistant secondary containment is strongly recommended. It is also advisable to use acid-resistant secondary containment for indoor storage. In addition, batteries should be placed on acid-resistant pallets and never stacked.

2.9 FUEL SAFETY AND STORAGE

Gasoline is very explosive. Expanding gasoline vapors are extremely dangerous and are present even in cold temperatures. In many vehicles, vapors that form in gasoline tanks are controlled, but vapors from gasoline storage may escape from the can, resulting in a hazardous situation. Therefore, gasoline storage containers should be placed in a well-ventilated space. Although diesel fuel is not as volatile as gasoline, the same basic rules apply to diesel fuel as to gasoline storage. These rules include the following:

1. Use storage cans that have a flash-arresting screen at the outlet. These screens prevent external ignition sources from igniting the gasoline within the can when someone pours the gasoline or diesel fuel.

2. Use only a red, approved gasoline container to allow for proper hazardous substance identification. ● **SEE FIGURE 2–8**.

FIGURE 2–8 This red gasoline container holds about 30 gallons of gasoline and is used to fill vehicles used for training.

3. Do not fill gasoline containers completely full. Always leave the level of gasoline at least 1 inch from the top of the container. This action allows for expansion of the gasoline at higher temperatures. If gasoline containers are completely full, the gasoline will expand when the temperature increases and force gasoline from the can to create a dangerous spill. If gasoline or diesel fuel containers must be stored, place them in a designated storage locker or facility.

4. Never leave gasoline containers open, except while filling or pouring gasoline from the container.

5. Never use gasoline as a cleaning agent.

6. Always connect a ground strap to containers when filling or transferring fuel or other flammable products from one container to another to prevent static electricity from building up that could result in a spark and a disastrous explosion and fire.

2.10 AIRBAGS

Airbag modules are pyrotechnic devices that can be ignited if exposed to an electrical charge or if the body of the vehicle is subjected to a shock. Airbag safety should include the following precautions:

1. Disarm the airbag(s) if you will be working in the area where a discharged bag could make contact with any part of your body. Consult service information for the exact procedure to follow for the vehicle being serviced. The usual procedure

is to deploy the airbag using a 12-volt power supply, such as a jump-start box, using long wires to connect to the module to ensure a safe deployment.

2. Do not expose an airbag to extreme heat or fire.

3. Always carry an airbag pointing away from your body.

4. Place an airbag module facing upward.

5. Always follow the manufacturer's recommended procedure for airbag disposal or recycling, including the proper packaging to use during shipment.

6. Wear protective gloves if handling a deployed airbag.

7. Always wash your hands or body well if exposed to a deployed airbag. The chemicals involved can cause skin irritation and possible rash development.

2.11 USED TIRES

Used tires are an environmental concern for several reasons, including the following:

1. In a landfill, they tend to "float" up through the other trash and rise to the surface.

2. The inside of tires traps and holds rainwater, which is a breeding ground for mosquitoes. Mosquito-borne diseases include encephalitis and dengue fever.

3. Used tires present a fire hazard and, when burned, create a large amount of black smoke that contaminates the air.

Used tires should be disposed of in one of the following ways:

1. Used tires can be reused until the end of their useful life.

2. Tires can be retreaded.

3. Tires can be recycled or shredded for use in asphalt.

4. Derimmed tires can be sent to a landfill (most landfill operators will shred the tires because it is illegal in many states to put whole tires in landfills).

5. Tires can be burned in cement kilns or in power plants where the smoke can be controlled.

6. A registered scrap tire handler should be used to transport tires for disposal or recycling.

2.12 AIR-CONDITIONING REFRIGERANT OIL

Air-conditioning refrigerant oil contains dissolved refrigerant and is therefore considered hazardous waste. This oil must be kept separated from other waste oil or the entire amount of oil must be treated as hazardous. Used refrigerant oil must be sent to a licensed hazardous waste disposal company for recycling or disposal. ● SEE FIGURE 2–9.

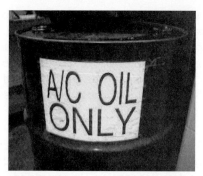

FIGURE 2–9 Air-conditioning refrigerant oil must be kept separated from other oils because it contains traces of refrigerant and must be treated as hazardous waste.

FIGURE 2–10 Placard near driver's door, naming what devices in the vehicle contain mercury.

  TECH TIP

Remove Components That Contain Mercury

Some vehicles have a placard near the driver's side door that lists the components that contain the heavy metal mercury. **Mercury** can be absorbed through the skin and once absorbed by the body, it does not leave. ● **SEE FIGURE 2–10.**

These components should be removed from the vehicle before the rest of the body is sent to be recycled to help prevent releasing mercury into the environment.

TECH TIP

What Every Technician Should Know

The Hazardous Material Identification Guide (HMIG) is the standard labeling for all materials. The service technician should be aware of its meaning. ● **SEE FIGURE 2–11.**

Hazardous Materials Identification Guide (HMIG)

TYPE HAZARD			DEGREE	
	○ HEALTH			4 - Extreme
	○ FLAMMABILITY			3 - Serious
	○ REACTIVITY			2 - Moderate
	○ PROTECTIVE EQUIPMENT			1 - Slight
				0 - Minimal

HAZARD RATING AND PROTECTIVE EQUIPMENT

Health	Flammable	Reactive
Type of Possible Injury	Susceptibility of materials to burn	Susceptibility of materials to release energy
4 Highly Toxic. May be fatal on short-term exposure. Special protective equipment required.	4 Extremely flammable gas or liquid. Flash Point below 73°F.	4 Extreme. Explosive at room temperature.
3 Toxic. Avoid inhalation or skin contact.	3 Flammable. Flash Point 73°F to 100°F.	3 Serious. May explode if shocked, heated under confinement, or mixed with water.
2 Moderately Toxic. May be harmful if inhaled or absorbed.	2 Combustible. Requires moderate heating to ignite. Flash Point 100°F to 200°F.	2 Moderate. Unstable, may react with water.
1 Slightly Toxic. May cause slight irritation.	1 Slightly Combustible. Requires strong heating to ignite.	1 Slight. May react if heated or mixed with water.
0 Minimal. All chemicals have a slight degree of toxicity.	0 Minimal. Will not burn under normal conditions.	0 Minimal. Normally stable, does not react with water.

Protective Equipment

A	Safety Glasses	E	Safety Glasses + Gloves + Dust Respirator	I	Safety Glasses + Gloves + Combination Dust & Vapor Respirator
B	Safety Glasses + Gloves	F	Safety Glasses + Gloves + Apron + Dust Respirator	J	Chemical Goggles + Gloves + Apron + Combination Dust & Vapor Respirator
C	Safety Glasses + Gloves + Apron	G	Safety Glasses + Gloves + Vapor Respirator	K	Apron + Gloves + Full Protection Suit + Boots
D	Faceshield + Gloves + Apron	H	Chemical Goggles + Gloves + Apron + Vapor Respirator	X	Ask your supervisor for guidance.

FIGURE 2–11 The Environmental Protection Agency (EPA) Hazardous Materials Identification Guide is a standardized listing of the hazards and the protective equipment needed.

All automotive service facilities create some waste and although most of it is handled properly, it is important that all hazardous and nonhazardous waste be accounted for and properly disposed of. See the following chart for a list of typical wastes generated at automotive shops, plus a checklist for keeping track of how these wastes are to be handled.

Typical Wastes Generated at Auto Repair Shops and Typical Method of Disposal for Each Category
(Hazardous or Nonhazardous)

Waste Stream	Typical Category If Not Mixed with Other Hazardous Waste	If Disposed in Landfill and Not Mixed with a Hazardous Waste	If Recycled
Used oil	Used oil	Hazardous waste	Used oil
Used oil filters	Nonhazardous solid waste, if completely drained	Nonhazardous solid waste, if completely drained	Used oil, if not drained
Used transmission fluid	Used oil	Hazardous waste	Used oil
Used brake fluid	Used oil	Hazardous waste	Used oil
Used antifreeze	Depends on characterization	Depends on characterization	Depends on characterization
Used solvents	Hazardous waste	Hazardous waste	Hazardous waste
Used citric solvents	Nonhazardous solid waste	Nonhazardous solid waste	Hazardous waste
Lead-acid automotive batteries	Not a solid waste if returned to supplier	Hazardous waste	Hazardous waste
Shop rags used for oil	Used oil	Depends on used oil characterization	Used oil
Shop rags used for solvent or gasoline spills	Hazardous waste	Hazardous waste	Hazardous waste
Oil spill absorbent material	Used oil	Depends on used oil characterization	Used oil
Spill material for solvent and gasoline	Hazardous waste	Hazardous waste	Hazardous waste
Catalytic converter	Not a solid waste if returned to supplier	Nonhazardous solid waste	Nonhazardous solid waste
Spilled or unused fuels	Hazardous waste	Hazardous waste	Hazardous waste
Spilled or unusable paints and thinners	Hazardous waste	Hazardous waste	Hazardous waste
Used tires	Nonhazardous solid waste	Nonhazardous solid waste	Nonhazardous solid waste

SUMMARY

1. Hazardous materials include common automotive chemicals, liquids, and lubricants, especially those whose ingredients contain *chlor* or *fluor* in their name.

2. Right-to-know laws require that all workers have access to Material Safety Data Sheets (MSDS).

3. Asbestos fibers should be avoided and removed according to current laws and regulations.

4. Used engine oil contains metals worn from parts and should be handled and disposed of properly.

5. Solvents represent a serious health risk and should be avoided as much as possible.

6. Coolant should be disposed of properly or recycled.

7. Batteries are considered hazardous waste and should be sent to a recycling facility.

1. List five common automotive chemicals or products that may be considered hazardous materials.

2. List five precautions to which every technician should adhere when working with automotive products and chemicals.

CHAPTER QUIZ

1. Hazardous materials include all of the following except _____.
   a. engine oil
   b. asbestos
   c. water
   d. brake cleaner

2. To determine if a product or substance being used is hazardous, consult _____.
   a. a dictionary
   b. an MSDS
   c. SAE standards
   d. EPA guidelines

3. Exposure to asbestos dust can cause what condition?
   a. Asbestosis
   b. Mesothelioma
   c. Lung cancer
   d. All of the above are possible.

4. Wetted asbestos dust is considered _____.
   a. solid waste
   b. hazardous waste
   c. toxic
   d. poisonous

5. An oil filter should be hot drained for how long before disposing of the filter?
   a. 30 to 60 minutes
   b. 4 hours
   c. 8 hours
   d. 12 hours

6. Used engine oil should be disposed of by all except the following methods:
   a. Disposed of in regular trash
   b. Shipped offsite for recycling
   c. Burned onsite in a waste-oil-approved heater
   d. Burned offsite in a waste-oil-approved heater

7. All of the following are the proper ways to dispose of a drained oil filter except _____.
   a. sent for recycling
   b. picked up by a service contract company
   c. disposed of in regular trash
   d. disposed of as hazardous waste

8. Which is not considered to be a hazardous solvent?
   a. Nonchlorinated hydrocarbon solvent
   b. Tetrachloroethylene
   c. MIBK
   d. Chlorinated hydrocarbon solvent

9. Gasoline should be stored in approved containers that include what color(s)?
   a. A red container with yellow lettering
   b. A red container
   c. A yellow container
   d. A yellow container with red lettering

10. What automotive devices may contain mercury?
    a. Rear-seat video displays
    b. Navigation displays
    c. HID headlights
    d. All of the above

INTRODUCTION TO TRANSMISSIONS

OBJECTIVES: **After studying Chapter 3, the reader will be able to:** • Explain the requirements for an automotive drivetrain. • Identify the major components of an automatic transmission and transaxle. • Explain how different gear ratios can be obtained in a planetary gear set. • Describe the systems within an automatic transmission and how they relate to each other.

KEY TERMS: All-wheel drive (AWD) 46 • Annulus gear 49 • Backlash 51 • Band 57 • Bevel gear 50 • Clutch 57 • Continuously variable transmission (CVT) 66 • Differential 63 • Drive axle 46 • Drivetrain 46 • Dual-clutch transmission (DCT) 47 • Final drive 62 • Four-wheel drive (4WD) 46 • Front-wheel drive (FWD) 46 • Gear ratio 48 • Gear reduction 49 • Gear set 48 • Helical gear 49 • Hybrid drive system 67 • Hydraulic 49 • Hypoid gear 50 • Idler gear 50 • Internal gear 49 • Longitudinal 46 • One-way clutch 57 • Overdrive 49 • Pinion 51 • Planetary gear set 55 • Rear-wheel drive (RWD) 46 • Regenerative 68 • Ring gear 49 • Servo 59 • Spiral bevel gear 50 • Spur bevel gear 50 • Spur gear 49 • Sun gear 55 • Synchronizer hub 54 • Synchronizer sleeve 54 • Torque 48 • Torque converter 61 • Torque converter clutch (TCC) 62 • Transaxle 46 • Transmission 46 • Transverse 46

3.1 TRANSMISSIONS: THEIR PURPOSE

A vehicle would be difficult to operate without a **transmission**. Every driver is familiar with the gear shift lever that is moved to control a vehicle's motion. This lever determines gear selection in the transmission, which determines the driving mode of the vehicle. The transmission provides the various gear ratios for forward and reverse operation as well as two methods for the engine to run without moving the vehicle. These selections are:

P: Park. Allows the engine to run without moving the vehicle and mechanically locks the drivetrain to prevent movement.

R: Reverse. Allows the vehicle to be driven backward.

N: Neutral. Allows the engine to run without moving the vehicle or locking the drivetrain.

O or OD: Overdrive. Allows the engine to run slower while cruising for improved fuel mileage and lower emissions, shifts automatically from first gear through OD.

D: Drive. Allows automatic shifts from first gear through D, drives high gear with a 1:1 ratio.

I: Intermediate. Prevents high-gear operation and provides compression braking.

L: Low. Multiplies the engine's torque so there will be enough power to move the vehicle in difficult conditions, prevents upshifts, and provides compression braking.

At one time, most vehicles had the transmission mounted behind the engine and used a *drive shaft*, also called a *propeller shaft* or drive line, to transfer power to the rear axle and driving wheels. This **drivetrain** is called **rear-wheel drive (RWD)**. • SEE FIGURE 3–1. Many vehicles use a transaxle to drive the front wheels, called **front-wheel drive (FWD)**.

Most FWD vehicles have the engine mounted in a **transverse** position, crosswise in the vehicle. Some are **longitudinal** mounted, in a lengthwise position as in RWD vehicles. • SEE FIGURE 3–2. A **transaxle** is a combination of the transmission and final **drive axle**. Two short driveshafts are used to connect the transaxle to the front wheels. Driving only two wheels is adequate for most driving conditions.

Vehicles that can drive all four wheels are called **four-wheel-drive (4WD)** vehicles. The driver has the option of selecting two- or four-wheel drive. 2WD is used for normal driving conditions; 4WD is normally used only for off-road driving or slippery conditions. Vehicles that drive all four wheels all of the time on all road surfaces are called **all-wheel-drive (AWD)** or full-time 4WD vehicles. 4WD and AWD are more complex, more expensive, and heavier than 2WD. Either 4WD or AWD is available on most pickups, sport-utility vehicles (SUVs), vans, and light trucks. AWD is available on some passenger cars, station wagons, vans, and SUVs. Because of the added traction, AWD can benefit winter and performance-oriented driving. A transfer case or transfer gear is required to deliver power to the second drive axle, and it is usually mounted in or on the transmission or transaxle.

Automatic and manual transmissions serve the same purpose—the difference is how they are shifted. The driver with a manual transmission selects the gear and performs each shift while depressing the clutch pedal. An automatic transmission has a self-releasing clutch, the torque converter, and upshifts and downshifts automatically. Some *manumatic* transmissions are designed so the driver has more control of the shift points. In the past, several manufacturers offered semiautomatic transmissions; Chrysler Corporation's Fluid Drive and Volkswagen's Automatic Stick Shift are examples of semiautomatic transmissions. The driver had to perform each of the upshifts and downshifts, but did not need to operate a clutch.

Some manufacturers offer an optional **dual-clutch transmission (DCT)**. This transmission uses a gear train similar to a manual transmission, but it has automatic shifts. Servos

move the synchronizers, two automatic clutches are alternately applied to transfer torque, and electronic controls operate the servos and clutches. There is a more complete description in a following section.

FREQUENTLY ASKED QUESTION

When Were Automatic Transmissions Developed?

Before the 1940s, most vehicles used a clutch and *manual*, also called a *standard*, transmission. A well-known exception was the Model T Ford, which used a planetary gear transmission; this transmission used foot pedals to change gears. The first automatic transmission was the Hydra-Matic Drive introduced on the 1940 Oldsmobile; this option cost an additional $57. Since the 1960s, most of the domestic (U.S.-produced) and import (foreign-produced) vehicles are equipped with automatic transmissions. Currently, over 90% of the vehicles manufactured and sold in the United States are equipped with an automatic transmission. Now, there is a variety of transmissions that shift automatically. ● **SEE FIGURE 3–3**.

FIGURE 3–1 (a) A RWD drivetrain uses a transmission to provide the necessary gear ratio and a single driveshaft to transfer power to the rear axle. (b) A FWD drivetrain uses a transaxle that combines the transmission, final drive, and differential. A driveshaft is used for each of the two front drive wheels.

Global Automatic Shifting Transmissions (Millions)		
Type	2009	2014
DCT	0.8	5
Hybrid Electric	0.4	1
CVT	2.5	4.5
6, 7, & 8 Speed	4	15
3, 4, & 5 Speed	14.5	11.5
Automated Manual	0.4	2

FIGURE 3–3 A variety of transmissions will shift automatically. Shown are the global production forecasts for years 2009 and 2014.

TRANSVERSE
(a)

LONGITUDINAL
(b)

FIGURE 3–2 (a) Transverse and (b) longitudinal mounted FWD drivetrains. Note that (b) can easily be redesigned to drive a shaft to the rear wheels of a 4WD or AWD vehicle.

FIGURE 3–4 Torque is a twisting force like that produced when you pull on a wrench.

3.2 TORQUE AND HORSEPOWER

Torque is a twisting force. ● **SEE FIGURE 3–4**. We exert torque on a nut or bolt when it is tightened or loosened. Torque must be exerted at the drive axle in order to turn the wheels and move the vehicle.

Torque is commonly measured in *foot-pounds (ft-lb), inch-pounds (in-lb)*, or *Newton-meters (N-m)*. A foot-pound of torque is created when we exert 1 pound of force on a wrench that is 1 foot long. Force (in pounds) times the wrench length (in feet) equals the torque in foot-pounds. One foot-pound of torque is equal to 12 inch-pounds, or 1.356 N-m.

Torque is a form of mechanical energy and, like all other forms of energy, it cannot be created or destroyed. It can and is transformed from one form of energy to another. A vehicle's engine converts the potential heat energy of gasoline into torque that rotates the flywheel. The transmission receives the torque and increases or decreases it according to the gear selected. The torque at the drive wheels is transformed into the kinetic energy of the moving vehicle.

Most of us are more familiar with the term *horsepower* than torque. Horsepower is a measurement of the energy developed in the engine. It is a product of torque and engine speed. To determine horsepower, an engineer uses a dynamometer to measure the amount of torque that the engine can produce at various points through its operating range. Then the formula

torque × revolutions per minute (RPM) / 5,252

is used to convert torque at a certain RPM into a horsepower reading. The various readings are then plotted into a curve, as shown in ● **FIGURE 3–5**. A typical horsepower and torque curve shows us that an engine does not produce very much torque at low RPM. The most usable torque is produced in the mid-RPM range. Torque decreases with an increase of horsepower at a higher RPM.

The torque from an engine can be increased or decreased through the use of gears, belts, and chains. ● **SEE FIGURE 3–6**. These are called *simple machines*. Gears are commonly used in transmissions. Transmissions of the future will probably make greater use of a belt with variable-size pulleys; this will be described later in this chapter. Gears, belts, or chains cannot increase horsepower; they can only modify its effect. A gear set

FIGURE 3–5 A typical automotive engine horsepower and torque chart. Note that the maximum horsepower (155) occurs at about 3400 RPM and that maximum torque occurs between 2000 and 2500 RPM. The RPM range and maximum power output will vary depending on engine size and design.

FIGURE 3–6 The common methods of transferring torque are belt, gear, and chain.

can increase torque, but it will decrease speed the same amount. A driver feels the torque increase when he or she steps on the throttle. The different ratios are felt when the transmission shifts.

The maximum torque that a transmission can handle is referred to as *torque capacity*. Larger engines and heavier vehicles require larger transmissions with greater torque capacity than lighter vehicles with smaller engines. A transmission's torque capacity is determined by the size and strength of its internal components. Some manufacturers identify their transmissions by torque capacity. ● **SEE FIGURE 3–7**.

3.3 GEAR RATIOS

Gear ratio refers to the relative size of two gears (a **gear set**). The ratio can be determined using either the diameter or the number of teeth on the two gears. A pair of gears of different size will have different numbers of teeth, and the number of teeth is directly related to the diameter of the gears. ● **SEE FIGURE 3–8**. A pair of

FIGURE 3–7 Transmissions and transaxles are designed with a torque capacity to match the engine with which it is used.

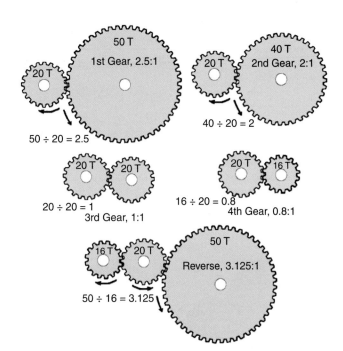

FIGURE 3–9 The gear ratio is determined by dividing the number of teeth on the driven (output) gear by the number of teeth on the driving (input) gear.

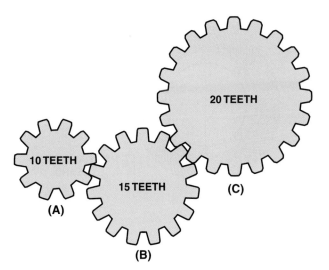

FIGURE 3–8 In a matched set of gears, the number of teeth on each gear is related to the diameter. Gear A is half the size of gear C and has half the number of teeth. Gear B is 1.5 times the diameter of gear A and has 1.5 times as many teeth.

gears has one gear that is turning the other, called the drive gear. The other gear is being turned and is called the driven gear. When the drive gear is smaller than the driven gear, the ratio between the two gears produces more torque but less speed at the output shaft, a process called **gear reduction**. When the drive gear is larger than the driven gear, this produces an **overdrive**. Overdrive increases the output speed but reduces the torque at the output shaft. The gear ratio is determined by dividing the driven gear by the driving gear.

The motoring public is attached to the term *overdrive*. It has helped to sell automobiles since the 1930s when a car with a three-speed transmission with overdrive was first introduced.

Gear ratios can be easily calculated. If, for example, a gear has 15 teeth and is meshed with a gear that has 30 teeth, the 30-tooth gear is exactly twice the diameter of the 15-tooth gear. If the 15-tooth gear is the input, drive gear, it has to rotate two

revolutions for each revolution of the 30-tooth-driven gear. This gear ratio is 2:1, and the output shaft has twice the torque and half the speed as the input shaft. ● SEE FIGURE 3–9. The first/left number of a ratio tells how far the driving gear turns for one revolution of the driven gear.

When calculating gear ratios, divide the number of teeth on the driven gear by the number of teeth on the drive gear:

gear ratio = driven gear / drive gear

If the drive gear has 12 teeth and the driven gear 36 teeth, the ratio will be 36 ÷ 12, or 3:1, a *reduction*, and the input shaft will turn three revolutions for each revolution of the output shaft. If we swap the driving and driven gears, then the ratio would be 12 ÷ 36, or 0.3:1, an *overdrive*. In this case, the input shaft would turn 0.3 turn for each revolution of the output shaft.

When power travels through more than one gear set, the overall ratio is determined by multiplying one gear ratio by the next. An example of this is the RWD, five-speed transmission. ● SEE FIGURE 3–10. A transmission with a first-gear ratio of 3.97:1 and a rear axle ratio of 3.55:1 produces an overall ratio of 3.97 × 3.55, or 14.09:1, in first gear. The engine will revolve 14.09 turns for each revolution of the drive axle. The overdrive ratio in fifth gear in this transmission is 2.84:1 (0.8:1 times the 3.55 rear-axle ratio). In fifth gear, the engine will revolve 2.84 turns for each drive axle revolution. This vehicle will have about one-fifth the torque it had in first gear but will be able to go about five times faster in fifth gear for each engine revolution.

Most gears have *external teeth*, where the teeth are cut around the outside of the gear. Some gears have the teeth cut on the inside of the gear's rim and are called **internal, ring,** or **annulus gears**. Most transmission gears are **helical gears** as compared with **spur gears**. ● SEE FIGURE 3–11. The teeth

Gear	Ratio	Final Drive Ratio	Overall Ratio	mph per 1000 rpm
I	3.97:1	3.55:1	14.09:1	4.5
II	2.34:1	3.55:1	8.31:1	9.2
III	1.46:1	3.55:1	5.18:1	14.7
IV	1:1	3.55:1	3.55:1	21.5
V	0.80:1	3.55:1	2.84:1	26.9

FIGURE 3–10 The forward gear ratios of a five-speed transmission are shown along with mph speed of the vehicle per 1000 RPM of engine speed. The overall gear ratio is determined by multiplying the transmission gear ratio by the final drive ratio. A final drive ratio of 3.55:1 and a first-gear ratio of 3.97:1 will produce an overall ratio of 14.09:1.

(a) Spur Gear Set   **(b)** Helical Gear Set

FIGURE 3–11 (a) The teeth of a spur gear are cut parallel to the shaft, which produces a straight pressure between the driving and driven gears. (b) The teeth of a helical gear are cut on a slant, which causes an axial or side thrust.

of a spur gear are cut in a straight line, parallel to the axis of the gear and the shaft on which the gear is mounted. The teeth of a helical gear are cut on a spiral helix shape; a helix spirals continuously if it is extended sideways. A spur gear is less expensive to make, but it is noisier and not as strong as a helical gear. A helical gear tends to be quieter and stronger, but it has a tendency to slide sideways, out of mesh. This is called *side thrust*. The other major gear type, a **bevel gear**, is used to transfer power between shafts that are not parallel. Bevel gears are made in both a **spur bevel** and **spiral bevel** form. ● SEE FIGURE 3–12. A **hypoid gear**, commonly used in drive axles, is a variation of the spiral bevel gear.

External gears reverse the direction of rotation when the drive gear transfers power to the driven gear. When it is necessary to change the ratio without changing the direction of power flow, an **idler gear** is added. An idler gear changes the rotational direction and does not affect the ratio. ● SEE FIGURE 3–13.

Some important rules to learn about gear sets are:

- Two mated external gears will always rotate in opposite directions.
- Mated internal and external gears will rotate in the same direction.
- An idler gear allows the drive and driven gears to rotate in the same direction.
- To find the ratio, divide the driven gear by the drive gear.
- When power transfers through an even number (two or four) of gears, the input and output gears will rotate in opposite directions.

A BEVEL GEARS

B SPIRAL BEVEL GEARS

C HYPOID GEARS   OFFSET

D WORM GEARS

FIGURE 3–12 The three major styles of bevel gears are (a) spur or plain bevel gears, (b) spiral bevel gears, and (c) hypoid gears. Note the differences in the shape of their teeth. A worm gear set (d) also transmits power between angled shafts. (*Reprinted with permission of General Motors*)

External gears
(a)

Idler gear

External gears
(b)

Internal gear

Internal and external
gears
(c)

FIGURE 3–13 External gears (a) rotate in opposite directions. An idler gear in an external gear set (b) changes the direction of rotation so the input and output gears turn in the same direction without changing the ratio. An internal and external gear set (c) rotate in the same direction.

- When power transfers through an uneven number (one, three, or five) of gears, the input and output gears will rotate in the same direction.
- To find the overall ratio of multiple gear sets, multiply the ratios of the gear sets.
- Two gears transferring power push away from each other in an action called gear separation. The gear separation force is proportional to the torque being transferred.
- All gear sets have **backlash** to prevent binding. ● **SEE FIGURE 3–14**.
- The smaller gear(s) in a gear set is often called a **pinion**.

Pitch diameter of driving gear

Point A   Point B   Point C

Backlash   Pitch diameter of driven gear

FIGURE 3–14 The pitch diameter is the effective diameter of a gear. Note how the contact points slide across the gear tooth. Backlash is the clearance on the nonloaded side of the gear tooth.

3.4 TRACTIVE FORCE

An engineer uses the term *tractive force* to describe the power in a vehicle's drivetrain. It is a product of the engine's torque multiplied by the gear ratio and can be plotted in a graph. ● **SEE FIGURE 3–15**. Note that a curve is shown for each of the transmission's gears. The second graph (b) shows driveshaft torque and engine speed relative to vehicle speed. It does not show engine RPM, but for each curve, the left end is plotted for 500 RPM and the right end for 4500 RPM. As shown, first gear produces the most torque and fourth gear the most speed.

When discussing vehicle speed, remember that the tire diameter will affect vehicle speed. The larger the tire, the faster the vehicle will go at a particular axle RPM. ● **SEE FIGURE 3–16**. You can use the following formula to determine the vehicle speed at a particular engine RPM or vice versa.

$$\text{Engine rpm} = \frac{\text{mph} \times \text{gear ratio} \times 336}{\text{tire diameter}}$$

$$\text{Vehicle rpm} = \frac{\text{rpm} \times \text{tire diameter}}{\text{gear ratio} \times 336}$$

3.5 MANUAL TRANSMISSION AND CLUTCH

A manual transmission, also called a standard transmission, has several sets of gears to produce the necessary gear ratios. ● **SEE FIGURE 3–17**. When a driver selects a gear, the power must flow through a specific path as it goes from the input shaft to the output shaft. A gear reduction or overdrive is produced when the power flows from the main drive gear on the input shaft to the cluster gear and from the cluster gear to a driven gear on the output shaft. ● **SEE FIGURE 3–18**. The cluster gear is also called a counter gear. The actual shift is made by moving

(a)

GEAR RATIOS— FIRST-2.4:1
SECOND-1.47:1
THIRD-1:1
FOURTH-0.67:1
FINAL DRIVE RATIO-3.27:1
TIRE SIZE-P215165SR-15

(b)

FIGURE 3–15 (a) Tractive force is determined by multiplying engine torque times the gear ratio. Note how it is greatest in first gear. (b) This chart shows the same curves related to engine and vehicle speed. The curve is based on a typical 5-liter V8 engine.

FIGURE 3–16 The speed of a vehicle is determined by the diameter of the drive tires and how fast the tires are turned.

FIGURE 3–17 A standard transmission provides several gear ratios and a method to shift them.

FIGURE 3–18 Power flows through each of the gear ranges of a five-speed, RWD, standard transmission. Note that the synchronizer sleeves are used to shift the power flow. (*Courtesy of Chrysler Corporation*)

(a)

(b)

FIGURE 3–19 (a) The shift fork slides the synchronizer sleeve into mesh with the dog teeth of the desired gear. This allows torque to be transferred between the speed gear and the synchronizer hub. (b) An exploded view of a synchronizer assembly shows all of the parts. (Figure (a) *Courtesy of Chrysler Corporation*)

Clutch Engaged – The flattened diaphragm spring pushes against the pressure plate.

(a)

Clutch Disengaged – Release bearing flexes the diaphragm spring and frees the clutch disc.

(b)

FIGURE 3–20 (a) A clutch cover (pressure plate assembly) is bolted onto the flywheel with the clutch disc between them. The release bearing and fork provide a method to release the clutch. (b) When the clutch is engaged, the disc is squeezed against the flywheel by the pressure plate. Releasing the clutch separates the disc from the flywheel and pressure plate.

a **synchronizer sleeve** to couple the desired driven gear to the **synchronizer hub** and the output shaft. ● **SEE FIGURE 3–19.** If the synchronizer assembly is on the cluster gear, the synchronizer will couple the drive gear to the cluster gear.

A shift cannot be made while the power is flowing in a manual transmission. The power flow must be interrupted or disengaged by depressing the clutch pedal. Pushing the clutch pedal releases the pressure on the clutch disc and disengages the power flow from the engine. ● **SEE FIGURE 3–20.** This allows the transmission gear being engaged to match the speed of the synchronizer sleeve during the shift, a process sometimes called a *nonpower* shift. The clutch is also needed so the transmission can be shifted from neutral to low or reverse.

A FWD transaxle is slightly different from a RWD unit in that power is always transferred through three or more shafts that are parallel to each other. ● **SEE FIGURE 3–21.** The input comes from the clutch to the first/input shaft. The second (main/intermediate) shaft transfers power through the pinion gear of the *final drive*. The third shaft is the ring gear of the final drive and the differential. The various transmission ratios are the different power paths between the first and second shafts. Like a RWD transmission, a synchronizer assembly is used to produce smooth shifts.

Unless it is important to be specific, most technicians will use the term *transmission* when referring to the transmission portion of a transaxle. Also, the front of a transmission

FIGURE 3–21 A FWD transaxle. Note that it combines a five-speed transmission with the final drive gears and differential. (*Courtesy of Chrysler Corporation*)

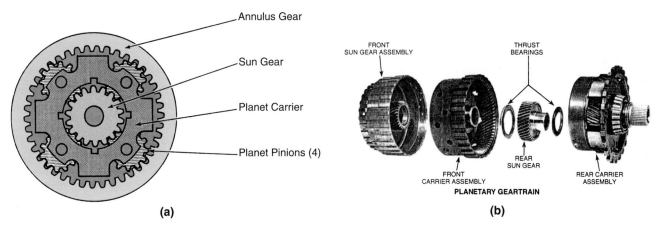

(a) (b)

FIGURE 3–22 (a) A simple planetary gear set is a combination of a sun gear, a planet carrier with a group of planet pinion gears, and an annulus/ring gear. (b) A transmission planetary gear train contains a combination of complex gear sets. (*Courtesy of Chrysler Corporation*)

or transaxle is the end closest to the engine, even though the engine might be mounted in a transverse or sideways position.

3.6 SIMPLE PLANETARY GEAR SETS

A **planetary gear set** is a combination of a **sun gear**, *ring gear*, and a *planet carrier* with two or more *planet gears/pinions*. The ring gear, also called an annulus gear, is an internal gear. All the other gears are external gears. The carrier holds the planet gears (also called *pinions*) in position and allows each of these gears to rotate on their own axis in the carrier. ● **SEE FIGURE 3–22.** When the gear set is assembled, the sun gear is in the center and meshed with the planet gears, which are located around it, somewhat like the planets in our solar system. The ring gear is meshed around the outside of the planet gears.

The three main members of the planetary gear set—the sun gear, ring gear, and planet carrier—have two possible actions: They can rotate or stand still.

The planet gears/pinions have the following three possible actions. ● **SEE ALSO FIGURE 3–23.**

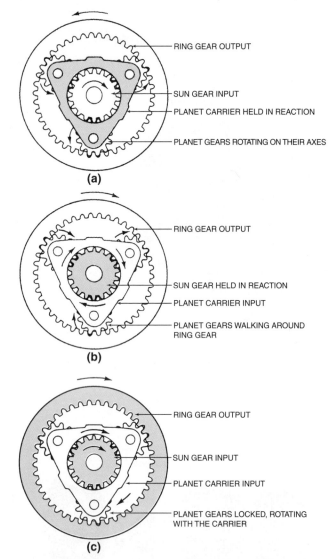

FIGURE 3–23 (a) If the planet carrier is held with the sun gear rotating, the planet gears simply rotate in the carrier and act as idler gears between the sun and ring gears. (b) If the sun or ring is held, the planet gears will walk around that stationary gear; they rotate on their shafts as the carrier rotates. (c) If two parts are driven and no parts are held, the planet gears are stationary on their shafts, and the whole assembly rotates as a unit.

1. They can rotate on their shafts in a stationary carrier and act like idler gears.

2. They can rotate on their shafts in a rotating carrier; the planet gears are *walking*.

3. They can stand still on their shafts and rotate with the carrier.

The planet gears can walk around the outside of a stationary sun or the inside of a stationary ring gear. The rotating carrier forces the planet gears to walk around the stationary sun or ring gear, which forces the planet gears to rotate on their shafts. This, in turn, will force the third member of the gear set to rotate.

Planetary gear sets are arranged so power enters one of the members and leaves through one of the other members while the third member is held stationary in reaction. One of the basic physical laws states that for every action, there is an equal and opposite reaction. In a gear set, the action is usually an increase in torque; the reaction is an equal amount of torque that tries to turn the gear box in a reverse direction. For example, watch a short-wheelbase truck-tractor pull a heavy trailer from a dead stop. The action needed is to turn the drive wheels and move the truck; the reaction is a lifting of the frame at the left front wheel. The front of the truck lifts in reaction to the drive axle torque, and the left side lifts in reaction to the driveshaft torque. Getting back to the planetary gear set, one of the three members has to be held stationary in reaction to obtain either the torque or speed increase in the gear box. There cannot be a ratio change without a reaction member.

Power flow through a planetary gear set is controlled by clutches, bands, and one-way clutches. One or more clutches will control the power coming to a planetary member and one or more reaction members can hold a gear set member stationary. The third planetary member will be the output. One simple planetary gear set can produce one of the following:

- A neutral if either the input clutch or reaction member is not applied
- A 1:1, direct-drive ratio if two gear set members are driven
- Two reduction ratios
- Two overdrive ratios
- Two reverse ratios, one a reduction and one an overdrive

The reduction, overdrive, and reverse ratios will require one driving member, one output member, and one reaction member in the gear set. ● **SEE FIGURE 3–24.**

Planetary gear sets offer several advantages over conventional gear sets. Because of the multiple planet gears, there is more than one gear transferring power, so the torque load is spread over several gear teeth. Because of this, planetary gear sets are quieter and stronger. Also, any gear separation forces (as gears transfer power, they tend to push away from each other) are contained within the ring gear, preventing this load from being transmitted to the transmission case. This allows the transmission case to be thinner and therefore lighter. Another advantage is the small relative size of the planetary gear set. Conventional gears are normally side by side, and for a 2:1 gear ratio, one gear has to be twice the size of the other. A planetary gear set can easily produce this same ratio in a smaller package. Also, planetary gear sets are in constant mesh; no coupling or uncoupling of the gears is required.

As illustrated in Figure 3–24, there can be seven possible power flow conditions and a neutral in a planetary gear set. A 1:1 ratio occurs if you drive any two members without a reaction member. Neutral occurs if there is no driving member or no reaction member. This effectively stops the power flow for the neutral condition. In the other six power flows, there is:

- One driving or input member
- One driven or output member
- One stationary or *reaction* member

(a) Neutral

No Drive Member

(d) Reduction, 1.43:1

$$\frac{18 + 42}{42} = 1.43$$

(g) Overdrive, 0.7:1

$$\frac{42}{18 + 42} = 0.7$$

Note: Ring gear has 42 teeth,
Sun gear has 18 teeth

Input Member:
Reaction Member:
Output Member:

(b) Direct Drive, 1:1

Two Drive Members

(e) Reverse, 2.33:1

$$42 \div 18 = 2.33$$

(h) Reverse, 0.43:1

$$18 \div 42 = 0.43$$

(c) Reduction, 3.33:1

$$\frac{18 + 42}{18} = 3.33$$

(f) Overdrive, 0.3:1

$$\frac{18}{18 + 42} = 0.33$$

(i) Neutral

No Reaction Member

FIGURE 3–24 Nine possible modes of operation for a simple planetary gear set. In all cases, solid black indicates the output member, the input is gray, and the output is blue.

3.7 COMPOUND PLANETARY GEAR SETS

Most automatic transmissions use a more complicated *compound planetary gear set* that combines a simple planetary gear set with portions of one or more planetary gear sets in such a way that three or more gear ratios are possible. In many four-speed transmissions, a simple planetary gear set is used along with a compound set to provide an additional overdrive or reduction ratio.

The most common compound planetary gear set used in three-speed transmissions is known as the *Simpson gear train*, named after its designer, Howard Simpson. This gear set uses one common sun gear with two ring gears and two planet carriers. ● **SEE FIGURE 3–25**. The rear ring gear and the front

carrier are attached to the output shaft, so they are the driven or output members. Three inputs are possible: either (1) the front ring gear, (2) the sun gear, or (3) both. Also, two reaction members are possible: either (1) the sun gear or (2) the rear carrier. In some transmissions, a stepped sun gear of two sizes is used. This allows lower first- and second-gear ratios. We will describe the power flow through this gear set as well as other common gear set arrangements in more detail in Chapter 5.

3.8 CONTROL DEVICES

Power flow through a gear set is accomplished by the *control devices*: the **clutches**, **bands**, and **one-way clutches**. They are also called *apply devices*. A gear set has several paths

FIGURE 3–25 A cutaway and an exploded view of a Simpson gear train. Note that the gear set uses a double sun gear with two carriers and ring gears. The two clutches allow either the forward ring gear or the sun gear to be driven. The two bands allow either the sun gear or the rear carrier to be held in reaction. The one-way clutch will keep the rear carrier from turning counterclockwise. (*Courtesy of Chrysler Corporation*)

for power flow, and each path provides a different gear ratio. ● **SEE FIGURE 3–26.** The control devices determine the power flow path through the gear set.

A control device is either a driving or a reaction member. A driving member connects two rotating parts and completes a path so power can transfer from one unit to another. A reaction member holds one of the gear set members from rotating so the power flow can occur. Because friction-type clutches and bands are used, the power flow does not have to be interrupted during a shift. This allows powered shifts to be made, and the drive wheels will have a constant flow of power during a shift.

Driving devices are multiple-disc clutches that connect the transmission's input shaft to the gear set input member. These clutches are applied by **hydraulic** force. This type of clutch is made up of plates that are lined with friction material and unlined steel plates. The plates are stacked in an alternating fashion, with half of the plates splined to the input and the other half splined to the planetary member. ● **SEE FIGURE 3–27**. When oil pressure is applied to the hydraulic piston, the clutch pack is squeezed together, applying the clutch. ● **SEE FIGURE 3–28**. When the oil pressure is released, a return spring pushes the piston away from the clutch pack, releasing the clutch. A reaction device can be a band, a one-way clutch, or a multiple-disc clutch. Some transmission manufacturers call their reaction members *brakes* because they stop a gear set member from turning. A band is also applied by hydraulic pressure and released by a spring or hydraulic pressure.

A band is a metal strap that is lined with friction material and wraps around a drum. ● **SEE FIGURE 3–29**. When a band is applied, it is tightened around the drum, bringing it to a stop; and when released, it allows the drum to rotate. The hydraulic device that applies a band is commonly called a **servo**; the servo is a hydraulic piston assembly.

A reaction clutch resembles a driving clutch except the unlined set of plates is connected to the transmission case. When it applies, the gear set member that it connects to will come to a stop.

FIGURE 3–26 A schematic view of a modern, six-speed, RWD transmission. It shows three driving clutches (C1, C2, C3) and two holding clutches (B1, B2) plus a one-way clutch (F1).

FIGURE 3–27 A multiple-disc clutch combines lined friction discs and unlined steel plates. (*Courtesy of Toyota Motor Sales USA, Inc.*)

FIGURE 3–29 A band is applied when fluid pressure forces the piston and rod inward (right). When the pressure is released, a spring pushes the piston back (left). (*Courtesy of Toyota Motor Sales USA, Inc.*)

FIGURE 3–28 Fluid pressure forces the piston against the clutch pack to apply a clutch (left). When the fluid pressure is released, the return springs push the piston away from the clutch pack (right). (*Courtesy of Toyota Motor Sales USA, Inc.*)

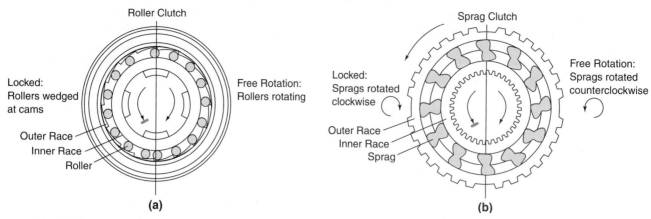

FIGURE 3–30 Two types of one-way clutches. (a) The roller clutch will release if the inner race turns clockwise and lock up if it turns counterclockwise. (b) The sprag clutch will operate in the same manner.

A one-way clutch is a device that allows rotation in only one direction. One-way clutches are either *roller clutches, sprag clutches*, or *mechanical diodes*. ● **SEE FIGURE 3–30**.

Hydraulic and electronically operated valves control the control devices. By the time we combine the gear set, control devices, and hydraulic and electronic controls, the transmission appears rather complex. After studying each of these transmission systems, much of the complexity and mystery will disappear.

3.9 TRANSMISSION HYDRAULICS

As soon as the engine starts, a *pump* driven by the torque converter sends fluid into the transmission's *hydraulic* passages. Fluid is pumped from the sump in the transmission pan into the hydraulic circuit where the pressure and flow is controlled by the valve body. ● **SEE FIGURE 3–31**. This fluid pressure is used to:

- Apply the clutches and bands
- Maintain a full torque converter so it can transmit power
- Lubricate and cool the internal parts of the transmission

A transmission has numerous passages that allow fluid to flow to the varied locations. ● **SEE FIGURE 3–32**.

The valve body contains most of the transmission's control valves. Sometimes, there are one or more valves elsewhere. The major valves used in nonelectronic transmissions are as follows:

- **Manual valve.** Operated by the shift linkage and used to select automatic forward gear ranges, nonautomatic forward gear ranges (manual first, second, etc.), reverse, as well as park and neutral.
- **Pressure regulator.** Controls fluid pressure.
- **Throttle or modulator valve.** Tailors the pressure regulator to the operation of the transmission and either delays upshifts or forces downshifts as the throttle is opened.

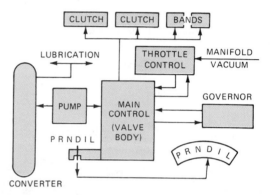

FIGURE 3–31 A simplified hydraulic control circuit for a nonelectronic transmission. The main control unit (valve body) sends oil pressure to the clutches and bands to control the shifts. It uses signals from the manual shift lever, governor, and throttle valve.

FIGURE 3–32 The end of this transmission case shows most of the fluid passages. These connect the valve body to passages in the case.

- **Governor.** Operated by the output shaft speed; causes upshifts.
- **Shift valves.** One for each shift; controls upshifts and downshifts.

FIGURE 3–33 The electronic controls for an electronic transmission include input sensor signals from the engine and the transmission to the PCM and output devices in the transmission. The test connector is the diagnostic link used to diagnose transmission problems.

- **Shift modifier valves.** Change the quality and timing of an upshift or downshift to ensure proper operation.

- **Torque converter clutch valve.** Controls the apply and release of the torque converter clutch.

Modern transmissions use electronic controls to improve shift timing and quality and to integrate transmission operation more closely with engine operation. Some vehicles electronically reduce engine torque during shifts to smooth out the shifts and increase transmission life. Electronic controls include *electronic sensors* that provide input to an *electronic control module (ECM)*, which operates *solenoids* inside the transmission that control hydraulic fluid flow. ● **SEE FIGURE 3–33**. Transmission electronics is described more completely in Chapter 8.

In reality, the hydraulic system is rather complex. It will be discussed more thoroughly in Chapters 6 and 7. A competent service technician has a good understanding of what the various valves do and what the fluid pressures should be at a specific location in a given gear range. The technician will often refer to a hydraulic diagram when trying to solve a problem. Many automatic transmission problems are caused by a loss of fluid pressure, sticky control valves, or faulty electronic controls.

3.10 TORQUE CONVERTERS

Most automatic transmissions use a **torque converter** to transfer power from the engine to the transmission. ● **SEE FIGURE 3–34**. It serves as an automatic fluid clutch as well as converting torque (as its name implies). It can multiply torque much like a gear set.

A torque converter is normally made up of four members: an *impeller*, a *turbine*, a *stator*, and a *clutch plate*. Early torque converters were three-member units with no clutch. To operate properly, it must be completely filled with transmission fluid. The impeller, also called a *pump*, is built into the housing that connects to the engine crankshaft. When the engine runs, the impeller produces fluid flow inside the converter.

The turbine is splined to the transmission input shaft. Oil flowing from the impeller causes the turbine to rotate and drive the transmission. The stator is splined to the *stator support*, a stationary shaft extending from the transmission case. In some transmissions the stator can rotate slightly to provide an engine load signal. A one-way clutch connects the stator to the stator

FIGURE 3–34 The torque converter transfers power from the engine to the transmission input shaft. It serves as an automatic clutch and multiplies torque during periods of engine load. This converter also has a clutch plate for the torque converter clutch.

FIGURE 3–35 A pair of helical gears provides the final drive reduction. The final drive ring gear is attached to the differential assembly. (*Courtesy of Chrysler Corporation*)

3.11 TRANSAXLE FINAL DRIVE AND DIFFERENTIAL

support so the stator can rotate in only one direction. The stator changes the direction of the fluid flow from the turbine back to the impeller.

At slow engine speeds, fluid flow inside the converter is not strong enough to rotate the turbine and the transmission input shaft. As the throttle is opened and engine speed increases, fluid flow becomes strong enough to rotate the turbine and move the vehicle. At this time, the fluid leaving the turbine will bounce back, but the stator will redirect the flow in the proper direction and increase the flow through the impeller. During slow turbine speeds, the stator redirects and increases the force of the fluid flow. This has the effect of increasing the torque, producing a ratio of about 2:1.

In a torque converter all of the power is transferred by fluid. Because of this, it always has some slippage; this slippage reduces the efficiency and fuel mileage. Modern torque converters have an internal clutch, called the **torque converter clutch (TCC);** it will produce torque converter lockup to eliminate slipping during cruising conditions. A TCC improves fuel mileage about 1 to 3 miles per gallon. Torque converter operation will be described in more detail in Chapter 9.

The difference between a transmission and a transaxle is the **final drive** unit and the output shafts. A RWD transmission has a single output shaft that connects to the driveshaft and rear-axle assembly. The differential of a transaxle has two output shafts, one for each front wheel. Also, the final drive gear reduction and the differential must fit into the area between the transmission's output and the two driveshafts.

The final drive is the gear reduction that determines the overall tractive force of the vehicle. It also determines the engine operating RPM at cruising speed. In an RWD vehicle, the final drive gears are the *ring* and *pinion* located in the rear axle. In an FWD vehicle, the ring and pinion are located inside the transaxle. The drive pinion gear is mounted on either the transmission mainshaft or a transfer shaft. The ring gear is mounted on the *differential case*, sometimes called a *carrier*. Helical gears are normally used in transverse-mounted transaxles because the transmission shaft is parallel to the differential. ● **SEE FIGURE 3–35.** Some transaxles use a planetary gear set to produce the final drive reduction. ● **SEE FIGURE 3–36.** The planetary members are arranged so the following occurs.

- The output shaft of the transmission drives a sun gear that is the input to the final drive.

9225   689   274   406   9746   873   536   6270   106   39   4083   588

FIGURE 3–36 Some transaxles use a planetary gear set for the final drive reduction. Part 274 is the internal gear (stationary), 536 is the sun gear (input), and 39 is the planet carrier (output). The carrier also contains the differential gears. (*Courtesy of Slauson Transmission Parts, www.slauson.com*)

FIGURE 3–37 Normally, an equal load from each wheel keeps the differential pinion gears stationary on their shaft (top). An equal load will cause the differential pinion gears to rotate and drive the axle shafts at unequal speeds (bottom).

- The ring gear is secured into the transmission case so it is the reaction member.
- The planet carrier is the output member and doubles as the differential case.

Longitudinal-mounted transaxles use either spiral bevel or hypoid final drive gears. The smaller final drive pinion gear driving the larger ring gear provides the desired gear reduction.

A **differential** is a device that allows the axle shafts to rotate at different speeds. When a vehicle turns a corner, the outer tires must travel farther and therefore must go faster than the inner tires. Most differentials use a set of bevel gears, as shown in ● **FIGURE 3–37**. The differential case is made with a differential pinion shaft running across it; this shaft also passes through a pair of differential pinion gears with the gears free to turn on the shaft. A pair of differential side gears is meshed with both differential pinions. One of these side gears is attached to each drive wheel through a driveshaft or drive axle.

When the vehicle is going straight ahead, the equal load of each side gear prevents rotation of the pinion gears on their shaft. The entire differential assembly rotates as a unit, and both wheels revolve at the same speed. When the vehicle turns a corner, one side gear rotates slower than the differential case. When this occurs, the pinion gears rotate on their shaft while walking around the slower axle side gear, causing the other side gear to rotate faster than the case. Both drive wheels receive the same torque, but they will rotate at different speeds.

3.12 FOUR-WHEEL DRIVE

Four-wheel drive (4WD) drivetrains can be based on any of the FWD or RWD engine-transmission variations. ● **SEE FIGURE 3–38**. 4WD vehicles are usually *part-time 4WD*, where the driver performs the shift between 2WD and 4WD. 2WD is used on a street with good traction, and 4WD is used in poor-traction conditions such as mud, sand, snow, or ice. These conditions usually cause enough tire slippage so that the speed difference between the front and rear tires is not a problem.

Full-time 4WD is also called all-wheel drive (AWD). Driving all of the wheels of a vehicle creates a few problems if driving on hard surfaces. One of the greatest is that all of the wheels rotate at different speeds when a vehicle turns corners (● **SEE FIGURE 3–39**), because each of the wheels travels around a circle that has a different radius and circumference. Vehicles normally drive only two wheels, and the differential in the drive axle provides for the speed difference between the inner and outer drive wheels. Vehicles with AWD need three differentials: one between the front and rear driveshafts and one in each of the front and rear drive axles between the two axle shafts. The center, or *interaxle*, differential allows the front wheels to travel faster than the rear wheels on corners.

AWD becomes more complex because the power that leaves the transmission must first go to the center differential and then split to the front and rear axles. Some center differentials are torque biasing: They have the ability to split the torque unequally and send more torque to the rear axle. Most center differentials include a lockout feature so both front and rear axles can be driven equally. This ensures that at least one front tire and one rear tire will be driven, and it is only used in poor-traction conditions.

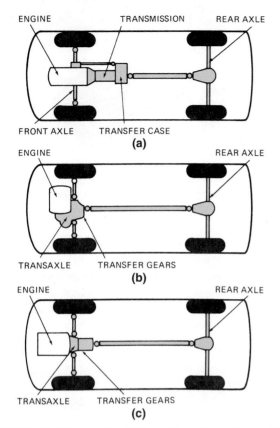

FIGURE 3–38 Three major 4WD configurations. The traditional form (a) uses a transfer case to split the torque for the front and rear drive axles. Both (b) and (c) are typical AWD configurations.

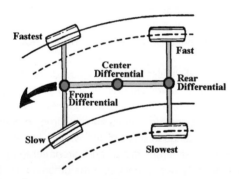

FIGURE 3–39 When a vehicle turns a corner, the front wheels must go faster than the rear, and the outside wheels must turn faster than the inside wheels.

FIGURE 3–40 The 4WD version of an RWD transmission often replaces the extension housing with an adapter and the transfer case.

FIGURE 3–41 This AWD transaxle has an output shaft to drive the rear wheels (at left). The interaxle differential is between the transfer gears for the rear and those that send power to the front final drive gears and differential. (*Courtesy of ZF Group North American Operations*)

The 4WD version of an RWD automatic transmission is basically the same as the transmission used in 2WD vehicles. A transfer case is attached to the rear of the transmission case by omitting the extension housing and using a shortened transmission output shaft. ● SEE FIGURE 3–40. The transfer case contains the mechanism to allow engagement and disengagement of 4WD and also the universal joint connection for the driveshaft to the front and rear drive axles. Gears or a chain and sprockets transfer the power flow to the front driveshaft.

There are two 4WD/AWD versions based on FWD vehicles, and these depend on the direction that the transmission shafts run. A few FWD/AWD vehicles use an engine and transmission that are positioned lengthwise in the vehicle. This makes it relatively easy to install a transfer clutch in the rear of the transmission. ● SEE FIGURE 3–41. The clutch can operate an output shaft that runs out the back of the transmission to connect with the driveshaft for the rear axle.

When the engine and transmission are mounted in a transverse position, 4WD becomes more complicated. The power flow must be turned 90 degrees to travel down the vehicle before turning another 90 degrees at the rear axle. The *power transfer unit* for a transverse transaxle must include a pair of bevel gears in order to change the direction of power flow. ● SEE FIGURE 3–42. The transfer case also includes a coupler to engage and disengage the power flow to the rear axle.

FIGURE 3–42 This transaxle has an output shaft for each of the front wheels plus a dog clutch and transfer gears to drive a rear axle (lower right).

FIGURE 3–43 This four-speed, automatic transaxle combines helical gears, as in a standard transmission, with four multiple-disc clutches and a torque converter. (*Courtesy of American Honda Motor Company*)

3.13 NONPLANETARY GEAR AUTOMATIC TRANSMISSIONS

3.13.1 AUTOMATIC LAYSHAFT TRANSMISSIONS
Honda and early Saturn automatic transmissions do not use planetary gear sets. The gear train used is much like that of a standard transmission with the gears in constant mesh. ● SEE

FIGURE 3–43. The major difference is that the synchronizer assemblies are replaced with multidisc clutches. The fully automatic shifts are made when the multiple-disc clutch for each gear is engaged. ● SEE FIGURE 3–44. The shifts are accomplished by hydraulic pressure using a hydraulic system like that of other automatic transmissions. Also like other automatic transmissions, a torque converter is used between the transmission and engine.

3.13.2 DUAL-CLUTCH TRANSMISSIONS
A dual-clutch transmission is essentially an automatically controlled manual

	1st CLUTCH	2nd CLUTCH	3rd CLUTCH	4th CLUTCH	SPRAG CLUTCH
DRIVE 1	APPLIED	RELEASED	RELEASED	RELEASED	ON
DRIVE 2	APPLIED	APPLIED	RELEASED	RELEASED	OFF
DRIVE 3	APPLIED	RELEASED	APPLIED	RELEASED	OFF
DRIVE 4	APPLIED	RELEASED	RELEASED	APPLIED	OFF
MANUAL 2	RELEASED	APPLIED	RELEASED	RELEASED	OFF
REVERSE	RELEASED	RELEASED	RELEASED	APPLIED	OFF

Power Flow

FIGURE 3–44 The power flows through this four-speed HondaMatic are controlled by applying the different clutches. (*Courtesy of American Honda Motor Company*)

transmission that uses two clutches and two countershafts. Gear section is determined by which clutch is applied. The clutches are applied, one at a time, to transfer power to the appropriate gear set. The shifts can occur very rapidly, being controlled by how fast the two clutches can be applied and released. This transmission is presently available in some models of the Audi TT and Volkswagen Golf and is called a direct-shift gearbox (DSG).

The gear arrangement shown in ● **FIGURE 3–45** illustrates how the odd-numbered gears, 1–3 and 5, are driven by clutch #1. The even-numbered gears, 2–4 and 6-reverse are driven by clutch #2. The two clutches are built into one DualTronic™ clutch assembly. Vehicle movement begins when the 1–3 synchronizer is shifted to first gear and clutch #1 is applied. The 2–4 synchronizer is then shifted into second gear by a hydraulic servo. The 1–2 upshift will occur when clutch #1 is released and clutch #2 is applied. The remaining upshifts occur in the same manner, with the synchronizer shifted early and the actual shift occurring when the clutches are cycled.

The driver can control the automatic operation by using a floor-mounted shifter or one of a pair of paddles mounted in front of the steering wheel. Clutches #1 and #2 are applied by hydraulic pressure, similar to automatic transmission clutches. As mentioned, the synchronizer sleeves are shifted by hydraulic servos. An electronic control module controls the hydraulic flow to the clutches and servos. The control module contains the hydraulic valve body, solenoids, a microprocessor, and the external electrical connectors. Sensors monitor shift lever position, upshift and downshift paddles, engine RPM, and fluid temperatures. The control module uses the information from these sensors to determine the proper clutch and servo operation.

3.13.3 CONTINUOUSLY VARIABLE TRANSMISSION

In some vehicles, the planetary gear transmission is replaced by a simpler **continuously variable transmission (CVT)**.

At this time, the CVT is used in small and midsize vehicles. It uses a metal V-belt and two variable-size pulleys to produce continuous gear ratios. ● **SEE FIGURE 3–46**. This transmission does not shift gears; the ratio gradually changes from the lowest ratio at a stop to the highest ratio for cruising speeds. While accelerating, the engine runs at almost a constant speed as the

(a)

(b)

(c)

FIGURE 3–45 (a) A dual-clutch transmission, also called an *automated manual transmission* (*AMT*), uses two clutches. (b) One of them drives the odd-numbered gears, and the other drives the even-numbered gears. (c) The actuators that apply the clutches and shift the synchronizers are operated by a control module.

FIGURE 3–46 A continuously variable transmission (CVT) uses a steel belt to transfer power from the drive pulley to the driven pulley. The two pulleys change effective diameter to obtain the various gear ratios. (*Courtesy of ZF Group North American Operations*)

transmission varies the ratio. For low gear, a small input pulley drives a large output pulley. ● **SEE FIGURE 3–47**. As the vehicle speed increases, the diameter of the input pulley becomes larger while the output pulley diameter becomes smaller. This is accomplished by moving the sides of each pulley together or apart. At cruising speeds (high gear), a large input pulley drives a small output pulley. Hydraulic controls are used to change the pulley diameter in response to throttle position (vehicle load) and output shaft speed (vehicle speed). A CVT uses an electronic magnetic clutch or a torque converter so the vehicle can be stopped and a planetary gear set for reverse.

3.14 HYBRID DRIVE SYSTEM

Hybrid drive systems were developed to help meet the demands for lower exhaust emissions and improved fuel economy. Hybrid drive combines an internal combustion engine, either gasoline or diesel, with an electric motor. An internal combustion engine is most efficient if it can be designed to run at a constant operating speed. Electrical-powered vehicles have a very limited operating range because they rely on batteries that need recharging. Combining the high torque at low RPM of an electric motor with the optimized, constant-speed, internal combustion engine to generate electricity produces a vehicle that has smooth, quiet acceleration with very low emissions.

Optimizing an internal combustion engine to constant RPM operation allows improvement of the following characteristics.

- Reduced strength and weight of the internal moving components

(a) Drive Pulley: Wide/Small Diameter

Driven Pulley: Narrow/Large Diameter
Low Ratio, about 2.5:1

(b) Drive Pulley: Narrow/Large Diameter

Driven Pulley: Wide/Small Diameter
High Ratio, about 0.5:1

FIGURE 3–47 CVTs in low (a) and high (b) ratios. The ratio changes to high ratio because the drive pulley squeezes together, moving it to maximum diameter; the driven pulley will spread apart for minimum diameter. When the vehicle is at rest, the drive pulley will be spread apart and the driven pulley will be squeezed together.

- Optimized air-fuel mixture
- Accurate ignition spark advance
- Variable intake and exhaust valve timing
- Reduced engine idling

Electric vehicles offer advantages in efficiency, but they have severely limited operating ranges, about 40 to 80 miles. Some electric vehicles can extend the operating range by using **regenerative** braking. This system slows the vehicle by converting the kinetic energy of the moving vehicle into electricity to recharge the batteries. A conventional brake system wastes this energy by converting it to heat and then dissipating the heat to air moving past the brakes.

General Motors recently introduced an electric vehicle that utilizes an engine to recharge the batteries as they run low. While parked, the vehicle is plugged into a household electrical outlet to recharge the batteries. With the batteries charged, it will run on the electric motor for the first 40 miles, then, as needed, the engine will start to recharge the batteries. This is an electric vehicle since the engine cannot mechanically drive the vehicle. This system should have a substantial impact on emissions and fuel economy since 78% of commuters drive less than 40 miles.

Another fuel-saving feature is called *idle-stop*. This feature saves the fuel the engine would normally use while waiting at a stoplight. When the vehicle comes to a stop with the driver's foot on the brake, the engine will shut off. When the driver depresses the accelerator, the electric motor will start the vehicle moving and restart the engine to accelerate.

Hybrid vehicles can be grouped into two categories; mild and true hybrid. Mild hybrids provide minimal electrical power to assist the internal combustion engine and recharge the batteries with regenerative braking and use idle-stop technology. True hybrids provide regenerative braking, idle-stop technology, engine generator for battery charging, and electric power to propel the vehicle.

3.14.1 HONDA HYBRID
Honda hybrid vehicles use a gasoline engine that has advanced variable valve timing coupled to a CVT or five-speed automatic transmission. This

FIGURE 3–48 The assist motor is sandwiched between the engine and the transmission.

system, called Integrated Motor Assist (IMA), uses an electric assist motor that is sandwiched between the engine and transmission. ● **SEE FIGURE 3–48.** As the name implies, the electric motor is used to assist the engine. When the vehicle is stationary the engine is off. During startup and acceleration the engine starts and powers the vehicle with the assist of the electric motor. Rapid acceleration will cause the engine to change valve timing to increase the engine's power, and the electric motor to provide additional assist. Under very light loads the engine will shut off and the electric motor will provide the power. While decelerating, the batteries are recharged by braking regeneration.

3.14.2 TOYOTA HYBRID
The Toyota hybrid drive system combines an internal combustion engine and an electric motor to improve economy and reduce emissions. This drive system uses the electric motor as the primary driving force. The gasoline engine powers a generator that produces electricity for the electric motor and charges the batteries, and acts as a supplementary driving force during acceleration. ● **SEE FIGURE 3–49.** The electric motor can be coupled directly to the

FIGURE 3–49 This hybrid drive system (HDS) combines a gasoline engine, an electric motor, and a generator with some rather complex electronic controls. The vehicle can be powered by the electric motor along with the engine as needed. The generator will help stop the vehicle using regenerative braking.

(a) Electric Motor

FIGURE 3–50 In this hybrid vehicle drivetrain, the engine drives the sun gear; motor/generator (M/G) A can drive or hold the carrier; and M/G B can drive the ring gear and the vehicle.

(b) Generator   **(c)** Power Split Device

FIGURE 3–51 (a) This HDS motor uses 274 volts to produce 44 horsepower. (b) The generator can be driven by the engine when electricity is needed or the drive wheels during braking. (c) The power split device allows the engine to drive either the rear wheels or the generator.

drive wheels through a set of reduction gears. Electric motors develop enough low-speed torque that a normal transmission is not required. Changing the polarity to the motor causes it to run backward for reverse. During deceleration, this motor is converted electrically to become a generator for regenerative braking to charge the batteries. The electric motor can also be electrically held stationary.

A large battery pack is required to store the electrical energy. Thirty-eight individual battery modules are wired in series for an operating voltage of 274 volts. Caution should be exercised with these systems, as the voltage is high enough to cause a fatal shock.

Toyota hybrid transaxles do not change gear ratios by shifting gears within the transmission.

A power divider, also called a power split device, is used to couple the engine to both the generator and the drivetrain to the wheels. ● **SEE FIGURE 3–50**. The power split device is a simple planetary gear set. The engine is connected to the planet carrier, the sun gear is connected to the generator, and the ring gear is connected to the drivetrain. ● **SEE FIGURE 3–51**. The power split device acts like a type of differential so the engine can run at its designed speed and add power to the drivetrain that might be turning at various speeds. The generator can operate at any speed, and its load can be adjusted electronically so the engine power can be split as needed for vehicle operation.

A complex set of electronic controls uses the shift lever position, accelerator position, and brake pedal position to

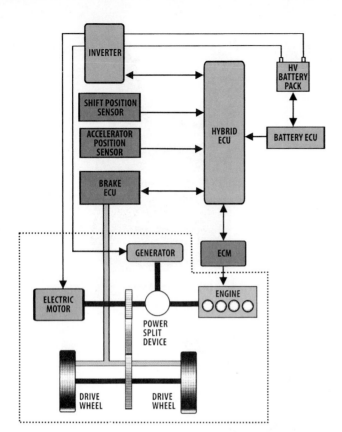

FIGURE 3–52 The HDS vehicle drive system and electrical system.

Normal Driving

FIGURE 3–53 When a vehicle is accelerating, the wheels are driven by the electric motor with an assist from the engine. The engine is also driving the generator through the power split device.

FIGURE 3–54 The motor/generator uses a rotor that is bolted to and turns with the crankshaft, and a stator that is sandwiched between the engine and transmission around the rotor.

control the motor and engine operation. ● **SEE FIGURE 3–52.** This includes an inverter to convert DC electricity of the batteries to AC current at the motor and generator.

The hybrid engine does not run when the ignition is turned to start, but a ready light will come on to inform the driver that the operating sequence has begun. When the shift selector is moved to drive and the accelerator is depressed, the vehicle can begin moving via the electric motor. The engine might start and run at its design speed as determined by the ECU. The determining inputs to the ECU for engine operation are the rate of acceleration being requested, the state of battery charge, the outside temperature, use of air conditioning, and if the vehicle is traveling over a level road or going uphill or downhill. If engine operation is required, the generator works as a starter; then after the engine starts, it becomes a load device providing electricity. ● **SEE FIGURE 3–53.** As soon as the engine is no longer needed, it is shut off, and the vehicle operates using the motor and batteries.

3.14.3 FORD HYBRID The Ford hybrid operation is similar to that of the Toyota system.

3.14.4 GENERAL MOTORS HYBRID General Motors has mild and true hybrid systems in production.

The parallel hybrid system uses a compact 14-kW electric motor/starter generator between the engine and transmission.

The electric motor's stator is positioned on dowels and clamped between the engine and transmission. ● **SEE FIGURE 3–54.** The rotor is bolted to the engine's crankshaft and extends over the torque converter. When slowing or stopping, the fuel to the engine is shut off. The electric motor is used to restart the engine. A 42-volt battery is used to store the electricity generated by the motor and provide electricity used to restart the engine. It is classified as a mild hybrid.

The belt alternator starter (BAS) system is another mild hybrid system that provides idle-stop, electrically controlled

(a)

Bright Orange Wires

(b)

FIGURE 3–55 The dual tensioner system allows the drive belt to turn the alternator/starter during charging mode and allows the alternator/starter to turn the crankshaft during starting (a). Note the three idlers (arrows) to keep the belt very tight. The controller and orange HV wires are shown in (b).

Bright Orange Wires

FIGURE 3–56 The two-mode hybrid transmission has two, three-wire sets of HV wires connected to the two electric motors/generators inside the transmission.

creep, and regenerative braking. The system uses a belt-driven alternator/starter that looks similar to an alternator. The reinforced belt that drives the alternator/starter utilizes a dual tensioner system that will control the bidirectional loads. ● **SEE FIGURE 3–55**. The alternator/starter is used to start the engine and provide some torque assist. During deceleration, power is passed back through the belt to turn the alternator/starter to recharge the batteries. The system provides idle-stop to conserve fuel and reduce exhaust emissions about 10% to 12%.

The General Motors two-mode system was developed jointly by General Motors, Chrysler, and BMW. ● **SEE FIGURE 3–56**. The system optimizes powertrain output and fuel economy at various driving conditions. The transmission can operate as a CVT with four fixed ratios, with power input from the engine and/or the two electric motors. There are two modes of operation. Mode 1 provides fuel savings in low speed, stop-and-go operation; mode 2 provides fuel savings at highway speeds as well as power for trailer towing or steep grades.

The two-mode hybrid transmission contains two internal 60-kW motors that operate from a three-phase, 288-volt power source, three planetary gear sets, and four clutches. ● **SEE FIGURE 3–57**. There are four fixed ratios: 3.7:1, 1.7:1, 1:1, and 0.07:1. The fixed ratios save battery power that would otherwise be used to keep the engine in its optimal operating range. Other advantages of the fixed ratios are overdrive and faster overall vehicle speed. The system provides a fuel improvement of up to 25%.

As the vehicle accelerates, the engine can be off and the electric motors will propel the vehicle and start the engine. Once the engine is running, the computer will control the engine and electric power to operate in the most efficient range.

One electric motor controls the speed ratio of the sun gear of the planetary set and the second motor generates electricity to power the first motor and can supply torque, if needed, to the output shaft. This allows the transmission to work like two transmissions interconnected: The first transmission is continuously variable and the other is a conventional transmission. The fixed ratios are used when the electric motors are ineffective for high-load and cruise conditions. When this happens, the motors can act as generators to recharge the batteries.

3.14.5 NISSAN HYBRID
The Nissan hybrid operation is similar to that of the Toyota system.

FIGURE 3–57 The two-mode hybrid transmission uses two motors/generators, three planetary gear sets, and four hydraulic clutches. This simplified, schematic view illustrates how the internal parts are connected.

SUMMARY

1. Transmissions provide the needed gear ratios for vehicle operation.

2. Gear ratios multiply torque and either reduce the speed or increase the speed as torque decreases.

3. Planetary gear sets are the most common automatic transmission gear trains.

4. A simple planetary gear set can provide seven driving modes and neutral.

5. Combinations of planetary gear sets provide two, three, four, or more forward gear ranges.

6. Clutches, bands, and one-way clutches are used to control planetary members.

7. Automatic transmissions are controlled hydraulically and/or hydraulically with electronic controls.

8. Torque converters provide the engine-to-transmission coupling and provide an automatic clutch.

9. In an effort to better control emissions and fuel economy, new automatic transmission drivetrains are being developed.

REVIEW QUESTIONS

1. The abbreviation used to describe front-wheel drive is _____, and the engine is usually mounted in a _____ position.

2. Torque is a twisting force that is commonly measured in _____, _____, and _____.

3. Five foot-pounds of torque equals _____ inch-pounds.

4. When the transmission increases torque, _____ is decreased.

5. Many transmission manufacturers include the _____ as part of the identifying code for the transmission.

6. If a transmission has a gear ratio of 3:1 in first gear and the final drive ratio is 4:1, the overall ratio would be _____.

7. Three names used to describe an internal cut transmission gear are _____, _____, and _____.

8. Two meshed external gears will rotate in the _____ direction. An external gear meshed with an internal gear will rotate in the _____ direction.

9. A vehicle with a tire diameter of 48 inches and a gear ratio of 12:1 is traveling at 30 mph. How fast is the engine turning?

10. How fast would a vehicle be traveling if the engine was turning at 3500 RPM, if the overall drive ratio was 10:1, and the tires were 45 inches in diameter?

11. A standard transmission will shift smoothly if the synchronizer sleeve and driven gear are turning at the same _____.

12. The front of the transmission is the part closest to the _____.

13. The three members of a simple planetary set are the _____, _____, and _____.

14. When the planet gears move around a stationary gear, the action is known as _____.

15. The most common compound planetary gear set is known as the _____ gear train.

16. The three types of control (apply) devices used in automatic transmissions are _____, _____, and _____.

17. List seven major valves used in a valve body of an automatic transmission.

18. The four major components of a typical, modern torque converter are _____, _____, _____, and _____.

19. Modern torque converters have a _____ that is applied during cruise conditions to eliminate torque converter slippage.

20. The _____ allows the drive wheels to rotate at different speeds when rounding a corner.

21. The two types of drivetrains that power all four wheels of a vehicle are _____ and _____.

22. _____ and _____ are vehicle manufacturers that do not use planetary gear sets in their automatic transmissions.

23. An alternative to the conventional automatic transmission for small vehicles is known as a _____ _____ _____.

24. The use of an internal combustion engine and an electric motor is known as a _____ drive system.

25. A gear set with a 12-tooth drive gear and a 24-tooth driven gear has a gear ratio of _____.

26. A gear set with a 10-tooth drive gear and a 24-tooth driven gear has a gear ratio of _____.

CHAPTER QUIZ

1. The transmission provides _____.
   a. Several gear ratios
   b. A means of backing up
   c. A neutral power path
   d. All of these

2. Student A says that the turning force produced in an engine is called horsepower. Student B says that the turning force produced by an engine is called torque. Who is correct?
   a. Student A
   b. Student B
   c. Both Students A and B
   d. Neither Student A nor B

3. Student A says that a 2:1 gear ratio will double the amount of torque. Student B says that a 2:1 gear ratio will reduce the speed by half. Who is correct?
   a. Student A
   b. Student B
   c. Both Students A and B
   d. Neither Student A nor B

4. A gear ratio of 0.75:1 _____.
   a. Is an overdrive ratio
   b. Will offer only a small amount of torque increase
   c. Is a very low gear ratio
   d. All of these

5. If the gear on the input shaft has 9 teeth and the gear on the output shaft has 27 teeth, the gear ratio will be _____.
   a. 2.5:1
   b. 0.33:1
   c. 3:1
   d. None of these

6. A vehicle has a transmission with a low gear ratio of 2.5:1 and a final drive ratio of 3.5:1. The overall gear ratio while operating in first gear will be _____.
   a. 2.5:1
   b. 3.5:1
   c. 6:1
   d. 8.75:1

7. When one external gear drives another external gear of the same size, the rotation of the driven gear will be _____.
   a. At a slower speed
   b. At a faster speed
   c. In the opposite direction
   d. All of these

8. The clearance between two meshed gears is called _____.
   a. Backlash
   b. Side clearance
   c. Side thrust
   d. End play

9. The speed of a vehicle is determined by the _____.
   a. Speed of the engine
   b. Gear ratio
   c. Tire diameter
   d. All of these

10. The amount of torque developed in a vehicle's drivetrain is called _____.
    a. Power
    b. Tractive force
    c. Powertrain torque
    d. All of these

11. A planetary gear set is made up of a _____.
    a. Sun gear
    b. Ring gear
    c. Carrier and planet gears
    d. All of these

12. When the carrier is held and the sun or ring gear is driven, the action of the planet gears will be to _____.
    a. Walk
    b. Be motionless in the carrier
    c. Idle
    d. None of these

13. When the carrier is driven while the sun gear is held, the action of the planet gears will be to _____.
    a. Walk
    b. Be motionless in the carrier
    c. Idle
    d. None of these

14. A Simpson gear train uses _____.
    a. Two ring gears, two carriers, and two sun gears
    b. Two ring gears, one carrier, and two sun gears
    c. One ring gear, one carrier, and one sun gear
    d. Two ring gears, two carriers, and one sun gear

15. Student A says that a clutch in an automatic transmission is applied by spring pressure and released by fluid pressure. Student B says that a band in an automatic transmission is applied by fluid pressure and released by fluid or spring pressure. Who is correct?
    a. Student A
    b. Student B
    c. Both Students A and B
    d. Neither Student A nor B

16. Student A says that a reaction member keeps a part of the gear set from rotating. Student B says that a reaction member is always applied by hydraulic pressure. Who is correct?
    a. Student A
    b. Student B
    c. Both Students A and B
    d. Neither Student A nor B

17. The transmission's hydraulic circuit _____.
    a. Controls clutch and band operation
    b. Produces upshifts and downshifts
    c. Controls shift quality and timing
    d. All of these

18. A lockup torque converter is used in transmissions to _____.
    a. Increase first-gear torque
    b. Improve fuel mileage
    c. Reduce engine operating speed
    d. All of these

19. Student A says that when a vehicle is going around a corner, the differential pinion gears are rotating on their shafts. Student B says that when a car is going around a corner, the differential pinion gears are in mesh with the axle side gears. Who is correct?
    a. Student A
    b. Student B
    c. Both Students A and B
    d. Neither Student A nor B

20. The job of the center differential of an AWD vehicle is to _____.
    a. Allow the front axle to go faster than the rear axle
    b. Force all four wheels to rotate at the same speed
    c. Work the same as in 2WD vehicles
    d. None of these

chapter 4

APPLY DEVICES: CLUTCHES AND BANDS

OBJECTIVES: **After studying Chapter 4, the reader will be able to:** • Describe the power flow through a planetary gear set. • Identify the components of a multiple-disc clutch and describe how it operates. • Identify a one-way clutch and describe how it operates. • Identify a band and servo and describe how they operate.

KEY TERMS: Asynchronous shift 89 • Belleville plate 88 • Belleville spring 77 • Clutch-to-clutch 75 • Cushion plate 88 • Diaphragm spring 77 • Direct clutch 75 • Directional grooving 79 • Double-wrap band 85 • Driving devices 75 • Drum 76 • Dynamic friction 81 • Flex band 85 • Freewheel shift 89 • Friction plate 77 • Front clutch 75 • Garage shifts 82 • High-reverse clutch 75 • Hub 76 • Lined plates 76 • Mechanical diode 84 • Nonsynchronous shift 89 • Power shifts 82 • Pressure balance 77 • Pressure plate 76 • Reaction devices 75 • Rigid band 85 • Separator plate 77 • Shift duration 81 • Shift feel 88 • Shift quality 81 • Shift timing 81 • Single-sided plate 80 • Static friction 81 • Steels 77 • Strut 85 • Synchronous 75 • Unlined plates 76 • Wave plate 88 • Wave spring 77

4.1 INTRODUCTION

There are several paths for power to flow through an automatic transmission, and each path provides a different gear ratio. These power paths are controlled by the driving and reaction devices, also called driving and reaction members. The **driving devices** connect the turbine shaft from the torque converter to a member of the planetary gear train. The **reaction devices** connect a member of the gear train to the transmission case. There are usually two or more driving devices and two or more reaction devices in a three- or four-speed automatic transmission. ● **SEE FIGURE 4–1**.

4.2 DRIVING DEVICES

The driving devices provide the input to the gear set. The turbine shaft (which transfers power into the transmission) is normally built as part of or splined to one or more of the driving devices. Driving devices are usually multiple-plate disc clutches. In most cases, they will be at the front of the transmission, just behind the pump.

A few transmissions have a one-way (roller or sprag) clutch positioned between the multiple-disc clutch and the input member of the planetary gear set. One-way clutches transfer power in only one direction. A one-way clutch in a driving

position will become effective and transfer power when the multiple-disc clutch is applied. It will release or overrun, becoming ineffective when the driving member for a higher gear applies, and this allows the part held by the roller clutch to increase speed.

A common problem that students and technicians have concerning automatic transmissions is the lack of common terms. Although the parts perform the same job, the driving clutches are often given different names by different manufacturers. An example of this involves the two clutches in front of a Simpson gear train transmission.

- Chrysler Corporation calls the first clutch the **front clutch**.
- Ford Motor Company calls it a **high-reverse clutch**.
- General Motors Corporation and Toyota call it a **direct clutch**.
- Toyota commonly calls it C2.

4.2.1 SYNCHRONIZING SHIFTS
Automatic shifts must be timed to happen quickly without the possibility of being in two gears at the same time. A gear set will lock up if it has two ratios at the same time. There are two strategies used by transmission manufacturers. One strategy is **synchronous**, *overlap*, or **clutch-to-clutch** shifting. This requires that one apply device be timed or synchronized with the application of the apply device for the next gear range. The other strategy is called *nonsynchronous, asynchronous*, or *freewheel shifts*. Nonsynchronous shifts use one or more one-way clutches as

FIGURE 4–1 The 4L60 (THM 700) has one band, five multiple-disc clutches, and two one-way clutches to control the power flow. The reverse input, overrun, forward, and 3–4 clutches along with the forward sprag clutch are driving members. The 2–4 band, low roller clutch, and low-reverse clutch are reaction members.

driving or reaction devices. A one-way clutch will self-release during a shift as soon as the next clutch applies, eliminating the need to synchronize the shifts.

4.3 MULTIPLE-DISC DRIVING CLUTCHES

The parts of a clutch assembly are the **drum**, **hub**, **lined plates**, **unlined plates**, **pressure plate**, apply piston, and piston return springs. The drum, also called a *housing*, has splines inside its outer edge for the externally lugged plates, usually the unlined plates. The inner diameter of the drum is machined for the apply piston and its inner and outer seals. ● **SEE FIGURE 4–2.** The drum of the rear, or forward, clutch is usually built as part of or splined to the input or turbine shaft. A clutch can be built as a single unit or combined with another drum or hub of a second clutch assembly. For example, the input drum of a General Motors 4L60 (THM 700-R4) transmission contains three different clutches as well as the hub for a fourth clutch. ● **SEE FIGURE 4–3.**

NOTE: The model designation for some transmissions has changed. In this text, the new designation for common transmissions will be given first and the older one will follow inside parentheses.

(a)

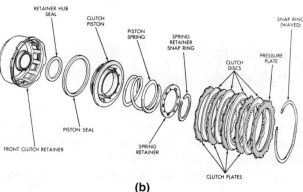

(b)

FIGURE 4–2 A sectioned view (a) and exploded view (b) of a multiple-disc clutch. Note the piston to apply the clutch and the spring(s) to release it. (Figure (b) *Courtesy of Chrysler Corporation*)

3116 85 591 3747 7611 61 267 853 7114 902 6526 335 202 9029

5331 105 928 662 583

4434 1892 211 607 281 633 3206 1575 228 309 228

FIGURE 4–3 A 4L60 input clutch assembly has three separate clutch packs: 202 is the overrun clutch; 607 is the forward clutch; and 228 is the 3–4 clutch. The input sprag assembly is at the bottom left. (*Courtesy of Slauson Transmission Parts, www.slauson.com*)

Check Ball: Seated

Return Spring

Fluid Pressure

Released **Applied**

FIGURE 4–4 The apply piston is released (left) by the coil springs. Fluid pressure moves the piston to apply the clutch (right).

A clutch hub is splined or lugged on its outer diameter to accept the internal lugs of the lined clutch plates. The clutch pack is made up by alternately stacked unlined and lined plates, and this stack is contained in the drum. Sometimes two steel plates will be stacked next to each other. The clutch pack is held in place by a thick pressure plate retained by a large retaining snap ring in the drum. The clutch hub is often built as part of the unit being driven, such as a ring gear or a carrier.

The doughnut-shaped apply piston is sealed at both its inner and outer diameter to trap the fluid entering the cylinder. During clutch application, fluid pressure forces the piston to squeeze the clutch pack against the pressure plate. ● **SEE FIGURE 4–4.** When the fluid pressure is released, one or more piston return springs push the piston back to its released position. Clutch assemblies use a group of small coil springs; a single, large coil spring; a single, large Belleville spring; or a wave spring. ● **SEE FIGURE 4–5.** When the clutch is released, the plates separate, creating a clearance between each plate.

A **Belleville spring**, also called a **diaphragm spring**, resembles a metal washer that is slightly cone shaped. Spring action occurs when this spring is flattened. A **wave spring** also resembles a large washer. It is not flat; it is bent back and forth. The action of a Belleville or wave spring cushions clutch application. Some clutches position a Belleville spring between the piston and the clutch pack so it serves as an apply lever as well as a return spring. The force increase from this leverage increases the strength of the clutch.

TECH TIP

If the fluid does not exhaust from the clutch apply chamber of a spinning clutch, centrifugal force will force the fluid to the outer edge of the chamber.
● **SEE FIGURE 4–6.** This trapped fluid can cause partial clutch apply and unwanted clutch drag.

PRESSURE BALANCED RELEASE. Traditionally, clutches are released by the spring(s), but this might be too slow for modern clutch-to-clutch transmissions. A clutch using **pressure balance**, also called a *compensator pressure* or *pressure cancel*, has a second fluid chamber on the spring side of the piston. ● **SEE FIGURE 4–7.** The clutch is applied when fluid pressure is sent to the apply side of the piston. Releasing pressure from the apply side and sending fluid pressure, also called compensator or cancel pressure, to the release side produces a precisely controlled clutch release. This is described more completely in Chapter 7.

4.3.1 CLUTCH PLATES

The unlined plates are called **steels**, or **separator plates**. They are flat pieces of steel stamped into the desired shape. A steel plate is usually about 0.070 to 0.100 inch (1.78 to 2.54 mm) thick. After being stamped, the plate is carefully flattened. An out-of-flat plate will use up clutch clearance and cause drag while released. A steel plate has a surface roughness of 12 to 15 microinches. ● **SEE FIGURE 4–8.** An unlined steel plate usually has lugs on its outer diameter to engage with the clutch drum/housing or transmission case. The steel plates used in current automatic transmissions are very smooth; some have a polished appearance. Steel plates have a secondary purpose of serving as heat sinks to help remove heat from the lined friction plates.

Lined plates are called **friction plates**, *friction discs*, or simply *frictions*. These plates are also made from stamped steel with lining material bonded to each side. The engagement lugs are usually on the inner diameter. A friction plate is about 0.063 to 0.086 in. (1.6 to 2.18 mm) thick, and the friction material is about 0.015 to 0.030 in. (0.38 to 0.76 mm) thick. The lining material can have a plain, smooth, flat surface or a grooved friction surface.

LIP SEALS

PISTON

RETURN SPRING RETAINER

FRONT CLUTCH RETAINER

PISTON RETURN SPRING

SNAP RING

(a)

DIRECT CLUTCH DRUM

DIRECT CLUTCH PISTON

O-RINGS

CLUTCH DRUM THRUST WASHER

CLUTCH PISTON SNAP RING

PISTON RETURN SPRINGS

CLUTCH PACK

RETAINER

DISC

PLATE

CLUTCH PACK SNAP RING

(b)

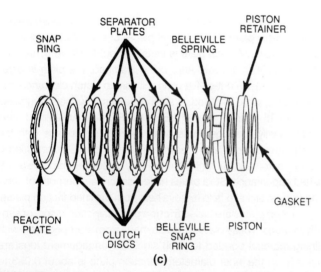

SNAP RING

SEPARATOR PLATES

BELLEVILLE SPRING

PISTON RETAINER

REACTION PLATE

CLUTCH DISCS

BELLEVILLE SNAP RING

PISTON

GASKET

(c)

FIGURE 4–5 Clutch piston return springs can be (a) a single large spring, (b) a group of small springs, or (c) a single Belleville spring. (*Courtesy of Chrysler Corporation*)

FLUID PRESSURE

CENTRIFUGAL FORCE

TRAPPED FLUID

FIGURE 4–6 Any fluid left in the apply chamber of a spinning clutch will be pushed outward by centrifugal force. This force can cause the fluid to push on the piston and partially apply a clutch.

PISTON

APPLY PRESSURE CHAMBER

RETURN SPRING

RELEASE PRESSURE CHAMBER

FIGURE 4–7 The baffle that supports the return springs also forms a chamber for release pressure. The clutch is released when fluid pressure enters this chamber as pressure is released from the apply side of the piston.

FIGURE 4–8 A close-up view of the surface finish on a steel plate. Note the small nicks and grooves that tend to hold fluid.

Smooth **Multiparallel**

Spiral **3-Pass Multiparallel**

Wagon Tracks **Sunburst**

Parallel **Waffle**

FIGURE 4–9 Friction plates often have a groove pattern to help wipe fluid away, dissipate heat, eliminate clutch noise, and change friction qualities during apply and release. A smooth plate is the coolest and slowest to apply; the waffle plate will apply the fastest. (*Courtesy of Raybestos*)

A grooved plate can have one of several grooving patterns cut or stamped into friction material, as shown in ● **FIGURE 4–9.** The grooves help fluid leave or enter between the unlined and lined plates during a shift. The different grooving patterns help

FIGURE 4–10 This friction plate has directional grooves. The lugs (center inset) are asymmetrical, so the plate cannot be installed incorrectly. (*Courtesy of Raybestos*)

control how fast the fluid leaves the friction area to produce different shift-quality characteristics. The faster the oil leaves, the faster the clutch can apply; but the longer the oil stays between the plates, the more heat can be absorbed by the oil. Different clutch packs for the same transmission will often use lined plates with different grooving patterns. Clutches that apply with the vehicle at rest can be smooth because apply rate is not important. Clutches that are used for upshifts will often have a groove pattern. Some new clutch designs use friction plates with **directional grooving**. ● **SEE FIGURE 4–10.** These are a slanted groove that must face the proper direction. Some have an inner spline shape that allows the plate to be installed only in the proper direction.

Clutch lining material is a mix of natural and man-made fibers, fillers, and binders. The exact mixture is selected to provide the desired clutch apply, duration, and heat resistance characteristics. The natural fibers come from cotton or wood. ● **SEE FIGURE 4–11.** The man-made fibers are aramid/Kevlar, glass, and carbon. Fillers help determine the density, porosity, and flexibility; common fillers are diatomaceous earth, graphite/carbon, and friction particles. Binders hold the mix together; the most common binders are thermosetting phenolic resins.

The clutches are flooded with transmission fluid while released, and during application this fluid prevents any heat generated by friction from overheating the lining. Theoretically, there will always be a film of fluid between the friction and steel plates.

Manufacturers often provide some means of adjusting the released clearance in a clutch pack. There must be sufficient clearance between the plates to ensure that there is no drag when released. This clearance should be about 0.010 to 0.015 in. (0.25 to 0.38 mm) between each friction surface-lined and unlined plate. Clutch pack clearance is also called *piston travel*.

FIGURE 4–11 A microscopic view of the surface of paper friction plate lining. Friction material is formed on the lined plate to establish a cross-linked matrix. Note the large cavities between the paper fibers that can store relatively large amounts of fluid. (*Courtesy of Raybestos*)

FIGURE 4–12 In this clutch assembly, clutch stack clearance is adjusted using either the large or small flange (backing plate). Other clutches may use a selective snap ring. (*Courtesy of Toyota Motor Sales USA, Inc.*)

Common methods of adjusting clutch pack clearance are selective size retaining rings, pressure plates, and steel plates. ● **SEE FIGURE 4–12.** A selective part is available in several thicknesses, and when a clutch is assembled, the correct width or thickness is selected.

DOUBLE- AND SINGLE-SIDED FRICTION PLATES. The clutch just described uses double-sided friction plates. **Single-sided plates** have friction material on one side only, and half of the plates have lugs on the inner diameter while the other half have lugs on the outer diameter. ● **SEE FIGURE 4–13.** Single-sided plates run cooler than two-sided plates, a feature that allows for more power transfer. The plates can be made thinner so that more plates can be put into a clutch pack. Single-sided plates have encountered problems of uneven heating because one side gets hotter, and the plate tends to deform into a conical shape. This problem has been cured by mechanically distorting the plates slightly or by specially designed grooves cut in the end plates.

(a)

(b)

(c)

FIGURE 4–13 (a) The ZPAK is a single-sided clutch design. (b) Both sides of the two different plates show a lined and unlined side. (c) The clutch pack requires proper placement of the end plates. (*Courtesy of Raybestos*)

4.3.2 CLUTCH OPERATION When a clutch is applied, the plates are squeezed together and torque is transferred from the friction plates to the steel plates. The amount of torque that can be transferred is determined by the following factors: diameter and width of the friction surfaces, number of friction surfaces (two per lined plate), and the amount of force being

FIGURE 4–14 When this transmission is in first gear, the sun gear and unlined plates of the front clutch rotate counterclockwise while the hub and lined plates of this clutch rotate clockwise. Any drag will produce heat that can cause clutch burnout.

FIGURE 4–15 If you push against a stationary book, you will notice the static friction that resists motion. Pushing against the same book while it is sliding is easier because the dynamic friction is somewhat less.

applied (hydraulic pressure times the piston area). The greater the plate area, number of plates, piston size, or hydraulic pressure, the greater the torque capacity. The formula used to determine clutch capacity is:

$$T = \frac{N\,[[D + d]\,F\mu]}{4}$$

where:

T = torque capacity (in inch-pounds)
N = number of active friction surfaces
D = outside diameter of clutch facings (in inches)
d = inside diameter of clutch facings (in inches)
F = total force on clutch pack (in pounds)
μ = coefficient of friction

A clutch with sufficient capacity will transfer torque without slipping. Many transmissions are made with varying torque capacities depending on the engine with which they will be used. Transmissions used with high-torque engines have more plates in the clutch packs.

When a clutch is released, there must be clearance between the plates. There is often a considerable speed differential between the friction and steel plates. For example, during first gear in a Simpson gear train, the sun gear revolves at a 2.5:1 ratio in reverse (counterclockwise). Imagine the speed difference in a released high-gear clutch with the input shaft, clutch hub, and lined plates revolving at an engine speed of 3000 RPM in a clockwise direction and the drum and the unlined plates turning 7500 RPM in a counterclockwise direction. ● SEE FIGURE 4–14. Without sufficient clearance and lubrication, these plates would surely drag, create friction, and burn up. The oil flow through the grooves and between the plates helps cool the friction surfaces.

A transmission engineer is concerned with three different friction conditions in a clutch:

- While the clutch is released, there should be no friction or drag.
- While applied, there should be sufficient **static friction** to transfer torque without slippage.
- While applying, there should be the proper **dynamic friction** to get a good, smooth shift.

An example of static and dynamic friction can be seen if we place a book on a table. With the book sitting still, the static (stationary) friction between the book and the table holds it in place. Push on the book, and you will notice the amount of force it takes to overcome this static friction. ● SEE FIGURE 4–15. Also notice how much force it takes to keep the book sliding; this is the dynamic or sliding friction. Static friction is always greater than dynamic friction.

Several terms are used to describe a shift. **Shift quality** describes how smooth or rough a shift feels. *Shift pattern* is used by General Motors to describe when the shift occurs—the vehicle speed and load to produce the upshift or downshift. The transmission industry uses the term **shift timing** for this same purpose. General Motors uses *shift timing* to describe the length of time required to completely apply or release the components involved in the shift. The transmission industry calls this **shift duration**.

The friction characteristics of a clutch are designed to work with the friction characteristics of the transmission fluid. The various types of automatic transmission fluid (ATF) use different friction modifiers. ● SEE FIGURE 4–16. A vehicle manufacturer specifies the fluid type to be used in its transmissions.

Some clutches in an automatic transmission are applied while the vehicle is at rest; the neutral-to-drive and neutral-to-reverse shifts are called **garage shifts**. The clutches for first or reverse gear need a high amount of static friction because of the amount of torque required to start the vehicle moving. The garage shifts can occur slowly so they are usually less severe than the 1–2, 2–3, or 3–4 shifts; they may take 3 or 4 seconds to apply. Clutches that are applied while the vehicle is in motion and are called **power shift** elements. They are applied under power and have to transfer substantial torque as they are applied. ● **SEE FIGURE 4–17**. These clutches must have a high dynamic coefficient of friction.

4.3.3 WET FRICTION
Wet friction occurs because ATF fills the space between the clutch plates. This ATF film transmits torque between the clutch plates as the clutch is being applied. The action of the film of fluid is called *fluid shear*.

As the clutch is applied, the clutch plate clearance reduces as the fluid is squeezed from between the plates, leaving a film of fluid. This hydrodynamic film begins transferring torque. Fluid shear, the resistance to motion, is the primary torque transmitting force at the start of a shift. As the plate clearance is reduced, fluid viscosity increases and its resistance to shear increases. The clutch plates make physical contact at the end of application. Since there is no movement between the plates at this time, friction lining wear is minimized.

OPEN PACK DRAG. Open pack drag refers to the torque that is required to spin a clutch that is released. Remember that during cruise operation, one or two of the clutch packs will be released, and any drag within the released clutches reduces transmission efficiency and fuel mileage. Fluid shear between the rotating plates increases parasitic drag. *Turbulator steels* have small holes drilled through them. The holes create a turbulence that tends to center the plate and separate the pack. ● **SEE FIGURE 4–18**. The turbulator holes also provide additional escape paths for fluid during clutch apply. Another design to reduce drag is a precision wave friction plate. The wave is very small, about 0.010 in. (0.0004 mm), just enough to help center the friction plate between the steels.

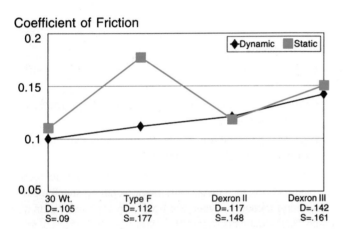

FIGURE 4–16 A comparison of the dynamic and static coefficients of friction with motor oil and three types of ATF. (*Courtesy of Raybestos*)

PROBLEM SOLVING 4–1

Imagine that you are working in a shop that specializes in transmission repair, and the following problems are brought to you.

Case 1:

A 1982 Chevrolet pickup starts okay in first gear, but the 1–2 shift is long and drawn out. A full-throttle shift has an engine speed flare with indications of slippage. What part of the transmission is faulty? What do you think is causing this problem?

Case 2:

A 1995 Nissan Sentra shifts good going into the forward ranges, but there is no reverse; it acts just like neutral. How can you determine the faulty part?

FIGURE 4–17 The clutch apply curves of five different clutches. The dynamic friction is the rate of torque increase, whereas the static friction is the amount of torque at the left. (*Courtesy of AFM*)

FIGURE 4–18 The four slots in this steel plate, called a turbulator plate, promote a fluid layer on each side of the stationary plate. (*Courtesy of Raybestos*)

(a)

(b)

FIGURE 4–19 (a) This overrunning clutch assembly is a roller clutch with the clutch cam secured to the transmission case. (b) It uses a set of spring-loaded rollers in the retainer. (*Courtesy of Chrysler Corporation*)

4.4 ONE-WAY DRIVING CLUTCHES

Two styles of one-way clutches are used in automatic transmissions: *roller clutches* and *sprag clutches*. One-way clutches are also called *overrunning clutches*. A one-way clutch is sometimes called a mechanical diode; like an electronic diode, it allows travel in one direction only.

4.4.1 ROLLER CLUTCH A roller clutch is made up of a smooth inner race, a ramped outer race, a series of rollers and energizing springs, and a cage or guide to locate the springs. ● **SEE FIGURE 4–19.** Some roller clutches are made with a ramped inner race and a smooth outer race. Each roller fits in the ramp or cam section of the race. ● **SEE FIGURE 4–20.** An energizing spring pushes the roller so there is a light contact between the roller, the ramp, and the smooth race. Counterclockwise rotation of the hub will wedge the rollers so they become locked between the inner and outer races. When locked, they will block any further rotation in that direction. Clockwise rotation will unwedge the rollers, and each roller will simply rotate, much like a roller bearing. The inner hub will rotate freely or overrun in a clockwise direction.

4.4.2 SPRAG CLUTCH A sprag clutch uses smooth, hardened inner and outer races and a series of sprags that are mounted in a special cage. A sprag is an odd-shaped part that somewhat resembles an hourglass or fat letter *S* when viewed from the end. A sprag has two effective diameters. The major diameter is greater than the space between the inner and outer

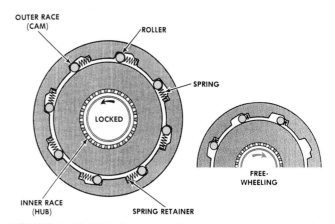

FIGURE 4–20 If this inner race tries to turn counterclockwise, the rollers will wedge at the narrow part of the cams and lock the clutch. Movement of the inner race in a clockwise direction will move the rollers to the wide part of the cams, where they will roll freely. (*Courtesy of Chrysler Corporation*)

races, and the minor diameter is smaller than this space. The sprags are mounted in a cage that spring loads each sprag in a direction to "stand up" or wedge the major diameter between the two races. A clockwise rotation of the inner race causes the

FIGURE 4–23 This clutch hub and sprag clutch should rotate freely in a clockwise direction but should lock up in the opposite direction. (*Courtesy of Toyota Motor Sales USA, Inc.*)

FIGURE 4–21 Each sprag has a major and minor diameter. The major diameter is greater than the distance between the two races (right); the minor diameter is smaller (left). (*Courtesy of Toyota Motor Sales USA, Inc.*)

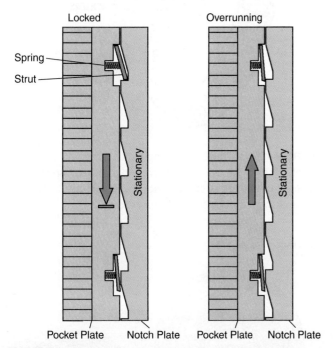

FIGURE 4–22 A mechanical diode. The struts can move out of the pocket plate to engage the notch plate, and this will lock the pocket plate. The pocket plate can overrun in the opposite direction.

sprags to rotate in the stand-up direction. This causes them to wedge firmly between the two races and lock the races together. A counterclockwise rotation of the inner race rotates the sprags in the opposite (laydown) direction. ● **SEE FIGURE 4–21**. Each sprag tends to lay down so its minor diameter is between the races, and the inner race rotates freely.

4.4.3 MECHANICAL DIODE A **mechanical diode** is a relatively new type of one-way clutch. It uses spring-loaded, rectangular struts in the face of one clutch ring, the pocket plate that can engage notches in the face of another ring, the notch plate. ● **SEE FIGURE 4–22**. The struts are pushed

into their pockets when the clutch is overrunning, and they can move outward, about 15 degrees, to engage the notch plate to lock up. Because the compressive forces though the strut are in the load direction, only one or two of the struts need to engage. A mechanical diode is much stronger than a roller or sprag clutch.

4.4.4 CLUTCH OPERATION A one-way clutch can be placed as an input to a gear set. In transmissions like the Ford 5R55E, a one-way clutch is always driving the forward planetary gear set at input shaft speed. In other transmissions, such as the General Motors 4T60-E, one-way clutches are driven through multiple-disc clutches to become effective in first and third gears. ● **SEE FIGURE 4–23**. One-way clutches will overrun as the transmission shifts into the next higher gear.

One-way clutches require continuous lubrication. In most automatic transmissions, one or more one-way clutches are overrunning in high gear. The constant motion would quickly cause overheating and wear if a good flow of fluid was not available at all times.

4.5 HOLDING/REACTION DEVICES

A holding member acts as a brake to hold a planetary gear set member in reaction. Three types of holding devices are used: multiple-disc clutches, bands, and one-way clutches. Multiple-disc clutches and bands are applied by hydraulic pressure and are controlled by the valve body. A one-way clutch is mechanically controlled; it allows rotation in one direction only. In most transmissions, a one-way clutch allows rotation in a clockwise direction but blocks counterclockwise rotation. Applying and holding in a one-way clutch is often referred to as holding or being *effective*, and releasing it is called ineffective or *noneffective*.

Although reaction devices do not rotate, there can be a substantial load on these devices. Remember that for every action, there is an equal and opposite reaction. A General Motors

FIGURE 4–24 The 41TE transaxle low/reverse clutch is a holding clutch. Note the splines in the case for the clutch plates. *(Courtesy of Chrysler Corporation)*

4L60 (THM 700-R4) transmission uses a 2:1 torque converter ratio and a 3.06:1 first gear. If the engine develops 100 ft-lb (135.6 N-m) of torque, there is 2 × 100, or 200, ft-lb (271 N-m) of torque coming from the torque converter and 200 × 3.06, or 612, ft-lb (829.8 N-m) of torque at the drive shaft. There will also be the same 612 ft-lb load on the reaction member, trying to turn it inside the transmission case.

4.6 MULTIPLE-DISC HOLDING CLUTCHES

A multiple-disc holding clutch is quite similar to a driving clutch. The difference is the transmission case is the drum, and the clutch plates splined to it do not rotate. Some manufacturers call these clutches a *brake*. The lugs on the outside of the unlined plates fit into slots built into the case. ● **SEE FIGURE 4–24**. Like a driving clutch, the lugs on the inner diameter of the lined plates fit over the hub, which is often a part of the gear train or the outer race of a one-way clutch.

The hydraulic piston can be built into the case, the back of the front pump assembly, or in a center support. ● **SEE FIGURE 4–25**. The stationary position of the piston and cylinder makes it relatively easy to provide fluid to it. Like a driving clutch, the piston is normally returned to a released position by springs.

4.7 ONE-WAY HOLDING CLUTCHES

One-way clutches are commonly used as reaction devices. The outer race is often secured directly to the transmission case so it cannot rotate. The one-way clutch (F2) in the transmission in Figure 4–25. has the ability to hold the rear carrier stationary in drive-1. The carrier can rotate clockwise in any of the other gears. This carrier can also be held stationary by the first and reverse clutch in manual-1 and reverse to provide compression (engine) braking.

4.8 BANDS

A band is a circular strip of metal that has lining bonded to the inner surface. It wraps around the smooth surface of a drum. There are three types: a single thick, heavy band; a single thin, light band; and a split, **double-wrap**, heavy **band**. The heavy, single-wrap band is also called a **rigid band**. The thin, single-wrap band is called a **flexible** or **flex band**. ● **SEE FIGURE 4–26**. A rigid band is strong and provides a good heat sink to absorb some of the friction heat during application. The disadvantage with a rigid band is that it is relatively expensive and does not always conform to the shape of the drum. A flex band is less expensive and, because of its flexibility, can easily conform to the shape of the drum. Double-wrap bands give more holding power, and are often used for reverse or manual first gears. Each band type has end lugs so it can be attached to the anchor and the servo. A small link, commonly called a **strut**, is often used to connect the lugs of the band to the anchor or the servo piston rod. ● **SEE FIGURE 4–27**.

The friction material used on a band is similar to that used on clutch plates. Paper- and cloth-based materials are normally used. Metallic and semimetallic materials tend to cause severe wear of the drum. The drum must be a smooth cylinder with straight sides in order to have complete contact with the band lining. The lining surface of the band is often grooved to help control fluid flow during apply and release operations. Similar to a clutch, band friction material and grooving are designed to operate with a specified fluid to ensure good shift quality and long life.

The band is anchored at the trailing end so drum rotation will tend to pull the band tightly into engagement. ● **SEE FIGURE 4–28**. A double-wrap band design takes advantage of this wrapping tendency and applies smoother and stronger than a single-wrap band. The band tries to rotate with its drum, and the band, anchor, and servo must be designed to absorb this load.

The anchor for the band can be a fixed or adjustable point in the transmission case. An adjustable anchor provides a method of adjusting the clearance between the band and the drum. There must be enough clearance to ensure there is no band-to-drum contact with the band released, but too much clearance might cause slippage if the band does not apply completely. A band that is too loose or too tight has an adverse effect on shift timing.

The servo is the hydraulic assembly that applies the band; its main components are a cylinder, piston, piston rod/pin, and return spring. ● **SEE FIGURE 4–29**. The piston rod pushes directly on the end of the band on most servos. Some servo

O/D Direct Clutch (Co)
O/D Brake (Co)
One-Way Clutch No.2 (F2)
First and Reverse Brake (B3)
Forward Clutch (C1)
Second Brake (B2)
Second Coast Brake (B1)
Direct Clutch (C2)

O/D One-Way Clutch No.2 (Fo)
O/D Planetary Gear
Counter Drive Gear
Intermediate Shaft
Rear Planetary Gear
One-Way Clutch No.1 (F1)
Front Planetary Gear
Input Shaft

FIGURE 4–25 The plates of the O/D brake, first and reverse brake, and the second brake are multiple-disc clutches that are splined to the transaxle case. (*Courtesy of Toyota Motor Sales USA, Inc.*)

(a)

(b)

FIGURE 4–26 (a) A flex band, and (b) a rigid band. Note the flex band has circumferential grooves for improved conformity, fluid flow, and performance. Note that this is a double-wrap rigid band. Single-wrap rigid bands are also used. (*Courtesy of Raybestos*)

TRANSMISSION CASE
ANCHOR
SERVO APPLY PISTON
BRAKE BAND
LINING (FRICTION MATERIAL)
STRUT
APPLY LEVER

(a)

LEVER RATIO

$$\text{LEVER RATIO} = \frac{A}{B}$$

(b)

FIGURE 4–27 (a) This band uses an adjustable anchor that allows the clearance to be easily adjusted. (b) Note that the apply lever will increase apply force. (*Courtesy of Chrysler Corporation*)

Released

Direction of Drum Rotation, Piston Rod, Piston, Brake Band, Transmission Case, Outer Spring

Applied

Piston Rod, Piston

FIGURE 4–28 A band is normally anchored at the trailing end so its rotation will pull the band tighter. Note that this servo is applied by fluid pressure and released by a spring. (*Courtesy of Toyota Motor Sales USA, Inc.*)

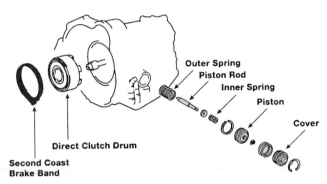

Outer Spring, Piston Rod, Inner Spring, Piston, Cover, Direct Clutch Drum, Second Coast Brake Band

FIGURE 4–29 Fluid pressure acting on the piston forces the piston and piston rod inward to apply the band. The band is released by the outer spring pushing outward on the piston. (*Courtesy of Toyota Motor Sales USA, Inc.*)

SST

FIGURE 4–30 Air pressure can be used to apply the band while the length of the piston stroke is measured. Piston stroke is used to determine the correct piston rod and adjust band clearance. (*Courtesy of Toyota Motor Sales USA, Inc.*)

pistons are connected to the band through a lever or linkage attached to the band strut.

A band lever provides a force increase because of the lever ratio. The ratio will require more piston travel to apply the band but increases the application force acting on the end of the band. Some manufacturers incorporate a band adjustment screw in the apply lever. Other manufacturers use selective-size servo piston rods for band adjustment. ● **SEE FIGURE 4–30.**

4.8.1 BAND OPERATION
When fluid pressure enters the servo, the servo piston strokes to tighten the band around the

PROBLEM SOLVING 4–2

Imagine that you are working in a shop that specializes in transmission repair, and these problems are brought to you.

Case 1:

A 1996 Dodge Ram pickup drives okay in all gears, but there is a bump, like a small bind-up, during the 2–3 shift. This transmission has a band-to-clutch operation during this shift. Would a worn band cause this problem? Could a sticking band servo cause it? How about a worn third-gear clutch? Could the band be out of adjustment?

Case 2:

A 1989 Chevrolet Caprice with a 200-4R transmission does not move forward with the shift selector in OD. It does work normally when shifted to manual-1, and then if shifted to OD, it works well. What do you think might be wrong with this transmission?

drum. The amount of torque that a band can absorb before slipping is determined by the band-to-drum contact area, type of band, drum diameter, fluid type, and the force squeezing the band onto the drum.

When a band releases, the servo piston backs off, and the springy, elastic nature of the band causes it to move away from the drum. A servo piston can be released by either spring pressure and/or hydraulic pressure.

- When the shift is to neutral, the release speed is not important. Normally, servos use only a release spring.

- During an upshift, the band release must be fast and carefully timed. The release of many bands is done by using fluid pressure from the clutch being applied. ● **SEE FIGURE 4–31.** For example, in a Simpson gear train transmission during a 2–3 shift, the fluid pressure to apply the third-gear clutch is also used to release the second-gear band.

- During a downshift, band apply must be quick and firm.

BAND APPLIED:
SECOND GEAR

APPLY PRESSURE FROM
1-2 SHIFT VALVE

RELEASE
PRESSURE FROM
2-3 SHIFT VALVE

BAND RELEASE:
THIRD GEAR
(FRONT CLUTCH DRUM
IN ROTATION)

FIGURE 4–31 This band is applied when 1–2 shift valve pressure pushes upward on the servo piston (top). It will release when 2–3 shift valve pressure pushes the piston downward (bottom). Note the larger area above the piston.

4.9 SHIFT QUALITY

As a power shift occurs, there must be a smooth transition from one apply device to the next. The smoothness of the shift is referred to as shift quality or **shift feel**. For example, when a Simpson gear train transmission starts a 2–3 (second [1.5:1 ratio] to third [1:1 ratio] gear) shift, the third-gear clutch drum is held stationary by a band, and the hub and lined plates are rotating at engine speed. During this shift, the band is released, and the clutch is applied to turn the clutch at engine speed. Imagine that as the shift begins, the engine is at 3000 RPM and the vehicle is going about 45 mph (72 km/h). In second gear, with a transmission ratio of 1.5:1, the driveshaft will be turning at 2000 RPM. The time duration of the shift must be gradual enough so the engine's RPM will be smoothly lowered (in this case, from 3000 to 2000 RPM). The resulting

BAND APPLIED   REAR CLUTCH
                 APPLIED

MECHANICAL POWER FLOW – SECOND GEAR
(a)

FRONT CLUTCH   REAR CLUTCH
APPLIED   APPLIED

MECHANICAL POWER FLOW – THIRD GEAR
(b)

FIGURE 4–32 (a) In second gear, the sun gear and front clutch drum are held stationary by the band. (b) In third gear, the clutch is applied so the drum and sun gear are rotating at engine speed. The driver feels this change as shift quality. (*Courtesy of Nissan North America, Inc.*)

1:1 third-gear ratio will have the input turning the same speed as the driveshaft. ● **SEE FIGURE 4–32.**

A shift should be smooth without any unusual noises. In order for this to occur, the clutches and bands must apply smoothly and quietly. The timing of the band releasing from second gear and the clutch applying for third gear must be precise. Any improper noises such as squeaks, squawks, or shrieks or operation such as engine RPM flare, jerks, bumps, or harsh application are considered faults that need to be corrected.

When one apply device is released as another one is applied it is called a synchronous shift. The release and application of the two elements, the intermediate band and the high clutch, must be synchronized.

Clutch shift quality is controlled by the type of lining material and grooving, the use of wave or Belleville plates, the type of fluid used, and the speed at which fluid moves the piston.

A **wave plate** is an unlined plate that is wavy, not flat. A **Belleville plate**, like a Belleville spring, is also not flat. ● **SEE FIGURE 4–33.** These are often called **cushion plates**. If either plate is used in a clutch pack, it will be placed between the piston and the first unlined plate or between the last unlined plate and the pressure plate. Both plates are designed to compress slightly under pressure during clutch application. The result is to slightly prolong the clutch apply time.

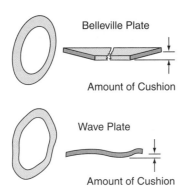

Belleville Plate

Amount of Cushion

Wave Plate

Amount of Cushion

FIGURE 4–33 Two cushion plates: The Belleville plate has a coned shape; the wave plate has a wavy shape. Both of them will flatten slightly as the clutch is applied.

Turn

Free

Lock

Hold

FIGURE 4–34 This one-way clutch allows the shaft to overrun in a clockwise direction. (*Courtesy of Toyota Motor Sales USA, Inc.*)

Again consider the time just before the 2–3 shift. The high clutch drum and unlined plates are stationary, and the hub and lined plates are revolving at about 3000 RPM. Transmission fluid enters the cylinder behind the clutch piston and starts the piston moving, reducing the clutch pack clearance. When the clearance has diminished, pressure will start squeezing the plates together. Suddenly, there is dynamic friction between the plates, and a power transfer takes place. If a cushion plate is used, clutch apply is slightly longer and a slight slippage occurs. This gives a smoother, less severe clutch application.

Many transmissions do not use Belleville or wave plates. Hydraulic controls (accumulators and orifices) are used to control piston movement and the desired shift quality. Electronically controlled transmissions have even greater ability to alter shift quality. The shift solenoids and hydraulic pressure control solenoids can be turned off and on, or cycled to produce the desired shifts. Electronic shift control will be described more completely in Chapter 8.

4.9.1 SHIFTS INVOLVING ONE-WAY CLUTCHES A one-way clutch is an ideal driving or reaction member for automatic shifts. It applies or holds when it is needed and self-releases or overruns when it is not needed. Its operation is controlled by the load direction on the inner or outer race so shift timing is automatic. When the transmission upshifts, the reaction or driving member for the next gear is applied, and the one-way clutch simply overruns.

This is called a **nonsynchronous** or **asynchronous shift**; the shift elements do not need to be synchronized. It is also called a **freewheel shift**.

4.9.2 DECELERATION WITH ONE-WAY CLUTCHES When the throttle is released while in a gear that uses a one-way clutch, the transmission will go into neutral as the one-way clutch overruns. This action is good if the vehicle is coasting to a stop, but can be a problem if going down a steep hill.

One-way clutches are normally used in the automatically selected drive gears, such as drive-1 or drive-2. The manually selected gears such as manual-1 or manual-2 will apply a reaction member like the low-reverse band or second-gear coast brake (a clutch). ● **SEE FIGURE 4–34.** This reaction member, like the intermediate band in a THM 350, is often called an *overrun band*. The overrun clutch in a 4L60 transmission bypasses the Forward Clutch and Sprag (see Figure 4–1.). The overrun band or clutch acts as a second reaction or drive member in manual gears to lock the gear set during deceleration or coasting.

The second reaction member locks the gear set into the desired gear during deceleration and coasting. This helps control vehicle speed while descending hills by using the engine's compression, commonly called compression braking. The added clutch or band also provides a stronger reaction member while pulling heavy loads such as a trailer.

SUMMARY

1. The power flow through a gear set is controlled by driving and reaction devices.
2. The driving and reaction devices are multiple-disc clutches, one-way clutches, and bands.
3. Multiple-disc clutches are the primary driving devices and are also used to hold planetary members in reaction.
4. One-way clutches primarily are used to hold planetary members in reaction, but can be used with a multiple-disc clutch to be a driving device.
5. Bands are used to hold a planetary member in reaction.
6. The timing of the apply and release of the apply devices has a direct effect on shift quality.

REVIEW QUESTIONS

1. The power flow through an automatic transmission is controlled by the _____ and _____ devices.

2. The most common driving member is the _____ _____ _____; a(n) _____ _____ is also used as a driving member.

3. List the seven major parts of a clutch assembly.

4. Usually the lined plates of a driving multiple-disc clutch are splined to the clutch _____, and the unlined plates are splined to the clutch _____.

5. List the four types of return springs used in a multiple-disc clutch.

6. Piston travel or clutch plate clearance can be adjusted by replacing the _____ or _____.

7. The multiple-disc clutch torque capacity can be increased by increasing the _____ area, number of _____, _____ size, or by increasing the _____ pressure.

8. *Shift quality* is a term used to describe the _____ of a shift.

9. The two types of one-way clutches used in an automatic transmission are the _____ and _____.

10. One-way clutches _____ when turned in one direction and _____ when rotated in the other direction.

11. One-way clutches can be used as a _____ or a _____ apply device.

12. List the three types of apply devices that can be used to hold a planetary member.

13. A one-way clutch that is holding is referred to as being _____.

14. A multiple-disc clutch that is used in reaction has the steel plates splined to the _____.

15. Bands are applied by _____ pressure and released by _____ or _____ pressure.

16. A _____ shift sequence is a shift where the apply and release of the apply devices must be carefully timed.

17. A shift sequence that does not need to be timed is known as a _____ or _____ shift.

18. One-way clutches are only used in the _____ gear ranges.

19. The disadvantage of one-way clutches is that they do not provide _____ on deceleration.

20. Manual gear ranges use an additional _____ or _____ to provide more holding power when pulling a heavy load.

CHAPTER QUIZ

1. Student A says that in order for a planetary gear set to change the ratio and transmit torque, there must be an input and a reaction member. Student B says that the turbine shaft is the primary input to the transmission. Who is correct?
   a. Student A
   b. Student B
   c. Both Students A and B
   d. Neither Student A nor B

2. Student A says that neutral in a planetary gear set can be obtained by releasing all of the driving clutches. Student B says that neutral in a planetary gear set can be obtained by not applying any reaction members. Who is correct?
   a. Student A
   b. Student B
   c. Both Students A and B
   d. Neither Student A nor B

3. The apply device that is most commonly used as a driving member is a _____.
   a. Cone clutch
   b. Multiple-disc clutch
   c. One-way clutch
   d. Band

4. Student A says that some of the plates used in a multiple-disc clutch are lined with paper friction material. Student B says that some of the plates used in a multiple-disc clutch are unlined steel plates. Who is correct?
   a. Student A
   b. Student B
   c. Both Student A and B
   d. Neither Student A nor B

5. The ideal unlined steel plates _____.
   a. Are perfectly flat
   b. Have many very small nicks in their surface
   c. Are not extremely smooth
   d. All of these

6. The lining of a friction plate is made from _____.
   a. Paper
   b. Asbestos
   c. Inorganic fibers
   d. Any of these

7. A multiple-disc clutch is applied by _____.
   a. One or more coil springs
   b. A piston and air pressure
   c. Hydraulic pressure pushing against a piston
   d. None of these

8. The grooves in the surface of a lined clutch plate _____.
   a. Help cool the friction material
   b. Allow oil to flow between the plates more easily
   c. Are cut using different patterns depending on the clutch
   d. All of these

9. The torque-carrying capacity of a clutch is determined by the _____.
   a. Number of plates
   b. Amount of lining area on the plates
   c. Amount of pressure squeezing the plates together
   d. All of these

10. Commonly used holding or reaction members are _____.
    a. Bands
    b. One-way clutches
    c. Multiple-disc clutches
    d. All of these

11. Student A says that a band is applied by a hydraulic servo and released by a spring or hydraulic pressure. Student B says that a clutch is applied by hydraulic pressure and released by a spring or hydraulic pressure. Who is correct?
    a. Student A
    b. Student B
    c. Both Student A and B
    d. Neither Student A nor B

12. When a multiple-disc clutch is used as a holding member, the lugs of the unlined plates are splined into _____.
    a. A very large drum
    b. The reaction carrier
    c. The transmission case
    d. The output shaft

13. The strongest of the band designs is the _____.
    a. Single wrap
    b. Heavy band
    c. Double wrap
    d. Flexible

14. Band clearance can be adjusted using a _____.
    a. Threaded adjuster at the band anchor
    b. Threaded adjuster at the servo lever
    c. Selective-size servo piston rod
    d. Any of these, depending on the transmission

15. Student A says that the inner and outer races of a sprag clutch are perfectly round and smooth. Student B says that one of the races of a roller clutch is perfectly round and smooth while the other one has a series of ramps in it. Who is correct?
    a. Student A
    b. Student B
    c. Both Students A and B
    d. Neither Student A nor B

16. When a sprag clutch locks, the sprags _____.
    a. Try to rotate but wedge between the two races
    b. Roll down the ramps and wedge into place
    c. Rotate into a position that unlocks them
    d. Rotate with the free or rotating race

17. When a roller clutch unlocks, the rollers _____.
    a. Are wedged between the two races
    b. Are free to rotate
    c. Rotate to a position where they allow both inner and outer races to rotate
    d. None of these

18. A one-way clutch in a reverse direction _____.
    a. Is applied by hydraulic pressure
    b. Is released by a group of springs
    c. Self-applies whenever one of the races tries to rotate in a reverse direction
    d. Any of these

19. The term used to describe when the apply devices do not need to be timed when shifting gears is _____.
    a. Shift feel
    b. Asynchronous
    c. Shift quality
    d. All of these

20. The term used to describe the condition when the engine is used to slow the vehicle is _____.
    a. Compression braking
    b. Compression gear
    c. Low gear
    d. Forced braking

chapter 5

POWER FLOW THROUGH TRANSMISSION GEAR SETS

OBJECTIVES: **After studying chapter 5, the reader will be able to:** • Explain how power can be transferred through a planetary gear set to produce the various ratios. • Identify the major components of simple, compound, and complex planetary gear sets. • Explain the role of the driving and reaction members in producing the different power flows. • Identify the basic gear train arrangements used in automatic transmissions. • Trace the power flow through various planetary gear trains.

KEY TERMS: CVT (continuously variable transmission) 126 • Direct-drive ratio 92 • Drive (1, 2, 3, 4) 101 • Driving member 94 • Forward clutch 101 • Forward sprag 117 • Gear reduction 92 • High-reverse clutch 102 • Input gear set 117 • Intermediate band 98 • Intermediate clutch 101 • LePelletier gear train 92 • Low-reverse band 101 • Low-reverse clutch 101 • Manual (1, 2, 3) 101 • Neutral 92 • Nonsynchronous 99 • One-way clutch 94 • Overdrive 92 • Park 97 • Primary sun gear 110 • Ravigneaux gear set 92 • Reaction gear set 117 • Reaction member 94 • Reverse 92 • Secondary sun gear 110 • Simpson gear train 92 • Synchronous 99 • Torque steer 96 • Variator 126

5.1 RULES OF POWER TRANSFER

The gear set in an automatic transmission must provide a **neutral**, one or more **gear reductions**, a 1:1 or **direct-drive ratio**, a **reverse**, and an **overdrive**. (Helical gear transaxles described in Section 5.11.1 and some planetary gear transmissions do not use a 1:1 direct-drive ratio.) Some manufacturers are currently using five-, six-, seven-, and even eight-speed transmissions.

To provide the various gear ratios, most automatic transmissions use planetary gear sets that are combined in different arrangements. The same gear set design can be found in more than one make or model of transmission. A simple planetary gear set has a sun gear, ring gear, and planet carrier with two or more planet gears. ● **SEE FIGURE 5–1**. Two or more simple gear sets can also be combined using different arrangements to provide more gear ratios. A compound or complex planetary gear set combines one or more of the planetary members. Two examples of compound gear sets are:

- **Simpson gear train.** which combines one sun gear with two carriers with planet gears and two ring gears (● **SEE FIGURE 5–2**)

- **Ravigneaux gear set.** which combines one carrier that has two sets of planet gears with two sun gears, and one ring gear (● **SEE FIGURE 5–3**)

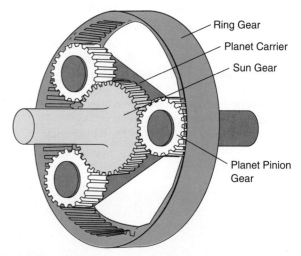

Ring Gear
Planet Carrier
Sun Gear
Planet Pinion Gear

FIGURE 5–1 A simple planetary gear set consists of a sun gear, ring gear, planet carrier, plus a group of planet pinion gears. To produce a power flow, one part is the input, one part is held in reaction, and one part becomes the output.

Gear sets can used in combination, which will result in additional ratios.

- A simple planetary gear set and a Simpson gear set can be combined to get four- and five-speed transmissions.

- A Ravigneaux gear set and a simple planetary gear set can be combined to get six, seven, and eight speeds. This arrangement is known as the **LePelletier gear train.**

FRONT PLANETARY GEAR SET
TURBINE
STATOR
IMPELLER
FRONT CLUTCH
REAR CLUTCH
REAR PLANETARY GEAR SET
LOW AND REVERSE (REAR) BAND
OIL PUMP
OVERRUNNING CLUTCH
OUTPUT SHAFT
LOCK-UP CLUTCH
GOVERNOR
BEARING
SEAL
BUSHING
EXTENSION HOUSING
PARKING LOCK ASSEMBLY
ENGINE CRANKSHAFT
INPUT SHAFT
VALVE BODY
OIL FILTER
KICKDOWN (FRONT) BAND
SUN GEAR DRIVING SHELL
FLEXIBLE DRIVE PLATE

FIGURE 5–2 A Simpson gear train transmission. Note that the two gear sets (front and rear) use the same sun gear. Also note that one carrier and the sun gear can be the reaction members. The sun gear and one ring gear can be input members, and the other carrier and ring gear can be output members. (*Courtesy of Chrysler Corporation*)

? FREQUENTLY ASKED QUESTION

How Many Speeds were Available in Early Automatic Transmissions?

At one time, Chevrolet used a transmission (the Turboglide) that had only a single forward speed. There were several two-speed transmissions: the Chrysler Powerflite, Ford Fordomatic and Merc-O-matic two-speed, General Motors Powerglide, Toyota Toyoglide, and Honda Hondamatic. These transmissions had a reduction and a direct drive. During the 1960s and 1970s, most automatic transmissions were three speeds, with high gear being a direct drive; early Hydramatic transmissions were four speeds. The demand in the 1970s and 1980s for improved fuel economy and reduced emissions resulted in four-speed transmissions, with fourth gear being an overdrive.

Annulus Gear   Planet Carrier   Large Sun Gear
Short Planet Pinion (3)
Small Sun Gear
Long Planet Pinion (3)

FIGURE 5–3 A Ravigneaux gear set has two sun gears (one small [sun gear 1] and one large [sun gear 2]), one carrier with a set of short pinions (planet pinions 1) and a set of long pinions (planet pinions 2), and a single ring gear. (*Courtesy of Chrysler Corporation*)

Knowledge of the arrangement or type of gear set will help to understand similar transmissions without memorizing the power flow for each transmission.

The power flow through the gear set (the gear ratio) is changed by applying or releasing the appropriate driving device(s) and reaction device(s). The following rules of power flow explain the power flow through a gear set.

- One planetary member must provide input (usually by applying a clutch). This **driving member** or input member will be turned by the engine through the torque converter.
- One planetary member must drive the output shaft; this will be the output member.
- To produce a ratio change, one planetary member must be a **reaction member** (usually by applying a band, holding clutch, or self-applying **one-way clutch**).
- To get a 1:1 ratio, two planetary members must be driven, and there can be no reaction device.
- Neutral occurs when none of the planetary members are driving or are held in reaction.

To understand the power flow through a particular automatic transmission, consider each part of the gear set as a simple planetary gear set. Identify which planetary member is driven for the input, which one is held in reaction, and which one is the output for each of the gear ratios. ● **SEE CHART 5–1.**

5.1.1 PLANETARY GEAR RATIOS
A simple planetary gear set can produce seven different gear ratios, plus neutral. Changing the gear ratios is done by changing the input (driving) and the reaction (held) member. These various conditions are illustrated in ● **FIGURE 5–4** and described as follows:

A. If the ring gear is held and the sun gear is driven, the planet gears are forced to rotate as they walk around inside the ring gear. The result is a torque increase and a speed reduction. The formula for calculating the gear ratio is (sun + ring) ÷ sun.

B. If the ring gear is held and the carrier is driven, the planet gears are forced to rotate as they walk around inside the ring gear. This is the reciprocal, or inverse (opposite), of A. The opposite of a reduction ratio is an overdrive ratio. The formula for calculating the gear ratio is sun ÷ (sun + ring).

C. If the sun gear is held in reaction and the ring gear is driven, the planet gears are forced to rotate as they walk around the sun gear. The result is a torque increase and a speed reduction. The formula for calculating the gear ratio is (sun + ring) ÷ ring.

D. If the sun gear is held and the carrier is driven, the planet gears are forced to rotate as they walk around the sun gear. The result is a speed increase and a torque reduction. The formula for calculating the gear ratio is ring ÷ (sun + ring). This ratio is the reciprocal of C.

E. If the carrier is held and the sun gear is driven, the planet gears will rotate and act as idlers; the planet gears drive the ring gear in a direction opposite to the sun gear. The result is a reverse with a torque increase and a speed reduction. The formula for calculating the gear ratio is ring ÷ sun.

F. If the carrier is held and the ring gear is driven, the planet gears will rotate and act as idlers, driving the sun gear in a direction opposite to the ring. The result is a reverse with a speed increase and a torque reduction. The formula for

NEUTRAL, FORWARD, OR REVERSE	REDUCTION, OVERDRIVE, OR DIRECT DRIVE	PLANETARY GEAR ACTION
Neutral		When there is no driving member or reaction member, neutral results.
Forward	Direct drive, 1:1	When there are two driving members, direct drive occurs.
Forward	Reduction	When the carrier is the output, a forward reduction occurs.
Forward	Overdrive	When the carrier is the input, an overdrive occurs.
Reverse	Reduction or OD	When the carrier is the reaction member, a reverse occurs.
F or R	OD	When the sun gear is the output, an overdrive occurs.
F or R	Reduction	When the sun gear is the input, a reduction occurs.
Reverse	Reduction or OD	When one external gear drives another, reverse rotation occurs.
Forward	Any	When an external gear drives an internal gear or vice versa, same-direction rotation occurs.

CHART 5–1

Planetary Rules

calculating the gear ratio is sun ÷ ring. This ratio is the reciprocal of E.

A technician rarely needs to calculate planetary gear set ratios. The gear ratio formulas are shown here for those who are interested or for reference.

When discussing transmission power flow, the input shaft usually turns in a clockwise direction. The direction of rotation for a rear-wheel-drive (RWD) transmission is normally viewed from the front of the transmission looking rearward. With a transaxle, this can become confusing because the front of the transmission is usually facing toward the right side of the vehicle. The right and left sides of a vehicle are determined by the driver's view of the vehicle from the driver's seat. When viewing a transaxle from the right side, the input shaft will turn in a clockwise direction. Some transmissions and transaxles use a drive

(a) $\dfrac{40 + 76}{40} = 2.9:1$

(b) $\dfrac{40}{40 + 76} = 0.34:1$

(c) $\dfrac{40 + 76}{76} = 1.53:1$

(d) $\dfrac{76}{40 + 76} = 0.65:1$

(e) $\dfrac{76}{40} = 1.9:1$

(f) $\dfrac{40}{76} = 0.53:1$

FIGURE 5–4 The gear ratio through a planetary gear set depends on which part is driven, which part is held, and which part is the output. The formula used to calculate the ratio is included with each illustration. Each gear set uses a 40-tooth sun gear and a 76-tooth ring gear.

chain to couple the torque converter and pump to the main gear section. On these units, the first input will be clockwise (viewed from the right), and the second input into the main case is considered to be counterclockwise, because it is normally viewed from the left. ● **SEE FIGURE 5–5**. (Imagine watching a clock's hands rotate from the back side.) An exception is that the engine and transaxle in some Honda and Hyundai vehicles rotate in a counterclockwise direction.

The following descriptions of transmission power flows also apply to transaxles. Most features of a transaxle are the same as those of a transmission; in the following discussions, we will treat them as the same and only refer specifically to a transmission or a transaxle when necessary. With the exception of CVTs that use an electromagnetic clutch, all automatic transmissions have the torque converter mounted on the input shaft at the front of the transmission. RWD transmissions have a single output shaft that connects to either the driveshaft of 2WD vehicles or transfer case for 4WD vehicles.

Most FWD vehicles have transverse-mounted engines, and the engine-transmission package must fit between the front suspension. A transaxle includes the transmission, final drive reduction gears, and the differential with its two output shafts. Ideally, these two shafts will exit the transaxle at the center of the vehicle to provide equal-length driveshafts.

Many transaxles have the differential mounted off center; the result is unequal-length driveshafts. ● **SEE FIGURE 5–6.** Unequal-length driveshafts can cause the vehicle to pull to one side during acceleration; this is called **torque steer.** Torque steer is caused by the unequal CV joint angles, by the length of the shafts, and by the tendency for the longer drive shaft to twist. The vehicle turns toward the side that has the longer driveshaft. Some vehicles use a short intermediate driveshaft to shorten the length of the long axle and equalize the CV joint angles.

Various designs are used to shorten transaxle length and equalize driveshaft length. One design mounts the torque converter, pump, and valve body above the main case, and a drive chain and sprockets connect the torque converter with the transmission input shaft. Some General Motors transaxles and the Ford AX4N and AX4S are examples of this arrangement. ● **SEE FIGURE 5–7.** The Chrysler 31TH uses a gear train at the output of the gear set and a short intermediate shaft to position the final drive closer to the center of the vehicle. ● **SEE FIGURE 5–8.** The Ford CD4E uses a drive chain and sprockets to connect the gear set output with the final drive and differential. ● **SEE FIGURE 5–9.**

FIGURE 5–5 When a transmission or transaxle is viewed from the engine end, the rotation of the torque converter and input shaft is in a clockwise direction. If the gear set is driven by a chain and sprockets, the rotation is counterclockwise.

FIGURE 5–6 This transaxle has a driveshaft for each front wheel. To reduce torque steer, the top unit has equal-length shafts; note the two-part right driveshaft. The lower unit uses a larger tubular shaft on the right side. *(Courtesy of Chrysler Corporation)*

FIGURE 5–7 This transaxle uses a drive chain and two sprockets to transfer torque from the torque converter at the left to the gear train. (*Courtesy of BorgWarner, Morse TEC*)

Some FWD vehicles mount the engine lengthwise, longitudinal, to allow a longer transaxle. Longitudinal transaxles are used exclusively by Subaru (the Justy is an exception) and in some Chrysler, Honda, Toyota, and Volkswagen vehicles.

Other important design features of new transaxles are lighter weight and reduced friction. Current engine designs tend to have smaller displacement with reduced torque output. All of these features improve vehicle efficiency. Improved fuel mileage and reduced emissions become more important every year.

5.3 PARK

Every automatic transmission and transaxle includes a **park** range. A shift into park prevents the transmission's output shaft from turning, thus holding the vehicle stationary. The parking gear has gearlike teeth and is mounted on the output member of the transmission. ● **SEE FIGURE 5–10**. The park pawl (sometimes called a lever) moves on a pivot pin in the case.

In all gear positions except park, the park pawl is held away from the park gear teeth by a spring. When the gear selector is moved to park, a circular cam on the end of the park actuating rod pushes the pawl into mesh with the gear teeth. This holds

FIGURE 5–8 This transaxle uses a pair of transfer gears to transfer torque to the transfer shaft and final drive gears. (*Courtesy of Chrysler Corporation*)

FIGURE 5–9 A CD4E transaxle uses a chain (3201) to transfer torque from the planetary gear set (3562) to the final drive (4031) and differential (4541). (*Courtesy of Aceomatic Recon*)

FIGURE 5–10 The park gear can be built into one of the planetary output members like this output ring gear (a) or as a separate member attached to the transmission output shaft (b). Note that (b) also supports the governor. (*Figure (a) Courtesy of Slauson Transmission Parts, www.slauson.com; (b) Courtesy of Chrysler Corporation*)

FIGURE 5–11 When the control rod is moved, the locking cam pushes the pawl into engagement with the parking gear. (*Courtesy of Chrysler Corporation*)

Type 1 Gear Train
Simpson 3-speed (A-727, A-904, C4)

FIGURE 5–12 Type 1 gear set is a three-speed Simpson gear train that uses bands to hold the sun gear and reaction carrier. Note that the reaction carrier can also be held by a one-way clutch.

the gear and output shaft stationary. ● **SEE FIGURE 5–11**. The actuating cam is spring loaded. If the gear teeth and pawl are not aligned, the gear selector lever can still be shifted into park. When the output shaft rotates slightly, the spring moves the cam, which in turn moves the pawl into engagement.

The shift into park is a mechanical connection that should be made with the driveshaft stopped. It is recommended that the shift to park should be made after the parking brake is applied. If the vehicle is rolling as park is engaged, damage to the park pawl or gear could result.

5.4 TRANSMISSION SCHEMATICS

Transmission parts and operation are often illustrated using pictures and cutaway drawings. They show the bare essentials of the transmission gear train in the simplest way possible. When you look at the typical cutaway view of a gear train, the transmission is usually split lengthwise through the middle. This shows the relationship of the parts, but in many cases, it is difficult to tell where one part stops and another begins, making it difficult to trace the path of the power flow. Many exploded views of the internal parts show the front or back of a clutch, carrier, or gear, but it is difficult to tell what the backside connects to unless a separate view is given. Exploded views are typically used by parts personnel to identify parts.

An easier way to view transmission operation is by using schematics. Transmission schematics resemble stick drawings. ● **SEE FIGURE 5–12**. Schematics use symbols for the parts and a line shows the link between the parts. Similar to electrical schematics, the major objective is to simplify the transmission as much as possible. ● **SEE FIGURE 5–13**.

A schematic is most useful when tracing the power flow. At this time, there is no industry-wide standard for automatic transmission symbols.

The Type 1 gear train schematic shows that the transmission input from the torque converter splits and goes to two clutches. One clutch can drive the front (left side) ring gear, and the other clutch can drive the sun gear that is common to both gear sets. The sun gear can also be held in reaction by the **intermediate band**. The other reaction member is the rear carrier, and it can be held by either the low-reverse band or the one-way clutch. The output of the gear set is either the front carrier or the rear ring gear because they both connect to the output shaft.

5.5 SIMPSON GEAR TRAIN TRANSMISSIONS

The Simpson gear train is a compound gear set commonly used in many three-speed transmission/transaxles. Most of the automatic transmissions used in domestic vehicles during the 1960s and 1970s used this gear train. The better known Simpson gear train transmissions are as follows:

Aisin-Warner: Three-speed models

Chrysler Corporation: 36 and 37 RH (Torqueflite A-727 and A-904) transmissions and the 31TH (A-404, A-413, A-415, and A470) transaxles

Ford Motor Company: Cruisomatic C3, C4, C5, and C6 and JATCO transmissions

General Motors: The 3L80 (THM 400), THM 200, 250, 350, 375, and 425 transmissions and 3T40 (THM 125) and THM 325 transaxles

JATCO: Three-speed models

Toyota: A40, A41, A130, A131, and A132

NOTE: Aisin-Warner (AW) and JATCO (Japanese Automatic Transmission Company) are independent transmission manufacturers. They manufacture transmissions that are used by various vehicle manufacturers.

FIGURE 5–13 Common symbols used in the transmission schematics to illustrate the various parts.

NOTE: Manufacturers occasionally change transmission model designations. In this book, the older designations are placed in parentheses, for example, current designation: 3T40; old designation: (THM 125). Appendix B provides information for identifying a transmission.

Although transmissions using a Simpson gear train are similar, they are not identical. The power flow through the gear set is essentially the same. They all have two input or driving clutches and a one-way reaction clutch, but the reaction members vary. ● **SEE FIGURE 5–14.** To help understand these different arrangements, we will group them into similar types, as follows:

- Type 1 transmissions use a band for both reaction members.

- Type 2 transmissions use a multiple-disc clutch for the reaction carrier and a band to hold the sun gear.

- Type 3 transmissions use a multiple-disc clutch, a one-way clutch, and an overrun band for the sun gear reaction member and a multiple-disc clutch to hold the reaction carrier. (When a one-way clutch is used for a reaction member, an overrun band or clutch is applied to hold the reaction member during deceleration.)

- Type 4 transmissions use a multiple-disc clutch, a one-way clutch, and an overrun band for the sun gear reaction member and a band to hold the reaction carrier.

The major difference between these transmissions is the type of reaction member. A multiple-disc clutch can handle more torque than a band. It has a much larger friction area and multiple case connections. A clutch is more complex than a band and requires more space. Type 3 and 4 units are **nonsynchronous** (asynchronous) designs. All four types use a nonsynchronous

1–2 shift in drive. The 2–3 upshift timing is less critical because the disc clutch is used with a one-way clutch; the clutch stays applied while the one-way clutch simply overruns as the upshift occurs. ● **SEE FIGURE 5–15.** The band used in **synchronous** designs must be released at an exact time for the upshift, and it must reapply at the exact time during a downshift.

The nonsynchronous arrangement is great for upshifts, but is ineffective during deceleration. Similar to the one-way clutch in first gear, the one-way clutch overruns during deceleration. An overrun band is used in manual-2 range for compression braking.

Type 4 transmissions, the 3L80 (THM 400), have the gear set turned end for end. In this arrangement, the input ring gear is at the back of the transmission, and the output ring gear is at the front. This transmission uses a center support to hold the inner race of the low-roller clutch and house the intermediate clutch piston. Type 4 units are nonsynchronous because of the two one-way clutches.

As mentioned, the Simpson gear set consists of a double sun gear that is meshed with the planet gears of the two carriers. ● **SEE FIGURE 5–16.** This sun gear is also called a compound or common sun gear. One of the carriers (usually the front) is attached to the output shaft, and the other carrier serves as a reaction member. It is called the reaction carrier in some transmissions. One ring gear (usually the front) is the input and is splined to a driving clutch. The other ring gear is the output ring gear, and it is attached to the output shaft. The sun gear is attached to a driving clutch through an input shell, making it an input member, but it can also be a reaction member, held stationary by a band or a multiple-disc holding clutch. ● **SEE CHART 5–2.** In most transmissions, the sun gear is the same size at both ends, but in some transmissions, the rear section has a smaller sun gear so first and reverse gears have lower ratios.

Type 2 Gear Train
Simpson 3-speed (C6)

Type 3 Gear Train
Simpson 3-speed (THM 350)

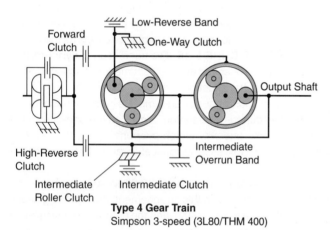

Type 4 Gear Train
Simpson 3-speed (3L80/THM 400)

FIGURE 5–14 These gear train types are all Simpson three-speed units that use different apply devices or, in the type 4, a different gear set arrangement.

FIGURE 5–15 The one-way clutch of this type 1 gear set serves as the reaction member in D1. The low-reverse band is applied in M1 to allow compression braking.

FIGURE 5–16 If both the high-reverse and forward clutches are released, then the transmission is in neutral. Note that the sun gear can be of two different sizes.

RING GEAR	SUN GEAR	PLANET CARRIER	RATIO
Held	Input	Output	Reduction
Held	Output	Input	Overdrive
Input	Held	Output	Reduction
Input	Output	Held	Reverse Overdrive
Output	Held	Input	Overdrive
Output	Input	Held	Reverse Reduction
Input	Input	Output	Direct Drive

CHART 5–2

Planetary Gear Actions

Manufacturers usually provide clutch and band application charts for their transmissions, and these charts show which apply devices are used for each gear range. Each apply device drives a particular gear set member or holds it in reaction. Clutch and band charts are very helpful in understanding the power flow through a transmission. They are also very helpful when diagnosing transmission failures. ● **SEE CHART 5–3.**

5.5.1 NEUTRAL Neutral is achieved by not applying the input clutches. Power enters the transmission from the torque converter but only travels as far as the released clutches. When shifted into neutral, some transmissions apply one of the clutches needed for first or reverse to prevent a harsh engagement when the vehicle is shifted into gear.

GEAR	FRONT RING	FRONT CARRIER	SUN	REAR CARRIER	REAR RING
First	Input	Reaction	Output/input	Reaction	Output
Second	Input	Output	Reaction	—	—
Third	Input	Output	Input	—	—
Reverse	—	—	Input	Reaction	Output

CHART 5–3

Simpson Gear Train Summary

(a)

(b)　　　　**(c)**

FIGURE 5–17 (a) In D1, the front ring gear is driven while the rear carrier is held by the one-way clutch. A reverse reduction occurs in both (b) the front unit and (c) the rear unit.

5.5.2 FIRST GEAR The Simpson gear set has two slightly different first gears—drive-1 and manual-1—the difference being in how the reaction carrier is held. In both gear ranges, power flows through the gear set when the front ring gear is driven and the reaction carrier is held. All Simpson gear sets use a clutch to drive the front (input) ring gear. Transmission types 1 and 4 use a one-way clutch and a band and types 2 and 3 use a one-way clutch and a holding clutch to hold the reaction carrier. In drive-1, the one-way clutch is used; it provides self-application and release. In manual-1, a band or holding clutch is applied to provide engine compression braking during deceleration.
● **SEE FIGURE 5–17.**

　　When manual-1 (low) is selected, the one-way clutch is assisted by either a band (types 1 and 4) or multiple-disc clutch (types 2 and 3). The band is called the *low and reverse* or **low-reverse band**. The multiple-disc clutch is called a **low-reverse clutch**. The power flow is exactly the same as drive-1 except that power can be transmitted from the drive shaft to the engine during deceleration. This provides engine (compression) braking as the vehicle slows. Engine braking is easily noticed by comparing the deceleration of a vehicle in drive-1 and manual-1. For simplicity, we will call this holding member either a low-reverse band or a low-reverse clutch in this text.

POWER FLOW: SIMPSON DRIVE-1. In drive-1 (low), the following occurs.

- The **forward clutch** is applied to drive the input ring gear in a clockwise direction.
- The output/front carrier will not rotate because it is connected to the driveshaft.

　　NOTE: The front carrier becomes a rotating reaction member when the vehicle starts moving.

- The front planet gears are driven clockwise.
- The sun gear is driven in a reverse direction (counterclockwise) at a reduction speed.
- The reaction carrier is held from turning counterclockwise by the one-way clutch (or the low-reverse band or clutch in manual-1).
- The rear planet gears are driven clockwise.

- The rear ring gear is driven clockwise at a reduced speed.
- The output shaft and driveshaft are driven clockwise at a reduced speed.

The gear set is producing two reverse reduction ratios, and the result is a forward (clockwise) rotation of the driveshaft. The overall ratio will be about 2.45:1 to 2.74:1 depending on the size of the gears.

5.5.3 SECOND GEAR The sun gear must be held stationary in second gear. This is done by a band in type 1 and 2 transmissions or a multiple-disc clutch plus a one-way clutch in type 3 and 4 transmissions. Type 3 and 4 transmissions use an **intermediate clutch** and an *intermediate one-way clutch*.
● **SEE FIGURE 5–18.** When the intermediate clutch is applied, it holds the outer race of the intermediate roller clutch stationary. The one-way clutch locks, holding the sun gear from rotating counterclockwise. Because the one-way clutch will only hold in one direction, these units have two slightly different power flows in second gear: **drive-2** and **manual-2**. Manual-2 applies an intermediate overrun band to provide engine compression braking during deceleration. For simplicity, we will call this reaction member either an intermediate band or intermediate clutch in this text.

FIGURE 5–18 The intermediate clutch and intermediate roller clutch hold the sun gear from rotating in second gear in the THM 350, type 3 gear set. The intermediate overrun band is used in manual-2 for compression braking. (*Reprinted with permission of General Motors*)

(a)   (b)

FIGURE 5–19 In second gear, the ring gear is driven while the sun gear is held, and the planet gears walk around the sun gear and force the carrier to revolve at a reduced speed.

POWER FLOW: SIMPSON DRIVE-2. In drive-2 (intermediate), the following occurs.

- The forward clutch stays applied to drive the input ring gear clockwise. ● **SEE FIGURE 5–19**.
- The intermediate band or clutch applies to hold the sun gear stationary.
- The front planet gears are driven clockwise and walk around the sun gear.
- The front carrier is driven clockwise.
- The front carrier drives the output shaft clockwise at about a 1.5:1 ratio.

5.5.4 THIRD GEAR
Third gear in this gear set is direct drive with a 1:1 ratio. It is produced by applying both driving clutches (forward and high-reverse) and either releasing the

FIGURE 5–20 In third gear, both driving clutches are applied so two members (the ring and sun gears) of the same gear set are driven. This locks the gears and produces a 1:1 gear ratio.

intermediate band in synchronous transmissions (types 1 and 2) or allowing the intermediate roller clutch to overrun in nonsynchronous transmissions (types 3 and 4). The gear set locks up because the ring gear is trying to turn the planet pinions clockwise while the sun gear is trying to turn them counterclockwise.

POWER FLOW: SIMPSON DRIVE-3. In drive-3 (high), the following occurs.

- The forward clutch stays applied to drive the input ring gear clockwise.
- The **high-reverse clutch** applies to drive the sun gear clockwise.
- The front planet gears become locked in the carrier.
- The front carrier is driven clockwise at the same speed as the ring and sun gears. ● **SEE FIGURE 5–20**.
- The front carrier drives the output shaft clockwise at a 1:1 ratio.

INTERMEDIATE
BAND—RELEASED

LOW-REVERSE
BAND—APPLIED

INPUT
SHAFT

OUTPUT
SHAFT

FORWARD CLUTCH—
RELEASED

HIGH-REVERSE
CLUTCH—APPLIED

(a)

(b)

FIGURE 5–21 In reverse, the sun gear is driven while the carrier is held. The planet gears act as idlers and cause the ring gear to revolve in a reverse direction at a reduced speed.

GEAR	FORWARD CLUTCH	HIGH-REV. CLUTCH	INTERMEDIATE BAND	LOW-REV. BAND	ONE-WAY CLUTCH
D1	Applied				Effective
D2	Applied		Applied		
D3	Applied	Applied			
M1	Applied			Applied	Effective
M2	Applied		Applied		
R		Applied		Applied	
Planetary	Drives Input	Drives	Holds	Holds Reaction	Holds Reaction
Member	Ring	Sun	Sun	Carrier	Carrier

CHART 5–4

Simpson Gear Train Band and Clutch Application, Type 1

5.5.5 REVERSE

Reverse in a Simpson gear train occurs when the high-reverse clutch and the low-reverse band or clutch are applied. The high-reverse clutch drives the sun gear while the carrier in the rear gear set is held stationary by the low-reverse band or clutch. ● **SEE FIGURE 5–21**. The planet gears act as idlers, reversing the power flow as they transfer power from the smaller sun gear to the larger ring gear. Gear action is shown in ● **FIGURE 5–4E**. A reverse reduction is produced at the output ring gear of about 2.07:1 to 2.22:1.

POWER FLOW: SIMPSON REVERSE. In reverse, the following occurs.

- The high-reverse clutch is applied to drive the sun gear clockwise.
- The low-reverse band or clutch is applied to hold the rear carrier.
- The rear planet gears are driven counterclockwise.
- The rear ring gear is driven counterclockwise at a speed reduction.

- The rear ring gear drives the output shaft counterclockwise at a 2.07:1 to 2.22:1 ratio.

A summary of the Simpson gear train members used to produce the two reduction ratios, one direct and one reverse, is provided in Chart 5–3. Clutch and band application charts for type 1 and 3 gear trains are provided in ● **CHARTS 5–4 AND 5–5**.

5.6 SHIFT TIMING

As a vehicle accelerates from a stop to cruising speed, the driving and reaction members have to apply and release in an exact operating sequence. When they apply, they must come on at a precise rate. To illustrate this, we will follow an upshift sequence during a hard acceleration with shift points occurring at 4800 RPM. ● **SEE FIGURE 5–22**.

In first gear, the ratio will be 2.5:1, so the vehicle driveshaft will be revolving at 1920 RPM (4800 ÷ 2.5) when the 1–2 upshift

GEAR	FORWARD CLUTCH	HI-REV. CLUTCH	INTER. CLUTCH	INTER. ONE-WAY CLUTCH	INTER. BAND	LOW-REV. CLUTCH	ONE-WAY CLUTCH
D1	Applied						Effective
D2	Applied		Applied	Effective			
D3	Applied	Applied	Applied	Overruning			
M1	Applied					Applied	Effective
M2	Applied		Applied	Effective	Applied		
R		Applied				Applied	
Planetary	Drives	Drives	Holds	Holds	Holds	Holds Reaction	Holds Reaction
Member	Input Ring	Sun	Sun	Sun	Sun	Carrier	Carrier

CHART 5–5

Simpson Gear Train Band and Clutch Application, Type 3

First Gear, 2.5:1

Second Gear, 1.5:1

Third Gear, 1:1

Reverse, 2.2:1

Triple 1 Shift Sequence

FIGURE 5–22 The full-throttle shift sequence for a type 1 transmission showing the apply devices and the output shaft speed at the 1–2 and 2–3 upshifts. Reverse is also shown.

occurs. Second gear has a ratio of 1.5:1, so the engine speed will drop from 4800 to 2800 RPM (1920 × 1.5) during the shift.

The forward clutch is used in all the forward gear ranges. It is applied when the driver makes the neutral-to-drive shift, and it will stay applied through all forward gears, driving the front ring gear at input shaft speed. In first gear, the sun gear is revolving in a reverse direction. During the 1–2 shift, the intermediate reaction member must apply gradually, smoothly, and firmly so the sun gear will come to a stop during the time duration required for the shift. If it stops too fast, the shift will be harsh. The shift will be long and drawn out if it stops too slowly. This shift is relatively easy to accomplish because the

one-way clutch will overrun and release the reaction carrier as the intermediate reaction member is applied (nonsynchronous shift). The duration or timing of this shift will be controlled by how fast the intermediate reaction member is applied. Some of the variables that affect application time are servo diameter, fluid feed orifice diameter, and use of an accumulator. These are described in Chapter 7. Shift timing can also be controlled electronically as described in Chapter 8.

When the 2–3 shift occurs, the vehicle driveshaft will be turning at 3200 RPM (4800 ÷ 1.5), and during the shift the engine speed will drop from 4800 to 3200 RPM. Remember that this is a 1:1 gear ratio, and the sun gear speed must

FIGURE 5-23 This A340E transmission sectional view shows the overdrive section between the pump and three-speed planetary gear section. (*Courtesy of Toyota Motor Sales USA, Inc.*)

PROBLEM SOLVING 5-1

Imagine that you are working in a shop that specializes in transmission repair, and these problems are brought to you.

Case 1:

A 1970 Dodge pickup with an A727 transmission (type 1) drives normally in all ranges, except there is an engine flare, indicating slippage, during a full-throttle 1–2 shift. Do you think a driving or reaction member could be faulty? If so, which one?

Case 2:

A 1986 Chevrolet with a THM 350C transmission (type 3) has no second gear. It has a delayed shift from first into third. There is a second gear if you shift manually from manual-1 to manual-2. What would be the cause of this problem? Which driving or reaction member is at fault?

increase from a stop to input shaft speed as the direct clutch is applied.

The synchronous type 1 and 2 transmissions that use a band for the intermediate reaction member have a potential timing problem during the 2–3 shift. The band must release as the direct clutch is applied. If the band releases too quickly, the transmission will fall back into first gear, and an engine overspeed or flare will occur ($3200 \times 2.5 = 8000$ RPM). If the band releases too slowly or the direct clutch applies too rapidly, the combination will try to bring the engine and the vehicle to a stop. This produces a very harsh shift.

The intermediate overrunning clutch in the type 3 or 4 transmission eliminates any timing problem. As the direct clutch applies, the sun gear picks up speed because the overrunning clutch simply overruns.

5.7 SIMPSON GEAR TRAIN PLUS AN ADDITIONAL GEAR SET

The Simpson gear train with an additional simple planetary gear set is used to produce a four-speed overdrive transmission or transaxle.

The overdrive planetary gear set provides two speeds: direct 1:1 and overdrive. When the overdrive planetary gear set is in direct drive it turns the Simpson planetary gear set input at engine speed. When the overdrive gear train is in direct drive 1:1, the Simpson gear train will shift from first to second and then to third. If the overdrive planetary gear set is in overdrive, it will turn the Simpson planetary gear set input faster than engine speed. The three-speed Simpson gear train will operate as described earlier. To get overdrive, the overdrive planetary gear set will be in overdrive and the Simpson gear set will be in direct 1:1. To get reverse, the overdrive gear set will be in direct and the Simpson will be in reverse.

Some transmissions and transaxles place the overdrive gear set at the back end of the main gear set so it increases the speed of the output shaft or gear. The more common transmissions using this gear set are as follows:

Chrysler 42RH (A-500), 46RH (A-518)

Ford 4R44E (A4LD), 5R55E, and E4OD

GM 4T80-E, THM-2004R, and 325–4L

Jeep AW-4

Nissan E4N7IB

Toyota A40 and A340 series

5.7.1 OVERDRIVE In most of these transmissions, the overdrive gear set is built into the area at the front of the case between the torque converter and the main gear set. ● **SEE FIGURE 5–23.**

FIGURE 5–24 This Chrysler 42RH transmission cutaway view shows a three-speed, Simpson type 1 gear set with an overdrive unit at the output end of the transmission. (*Courtesy of Chrysler Corporation*)

FIGURE 5–25 An exploded view of the A340E overdrive unit. The O/D one-way clutch provides a 1:1 ratio in D1, D2, and D3. The O/D direct clutch is used in manual gear ranges. The O/D brake pack is applied in D4. (*Courtesy of Toyota Motor Sales USA, Inc.*)

The input shaft from the torque converter is connected to the carrier of the overdrive gear set, and the ring gear of the overdrive gear set is arranged so it becomes the input of the main gear set. The Chrysler 42RH and 46RH have the overdrive gear set built into the transmission extension housing to cause a speed increase between the main gear set and the output shaft. ● **SEE FIGURE 5–24.** Each of these transmissions uses a different arrangement of bands and clutches so they fall into a different transmission category or type.

The input member for the overdrive gear set (a simple planetary gear set) is the planet carrier, and the output is the ring gear. ● **SEE FIGURE 5–25.** The sun gear is a reaction member and can be held stationary by either a band or a multiple-disc clutch. There is also a multiple-disc clutch that can lock the carrier to the sun gear and a one-way clutch. In the 4R44E/5R55E, the one-way clutch is placed so the carrier can drive the ring gear. In the others, the one-way clutch is placed so the sun gear cannot turn faster than the carrier. The overdrive friction

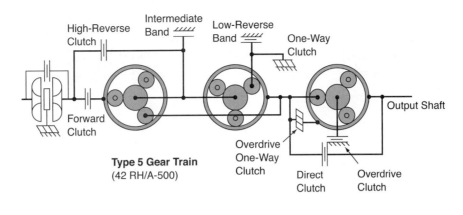

Type 5 Gear Train
(42 RH/A-500)

Type 6 Gear Train
(4R44E/A4LD, 5R55E)

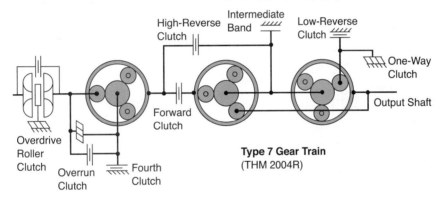

Type 7 Gear Train
(THM 2004R)

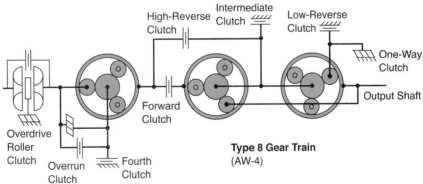

Type 8 Gear Train
(AW-4)

FIGURE 5–26 Types 5, 6, 7, and 8 gear sets illustrate the different four-speed gear train arrangements that combine a Simpson three-speed gear set with an overdrive unit.

members have different names depending on the transmission manufacturer.

Power is transmitted through the overdrive gear set at a 1:1 ratio by the one-way clutch in drive-1, D2, and D3. ● **SEE FIGURE 5–26**.

The 42RH and 46RH are a little unusual in that one hydraulic piston and return spring is used for both the direct clutch and the overdrive clutch (type 5 gear train). The very strong return spring is used to release the overdrive clutch and apply the direct clutch. Hydraulic pressure at the piston releases the

First Gear, 2.47:1

Input: 4,800 rpm
One-Way Clutch Effective
Forward Clutch Applied
One-Way Clutch Effective
Output: 1,943 rpm

Second Gear, 1.47:1

One-Way Clutch Effective
Intermediate Band Applied
Forward Clutch Applied
Input: 4,800 rpm
Output: 3,265 rpm

Third Gear, 1:1

High-Rev. Clutch Applied
One-Way Clutch Effective
Forward Clutch Applied
Input: 4,800 rpm
Output: 4,800 rpm

Fourth Gear, 0.75:1

High-Rev. Clutch Applied
Front/OD Band Applied
Forward Clutch Applied
Input: 4,800 rpm
Output: 6,400 rpm

Reverse, 2.1:1

High-Rev. Clutch Applied
One-Way Clutch Effective
Low/Rev. Band Applied
Input: 4,800 rpm
Output: 2,286 rpm

FIGURE 5–27 The full-throttle shift sequence for a type 6 transmission showing the apply devices and the output shaft speed at the 1–2, 2–3, and 3–4 upshifts. Reverse is also shown.

direct clutch and then almost immediately applies the overdrive clutch. With this arrangement, the gear set is locked in either direct drive or overdrive with the overrunning clutch transferring power while the upshift or downshift is made.

In the 4R44E/5R55E (type 6), the power is transferred directly from the carrier to the ring gear. In the 2004R (type 7), the gear set is locked because the one-way clutch does not allow the sun gear to overrun the carrier. The type 8 gear train illustrates the power flow through a Jeep AW-4 transmission.

Like other power flows using a one-way clutch, these gear sets overrun during deceleration and do not produce engine (compression) braking. To prevent this in manual-1, M2, or M3, the overdrive clutch in the 4R44E/5R55E, overrun clutch in the 200–4R, or the O/D direct clutch in the AW-4 are applied. This locks the overdrive gear assembly so it operates in direct drive in both acceleration and deceleration.

A shift sequence for a type 6 transmission is illustrated in ● **FIGURE 5–27**, and a band and clutch chart is shown in ● **CHART 5–6**. A summary of the input, reaction, and output members of the overdrive gear sets to produce the various ratios is given in ● **CHARTS 5–7 AND 5–8**.

POWER FLOW: OVERDRIVE GEAR SET. In the overdrive gear set, the following occurs.

- The overdrive carrier is driven by the input shaft.
- The band or clutch is applied to hold the overdrive sun gear.
- The overdrive planet gears are driven clockwise and walk around the sun gear.

GEAR	FORWARD CLUTCH	HIGH-REVERSE CLUTCH	OVER-DRIVE CLUTCH	O/D ONE-WAY CLUTCH	OVER-DRIVE BAND	INTERMEDIATE BAND	LOW/REV. BAND	REAR ONE-WAY CLUTCH
D1	Applied			Effective				Effective
D2	Applied			Effective		Applied		
D3	Applied	Applied		Effective				
D4	Applied	Applied		Overrunning	Applied			
M1	Applied		Applied	Effective			Applied	Effective
M2	Applied		Applied	Effective		Applied		
M3			Applied	Effective				
R		Applied					Applied	
Planet	Drives	Drives	Locks	Drives	Holds	Holds	Holds	Holds
Member	Input Ring	Forward Sun	Front Sun & Ring	Center Shaft	Front Sun	Forward Sun	Reaction Carrier	Reaction Carrier

CHART 5–6

Simpson Gear Train Plus Overdrive Band and Clutch Application, Type 6

GEAR	MAIN GEAR SET	O/D GEAR SET	RATIO
1	1st gear	Direct	2.47:1
2	2nd gear	Direct	1.47:1
3	3rd gear	Direct	1:1
4	3rd gear	Overdrive	0.75:1

CHART 5–7

Shift Strategy: Four Speed

GEAR	MAIN GEAR SET	O/D GEAR SET	RATIO
1	1st gear	Direct	2.47:1
2	1st gear	Overdrive	1.87:1
3	2nd gear	Direct	1.47:1
4	3rd gear	Direct	1:1
5	3rd gear	Overdrive	0.75:1

CHART 5–8

Shift Strategy: Five Speed

- The overdrive ring gear is driven clockwise at an overdrive speed.
- The overdrive ring gear drives the main gear set at a 0.69:1 to 0.75:1 ratio.

5.8 RAVIGNEAUX GEAR SETS

The Ravigneaux gear set uses a single carrier that has two sets of intermeshed planet gears, two sun gears, and a single ring gear. The planet gears are different lengths. The two sun gears

PROBLEM SOLVING 5–2

Imagine that you are working in a shop that specializes in transmission repair, and these problems are brought to you.

Case 1:

A 1998 Ford Ranger pickup with a 4R44E transmission (type 6) drives normally in all ranges, except there is an engine flare, indicating slippage, during a full-throttle 1–2 shift. Do you think one driving or reaction member could be faulty? If so, which one?

Case 2:

A 1990 Chevrolet Caprice with a TH 200-4R transmission (type 7) does not move when in drive. It has manual-1, and there is a second gear if you shift manually from manual-1 to manual-2. What would be the cause of this problem? Which driving or reaction member is at fault?

have different diameters and are independent of each other. The long pinion gears mesh with the large sun gear, short pinions, and ring gear. The short pinions mesh with the small sun gear and the long pinion gears (see Figure 5–3). In some transmissions, the ring gear is in mesh with the short pinions. The Ravigneaux gear set is used in the following.

Two-speed transmissions. Chrysler Powerflite, the Ford two-speed, and the General Motors Powerglide, Dynaflow, and THM 300

Three-speed transmissions. Ford FMX and General Motors 3L30 (THM 180)

Three-speed transaxles. Ford ATX, KM 171 to 175 versions

Four-speed transmission. Ford 4R70W (AOD)

Four-speed transaxles. Ford 4EAT, KM 175 to 177, and ZF-4

FIGURE 5–28 Types 9, 10, 11, and 12 gear sets illustrate the different three- and four-speed gear train arrangements that use a single Ravigneaux gear set.

NOTE: KM (Kyoto Transmission) and ZF (Zahnradfabrik Freidrichshafen) are independent transmission manufacturers. They manufacture transmissions that are used by various vehicle manufacturers.

The exact arrangement of the gear set varies depending on the usage. ● **SEE FIGURE 5–28**.

5.8.1 TWO-SPEED RAVIGNEAUX ARRANGEMENT AND OPERATION

POWER FLOWS: POWERGLIDE. In drive low, the following occurs.

- The primary sun gear is driven by the input shaft.
- The low band is applied to hold the secondary sun gear.
- The primary sun gear drives the long planet pinion gears counterclockwise.
- The long planet pinions drive the short planet pinions clockwise.
- The short planet pinions walk around the secondary sun gear.
- The planet carrier is driven clockwise at a reduction speed.
- The output shaft is driven clockwise at a 1.76:1 or 1.82:1 ratio.

FIGURE 5–29 When a Powerglide is in low gear, the low band is applied to hold the low sun gear stationary; at this time, the long pinions will be driven by the input sun gear and walk around the low sun gear to drive the carrier. (*Reprinted with permission of General Motors*)

In drive high:

- The primary sun gear is driven by the input shaft.
- The low band releases.
- The high clutch is applied to drive the secondary sun gear.
- The long and short planet pinion gears become locked.
- The carrier is driven at input shaft speed.
- The output shaft is driven clockwise at a 1:1 ratio.

In reverse:

- The primary sun gear is driven by the input shaft.
- The reverse clutch is applied to hold the ring gear.
- The primary sun gear drives the long planet pinion gears counterclockwise.
- The long planet pinions drive the short planet pinions clockwise.
- The short planet pinions walk around inside the ring gear.
- The planet carrier is driven counterclockwise at a reduction speed.
- The output shaft is driven counterclockwise at a 1:76 to 1.82:1 ratio.

5.8.2 THREE-SPEED RAVIGNEAUX ARRANGEMENT AND OPERATION: FIRST VERSION
There are two three-speed versions of the Ravigneaux gear set. The Ford FMX (type 10 gear set) is the first version. It uses two driving clutches, two bands, and a one-way clutch. The ring gear is the output member, and the carrier with its two sets of planet pinion gears can be a reaction member held by either a band or the one-way clutch. The inner one-way clutch race is secured by a stationary transmission part called a *center support*. One sun gear (the smaller, rear, primary one) is driven by the front, *forward clutch*. The larger secondary sun gear is driven by the high-reverse clutch or held stationary by the intermediate band.

In neutral, both driving clutches are released, and the power flow from the torque converter goes no farther than the clutches.

POWER FLOWS: FMX. In drive-1 (low), the following occurs.

- The forward clutch applies to drive the primary sun gear.
- The primary sun gear drives the short planet pinion gears counterclockwise.
- The carrier is held from turning counterclockwise by the one-way clutch (rear band in manual-1).
- The short planet pinions drive the long planet pinions clockwise.
- The long planet pinions drive the ring gear clockwise at a reduction speed.
- The output shaft is driven clockwise at a 2.4:1 ratio.

In drive-2 (intermediate):

- The forward clutch stays applied to drive the primary sun gear.
- The intermediate band applies to hold the secondary sun gear.
- The primary sun gear drives the short planet pinion gears counterclockwise.
- The short planet pinions drive the long planet pinions clockwise.

- The long planet pinions walk around the secondary sun gear.
- The long planet pinions drive the ring gear clockwise at a reduction speed.
- The output shaft is driven clockwise at a 1.47:1 ratio.

In drive-3 (high):

- The forward clutch stays applied to drive the primary sun gear.
- The intermediate band is released.
- The high-reverse clutch is applied to drive the secondary sun gear.
- The long and short planet pinion gears become locked.
- The ring gear is driven at input shaft speed.
- The output shaft is driven clockwise at a 1:1 ratio.

In reverse:

- The high-reverse clutch is applied to drive the secondary sun gear.
- The low-reverse band is applied to hold the carrier.
- The secondary sun gear drives the long planet pinion gears counterclockwise.
- The long planet pinions drive the ring gear counterclockwise at a reduction speed.
- The output shaft is driven in a reverse direction at a 2:1 ratio.

5.8.3 THREE-SPEED RAVIGNEAUX ARRANGEMENT AND OPERATION: SECOND VERSION

The General Motors 3L30 (THM 180) transmission (type 11 gear set) and the Ford ATX transaxle use a slightly different arrangement of the Ravigneaux three-speed gear set. Both use two driving clutches, one holding clutch, a one-way clutch, and a band. The carrier with its two sets of planet pinion gears is the output member. The ring gear is meshed with the long planet pinion gear set and is arranged so it can be an input or a reaction member. We will use the 3L30 as an example while describing power flow through this gear set. Remember that power flow through an ATX is very similar.

The ring gear can be held stationary by the *reverse clutch*, or it can be driven by the *second clutch*. ● **SEE FIGURE 5–30.** The smaller sun gear, called the input sun gear, can be driven by a clutch called the *third clutch*. There is also a one-way clutch in this sun gear drive arrangement that allows the sun gear to overrun the speed of the input shaft. The larger sun gear can be a reaction member. It is called the reaction sun gear and can be held by the *low band*.

POWER FLOW: 3L30.   In drive-1 (low), the following occurs.

- The third clutch is applied to drive the input sun gear.
- The input sun gear drives the short planet pinion gears counterclockwise.
- The short planet pinions drive the long planet pinions clockwise.
- The low band is applied to hold the reaction sun gear.
- The long planet pinions walk around the reaction sun gear.
- The long planet pinions drive the carrier clockwise at a reduction speed.
- The output shaft is driven clockwise at a 2.4:1 to 2.8:1 ratio.

In drive-2 (intermediate):

- The second clutch is applied to drive the ring gear.
- The low band stays applied to hold the reaction sun gear.
- The ring gear drives the long planet pinions clockwise.
- The long plant pinions walk around the reaction sun gear.
- The long planet pinions drive the carrier clockwise at a reduction speed.
- The output shaft is driven clockwise at a 1.48:1 to 1.6:1 ratio.

In drive-3 (high):

- The second clutch stays applied to drive the ring gear.
- The third clutch is applied to drive the input sun gear.
- The long and short planet pinion gears become locked.

(a)

(b)

FIGURE 5–30 Exploded views of (a) a Ford ATX transaxle and (b) a GM 3L30 transmission gear set. Note the difference in the carriers (27). (*Courtesy of Slauson Transmission Parts, www.slauson.com*)

- The carrier is driven at input shaft speed.
- The output shaft is driven clockwise at a 1:1 ratio.

In reverse:

- The third clutch is applied to drive the input sun gear.
- The reverse clutch is applied to hold the ring gear.
- The input sun gear drives the short planet pinion gears counterclockwise.
- The short planet pinions drive the long planet pinions clockwise.
- The long planet pinions walk around inside the ring gear.
- The long planet pinions drive the carrier counterclockwise at a reduction speed.
- The output shaft is driven counterclockwise at a 1.9:1 to 2.1:1 ratio.

5.8.4 FOUR-SPEED RAVIGNEAUX ARRANGEMENT AND OPERATION

The Ford 4R70W (AOD) (type 12 gear set) uses a four-speed version of the Ravigneaux gear train. The gears in the 4R70W are arranged in a manner similar to the type 10 Ford FMX. The first version of this transmission, the AOD, has an additional input shaft (the direct driveshaft) and an additional clutch (the direct clutch). These are arranged so the carrier can be an input member in third and fourth gears as well as a reaction member in first and reverse. The direct driveshaft is driven by a damper assembly at the front of the torque converter so it is a purely mechanical input into the gear set. ● **SEE FIGURE 5–31.** Newer versions, such as the 4R70W, use

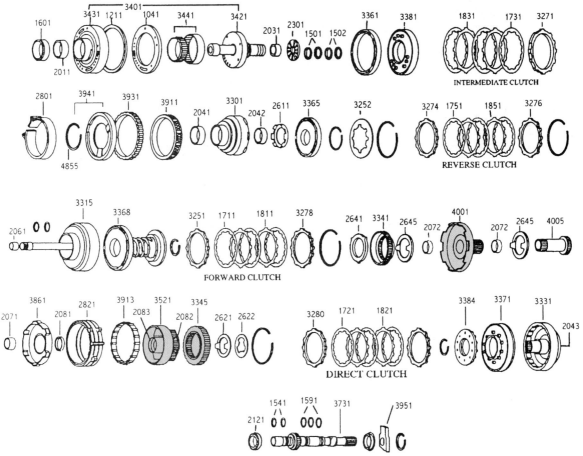

FIGURE 5–31 A stub shaft (not shown) is used to connect the turbine shaft and forward drum (107) of the Ford 4R70W transmission to the direct clutch housing (98). The direct clutch is used in third and fourth gears. (*Courtesy of Aceomatic Recon*)

a more conventional torque converter with a converter clutch and connect the direct clutch to the forward clutch by a short stub shaft.

The first-, second-, and reverse-gear power flows in the 4R70W are the same as those in the FMX, with the exception that the intermediate clutch is used to hold the carrier for a reaction member in second gear. In third gear, the direct-drive clutch is applied to drive the carrier while the forward clutch remains applied to drive the small, forward sun gear. This locks the planet gears and drives the ring gear in direct drive. The intermediate clutch remains applied, but it becomes ineffective because the intermediate one-way clutch overruns.

In summary, the input, reaction, and output members for the various power flows are shown in ● **FIGURE 5–32**. A clutch and band chart is shown in ● **CHART 5–9**.

POWER FLOW: 4R70W. The 4R70W power flows for drive-1, D2, D3, and reverse are very similar to those of the FMX described in Section 5.8.2. The exception is that the D3 applies the forward and direct clutches.

In drive-4 (overdrive), the following occurs.

- The direct clutch stays applied to drive the carrier.
- The carrier drives the long planet pinion gears counterclockwise.

First Gear, 2.84:1

Second Gear, 1.56:1

Third Gear, 1:1

Fourth Gear, 0.7:1

Reverse, 2.33:1

FIGURE 5–32 The full-throttle shift sequence for a type 12 transmission showing the apply devices and the output shaft speed at the 1–2, 2–3, and 3–4 upshifts and reverse.

GEAR	FORWARD CLUTCH	REVERSE CLUTCH	INTER. CLUTCH	INTER. ONE-WAY CLUTCH	DIRECT CLUTCH	O/D BAND	LOW-REV. BAND	PLANETARY ONE-WAY CLUTCH
D1	Applied							Effective
D2	Applied		Applied	Effective				
D3	Applied		Applied	Overruning	Applied			
D4			Applied	Overruning	Applied	Applied		
M1	Applied						Applied	Effective
M2	Applied			Effective	Applied			
R		Applied					Applied	
Planet	Drives	Drives	Holds	Holds		Holds		
Member	Forward Sun	Reverse Sun	Reverse Sun	Reverse Sun	Drives Carrier	Reverse Sun	Holds Carrier	Holds Carrier

CHART 5–9

Four-Speed Ravigneaux Gear Train Band and Clutch Application, Type 12

- The overdrive band is applied to hold the front sun gear.
- The long planet pinions walk around the front sun gear.
- The long planet pinions drive the ring gear clockwise at an overdrive speed.
- The output shaft is driven clockwise at a 0.67:1 ratio.

5.8.5 FOUR-SPEED RAVIGNEAUX ARRANGEMENT AND OPERATION: SECOND VERSION

The General Motors 4L30-E transmission is a dual-unit transmission that is a combination of the type 11 gear train with an overdrive unit at the front. This combination is similar to the type 6, 7, and 8 gear trains. Like these other gear sets, the overdrive unit is kept in its lower ratio in first, second, and third and shifted into overdrive for fourth gear. ● **SEE FIGURE 5–33.**

5.8.6 LE PELLETIER GEAR TRAIN

The LePelletier gear train (type 13 gear set) is a recent development and combines a simple planetary gear set with a Ravigneaux gear set providing six forward speeds. ● **SEE FIGURE 5–34.** The combination is fairly simple, using only five multiplate clutches and, in some transmissions, a one-way clutch. Three of the clutches are driving members and the other two are used in reaction. This gear set is used in the Ford 6R60 and 6R80 and General Motors 6L80E transmissions, and transmissions produced by Aisin and ZF.

Because the ring gear is always an input and the sun gear is always a reaction member (it is splined to the back of the pump), the simple gear set is always in reduction. The C1 and C3 clutches can provide a reduced speed input to the Ravigneaux gear set. The Ravigneaux gear set is arranged like a type 12 gear set, with three possible inputs and two reaction members.

This gear set has four reduction ratios and two overdrive ratios, with a gear ratio spread of over 6:1. ● **SEE FIGURE 5–35.** Compared to current five-speed transmissions, these six-speed transmissions have fewer control devices and weigh about 13% less. Because of the close gear ratios and lighter weight, they also promise fuel mileage increases of 5% to 7%, and provide faster acceleration.

FIGURE 5–33 This cutaway view of a GM 4L30 transmission shows an overdrive unit as the input of a type 11, three-speed Ravigneaux gear set.

PROBLEM SOLVING 5–3

Imagine that you are working in a shop that specializes in transmission repair, and these problems are brought to you.

Case 1:

A 1995 Ford Thunderbird with a 4R70W transmission (type 12) drives normally in all ranges, except there is an engine flare, indicating slippage, during a full-throttle 1–2 shift. Do you think a driving or reaction member could be faulty? If so, which one?

Case 2:

A 1978 Chevrolet Chevette with a TH 180C transmission (type 11) has noisy first and second gears. It is okay in third gear. What would be the cause of this problem? Which driving or reaction member is at fault?

Type 13 Gear Train
Lepelletier Principle
(a)

	Lepelletier Gear Ranges						
Range	C1	C2	C3	B1	B2	F1	Ratio
1	X					X	4.15:1
Manual 1	X				X		4.15:1
2	X			X			2.37:1
3	X		X				1.56:1
4	X	X					1.15:1
5		X	X				0.86:1
6		X		X			0.69:1
Reverse			X		X		3.39:1

(b)

FIGURE 5–34 A schematic view of a type 13, LePelletier six-speed gear set (a) and a clutch application chart (b).

First Gear, 4.15:1 — C1 Applied, F1 Effective B2 Applied

Second Gear, 2.37:1 — C1 Applied, B2 Applied

Third Gear, 1.56:1 — C3 Applied, C1 Applied

Fourth Gear, 1.15:1 — C1 Applied, C2 Applied

Fifth Gear, 0.86:1 — C3 Applied, C2 Applied

Sixth Gear, 0.69:1 — B1 Applied, C2 Applied

Reverse, 3.39:1 — C3 Applied, B2 Applied

FIGURE 5–35 A type 13 shift sequence.

FIGURE 5–36 A schematic view of a type 14, GM 4L60 four-speed gear set.

5.9 FOUR-SPEED OVERDRIVE GEAR SET

A four-speed gear set was developed by General Motors and introduced in the 4L60 (THM 7004R). ● **SEE FIGURE 5–36**. It has two simple planetary gear sets that have the ring gears interconnected with the carriers of the other set. A second version of this gear set is used in the Chrysler 41TE (A-604) and 42LE and Ford AX4N, AX4S (AXOD), and CD4E units. General Motors uses this type of gear set in the 4T60E (THM 440), 4T65-E, and 4T80-E transaxles. The operation of the second version will be described later in this chapter.

The 4L60E (THM 7004R) is a type 14 gear train and uses four multiple-disc clutches plus a one-way clutch as driving members and one multiple-disc clutch, a one-way clutch, and a band for holding members. The driving clutches are arranged so they can drive the sun gear and ring gear in the front gear set, called the **input gear set**, and the sun gear and carrier in the rear gear set, called the **reaction gear set**. The input housing contains three of the driving clutches and the hub for the fourth. There are two ways that the front sun gear can be driven. One way is through the *forward clutch* and forward one-way clutch, called a **forward sprag**, and the other way is through the *overrun clutch*. The overrun clutch is used in manual-1, M2, and M3 to provide engine braking during deceleration.

The rear carrier (and front ring gear) can be held by the one-way clutch, *low-roller clutch*, or the multiple-disc *low and reverse clutch*. The rear sun gear can be held by the *2–4 band* to serve as a reaction member as well as a driving member.

In neutral, all clutches are released so the power flows no farther than the input housing. ● **FIGURE 5–37** shows the shift sequence for the various power flows.

5.9.1 POWER FLOW: 4L60E
In drive-1 (low), the following occurs.

- The forward clutch is applied to drive the front sun gear.
- The front sun gear drives the front planet pinion gears counterclockwise.

- The front ring gear/rear carrier is held from turning counterclockwise by the low-roller clutch (low and reverse clutch in manual-1).
- The front planet pinions walk around inside the ring gear.
- The front carrier/rear ring gear is driven clockwise at a reduction speed.
- The output shaft is driven clockwise at a 3.06:1 ratio.

In drive-2:

- The forward clutch stays applied to drive the front sun gear.
- The 2–4 band applies to hold the rear sun gear.
- The front sun gear drives the front planet pinion gears counterclockwise.
- The front planet pinions drive the front ring gear/rear carrier clockwise.
- The rear planet pinions walk around the sun gear.
- The rear ring gear is driven clockwise at a reduction speed.
- The output shaft is driven clockwise at a 1.63:1 ratio.

In drive-3:

- The forward clutch stays applied to drive the front sun gear.
- The 2–4 band is released.
- The 3–4 clutch applies to drive the front ring/rear carrier.
- The front planet pinion gears become locked.
- The front carrier is driven at input shaft speed.
- The output shaft is driven clockwise at a 1:1 ratio.

In drive-4 (overdrive):

- The 3–4 clutch stays applied to drive the front ring/rear carrier.
- The 2–4 band applies to hold the rear sun gear.
- The rear planet pinion gears walk around the sun gear.
- The rear planet pinion gears drive the carrier clockwise at an overdrive.
- The output shaft is driven clockwise at a 0.7:1 ratio.
- The forward clutch stays applied, but the front sprag allows the sun gear to overrun.

In reverse:

- The reverse clutch applies to drive the rear sun gear.
- The low and reverse clutch applies to hold the rear carrier.
- The rear planet pinion gears are driven counterclockwise.
- The rear ring gear is driven counterclockwise at a reduction speed.
- The output shaft is driven counterclockwise at a 2.3:1 ratio.

5.9.2 FOUR-SPEED OVERDRIVE GEAR SET: SECOND VERSION
The 41TE (A-604) and 42LE (Type 15) use a similar gear set to the 4L60 (THM 700R4), with different input and output members and a reversal of the gear set so the front

FIGURE 5–37 The full-throttle shift sequence for a type 14, 4L60 transmission showing the apply devices and the output shaft speed at the 1–2, 2–3, and 3–4 upshifts and reverse.

FIGURE 5–38 A schematic view of a type 15, Chrysler 41TE four-speed gear set.

ring gear and the rear carrier are the output members. ● **SEE FIGURE 5–38.** This produces slightly different power flows. The 41TE transmission is also unique in that no bands or one-way clutches are used.

Three of the multiple-disc clutches used in the 41TE are driving members and the other two clutches are holding members. ● **SEE FIGURE 5–39.** The driving clutches are arranged so they can drive the front sun gear (closest to the engine), the front carrier, or the rear sun gear. Remember that driving the carrier in the front gear set also drives the ring gear in the rear gear set. The holding clutches are arranged so one clutch can hold the sun gear in the front gear set. The other clutch can hold the ring gear in the rear gear set as well as the carrier in the front set.

Clutch application is controlled by the manual valve and four solenoid valves. The solenoid valves are controlled by the transaxle electronic control module, and they are opened and closed to produce the automatic upshifts and downshifts. They are also operated at the exact rate to produce the proper clutch application and release for good shift quality. These valves will be explained in more detail in Chapter 8.

In neutral, the three driving clutches are released. The low-reverse clutch is applied to hold the reaction member as soon as the transmission is shifted into first or reverse gear.

FIGURE 5–39 (a) A 41TE and (b) a 42LE transaxle use essentially the same transmission gear train with different final drives. The 41TE is mounted transversely, and the 42LE is mounted longitudinally. (*Courtesy of Chrysler Corporation*)

POWER FLOW: 42LE. In drive-1 (first), the following occurs.

- The underdrive clutch is applied to drive the rear sun gear.
- The low-reverse clutch is applied to hold the rear ring gear/front carrier.
- The rear planet pinion gears are driven counterclockwise.
- The rear planet pinions drive the rear carrier/front ring gear clockwise at a reduction speed.
- The output shaft is driven clockwise at a 2.84:1 ratio.
  - ● **SEE FIGURE 5–40**.

In drive-2 (second):

- The underdrive clutch stays applied to drive the rear sun gear.
- The low-reverse clutch is released.
- The 2–4 clutch is applied to hold the front sun gear.
- The rear planet pinion gears are driven counterclockwise.
- The rear planet pinions drive the rear carrier/front ring gear clockwise.

FIGURE 5–40 In first gear, the 41TE rear sun gear is driven by the underdrive clutch while the rear ring and front carrier are held by the low-reverse clutch. This forces the rear planet gears to walk around the inside of the ring gear and the rear carrier to rotate at a reduced speed. (*Courtesy of Chrysler Corporation*)

FIGURE 5–41 In second gear, the 41TE rear sun gear is driven by the underdrive clutch and the front sun gear is held by the 2–4 clutch. This forces the front planet gear to walk around the stationary sun gear and drive the front carrier and rear ring gear at a reduced speed. (*Courtesy of Chrysler Corporation*)

- The front planet pinions are forced to walk around the front sun gear.
- The front ring gear is driven clockwise at a reduction speed.
- The output shaft is driven clockwise at a 1.57:1 ratio.
  - ● **SEE FIGURE 5–41**.

In drive-3 (third):

- The underdrive clutch stays applied to drive the rear sun gear.
- The 2–4 clutch is released.
- The overdrive clutch is applied to drive the front carrier/rear ring gear.
- The front planet pinion gears become locked.

FIGURE 5–42 In third gear, the 41TE rear sun gear is driven by the underdrive clutch and the front carrier/rear ring gear is driven by the overdrive clutch. This locks the front gear set and produces a 1:1 ratio. (*Courtesy of Chrysler Corporation*)

FIGURE 5–43 In fourth gear, the 41TE rear sun gear is driven by the overdrive clutch and the front sun gear is held by the 2–4 clutch. This forces the front planet gears to walk around the stationary sun gear and drives the front carrier at an overdrive ratio. (*Courtesy of Chrysler Corporation*)

- The front carrier is driven at input shaft speed.
- The output shaft is driven clockwise at a 1:1 ratio. ● **SEE FIGURE 5–42.**

In drive-4 (overdrive):

- The overdrive clutch stays applied to drive the front carrier/rear ring gear.
- The underdrive clutch is released.
- The 2–4 clutch is applied to hold the front sun gear.
- The planet pinions are forced to walk around the sun gear.
- The front planet pinions drive the ring gear clockwise at an overdrive.
- The output shaft is driven clockwise at a 0.69:1 ratio. ● **SEE FIGURE 5–43.**

FIGURE 5–44 In reverse, the 41TE front sun gear is driven by the reverse clutch while the front carrier/rear ring gear is held by the low-reverse clutch. The front planet gears act as idlers, driving the front ring gear at a reverse, reduction ratio. (*Courtesy of Chrysler Corporation*)

In reverse:

- The reverse clutch is applied to drive the front sun gear.
- The low-reverse clutch is applied to hold the rear ring gear/front carrier.
- The front planet pinion gears are driven counterclockwise.
- The front ring gear is driven counterclockwise at a reduced speed.
- The output shaft is driven counterclockwise at a 2.21:1 ratio. ● **SEE FIGURE 5–44.**

The shift sequence for the 42LE transaxle is shown in ● **FIGURE 5–45**. A clutch and band chart is shown in ● **CHART 5–10**.

5.9.3 FOUR-SPEED OVERDRIVE GEAR SET: VARIATION OF SECOND VERSION

The General Motors 4T60-E (THM 440), 4T65-E, and 4T80-E and the Ford AX4N (AXOD), AX4S, and CD4E transaxles use gear sets that are very similar to the arrangement in the 41TE. ● **SEE FIGURE 5–46.** These transaxles have the front carrier and the rear ring gears combined and are the output members. The rear carrier and the front ring gear can be a driving member, a reaction, or neither. The rear sun gear can only be a reaction member. The 4T60 is illustrated as a type 16 gear train. ● **SEE FIGURE 5–47.**

POWER FLOW: 4T60E. In drive-1 (low), the following occurs.

- The input clutch is applied to drive the input sun gear.
- The input sun gear drives the front planet pinion gears counterclockwise.
- The reaction sun gear is held by the 1–2 band (low and reverse clutch in manual-1).
- The reaction planet pinions walk around the reaction sun gear.

First Gear, 2.84:1

Underdrive Clutch Applied
Low–Rev. Clutch Applied
Input: 4,800 rpm
Output: 1,690 rpm

Second Gear, 1.57:1

Underdrive Clutch Applied
2–4 Clutch Applied
Input: 4,800 rpm
Output: 3,057 rpm

Third Gear, 1:1

Underdrive Clutch Applied
Input: 4,800 rpm
Overdrive Clutch Applied
Output: 4,800 rpm

Fourth Gear, 0.69:1

2–4 Clutch Applied
Overdrive Clutch Applied
Input: 4,800 rpm
Output: 6,957 rpm

Type 14 Shift Sequence

Reverse Clutch Applied
Low-Rev. Clutch Applied
Input: 4,800 rpm
Output: 2,172 rpm

FIGURE 5–45 The full-throttle shift sequence for a type 15, 41TE transmission showing the apply devices and the output shaft speed at the 1–2, 2–3, and 3–4 upshifts and reverse.

GEAR	UNDERDRIVE CLUTCH	LOW-REV. CLUTCH	2–4 CLUTCH	OVERDRIVE CLUTCH	REVERSE CLUTCH
D1	Applied	Applied			
D2	Applied		Applied		
D3	Applied			Applied	
D4			Applied	Applied	
R		Applied			Applied
Planetary	Drives Rear	Holds Front	Holds	Drives Front	Drives
Member	Sun	Carrier & Rear Ring	Front Sun	Carrier & Rear Ring	Front Sun

CHART 5–10

Four-Speed Gear Train Band and Clutch Application, Type 15

- The input carrier assembly is driven clockwise at a reduction speed.
- The output shaft is driven clockwise at a 2.92:1 ratio.
  - ● **SEE FIGURE 5–48.**

In drive-2:

- The second clutch is applied to drive the rear ring gear (input carrier assembly).
- The 1–2 band stays applied to hold the reaction sun gear.

FIGURE 5–46 An exploded view of the type 16 gear train used in an AXOD/AX4N transaxle.

FIGURE 5–47 A schematic view of a type 16, GM 4T60 four-speed gear set. The Ford AX4N gear set is similar.

- The rear ring gear drives the rear planet pinion gears clockwise.
- The rear planet pinions walk around the sun gear.
- The rear planet pinions drive the front ring gear/rear carrier clockwise at a reduction speed.
- The output shaft is driven clockwise at a 1.57:1 ratio.
  ● **SEE FIGURE 5–49.**

First Gear

FIGURE 5–48 In first gear, the AXOD front sun gear is driven by the forward clutch and low one-way clutch while the rear sun gear is held by the low-intermediate band.

Second Gear

FIGURE 5–49 In second gear, the AXOD front carrier is driven by the intermediate clutch while the rear sun gear is held by the low-intermediate band.

In drive-3:

- The second clutch stays applied to drive the rear ring gear (input carrier assembly).
- The 1–2 band is released.
- The third clutch applies to drive the front sun gear.

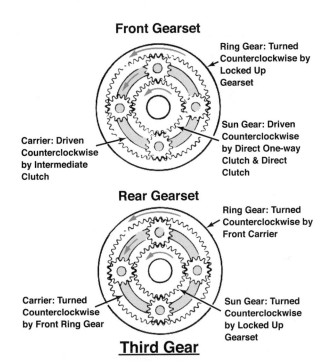

Front Gearset

Ring Gear: Turned Counterclockwise by Locked Up Gearset

Carrier: Driven Counterclockwise by Intermediate Clutch

Sun Gear: Driven Counterclockwise by Direct One-way Clutch & Direct Clutch

Rear Gearset

Ring Gear: Turned Counterclockwise by Front Carrier

Carrier: Turned Counterclockwise by Front Ring Gear

Sun Gear: Turned Counterclockwise by Locked Up Gearset

Third Gear

FIGURE 5–50 In third gear, the AXOD front gear is driven by the intermediate clutch while the front sun gear is driven by the forward clutch and low one-way clutch, and this locks up both gear sets to produce a 1:1 ratio.

Front Gearset

Pinions: Turned Counterclockwise by Carrier

Ring Gear: Turned Counterclockwise by Pinions

Carrier: Driven Counterclockwise by Intermediate Clutch

Sun Gear: Held by Overdrive Band

Rear Gearset

Pinions: Turned Counterclockwise by Front Ring Gear

Ring Gear: Turned Counterclockwise by Front Carrier

Carrier: Turned Counterclockwise by Front Ring Gear

Sun Gear: Turned Counterclockwise by Pinions

Fourth Gear

FIGURE 5–51 In fourth gear, the AXOD front carrier is driven by the intermediate clutch while the front sun gear is held by the overdrive band.

- The front planet pinions become locked.
- The front carrier is driven at input shaft speed.
- The output shaft is driven clockwise at a 1:1 ratio.
  - ● **SEE FIGURE 5–50.**

In drive-4 (overdrive):

- The second clutch stays applied to drive the rear ring gear (input carrier assembly).
- The fourth clutch applies to hold the front sun gear.
- The front planet pinion gears walk around the sun gear.
- The front planet pinion gears drive the carrier clockwise at an overdrive.
- The output shaft is driven clockwise at a 0.7:1 ratio.
  - ● **SEE FIGURE 5–51.**
- The third clutch stays applied, but the third sprag allows the sun gear to overrun.

In reverse:

- The input clutch applies to drive the front sun gear.
- The reverse band applies to hold the front carrier.
- The front planet pinion gears are driven counterclockwise.
- The front ring gear is driven counterclockwise at a reduction speed.
- The output shaft is driven counterclockwise at a 2.38:1 ratio. ● **SEE FIGURE 5–52.**

Front Gearset

Pinions: Turned Clockwise by Sun Gear

Ring Gear: Turned Clockwise by Pinions

Carrier: Held by Reverse Clutch

Sun Gear: Driven Counterclockwise by Low One-way Clutch & Forward Clutch

Rear Gearset

Pinions: Turned Counterclockwise by Carrier

Ring Gear: Held by Front Carrier

Carrier: Turned Clockwise by Front Ring Gear

Sun Gear: Turned Clockwise by Pinions

Reverse

FIGURE 5–52 In reverse, the AXOD front sun gear is driven by the forward clutch and low one-way clutch while the carrier is held by the reverse clutch.

5.9.4 FOUR-SPEED OVERDRIVE GEAR SET: VARIATION TWO
The Ford CD4E is another version of the four-speed gear set; it is illustrated as a type 17 gear train. ● **SEE FIGURE 5–53.** It is a compact transaxle with a chain drive between the transmission

FIGURE 5–53 A schematic view of a type 17, Ford CD4E four-speed gear set.

gear set and the planetary reduction gears and differential of the final drive. The power flows through this gear set are quite similar to that of the other four-speed gear sets.

5.10 JOINT VENTURE, SIX-SPEED GEAR SET

The type 18 gear set was developed jointly by Ford (6F50) and General Motors (6T70 and 6T75). It uses three simple planetary gear sets and has each carrier connected to the ring gear of another set. ● SEE FIGURE 5–54. The sun gear of the center gear set is connected to the input shaft, so it is always driven. It uses two driving clutches, three reaction clutches (brakes), and one mechanical diode (one-way clutch). The front carrier and rear ring gear are the output.

Except for first gear with the one-way clutch, it uses clutch-to-clutch shifts. It has a low 4.48:1 first gear, and an overdrive 0.74:1:1 sixth gear. ● SEE FIGURE 5–55.

5.11 NONPLANETARY GEAR SETS

Several automatic transmission designs do not use planetary gear sets. These designs are attempts to produce a smaller, simpler, lighter, and less expensive transmission that will produce better fuel mileage with lower exhaust emissions. Many consider the dual clutch transmissions to be automatic transmissions.

5.11.1 HELICAL GEAR TYPES   The Hondamatic and the Saturn TAAT use constant-mesh helical gears, much like those in a manual transmission. The major difference is that manual

Joint Venture 6-Speed Gearset
(a)

Joint Venture Gearset							
Range	C1	C2	B1	B2	B3	F1	Ratio
1			X			X	4.48:1
Manual 1			X		X		4.48:1
2			X	X			2.87:1
3	X		X				1.84:1
4		X	X				1.41:1
5	X	X					1:1
6		X		X			0.74:1
Reverse	X				X		2.88:1

(b)

FIGURE 5–54 A schematic view of (a) a type 18, joint venture six-speed gear set and (b) a clutch application chart.

PROBLEM SOLVING 5–4

Imagine that you are working in a shop that specializes in transmission repair, and these problems are brought to you.

Case 1:

A 1992 Camaro with a TH 700-R4 transmission (type 14) drives normally in all ranges, except there is an engine flare, indicating slippage, during a full-throttle 1–2 shift. Do you think a driving or reaction member could be faulty? If so, which one?

Case 2:

A 1996 Dodge Intrepid with a 42LE transaxle (type 15) has no second or fourth gear. With enough throttle, it will skip second and make a 1–3 shift. What would be the cause of this problem? Which driving or reaction member is at fault?

transmissions use a mechanical clutch and synchronizer assemblies that are shifted through manual linkage, and the automatic transmissions use a torque converter and hydraulically applied clutch packs. ● SEE FIGURE 5–56. The power flow for each gear range goes through a pair of gears and each gear range uses a different gear set. ● SEE FIGURE 5–57.

A garage shift into first or reverse is made by applying that particular clutch pack. Upshifts and downshift timing and ratio changes are made by applying the next clutch pack while releasing the previous one. ● SEE FIGURE 5–58. All shifts, with one exception, occur with the application of a

FIGURE 5–55 A type 18 shift sequence (6T70/6F50 series).

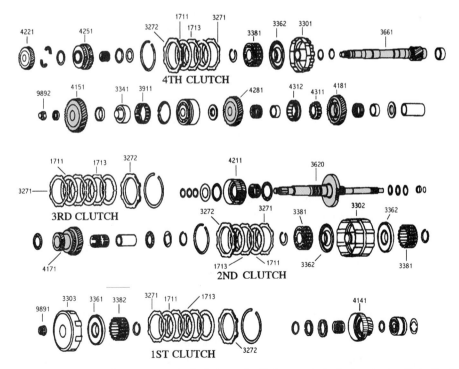

FIGURE 5–56 This parts catalog page shows an exploded view of a Saturn automatic transaxle. Note the helical gear set and the clutches for shift control. (*Courtesy of Aceomatic Recon*)

Type 19 Gear Train
Nonplanetary

FIGURE 5–57 A schematic view of a type 19, Honda four-speed gear set.

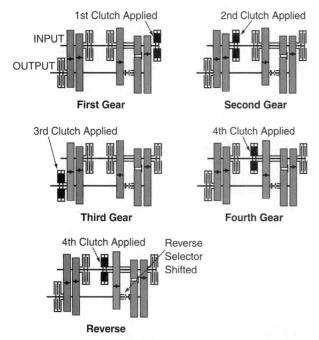

FIGURE 5–58 The shift sequence for a type 19, four-speed transmission showing the apply devices.

single clutch pack. The exception is reverse, which requires the movement of the reverse selector and the engagement of the fourth clutch.

5.11.2 CVT TYPES A **CVT (continuously variable transmission)** has an infinite number of gear ratios between its lowest ratio, about 3.7:1, and its highest ratio, which is a 0.27:1 overdrive. Ideally, it can keep the engine at the most efficient RPM. As the vehicle accelerates from a stop, the engine speed rises quickly from idle to the desired RPM. From that point on, the engine stays at the same speed, while the transmission ratio continuously changes to provide acceleration. CVTs are commonly used in snowmobiles. The clutch used in top-fuel dragsters and "funny" cars could be considered a type of CVT. These transmissions have been used in the Subaru Justy and are now used by Audi, Dodge, Honda, and Nissan.

Automotive CVTs are used with multiplate clutches, magnetic particle clutches, and torque converters. A pair of hydraulically controlled, variable-size pulleys is used with a steel-link drive belt. ● **SEE FIGURE 5–59**. This belt is often called a push belt because torque is transferred by the driving pulley pushing on the belt, which in turn pushes the driven pulley. At start, the pulley halves/discs on the primary input shaft are spread apart, and the pair of pulley halves on the secondary output shaft are pushed together. This produces a small pulley driving a large pulley, which produces the lowest drive ratio. When a ratio change is required, the primary pulley halves are pushed together, producing a bigger pulley diameter, and the secondary pulley halves separate, producing a smaller diameter. ● **SEE FIGURE 5–60**. This produces a higher gear ratio. Both pulleys must maintain enough pressure on the drive belt to transfer the required torque.

A reverse gear set, controlled by a multiplate clutch pack, is used to produce reverse.

A CVT offers the following advantages over a planetary-gear automatic transmission.

- Compact, very short
- Lighter weight
- Constant, stepless acceleration with engine staying at the RPM for maximum power
- Efficient fuel use and emissions, cruise with engine staying at the RPM for maximum efficiency
- Lower internal power loss

One method used to compare transmissions is the engine revolutions for a specific driving cycle. A test vehicle using a 3.0-L engine and a CVT showed 3% fewer revolutions than the same vehicle with a five-speed transmission and 11% less than with a four-speed transmission. This should equal a gain of about 12% in fuel economy.

CVT COMPONENTS, PULLEYS. A CVT improves efficiency by changing ratios from underdrive/reduction to overdrive in a gradual, continuous manner. Two pulleys, also called **variators**, and a steel drive belt are used.

The primary/drive pulley is attached to the input shaft. The secondary/driven pulley is on the output shaft and drives the final drive gears. Each pulley, also called a **sheave**, has two sides: One is fixed so it cannot move, and the other can float sideways to change pulley width. When the vehicle is at rest, the primary pulley is wide so the belt sits low on the pulley, and

RING GEAR

STEEL BELT

FLYWHEEL

START CLUTCH

INPUT SHAFT

DRIVE PULLEY

DRIVEN PULLEY

FORWARD CLUTCH

REVERSE BRAKE

PLANETARY GEAR SET

ATF FILTER

FIGURE 5–59 Forward ratios in this CVT are changed as the two halves of the drive pulley are forced together, increasing the diameter. At the same time, the two halves of the driven pulley spread apart to reduce its diameter. The planetary gear set at the rear of the input shaft is used to produce reverse. (*Courtesy of American Honda Motor Company*)

the secondary pulley is narrow so the belt sits high. ● **SEE FIGURE 5–61**. This produces the lowest underdrive ratio.

As the vehicle moves, the floating side of the primary pulley moves inward, making the pulley narrower and forcing the belt to move out to a wider diameter. The belt is steel so it cannot stretch, so it will be forced deeper into the secondary pulley, forcing that pulley to become wider.

The floating side of each pulley can be thought of as a hydraulic piston. Fluid pressure is used to force the drive piston/pulley to a narrower position and the driven pulley to a wider position. The secondary pulley is spring loaded to force it to a narrow position. The primary pulley is adjusted to control the gear ratio, and the secondary pulley is adjusted to maintain tension on the belt. The belt must never be loose between the pulleys.

CVT COMPONENTS, DRIVE BELT. Two different styles of fixed-length steel belts are used. ● **SEE FIGURE 5–62**.

■ One type is a push-belt made up of about 400 wedge-shaped segments that are held together by two steel bands. Each band is made from multiple layers to allow

flexibility. The segment sides contact the pulley sides. A push-belt is often called the *Van Doorne design*. This style of belt is directional, and it usually is marked with an arrow to show belt direction.

■ The other type is a pull-belt that is made up of links and link pins, much like a silent chain. The ends of the link pins contact the pulley sides. This style is also called a *Luk chain drive*.

CVT OPERATION. With no fluid pressure, the secondary pulley spring forces the floating side to a narrow, high-belt position, which in turn moves the primary pulley to a wide, low-belt position. This produces an underdrive that is always used as the vehicle starts moving. ●**SEE FIGURE 5–63**.

As the vehicle begins moving, the ratio control valve moves to send fluid pressure to the primary piston, and this forces the floating side to a more narrow position. The belt is forced outward, which in turn forces the secondary pulley to a lower-belt position. Continued fluid flow to the primary piston will change the ratio from an underdrive/reduction through 1:1 to an overdrive.

FIGURE 5–60 The shift sequence for a CVT is a very smooth, stepless transition from a low ratio to a high ratio as the pulleys change diameter. The engine speed can stay constant as the vehicle's speed increases. (*Courtesy of American Honda Motor Company*)

(a)

(b)

FIGURE 5–62 (a) A push-belt is made from a few hundred steel segments held together by two bands that have multiple layers of thin steel. (b) A pull-belt resembles a silent chain with exposed end links that grip the pulley sides.

FIGURE 5–61 The drive pulley is wide while the driven pulley is narrow for low ratio, vehicle start (left). The ratio changes by making the drive pulley narrow and the driven pulley wider.

FIGURE 5–63 The ratio control valve and motor control the drive pulley fluid pressure, which in turn controls the pulley widths and ratio.

CVT REVERSE. A planetary gear set is needed for reverse-direction operation, and this is a simple planetary with a carrier that can be held by the reverse clutch (see FIGURE 5–60). The input shaft drives the ring/internal gear, and the sun gear drives the shaft to the primary pulley. Reverse gear ratio depends on the gear sizes; one transaxle has a planetary reverse ratio of 0.74:1.

CVT FORWARD OPERATION. A forward clutch is mounted on the input shaft from the torque converter; it is mounted inside a clutch drum that also contains the planetary ring gear. When it applies, the forward clutch drives the planetary sun gear so both the sun and ring gears are driven. This locks the gear set to produce a 1:1 ratio.

SUMMARY

1. An understanding of the rules of power transfer through a planetary gear set is needed to trace the power through any planetary gear set.

2. A simple planetary gear set can produce seven different gear ratios.

3. Transmission schematics are helpful tools for understanding gear train power flow.

4. There are two basic types of planetary gear sets used: Simpson and Ravigneaux.

5. Combinations of Simpson or Ravigneaux gear sets with a simple planetary gear set will produce four, five, six, eight, or more gear ratios.

6. CVTs offer unique advantages, better fuel economy, lower emissions, and smoother operation.

REVIEW QUESTIONS

1. A simple planetary gear set has a _____ _____, a _____ _____, and a _____ that has two or more planet gears.

2. A Simpson gear train combines one _____ _____ with _____ planet gear sets and two _____ gears.

3. The right and left sides of a vehicle are determined by viewing from the _____ _____.

4. The transmission/transaxle can be mounted in either a _____ (lengthwise) or _____ (crosswise) position.

5. The lever or arm used to hold the vehicle stationary in park is called a parking _____.

6. _____ transmission designs require that during an upshift, the application of a clutch must be carefully timed with the release of a reaction member.

7. A _____ and _____ application chart shows the relationship between the apply devices used in each of the gear ranges.

8. Complete the following for a Simpson, type 1 transmission.
   a. The forward clutch _____ the input ring gear.
   b. The one-way clutch holds the _____ _____.
   c. The high-reverse clutch _____ the _____ _____.
   d. The intermediate band holds the _____ _____.
   e. The low-reverse band _____ the _____ _____.

9. Which apply devices are working when a three-speed Simpson gear train is in third gear?

10. Variables that affect the speed of a band engagement include:
    a. _____ diameter.
    b. Fluid feed _____ diameter.
    c. Use of a(n) _____.

11. When an overdrive Simpson gear train is in third gear, what is the gear ratio in the overdrive planetary gear set? The main gear set?

12. A Ravigneaux gear set uses a _____ carrier that has _____ and _____ planet pinions, a _____ and a _____ sun gear, and a single _____ gear.

13. A single _____ gear set can be used in a two-, three-, or four-speed transmission or transaxle.

14. The gear train in the GM 4L60 has two _____ gear sets and has _____ apply devices.

15. The automatic transmissions used in most Honda and Saturn vehicles use _____ mesh _____ gears similar to conventional standard transmissions. In place of synchronizers, they use _____ disc _____.

16. A _____ _____ _____ has an infinite number of _____ ratios that should keep the engine at its most efficient _____.

CHAPTER QUIZ

1. Student A says that if the carrier is the input and the sun gear is the reaction member, the ring gear will rotate in a gear reduction. Student B says that if the carrier is the input and the sun gear is the reaction member, the ring gear rotates in reverse. Who is correct?
   a. Student A
   b. Student B
   c. Both Students A and B
   d. Neither Student A nor B

2. Student A says that a simple planetary gear set operates in neutral if there is no input member. Student B says that it will operate in neutral if there is no reaction member. Who is correct?
   a. Student A
   b. Student B
   c. Both Students A and B
   d. Neither Student A nor B

3. Student A says that driving the ring gear while the sun gear is held will make the planet gears walk around the sun gear. Student B says that driving the ring gear while holding the sun gear will force the carrier to rotate at a reduction speed. Who is correct?
   a. Student A
   b. Student B
   c. Both Students A and B
   d. Neither Student A nor B

4. Student A says that if the sun gear is driven while the ring gear is held, the planet gears will walk around the inside of the ring gear. Student B says that if the sun gear is driven while the carrier is held, the ring gear is forced to rotate at a slower speed than the sun gear. Who is correct?
   a. Student A
   b. Student B
   c. Both Students A and B
   d. Neither Student A nor B

5. If the ring gear is driven while the sun gear is held, the planet gears will _____.
   a. Merely rotate in the carrier
   b. Rotate as they walk around the sun gear
   c. Rotate with the carrier but not on their axis
   d. Be stationary in the carrier

6. The term referring to the steering pull of a FWD vehicle under a hard acceleration is _____.
   a. Torque pull   c. Torque steer
   b. Steer pull   d. Acceleration steer

7. In a three-speed Simpson gear train, if the sun gear is stationary, the transmission is in _____.
   a. First gear   c. Second gear
   b. Third gear   d. Reverse

8. When a three-speed Simpson gear train is in first gear, the sun gear is _____.
   a. Rotating clockwise
   b. Stationary
   c. Rotating counterclockwise
   d. Freewheeling

9. In a three-speed Simpson gear train, third gear occurs when the forward clutch is applied along with the _____.
   a. Rear band
   b. One-way clutch
   c. Front band
   d. None of these

10. In a three-speed Simpson gear train, the reaction carrier is held stationary by a _____.
    a. One-way clutch
    b. Multiple-disc clutch
    c. Band
    d. Any of these

11. Student A says that when a one-way clutch is used for a reaction member, the clutch will release if the vehicle decelerates in that gear. Student B says that when a one-way clutch is used for a reaction member, the clutch self-applies when the throttle is opened. Who is correct?
    a. Student A
    b. Student B
    c. Both Students A and B
    d. Neither Student A nor B

12. Driving two members of a planetary gear set while there is no reaction member will result in a _____ ratio.
    a. Overdrive   c. 1:1
    b. Reduction   d. Reverse, reduction

13. Student A says that in a four-speed Simpson gear train, the sun gear is the input member for the overdrive gear set. Student B says the ring gear is the overdrive gear set's output member. Who is correct?
    a. Student A
    b. Student B
    c. Both Students A and B
    d. Neither Student A nor B

14. Student A says that in types 5, 6, 7, and 8 transmissions, both driving clutches in the main gear set are applied in third gear. Student B says that the overdrive gear set reaction member is applied in third gear. Who is correct?
    a. Student A
    b. Student B
    c. Both Students A and B
    d. Neither Student A nor B

15. A Ravigneaux gear set uses _____.
    a. Two sun gears
    b. One ring gear
    c. Two sets of planet pinion gears
    d. All of these

16. Student A says that in a two-speed Ravigneaux gear train, one sun gear is driven whenever the turbine shaft turns. Student B says that it will always be in neutral if there is no reaction member. Who is correct?
    a. Student A
    b. Student B
    c. Both Students A and B
    d. Neither Student A nor B

17. The Ravigneaux gear train can be arranged so it produces _____ forward speeds.
    a. 2
    b. 2 or 3
    c. 2, 3, or 4
    d. 2, 3, 4, or 5

18. Student A says that in a Ravigneaux gear train, the long pinion gears are meshed with the large sun gear. Student B says that the long pinion gears are meshed with the short pinion gears. Who is correct?
    a. Student A
    b. Student B
    c. Both Students A and B
    d. Neither Student A nor B

19. Student A says that in a Ravigneaux gear train, fourth gear, the sun gear is driven. Student B says the carrier is held stationary in fourth gear. Who is correct?
    a. Student A
    b. Student B
    c. Both Students A and B
    d. Neither Student A nor B

20. Student A says that when a Simpson gear set is in reverse, the output/rear carrier is held stationary. Student B says the rear ring gear is the output member in reverse. Who is correct?
    a. Student A
    b. Student B
    c. Both Students A and B
    d. Neither Student A nor B

HYDRAULIC SYSTEM THEORY

OBJECTIVES: **After studying Chapter 6, the reader will be able to:** • Discuss hydraulic principles. • Describe how a hydraulic system operates. • Identify the parts of a transmission hydraulic system and explain each of their purposes. • Explain the requirements for a transmission hydraulic system. • Identify the requirements for automatic transmission fluid and the differences between fluids.

KEY TERMS: Accumulator 151 • Actuator 136 • Area 133 • Automatic transmission fluid (ATF) 152 • Check ball 143 • Crescent pump 137 • Depth filter 139 • Detent valve 143 • Dynamic seal 146 • Elastomer 149 • Electronic control module (ECM) 142 • Filter 135 • Fluid power 132 • Fluid supply 134 • Force 132 • Gasket 146 • Gerotor pump 137 • Governor valve 142 • Hydraulics 132 • Internal-external gear 137 • Kilopascal 132 • Land 141 • Mainline pressure 138 • Manual valve 136 • Metal-clad lip seal 147 • Micron 139 • Modulator valve 143 • Orifice 151 • O-ring 146 • Paper filter 139 • Positive displacement pump 138 • Pounds per square inch (PSI) 132 • Pressure 132 • Pressure regulator valve 135 • Pressure relief valve 136 • Pump 135 • Reaction surface 141 • Separator plate 143 • Shift quality 151 • Shift timing 142 • Shuttle valve 144 • Side loaded 142 • Spool valve 141 • Static seal 146 • Supply pressure 138 • Surface filter 139 • Throttle position sensors (TPS) 142 • Throttle valve 142 • Vane pump 137 • Variable displacement 136 • Vehicle speed sensors (VSS) 142 • Worm track 146

6.1 INTRODUCTION

The automatic transmission's hydraulic system has several important functions. ● **SEE FIGURE 6–1.** It must be able to:

- Apply the clutches and bands and therefore control the transmission power flow
- Transmit sufficient force and motion to completely apply the control units to prevent slippage
- Maintain fluid flow through the torque converter for its proper operation
- Maintain fluid flow to lubricate and cool the moving parts of the gear train

6.2 HYDRAULIC PRINCIPLES

Hydraulics, often called **fluid power**, is a method of transmitting motion and/or **force**. Hydraulics is based on the fact that liquids can flow easily through complicated paths, but they cannot be compressed. All the components in a hydraulic system

are connected so that fluid pressure can be transmitted and allowed to work. Another important feature is that when fluids transmit pressure, that pressure is transferred equally in all directions and acts on all parts of a circuit at the same time with the same pressure. ● **SEE FIGURE 6–2.** This is a simplified version of Pascal's law, which was developed by Blaise Pascal. It states that pressure applied to a confined fluid is transmitted equally throughout the fluid in all directions and acts equally upon equal areas.

If we were to fill a strong container with a liquid, it would be impossible to add more liquid, even by force. ● **SEE FIGURE 6–3.** Once the container is full, any added force becomes fluid pressure. **Pressure** is defined as the amount of force applied to a given area. In the United States, pressure is commonly measured using **pounds per square inch (PSI)**. Ten pounds per square inch is equal to a force of 10 pounds pushing on an area of 1 square inch. In other parts of the world, the metric system is used. The metric system measures pressure using kilograms per square centimeter (kg/cm^2), or bars (1 bar is equal to 14.5 PSI). Today, pressure is also measured in kilopascals (kPa); 1 PSI is equal to 6.895 kPa, 0.07 kg/cm^2, or 0.0689 bar. The **kilopascal** is an international unit for measuring pressure.

Pressure can be created in a hydraulic system in several ways. It is easier to describe and understand if we use a piston as the pressure input and one or more pistons for the output. System pressure is a product of three things: the ability of the system to contain the pressure, the surface area of the input

FIGURE 6–1 A hydraulic diagram for a four-speed transmission with electronic controls. Diagrams are used to determine the relationship of the components. They are often color-coded to help locate the circuits. (*Courtesy of Chrysler Corporation*)

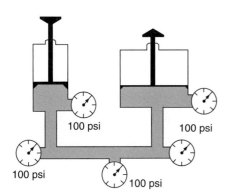

FIGURE 6–2 Fluid pressure is transmitted undiminished in all directions. Note that the pressure is equal throughout the system.

FIGURE 6–3 Fluids flow freely and will assume the shape of their container (a), yet they are virtually noncompressible (b).

piston, and the amount of force applied to the piston. ● **SEE FIGURE 6–4.** The strength of the system is important because if the pressure gets too high for the system, the system will rupture and release the pressure.

When force is exerted on the piston of a closed system, that force becomes fluid pressure. Pressure is equal to the force

divided by the **area** of the piston. A 100-lb (90.9-kg) force on a piston that is 10 in² (64.5 cm²) in area will generate a pressure of 10 PSI (1.4 kg/cm²). The pressure can be converted to kilopascals by multiplying 6.895 by 10 PSI (6.895 × 10). The pressure would be 68.95 kPa. The amount of pressure is determined by dividing the force by the area of the piston.

FIGURE 6–4 A 100-lb force applied on an input piston that has an area of 1 in. will produce a fluid pressure of 100 PSI.

● **SEE FIGURE 6–5.** This same 100-lb force acting on a 0.5-in² (3.2 cm²) piston generates a pressure of 100 ÷ 0.5, or 200, PSI (28 kg/cm²) (1,399 kPa).

Fluid pressure is never greater than what is needed to overcome resistance to fluid flow. Using a vehicle's brake system as an example, it takes only a few pounds of force to push the brake pedal downward, and then after the pedal has moved an inch or so, it will not move any farther. During the first part of the pedal travel, the brake shoes or pads were moving to make contact with the rotors and drums. The only resistance was the seals and brake shoe return springs. Only a relatively low pressure is needed to overcome the resistance and produce this movement, about 10 to 150 PSI. After the shoes touch their friction surfaces, the pistons can move no farther; now the hydraulic system pressure will increase to whatever the driver demands through the amount of force applied to the pedal.

When discussing hydraulic pistons and computing fluid pressures and forces, it is important to use the area of the piston and not the diameter. The area of a piston or any circle can be determined using the following formula.

$$\pi r^2 \text{ or } \pi (0.785 d^2)$$

where:

$\pi = 3.1416$
r = one-half the diameter
d = diameter

The pressure in a hydraulic system becomes a force to produce work, and the amount of force can be determined by multiplying the area of the output piston by the system pressure. A pressure of 200 PSI pushing on a piston with an area of 1 in² produces a force of 200 lb (200 × 1). This same pressure on a 4-in² (26.17-cm²) piston produces a force of 200 × 4, or 800 lb (363.6 kg). Application force is multiplied whenever the output piston is larger than the input. Force will decrease if the input piston is larger than the output piston. A simple memory triangle can be used as an aid to determine area, force, or pressure. ● **SEE FIGURE 6–6.**

A hydraulic system can only transmit the energy, force, and motion that is put into it; it cannot create energy. What goes in one end is all that can come out of the other. However, it is

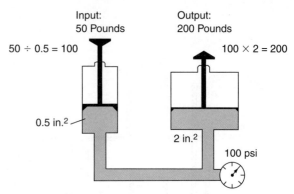

FIGURE 6–5 System pressure can be determined by dividing the input force (50 lb) by the area of the input piston (0.5 in²). Output force can be determined by multiplying the area of the output piston (2 in²) by the fluid pressure (100 PSI).

FORCE = PRESSURE × AREA
PRESSURE = FORCE ÷ AREA
AREA = FORCE ÷ PRESSURE

FIGURE 6–6 A simple memory triangle will help you remember the commonly used hydraulic formulas.

possible to change force to motion or vice versa. Most automotive brake systems multiply force with a loss in travel; other hydraulic systems are used to increase travel.

As the input piston moves, it displaces or pushes fluid through the passages or tubing of the system. The volume of fluid displaced is equal to the piston area times the length of piston stroke. A 1-in. (2.54-cm) diameter piston has an area of 0.785 in² (5.067 cm²); if this piston strokes 2 in. (5.08 cm), 1.57 in³ (25.7 cm³) of fluid is displaced (0.785 in² × 2 in.) (5.067 cm² × 5.08 cm). This much fluid can move a 1-in. diameter output piston 2 in. If the output piston is larger, its larger area requires a larger volume of fluid, so its travel will be shorter.

6.3 SIMPLE HYDRAULIC SYSTEMS

Many hydraulic systems use an engine- or motor-driven pump to produce fluid movement. These systems normally consist of the pump, a fluid intake system usually equipped with a filter, a **fluid supply** (sump), control valves, and the actuators that provide the system output. ● **SEE FIGURE 6–7.** In these systems, the pressure is determined by the amount of power turning the pump and the resistance to the fluid flow.

The power needed for the transmission's hydraulic system is determined by how much fluid is being pumped and the system pressure.

FIGURE 6–7 The basic components of a simple hydraulic system.

SOURCE OF PRESSURE (PUMP)

HYDRAULIC OPERATING UNITS

FLUID SOURCE (PAN)

PRESSURE REGULATION SYSTEM
(VALVE BODY)

FIGURE 6–8 In many transmissions, the oil pump is at the front of the transmission and is driven by the torque converter hub. (*Courtesy of Chrysler Corporation*)

6.4 BASIC AUTOMATIC TRANSMISSION HYDRAULICS

In most automatic transmissions, the **pump** is built into the front or engine end of the transmission and is driven by the back of the torque converter. ● **SEE FIGURE 6–8**. In some units, the pump is mounted deeper into the case and is connected to the torque converter housing. ● **SEE FIGURE 6–9**. In either case, the pump begins moving fluid as soon as the engine starts. The pump is sized to produce enough fluid flow to fill the actuators and stroke the pistons during each shift in addition to keeping the torque converter filled and the transmission lubricated at all engine speeds.

The pump intake begins at the **filter**, which is positioned in the transmission's pan; in many cases, the filter is attached to the bottom of the valve body. The pan is the *fluid reservoir* or *sump,* and it contains more than enough fluid for normal operation.

All automatic transmissions use a variable **pressure regulator valve** that controls or adjusts the operating pressure, and provides the appropriate hydraulic pressure for the various operating conditions. ● **SEE FIGURE 6–10**. The pressure regulator is normally found in the valve body, although in some

FIGURE 6–9 This pump assembly (20) is attached to the valve body (51) and channel plate (280). The pump is driven by the oil pump driveshaft (340). (*Courtesy of Slauson Transmission Parts, www.slauson.com*)

FIGURE 6–10 A pressure regulator valve. When fluid pressure acting on the right end of the valve exceeds spring tension, the valve will move to the left and open the passage back to the pump inlet. (*Courtesy of Chrysler Corporation*)

FIGURE 6–12 The manual valve is connected to the gear shift lever so movement of the lever will slide the valve along its bore. (*Courtesy of Nissan North America, Inc.*)

FIGURE 6–11 This valve body has two sections that contain 11 sets of valves.

Downshift

Upshift

FIGURE 6–13 A typical shift valve has a spring to move the valve to a downshift position; throttle pressure works with this spring. When governor pressure gets high enough, the valve will move to an upshift position.

transmissions it is located in the pump body. In addition to the pressure regulator, some transmissions use a **pressure relief valve** to release excess pressure that might occur under certain operating conditions. Some transmissions use a **variable displacement** vane pump or a two-stage pump. These pumps can reduce their displacement and therefore the amount of fluid that is pumped when fluid demands are low.

Fluid flow through a transmission's hydraulic system is controlled by various valves, most of which are in the *valve body*. ● **SEE FIGURE 6–11**. All transmissions have a **manual valve**. This valve is connected to the shift lever in the driver's compartment. ● **SEE FIGURE 6–12**. Nearly all transmissions also have one *shift valve* for each automatic upshift. ● **SEE FIGURE 6–13**. A two-speed transmission has one shift valve; a four-speed has three shift valves. Additional valves are used to tailor the timing, speed, and quality of the upshifts and downshifts.

The greatest fluid flow is to the **actuator**, which is usually a hydraulic piston. The hydraulic actuators of an automatic

(a)

Valve Closed: Fluid flow is blocked

(b)

Valve Open: Fluid pressure moves piston to right

Valve Open: Springs move piston to left

Exhaust

(c)

FIGURE 6–14 Operation of the valve controls fluid flow to the actuator. It can (a) block operation, (b) cause apply, or (c) cause release.

transmission are the servos that apply and release the bands and the pistons that apply the clutches.

In automatic transmissions, the valves are positioned so that fluid pressure is exerted on the actuator piston all the time that the actuator is applied. When the actuator is released, fluid pressure is exhausted. ● **SEE FIGURE 6–14.** Many valves shuttle back and forth between the apply and exhaust ports.

6.5 PRODUCING FLUID FLOW AND PRESSURE

Three common types of rotary pumps are used to produce the fluid flow and resulting pressure in an automatic transmission. They are the **internal-external gear** with **crescent** (or *gear*) **pump**, the **gerotor** (*rotor*) **pump**, and the **vane pump**. ● **SEE FIGURE 6–15.** The pumping action in each of these is essentially the same. The inner pumping member (external gear or inner rotor) is driven by the torque converter hub or a driveshaft, and the outer pumping member (the internal gear, outer rotor, or vane housing) is offset or eccentric relative to the inner gear or rotor.

(a)

(b)

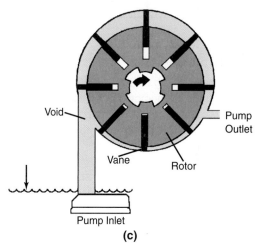

(c)

FIGURE 6–15 (a) An internal-external gear pump, (b) gerotor pump, and (c) vane pump.

As the inner member rotates, a series of chambers (between the gear teeth, the rotor lobes, or vanes) increase in volume in one area and decrease in another. A low-pressure area is created in the void area where the chamber volume increases. This area is connected to a passage leading to the filter that is submerged in fluid near the bottom of the sump. Atmospheric pressure inside the transmission pushes fluid into the filter, through the intake passage, and into the pump inlet. ● **SEE FIGURE 6–16.** As the pump rotates, fluid fills the chambers just as fast as they enlarge.

On the other side of the pump the chambers get smaller, and the outlet port of the pump is positioned in this area. Here, the fluid is forced out of the pump and into the passage leading to the pressure control valve and the rest of the hydraulic system. The pressure-regulated fluid is often called **supply** or **mainline pressure**.

Many automatic transmissions use a fixed-size **positive displacement pump**. Every revolution of the pump will move the same volume of fluid. The faster the pump is turned, the more fluid will be pumped during a given time period. Both the gear pump and the rotor pump are positive displacement pumps. Variable vane pumps are also positive displacement in that they will pump a certain volume on each revolution, but the displacement, and therefore the fluid volume, can be changed. This is done by moving the vane housing to reduce the size of the pumping chambers. ● **SEE FIGURE 6–17**. Variable displacement pumps allow a large output to produce the fluid volume needed for shifts and lubrication and a reduced output when it is not needed.

Some transmissions use a dual-stage gear pump—a combination of two positive displacement pumps. Both pumps supply fluid when demands are high. The output of the second-stage pump is released or vented when the primary stage can supply the needed flow and pressure. This system provides the volume of a large displacement pump at low speeds plus the economy of a small displacement pump at higher, cruising speeds. ● **SEE FIGURE 6–18**.

The parts in a pump must fit together with very little clearance to prevent the fluid from leaking across the pump from the high-pressure area to areas of lower pressure. The fit provides just enough clearance for the parts to move without excess drag.

FIGURE 6–16 As a pump rotates, a low pressure/vacuum is created as the pumping members move apart in one area, and atmospheric pressure will force fluid into this area. Pressure is created where the pumping members move together.

6.6 PROVIDING CLEAN FLUID

A filter is located at the pump inlet to trap dirt, metal, and other foreign particles that might cause wear in the pump, bearings, bushings, and gear train or cause sticking of the various valves.

FIGURE 6–17 A variable displacement vane pump in maximum and minimum output positions. The slide is moved to the high-output position by the spring moving the slide. Decreased pressure comes from the pressure regulator valve. (*Reprinted with permission of General Motors*)

Three types of filters are used: surface, depth, and paper. ● **SEE FIGURE 6–19**. Filters offer a potential problem in that as they do their job, they will eventually plug up. This might cause an excessive pressure drop across the filter and fluid starvation to the pump.

A **surface filter** traps the foreign particles at the outer surface. ● **SEE FIGURE 6–20**. This filter can be a woven screen of metal or synthetic material such as dacron or polyester. Some sources consider a **paper filter** to be a surface filter. With a metal or synthetic screen, the size of the openings varies from rather large to very fine, in the range of 50 to 100 microns (or micrometers). A **micron** is 1 millionth of a meter or 39 millionths of an inch. The symbol for micron is μm. The disadvantage of a surface filter is its limited surface area, which in turn limits its capacity. The mesh openings are the usable area. A large portion of a filter's surface is the fibers or wires that make up the filter, with the remainder being the openings. ● **SEE FIGURE 6–21**. The filter can quickly become plugged. The filter material must be strong enough to prevent collapse or tearing of the filter.

A **depth filter** traps particles as they try to pass through the filter material. Depth filters use felt or a synthetic material of various thickness. ● **SEE FIGURE 6–22**. The depth of the material allows room to trap particles as well as room for fluid flow.

FIGURE 6–18 This transmission uses a dual-stage, external gear pump. Both stages are used at low engine speeds to produce enough fluid for the transmission's needs. At higher engine speeds, the secondary stage is vented. (*Courtesy of Chrysler Corporation*)

FIGURE 6–20 A surface filter traps particles that are too big to pass through the openings in the screen. (*Courtesy of SPX Filtran*)

FIGURE 6–19 Two filters: (a) a surface/screen filter, and (b, c) a depth/felt filter.

It also offers the ability to trap smaller particles, more capacity to trap particles, and the ability to flow better for a longer period of time. ● **SEE FIGURE 6–23**. Some depth filters trap particles as small as 10 µm.

Particle size is important when we consider the space between a bushing and the shaft. This clearance is about 0.001 to 0.003 in. (0.025 to 0.076 mm), but if the shaft is loaded to one side by gear pressure, this clearance might be only the width of two or three oil molecules. A hard, abrasive particle in this area will produce wear that, in turn, will produce small metal particles that cause more wear. Dirt or other particles that enter the valve body may cause a valve to stick in its bore. This can cause a no-shift problem or a partial shift with low pressure. A recent study of the fluid from eight different transmissions used less than 3,000 miles showed the following:

- 1 to 20 particles in the 50-µm size
- 800 to 8,000 particles in the 15-µm size
- More than 50,000 particles in the 5-µm size

FIGURE 6–21 The surface area of a surface filter is reduced somewhat by the material that makes up the screen. The size of the screen openings determines how small of a particle can be filtered.

FIGURE 6–22 A depth filter is a group of woven fibers of a certain thickness. Foreign particles are trapped at different levels as they try to flow through. (*Courtesy of SPX Filtran*)

A ——— Felt per SPFM-86 - Rated 60 Micron @ 90%
B ••••• Paper per AC 9025
C ········ Polyester Mesh HC-7-59 rated 59 Micron
D – – – Polyester Mesh HC-7-105 rated 105 Micron

FIGURE 6–23 Comparison of the filtering ability of four types of filters. (*Courtesy of SPX Filtran*)

FIGURE 6–24 General Motors transaxles have two fluid reservoirs. One is the lower pan, and one is the valve body cover. The thermostatic element closes when the fluid heats up to raise the fluid level in the upper pan. (*Reprinted with permission of General Motors*)

FIGURE 6–25 A spool valve resembles a spool for thread (top).

Normally, the pan is the sump or reservoir for the fluid, and the filter is positioned close to the bottom of the pan. General Motors transaxles use two reservoirs; one is the bottom pan and the other is the valve body cover or side pan. ● **SEE FIGURE 6–24.** When the unit is cold, all the fluid is kept in the bottom pan. As the transaxle warms up, the thermostatic element closes to retain fluid in the side pan.

6.7 CONTROLLING FLUID FLOW

The fluid flow from the pressure regulator valve to the manual valve and into the control circuit is called *mainline, line,* or *control pressure.* Flow to and from a transmission hydraulic actuator is controlled by one or more valves. Spool valves sliding in a round bore are used for this purpose. A **spool valve** gets its

FIGURE 6–26 A spool valve and its bore. Note the names of the various parts. (*Courtesy of Chrysler Corporation*)

PROBLEM SOLVING 6–1

Imagine that you are working in a shop that specializes in transmission repair, and these problems are brought to you.

Case 1:

A 1996 Toyota Camry drives okay in all gears, but it seems to go into neutral when it makes sharp turns. What could cause this problem? What should you first check?

Case 2:

A 1989 Chevrolet Caprice with a 200–4R transmission does not move, forward or backward, with the shift selector in any position. What do you think might be wrong with this transmission? Where would you begin your checks?

name from its resemblance to a spool used for thread. ● **SEE FIGURE 6–25.** A spool valve can have two or more **lands** that fit the valve bore tightly enough so that fluid cannot escape past the valve land but loosely enough so that the valve can slide freely in the bore. ● **SEE FIGURE 6–26.** The annular grooves (valleys) between the lands is where the fluid flows through the valve. Typically the valve-to-bore clearance is about 0.003 to 0.004 in. (80 to 100 µm). The close fit requires the valve to expand and contract at the same rate as the valve body. This prevents the valve from sticking or having excessive leakage. The outer edges of the lands have sharp corners to help prevent debris from wedging between the land and the valve bore. The valleys or grooves between the lands serve as fluid passages. The faces serve as pressure surfaces, called **reaction surfaces**, to produce valve movement. Some valves are relatively long with a series of lands and grooves so fluid flow through two or more passages are controlled at the same time. The lands of a spool

FIGURE 6–27 The sleeve allows the larger primary regulator valve to enter its part of the bore and also provides the bore for the smaller No. 1 and No. 2 plungers. (*Courtesy of Toyota Motor Sales USA, Inc.*)

FIGURE 6–28 When a valve moves in its bore, the side passages are opened or closed to control fluid flow. (*Courtesy of Chrysler Corporation*)

valve often have different diameters in order to provide different-size reaction areas. Some valves are used with bushings, also called sleeves, that allow the manufacturer to easily change valve diameter and fluid passages. ● SEE FIGURE 6–27.

A spool valve bore has fluid passages entering from the sides, which connect to the grooves (valleys) that extend clear around the valve. This is done to produce the same pressure entirely around the valve. If pressure were exerted on only one side of the valve, the valve would be **side loaded**. This can force the valve sideways and lock the valve in the bore. Only a very few manual valves are designed with side loading. These valves have one or more grooves running along part of the valve's length. As a spool valve is slid along the bore, the lands open up or close off the side passages and block or allow fluid flow from one place to another or to the sump to allow pressure to be exhausted.

FIGURE 6–29 Fluid pressure acting on the surface area of the valve face can move the valve along the bore.

The position of a valve can be controlled by the following:

- Mechanical linkage
- Hydraulic pressure
- Spring
- Centrifugal force
- Engine vacuum
- Electric solenoids

The manual valve (a spool valve) is moved mechanically by the shift lever. Movement of the shift lever slides the manual valve along its bore, opening or closing the desired passages. Fluid will be sent to the appropriate apply devices and valves for the selected gear range.

Most of the spool valves in a valve body are positioned by a spring at one end and fluid force (pressure × area) at the other. ● SEE FIGURE 6–28. The spring tries to hold the valve in one position, and when fluid pressure at the other end gets stronger than the spring, the valve will move. ● SEE FIGURE 6–29. Some valves act as a servo to produce motion (usually of another valve), redirect fluid flow, or regulate fluid pressure. They will be described more completely in Chapter 7.

Nonelectronic transmissions use a mechanical **governor valve** and either a mechanical or vacuum-operated throttle valve. **Shift timing**, also called *shift points,* is controlled by the governor and throttle valves. Newer transmissions use electronic controls with **vehicle speed sensors (VSS)** and **throttle position sensors (TPS)** for this purpose. An **electronic control module (ECM)** uses signals from these two sensors as well as other sensors to determine shift points, and the ECM activates electronic *solenoid valves* to produce the shifts. Electronic shift control is described more completely in Chapter 8.

Governor valves are spun by the transmission output shaft so the valve is thrown outward by centrifugal force. Hydraulic pressure from the governor and a light spring is used to oppose centrifugal force. ● SEE FIGURE 6–30. The output of this valve is a gradual fluid pressure increase that is roughly proportional to vehicle speed. ● SEE FIGURE 6–31. The pressure produced by the governor is called *governor pressure*. Many transmissions use a **throttle valve** to produce hydraulic pressure that is proportional to vehicle load. ● SEE FIGURE 6–32. A throttle valve can be controlled either mechanically or by vacuum.

FIGURE 6–30 The governor valve produces a fluid pressure that is proportional to the speed of the vehicle. (*Courtesy of Nissan North America, Inc.*)

FIGURE 6–31 Ideally, governor pressure increases with speed so the pressure in PSI matches the speed in mph. There should be about 40 PSI at 40 mph.

FIGURE 6–32 (a) A vacuum-operated throttle valve uses a vacuum modulator to produce an engine-load-sensitive signal at the transmission. (b) A mechanical-controlled throttle valve (in this case, a cable) transfers an engine-load-sensitive signal through mechanical linkage. (*Reprinted with permission of General Motors*)

Some transmissions use a rod or cable to make a mechanical connection to the engine's throttle linkage. Other transmissions use a **modulator valve** with a vacuum signal from the intake manifold that acts on the diaphragm of a vacuum motor. The valve is balanced between a mechanical pressure from a spring-versus-vacuum-diaphragm pressure at one end and fluid pressure at the other. The pressure produced by sensing engine load is known as throttle pressure or throttle valve (TV) pressure.

The vacuum motor (modulator) has a spring that is always pushing against the hydraulic valve, and the engine manifold vacuum reduces the power of the spring. TV pressure is very low at idle speed and very high at wide-open throttle (WOT). A **detent valve** is used in some circuits to increase TV pressure and force downshifts at WOT. The maximum pressure that a governor or a throttle valve can produce is line pressure.

Another way to control the position of a spool valve is to use an electric solenoid. The solenoid can be switched on or off by an electric switch or an electronic control module (ECM). The ECM can be programmed to react to inputs from many different sensors. Electronic transmissions can use several solenoids to control the torque converter clutch, line pressure, and shift valve operation. The solenoid can control a shift valve by exhausting the fluid pressure at one end, and a spring or fluid pressure at the other end causes the spool valve to move and change the fluid path through the valve. ● **SEE FIGURE 6–33.** Some valves consist of a steel ball that is moved mechanically by the solenoid.

A **check ball** is the simplest method of controlling fluid flow. A *one-way check valve* resembles a steel bearing or plastic ball over a hole in the **separator plate**. The separator plate, also called a *transfer plate* or *restrictor plate,* is positioned between valve body sections or between the valve body and transmission case. ● **SEE FIGURE 6–34.** An upward fluid flow moves the ball aside and fluid flows around it. A downward fluid flow forces the ball against the hole and stops the flow. The flow of fluid is only possible in one direction, upward.

FIGURE 6–33 (a) This kickdown valve is controlled by the electric solenoid and is closed when there is no electrical signal. (b) The valve opens when the solenoid is energized. (*Courtesy of Nissan North America, Inc.*)

FIGURE 6–34 A check valve is opened by fluid flow in one direction (left) and closes when the fluid tries to flow in the other direction.

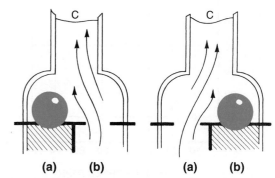

FIGURE 6–35 When fluid flows through this shuttle valve from port B to port C, the check ball moves over to close port A (left). Fluid flow from port A will close port B (right).

Some transmissions use a *two-way check valve,* also called a **shuttle valve.** The ball is positioned above two side-by-side holes with another flow passage extending upward or to the side. Upward flow through one of the holes in the plate causes the ball to move over and seat against the other hole. ● **SEE FIGURE 6–35.** Fluid flow upward through the second hole causes the ball to move over and seal the first hole.

A pressure relief valve resembles a check valve, but it is spring loaded. ● **SEE FIGURE 6–36.** Sometimes a flat disc or spool valve is used in place of a ball. The fluid pressure required to unseat this valve is determined by the strength of the spring and the size of the opening at the seat. Fluid pressure acting on the exposed area of the ball pushes against the spring. When fluid pressure exceeds spring pressure, the ball moves off its seat, the pressure is relieved through the opening, and the spring closes the passage again. This can happen many times a second. The rate of fluid flow can be controlled by a

A X P = Spring Force

FIGURE 6–36 (a) A pressure relief valve. (b) When fluid pressure acting on the area of the ball exceeds the spring force, the ball will move off of its seat and allow excess pressure to escape.

restriction called an orifice. Orifices are described more completely in Section 6.11.

6.7.1 VALVE HYDRAULIC FORCES Think of a valve as a hydraulic actuator. The hydraulic force exerted by a valve is simply the valve land area multiplied by fluid pressure. The valve area is determined using the formula for the area of a circle, πr^2.

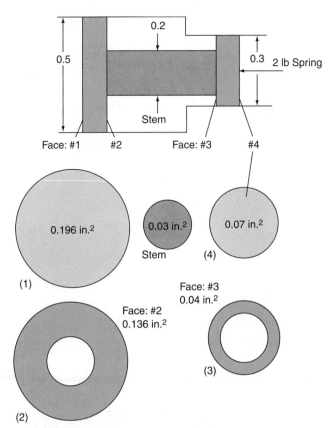

FIGURE 6–37 This valve spool has four possible hydraulic reaction faces. The areas are calculated like those of any other circular surface using the formula πr^2.

Let us imagine a valve with a 2-lb (0.9-kg) spring pressing on one end and a 0.5-in. (12.67-mm) diameter land at the other end. ● **SEE FIGURE 6–37.**

- The area of the 0.5-in. land is $0.25 \times 0.25 \times 3.1416 = 0.196$ in^2 (1.26 cm^2).
- A fluid pressure of 10.2 PSI (70.33 kPa) acting on an area of 0.196 in^2 (1.26 cm^2) generates a force of 2 lb.

Fluid pressure greater than 10.2 PSI will cause the valve to move and compress the spring.

In some cases, pressure is exerted between two different-size land faces; fluid pressure acting on a larger face develops a greater force that will move the valve in that direction. If the diameter of one land is 0.5 in., the other land is 0.3 in. (7.6 mm), and the stem or shank of the valve is 0.2 in. (5.1 mm). There are three diameters and two important areas, as follows:

- Face 1: 0.5-in. diameter has an area of 0.196 in^2.
- Stem: 0.2-in. diameter has an area of $0.1 \times 0.1 \times 3.1416 = 0.031$ in^2.
- Face 2: has an area of $0.196 - 0.030 = 0.166$ in^2.
- Face 3: has an area of $0.070 - 0.030 = 0.040$ in^2.
- Face 4: 0.3 diameter has an area of $0.15 \times 0.15 \times 3.1416 = 0.070$ in^2.

TECH TIP

Usually a pressure regulator valve produces the correct pressure, but a valve that does not slide easily in its bore can stick and then overtravel. This can cause the pressure to drop; the valve then moves back to its original position, and the cycle soon repeats. A pressure regulator valve can move back and forth quite rapidly, probably several thousand times a second. This movement follows the pressure pulsations from the pump. At times this makes a whining or buzzing sound in some transmissions, especially when they are cold.

- Area difference between face 2 and face 3: $0.136 - 0.040 = 0.096$ in^2.
- A fluid pressure of 10 PSI (68.95 kPa) will develop a force of 0.96 lb (0.75 kg) pushing in the direction of face 2, the larger land.

6.8 CONTROLLING FLUID PRESSURE

Fluid pressure in an automatic transmission is controlled by a variable pressure regulator valve. Fluid pressure must be high enough to apply a clutch or band tightly enough to prevent slippage. Excessive fluid pressure will produce heat and fluid foaming as well as more drag on the engine. In most transmissions, the pressure regulator valve is positioned close to the outlet of the pump. This valve is usually arranged so fluid pressure is at one end and a spring is at the other end. An additional passage from the pump enters the valve at one valley, and a passage leading back to the pump inlet is located at an adjacent valley.

When fluid pressure is multiplied by the reaction area of the valve, a force greater than that of the spring's strength is created, and the valve will move to allow flow back to the pump inlet. The valve finds a balanced position where the fluid pressure acting on the reaction area of the valve and working against the spring releases enough fluid to maintain the correct pressure.

Transmissions with a vane pump use a different style of pressure regulator. The pressure regulator valve works like those with other pumps, but the passage from the valve goes to the pump's vane housing instead of back to the pump inlet. This pressure moves the pump slide to reduce the displacement and output of the pump (see Figure 6–17). High fluid pressure causes the pressure regulator to send a calibrated pressure to the pump slide, which reduces pump output and thus pressure. When fluid pressure drops, the priming spring returns the pump slide back to the high-output position.

Regulator valves have additional lands and valleys or another valve in the same bore to provide boost pressures for medium- to full-throttle operation or while in reverse. Sometimes

Imagine that you are working in a shop that specializes in transmission repair, and these problems are brought to you.

Case 1:

A 1996 Dodge Ram pickup drives okay in first and second gears, but there is no 2–3 shift. There is no third gear; it just stays in second. The fluid level is okay, but it is almost black. Would a worn band cause this problem? Could a sticking valve cause it? How about a worn third-gear clutch?

Case 2:

A 1994 Ford Mustang has very harsh upshifts in all gears. The shifts are severe with all throttle positions. The fluid level is slightly low but within the range on the dipstick, and the fluid condition appears good. What do you think might be wrong with this transmission? What would you check next?

FIGURE 6–38 This valve body uses upper (at bottom) and lower sections (at top) that are separated by the separator plate. Note how the separator plate can restrict a passage so it becomes a port or orifice for flow into the other section. (*Courtesy of Chrysler Corporation*)

manual low and intermediate gears require additional pressure because of the probable increased torque requirement. Boosted mainline pressure is used to provide additional holding power at the clutches and bands. A firmer shift occurs when operating under wider throttle openings (increased load).

6.9 SEALING FLUID PRESSURE

The fluid passages run throughout the valve body, transmission case, shafts, and tubes of the transmission. Remember that fluid transmits pressure equally through a passage, regardless of its size or shape. The many passages in the valve body and the transmission case resemble **worm tracks** (a nickname used by transmission rebuilders). ● **SEE FIGURE 6–38**. The passages in the transmission case can be worm tracks or simply holes drilled to form passages. Metal plugs are commonly used to seal unwanted openings. Some transmission shafts have several different passages for apply pressure to various clutches or lubrication. ● **SEE FIGURE 6–39**. Gaskets and seals are used to keep the pressure from escaping where fluid flows between parts. Seals fall into two categories: **static** and **dynamic**.

A static seal is used to seal the space between two parts that are stationary relative to each other. Static seals include **gaskets** and **O-rings** that are placed between the two parts and squeezed tightly as the parts are fastened together. A static seal must provide enough compression to fill any possible voids between the two surfaces. ● **SEE FIGURE 6–40**. The compression needed for a seal to work properly depends greatly on the flatness and rigidity of the sealing surfaces. Wavy or weak surfaces need a thick, resilient seal or gasket. Aluminum transmission cases move quite a bit as they expand and contract during heating and cooling cycles, so a resilient gasket and seal material are required.

A dynamic seal has a much harder job because one of the surfaces to be sealed is moving relative to the seal. The movement can be rotating (e.g., the torque converter enters the front of the transmission or the fluid flows from the pump housing into a clutch assembly) or a sliding motion (e.g., the stroking of a clutch piston). ● **SEE FIGURE 6–41**.

At each end of the transmission, a rotating shaft enters or leaves the transmission, and the opening through which the shaft runs must be sealed to keep the fluid in and the dirt and water out. At these openings the torque converter enters the

FRONT ANNULUS GEAR

DRIVING SHELL

REAR ANNULUS GEAR

FRONT PLANETARY GEAR ASSEMBLY

REAR PLANETARY GEAR ASSEMBLY

LOW/REVERSE DRUM

INTERMEDIATE SHAFT

LUBRICATION HOLES

FIGURE 6–39 This intermediate shaft has fluid passages to transfer lubricating oil to the planetary gear sets. (*Courtesy of Chrysler Corporation*)

Dynamic Seals (Sliding)

Static Seal

Dynamic Seals (Rotating)

Fluid Passage

Dynamic Seal

Static Seal

FIGURE 6–40 Static seals prevent fluid from passing between two stationary surfaces. Dynamic seals keep fluid from passing through when one of the surfaces is moving. (*Courtesy of Toyota Motor Sales USA, Inc.*)

CASE

FLUID

SEALING MEMBER

GARTER SPRING

METAL CASE

FIGURE 6–41 The sealing member of a metal-clad lip seal makes a dynamic seal with the rotating shaft while the metal case forms a static seal with the transmission case. (*Courtesy of Chrysler Corporation*)

front pump and the output shaft(s) leaves the extension housing. In both cases, a **metal-clad lip seal** is used. A lip seal has a flexible rubber sealing lip that rubs against the revolving shaft with enough pressure so fluid cannot flow between the shaft and the seal lip. A garter spring is often used to increase this sealing pressure. The lip is molded into the seal's case or outer housing, which forms a static seal with the transmission case or extension housing.

Another type of seal is used to seal the fluid passages where fluid leaves a stationary member and transfers to a rotating member such as the turbine shaft, front clutch assembly, or governor support. ● **SEE FIGURE 6–42**. This seal is a metal, plastic, or Teflon ring that fits tight in its bore to make a seal while the side seals against the side of its groove. ● **SEE FIGURE 6–43**. A seal with a small leak is sometimes desirable to lubricate a bearing area close to the sealing ring. Metal and plastic sealing rings can be a full-circle *hook ring* or a *butt-cut ring* with a small gap. Teflon rings can be *scarf cut* (have the ends cut at an angle so they overlap), *butt cut,* or *uncut.* ● **SEE FIGURE 6–44**. Teflon seals can change size. When a Teflon ring is stretched over a shaft, it must be resized smaller to fit into the groove and bore. Special installing and resizing tools are recommended when installing Teflon sealing rings.

The sliding seals for the clutch and band servo pistons are made of rubber in an O-ring, D-ring, lathe-cut seal, or lip seal

FIGURE 6–42 Sealing rings are used to seal the passages between stationary and rotating members. For example, the seal rings at the right keep the fluid flows from the pump to the front clutch from escaping. (*Courtesy of Chrysler Corporation*)

FIGURE 6–43 Fluid pressure forces a sealing ring outward in both directions to make firm contact with the side of the groove and outer diameter of the bore.

FIGURE 6–44 Metal seal rings (bottom) have plain or hooked ends. Teflon rings (top) are either uncut, scarf cut, or butt cut.

FIGURE 6–45 Clutch and servo piston seals are usually O-rings, lathe-cut rings, or lip seals.

shape. An O-ring is a rubber ring with a round cross section. A D-ring is rounded on the sealing side and square on the side where it is retained; the square portion prevents the seal from rotating. A lathe-cut seal, also called a *square-cut seal* or *quad-ring,* is a rubber ring with a square cross section. A lip seal has a sealing lip much like that of the metal-clad seal described earlier. ● **SEE FIGURE 6–45.**

The type of seal used on a piston is determined by the shape and size of the seal groove. By its nature, a lip seal provides the best pressure retention as well as the ability to adapt to piston-to-bore clearance. ● **SEE FIGURE 6–46.** The lip seal is bonded to the servo or clutch piston in some transmissions to give more consistent operation and lower drag. ● **SEE FIGURE 6–47.** The bore in the clutch assembly as well as the center seal area must have straight, smooth sides to provide a good sealing surface and keep seal wear to a minimum. The outer ends of the piston bores are normally chamfered to make piston and seal installation easier. The close fit of bushings also serves to limit fluid flow along a shaft.

FIGURE 6–46 Two lip seals (blue) form fluid-tight seals between the front clutch piston and its bore. (*Courtesy of Chrysler Corporation*)

6.9.1 SPECIAL NOTES ON ELASTOMERS

The rubber seal materials used for seals are called **elastomers** because of their elastic nature. A dynamic seal must remain flexible and maintain its size and shape in order to work properly. Plain rubber is not used in a transmission because it is adversely affected by heat and contact with ATF. Natural rubber has an operating range of −58°F (−50°C) to 212°F (100°C). Higher temperatures cause rubber materials to harden, and exposure to transmission fluid causes it to swell excessively. A hardened seal may leak and cause a pressure loss, which in turn will cause clutch slippage and failure.

Synthetic rubber compounds are blends of various rubber-like materials. Those used in automatic transmissions include *Buna N* or *nitrile rubber* (to 230°F), *polyacrylate* (to 320°F), *ethyleneacrylic* (to 375°F), *fluoroelastomer* (to 400°F), and *silicone* (above 400°F). ● **SEE FIGURE 6–48**. Another major difference between these compounds is cost; as the operating temperature range increases, the cost of the material goes up many times. A manufacturer usually selects the lowest-cost seal material that will do the job, and we should realize that different seals in a transmission have different working conditions. For example, the high-reverse clutch in a Simpson gear train transmission is subjected to about 30 to 35 times as much activity as the forward clutch. One seal material might work well in one clutch but not stand up to the load or movement requirements of another.

When a transmission rebuilder purchases a gasket and seal kit, cost should not be the only concern. The use of better-quality materials will lead to an overhaul that will perform better and last longer. The price of the correct seal material can be many times greater than a cheaper Buna N seal. The following methods can be used in the field to identify the quality of a particular seal.

- A letter code is molded into the seal surface. The code is registered with the Rubber Manufacturers Association (RMA) to identify the manufacturer. The original equipment manufacturer (OEM) of a transmission seal normally supplies the same OEM seal to the aftermarket. ● **SEE FIGURE 6–49**. These are the best-quality seals.

- Ignite the seal with a match, let it burn for 2 or 3 seconds, and then extinguish the fire. If the smoke odor is like

FIGURE 6–47 The seal was bonded onto this servo piston, and the seal is replaced by replacing the piston.

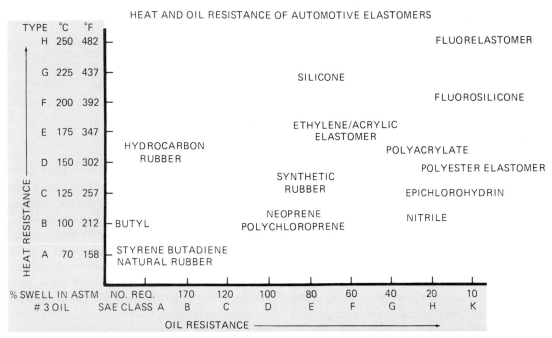

HEAT AND OIL RESISTANCE OF AUTOMOTIVE ELASTOMERS

FIGURE 6–48 This chart compares the ability of seal materials to withstand heat and fluid. Note that natural rubber is very low in both cases.

FIGURE 6–49 The code letters cast into the surface of this seal identify the manufacturer of the seal.

a burning tire, the material is Buna N; if it has a sweet smell, it is polyacrylic material. This destroys the seal, but it gives you a good idea of the material.

- Feel the material. Polyacrylic is harder and less elastic than rubber.

6.10 APPLYING FLUID PRESSURE

An automatic transmission shifts when hydraulic pressure applies or releases a clutch or band. Hydraulic pressure causes the clutch or servo piston to stroke, taking up the clearance, and then squeezes the parts together. Both bands and clutches are released by spring pressure. Band servos can also be released by hydraulic pressure.

The force that a clutch piston exerts on the clutch plates is a product of piston area multiplied by hydraulic pressure. A rotating, driving clutch has a piston with an outside diameter (OD) of about 6 in. (152 mm), and an inner diameter (ID) that can vary from 2 to 5 in. (102 to 127 mm). ● **SEE FIGURE 6–50.** Most stationary, holding clutches have a larger diameter; the intermediate clutch piston in some transmissions has an OD of 10 in. (254 mm). A piston with an OD of 6 in. (152 mm) and an ID of 3 in. (76 mm) has an area of 21.27 in². A hydraulic pressure of 80 PSI (551.6 kPa) will generate a force of 9,697 lb (4,408 kg), a fairly significant force. This piston will require about 2 cubic in. (in³) of fluid to complete its stroke of 0.1 in. (0.254 mm).

Some clutches have two piston areas, and a lip seal is located between these two areas. ● **SEE FIGURE 6–51.** In high gear, the inner, smaller area is used; it fills faster and provides sufficient force for the torque requirements of high gear. In reverse, fluid enters the outer area and leaks past the lip of the center seal to fill both areas. This produces a very strong clutch application force, and since reverse is a garage shift, there is ample time to fill the clutch.

Piston Area:	6" OD	=	28.27 in.²	(3 × 3 × 3.1416)
	3" ID	=	−7 in.²	(1.5 × 1.5 × 3.1416)
	Area	=	21.27 in.²	

FIGURE 6–50 A typical clutch piston area is determined by subtracting the area of the inner diameter from the area of the outer-circle diameter.

Outer Piston Area:			Inner Piston Area:		
6" OD	=	28.27 in.²	4" MD	=	12.56 in.²
4" MD	=	−12.56 in.²	3" ID	=	−7 in.²
Area	=	15.71 in.²	Area	=	5.56 in.²

FIGURE 6–51 Some clutch pistons use a middle seal so the piston will have two working areas.

Most bands use fairly small servo pistons, which generate less force than a clutch piston; a typical servo piston has an OD of a few inches. Some transmissions are designed so that several different servo piston diameters can be used. The different servos will tailor the transmission to suit vehicles with larger or smaller engines and torque requirements. More engine horsepower or heavier loads require more band application force. Some servos are released by clutch apply pressure. For example, in some transmissions the intermediate servo is applied by hydraulic pressure in second gear. As the transmission shifts into third gear, it is released by third-gear oil pressure; when the vehicle slows for a stop, the servo is released by the spring.

Variable	Softer	Firmer
Line pressure	lower	higher
Flow rate	slower	faster
Accumulator stroke rate	faster	slower
Clutch cushion springs	more	less
Friction plate grooving	less grooving less aggressive pattern	more aggressive pattern
Friction plate composition	less aggressive compound	more aggressive compound
Steel plate/drum surface	smoother	rougher
Fluid type	lower dynamic friction	higher dynamic friction

FIGURE 6–52 Shift quality can be modified by changing any of these variables.

6.10.1 DETERMINING PISTON FORCE The force exerted by a piston is simply the piston area multiplied by fluid pressure. Like a valve, piston area is determined using the formula πr^2.

Piston A: A 5-in. diameter piston has a radius of 2.5 in.

- Radius squared: $2.5 \times 2.5 = 6.25$.

- 6.25 multiplied by π: $6.25 \times 3.1416 = 19.635$ (round up to 20 in^2).

- A fluid pressure of 80 PSI acting on this piston will produce $80 \times 20 = 1,600$ lb of force.

- If this piston travels 0.100 in., it will require $20 \times 0.1 = 2$ in^3 of fluid.

Piston B: A clutch piston is slightly different because we must subtract the area of the center hole.

- If this piston has a 5-in. OD and a center hole diameter of 2.4 in., the center hole radius is 1.2 in.

- Radius squared (r^2): $1.2 \times 1.2 = 1.44$.

- The area of the center hole: $1.44 \times 3.1416 = 4.524$.

- 5-in. piston area: 19.635 in^2.

- 5-in. clutch piston area: $19.635 - 4.524 = 15.1$ in^2 (round off to 15 in^2).

- A fluid pressure of 80 PSI acting on this piston will produce a force of $80 \times 15 = 1,200$ lb of force.

- If this piston travels 0.100 in., it will require $15 \times 0.1 = 1.5$ in^3 of fluid.

6.11 MODIFYING FLOW AND PRESSURE

During a shift, it is desirable to provide a gradual pressure increase to the clutch pistons or band servos. This improves the **shift quality**, producing the desirable *shift feel*. Shift feel is a "seat-of-the-pants" response the driver experiences during shifts. As the piston is stroking to take up the clutch or band clearance, the pressures in the circuit are relatively low. But the instant the

FIGURE 6–53 (a) An orifice will cause a pressure drop as fluid flows through; (b) when the flow stops, the pressure on both sides of the orifice will be the same.

clearance disappears and the piston stops moving, the pressure rises very rapidly, causing a sudden and possibly very harsh application. Shift quality can be adjusted mechanically by changing the friction material or hydraulically by controlling fluid pressure. There are many variables that affect shift quality. ● **SEE FIGURE 6–52.**

The two commonly used devices to control band or clutch application are an **orifice** and an **accumulator**. Different versions of a particular transmission often have different orifice sizes and accumulator settings to adjust the transmission to the engine, vehicle weight, and intended use.

An orifice is simply a small hole, usually in the separator plate. ● **SEE FIGURE 6–53.** An orifice produces a resistance to fluid flow and therefore causes a pressure drop as long as fluid is flowing through it. The amount of pressure drop is relative to the size of the orifice and the flow volume. The smaller the orifice, the greater resistance to flow and the larger the pressure drop. As soon as the flow stops, the orifice no longer has an effect on the flow, and the pressure on both sides becomes equal. An orifice is also used to dampen fluid flow to the control valves. There is usually one in the passage between the pump and reaction land

BOTTOMED AGAINST
ACCUMULATOR PLATE

LINE
PRESSURE

NEUTRAL AND DRIVE POSITIONS

ACCUMULATOR

FRONT SERVO

BOTTOM IN BORE

SECOND GEAR

FIGURE 6–54 In neutral, the accumulator piston is moved to the top of its stroke by line pressure (top). Front servo apply pressure strokes the accumulator piston downward, delaying the pressure rise at the servo. (*Courtesy of Chrysler Corporation*)

FULL LINE PRESSURE
WITH CLUTCH APPLIED

APPLY PRESSURE

PRESSURE

STROKE OF CLUTCH PISTON
PRESSURE RISE TO FILL CLUTCH CIRCUIT

TIME

(a)

FULL LINE PRESSURE
WITH CLUTCH APPLIED

PRESSURE

STROKE OF ACCUMULATOR PISTON

STROKE OF CLUTCH PISTON
PRESSURE RISE TO FILL CLUTCH CIRCUIT

TIME

(b)

FIGURE 6–55 (a) When a clutch applies, fluid pressure rises gradually until the circuit is filled and the piston strokes to take up the clearance; then there is a rapid increase to line pressure. (b) An accumulator can be placed into the circuit to slow this pressure rise and soften clutch application.

of the pressure regulator valve; this orifice helps soften pressure pulses from the pump that can cause the valve to overreact.

Fluid flow rate through an orifice requires a rather complex formula; calculating the actual flow is beyond the scope of this book, but understanding the effect of an orifice is important. Imagine a clutch with a piston that requires 1.5 in³ of fluid to apply. Transmission engineers will determine the orifice diameter that allows a flow of 1.5 in³ of fluid in about one-fifth of a second to apply the clutch at about 80 PSI. Increased fluid pressure, from boost, will produce increased flow, quicker clutch filling, and a faster, firmer shift.

An orifice keeps the supply side of the circuit from having a pressure drop during a clutch or band application. In a simple shift circuit, when the shift valve moves to send fluid to a clutch piston, the fluid pressure will drop at the shift valve. It might also drop in the circuit that feeds the shift valve, which could cause an unwanted operation.

An accumulator is a piston or valve that is not attached to anything; all it does is stroke in its own bore. ● SEE **FIGURE 6–54**. The pressure required to stroke the accumulator is controlled by a spring or by opposing fluid pressure. An accumulator is tied to an apply piston by a branch of the fluid passage used for apply pressure. It is adjusted to stroke at a pressure just above that needed to stroke the apply piston.

Just after the apply piston takes up the clutch or band clearance and the fluid pressure starts to increase, the accumulator strokes and absorbs some of the fluid flow. This causes a lag in the pressure increase at the band servo and clutch. ● SEE **FIGURE 6–55**. The effect is a slightly longer and smoother shift. If we were to add an accumulator with the capacity of 0.75 in³ to the circuit previously described, the clutch would now take 50% longer, about 3/4 second, to fill. Some transmissions vary the pressure behind the accumulator to provide different shift characteristics depending on the throttle position or load. Full-throttle shifts are usually firmer than part-throttle shifts.

6.12 AUTOMATIC TRANSMISSION FLUID

Automatic transmission fluid (ATF) is one of the most complex fluids used in a vehicle. It must do the following:

- Transfer *hydrodynamic* energy in the torque converter
- Transfer *hydrostatic* energy at the clutch and servo pistons as well as at the valve body

- Help transfer sliding friction energy as the clutches and bands apply

- Transfer excess heat away from high-temperature locations such as the torque converter's friction surfaces, gears, and bushings

- Lubricate the various moving parts

Early automatic transmissions used engine oil for a transmission fluid. Since the internal operating conditions in an engine and automatic transmission are significantly different, a special transmission fluid was developed in the late 1940s. At first, the ATF was simply a mineral oil much like motor oil but dyed red. Newer ATFs can be mineral oil or synthetic lubricant with a number of additives to make it more suited to the needs of a transmission. The first transmission fluid was developed by General Motors and was labeled *Type A* transmission fluid. As transmission fluid was improved, Type A was replaced with *Type A, Suffix A; Dexron;* and then *Dexron II, Dexron IIE,* and *Dexron III.* ● **SEE FIGURE 6–56.** The Dexron fluids are compatible, and Dexron III can be used in most older transmissions that specify one of the older fluid types.

Like other vehicle manufacturers, Ford Motor Company has developed fluids for use in its vehicles. *Types F, CJ, Mercon,* and *Mercon V* are required for various Ford transmission models. Mercon can be used in place of older Ford fluids. Mercon V should be used only in transmissions that specify its use. ● **SEE FIGURE 6–57.** Some fluids meet both Mercon and Mercon V specifications. Mercon V and Dexron III are very

	General Motors	Ford Motor Company	Chrysler	Toyota
1940				
1950	Type A			
1960	Type A Suffix A	M2C33 A-B		
		M2C33 C-D		
1970	Dexron	M2C33-F (Type F)		
	Dexron II	M2C33-G		Type F
1980		M2C138-CJ M2C166-H	ATF+ ATF+1	Dexron II
		Mercon		Type T
1990	Dexron IIE Dexron III		ATF+2 ATF+3	Dexron III
2000		Mercon V	ATF+4	
	Dexron VI	Mercon SP		ATF-WS
2010				

FIGURE 6–56 The first special ATF was developed in the late 1940s. Since that date, advanced, special fluids have been developed by domestic as well as foreign vehicle manufacturers.

(a)   (b)   (c)

FIGURE 6–57 The markings on ATF containers show the fluid types. *(Figures (b) and (c) Courtesy of Pennzoil)*

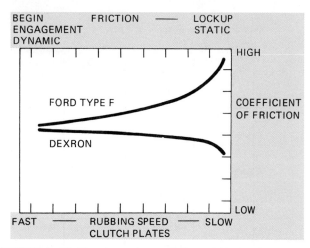

FIGURE 6–58 The dynamic coefficient of friction for these two fluids is almost the same, but the static friction is very different.

similar, and some fluids meet both specifications. Other manufacturers have developed specific fluids to meet the needs of their transmissions. Always use the specified fluid when adding or replacing transmission fluid. At least one vehicle manufacturer has stated that it will not reimburse dealers for repair costs if the wrong transmission fluid was used. Many transmission shops are forced to keep a large variety of fluid types on hand, but they have discovered that the OEM-specified fluid makes the transmission operate the way that it was designed to operate.

Manufacturers introduce new transmission fluids as they develop new transmissions with more speed ranges, improved fuel economy, and reduced maintenance costs. The increased fluid durability has made it possible to eliminate or reduce scheduled fluid changes. Another trend with new fluids is to lower the viscosity to help cool the transmission. More torque is going through smaller, thinner, and lighter transmissions, and lower viscosity fluids flow and cool better.

General Motors introduced Dexron® VI. It has a more consistent viscosity to produce more consistent shift performance during extreme conditions and less degradation over time. This fluid has more than twice the durability and stability in tests compared to previous ATFs. Toyota uses world standard (WS) fluid. It is formulated to provide lower viscosity at normal operating temperatures, which helps improve fuel economy. At higher temperatures, this ATF provides greater durability. Ford introduced Mercon SP fluid, which has the same characteristics as Dexron® VI and Toyota WS. Although these fluids are similar, they are not interchangeable.

Some fluids are similar but have different friction characteristics. Normally a fluid has a *higher static coefficient of friction* than *dynamic coefficient of friction*. In a nonmodified fluid, the coefficient of friction increases as a clutch or band locks up. A *friction-modified* fluid does just the opposite. It has a much lower static coefficient of friction than the dynamic coefficient of friction. ● **SEE FIGURE 6–58**. A transmission designed for a friction-modified fluid must have more friction area in the clutches and bands or use higher apply pressure

to compensate for the lower friction; but the lockup portion of the shift is less harsh, and the shifts are smoother. Use of the wrong fluid can produce a harsh shift with higher shock loads to the driveline components or a slipping shift with possible transmission damage. Service information should be consulted when selecting the fluid for a particular transmission, and the fluid container should be checked to ensure that it meets the transmission's fluid requirements.

Transmission fluid is formulated with various additives to produce the favorable operating characteristics. A fluid contains about 10% to 15% additives. These additives are chemical compounds, and the reasons for their use are as follows:

Detergents-dispersants. Keep the transmission clean and the valves free from sticking by keeping foreign items in suspension until they are removed by the filter or by draining.

Oxidation inhibitors. Reduce oxidation and decomposition of the fluid, which can produce varnish and sludge.

Viscosity index improvers. Reduce the fluid viscosity change relative to temperature so fluid thickness and shift characteristics remain stable.

Friction modifiers. Change the fluid's coefficient of friction.

Foam inhibitors. Prevent formation of air bubbles and foam in the fluid.

Seal swellers. Produce a slight swelling of the elastomers to compensate for any wear that occurs.

Antiwear agents. Reduce friction and prevent scoring and seizure of metal parts running against each other.

Rust inhibitors. Prevent rust from forming on the iron and steel parts.

Corrosion inhibitors. Prevent corrosion of the nonferrous parts.

Metal deactivators. Form a protective film to inhibit oxidation of metal surfaces.

The transmission fluid that is blended by different companies must meet specifications established by the transmission manufacturers and the American Petroleum Institute (API). Fluids that meet a particular specification are allowed to show that specification or type label on the container.

Synthetic fluids are man-made in that chemists have rearranged the oil molecule. Generally, synthetic fluids offer better high-temperature lubrication, better resistance to oxidization, and have a lower cold viscosity. They are more stable with temperature changes, with better cold and hot lubrication. Synthetic fluids often have a longer life. Some modern ATFs use a synthetic base.

Transmissions are expected to perform over a wide range of temperatures. Cold fluids are much thicker than hot fluids. On a cold day, the first shifts tend to be sluggish because the fluid moves slowly through the orifices and small openings. The best operating temperature for an automatic transmission is in the range of 150°F to 250°F (65°C to 120°C). This produces good fluid viscosity without excessive fluid degradation. Some transmissions use fluid heaters to improve cold operation.

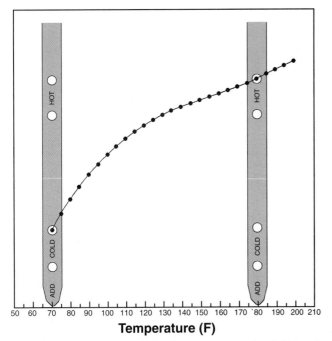

FIGURE 6–59 As the transmission warms up, the fluid level increases from the cold mark at 70°F (21°C) to the hot mark at 180°F (82°C).

Like other fluids, ATF expands with heat. ● **SEE FIGURE 6–59**. The coefficient of expansion is about 0.004% per degree Fahrenheit. This means that a temperature increase from 32°F (0°C) to 180°F (82°C) will cause the fluid to expand 148 × 0.0004 = 0.0592%. If the transmission holds 10 quarts (9.5 L) of fluid, the volume will increase to 10.592 qt (10 × 0.0592). This volume increase is slightly more than 0.5 qt (1 pint; 0.5 L), which is about the distance between the cold/low point on the dipstick to the higher hot point.

Probably the greatest problem for transmission fluid is heat. Excess heat significantly shortens the fluid's life. Excess temperatures cause the fluid to break down and form gum or varnish. This in turn can cause valve sticking or reduce the fluid flow in certain circuits. All transmissions use a cooler to help remove excess heat. The fluid should be changed more frequently than normal if it operates at temperatures above 175°F (79°C). Adverse driving conditions that produce higher fluid

PROBLEM SOLVING 6–3

Imagine that you are working in a shop that specializes in transmission repair, and these problems are brought to you.

Case 1:

A 1986 Ford LTD has just had a fluid change (by the owner). It drives okay, but there is a very soft 2–3 upshift, almost a slipping condition. The owner says that it drove okay before the fluid change. Could a worn band cause this problem? Where should you begin to find the cause of this problem?

Case 2:

A 1993 Chrysler New Yorker has a harsh 2–3 shift. It operates normally in all gear ranges, but the problem began one day and has been the same ever since. What do you think might be wrong with this transmission? Could this be a misadjusted throttle valve?

temperatures are trailer towing, driving on hills, and stop-and-go driving. The torque converter is the primary source of heat in an automatic transmission. The greater the speed difference between the torque converter input and output, the greater the temperature increase.

Experience has shown that a temperature increase of 17°F (8°C) will double the rate of fluid oxidation and cut the fluid life in half. A transmission operating at 250°F (121°C) should have a fluid life of about 75,000 miles (120,700 km). The same transmission operating at a temperature of 267°F (131°C) will have a fluid life reduced to about 37,500 miles (60,350 km).

Another heat-related problem occurs at contact areas between the friction surfaces of an applying band or clutch. The friction can cause the fluid temperature to increase to its oxidation point, and some fluids will burn and leave an abrasive ash on the friction surfaces.

Automatic transmission fluid is a complex and sophisticated product that has become highly specific to each transmission model and vehicle manufacturer. The technician and vehicle owner should be aware that transmission operation and life is dependent on having the correct fluid.

SUMMARY

1. The hydraulic system applies the band and clutches, transmits force and motion, maintains fluid flow to the torque converter, and provides lubrication and cooling to the moving parts of the transmission.

2. Pumps produce the fluid flow in a transmission and the restriction to the flow results in the system pressure.

3. The mainline pressure is controlled by a variable pressure regulator. Other valves and orifices are used to modify mainline pressure for various purposes.

4. The flow of fluid through a transmission is controlled by valves that are moved by hydraulic pressure, spring force, centrifugal force, and engine vacuum, electrically or manually.

5. Seals are used to confine the fluid to the appropriate passages. Metal, rubber, Teflon, and various synthetic materials are used for this purpose.

6. Automatic transmission fluid is the lifeblood of an automatic transmission, and only the specified fluid should be used.

REVIEW QUESTIONS

1. The important functions of the automatic transmission's hydraulic system are to _____ the clutches and bands, transmit _____ and _____, maintain _____ _____ through the torque converter, and cool and _____ the moving parts.

2. Pressure is defined as _____ pushing on a specified area and is commonly measured in _____.

3. Hydraulic systems usually have a _____ valve or a _____ _____ to prevent damage from excessive pressure.

4. The automatic transmission pump turns whenever the _____ is running.

5. Regulated pump output pressure is called _____ pressure.

6. Pump output volume changes relative to engine _____.

7. The main transmission filter is designed to trap _____, metal, and other foreign _____.

8. A micron is approximately _____ of an inch.

9. The position of a valve can be controlled by: (List five)

10. Identify a transmission valve that is controlled
    a. mechanically.
    b. by centrifugal force.
    c. by vacuum.

11. Older automatic transmissions use a _____ and a _____ _____ to control shift timing and quality.

12. Electronically controlled automatic transmissions use a _____ _____ _____ and a _____ _____ _____ to help the ECU determine when the shift should occur.

13. A typical application for a ball check valve is to act as a _____ relief valve.

14. Three types of seals are used to seal clutch pistons. Which one provides the best pressure retention?

15. Clutches are applied by a _____ in the clutch assembly and bands are applied by a _____ piston.

16. If a clutch piston has a diameter of 5 in. and 80 PSI of pressure is applied, the apply force is _____ pounds.

17. The rate that pressure is applied to a clutch will affect shift _____ and shift _____.

18. Two devices that can be used to control shift feel and quality are an _____ and an _____.

19. Driving conditions that produce higher temperatures are _____ towing, driving up _____, and stop-and-_____ driving.

20. Always use the automatic transmission fluid that is recommended by the _____ when adding or replacing the fluid.

CHAPTER QUIZ

1. Fluid under pressure can be used to transmit motion and force because _____.
   a. Fluids cannot be compressed
   b. Fluid conforms to the shape of its container
   c. Fluids under pressure will apply pressure equally in all directions
   d. All of these

2. Student A says that fluid pressure is measured in kilopascals or pounds per square inch. Student B says that 1 PSI is equal to about 7 kPa. Who is correct?
   a. Student A
   b. Student B
   c. Both Students A and B
   d. Neither Student A nor B

3. If a fluid pressure of 50 PSI is exerted on a piston area of 10 in², it will generate a force of _____ lb.
   a. 10
   b. 50
   c. 100
   d. 500

4. Student A says that to increase hydraulic force, the amount of fluid flow should be increased. Student B says that to increase hydraulic force, the length of the piston stroke should be increased. Who is correct?
   a. Student A
   b. Student B
   c. Both Students A and B
   d. Neither Student A nor B

5. The pressure regulator valve _____.
   a. Directs flow in the valve body
   b. Regulates flow to match the driving conditions
   c. Regulates pressure to match transmission requirements
   d. Controls the pump speed

6. Positive displacement pumps _____.
   a. Maintain a constant pressure
   b. Move a constant volume of fluid
   c. Vary the flow with RPM
   d. Vary the flow with gear changes

7. Fluid is forced through the pump intake by _____.
   a. Pump suction
   b. Inner case pressure
   c. Atmospheric pressure
   d. Gravity

8. Student A says that some automatic transmissions use an internal-external pump. Student B says that some automatic transmissions use a gerotor or vane-type pump. Who is correct?
   a. Student A
   b. Student B
   c. Both Students A and B
   d. Neither Student A nor B

9. Variable displacement pumps change the output volume based on _____.
   a. Torque converter demands
   b. Transmission temperature
   c. Gear range and shift demands
   d. Engine speed

10. Student A says that a depth filter can trap smaller particles than a surface filter. Student B says that a depth filter has more filter capacity than a surface filter. Who is correct?
    a. Student A
    b. Student B
    c. Both Students A and B
    d. Neither Student A nor B

11. Excessive mainline pressure loss could be caused by _____.
    a. Too much fluid
    b. A plugged filter
    c. The wrong transmission fluid
    d. A plugged cooler line

12. The part of a spool valve where pressure is applied to cause the valve movement is called the _____.
    a. Land   c. Valley
    b. Bore   d. Face

13. The throttle valve is designed to produce a fluid pressure signal that is proportional to the _____.
    a. Speed of the vehicle
    b. Gear selector position
    c. Load on the engine
    d. All of these

14. A governor's output pressure increases gradually and in proportion to _____.
    a. Engine speed
    b. Vehicle speed
    c. Gear range
    d. Road conditions

15. A shift valve is moved to the upshift position by _____.
    a. Throttle valve pressure
    b. A spring
    c. Governor pressure
    d. Any of these

16. The metal balls are used in a valve body to _____.
    a. Allow fluid flow in only one direction
    b. Close one passage while fluid is flowing in another
    c. Relieve excess pressure
    d. Any of these

17. Student A says that an accumulator in a hydraulic circuit is used to increase the fluid flow through the circuit. Student B says that an accumulator in a hydraulic circuit is used to cushion a shift by absorbing some of the fluid flow. Who is correct?
    a. Student A
    b. Student B
    c. Both Students A and B
    d. Neither Student A nor B

18. An orifice in a fluid passage _____.
    a. Reduces the pressure in a servo while it is in the applied position
    b. Causes a servo to apply faster than normal
    c. Causes a pressure drop in the circuit while there is fluid flow
    d. Reduces the chance that a leak will develop

19. Which type of seals require special tools to properly install and resize?
    a. Lip
    b. O-ring
    c. Teflon
    d. Square cut

20. Automatic transmission fluid contains additives designed to _____.
    a. Change the friction characteristics of the fluid
    b. Clean the transmission
    c. Reduce the rate of oxidation
    d. All of these

21. Clutches are applied by hydraulic pressure and released by _____.
    a. Hydraulic pressure
    b. A spring
    c. Centrifugal force
    d. Neither a nor b

22. Bands are applied by hydraulic pressure and released by _____.
    a. Hydraulic pressure
    b. A spring
    c. Centrifugal force
    d. Both a and b

23. Student A says that all transmission fluids are the same and a universal type of fluid can be used in any automatic transmission. Student B says that all transmission fluids are not the same and only the fluid recommended by the manufacturer should be used. Who is correct?
    a. Student A
    b. Student B
    c. Neither Student A nor B
    d. Both Students A and B

24. When automatic transmission fluid is overheated, _____.
    a. It will turn pink
    b. Nothing will happen
    c. Varnish will form
    d. Tar will form

25. Using the wrong fluid could _____.
    a. Shorten the life of the transmission
    b. Cause shift-quality problems
    c. Cause the clutches to slip excessively
    d. All of these

HYDRAULIC SHIFT CONTROL

OBJECTIVES: **After studying Chapter 7, the reader will be able to:** • Explain how an automatic transmission hydraulic system operates. • List the valves used in an automatic transmission. • Describe the operation of the valves in an automatic transmission. • Describe how vehicle speed and load affect automatic shifts. • Follow an upshift or downshift sequence through a hydraulic schematic.

KEY TERMS: Accumulator 177 • Asynchronous 175 • Control pressure 159 • Cooler 165 • Detent valve 168 • Downshift valve 168 • Drain down 163 • Electronic pressure control (EPC) 162 • Exhaust 159 • Governor valve 171 • Kickdown valve 168 • Line pressure 159 • Mainline pressure 159 • Manual valve 171 • Modulated pressure 168 • Nonsynchronous 175 • Orifice 177 • Pressure balanced clutch 176 • Regulator valve 159 • Reverse boost valve 161 • Rooster comb 171 • Servo valve 158 • Slide-bump shift 177 • Supply pressure 159 • Switch valve 164 • Synchronous 175 • Turbulator 165 • TV pressure 160 • Vacuum modulator 169

7.1 INTRODUCTION

The hydraulic system enables an automatic transmission to operate automatically. It supplies the force to apply the clutches and bands and the valves that control pressure and direct the fluid for automatic shifts. ● **SEE FIGURE 7–1**. Most of these valves are contained in the valve body. ● **SEE FIGURE 7–2**. The valve body in most transmissions and many transaxles is attached to the bottom of the transmission case, inside the pan. ● **SEE FIGURE 7–3**. Some transaxles mount the valve body in other locations. With experience, you will gain the ability to identify the valves, determine if they are working correctly, and repair any faults.

The basic functions of the hydraulic control system include the following:

- Schedule shifts to optimize engine performance
- Provide the best gear ratio for the driving conditions
- Safely shift into reverse when requested
- Provide driver control of the operating ranges
- Provide engine braking to help control vehicle speed on downgrades
- Lock or unlock the torque converter clutch

Most of the valves used in an automatic transmission are spool valves, and each valve has a specific purpose. Most of the valves are controlled by fluid pressure. Some valves, like the manual valve, are operated mechanically. The mass/weight of a spool valve is kept as low as possible so the valve will move

quickly. Most valves are made from aluminum for this reason, and they are anodized to reduce wear. Valves can be divided into three categories: switch, servo, and regulator. A switch valve controls fluid flow into the different circuits; it is also called a *flow control valve*. A **servo valve** is used to move another valve. Some servo valves operate switch valves, and some help control pressure regulator valves. Control of the fluid pressure at various locations in the transmission allows for shifts that are tailored to the driving conditions. Various types of pressure regulating valves handle this job.

Most switch- or servo-type valves are kept in one of two positions. For example, a shift valve (switch-type valve) is spring loaded in the downshift position, and when there is sufficient fluid pressure from the governor, the valve moves to the upshift position. ● **SEE FIGURE 7–4**. There should be no in-between position with a shift valve; a halfway shift can cause slippage and wear.

Regulator-type valves will operate anywhere along their bore, and some pressure regulator and throttle valves move to a balanced position to produce a modulated pressure. (This is explained in the next section.) Some pressure regulators and most pressure relief valves cycle rapidly. Pressure builds up and causes the valve to open and release pressure, and as soon as this happens, the valve closes and the cycle soon repeats.

The hydraulic system begins at the filter and ends as pressure at the clutch and servo pistons or as lubricating oil. In this chapter, we trace the fluid flow through a hydraulic system. A hydraulic circuit diagram is a useful tool for this purpose. Later, when diagnosing transmission problems, you will use a hydraulic circuit diagram as a tool to locate fluid routes and the possible cause of a problem.

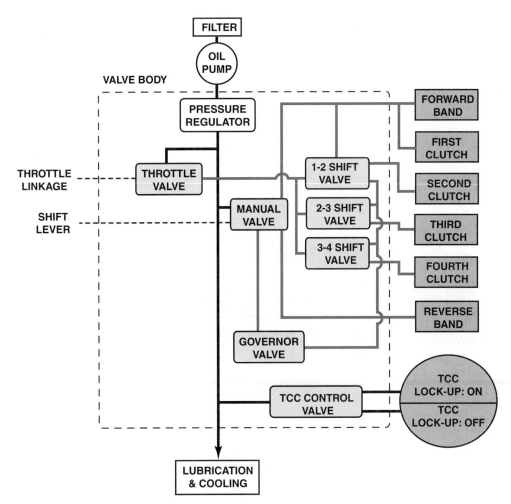

FIGURE 7–1 The valve body contains valves that control fluid pressure and flow to various apply devices that, in turn, produce proper shifts at the proper time.

The hydraulic system is easier to understand if it is divided into subcircuits. ● **SEE CHART 7–1.** A flow control valve is the dividing point as supply pressure enters the different circuits. Also note that each circuit serves a particular purpose.

7.2 PRESSURE DEVELOPMENT AND CONTROL

As soon as the engine starts, the torque converter hub drives the transmission pump to produce fluid flow. Pressure is created by resistance to fluid flow. This pressure is called *line, mainline, supply,* or **control pressure.** Some sources identify **supply pressure** as the fluid in the passage between the pump and the pressure regulator valve. **Line pressure,** also called **mainline pressure,** usually refers to regulated fluid pressure. As soon as the supply passages fill with fluid, the fluid pressure

acts on one end or one large land of the regulator valve acting in opposition to a spring positioned at the other end. When line pressure increases, the regulator valve moves and opens a passage that directs fluid back to the pump intake or sends a pressure signal to the housing of a vane pump to decrease pump volume. ● **SEE FIGURES 7–5 AND 7–6.** During start-up, the pressure will build up rapidly because the manual valve is blocking the flow to the clutches and bands; the only flow is to the **regulator valve,** a few other valves, and the torque converter. It should be noted that some transmissions do not build fluid pressure in park because the manual valve opens line pressure to exhaust; fluid flow is through the manual valve and back to the sump. ● **SEE FIGURE 7–7.** The term **exhaust** refers to fluid flow back to the pan to empty or drain a circuit.

Pressure regulator valves balance line pressure against the strength of a spring. The spring has a predetermined strength to maintain fluid pressure at about 50 to 60 PSI (345 to 414 kPa). In some transmissions, this spring is adjustable by turning a screw; in others, it is adjustable by adding or removing shims. ● **SEE FIGURE 7–8.**

Fluid pressure during mid-throttle to full throttle and reverse is boosted by one or more boost areas of the regulator

FIGURE 7–2 (a) This electronic transmission valve body has only five valves. (b) Four solenoids in the solenoid assembly control shifts and torque converter clutch (TCC) apply and release. (*Courtesy of Chrysler Corporation*)

valve. Some transmissions also *boost pressure* in manual low and intermediate gears. ● **SEE FIGURE 7–9**. The throttle valve (TV) circuit produces a pressure signal relative to the throttle opening (engine load). **TV pressure** will be somewhere between

zero and line pressure depending on throttle position, and it acts on the regulator valve in the same direction as the valve's spring. This will increase spring pressure, causing the regulator valve to modulate to a higher pressure. Throttle boost is used

CONTROL
VALVE
BODY

CONTROL
VALVE
BODY

FIGURE 7–3 (a) The valve body is mounted to the bottom of the main case of transmissions and some transaxles. (b) It is also mounted at the end or top of some transaxles. (*Reprinted with permission of General Motors*)

(a)

Circuit 1   Circuit 2

Controlling   Mainline   Spring
Pressure   Pressure

(b)

TV Boost   D2 & Rev. Boost
Valve   Valve   Spring

Mainline
Exhaust   Pressure
                    Regulator Valve

(c)

Exhaust

TV   D2   REV   Supply

FIGURE 7–4 (a) The switch valve will shift the fluid flow from circuit 1 to circuit 2 when the controlling pressure increases. (b) This regulator valve has two servo valves (TV boost, and D2 and reverse boost), which cause a pressure increase when the throttle is opened or when the transmission is shifted into D2 or reverse. (c) This regulator valve controls supply pressure to become mainline pressure.

NAME OF CIRCUIT	PURPOSE
Supply	Provides fluid to pressure regulator valve and transmission.
Main control pressure	Supplies fluid at a controlled pressure to transmission and converter when the engine is running.
Converter and cooler	Regulates converter pressure; provides gear train lubrication and cooling of the fluid.
Drive	Applies forward clutch and supplies control systems in forward-gear ranges.
Manual-1	Applies low and reverse band and locks out second gear.
Manual-2	Prevents upshift from second-gear range.
Reverse	Increases control pressure and supplies reverse-high clutch and low-reverse band.
Shift valve	Controls switch pressure and exhaust pressure to servos and clutches for upshifts and downshifts.
Kickdown (downshift, detent)	Forces downshifts by overriding governor and/or throttle valve control of shift valves.
Governor	Provides a pressure proportional to road speed for upshifts.
Throttle valve (TV)	Provides a pressure proportional to engine load and vacuum for shift timing and quality.
Accumulator	Cushions shift by softening clutch or band apply.
Converter clutch	Controls the converter clutch to time clutch lockup.

CHART 7–1

Hydraulic System Subcircuits

to produce firmer shifts, improve shift feel, and increase clutch and band holding power at higher throttle openings. Full throttle in forward gears causes line pressure to increase to about 90 to 150 PSI (621 to 1,034 kPa).

Line pressure is increased in reverse because the reverse passage at the manual valve sends pressure to the **reverse boost valve.** ● SEE FIGURE 7–10. Line pressure acts with the spring to increase control pressure. Reverse boost produces line pressures of between 150 and 300 PSI (1,034 and 2,068 kPa), depending on the transmission and the throttle opening. The purpose for boosting pressure in reverse is to ensure sufficient force to the clutch and band to prevent slipping.

Some transmissions boost pressure in manual-1 and sometimes manual-2 to ensure strong clutch and band application while operating in these gears. When used, another boost

(a) Engine startup, filling lines and building pressure

(b) Filling the converter and lube passages

(c) Regulating line pressure

FIGURE 7–5 Many pressure regulator valves have three positions. (a) The spring has moved the valve to the bottom of the bore. (b) Line pressure is moving the valve upward, opening the passage to the torque converter (circle). (c) Increased line pressure has moved the valve upward to where it can release pressure to the pump inlet (circle). Note that boost pressure in either of the two upper ports can cause a pressure increase.

FIGURE 7–6 The pressure regulator of this variable displacement vane pump can send fluid pressure to the DECREASE passage. This pressure will move the pump slide to the right and reduce pump output. (*Reprinted with permission of General Motors*)

FIGURE 7–7 This manual valve is arranged so it dumps line pressure to the sump in park (circle). This reduces line pressure to below 30 PSI. (*Courtesy of Chrysler Corporation*)

area of the regulator valve is pressurized by the manual valve in a manner similar to reverse boost. Low-gear boost increases line pressures to about 150 PSI (1,034 kPa).

Fully electronic transmissions use an **electronic pressure control (EPC)** solenoid to control the pressure regulator valve. Early *electronic transmissions* used a hydraulic pressure

FIGURE 7–8 Some pressure regulators use an adjusting screw that allows adjustment of line pressure. Others use a shim/spacer to allow an adjustment.

FIGURE 7–9 Hydraulic pressure moves this regulator valve to the left against spring tension. Pressure in the manual valve circuit will work against hydraulic pressure to increase/boost line pressure. Pressure in the overdrive clutch circuit will reduce/cut back line pressure. (*Courtesy of Chrysler Corporation*)

FIGURE 7–10 Fluid from the manual valve reverse circuit acts on the primary regulator valve to increase line pressure in reverse.

regulator valve. As we will see in Chapter 8, the EPC in most instances is controlled by either the transmission control module (TCM) or engine control module (ECM).

7.3 TORQUE CONVERTER, OIL COOLER, AND LUBRICATION CIRCUIT

As soon as the supply circuit begins to develop pressure, the regulator valve moves slightly and opens a passage to the torque converter. This fluid flow serves several purposes.

- It ensures that the torque converter is filled so it can transmit torque from the engine to the transmission's input shaft.
- It helps control converter fluid temperature.
- It provides lubrication for the moving parts inside the transmission. ● **SEE FIGURE 7–11**.

It should be noted that this feature can shut off the fluid flow to the torque converter, cooler, and lubrication circuit whenever line pressure drops below the regulated pressure point. There are several possibilities in which a transmission with a slightly worn pump running at idle, very low engine speeds, or under conditions calling for high line pressures (full throttle, low vacuum, reverse gear, etc.) can be operated without converter, cooler, and lubrication flow. This can cause severe wear of the thrust washers, bushings, and gear train if it is allowed to continue for any length of time.

7.3.1 TORQUE CONVERTER PRESSURE CONTROL

A potential problem with torque converters is **drain down**, or a partial emptying while the engine is off. This causes slippage and delay in power flow until the converter is refilled. The possibility of drain down is reduced by shutting the fluid passage to the converter at the regulator valve as soon as the pressure drops or when the engine is off. ● **SEE FIGURE 7–12**. Some transmissions have an additional valve in the passage leaving the converter to prevent drain down through the cooler circuit. The simple, spring-loaded check valve, often called an anti-drainback valve, closes off the passage as soon as fluid flow through the converter stops.

Pressure inside the converter is controlled by how fast the fluid enters and how fast it can leave. This flow is controlled by the size of restriction in the two passages. Since there is not much restriction on a converter's outlet passages, normal internal pressures do not get too high, about 15 to 75 PSI (103 to 517 kPa). ● **SEE FIGURE 7–13**.

Another potential converter problem is ballooning, which is a swelling of the outer shell of the converter that can result from excessive internal pressure. Some transmissions use a pressure relief valve or a torque converter pressure regulator valve to limit the pressure to about 100 PSI (689 kPa) maximum.

FIGURE 7–11 The converter and cooler feed circuit begins at the pressure regulator, goes through the converter and cooler, and then into the lube passages. Note that the cooler and the lines connecting it to the transmission are outside of the transmission. (*Courtesy of Chrysler Corporation*)

FIGURE 7–12 When the engine is not running, the regulator valve spring moves the T/C control valve to the right, blocking the cooler passage and reducing the chance of converter draindown. Note the bypass valve that will open if the cooler becomes plugged. (*Courtesy of Chrysler Corporation*)

7.3.2 TORQUE CONVERTER CLUTCH CONTROL

A torque converter clutch (TCC) is applied by redirecting the flow inside the converter. Depending on the transmission, this valve is called a *converter clutch control valve,* a **switch valve**, or a *converter clutch apply valve* (see Figure 9–17). When the TCC valve moves, the fluid flow through the converter is reversed. In some transmissions, this valve is controlled completely by transmission fluid flow, but in most transmissions, it is controlled electronically by the ECM. The ECM uses input signals from the various engine sensors, vehicle speed sensor, and brake pedal switch to determine if the torque converter clutch should be applied or released. Electronic TCC control is described in Chapter 8.

FIGURE 7–13 With the torque converter clutch (TCC) released, fluid enters this converter through the input shaft. It leaves through the area between the input shaft and the stator support. (*Courtesy of Chrysler Corporation*)

In older Chrysler Corporation transmissions, the switch valve is operated by fluid pressure from the drive circuit acting on one end of the valve and a spring at the other end that tries to hold the valve in a non-lockup position. The valve moves to the lockup position after the lockup valve (moved by pressure in the governor circuit) and fail-safe valve (moved by pressure from the third-gear circuit) move to upshift positions. In these transmissions, torque converter clutch lockup only occurs above a certain speed and coolant temperature and after the transmission has shifted into third gear. ● **SEE FIGURE 7–14.** It releases when the vehicle slows down, the transmission downshifts out of third gear, or when there is enough throttle pressure to move the fail-safe valve to a non-lockup position.

FIGURE 7-14 The lockup valve and fail-safe valve control the switch valve. This in turn controls fluid flow through the converter and, therefore, converter lockup. (*Courtesy of Chrysler Corporation*)

FIGURE 7-15 The transmission cooler is normally mounted in the colder, outlet tank of the radiator. Steel lines are normally used to connect the transmission to the cooler. (*Courtesy of Chrysler Corporation*)

FIGURE 7-16 (a) This cooler has a large, flat passage from its inlet to its outlet. (b) Note the screenlike turbulator.

7.3.3 COOLER FLOW

The fluid leaving the torque converter is routed out of the transmission case and through a steel line to the *transmission cooler*. The cooler is positioned in the colder (outlet) tank of the radiator. ● **SEE FIGURE 7-15**. Another steel line is used to return the fluid to the transmission. A **cooler** is often called a heat exchanger because it moves heat from one location to another. Heat from the transmission fluid is transferred to the engine coolant. The cooler is either a flat or a tubular-shape plate-type cooler that is simply two outer metal surfaces with a **turbulator** between them. ● **SEE FIGURE 7-16**. The outer surfaces are in contact with the relatively cool coolant in the radiator tank. The screenlike turbulator causes a turbulence in the fluid flow to ensure constant mixing and thorough cooling of the fluid.

A plain-tube cooler is not very effective for cooling fluid because fluid tends to increase its viscosity and slow down as it cools. The cooler oil then tends to become stationary on the outer, cooler areas of the cooler while the hotter, thinner-viscosity fluid flows through the center. ● **SEE FIGURE 7-17**.

FIGURE 7-17 Cold fluid tends to stick to the walls of a plain tube cooler (top). The turbulator causes fluid turbulence to promote mixing so all of the fluid cools (bottom).

The turbulator in a well-designed oil cooler continuously mixes the fluid. It also causes some restriction to the fluid flow, but most coolers are sized properly to allow for this.

The transmission cooler tends to trap foreign particles and can become plugged, especially when the fluid is extremely dirty, contains metal particles, or there is a torque converter clutch

(a)

(b)

FIGURE 7–18 (a) An auxiliary filter can be installed in one of the cooler lines to help trap contaminants. (b) The cutaway view shows the internal magnet and folded paper filter element. (*Courtesy of SPX Filtran*)

mechanical failure. The procedure for checking cooler flow and cleaning of the cooler is described in Chapter 11. At least one aftermarket manufacturer markets a filter that can be installed in the transmission-to-cooler line. ● **SEE FIGURE 7–18.** This filter provides added protection by removing foreign particles from the fluid and preventing cooler blockage; many filters contain a magnet to remove iron particles. If the filter gets plugged, fluid flow will be restricted or blocked completely, which then shuts off transmission lubrication. Supplementary filters must include a bypass valve to maintain fluid flow if the filter becomes plugged.

Supplementary coolers are also available that can be placed in series with the original equipment manufacturer (OEM) cooler to ensure adequate cooling. These are fluid-to-air coolers, whereas the OEM cooler is normally a fluid-to-coolant cooler. The heat in the supplementary cooler flows directly to the air passing through the cooler. The supplementary cooler is normally positioned where there is an adequate airflow, which is often in front of the radiator or air-conditioning condenser. This location is not ideal because the new cooler tends to block the airflow through the other heat exchangers and increases their operating temperatures. The supplementary cooler is connected to one of the transmission's cooler lines and then to the OEM cooler. The hot fluid from the transmission can be routed through the supplementary cooler first, then through the OEM cooler and back to the transmission. ● **SEE FIGURE 7–19.** Running the fluid through in this manner improves the efficiency of the supplementary cooler by operating it at the highest possible temperature. When operating in very cold temperatures,

FIGURE 7–19 An auxiliary cooler is mounted so the fluid flows through it and then through the standard cooler in the radiator. (*Courtesy of Chrysler Corporation*)

FIGURE 7-20 Transmission lube passages. Note how the passage leads to gears and bushings. (*Courtesy of Toyota Motor Sales USA, Inc.*)

FIGURE 7-21 This planet carrier burned out from lack of lubrication; note the excess clearance and dark coloration at the planet gear shafts.

the OEM cooler reduces the chance of overcooling the fluid by warming the fluid before returning it to the transmission. Raising the fluid's operating temperature helps ensure an adequate lubrication flow.

7.3.4 LUBRICATION FLOW
In most transmissions, the fluid returning from the torque converter lubricates the transmission. The fluid from the cooler enters the lubrication passages at the case. It flows through holes drilled in the case to the main shaft bushings, where it passes into holes drilled in the input or output shaft. **SEE FIGURE 7-20.** From here, it flows through the shaft to side holes that align with support bushings, thrust washers, planetary gear sets, clutch drum bushings, and clutch packs. Most transaxle final drive gears and differential are also lubricated by this circuit.

A vehicle with an automatic transmission should not be towed or pushed very far because there will be no lubricating fluid flow without the engine running. The gear sets and bushings will run dry, wear, and overheat or burn out without a constant flow of lubricating oil. ● **SEE FIGURE 7-21.** Most manufacturers recommend towing only when absolutely necessary. They caution that towing should be limited to a few miles with a maximum speed of 20 to 25 mph (32 to 40 km/h). If possible, the drive wheels should be lifted off the ground or the driveshaft removed from a rear-wheel-drive (RWD) vehicle. Special cautions also should be taken when towing an all-wheel-drive (AWD) vehicle.

TECH TIP

At least one new transmission design has a lube scoop and trough that allows lubrication while being towed. The vehicle can be towed with all four wheels on the ground at speeds up to 65 mph. All-wheel-drive (AWD) vehicles must be towed with all four wheels either on or off the ground.

PROBLEM SOLVING 7-1

Imagine that you are working in a shop that specializes in transmission repair, and these problems are brought to you.

Case 1:

A 1982 Corvette starts out okay in first gear, but the 1–2 shift is long and drawn out. A full-throttle shift has an engine speed flare with indications of slippage. What part of the transmission is faulty? What do you think is causing this problem?

Case 2:

A 1995 Ford Thunderbird had a badly worn gear train; the gears were blue from overheating. The gear set was replaced while rebuilding the transmission. Are there any special checks that should be made before replacing this transmission into the car?

FIGURE 7–22 The throttle valve produces a pressure signal that is directly related to throttle opening or engine load. This pressure signal is used to control line pressure so that line pressure increases as the throttle is opened.

FIGURE 7–23 In this hydraulically controlled transmission, the shift valves are positioned by a spring and hydraulic pressures from the throttle valve and governor. (*Courtesy of Chrysler Corporation*)

7.4 THROTTLE PRESSURE

A circuit carrying a throttle pressure signal is always available while the engine is running in most transmissions. Throttle valves are pressure regulating/pressure control valves that provide a pressure signal in proportion to engine load. ● SEE FIGURE 7–22. This controlled, variable pressure is also called **modulated pressure.** Modulated pressures are regularly readjusted. The throttle signal can be brought to the transmission by three commonly used methods: mechanical, vacuum, and electrical.

Transmissions with hydraulic shift controls have hydraulic TV pressure working against governor hydraulic pressure to control shift valve movement. ● SEE FIGURE 7–23. Shift feel is also controlled hydraulically with clutch or servo feed orifices and TV pressure modifying accumulator pressure. As you

FIGURE 7–24 Application speed of this front band is controlled by the accumulator stroke rate, and this is controlled by the shuttle valve and the 1–2 shift control valve. (*Courtesy of Chrysler Corporation*)

will learn in Chapter 8, electronic transmissions use electronic devices for these same purposes.

The transmission control system uses throttle pressure to reprogram or reschedule the following areas of operation.

- **Shift quality.** The friction devices should apply firmly while under full throttle to handle the increased torque. This is accomplished by boosting line pressure.

- **Shift timing.** A full-throttle, full-load upshift should occur at a higher speed than a part-throttle, partial-load shift. This is accomplished by throttle pressure working against governor pressure at the shift valves.

- **Shift feel.** A full-throttle, high-load upshift should have a firmer, faster quality to reduce slippage during a shift. This is accomplished by changing the accumulator rate used to cushion a shift. ● SEE FIGURE 7–24.

- **Torque converter clutch control.** The TCC should be released during full-throttle operation so the converter is able to multiply the torque needed for acceleration and power. This is accomplished by the throttle pressure acting on the TCC control valve.

Most older transmissions use either a double-throttle valve (mechanical operation) or two separate units (vacuum and mechanical or electrical) to sense engine load and throttle position. ● SEE FIGURE 7–25. The second throttle valve is called a **detent, downshift,** or **kickdown valve,** and it signals full-throttle operation, also called *wide-open throttle* (*WOT*). Other transmissions use a mechanical throttle and detent valve to control shift timing and a vacuum unit to control line pressure and shift feel.

FIGURE 7–25 This mechanical throttle valve is operated by a cable that is connected to the engine throttle body and accelerator pedal. (*Courtesy of Chrysler Corporation*)

FIGURE 7–26 At wide-open throttle, the kickdown valve pushes the throttle valve to the end of the bore. At this position, TV pressure is equal to line pressure in both the TV and kickdown passages. (*Courtesy of Chrysler Corporation*)

TV pressure is modified in some transmissions by one or more of the valves in order to achieve precise shift timing. The 3–4 modified throttle valve (MTV) and 4–3 MTV act to reduce TV pressure at low throttle openings.

7.4.1 MECHANICAL THROTTLE VALVES
A mechanical throttle valve and a detent valve are used in many transmissions. These valves are in the same bore, with the kickdown valve positioned by a spring to rest against the throttle lever assembly. ● SEE FIGURE 7–26. The throttle valve is positioned at the opposite end of the kickdown valve spring. The throttle lever is connected to the throttle linkage by a metal rod or cable; the lever moves as the throttle is opened or closed. The throttle valve is also positioned by pressure in the throttle pressure passages. As throttle pressure moves the valve against the spring, the valve moves to cut off throttle pressure. The mechanical force of the throttle linkage tends to increase throttle pressure, but throttle pressure tries to reduce itself. The throttle valve will be balanced between the mechanical throttle pressure (the strength of the spring controlled by the kickdown valve position) and the amount of throttle fluid pressure. At the WOT position, the throttle valve is pushed to the end of the bore by an extension of the kickdown valve. At this time, throttle pressure increases to equal line pressure, and the kickdown valve opens the kickdown passages to allow fluid pressure to enter the valve.

7.4.2 VACUUM THROTTLE VALVES
Many transmissions use a throttle valve operated by a vacuum unit called a **vacuum modulator.** The modulator is secured to the outside of the transmission case and is connected to the engine's intake manifold by a metal tube or rubber hose. ● SEE FIGURE 7–27.

FIGURE 7–27 With high manifold vacuum, the modulator diaphragm and modulator valve are to the left, and modulator pressure is low. When manifold vacuum drops, the spring moves the diaphragm toward the right, and modulator pressure will increase. Note the bellows used in this modulator. (*Reprinted with permission of General Motors*)

The vacuum unit contains a flexible diaphragm and a spring. The spring pushes the diaphragm and its extension toward the transmission. Manifold vacuum acts on the diaphragm, compresses the spring, moving the diaphragm and its extension away from the transmission. A vacuum is simply a pressure that is lower than atmospheric, and atmospheric pressure pushes against the opposite side of the diaphragm to cause movement. Vacuum is commonly measured in inches of mercury (in. Hg).

The output of the vacuum modulator is a product of the area of the diaphragm, the pressure differential across the diaphragm (atmospheric pressure minus the lower vacuum pressure), and the strength of the spring. ● SEE FIGURE 7–28. Vacuum

Diaphragm Diameter (in.)	Diaphragm Area (SI)	Manifold Vacuum			(1.76 SI Diaphragm) Force (lb)
		in. Hg.	psia	Pressure Difference	
$1\frac{1}{4}$	1.227	0	14.7	0	0
$1\frac{9}{32}$	1.289	5	12.2	2.5	4.4
$1\frac{1}{2}$	1.767	10	9.7	5	8.8
$1\frac{9}{16}$	1.917	15	7.2	7.5	13.25
$1\frac{11}{16}$	2.23	20	4.7	10	17.7
2	3.1416				

FIGURE 7–28 Vacuum modulators have different diameters, which change the relative strength of the modulator.

modulators are made with different sizes of diaphragms and with springs of different strengths to suit the operating conditions in vehicles of different sizes or engines with different torque outputs. A stronger spring or smaller diaphragm area produces a stronger outward force and higher TV pressure; a weaker spring or a larger diaphragm produces a weaker force and lower TV pressure. The stem of the vacuum modulator pushes against one end of the throttle valve while throttle pressure acts against the opposite end, much like in a mechanical throttle valve.

Vacuum-operated throttle valves produce a throttle pressure that is more relative to engine load than a mechanically operated valve. Engine manifold vacuum is a product of throttle position, engine load, and engine speed. At idle speed and while operating at light throttle, intake manifold vacuum is relatively high, about 18 to 20 in. Hg. At this time, the pumping action of the pistons pulls air out of the manifold faster than it can flow in past the closed throttle plates. ● **SEE FIGURE 7–29.** At WOT, manifold vacuum is usually lower than 1 in. Hg because air can easily flow past the open-throttle plates. During cruise conditions, the throttle is partially open, and manifold vacuum is somewhere in the range of 10 to 15 in. Hg. Cruise vacuum will vary greatly depending on engine size, vehicle weight, and gear ratio. During cruise conditions, an increase in engine load such as a head wind or going up an incline slows the engine relative to the throttle opening and thus causes a drop in vacuum, from 10 to 15 in. Hg down to 6 to 8 in. Hg.

Some vacuum modulators contain an evacuated bellows assembly. This unit acts against the spring to produce more consistent shift response at differing altitudes. When a vehicle is operated at higher altitudes, the air is thinner and atmospheric pressure is lower. This produces less torque in the engine, and the transmission pressures should be lowered slightly to prevent harsh shifts. At this time, the reduced atmospheric

FIGURE 7–29 Manifold vacuum varies with load. Cruising at light load produces about 15 to 20 in. Hg. A high load produces zero vacuum, 0 in. Hg. (*Courtesy of Nissan North America, Inc.*)

pressure acting on the bellows allows the bellows to lengthen and increase the pressure acting against the diaphragm spring. This has the effect of reducing the spring's strength, which reduces the force acting on the throttle valve and therefore the throttle pressure.

7.4.3 WIDE-OPEN THROTTLE KICKDOWN VALVE

A vacuum modulator cannot accurately indicate the exact throttle opening. The WOT signal can be brought to the transmission by a mechanical linkage, a rod or a cable, or an electric current. A WOT kickdown valve is also called a detent valve. A mechanical detent valve resembles the mechanical throttle and detent valve combination described earlier. Throttle movement is transmitted to the detent valve so it can produce a full pressure in the detent passages at WOT.

FIGURE 7–30 The manual valve is moved by the shift lever and held in position by the detent lever (cam).

PROBLEM SOLVING 7–2

Imagine that you are working in a shop that specializes in transmission repair, and these problems are brought to you.

Case 1:

A 1982 Chevrolet pickup starts out okay in first gear, but the 1–2 shift is long and drawn out. A full-throttle shift has an engine flare. What part of the transmission is at fault? What do you think is causing this problem?

Case 2:

A 1988 Dodge Diplomat (RWD) drives okay, but the shifts are very harsh. What could be wrong? How can you determine which part is faulty?

An electric detent valve is controlled by a switch in the throttle linkage and a solenoid at the valve body. When the throttle is opened to a point close to WOT, the switch is closed to complete the circuit. Battery voltage energizes the solenoid, causing it to stroke a metal rod or move a metal plate that either moves a valve or opens a passage. In either case, fluid pressure is sent to the detent passages.

7.5 MANUAL VALVE

The **manual valve** controls fluid flow to the band servos; to clutch apply pistons for drive, low, and reverse gears; and to the shift valves. This valve is also called a *selector valve*. It receives the fluid from the pump at line pressure. The manual valve is moved by mechanical linkage when the driver moves the shift lever. It is held in position by the detent cam at the valve body. ● **SEE FIGURE 7–30.** This detent is a spring-loaded roller or ball that drops into notches in the cam to position the manual valve properly in its bore. The detent cam is commonly called a **rooster comb.**

When the gear selector is in neutral or park, fluid flow through the manual valve is blocked by a land or trapped between two lands. Many transmissions send line pressure to the throttle valve in neutral so the TV circuit is ready to operate as soon as the neutral–drive or neutral–reverse shift is made.

In the other gear selector positions, the valve is moved to allow fluid flow through the valve to various valves and friction-apply circuits. Most three- and four-speed transmissions have six gear selector positions. Some four-speed transmissions have seven positions that allow fourth-gear operation in overdrive and limit the transmission to first- through third-gear operation in drive. For simplicity, the following descriptions are for a three-speed transmission. In general, the fluid flows are as follows:

- **Drive.** Fluid is directed to the forward clutch, the 1–2 shift valve, and the governor. ● **SEE FIGURE 7–31.** Automatic upshifts and downshifts will occur.

- **Intermediate.** Same as drive but the 2–3 shift valve is either blocked from moving or fluid is not fed to it.

- **Low.** Fluid is directed to the forward clutch, the low-reverse clutch or band, and the governor; and the 1–2 shift valve is blocked from moving. A pressure signal may also be sent to the pressure regulator to boost line pressure.

- **Reverse.** Fluid is directed to the high-reverse clutch, the low-reverse clutch or band, and the pressure regulator to boost fluid pressures.

The various fluid flows leaving the manual valve are labeled drive oil, manual-2, manual-1, and reverse.

7.6 GOVERNOR VALVE

The transmission will begin transferring power and rotating the output shaft when the selector lever is moved to drive, intermediate, or low. When the output shaft starts turning, the governor spins with it. The governor is either shaft mounted (attached directly onto the output shaft) or case mounted (driven by a gear on the output shaft). ● **SEE FIGURE 7–32.**

The **governor valve** produces a pressure signal that is proportionate to the vehicle speed; it is used to move the shift valves to an upshift position. The governor pressure should be zero when the vehicle is at rest. When the vehicle is moving, governor output pressure should roughly equal vehicle speed. There should be a steady pressure increase as the vehicle accelerates. ● **SEE FIGURE 7–33.** Governor pressure is routed to one end of each shift valve. It is also sent to any other valve that requires a speed-related input, such as a TCC control valve or a downshift inhibitor valve.

A governor uses the centrifugal force acting on a pair of weights to measure speed. The weights try to move outward as speed increases, moving the valve to increase governor pressure. Centrifugal force moves the governor valve, allowing drive oil into the governor oil passages. Somewhat like a throttle

FIGURE 7–31 The manual valve is in drive and the transmission is in first gear. Fluid is being sent to the rear clutch, accumulator, 1–2 shift valve, throttle valve, and governor. (*Courtesy of Chrysler Corporation*)

valve, governor pressure acts on a reaction area of the governor valve trying to reposition the valve and exhaust governor pressure. Governor pressure is balanced between output shaft RPM and governor pressure.

All governor assemblies share the same basic engineering problem: Centrifugal force increases at an ever-increasing rate; the force more than doubles as RPM doubles. This produces an output that is not properly aligned with speed. Most governor

FIGURE 7–32 A case-mounted governor is driven by a gear on the output shaft. It provides a pressure signal relative to vehicle speed.

FIGURE 7–33 The ideal governor pressure signal increases in exact proportion to vehicle speed, but a simple governor produces a signal that is too low at intermediate speeds or too high at higher speeds. The pressure signal from a two-stage governor comes closer to matching vehicle speed.

FIGURE 7–34 As the vehicle speeds up, centrifugal force acting on the governor weight tries to move the weight and valve toward the right to increase governor pressure. This is opposed by governor pressure at the valve, which tries to move the valve toward the left and reduce governor pressure. *(Courtesy of Chrysler Corporation)*

assemblies use two or more stages to produce a more straight-line pressure increase.

Governor valve assemblies are manufactured in four basic styles. Two are shaft mounted, and two are case mounted.

- **Shaft mounted with the weight(s) opposing the valve.** The valve is on one side of the shaft and the weight(s) on the other, and they are connected by a pin that passes through the shaft. ● SEE FIGURE 7–34.

- **Shaft mounted with a primary and secondary valve.** These two valves, which also act as the weights, are

mounted so the output of one valve acts to help control the movement of the other valve. ● SEE FIGURE 7–35.

- **Case mounted with a pair of primary and secondary weights.** The valve is operated by a pair of levers (weights) that move the valve.

- **Case-mounted bleed-off system.** Two governor pressure balls bleed off pressure. With the vehicle at rest, pressure escapes past these balls. They are seated by a pair of levers extending from the weights. An increase in governor pressure occurs as speed increases. ● SEE FIGURE 7–36.

In all of these governor assemblies, governor pressure acts on the valve(s) or balls to allow the pressure to escape or bleed off to exhaust. This occurs as the vehicle slows to a stop. As the vehicle speed increases, the centrifugal force acting on the weights causes the exhaust flow to decrease. In the valve, a flow is opened between the drive oil and governor pressure passages. Governor pressure is a balance between governor pressure trying to open the valve to exhaust and centrifugal force trying to open the valve to drive oil as it closes the exhaust port. ● SEE FIGURE 7–37.

In two-stage governors, the primary governor weight is heavier so centrifugal force begins to act on it as soon as the vehicle starts moving. This weight is the major control for slow-speed operation. The primary weight is designed so it reaches a limit and bottoms out at middle operating speeds, and any further centrifugal force from that point is blocked. As the vehicle speed increases, the secondary weight becomes the controlling factor in the governor.

The governor valve is the least-reliable valve in a transmission because of its tendency to stick in its bore. This is basically a result of the very gradual movement of the valve in normal operation; most of the other valves in a transmission "snap" from one end of their bore to the other. A governor valve must move freely to respond to every change in speed. A very fine screen is normally placed in the fluid passage leading to the governor to trap dirt and debris that might cause a valve to stick. A stuck governor valve can cause a no-upshift condition or high gear starts.

FIGURE 7–35 This two-stage, shaft-mounted governor uses both a primary and secondary valve. (*Courtesy of Chrysler Corporation*)

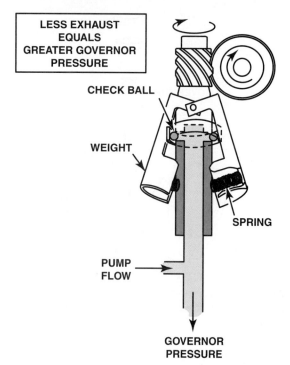

FIGURE 7–36 Centrifugal force will cause the two weights to move outward. This pushes the two balls against their seats, reducing the amount of exhaust and increasing governor pressure.

FIGURE 7–37 Centrifugal force produces an upward force on the valve that will increase governor pressure if the valve moves. Governor pressure at the top of the valve opposes this action. The governor valve is positioned between these two forces.

7.7 SHIFT VALVES

An upshift or downshift occurs when the shift valves move. Shift valves are balanced between the governor pressure trying to move the valve to cause an upshift and the spring plus throttle pressure trying to resist an upshift. ● **SEE FIGURE 7–38**. Shift valves are placed in one of two positions and are moved to the desired position by an increase or decrease of fluid pressure at one end. At rest or very slow speeds, the spring moves the valve to the downshift position. A typical shift valve has a land for the

governor reaction area at one end and a spring at the other. Throttle pressure enters from the side, crosses through a valve valley, and reenters at the end with the spring. The controlled

FIGURE 7–38 Governor pressure can move this 1–2 shift valve from the downshift position (left) to the upshift position.

FIGURE 7–39 The 1–2 shift valve has moved to upshift, allowing drive oil to flow into the second-gear passages. Fluid pressure moves the front servo to apply the band and also strokes the accumulator piston. (*Courtesy of Chrysler Corporation*)

flow to the next gear's apply device also enters from the side and is blocked by a land or a closed valley while the passage to the apply device is open to exhaust.

As the vehicle is accelerating, governor pressure gradually increases until the force at that end of the shift valve becomes stronger than the spring plus the force created by throttle pressure. At this time, the shift valve should move, but we want the valve to snap from one end to the other to ensure a complete application of the controlled apply device. This happens in most shift valves because the first valve movement cuts off the throttle (TV or STV) pressure at the end of the valve and opens this chamber to exhaust. This unbalances the forces on the valve, and the valve then quickly completes its movement to an upshift position.

The governor land on the 1–2 shift valve is usually larger than the 2–3 shift valve governor land, to guarantee that the 1–2 valve moves before the 2–3 valve. When the 1–2 shift valve moves to upshift, it opens a passage so that drive oil can flow through the valve and to the intermediate band or clutch applying second gear. ● **SEE FIGURE 7–39.** When the 2–3 shift valve moves to upshift, it opens a passage sending pressure to the high-reverse clutch and the intermediate band. This pressure will release the band and apply the clutch. ● **SEE FIGURE 7–40.**

FIGURE 7–40 The 2–3 shift valve has moved to upshift. Fluid pressure will apply the front clutch and also move the front servo to release the band. (*Courtesy of Chrysler Corporation*)

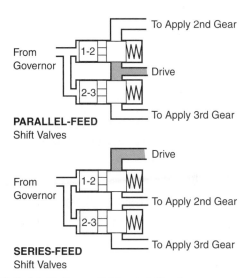

FIGURE 7–41 Both parallel-feed shift valves are connected to drive oil (top); an upshift will occur when governor oil moves either one to the right. With series-feed shift valves, drive oil feeds only the 1–2 shift valve, and the 2–3 shift valve is fed from the 1–2 valve (bottom).

Fluid flow into the shift valves also affects shift sequence. Most shift valves are *series fed*. ● **SEE FIGURE 7–41.** With series-fed valves, the 2–3 shift valve receives its fluid for the upshift from the 1–2 shift valve; the 1–2 upshift must occur before the 2–3 shift. *Parallel-fed* shift valves are connected to the same fluid supply source. It is possible for the 1–2 and 2–3 shifts to occur at the same time, producing a 1–3 upshift.

7.7.1 SHIFT OVERLAP

To shift from one gear range to another, transmissions apply and release clutches or bands—a process often called *shift calibration*. Some transmissions are designed to apply a clutch or a band without having to release another one. These are called **nonsynchronous** or **asynchronous** transmissions. **Synchronous** transmissions require a clutch or band to release during the clutch or band apply for the next gear range, and these must be carefully synchronized. For example, during a 2–3 shift in many Simpson three-speed transmissions, the intermediate band releases while the high-reverse clutch applies. ● **SEE FIGURE 7–42.** The band must be released as the clutch is applied. An early

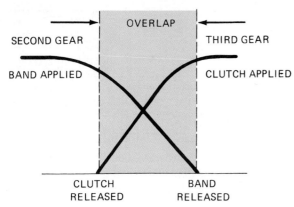

FIGURE 7–42 Shift overlap is the time period as the band releases and the direct clutch applies between second and third gears.

PROBLEM SOLVING 7–3

Imagine that you are working in a shop that specializes in transmission repair, and these problems are brought to you.

Case 1:

A 1982 Chevrolet Impala starts out okay in first gear, but the 1–2 and 2–3 shifts are late. What part of the transmission is faulty? What do you think is causing this problem?

Case 2:

A 1986 Toyota Celica starts out okay in drive, but it stays in first, and at about 20 to 30 mph, it makes a 1–3 shift. There is no second gear. What do you think might be wrong? How can you determine what part is faulty?

FIGURE 7–43 When a clutch is applied, fluid pressure keeps the exhaust check ball tightly seated (right). When the pressure is released, centrifugal force moves the check ball off its seat and allows a fluid flow out of the clutch (left).

FIGURE 7–44 Centrifugal force in the balance/release cavity (a) generates the same fluid force as that in the apply chamber (b). This balanced force allows the springs to return the piston and release the clutch.

application of the clutch or a late release of the band produces a "fight" or "bind" between these two parts, which produces a harsh shift and probable damage to the clutch or band. A late application of the clutch or an early release of the band produces an engine overspeed (also called a "flare" or "buzzup") as the transmission falls back to first gear before the shift to third is completed.

Timing these two apply devices occurs by using the upshift fluid pressures from the shift valve to apply the clutch and also release the band. In some units, band-release fluid flow is used as an accumulator control for the clutch apply. Accumulators are also used to control shift quality, as described in the next section.

During a 3–2 downshift, the clutch must release as the band reapplies, and this action must be carefully coordinated, just like an upshift. An additional problem occurs at this time because centrifugal force in the spinning clutch tends to inhibit the fluid from flowing back to the entrance port at the center. The clutch exhaust check ball is designed to allow the fluid to leave from the outer area of the clutch chamber.

● **SEE FIGURE 7–43**. When the clutch applies, fluid pressure seats the check ball to prevent losing pressure. When the clutch releases and the pressure drops, centrifugal force moves the ball outward to an unseated position. This allows the fluid in the clutch assembly to escape so the clutch can release quickly and completely.

Some newer transmissions use a pressure balanced clutch, also called a *centrifugal force balanced clutch* or *centrifugal fluid pressure cancelling*. ● **SEE FIGURE 7–44**. This clutch has a second fluid chamber on the spring/release side of the clutch piston. Fluid in this chamber develops the same pressure from centrifugal force as that on the apply side of the piston. The springs can now move the piston to release the clutch, and both the apply and release chambers stay filled with fluid. This style of clutch gives more precise clutch apply and release characteristics than a clutch that uses a check ball and is becoming more popular with electronic shift control.

With a **pressure balanced clutch**, both the apply and release fluid chambers can be kept filled. When the clutch is applied, very little fluid needs to enter the apply chamber, and when the clutch is released, very little fluid needs to leave. This allows much more precisely timed clutch apply and release that is necessary for clutch-to-clutch, synchronous shifts.

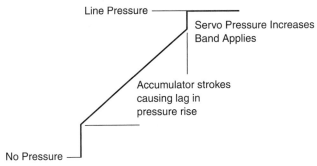

FIGURE 7–45 The pressure rise in this servo is delayed as the accumulator strokes.

Clutch Apply   Clutch Release

FIGURE 7–46 Clutch apply pressure seats the check ball so apply fluid must pass through the orifice (left). When the clutch releases, the check ball moves off its seat, allowing a faster clutch release because the fluid can bypass the orifice (right).

VARIABLE	CHANGE	EFFECT
Line pressure	Increase	Firmer shift
Flow rate	Increase	Firmer shift
Orifice size	Increase	Faster flow rate
Accumulator rate	Increase	Firmer shift
Accumulator spring	Softer	Faster accumulator rate
Accumulator back pressure	Reduce	Faster accumulator rate
ATF type	More aggressive	Firmer shift

CHART 7–2

Shift Quality

7.7.2 SHIFT MODIFIERS Many automatic transmissions contain valves to adjust the quality (speed and firmness) of the shift. A light-throttle shift, made while the engine is not producing much torque, can be fairly slow and at a light pressure. At heavy throttle, the engine is producing more torque so higher pressures are needed for the shift in order to lock the band or clutch being applied and prevent excessive slippage. Too slow of a shift at pressures that are too low will cause slippage and burning of the friction material. Too fast of a shift at pressures that are too high produces an aggressive, harsh shift that can cause mechanical damage to the drive train. Several methods are used to tailor a shift to the throttle opening or speed of the vehicle. ● **SEE CHART 7–2.**

An **accumulator** is tied hydraulically to the clutch or band servo, and absorbs fluid during the pressure buildup stage when a clutch or band applies. This has the effect of slowing the pressure increase and lengthening the time it takes for the friction device to lock up. ● **SEE FIGURE 7–45.** As clutch or band apply pressure is entering the apply side of the accumulator, fluid must leave the opposite, exhaust side of the accumulator piston. The pressure on the apply side and rate of stroke can be controlled by how easily the fluid leaves the exhaust side. An accumulator valve or shift control valve is often placed in the accumulator exhaust passage. The accumulator valve is usually balanced between throttle pressure and accumulator pressure in such a way that high throttle pressure closes down the accumulator exhaust flow. This produces higher accumulator pressure and therefore a firmer, quicker shift. The shift must be completed before the accumulator completes its stroke. If the accumulator piston bottoms before the shift is complete, there will be a sudden pressure increase that will cause a **slide-bump shift**. This is a shift with poor quality that starts smooth, but ends harsh.

Another method of changing upshift speed relative to downshift speed is to use an **orifice** in parallel with a one-way check ball. During upshifts, the ball seats so the flow passes through the orifice, and the diameter of the orifice controls the apply rate. During a downshift, the fluid flow unseats the ball, allowing a fast release. ● **SEE FIGURE 7–46.**

Still another method of changing shift speed is to position a valve to open a circuit bypassing an orifice. Under high throttle pressures, the valve opens the bypass so that a higher flow and pressure reaches the clutch or band apply piston, producing a faster shift. Low throttle pressures will close the bypass valve so the apply fluid must pass through the orifice and be controlled by the small size of the orifice opening.

7.7.3 DOWNSHIFTS The shift valves move to the downshift position under four operating conditions.

1. **Coasting downshift.** What normally occurs as a vehicle is brought to a stop. The spring moves the valve as governor pressure drops.

2. **Part-throttle downshift.** When the throttle is opened slightly to accelerate slowly and the rise in throttle pressure plus the spring can overcome governor pressure.

3. **Detent downshift.** Full-throttle/kickdown operates the detent valve and sends pressure through the detent passages to the shift valve. This pressure plus the spring will overcome governor pressure (see Figure 7–23).

4. **Manual downshift.** Movement of the shift lever to the M1 or M2 position sends pressure to a reaction area on the shift valve or governor plug that works against governor pressure. ● **SEE FIGURE 7–47.**

FIGURE 7–47 The manual valve has been moved to manual-2 to send line pressure to the 2–3 shift valve and governor plug. This moves both of them to the left and forces a downshift.

PROBLEM SOLVING 7-4

Imagine that you are working in a shop that specializes in transmission repair, and these problems are brought to you.

Case 1:

A 1983 Ford Ranger pickup starts out in second gear. The 2–3 and 3–4 shifts are normal. What part of the transmission is faulty? What do you think is causing this problem?

Case 2:

A 1993 Buick Regal drives okay most of the time, but the 3–4 part-throttle upshift is harsh. Could this be an accumulator or shift modifier valve problem? How can you determine if either of these parts is used in this transmission?

Coasting downshift is 4–1 or 3–1, not 3-2-1. A 3–1 downshift cannot be felt because the one-way clutch (the first-gear reaction member) overruns. Under most driving conditions with easy stops, we do not really need the compression braking that a 3–2 shift provides because there is adequate power in the vehicle's braking system. A 3–2 shift causes more wear in the transmission and an unnecessary downshift "bump."

If the shift selector is moved to manual-1 at speeds above 30 mph (48 km/h), the 1–2 shift valve normally stays in the upshift position until the speed drops off. A downshift at too high of a speed causes the engine to overrev and possible engine damage. This delay in a manual downshift is obtained by the relative sizes of the governor and manual-1 reaction areas. Some transmissions include an *inhibitor valve* that blocks this type of action, which can cause unsafe conditions and possible damage.

7.8 CVT HYDRAULIC CONTROL

Several hydraulic valves are used in a CVT to control the pulley positions and the fluid pressure for other systems, including:

- Ratio control valve
- Secondary pulley pressure
- Reverse and, if used, forward clutch apply pressure
- Torque converter clutch apply and release pressures
- Lubrication pressure

The ratio control valve is a three-position valve that can feed fluid to the primary piston, hold that fluid, or bleed fluid from the piston. The valve is connected at the center of a link between the floating pulley side and a stepper motor. When the TCM desires a higher ratio, the stepper motor is commanded to move, and this moves the ratio control valve to feed fluid to the primary piston. ● **SEE FIGURE 7–48**. The primary piston will then move, and the pulley movement will move the ratio control valve to a hold position. If the TCM desires a lower ratio, the stepper motor will be driven inward, and the ratio control valve will bleed fluid from the primary piston until the pulley moves to the proper position.

The drive belt must be clamped tight enough between the pulley sides and the two pulleys to prevent slippage. The primary pulley must be able to overcome the clamping force of the secondary pulley. This is done by giving the primary a larger piston area, higher fluid pressure, or both. The secondary pulley pressure valve controls the fluid pressure to the secondary piston, and this pressure provides belt-clamping pressure. Primary and secondary piston pressure can be as high as 900 PSI (6.2 megapascal [Mpa]).

The forward and reverse clutches are hydraulically operated, multiplate clutches, like those used in other transmissions. Their operation is controlled by a manual valve. Clutch apply pressure ranges up to 220 PSI (1.5 Mpa).

Some CVTs use an offset, chain-driven pump to reduce transaxle length. ● **SEE FIGURE 7–49**. Others mount the pump in a normal position. A gerotor and a balanced vane-type pump can be used.

FIGURE 7–48 Movement of either the stepper motor or primary floating sheave will move the ratio control valve to add or remove fluid from the primary pulley. The secondary valve maintains the necessary pulley pressure on the drive belt.

FIGURE 7–49 This pump is mounted off to the side and driven by a chain from the transmission input shaft.

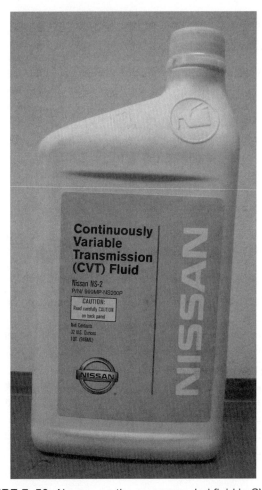

FIGURE 7–50 Always use the recommended fluid in CVT transmissions.

TCC and lube circuits are similar to those of other transaxles. TCC control is by a solenoid-controlled spool valve. These circuits have pressures from 0 to 145 PSI (0 to 1 Mpa).

CVT transmission requires a special fluid; even a small amount of another fluid, such as ATF, can cause belt-to-pulley slippage and serious damage. ● **SEE FIGURE 7–50.**

SUMMARY

1. An automatic transmission monitors vehicle load and speed to determine shift timing and quality.

2. Various types of valves are used to direct the fluid flow and regulate the pressures used to operate the transmission.

3. The torque converter is a hydraulic coupling that connects the engine to the transmission. It also has a hydraulically operated lockup clutch that, when applied, makes a mechanical connection between the engine and transmission.

4. A governor valve is used to monitor vehicle speed, and a vacuum or mechanically controlled throttle valve regulates pressure that is applied to the ends of the shift valves to control when the shifts will occur.

5. Additional valves are used to control the shifts needed for other driving conditions. A kick-down valve is used to force a downshift, and shift-modifying valves are used to improve the quality and timing of both the upshifts and downshifts.

1. Valves can be placed into three categories. What are they?

2. Servo valves are used to _____ another valve and switching valves are used to _____ flow.

3. The term *exhaust* when used with an automatic transmission means that the fluid is being directed to the _____ to empty a circuit.

4. The typical spring-balanced pressure regulator valve maintains mainline pressure at about _____ to _____ PSI.

5. Under certain driving conditions, _____ pressure will increase and be used to _____ mainline pressure.

6. Full-throttle pressure will increase mainline pressure to about _____ to _____ PSI.

7. Mainline pressure in reverse should be between _____ and _____ PSI.

8. The torque converter must have continual flow to maintain _____ temperature.

9. Typical torque converter pressure is _____ to _____ PSI.

10. Most lockup torque converters are controlled _____ by the ECM.

11. Fluid leaving the torque converter is directed to the _____ exchanger.

12. Fluid returning from the heat exchanger is used to _____ the transmission.

13. Throttle valves are _____ regulating valves that provide a pressure _____ relative to the vehicle _____.

14. Throttle valves can be controlled by _____, _____, or _____ connections to the throttle linkage.

15. As vehicle load _____, engine vacuum will _____, and throttle valve pressure will _____.

16. The detent valve is used to produce full-throttle pressure at _____ _____ _____.

17. The governor produces a signal that is proportionate to vehicle _____.

18. Shift valves are positioned by a spring and _____ pressure at one end and _____ pressure at the other end.

19. A coasting downshift results when _____ pressure drops.

20. A part-throttle downshift results because of a rise in _____ _____ pressure.

1. Automatic transmission hydraulic pressure is created by _____.
   a. The pump
   b. The pressure regulator valve
   c. Restrictions to fluid flow
   d. All of these

2. Three categories of valves found in a hydraulic circuit are _____.
   a. Switching, servo, and pressure regulating
   b. Accumulator, flow control, and pressure regulating
   c. Switching, manual, and flow control
   d. Manual, shift, and accumulator

3. Hydraulic diagrams are useful to _____.
   a. Trace the power flow
   b. Trace the fluid flow
   c. Understand the gear train
   d. All of these

4. A switching valve can be moved _____.
   a. Hydraulically
   b. Mechanically
   c. By another valve
   d. All of these

5. Normal unboosted line pressure is about _____ PSI.
   a. 10 to 15   c. 50 to 60
   b. 25 to 35   d. 125 to 135

6. Student A says that most pressure regulator valves are arranged so that line pressure tries to move the valve in one direction while a spring tries to move the valve in the other. Student B says that most pressure regulator valves are arranged so line pressure tries to move the valve in one direction while boost valve pressure increases spring force. Who is correct?
   a. Student A
   b. Student B
   c. Both Students A and B
   d. Neither Student A nor B

7. An increase in mainline pressure is desirable to _____.
   a. Produce firmer shifts
   b. Produce a quicker shift
   c. Increase holding power
   d. All of these

8. Fluid leaving the torque converter is sent to the _____.
   a. Lubrication passages
   b. Manual valve
   c. Pump
   d. Pressure regulator

9. In many transmissions, torque converter clutch lockup occurs when the _____.
   a. Fluid flow through the converter is reversed
   b. Fluid flow to the cooler is shut off
   c. Converter pressure is raised to 125 PSI
   d. All of these

10. The transmission cooler is usually located in the _____.
    a. Oil pan
    b. Coolest tank of the radiator
    c. Area in front of the air-conditioning condenser
    d. Hottest part of the radiator

11. An automatic transmission can be damaged by towing a vehicle because _____.
    a. It will not be lubricated unless the engine is running
    b. The torque converter will seize up
    c. The clutches and bands will not apply
    d. All of these

12. A supplemental transmission cooler should typically be installed _____.
    a. Before the cooler in the radiator
    b. After the cooler in the radiator
    c. Behind the radiator
    d. Behind the condenser

13. The throttle valve is used to sense _____.
    a. Vehicle speed
    b. Engine load
    c. Engine speed
    d. Transmission load

14. Higher throttle openings cause the transmission to _____.
    a. Shift at higher speeds
    b. Produce firmer upshifts
    c. Increase the line pressure
    d. All of these

15. The governor valve is used to sense _____.
    a. Vehicle speed
    b. Engine load
    c. Engine speed
    d. Transmission load

16. A vacuum modulator transmission also has a throttle-controlled valve that can produce _____.
    a. Reduced line pressure
    b. Full-throttle downshifts
    c. Slightly earlier shift timing
    d. All of these

17. A stronger spring in the vacuum modulator produces _____.
    a. Less part-throttle line pressure
    b. Greater part-throttle line pressure
    c. Earlier upshifts
    d. Softer upshifts

18. Student A says that the manual valve position is controlled by the shift lever. Student B says that the manual valve position is controlled by a detent cam and spring-loaded ball or roller. Who is correct?
    a. Student A
    b. Student B
    c. Both Students A and B
    d. Neither Student A nor B

19. The pressure signal from the governor is used to _____.
    a. Produce higher line pressure at higher speeds
    b. Move the shift valves to the upshift position
    c. Produce firmer shifts at higher speeds
    d. Move the shift valves with the vehicle stopped

20. Student A says that as the speed increases, centrifugal force acting on the governor weights will move the valve to increase governor pressure. Student B says that as the speed increases, centrifugal force acting on the governor weights will balance the output shaft to prevent vibrations. Who is correct?
    a. Student A
    b. Student B
    c. Both Students A and B
    d. Neither Student A nor B

21. Most shift valves use _____ to move them to a downshift position when the vehicle stops.
    a. Throttle pressure
    b. Governor pressure
    c. Spring pressure
    d. Any of these

22. When a shift valve overcomes the spring pressure and moves, the transmission will _____.
    a. Upshift
    b. Downshift
    c. Increase the line pressure
    d. Shift to neutral

23. Student A says that an accumulator is used to reduce fluid pressure in a servo that is applying to produce a softer upshift. Student B says that an orifice is used to reduce fluid pressure in a servo that is applying to produce a softer upshift. Who is correct?
    a. Student A
    b. Student B
    c. Both Students A and B
    d. Neither Student A nor B

24. Student A says that an orifice causes a fluid pressure drop while fluid is flowing through it. Student B says that an orifice does not change fluid pressure when there is no flow. Who is correct?
    a. Student A
    b. Student B
    c. Both Students A and B
    d. Neither Student A nor B

25. A manual-1 downshift above 30 mph can cause the _____.
    a. Engine to overrev
    b. Transmission to shift into second
    c. Transmission to shift into neutral
    d. Vehicle to set off an alarm

chapter 8
ELECTRONIC TRANSMISSION CONTROLS

OBJECTIVES: After studying Chapter 8, the reader will be able to: • Describe the operation of an electronic transmission. • Explain how electronic controls are used for transmission operation. • Identify the major automatic transmission electronic control components. • Describe the relationship between volts, amperes, and ohms. • Explain the circuit required for an electrical system to operate.

KEY TERMS: Adaptive control 183 • Adaptive learning 183 • Ampere 185 • Analog 194 • Break 187 • Circuit 185 • Clamping diode 191 • Close 187 • Digital 194 • Gauge 187 • Ground 185 • Ground control 200 • Infinite resistance 187 • Load 185 • Make 187 • Malfunction indicator lamp (MIL) 189 • Multiplexing 197 • Ohm 185 • On-Board Diagnostics, Second Generation (OBD-II) 203 • Open 187 • Resistance 185 • Scan tool 184 • Solenoid 184 • Strategy base 207 • Switch 187 • Torque management 183 • Transmission control module (TCM) 182 • Voltage 184

8.1 INTRODUCTION

Once automotive engineers determined that electronic devices could be used to accurately control engine performance, the devices have been used to operate and control almost every vehicle's electrical system. The first electronic transmissions were introduced in the early 1980s. These were relatively simple applications that controlled only the torque converter clutch, and the operation was similar to a typical nonelectronic transmission. A speed sensor was used in place of a governor, and the throttle position sensor, as part of the engine electronic controls, was used to detect vehicle load. An electronic control unit would process the sensor information and then operate solenoids to produce transmission shifts and torque converter clutch apply or release.

Engineers have steadily redesigned electronic systems to improve transmission operation and its interaction with other vehicle systems. Current electronic automatic transmissions are able to provide diagnostic information and to accurately control the following:

- Shift timing and quality
- Mainline pressure
- Application and release of apply devices
- Apply-device pressures
- Application and release of the torque converter clutch
- Engine torque during shifts

In addition, the two-mode hybrid transmission has two electric motor/generators that provide torque to drive the

vehicle and generate electricity during braking (see Figures 3–56 and 3–57). There is also an electric motor driven pump to provide fluid pressure while the engine is shut off during idle-stop. Automatic transmissions normally go into neutral because of the pressure loss when the engine stops.

An automatic transmission can be controlled by its own computer, called a **transmission control module (TCM)**, or a *transmission control unit (TCU)*. The transmission can also be controlled through either the vehicle's body control module (BCM) or the powertrain control module (PCM). Each manufacturer has its own design criteria and terminology. For consistency in this text, we will call the controlling unit a TCM.

The TCM is normally located outside the transmission in a protected, relatively cool and clean location. Some newer transmissions have the TCM mounted on the valve body inside the transmission. The primary advantage is the reduction of wiring and the elimination of electrical connectors, both sources of potential problems.

Electronic transmissions need to sense the same basic information for operation as a traditional hydraulic transmission: engine load and vehicle speed. ● **SEE FIGURE 8–1.** The governor is replaced by a *vehicle speed sensor (VSS)*, and engine load is sensed using a *throttle position sensor (TPS)*, manifold air pressure (MAP) sensor, or a mass airflow (MAF) sensor. Computer logic gives electronic transmissions a big advantage over hydraulically controlled transmissions that could only use mechanical, hydraulic, or vacuum to determine fluid pressure, shift timing, and quality. Additional information is available from other control modules to the TCM that can be used to more precisely determine when and how the transmission will shift.

FIGURE 8–1 An electronic transmission has electronic sensors and actuators and is integrated electronically with other phases of vehicle operation.

Data inputs to the TCM include:

- Mainline pressure
- Input shaft speed
- Vehicle speed
- Fluid temperature
- Gear range
- Coolant temperature
- Engine speed and load
- Brake apply
- Air conditioning, on-off
- Cruise control, on-off

Accurate control of shift timing and quality provides a smoother driving experience. In addition to improving shift quality, altering the ignition timing during the shift decreases the load on the transmission and increases transmission life. ● SEE FIGURE 8–2. This is called **torque management** or *torque reduction*. Another benefit is that the driver may not notice the shift occurring. Shift feel is controlled by the TCM and PCM.

Another shift improvement is **adaptive control**, or **adaptive learning**, which keeps shift duration within a certain time period as determined by the driver's habits. The TCM learns shift duration by monitoring the input and output speed sensors and the pressure sensors. It can easily calculate the transmission gear ratio at any point in time; some TCMs make this calculation every 4 milliseconds. A solenoid can be cycled (pulsed on and off) or line pressure can be increased to correct a shift that is taking too long. Fluid is sent to an applying member at the rate needed to produce the desired shift quality, by adjusting the electrical signal to the electronic pressure control (EPC) or shift

FIGURE 8–2 When the transmission control module (TCM) is ready to begin an upshift, it signals the powertrain control module (PCM) to reduce engine torque. This produces a smoother shift with less wear in the transmission.

solenoid. ● SEE FIGURE 8–3. One system can adjust a slipping shift in 400 milliseconds, less than 0.5 second.

Some vehicles have additional shift control modes, and these provide earlier or later and smoother or faster shifts. The driver can choose economy mode, which causes the transmission to shift early with a smooth shift feel. When switched to power mode, the transmission shifts later and more firmly.

Another feature for improved shift timing is through a process called *fuzzy logic*. In most situations, shifts simply match vehicle speed and throttle position. Fuzzy logic adapts shifts to driving conditions such as mountains, upgrades and downgrades, and while turning corners. The shifts will be delayed and firmer because of increased load and multiple changes in throttle position. Fuzzy logic and advanced electronics allow improved shifts for many different situations. ● SEE FIGURE 8–4.

FIGURE 8–3 Using data from the various sensors, the TCM can apply or release the clutches. During an upshift, solenoid 1 can control how fast clutch 1 releases as solenoid 2 controls how fast clutch 2 applies to keep the shift time at the proper speed.

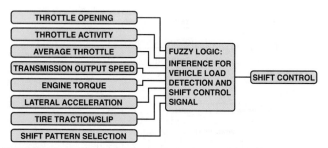

FIGURE 8–4 The fuzzy logic part of the TMC receives input signals, compares what the driver is doing with the throttle and what the vehicle is doing with normal operation, and adapts shift timing.

An electronic transmission controls the shift points by turning a **solenoid**(s) on and off. The solenoids in turn control the hydraulic pressure that moves the shift valves or operates the torque converter clutch. ● **SEE FIGURE 8–5.** Some shift solenoids apply using *pulse width modulation (PWM)*; the solenoids cycle on and off during apply to adjust shift apply. In some transmissions the solenoids completely replace the shift valves.

An automatic transmission technician needs a working knowledge of electricity, basic electronics, and hydraulics. In the past, diagnosing and repairing simple electrical circuits could often be accomplished with a limited knowledge of electrical circuits and a simple test light. The introduction of solid-state computerized electronics presented the need to have an understanding of the system and electrical test procedures, the ability to measure electrical values, and knowledge to interpret their meaning. Specialized electronic test equipment and **scan tools** are required to read diagnostic trouble codes and diagnose the problem.

Solid-state electronics is at the heart of computerized circuits. Electronic components include transistors, diodes, and integrated microchips. These devices are quite fragile relative to other automotive components. They are also relatively trouble free and usually have a long life because they have no moving parts except electrons, so nothing should wear out.

8.2 BASIC ELECTRICITY

A course in basic automotive electronics is necessary to thoroughly understand electricity, how to measure it, and how to diagnose electrical problems. The following is a brief review of basic electricity.

In the future, vehicles will depend more on electricity for driving power and the operation of accessories (air conditioning, power steering, power brakes, etc.). Originally, vehicles used 6-volt electrical systems. These systems gave way to 12-volt systems to meet customer demands for more power and convenience. Now hybrid vehicles use high-voltage electrical systems—some are over 300 volts. As a result of the changes in electrical power, it is becoming more important for every automotive technician to have at least a basic understanding of electrical circuit characteristics and Ohm's law.

The three measurable aspects of electricity that concern an automotive technician are electrical pressure (voltage), current flow (amperage), and resistance to current flow (ohms).

- Voltage (volts) is comparable to the pressure in a hydraulic system. **Voltage**, also called *electromotive force (EMF)*, is the force that causes electron flow—much like hydraulic pressure forces the fluid to flow in a hydraulic circuit. ● **SEE FIGURE 8–6.** In a vehicle, the voltage source is the battery or alternator.

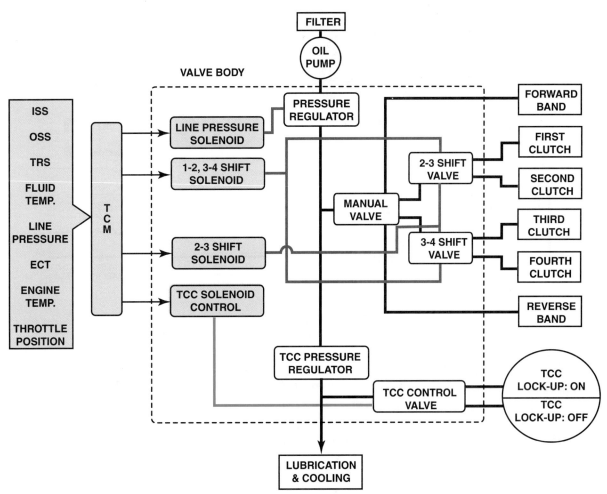

FIGURE 8–5 This diagram shows the relationship between the electronic and hydraulic controls.

- **Amperes (amps)** is the measurement of electron (current) flow through a circuit. One amp is equal to 6.28 billion electrons flowing past a point in 1 second. Current flow can be compared to the quantity of hydraulic fluid flowing into a clutch or servo.

- **Ohm** is the measurement of electrical resistance. The **resistance** in an electrical circuit controls how much current flows—much like an orifice restricts fluid flow in a hydraulic circuit. The higher the circuit resistance, the lower the current flow. The symbol Ω (omega) indicates ohms.

For current to flow, there must be a complete **circuit**. The circuit starts at the power supply, travels through the wires (conductors) to the working component(s) (often called the **load**), and then returns to the power supply. The positive side of the circuit, often called battery positive (B+), is routed through insulated wires. The negative side, **ground** (B–), can be run through wires or the metal parts of the vehicle. ● **SEE FIGURE 8–7.** A component that is grounded by being bolted to the ground circuit is called *case grounded*.

Vehicles have many different electrical circuits, and it is common for a vehicle to have well over 1 mile (1.6 km) of wiring. Each circuit starts at the battery/alternator positive connection

(B+) and ends at the battery/alternator negative connection (B–). A simple circuit has only one load. Following are other types of circuits.

- **Series.** The loads are connected one after the other in a series circuit. This causes all the current to flow through all of the loads. ● **SEE FIGURE 8–8.**

- **Parallel.** There are branches in a parallel circuit. Each branch is connected to the same power source, and the branches allow the current to flow through separate paths.

- **Series/parallel.** The series/parallel circuit is a combination of series and parallel circuits in one complex circuit.

Vehicle manufacturers publish *wiring diagrams* as road maps of the electrical circuits. These maps help the technician understand the electrical circuits, the location of the components, and how the circuits are related. Wiring diagrams or *schematics* use symbols for the components to help simplify the drawings. ● **SEE FIGURE 8–9.**

Automotive electrical circuits commonly use *direct current* 12-volt systems, which are actually 12.6 volts. Direct current (DC) always travels in one direction, and electron flow is believed to be from negative to positive. Household electricity is *alternating current*, and alternating current (AC) switches direction

FIGURE 8–6 If we compare electricity with (a) hydraulics, voltage, and pressure, (b) current flow and fluid flow, and (c) a resistor and orifice, they are very similar.

FIGURE 8–7 Insulated wires conduct electricity to the lights. The body metal forms the ground circuit to complete the circuit back to the battery. This is shown in (a) a diagram and (b) a schematic.

(a) **(b)**

FIGURE 8–8 (a) A series circuit, and (b) a parallel circuit.

many times a second. Hybrid vehicles use alternating current to operate some of their circuits.

Some automatic transmission technicians may find understanding electricity easy because it bears a strong resemblance to hydraulic systems.

- Hydraulic pressure and voltage are both forces that cause something to move.
- The flow of hydraulic fluid and amperage are the movement in the circuits.
- The hydraulic circuit and the electrical circuit wiring are both the paths that the flow must follow.
- The orifice and the resistor both reduce the flow in the circuit.
- The hydraulic check valve and a diode are one-way check valves.
- An accumulator and a capacitor are used to absorb and hold some of the circuit flow.

8.2.1 SYSTEM COMPONENTS
A typical automotive circuit has the following components. ● **SEE FIGURE 8–10**.

- Power source: the battery or alternator
- Circuit protection: fuse, fusible links, and circuit breakers
- Circuit control: switches
- Conductor: wires and connectors
- Load: components that do the work

POWER SOURCE. The automotive power source is either the battery or the alternator. The battery is primarily used to start the engine. It also provides the electrical power when the engine is not running or the electrical demands exceed the output of the alternator. The alternator not only provides electrical power while the vehicle is running but also must be able to recharge the battery if it is low. A fully charged battery will measure 12.6 volts at 80°F (27°C). When the engine is running, the alternator raises the system voltage to between 13.6 and 15.6 volts.

CIRCUIT PROTECTION. Circuit protection is the weak link in a circuit and will burn out or blow if excess current flows in the circuit. Serious damage can result if too much current is allowed to flow through a circuit. Circuit protection devices are used to stop the current flow in a circuit if the current exceeds the rated capacity of the circuit. The circuit protection devices

used in vehicles are fuses, fusible links, and circuit breakers. ● **SEE FIGURE 8–11**. Protection devices are rated to allow a current flow of about twice that needed for the load.

A *fuse* is a device that melts at a predetermined current flow. Fuses are designed to be easily tested and quickly replaced if they melt or blow. They are available in different shapes, sizes, and amp ratings to meet the requirements of the circuit. Color-coding provides a means for easy identification.

A *fusible link* is a short piece of wire that is about four wire gauge sizes smaller than the wire used in the circuit. If the circuit is overloaded, the fusible link will burn open to stop the flow of current.

A *circuit breaker* senses the current flow; if the amperage (heat) becomes excessive, then a set of contacts cycles open, stopping the current flow. Some circuit breakers are designed to be self-resetting, and they will reset automatically after the circuit breaker has cooled, allowing the circuit to operate again. Other circuit breakers must be reset manually.

A *positive temperature coefficient (PTC)* thermistor acts like a self-resetting circuit breaker. The circuit is opened by the temperature increase as the current reaches the maximum value. The circuit will reset when the cause of the excess current flow is corrected.

SWITCHES. A **switch** is used to control a circuit. It will **break** (**open**) the circuit to stop current flow or **make** (**close**) the circuit to allow current to flow. ● **SEE FIGURE 8–12**. An open switch has **infinite resistance** and will not allow electricity to pass through it. A closed switch should have no resistance to electrical flow. Switches come in many sizes and shapes, but they all do the same job: They control the circuit. Switches can be *normally open (NO)* or *normally closed (NC)*. Normally open switches are open at rest and closed as needed to complete a circuit. Normally closed switches are closed at rest and opened as needed to stop current flow. Automatic transmissions may have one or more switches that are opened or closed by fluid pressure, and they may be mounted on the inside or outside of the transmission. A switch can control a circuit directly or indirectly through a relay. Switches are also used as an input to the TCM.

A *relay* is an electromagnetic switch. ● **SEE FIGURE 8–13**. It is made up of a switch and a coil. When current passes through the coil, a magnetic field is produced, and the magnetic field can close or open the switch contacts. The horn circuit is a good example of how a relay is used, and the horn button is the control switch. When the button is depressed, it closes the circuit, current passes through the relay coil, and the relay contacts close. This completes the circuit, allowing current to pass to the horn. Relays are used to reduce the current flow through the controlling switch.

WIRING. Wire is used to connect the components of the circuit. Automotive wire typically is a multistrand copper wire surrounded by a plastic *insulator*. Copper is a very good conductor, bends easily, and offers a relatively small resistance to the circuit. The size of the conductor in a wire determines the amount of current it can safely carry. A **gauge** number is used to identify the size of the wire conductor. ● **SEE FIGURE 8–14**.

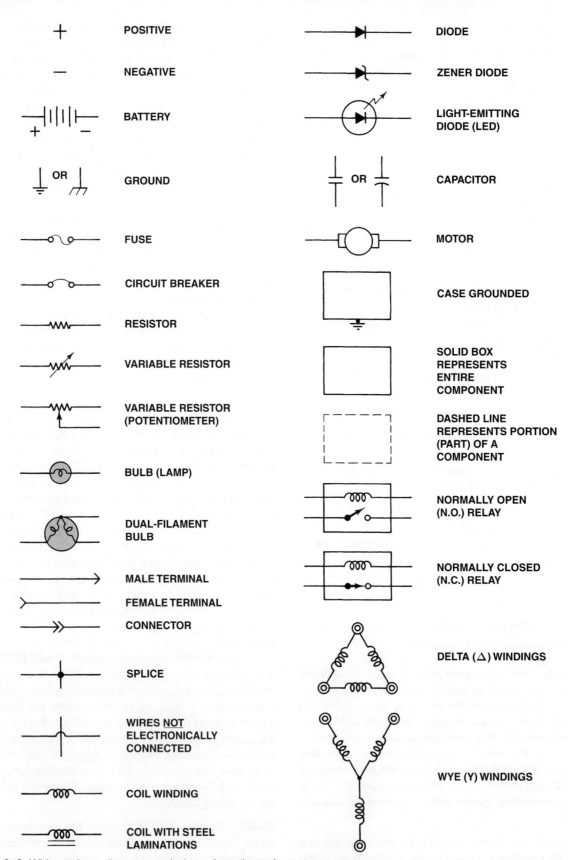

FIGURE 8–9 Wiring schematics use symbols to show the various components.

FIGURE 8–10 This diagram for a backup light circuit shows the power source (battery), a fuse for protection, a control switch, two output devices (the lights), and the wires that connect them.

FIGURE 8–11 Circuit protection can be (a) fuses with tubular or flat-blade connections, (b, c) a circuit breaker, or (d) a fusible link. (*Courtesy of Chrysler Corporation*)

Brake Pedal	STP Terminal Voltage
Depressed	12 V
Released	0 V

FIGURE 8–12 This stop light switch is a normally open switch. When the brake pedal is depressed, battery voltage is sent to the ECT ECU. (*Courtesy of Toyota Motor Sales USA, Inc.*)

The gauge number is inversely proportional to the wire size; therefore, the larger the conductor, the smaller the gauge number. The conductor can also be identified by the cross-sectional diameter of the wire measured in inches or millimeters. The insulation prevents unwanted connections to keep the electricity in that wire.

LOADS. Loads are components that do the work. Typical loads are lights, motors, relay coils, and solenoids. Solenoids are the most common load in automatic transmission circuits. ● **SEE FIGURE 8–15.** Another load is the instrument panel **malfunction indicator lamp (MIL)** that warns the driver of transmission problems. A solenoid is an electromagnet with a movable core or plunger, and the plunger is held in one position by a spring. When current passes through the solenoid windings, a magnetic field is produced that moves the plunger to the other position. The plunger, in turn, opens or closes a fluid passage. The strength of the solenoid magnet is determined by the amount of current flowing through the coil and the number of wire turns (length). The current flow is determined by the resistance of the wire in the coil, and increasing the wire size or making the wire shorter will increase the current flowing through the coil and the strength of the magnetic field.

A solenoid can be turned on and off many times a second. The cycle speed, or on-off time, also called the *duty cycle*, can be used to control fluid pressure or how fast fluid moves to fill a clutch. Solenoids can be normally on or normally off, and they are designed to allow a fluid flow when they are either on or off. ● **SEE FIGURE 8–16.**

Electromagnetic devices can cause a problem for electronic circuits that cannot handle large increases in voltage or current. When the current stops flowing in a coil of wire, the magnetic field collapses, and it will collapse inward, passing

Bottom View of Relay

De-Energized Relay

FIGURE 8–13 A deenergized relay. Relays use a magnetic coil to either close or open switch contacts. Note that terminals 85 and 86 are for control, terminals 30 to 87 are normally open, and terminals 30 to 87A are normally closed. (*Courtesy of Chrysler Corporation*)

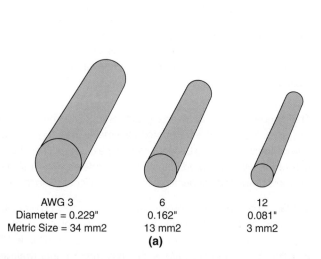

AWG 3
Diameter = 0.229"
Metric Size = 34 mm2

6
0.162"
13 mm2

12
0.081"
3 mm2

(a)

Wiring Color Code Chart					
Color Code	Color	Standard Tracer Color	Color Code	Color	Standard Tracer Code
BK	Black	WT	PK	Pink	BK or WH
BR	Brown	WT	RD	Red	WT
DB	Dark Blue				
DG	Dark Green	WT	VT	Violet	WT
GY	Gray	BK	WT	White	BK
LB	Light Blue	BK	YL	Yellow	BK
LG	Light Green	BK	•	With Tracer	
OR	Orange	BK			

(b)

FIGURE 8–14 (a) Electrical wire is sized by gauge sizes or cross section in millimeters; three American wire gauge (AWG) sizes are shown for comparison. (b) Wire colors with tracers are used to identify particular wires. (*Figure (b) Courtesy of Chrysler Corporation*)

Overdrive Solenoid (Black Wire)

Lockup Solenoid (White Wire)

(a)

(b)

FIGURE 8–15 Transmission solenoids can take different shapes, but they all include an electromagnet and a valve. The style shown in (b) is the most common. (*Figure (a) Courtesy of Chrysler Corporation; (b) Courtesy of Toyota Motor Sales USA, Inc.*)

FIGURE 8–16 This normally closed solenoid is on, and magnetic force has pulled the plunger to the right. Fluid pressure has moved the metering ball off its seat, and fluid is passing through the valve. (*Courtesy of Toyota Motor Sales USA, Inc.*)

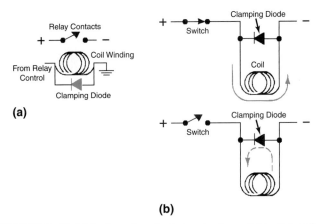

(a)

(b)

FIGURE 8–17 (a) A clamping diode is wired parallel to the coil winding. (b) It blocks current flow when the switch is closed, but it allows induced current to dissipate when the switch opens.

through the coil. The collapsing field induces a high voltage in the coil, and this voltage is high enough to damage electronic devices. To prevent this, a **clamping diode**, also called an *isolation diode*, is included in many circuits that use a coil. A diode is an electronic check valve that will allow current to move in only one direction. A clamping diode is connected to each end of the coil, and during operation, the diode will block current from bypassing the coil. ● **SEE FIGURE 8–17**. When the system is shut off, the diode will allow the induced current to bleed off through the coil, eliminating the high-voltage spikes.

8.3 BASIC ELECTRONICS

Solid-state electronics is the basis of automotive computers and control modules. These devices are constructed from diodes, transistors, capacitors, resistors, integrated circuits, and microchips. Solid-state devices, for all practical purposes, do not wear out because there are no moving parts. A major difference between electrical and electronic circuits is the quantity of electrical flow. Current flow in electronic circuits is very small,

FIGURE 8–18 This PCM receives sensor input (at left) and controls actuators (outputs) inside the transmissions.

PROBLEM SOLVING 8–1

Imagine that you are working in a shop that specializes in automatic transmission repair. You are asked to repair vehicles with the following concerns.

Case 1:

A 1995 Thunderbird has no backup lights. You find a blown fuse for the backup lights. You replace the fuse, but as soon as you shift into reverse, the new fuse blows. What do you think is the cause? Where would you begin checking for the cause of the problem?

Case 2:

A 1987 Citation has no TCC lockup. The converter clutch does not engage at any speed or under any driving condition. Could this be caused by a broken wire? How would you check for a broken wire?

so the voltage requirement is low (about 5 volts) and circuit resistance must be kept to a minimum.

Electronic devices can, however, be easily damaged by rough handling, vibration, and high temperatures. High current or voltage spikes will easily damage electronics. Voltage spikes can result from circuit problems or *electrostatic discharge (ESD)*. High resistance can also limit the current to the point that the electronics will not operate. Well-maintained circuits and proper handling are essential for proper operation.

Electronic devices are used for sensing and controlling circuits, and an automatic transmission is a good candidate for electronically controlled circuits. ● **SEE FIGURE 8–18**. An electronically controlled system can be divided into three parts: *inputs (sensors)*, the *transmission control module (TCM)*, and *outputs (actuators)*. Remember that the TCM is also called an *electronic control module (ECM)* and in some vehicles the TCM is a part of the *powertrain control module (PCM)* or *body control module (BCM)*.

8.3.1 SENSORS

Sensors are the TCM inputs. They monitor the things that can affect transmission operation: vehicle speed, input shaft speed, transmission fluid temperature, the selected gear range, and engine coolant temperature, RPM, and load. A typical transmission sensor can be a switch that is made to open or close at certain pressures or temperatures, a transducer that senses pressure, a thermistor that senses temperature, or a speed sensor that measures vehicle speed or shaft RPM. The various sensor types (organized by the type of electrical signal) are as follows:

- Frequency generators (creates an AC signal with a frequency relative to speed and the TCM monitors the signal frequency)
- Voltage generator (creates a voltage signal that is relative to speed and the TCM monitors the voltage)
- Potentiometer or variable resistor (alters resistance)
- Switches (an on-off signal)
- Thermistor (changes resistance relative to temperature)
- Transducer (changes resistance relative to pressure)
- Serial data (an on-off signal coming from another control module)

The vehicle speed sensor is located next to the output shaft, similar to the governor. ● **SEE FIGURE 8–19**. Most speed sensors use a coil of wire that is wrapped around a magnetic core. This sensor is mounted next to a toothed ring or wheel. ● **SEE FIGURE 8–20**. As the toothed ring revolves, an alternating voltage is produced in the sensor.

Another style of speed sensor consists of a normally open reed switch. The switch is mounted next to a rotor that has a magnet built into it or a gearlike reluctor. ● **SEE FIGURE 8–21**. When the vehicle starts moving, the magnet passes by the reed switch and momentarily pulls the contacts closed. The TCM can accurately determine how fast the vehicle is going by the voltage change frequency. The rate of this pulsating voltage determines transmission shaft speed. Most RPM or speed sensors are frequency generators.

Newer transmissions use an input and an output speed sensor. By comparing the signals, the TCM can determine the gear ratio and how long it takes to make the shift. ● **SEE FIGURE 8–22**. Chrysler refers to this as the *clutch volume index (CVI)*, the length of time it takes to fill the clutches with fluid.

FIGURE 8–19 This transmission uses an input (left) and output (right) speed sensor. The sensors generate a signal frequency that is relative to the speeds of the reluctor rings. (*Courtesy of Toyota Motor Sales USA, Inc.*)

FIGURE 8–20 (a) The speed sensor switch will close as the magnet moves past it. (b) It will generate a square wave/on-off signal.

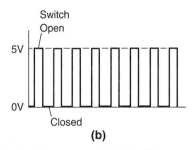

FIGURE 8–21 (a) The reluctor tooth will pull the magnetic field across the coil windings as it moves past. (b) It will generate a sine wave/AC signal.

FIGURE 8–22 An input speed sensor along with an output speed sensor allows the TCM to calculate the gear ratio and determine how long it takes to complete a shift or if there is internal slippage in the gear train. (*Courtesy of Chrysler Corporation*)

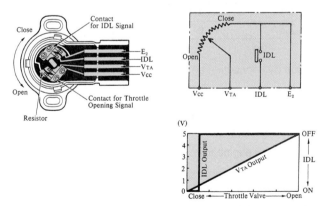

FIGURE 8–23 A TPS (throttle position sensor) is mounted at the throttle body. It provides an electronic signal of the throttle operation to the ECM.

The throttle position sensor (TPS) is attached to the engine throttle shaft. ● **SEE FIGURE 8–23**. It changes resistance as the throttle is opened and closed. By measuring the voltage, the TCM can accurately determine the throttle position and produce correctly timed upshifts or downshifts. The TPS takes the place of the throttle/vacuum modulator valve in hydraulically controlled transmissions.

Most temperature sensors are thermistors, a type of variable resistor that changes electrical resistance relative to temperature. These are called negative temperature coefficient (NTC) thermistors. The signal from a thermistor is the inverse of the temperature; it has high resistance at low temperatures and a low resistance at high temperatures. For example, a particular transmission fluid temperature sensor has a resistance of 37 to 100 Ω at 32°F to 58°F (0°C to 20°C) and 1.5 to 2.7 kilohms (kΩ) at 195°F to 230°F (91°C to 110°C). The *engine coolant temperature (ECT) sensor* tells the TCM when the engine is at operating temperature. ● **SEE FIGURE 8–24**. The temperature signal is used to prevent TCC lockup while the engine is cold. In some transmissions, this signal is used to produce earlier-than-normal converter clutch lockup if the engine temperature rises too high. A cold engine temperature signal can also be used to delay upshifts or prevent an upshift until the engine is at operating temperature.

A *transmission oil temperature (TOT)* sensor is used in some transmissions. The TOT can be a thermistor or a bimetal switch that opens or closes at a specific temperature. ● **SEE FIGURE 8–25**.

A *transducer* is a variable resistor; it produces a variable signal that is relative to pressure, allowing the control module to monitor pressure. The *line pressure sensor (LPS)* is a transducer that converts line pressure to a variable resistance.

Many transmissions include pressure switches at the valve body. ● **SEE FIGURE 8–26**. This signal tells the TCM that the circuit has pressure. The TCM uses this along with other information to determine TCC lockup and shift timing.

The *manifold air pressure (MAP)* sensor is a type of transducer that provides an "engine load" signal to the ECM.

A commonly used variable resistor found in automotive applications is the *potentiometer*, a type of variable resistor. The control module sends a low-voltage signal (about 5 volts) to the potentiometer, and the sensor returns a voltage that is relative to the condition that the sensor is monitoring (see Figure 8–23). If sensor resistance increases, the voltage returning from the sensor to the control module will be lower; and if the resistance decreases, the returning voltage will be higher. These sensors are normally used to monitor position. A common example is the throttle position sensor (TPS). It is often called a three-wire sensor. A switch-type sensor or variable resistor needs only two wires.

(a)

(b)

(c)

(d)

FIGURE 8–24 (a) The ECT (engine coolant temperature) sensor is mounted close to the engine's thermostat. (b) It is a thermistor that provides (c, d) a coolant temperature signal to the ECM.

Temperature		Resistance (Ohms)
°C	°F	
140	284	0.6 K
120	248	1.1 K
100	212	2.1 K
80	176	3.8 K
50	122	10 K
30	86	27 K
10	50	69 K
-10	14	193 K
-30	-22	600 K

(a)

(b)

FIGURE 8–25 (a) A transmission fluid temperature sensor can be checked by connecting an ohmmeter to the harness connector terminals. (b) The resistance should change as the temperature changes.

Frequency and voltage generators develop an **analog** AC electrical wave that is continuously varying in frequency and intensity. The control module operates using a **digital** signal that is essentially an on-off pulse of electricity. It reads the signal by the length of time that the input is on or off. ● **SEE FIGURE 8–27**. Most control modules use an analog-to-digital (AD) converter to modify the analog signal to a digital signal.

The transmission *manual lever position (MLP)* switch, sometimes called a neutral start switch, is usually mounted on the transmission. ● **SEE FIGURE 8–28**. It is operated by the shaft connecting the gear selector and manual linkage to the manual valve. It is a multiposition switch that has multiple inputs to the TCM. ● **SEE FIGURE 8–29**. As the gear range selector is moved, the MLP switch can make a variety of switch connections for each gear range. These inputs allow the TCM to

determine which gear range has been selected. The MLP switch is used by the TCM to:

- Keep the engine from starting in any gear position except park or neutral
- Allow a progressive 1–2–3–4 shift sequence in drive
- Limit upshifts in manual ranges
- Operate the backup lights in reverse

Another important switch is *brake on/off (BOO)* switch, commonly called the stop light switch. It is mounted at the brake pedal, and its signal is used to release the TCC when the brakes are applied. ● **SEE FIGURE 8–30**.

Some vehicles use a comfort-power switch. This switch allows the driver to select one or more operating modes programmed into the TCM. In the "comfort" mode, the upshifts and downshifts are made at normal shift points, producing quiet,

FIGURE 8–26 This hydraulic circuit shows three fluid pressure switches that signal the TCM when there is pressure in their circuits. (*Courtesy of Chrysler Corporation*)

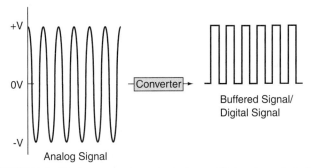

FIGURE 8–27 Some systems include an AD (analog–digital) buffer to convert the AC analog speed sensor signal so it can be read by the ECM.

economical operation. This is also called the economy mode. In the "power" mode, the upshifts are made later and the downshifts occur at higher speeds. Delaying the shifts allows higher engine RPM at wider throttle openings for added performance. Some newer vehicles use a five-position manual lever with the rear position a manual shift mode. ● **SEE FIGURE 8–31.** This mode uses a pair of buttons/switches (+ and −) to produce upshifts or downshifts, and these buttons are mounted on the steering wheel (often called paddles), shift lever, or console.

The following are commonly used transmission sensors.

NOTE: Sensor terminology can be confusing because different transmission manufacturers use different names for similar items. A listing of SAE J1930 terminology pertaining to an automatic transmission is given in Appendix D.

Brake on/off (BOO) switch. This switch mounted at the brake pedal provides a signal when the brake is depressed. It signals the TCM that the brake is applied, and the TCC should be released.

Engine coolant temperature (ECT). This variable resistor (thermistor) monitors engine temperature. It signals the TCM that the engine is at operating temperature or approaching overheat temperatures.

Line pressure sensor (LPS). This transducer monitors line pressure. It allows the TCM to determine the actual line pressure.

Manifold absolute pressure (MAP), mass airflow sensor (MAF). It provides an engine load signal to the PCM.

Transmission control switch (TCS), park reverse neutral, park/neutral position (PNP) switch. This multicontact switch provides a park or neutral gear range position signal. It signals the TCM of the driver's request for neutral or park.

Manual lever position (MLP) switch, park reverse neutral drive low (PRNDL) switch. This multicontact switch provides a gear range position signal. It signals the TCM of the driver's request for a particular gear range.

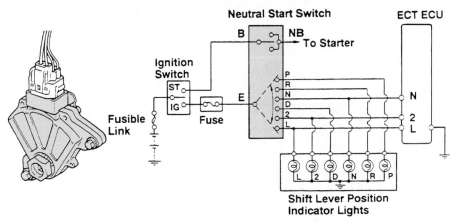

FIGURE 8–28 This MLP (manual lever position) sensor/neutral start switch is mounted at the transmission. It provides a shift lever position signal to the ECM.

Range	Terminal A	Terminal B	Terminal C
P	OFF	ON	OFF
R	ON	ON	OFF
N	OFF	ON	OFF
D4	OFF	ON	ON
D3	OFF	OFF	ON
D2	OFF	OFF	OFF
D1	ON	OFF	OFF

ON = 0 volts; OFF = B+

FIGURE 8–29 The voltage at the three MLP switch terminals change depending on the position of the shift lever.

FIGURE 8–30 The stop light switch is mounted at the brake pedal. It provides a brake-apply signal to the TCM. (*Courtesy of Toyota Motor Sales USA, Inc.*)

Mode switch. It allows the driver to select the desired transmission operating mode and gear range.

Pressure sensor or switch. This hydraulically operated switch or pressure transducer allows the TCM to determine the fluid pressure in one or more circuits.

Power-economy switch. This switch allows the driver to raise or lower the shift points. Raising the shift points delays the shifts and increases performance. Lowering the shift points produces earlier shifts to increase fuel economy.

Throttle position sensor (TPS). This variable resistor (potentiometer) provides a voltage signal that is relative to throttle opening. It provides a throttle position signal to the TCM.

Transmission oil temperature (TOT). This variable resistor (thermistor) monitors transmission temperature. It signals the TCM that the transmission is at operating temperature or approaching overheat temperatures.

Transmission range drive (TRD), transmission range low (TRL), transmission range overdrive (TROD), transmission range reverse (TRR), fourth-gear/OD lockout switch. It limits transmission operation to specific ranges by signaling the TCM of the driver's request for a particular gear operating strategy.

Transmission speed sensor (TSS), turbine speed sensor (TSS), output speed sensor (OSS). This magnetic pickup, frequency generator determines the speed of the input and output shafts. It allows the TCM to determine what gear the transmission is in and if there is excessive slippage in that gear range.

Vehicle speed sensor (VSS). This switch (a digital, on-off) or sensor (AC frequency) counts the revolutions of the output shaft. It provides a voltage or frequency signal that is relative to vehicle speed. The TCM uses this signal to determine vehicle speed.

8.3.2 ELECTRONIC TRANSMISSION SHIFT CONTROLS

TRANSMISSION CONTROL MODULE. Many features of an electronic transmission, such as shift timing and quality, torque converter clutch apply timing, and quality, are software driven. A vehicle manufacturer can use the same transmission and adjust the operating characteristics with the software for variations of particular vehicles. Some control modules allow calibration values to be reprogrammed by technicians in the field.

The TCM receives data from the sensors and other control modules, and when these signals match the program stored in the TCM's memory, the TCM sends a signal to one or more actuators. The TCM can be programmed to incorporate several

FIGURE 8–31 Moving the shift lever to the M (manual) position (a) activates the up/down, +/− switches that will cause an upshift or downshift.

different operating strategies that are stored in the memory, including the following:

- **Random access memory (RAM).** This is temporary memory that is cleared every time the vehicle is turned off.

- **Read-only memory (ROM).** The TCM/processor can read from ROM but cannot save any information to ROM.

- **Programmable read-only memory (PROM).** This is similar to a ROM but is programmed for a specific vehicle.

- **Electronically erasable programmable read-only memory (EEPROM).** This is similar to PROM but can be erased and reprogrammed. This is often called *reflashing*.

- **Keep alive memory (KAM).** ROM that is always connected to power so it retains memory. This can store information such as transmission adaptive strategies and radio station presets; such data will be lost if a battery becomes discharged or is disconnected.

SERIAL DATA. An advantage of electronic controls is that digital control modules can communicate with each other using *serial data streams*. The TCM can share information with other control modules such as the ECM and BCM. The data stream is a series of low-voltage, on-off electrical signals. The length of the on- and off-time becomes the message.

Multiplexing allows one sensor or wire to work for more than one circuit; in older vehicles, every circuit uses a separate wire or electronic device. Multiplexing uses a pair of wires to complete multiple circuits, which greatly reduces the number of wires in a vehicle. Multiplex circuits include the serial data stream between two control modules, for example, the PCM and the BCM. The two modules share the same sensors, and

the output of one often affects the output of the other. ● **SEE FIGURE 8–32.** For example, a transmission upshift or downshift will change the speed of the engine, and the power from the engine definitely affects the quality of the shift.

Multiplexing is also called a *bus information system*, and besides reducing the amount of wire and connections, it also eliminates some switching hardware, reduces current flow through the sensors, and improves diagnostics. A microprocessor is required in each control module and bus + and bus − wires connect the control modules. The bus + and bus − wires are twisted together to prevent stray electromagnetic signals from altering signal transmission. These wires are often called a *twisted pair*.

Probably the biggest impact of multiplexing on the transmission technician is that seemingly unrelated problems can affect the operation of the transmission. If the multiplex system does not operate properly, strange faults can occur. A technician has to be more aware than ever of all the branches of the circuit.

The TCM processes the input signals from the sensors and serial data from the network with other control modules.

NETWORKS. Networks connect control modules so they can share data at speeds up to 1 million bits per second (bps). Networks reduce the number of sensors, connectors, and wire. The most common are as follows:

- **Local area network (LAN)** is used to connect computers in a limited area. LAN can be interconnected using different configurations (e.g., ring or star connections).

- **Controller area network (CAN)** is required for all OBD-II vehicles since 2008.

CONTROLLER AREA NETWORK. CAN is a system that determines how the various control modules communicate with each

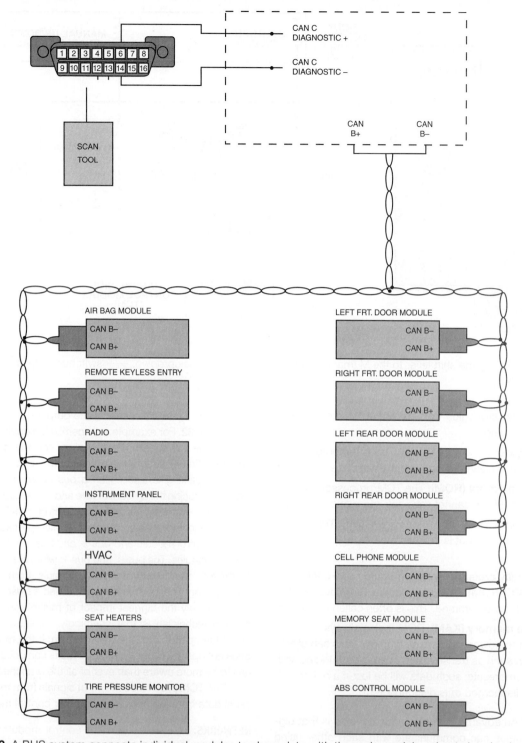

FIGURE 8–32 A BUS system connects individual modules to share data with the main module using twisted pairs of wires.

other, share sensor information, and determine which ECMs have operating priority. ● **SEE FIGURE 8–33**. CAN was used on a few 2003 vehicles, and all new vehicles sold in the United States since the 2008 model year use CAN. CAN is a very-high-speed system, much faster than earlier multiplex systems. CAN also is better at operating the critical safety systems such as ABS, electronic steering control, and stability and traction control systems.

The biggest impact on automatic transmission service is the need for upgraded or enhanced scan tools or cartridges that will allow current scan tools to communicate with the system. The best practice is to always use the correct tool for the job.

TCM FUNCTIONS. The primary task of the processor in the TCM is to control the actuators, and it uses transistors to turn them on and off. The TCM can operate relays for the relatively high

FIGURE 8–33 The CAN bus connects the most critical control modules using a twisted pair of wires that has a 120-Ω resistor at each end. The TCM can be a separate module or integrated into the PCM as shown.

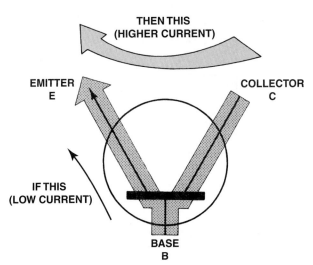

FIGURE 8–34 A large current flow from the collector to the emitter of this transistor is controlled by a small current flow from the base to the emitter.

current requirements of motors and some solenoids. When the processor turns a transistor on, the circuit for an actuator is completed, and the actuator will operate. ● **SEE FIGURE 8–34**.

The TCM can be programmed to incorporate the following operation strategies.

- **Adaptive learning/shifts.** The TCM maintains a consistent shift feel by adjusting fluid pressure and/or solenoid duty cycle to compensate for internal wear. A closed loop from a pressure sensor in the clutch circuit lets the TCM know when the clutch is applied, and the TCM adjusts solenoid so the clutch apply occurs in the proper time span. ● **SEE FIGURE 8–35**.

- **Driver shift request.** If the driver has selected manual gears, then the TCM notes the requested gear and if an upshift or downshift is requested.

- **Closed-loop pressure control.** The TCM can modify apply pressure by adapting solenoid current to signals from the pressure sensor.

- **Reverse/drive lockout.** If the TCM detects a manual shift request while in the opposite direction, then it can block the shift and go into neutral to prevent transmission damage.

- **Rocking.** If the TCM detects repeated shifts between drive and reverse, then it can adjust the current to the EPC solenoid, raising the line pressure to reduce slippage and prevent transmission damage.

FIGURE 8–35 The second pressure/bottom sensor provides feedback to the TCM's solenoid driver circuit concerning the pressure increase in the clutch hydraulic circuit.

FIGURE 8–36 Power supply for the electrical circuits of a modern vehicle begins at the power distribution center. It usually includes major relays and the fuses. (*Courtesy of Chrysler Corporation*)

- **Failure mode.** If the TCM detects a sensor signal that is significantly out-of-value, then it can ignore that signal and default to a programmed strategy. It will illuminate the MIL. The vehicle will operate, and the driver should be aware that service is required.
- **Limp-home mode.** If the TCM detects a condition that can cause transmission damage, then it will illuminate the MIL and shut off solenoid operation. In this case, the transmission will operate in only one forward gear with high line pressure. The driver should be aware that service is required.

The electrical circuit for the TCM is fairly complex. It must be connected to the power source, B+, and a good ground, B−. The power feed is usually a relay controlled by the ignition switch and a fuse for protection. ● **SEE FIGURE 8–36**. The TCM can switch on B+ power to a solenoid that is grounded at the transmission, called *hot-side switching* or *feed control*. ● **SEE FIGURE 8–37**. With some designs, the solenoids receive B+ through a power relay. The TCM switches on the ground path to activate the solenoid, called *ground-side switching* or **ground control**. Actuators with small current flows such as the MIL, a light-emitting diode (LED), or a digital display operate directly from the control module. ● **SEE FIGURE 8–38**.

FIGURE 8–37 Solenoid control occurs when the ECM completes the circuit to ground (top) or switches on B+ (bottom). The ground connection is also B−.

Many control modules are programmed to run a test sequence at engine start-up. If out-of-range electrical values are found, the TCM will indicate a failure by turning on the MIL. The system is also monitored during operation, and if a failure should occur, the TCM will revert to *default* or *limp-in mode*. In limp-in mode, the operation of most transmissions will be limited to one gear, often third gear, to protect the transmission. The limp-in gear is usually the one with no solenoids activated. There will be no upshifts or downshifts, but the driver will not be stranded. At the same time, the TCM will set a *diagnostic trouble code (DTC)*.

FIGURE 8–38 This electrical schematic shows the various inputs and outputs of the transmission control module for a 42LE transaxle. (*Courtesy of Chrysler Corporation*)

A technician can read the DTC by following the proper procedure. A scan tool can be used to pull/read codes from the TCM. Service information is used to identify the code(s), the problem circuit, and what tests are needed to determine the exact cause of the failure. ● **SEE FIGURE 8–39**. Scan tools and DTCs are described more completely in Section 13.3.5.

Wire connections at the sensors and control module must be clean and tight to prevent any change in voltage. A small amount of corrosion can produce enough resistance to cause a significant change in low-voltage, low-current circuits. The connection is made when a round or square male pin/terminal enters a female terminal, and the connectors usually have multiple cavities for the wire terminals. These cavities determine the "way" number for the connector; a four-way connector will make four connections. The cavities are often identified by a number or letter to help identify a particular wire or terminal. Quite often, all of the connection's cavities will not be used. Most vehicles use mechanical-locking, weathertight connectors. They may also use waterproof conductive compound (dielectric silicon) on these connections. ● **SEE FIGURE 8–40**. A multiterminal connector connects the external wiring harness to the transmission's internal harness. The internal harness is connected to each of the electrical components inside the transmission. ● **SEE FIGURE 8–41**.

The TCM, like other automotive computers, is somewhat fragile and relatively expensive. It is normally mounted in a relatively clean and cool location where it is protected from possible damage. A fairly standard location is in the passenger compartment, under the instrument panel or the center console.

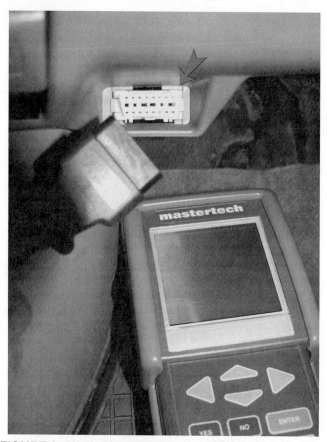

FIGURE 8–39 The scan tool is being plugged into the diagnostic connector (arrow) under the instrument panel. It can read any DTCs and sensor outputs, and operate the solenoids inside the transmission.

(a)

Pressure Switch

Latching Tab

Electrical Connector

(b)

Switch

Seal

Connector

FIGURE 8–40 (a) A weathertight connector is used at this pressure switch. (b) Opening the latch allows the connector to be removed.

FIGURE 8–41 One of the solenoids is wired directly to this internal electrical harness. Note the case connecter near the bottom.

FIGURE 8–42 (a) This control solenoid assembly contains four transmission fluid pressure (TFP) switches, a line pressure control (PC) solenoid, four pressure control (PC) solenoids, two shift solenoids (SS), a torque converter clutch (TCC) solenoid, a transmission fluid temperature (TFT) sensor, and the transmission control module (TCM). It also has a vehicle harness connector and connectors to the shift position switch and the input and output speed sensors. (b) A simplified view is also shown.

TRANSMISSION-BASED CONTROL MODULE. Many vehicles using CAN electronics integrate the TCM into the transmission. ● **SEE FIGURE 8–42.** This is called *control solenoid valve assembly, mechatronic,* and *solenoid body.* The assembly greatly reduces the number of wires entering the transmission because of the following:

- Input and output shaft speed sensors
- Transmission range sensor
- Fluid pressure sensors
- Fluid temperature sensor
- Shift and pressure control solenoids are connected directly to the TCM

The wire connections to the rest of the vehicle include:

- Hi and Lo CAN bringing data to and from the ECM, BCM, and PCM
- Ignition on
- Diagnostic connection
- Ground

The TCM in some transmissions is about the same size as a common credit card. A concern with an internal TCM is the possibility of overheating the electronic components. One design has a thermocouple temperature sensor(s) mounted in the TCM circuit board, and if the temperature rises above 288°F (142°C), it will go into failure mode/default. The TCM normally keeps relatively cool by contact with the transmission case, and a spring bracket is used to ensure tight contact.

OBD-II. On-Board Diagnostics, Second Generation, commonly called **OBD-II,** is a set of standards required for all 1996 and newer vehicles. OBD standards were first established in 1988 by the California Air Resources Board (CARB) and the Society of Automotive Engineers (SAE) for vehicle control systems. The purpose is to simplify and standardize vehicle diagnosis. These standards are designed to improve diagnosis and repair of malfunctioning vehicles in order to reduce vehicle emissions. Improper transmission operation can increase emissions. OBD-II standards require the following commonalities between vehicle manufacturers.

- Terms and definitions (SAE J1930)
- Diagnostic trouble codes and definitions (SAE J2012)
- Diagnostic connector and connector location (SAE J1962)
- Diagnostic scan tool (SAE J1978)
- Diagnostic test modes (SAE J1979 and 2190)
- Procedure for technicians to obtain service information (SAE J2008)

- SAE-recommended serial data communication system (SAE J1850)
- International serial data communication system (ISO 9141)

A technician reads the DTC of an OBD-II vehicle by connecting a scan tool to the *diagnostic connector* and requesting the DTCs. The diagnostic connector is mounted in the instrument panel within reach of the driver. It should be visible when kneeling next to an open driver's door. This process is described in Chapter 13. A listing of the OBD-II powertrain DTCs is given in Appendix C.

8.3.3 ACTUATORS
Actuators are the outputs for an electronically controlled system. They do the mechanical work for the TCM. The various types of outputs are diagnostics (MIL and DTCs), display and indicator lights, motors, relays, serial data (sent to another control module), and solenoids. The TCM controls the transmission actuators, usually solenoids. Modern electronic transmissions use a solenoid to control fluid flow for torque converter lockup, shift solenoids to control shifts, and electronic pressure control (EPC) solenoids to control fluid pressure.

SHIFT SOLENOIDS. Shift solenoids open or close an oil passage(s) so fluid pressure will be trapped drain and escape, or pass through to apply a clutch or servo. A solenoid is a coil of wire that becomes an electromagnet when current flows through it. It loses its magnetism when the current flow is shut off. An iron plunger, also called an *armature* or *core*, is located inside the coil and is spring loaded to one position. When the solenoid is energized/on, the plunger moves to the other position. ● **SEE FIGURE 8–43.** Plunger movement opens or closes a hydraulic valve.

Many solenoids have two positions, either on or off, and they are sometimes called *on/off solenoids*. The solenoid can be normally closed, opened by current flow, or normally open. Some solenoids are pulsed on and off, and this is called *duty cycle* or *pulse width modulation (PWM)* (see Figure 8–51). A 100% duty cycle means the current is on all of the time. A duty cycle of 50% means the current is on for 50% of the time and off for 50% of the time. With a 50% duty cycle, the flow through the solenoid will be about one-half of when it is completely on. Other solenoids are a current-controlled, linear type. In this case, one solenoid is closed with 0.1 amp or less and fully open with 1 amp.

Some shift solenoids are also pulsed to obtain more precise shift quality. The basic operation of an electronic-shifted transmission is the same as that of a hydraulically controlled transmission. The major difference is that the shift valves are balanced between hydraulic pressure from the governor and throttle valve in a standard unit, and in an electronic-shifted unit, the shifts are controlled by the TCM operating the shift solenoids.

Other actuators include:

- DC motors, turned to provide fluid pressure with the engine off (some hybrid vehicles)
- Relays, used to control a relatively high-current circuit needed to power a solenoid
- Lights, such as the malfunction indicator light (MIL), to alert the driver of a transmission problem

Solenoids can be mounted so they open or close a passage that is fed through a small orifice from line or drive pressure. When the solenoid is off, fluid pressure drains from the passage, and when the solenoid is on, pressure builds. ● **SEE FIGURE 8–44.** The orifice prevents a large pressure loss from the main circuits when the solenoid is open. The pressure controlled by the solenoid acts on one or more shift valve(s) while a spring acts on the other end. Shift valve position can be easily controlled with this arrangement.

SHIFT SOLENOID OPERATION. In some transmissions, the shift solenoid is usually turned completely on or off. Some might cycle a few times during a shift to prevent a too-rapid clutch apply with a harsh shift. The example shown in ● **FIGURE 8–45** shows an electronically controlled shift circuit. In first gear, (1) it uses a normally closed solenoid valve that is on, while (2) the normally closed solenoid is off. This produces a pressure at the end of the 1–2 shift valve that compresses the spring and keeps the valve downshifted. This combination also allows the springs to hold the 2–3 and the 3–4 shift valves downshifted.

The 1–2, 2–3, and 3–4 shifts in this transmission occur as follows:

- **1–2 shift.** Activate solenoid 2 to drain shift pressure; the spring moves the 1–2 shift valve to upshift.
- **2–3 shift.** Turn solenoid 1 off. The shift pressure moves the 2–3 shift valve to upshift.
- **3–4 shift.** Turn solenoid 2 off. The shift pressure moves the 3–4 shift valve to upshift.

A summary of the relationship of the transmission gear range and the solenoids for this transmission is as follows:

TCM Commanded Gear	Solenoid 1	Solenoid 2
First	On	Off
Second	On	On
Third	Off	On
Fourth	Off	Off (limp-in gear)

Downshifts occur in exactly the reverse manner as upshifts. For example, a 4–3 kickdown occurs from fourth gear if solenoid 2 is turned on.

- **4–3 shift.** Turn solenoid 2 on. The 3–4 shift valve spring moves the valve to downshift.
- **3–2 shift.** Turn solenoid 1 on. The 2–3 shift valve spring moves the valve to downshift.
- **2–1 shift.** Turn solenoid 2 off. Fluid pressure moves the 1–2 shift valve to downshift.

Note that some transmissions will make a second- or third-gear start if a solenoid fails. The Toyota transmission shown in Figure 8–45 will make a third-gear start because the TCM has a fail-safe program that turns on solenoid 2 if solenoid 1 fails. If both solenoids or the power supply fails, this unit will start out in fourth gear.

The Chrysler 41TE transaxle does not use shift valves. The relatively simple valve body contains only a pressure regulator

FIGURE 8–43 (a) The normally closed solenoid blocks fluid flow when it is off while opening the exhaust; and when it is on, it opens the valve. (b) The normally open solenoid allows fluid flow when it is off; and when it is on, it closes the valve while opening the exhaust.

FIGURE 8–44 The No. 1 solenoid is on. Fluid pressure is exhausted at the drain, and the 2–3 shift valve is upshifted. The No. 2 solenoid is off, so fluid pressure has the 1–2 shift valve in downshift position. (*Courtesy of Toyota Motor Sales USA, Inc.*)

valve, manual valve, solenoid switch valve, lockup (TCC) switch valve, and the torque converter (T/C) control valve. ● **SEE FIGURE 8–46**. The gear ranges are controlled by the manual valve and the operation of four solenoids. Each of the four solenoids operates a check ball, and two solenoids also operate a vent valve. The low-reverse/lockup and the overdrive solenoids are *normally vented*. When they are not energized, the check ball is allowed to operate in a normal manner, and the vent is opened. Opening the vent allows residual pressure to bleed from the circuit. When they are energized, the check ball is held open, off its seat, and the vent is closed.

The GM 4T65-E is another four-speed transmission that uses two shift solenoids. ● **SEE FIGURE 8–47**. It uses two rather complex valves, the 2–3 shift valve/3–2 manual downshift valve and 3–4 shift valve/4–3 manual downshift valve, that are moved by both solenoids. ● **SEE FIGURE 8–48**. These two valves are moved to apply or release the four clutches.

FIGURE 8–45 The hydraulic diagram of a Toyota A240E transaxle in second gear. Both the No. 1 and No. 2 solenoids are turned on.

FIGURE 8–46 The hydraulic diagram of a 41TE transaxle in first gear. The shift to second occurs when the 2–4/LR solenoid is turned on to allow pressure to flow to the 2–4 clutch. (*Courtesy of Chrysler Corporation*)

Gear	1-2, 3-4 SS	2-3 SS	Input Clutch	2nd Clutch	3rd Clutch	4th Clutch
D1	ON	ON	Applied			
D2	OFF	ON	Applied*	Applied		
D3	OFF	OFF		Applied		
D4	ON	OFF		Applied	Applied	
					Applied*	Applied

Note: SS = Shift Solenoid
* = Applied but ineffective, Sprag clutch is overrunning
Forward band is applied in all drive ranges

FIGURE 8–47 The solenoid and clutch schedule for a 4T65-E transmission.

The Ford 6F50 and GM 6T70 are six-speed transmissions that use two shift solenoids and four pressure control solenoids. ● **SEE FIGURE 8–49.**

PRESSURE CONTROL SOLENOIDS. Some transmissions control line pressure using an *electronic pressure control (EPC)* solenoid. ● **SEE FIGURE 8–50.** It is also called a force motor, also called a *linear solenoid.* The pressure is controlled by the amount of current sent to the solenoid and how far the solenoid moves. ● **SEE FIGURE 8–51.**

Some EPC solenoids use pulse-width modulation; the current is pulsed on and off so solenoid is constantly stroking when it goes into operation. This is called *duty cycle.* A longer duty cycle produces lower line pressure in most systems because the open solenoid releases line pressure. A longer duty cycle (e.g., 75%) means the system is draining 75% of the time and holding pressure 25% of the time.

Transmissions with **strategy-based** pressure control adjust line pressure to control shift duration. Adaptive strategy uses previous shift times, vehicle load, and throttle position to

FIGURE 8–48 The 1–2, 3–4, and 2–3 shift solenoids of the 4T65-E control the positions of the 1–2, 2–3/3–2 MDS, and 3–4/4–3 MDS shift valves.

Gear	SS 1	SS 2	PC 2	PC 3	PC 4	PC 5
D1	OFF	ON				ON
D2	OFF	ON			ON	ON
D3	OFF	ON	ON			ON
D4	OFF	ON		ON		ON
D5	OFF	ON	ON	ON		
D6	OFF	ON		ON	ON	

Note: SS 1 is ON in P, R, N, and M1
SS 2 is OFF in R

FIGURE 8–49 The solenoid schedule for a 6T70 transmission.

FIGURE 8–50 The signal from the TCM can cause the EPC solenoid to change the pressure regulator valve to adjust line pressure.

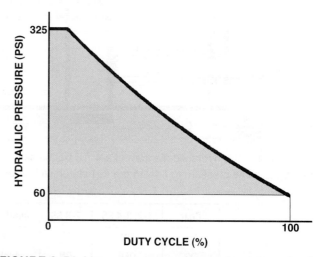

FIGURE 8–51 Line pressure increases as the duty cycle of the EPC solenoid decreases.

determine proper pressure. The TCM adjusts fluid pressure to keep future shifts within the same parameters as a new vehicle. Other transmissions use *torque-based* or *pressure-based* control of line pressure. A line pressure sensor is used to measure the actual line pressure during a shift, and the TCM keeps line pressure at a preset level (100 to 120 PSI) during shifts.

A serious potential problem is created when an electromagnet (solenoid) is mounted inside a transmission. The magnetism will attract fine metal particles worn from the moving parts, and this contamination can cause a sticking solenoid or a leaking valve. If this solenoid valve has problems, it can cause line pressure that is too low, with possible clutch and/or band slippage, or too high, causing harsh shifts. Some transmissions have a TCM strategy that pulses the solenoid completely open at regular intervals. The resulting full fluid flow should flush out any debris.

TCC SOLENOID. The TCC solenoid in most transmissions performs like a shift solenoid—it is either on or off. Some transmissions vary the TCC apply signal to gradually increase or *ramp* the apply and release pressures. Ramping produces a smoother operation and is done by using pulse-width modulation.

Problem solving and diagnosis are described more completely in Chapter 13.

8.3.4 CVT ELECTRONIC CONTROLS
The TCM of a CVT uses direct and indirect inputs to monitor transmission and engine operation. ● **SEE FIGURE 8–52.**

Direct inputs are as follows:

- **Transmission range sensor (TRS)**—a multicontact switch operated by the manual shift lever
- **Input speed sensor (ISS)**—a Hall-effect sensor
- **Output speed sensor (OSS)**—a Hall-effect sensor
- **Primary pressure sensor**—a pressure transducer to monitor primary pulley pressure
- **Secondary pressure sensor**—a pressure transducer to monitor secondary pulley pressure
- **Transmission temperature sensor (TTS)**—a NTC thermistor

Indirect inputs (from CAN bus) are as follows:

- PCM requests
- Engine output torque
- Brake switch
- ABS status signals

PROBLEM SOLVING 8–2

Imagine that you are working in a shop that specializes in transmission repair, and these problems are brought to you.

Case 1:

A 1997 Dodge van drops back into second gear when it gets hot and will not upshift or downshift in drive. The transmission MIL begins blinking at this time. Reverse feels good. Is this a mechanical, hydraulic, or electrical problem? Where would you start looking for the cause?

Case 2:

A 1987 Camry was driving down the freeway and the transmission downshifted unexpectedly; at the same time, the speedometer stopped operating. What could have caused this? Where would you start looking for the cause?

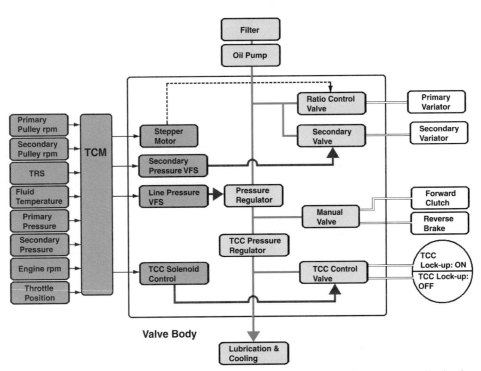

FIGURE 8–52 This block diagram shows the relationship between the TCM, electrical actuators, valve body, and hydraulic actuators for a CVT transmission.

- Charging system voltage
- Engine RPM
- Engine coolant temperature
- Accelerator pedal position
- Vehicle speed
- A/C system requests

TCM outputs include:

- Stepper motor to control ratio control valve
- Line pressure solenoid
- Secondary pressure solenoid
- TCC lockup solenoid

The TCM controls the drive ratio to match vehicle needs. It can adjust the ratio during vehicle cruise to produce the maximum fuel economy, best emissions, or maximum pulling power. It continuously monitors ISS and OSS signals to ensure that the speeds match the desired ratio.

The stepper motor, also called a ratio control motor, is a linear position motor that changes the position of the upper end of the pulley ratio link. ● **SEE FIGURE 8–53**. The lower end of this link moves with the floating side of the primary/ drive pulley; the ratio control valve is connected to the center of this link. Movement of the stepper motor or the floating

FIGURE 8–53 (a) The stepper motor and pulley ratio link with the CVT in low ratio. (b) The stepper motor has extended, moving the ratio link and ratio control valve; this should cause the primary pulley to become narrower to produce a higher ratio.

sheave will move the ratio control valve to produce a ratio change.

The TCM also controls fluid pressure to the secondary/ driven pulley and torque converter as well as TCC lockup. Some vehicles use predetermined stepper motor position to mimic upshifts and downshifts.

SUMMARY

1. Electronic controls are used for more accurate automatic operation of the transmission.

2. A basic understanding of electricity and electronic devices is essential to understanding and repairing electronically controlled transmissions.

3. Electronic controls use sensors to monitor various operational inputs that will be used to control the operation of the transmission.

4. The hydraulic operation of the transmission is controlled by solenoids that are switched to redirect pressurized fluid to move shift valves or change the operational pressures.

5. The TCM receives the signals from the sensors and operates the solenoids to produce upshifts and downshifts at the proper speed.

6. CVT transmissions use similar logic for transmission control as conventional electronic transmissions.

REVIEW QUESTIONS

1. Electronic control of the automatic transmission provides for accurate control of shift _____ and _____.

2. Electronic transmissions replace the governor with a _____ _____ _____ and the throttle valve with a _____ _____ _____.

3. Match the electrical terms with the appropriate definition

   a. Ohms   _____ controls flow

   b. Amp   _____ changes direction

   c. Volts   _____ plastic

   d. Battery   _____ flows in one direction

   e. Watt   _____ connected in a string

   f. Series   _____ conductor

   g. Parallel   _____ power source

   h. Ground
   circuit   _____ separate branches

   i. Direct
   current   _____ resistance

   j. Alternating
   current   _____ current flow

   k. Switch   _____ electrical work

   l. Copper   _____ pressure

   m. Insulator   _____ frame

4. A complete electrical circuit has a _____ source, circuit _____, _____, conductors, and an electrical _____.

5. Three types of electrical protection devices are _____, _____, and _____.

6. When the circuit is _____, current will stop flowing.

7. A _____ controls a switch by electromagnetism.

8. A _____ controls fluid flow by electromagnetism.

9. The three major parts that an electronic control system can be divided into are _____, _____, and _____.

10. Identify the six inputs that an electronically controlled transmission might use for each of the following:
    a. Vehicle _____
    b. Input shaft _____
    c. Engine coolant _____
    d. Engine _____
    e. Driver _____
    f. Transmission _____ temperature

11. A thermistor is a _____ resistor that changes resistance relative to _____.

12. Identify each of the following abbreviations.
    a. BOO
    b. PRNDL
    c. ECT
    d. MAP
    e. MAF
    f. MLP

g. PNP
h. TOT
i. TSS
j. TPS
k. VSS
l. TCC
m. ECM
n. PCM

13. Good ground connections are essential for proper operation of _____ circuits.

14. A diagnostic _____ code (DTC) will set if an electrical problem is identified by the electronic control unit (ECU). DTCs can be read with a _____ tool.

15. Six actuators that are computer controlled are _____, _____, _____, _____, serial data, and _____.

16. Shift solenoids are controlled by the ECU to control the fluid pressure in the _____ valve circuits.

17. If both shift solenoids on a typical Toyota transmission are inoperative, what gear will the transmission be in?

18. If the shift solenoids fail in a Chrysler 41TE transmission, what gear will the transmission be in?

19. EPC solenoids use _____ _____ to cycle a circuit on and off.

20. Ramping a torque converter clutch (TCC) solenoid produces a _____ lockup clutch apply.

CHAPTER QUIZ

1. Student A says that it is important to have an understanding of electricity to understand an electronic automatic transmission. Student B says that in most electronically controlled transmissions, the shift valves are controlled by solenoids. Who is correct?
   a. Student A
   b. Student B
   c. Both Students A and B
   d. Neither Student A nor B

2. Electrical pressure is measured in _____.
   a. Amperes
   b. Ohms
   c. Volts
   d. Watts

3. The current flowing through a circuit is measured in _____.
   a. Amperes
   b. Ohms
   c. Volts
   d. Watts

4. The resistance to electrical flow through a component is measured in _____.
   a. Amperes
   b. Ohms
   c. Volts
   d. Watts

5. The controlling unit for an electronically shifted transmission is the _____.
   a. Vehicle speed sensor
   b. TCM
   c. Throttle position sensor
   d. None of these

6. A _____ is an electromagnetic device that can be used to control fluid pressure in a hydraulic circuit.
   a. Neutral start switch
   b. TCM
   c. Solenoid
   d. Vehicle speed sensor

7. A normally vented solenoid _____ allow fluid to flow to the sump when it is not energized.
   a. Will
   b. Will, but at a reduced flow,
   c. Will not
   d. Any of these

8. Student A says that a transmission with electronic shift controls senses engine load using a throttle position sensor in place of a throttle valve. Student B says that a vehicle speed sensor is used in place of a governor. Who is correct?
   a. Student A
   b. Student B
   c. Both Students A and B
   d. Neither Student A nor B

9. If the solenoids fail in a transmission with electronic shift controls, the transmission will _____.
   a. Be ruined if the car is driven
   b. Not have any forward gears
   c. Operate in reverse only
   d. Operate in only one forward gear and reverse

10. Student A says that the neutral start switch in a transmission with electronic shift controls is the same as the ones in all other transmissions. Student B says that the neutral start switch in a transmission with electronic shift controls is operated by the manual shift linkage. Who is correct?
    a. Student A
    b. Student B
    c. Both Students A and B
    d. Neither Student A nor B

11. Student A says that if a transmission uses a comfort power switch, the switch will raise the shift points when it is in the power position. Student B says that if a transmission uses a comfort power switch, it will produce firmer shifts when it is in the comfort position. Who is correct?
    a. Student A
    b. Student B
    c. Both Students A and B
    d. Neither Student A nor B

12. The TCC should not apply if (A) brakes are applied and/or (B) the engine coolant sensor senses a cold engine.

    Which is correct?
    a. A
    b. B
    c. Both A and B
    d. Neither A nor B

13. An electrical circuit must have which of the following to operate?
    a. Power source, conductors, load
    b. Circuit protection, conductor, load
    c. Power source, switch, load
    d. Conductor, load, ground

14. Student A says that diagnostic trouble codes can be read from a light on the dash. Student B says that the diagnostic trouble codes will help to pinpoint the problem. Who is correct?
    a. Student A
    b. Student B
    c. Both Students A and B
    d. Neither Student A nor B

15. The vehicle speed sensor is driven by the _____.
    a. Front wheel
    b. Speedometer
    c. Transmission output shaft
    d. Drive shaft

16. The throttle position sensor is located on the _____.
    a. Throttle cable
    b. Throttle body
    c. Gas pedal
    d. Transmission case

17. The throttle position sensor is typically a _____.
    a. Thermistor
    b. Rheostat
    c. Potentiometer
    d. Switch

18. A pulse-width modulated solenoid can be used to _____.
    a. Modulate the engine pulses
    b. Smooth the application of the clutches
    c. Signal the computer of a problem
    d. Give the technician information about a problem

19. If a conductor has a very large amount of resistance, it is _____.
    a. Shorted
    b. Open
    c. Closed
    d. Grounded

20. A _____ is used to prevent high-voltage spikes from a collapsing electromagnetic field.
    a. Transistor
    b. Relay
    c. Diode
    d. Potentiometer

chapter 9

TORQUE CONVERTERS

OBJECTIVES: **After studying Chapter 9, the reader will be able to:** • Identify the components of a torque converter. • Explain the purpose for each torque converter component. • Describe the fluid flow inside a torque converter. • Explain the operation of a torque converter clutch.

KEY TERMS: Converter clutch 213 • Coupling 216 • Coupling phase 218 • Damper assembly 219 • Flexplate 214 • Fluid coupling 213 • Hydrodynamic 215 • Impeller 213 • Rotary flow 216 • Stall 216 • Stall speed 220 • Stator 213 • Torque converter clutch (TCC) 216 • Torsional vibrations 219 • Turbine 213 • Viscous converter clutch 220 • Vortex flow 216

9.1 INTRODUCTION

The torque converter, commonly called a *converter*, is a type of **fluid coupling** that transmits power from the engine's crankshaft to the transmission input (turbine) shaft. ● **SEE FIGURE 9–1.** It has two important purposes as it transfers the engine torque to the transmission.

1. It serves as an automatic clutch so the vehicle can be stopped with the engine running and the transmission in gear.

2. It multiplies torque while the vehicle is accelerating to improve acceleration and pulling power.

A driver uses the throttle to control the converter's output. At idle, there is not enough power transfer through the torque converter to move the vehicle. This is especially true if the brakes are applied. Opening the throttle increases engine speed and causes the converter to begin transferring power. At this time the converter begins multiplying engine torque to move the vehicle. Since the power transfer is through fluid, it will be very smooth and free from the severe shocks sometimes found with standard transmissions and clutches. Note that the fluid coupling shown in ● **FIGURE 9–2** has only two internal parts, a turbine and an impeller.

9.1.1 WET CLUTCH, NO CONVERTER ZF has developed a multiplate wet clutch assembly to replace the torque converter. It is used with transmissions in some European vehicles. ● **SEE FIGURE 9–3.** The clutch assembly contains six single-sided friction plates with an elaborate torsional vibration dampening system. This assembly is contained in a housing

FIGURE 9–1 The torque converter is mounted on the engine's crankshaft and transfers power to the transmission.

filled with fluid to cool the plates. It has a smaller diameter than the normal converter, which reduces inertia and provides quicker vehicle acceleration.

9.2 CONSTRUCTION

Most torque converters have four major elements: an **impeller, turbine, stator,** and **converter clutch.** ● **SEE FIGURE 9–4.** Before the late 1970s, most torque converters had three elements. ● **SEE FIGURE 9–5.** Three-element converters did not

FIGURE 9–2 A fluid coupling transfers power through fluid, from one set of vanes to the other.

FIGURE 9–3 This clutch assembly replaces the converter, and the clutch is applied at the proper rate for smooth vehicle starts. Note the large damper springs to remove engine pulsations. (*Courtesy of ZF Friedrichshafen AG*)

FIGURE 9–4 The major parts of a four-element torque converter are the clutch disc, turbine, stator, and impeller shown in this cutaway view. The turbine is splined to the transmission input shaft, and the stator is splined to the stationary reaction shaft at the front of the transmission. (*Courtesy of Chrysler Corporation*)

FIGURE 9–5 A three-element torque converter has a turbine, stator, and pump or impeller. (*Courtesy of Chrysler Corporation*)

have a lockup clutch. The torque converter clutch (TCC) was added to increase fuel economy. Each of the members in a three-element torque converter has a set of vanes that serve to control the fluid flow.

Some sources call the impeller a pump. To prevent confusion with the transmission's pump, the term *impeller* will be used.

The impeller is a converter's input. The vanes/fins are attached to the rear of the impeller, transmission end, of the converter housing or cover. ● **SEE FIGURE 9–6**. This assembly is bolted to the **flexplate,** which connects to the crankshaft. The flexplate and converter replace the flywheel used with standard transmissions. When the engine is running, the flexplate and converter rotate with the crankshaft. ● **SEE FIGURE 9–7**. The flexplate is flexible enough to allow the front of the converter to move forward or backward if the converter expands or contracts slightly from heat or pressure. The pilot of the converter slides into the end of the crankshaft and centers the converter to the crankshaft.

FIGURE 9–6 This cutaway view of a four-element torque converter shows the relationship of the internal parts.

FIGURE 9–7 The flexplate connects the converter to the crankshaft. The pilot of the converter fits the end of the crankshaft to center the converter to the crankshaft. (*Courtesy of Chrysler Corporation*)

The cross-sectional area of the impeller, turbine, and stator of most torque converters is round to give an efficient flow. The converter used with many newer transaxles has an elliptical cross-sectional shape that reduces the width of the converter. ● **SEE FIGURE 9–8**. A shorter, low-profile converter, often

FIGURE 9–8 Most torque converters have a round cross section (top). Some new transmissions use a shorter, elliptical, squashed converter (bottom) that is about 13% shorter than a round style.

called a *squashed* converter, makes the engine and transaxle shorter and easier to fit transversely in a vehicle.

The turbine is the converter's output member. The center hub of the turbine is splined to the transmission input shaft. The turbine is positioned in the front, engine end, of the converter housing so the turbine vanes face the impeller vanes.

The stator is the reaction member of the torque converter. The stator assembly is about one-half the diameter of the impeller or turbine. The outer edge of the stator vanes forms the inner edge of the three-piece fluid guide ring that is also part of the impeller and turbine vanes. The stator is mounted on a one-way clutch that is attached to the stationary reaction shaft splines. The reaction shaft extends from the front of the transmission, around the turbine shaft. The one-way clutch allows the stator to rotate clockwise but blocks counterclockwise rotation. ● **SEE FIGURE 9–9**.

9.3 OPERATION

A torque converter is a **hydrodynamic** unit. It transfers power through the dynamic motion of the fluid. Most other hydraulic units transfer power through the static pressure of the fluid.

FIGURE 9–9 The stator one-way clutch allows the stator to rotate freely during the coupling phase, but stops counterclockwise rotation during torque multiplication. (*Courtesy of Toyota Motor Sales USA, Inc.*)

What Does Four or Five Element Mean?

In the late 1940s and 1950s, some transmissions used four- and five-element torque converters. The fourth or fifth part or element was either a second turbine, stator, or impeller assembly. In a few cases, the five elements were three separate turbines along with one impeller and stator. The reason for the additional elements was to obtain a torque converter with a wider range, a lower reduction ratio, with the ability to smoothly change ratios inside the converter.

What Is an Air-Cooled Torque Converter?

Some early torque converters used with smaller engines were air cooled. They had a shroud with fins attached to the rear of the converter cover, to force cooling airflow past the converter.

Torque converters must be cooled because of the heat they generate during torque multiplication.

When the engine is running, the converter impeller acts as a centrifugal pump. Fluid is thrown from the outer edge of the impeller vanes, and because of the curved shape of the converter cover, the fluid is thrown forward into the turbine. The impeller is turning in a clockwise direction, and the fluid also rotates in a clockwise direction as it leaves the impeller vanes. ● SEE FIGURE 9–10. The mechanical power entering the converter is transformed in the fluid as fluid motion.

The torque converter operates at two very different conditions: **stall** and **coupling.** ● SEE FIGURE 9–11. Stall occurs

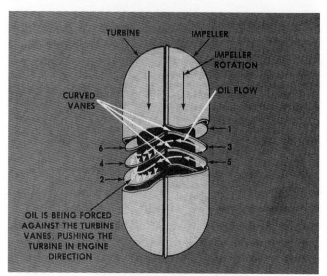

FIGURE 9–10 When the engine is running, fluid in the impeller is thrown outward and into the vanes of the turbine. (*Courtesy of Chrysler Corporation*)

Stall	Coupling
←——————————————→	
Torque Multiplication	1:1 Ratio
Vortex Flow	Rotary Flow
Vehicle Stopped	Constant Vehicle Speed

FIGURE 9–11 The two major operating conditions of a converter are stall and coupling. These conditions shift back and forth depending on throttle opening and vehicle load.

with the turbine stopped and the impeller turning at engine speed. Coupling normally occurs while the vehicle maintains a steady speed and the turbine and impeller are turning at the same speed. A gradual shift from stall to coupling occurs as vehicle speed increases. The **torque converter clutch (TCC)** applies during the coupling phase.

At stall, the rotating fluid from the impeller tries to turn the turbine in a clockwise direction. If the turbine is stationary or turning at a speed substantially slower than the impeller, only part of the energy leaves the fluid to drive the turbine. Most of the fluid energy is lost as the fluid bounces off the turbine vanes. The fluid moves toward the center of the turbine, driven there by the continuous flow of fluid from the impeller. As energy leaves the fluid, the flow slows down and returns to the center of the impeller vanes, where the impeller will pick it up and keep it circulating. This flow is called a **vortex flow.** The vortex flow is a continuous circulation of fluid outward from the impeller, around the guide ring, inward into the turbine, through the stator, and back to the impeller. ● SEE FIGURE 9–12. The guide ring directs the vortex flow, creating a smooth, turbulence-free flow. The clockwise flow of fluid leaving the impeller, in the direction of engine rotation, is called **rotary flow.**

When the impeller is rotating substantially faster than the turbine, the fluid tends to bounce off the turbine vanes and change the rotary flow to a counterclockwise direction. The fluid flow still has quite a bit of energy. It can be compared with

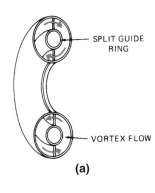

SPLIT GUIDE RING

VORTEX FLOW

(a)

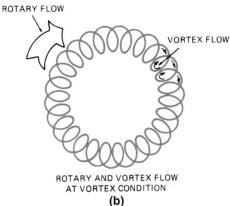

ROTARY FLOW

VORTEX FLOW

ROTARY AND VORTEX FLOW
AT VORTEX CONDITION

(b)

FIGURE 9–12 (a) The fluid flowing around the guide ring is called vortex flow. (b) The fluid flow around the converter is called rotary flow. (*Courtesy of Chrysler Corporation*)

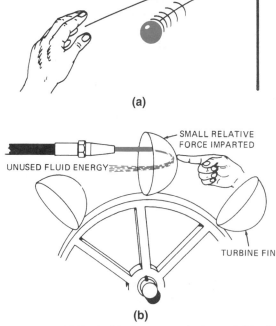

(a)

SMALL RELATIVE
FORCE IMPARTED

UNUSED FLUID ENERGY

TURBINE FIN

(b)

FIGURE 9–13 (a) If a ball is thrown against a wall, kinetic energy in the ball will cause it to bounce back. (b) The energy remaining in the fluid striking the turbine vanes will cause the fluid to bounce back in a similar manner.

a tennis ball thrown against a wall. The ball bounces back and travels in a different direction, but it still has most of its energy of motion. ● **SEE FIGURE 9–13.** A strong counterclockwise fluid flow from the turbine would tend to work against the clockwise rotation of the impeller.

9.3.1 TORQUE MULTIPLICATION

The stator redirects the fluid flow in the torque converter. It returns the fluid from the turbine back to the impeller in a clockwise direction. This action helps recover any energy remaining in the fluid. The curved shape of the stator vanes and a one-way clutch make this possible. Fluid leaving the turbine in a counterclockwise direction tries to turn the stator counterclockwise. This causes the stator one-way clutch to lock up and hold the stator stationary. The smooth, curved shape of the stator vanes redirects the fluid flow in a clockwise direction. ● **SEE FIGURE 9–14.** This fluid leaving the stator is picked up by the impeller. The leftover energy in the fluid produces the torque increase in a torque converter. The term *K-factor* is used by automotive engineers as they match torque converter design to the amount of torque of the engine. The K-factor is calculated by dividing the square root of engine torque by the torque converter stall speed. Another engineering term is *stall torque ratio (STR)*, which is the torque converter's ability to multiply torque. Most passenger car converters have a STR between 1.68:1 and 2.1:1.

A version of Newton's Law states that for every action, there is an equal and opposite reaction. The action is the flow

To Rear of
Pump Impeller

Curved
Vane

From Turbine
Runner

Path of Fluid
If There Was
No Stator

FIGURE 9–14 The fluid flow from the turbine is turned in the same direction as the impeller by the stator vanes.

of fluid pushing on the turbine vanes; the reaction is the fluid bouncing back. A converter cannot multiply torque without the reaction of the stator.

A way to view the stator operation is to imagine what would occur if the stator was not in the converter. The fluid flow leaving the turbine would be in a counterclockwise direction, opposite that of the impeller. This flow would fight, not help, the impeller rotation, and the opposing fluid flows would cause a power loss and slow the impeller. Torque multiplication occurs because the stator redirects the fluid flow. This occurs only when the impeller is rotating faster than the turbine. As the turbine speed increases, the direction of flow becomes more rotary. The stator clutch overruns and the converter becomes more of a coupling, transferring power from the engine to the transmission. ● **SEE FIGURE 9–15.**

Engine & Impeller Speed	1,800 rpm				
Turbine Speed	0	300	900	1,500	1,800
Vortex Flow	Very High	High	Low	None	None
Torque Multiplication	2.25:1	2:1	1.5:1	1:1	1:1
Efficiency	0%	40%	80%	90%	100%
	Torque Multiplication Phase			Coupling Phase	Lockup

FIGURE 9–15 The vortex flow, torque multiplication, and efficiency of a torque converter change as the turbine speed increases relative to the impeller.

9.3.2 COUPLING PHASE

The vehicle starts moving when the turbine begins rotating. As the vehicle speed increases, the turbine speed increases relative to the impeller. The fluid flow is redirected as the turbine speed increases.

The rotation of the turbine causes the fluid to leave the turbine in a clockwise direction. This moves the fluid force from the front to the back of the stator vanes. The stator is now pushed in a clockwise direction. Because of this action, the stator one-way clutch releases (overruns), and the stator is now free to move along with the impeller and turbine. The fluid flow from the turbine back to the impeller is now smooth and undisturbed.

When the turbine speed reaches 90% to 95% of impeller speed, *coupling* occurs. The **coupling phase** occurs when the speeds of the impeller and turbine are nearly equal. Centrifugal force acting on the fluid in the spinning turbine is great enough to stop the vortex flow. At this point, there is no torque multiplication. It should be noted that this coupling speed is a relative point between the speeds of the impeller and turbine. Therefore, the coupling phase occurs at various vehicle speeds depending on throttle position and speed.

Some slippage occurs during the coupling phase. If power and load demands require it, the converter can return to the torque multiplication phase. In a non-lockup converter, the turbine almost never turns at the same speed as the engine and impeller, a condition commonly referred to as converter slippage.

A torque converter is a relatively simple and inexpensive device for transferring power, but it is not a completely efficient device. In fact, at stall speeds it is totally inefficient; of the power that enters it, no power leaves to the transmission. At stall, all the power entering the converter is lost to the fluid as heat. The converter's efficiency steadily improves during torque multiplication and the coupling phases to about 90% to 95%.

9.4 TORQUE CONVERTER CLUTCHES

Since the late 1970s, most torque converters include an internal clutch called a torque converter clutch (TCC). The clutch is applied to eliminate the slippage during the coupling phase. Eliminating this slippage makes a significant improvement in fuel mileage. Most transmissions apply the clutch hydraulically,

FIGURE 9–16 The clutch disc of a TCC has lining on the outer edge where it can contact the inner side of the cover. While released, there is a fluid flow between the disc and the cover. Note that the clutch disc is splined to the turbine. (*Courtesy of Chrysler Corporation*)

but a few use centrifugal force. When the TCC applies, the converter locks up, connecting the transmission input shaft directly to the engine, much like a vehicle with a standard transmission and clutch.

The converter clutch is a large clutch disc called a *pressure plate* or *clutch disc*. It has friction material and a damper assembly attached to it and it is splined to the turbine. ● **SEE FIGURE 9–16.** When the friction material is forced against the torque converter cover, the turbine is driven mechanically by the engine.

The TCC is applied and released when the fluid entering the converter changes from the rear or front. Normal torque converter action occurs when the TCC is released, and the fluid flows from the front to the rear, past the clutch plate. TCC lockup occurs when the fluid enters the rear of the torque converter and forces the clutch plate against the front cover. TCC apply forces the fluid in front of the clutch outward, and this fluid acts like an accumulator to soften clutch application. ● **SEE FIGURE 9–17.**

FIGURE 9–17 TCC release fluid flows through the center of the turbine shaft to the front of the clutch disc (left). Pressure to apply the clutch enters between the converter hub and the stator support (right).

? FREQUENTLY ASKED QUESTION

What Is a CLC Torque Converter?

Some torque converters use a centrifugally applied clutch with the friction material attached to a group of shoes arranged around the outer diameter of the clutch disc. Each shoe is spring loaded to move toward the center of the disc to release the clutch. As the turbine speed increases, centrifugal force pushes the shoes and friction material outward. The friction material contact produces a mechanical transfer of torque from the converter cover to the clutch disc. Ford Motor Company calls this converter a centrifugal lockup converter (CLC).

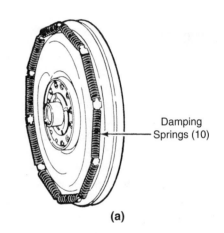

Damping Springs (10)

(a)

TCC fluid flow is controlled by a TCC control valve that is in turn controlled by a solenoid. TCC apply blocks the flow of fluid through the torque converter and cooler. The torque converter does not generate heat when TCC is applied, but some heat is generated by the rest of the transmission. Some fluid will be directed past the TCC control valve to provide cool fluid for transmission lubrication.

Most TCCs use paper friction material. It can be secured to the front of the clutch disc, to the inside of the converter cover, or left free between the two. Some vehicles use a modulated or pulsed TCC apply pressure to smooth out TCC apply. This produces a lot of slipping that can burn out paper clutch lining fairly rapidly. These converters use graphite or paper-graphite lining material for greater endurance under these more severe operating conditions.

Clutch discs include a **damper assembly** that transfers the power through a group of coil springs. ● **SEE FIGURE 9–18**. In most converters, the damper springs are grouped at the center; in others they are grouped around the outer edge. These springs are used to dampen **torsional vibrations** from the engine. All automotive engines produce

(b)

FIGURE 9–18 (a) The turbine has a series of damper strings that connect to the clutch disc. (b) Many clutch discs have a damper assembly at the center. (*Figure (a) Courtesy of Chrysler Corporation; (b) Courtesy of Tribco, Inc.*)

ENGINE ROTATION WITH TORSIONAL VIBRATIONS

SMOOTH ROTATION AT TURBINE SHAFT

DAMPER ASSEMBLY

FIGURE 9–19 A 4-cylinder engine has two power impulses every revolution, and these impulses cause the crankshaft to speed up momentarily. During this time, the damper springs will compress to absorb the speed fluctuation.

? FREQUENTLY ASKED QUESTION

Why Do Some Torque Converters Have a Viscous Coupling?

A **viscous converter clutch** was used in some vehicles to smooth TCC application. The operation is the same as the hydraulically applied converter clutch, except that a viscous element is built into the clutch disc. The viscous element, much like that in a cooling fan clutch, includes a rotor, a body, the clutch cover, and silicone fluid. The rotor and the body have a series of concentric, intermeshed ridges that provide two large surface areas. The viscous drag of the thick silicone fluid transfers power from the body to the rotor. The viscous clutch smoothly transfers power, minimizing engagement shock.

torsional vibration at some operating speed. Torsional vibrations are small speed increases and slowdowns as the crankshaft revolves. These vibrations can produce gear noise in the transmission and drivetrain as well as a noticeable vibration and harshness in the vehicle. ● SEE FIGURE 9–19.

TCC application tends to be harsh in some vehicles. Some drivers dislike the bump that occurs during application. One method used to smooth TCC apply is to delay the rate of pressure increase by cycling or pulsing the TCC solenoid, as described in Chapter 8.

9.4.1 CONTROLLED TCC CAPACITY The TCC can be used to provide a gradual transition into higher gear ranges by slipping or easing into lockup. Controlling TCC capacity has improved vehicle driveability. Early TCC lockup improves fuel mileage, but it can drop engine RPM to the point where misfire and vibration occur.

A TCC solenoid controls TCC apply and release; this is a normally open solenoid that is either open (release) or closed (apply). Controlled-capacity systems use a pulse-width modulated (PWM) solenoid to control TCC apply pressure. When the TCC is first applied, the TCC PWM solenoid will operate at a duty cycle of about 25%. Apply pressure will be very low and the clutch will have a high slip rate. Depending on the vehicle speed and load, the duty cycle gradually increases, causing the slip rate to gradually reduce until full lockup is achieved.

We would expect that fluid flow through the converter would stop during lockup, but any clutch slippage will generate heat. Because of this, some converters have a small orifice drilled in the turbine or clutch disc to allow a constant flow for cooling; others have passages/grooves in the thrust washers for this same purpose.

9.5 CVT TORQUE CONVERTER

Most CVT transmissions use a low-profile elliptical torque converter with a lockup clutch. Since CVTs are infinitely variable, the torque converter is not needed once the vehicle is moving. Therefore, the converter is used to multiply the torque to get the vehicle moving from a stop, and then becomes a mechanical connection between the engine and the CVT. The torque converter clutch apply will occur at about 12 mph (20 kph) and stay locked until the vehicle comes to a stop.

Some small vehicles with CVTs do not use a torque converter. The forward and reverse clutches are released for stops and one will be applied to start the vehicle moving.

9.6 STALL SPEED

Stall is when the turbine is held stationary while the converter housing and impeller are spinning. This is done by shifting the transmission into gear and applying the brakes to hold the drive wheels stationary. The importance of stall speed is that an engine must be able to reach an RPM where enough torque is available to accelerate the vehicle, but not running so fast that there is poor fuel economy and excessive noise. Stall occurs to some degree each time a vehicle starts moving, either forward or backward, and each time a vehicle stops at a stop sign. **Stall speed** is the fastest RPM that an engine can reach while the turbine is held stationary. ● SEE FIGURE 9–20.

A *stall test* measures stall speed in each of the gear positions. It is an important diagnostic test to determine transmission and torque converter condition. This test should be performed with caution because it operates the vehicle in a potentially dangerous situation: The vehicle is in gear with the throttle wide open. It is recommended that both the parking brake and the service brake be firmly applied, the wheels be blocked, and the throttle be held open for a maximum of 5 seconds.

A stall test can severely damage the transmission if done incorrectly. During a stall test, the dynamic fluid pressures inside a converter become very high, because there is a lot of turbulence. Fluid temperatures also become very high. All of the power the engine can produce is going into the converter, and no mechanical power is being delivered to the transmission. The natural law of energy conservation says that energy cannot be created or destroyed. The energy going into the converter must go somewhere; it is converted to heat. Because so much heat is generated, stall tests should be no longer than 5 seconds and followed by a cooling period.

9.6.1 STALL FACTORS
The actual stall speed of a torque converter is determined by the following factors.

- Amount of engine torque
- Diameter of the converter
- Angle of the impeller vanes
- Angle of the stator vanes

Firmly depress the brake pedal.

FIGURE 9–20 A technician measures stall speed while testing a transmission. This test is performed using extreme caution because of the potentially dangerous conditions. The test period is limited to 5 seconds because of potential transmission damage.

We will refer to a high stall speed as a *loose converter* and a low stall speed as a *tight converter*. When a vehicle is standing still, the turbine is not rotating. As the vehicle accelerates, the engine RPM rises quickly to the torque capacity of the converter (stall speed); then it stabilizes to a speed above turbine RPM. As the turbine speed increases, the engine speed also increases. A loose converter allows a higher engine RPM relative to the turbine RPM.

A high-torque engine has the ability to turn the impeller faster against a stalled turbine than a small or weak engine. ● **SEE FIGURE 9–21.** A low-torque engine is normally equipped with a looser converter. If the converter is too tight, the engine RPM cannot increase to the point of usable power, and the vehicle would lose acceleration and overall performance. A converter that is too loose will cause the engine to operate at excessive speed. The result will be poor fuel economy, excessive noise, and reduced performance because of the

---

? FREQUENTLY ASKED QUESTION

How Is a THM Super 400 Different?

In the 1960s, the THM Super 400 and Super 300 transmissions were produced with variable-pitch stator vanes. A hydraulic piston was built into the stator assembly, and fluid to this piston was controlled by an electric solenoid–controlled valve. At very low vehicle speeds or high-throttle openings, the stator vanes were moved to a high angle for maximum stall speed, torque multiplication, and acceleration. Otherwise, the stator vanes are kept at a low-angle position for maximum fuel economy and quiet, smooth vehicle operation. The switch to control stator fin position is mounted in the speedometer or throttle linkage, depending on the vehicle application.

COMPARING STALL SPEED				
Example	Engine Size	Maximum Torque: lb-ft @ rpm	Stall Speed: 11" Converter	Effect
#1	2L, I4	140 lb-ft @ 5,000	1,300 rpm	Engine stall speed is below power; vehicle will show power loss
#2	3L, V6	202 lb-ft @ 3,800	1,600 rpm	Engine stall speed is below power band; vehicle will show power loss
#3	4.2L, V8	303 lb-ft @ 3,100	2,000 rpm	OK combination
#4	5.4L, V8	350 lb-ft @ 2,500	2,500 rpm	Engine stall speed is at maximum torque; good combination
#5	5.9L, I6, Diesel	610 lb-ft @ 1,600	3,100 rpm	Stall speed is too high, above engine power band; vehicle will show power loss and poor fuel economy

FIGURE 9–21 The stall speed of a torque converter must match the engine for good vehicle driveability.

FIGURE 9–22 Converter diameter helps determine stall speed. Along with other factors, it is used to help select the correct replacement converter.

FIGURE 9–23 On some converters, it is possible to see the impeller fin angle from the outside. The converter on the right has rearward or negative fin angles that will produce a higher stall speed than the one on the left, which has forward or positive fin angle.

excessive slippage. In production, the torque converter capacity/stall speed is matched to the engine size and vehicle weight to produce the best vehicle performance and fuel economy. Depending on the engine, different converters are used with a transmission model. One manufacturer uses eight different converters with one transmission model. The technician must ensure that the correct replacement converter is used.

Diameter is a major factor in determining converter stall speed. Passenger car converters vary in size from about 8 to 12 in. (20.3 to 30.5 cm). ● SEE FIGURE 9–22. The rotary speed of the fluid in the impeller is almost the same speed as the converter's outer diameter. The circumference of a circle is a product of the diameter times π (pi), which is equal to 3.1416. The

PROBLEM SOLVING 9–1

Imagine that you are working in a shop that specializes in transmission repair, and these problems are brought to you.

Case 1:

A 1995 Ford van has a bump and shudder that occurs in drive at 20 to 40 mph. The shudder occurs once in every shift cycle. Could this be a torque converter problem? Would this be a mechanical, hydraulic, or electrical problem? Where would you start looking for the cause?

Case 2:

A 1987 Chevrolet Citation transaxle was rebuilt, and a rebuilt torque converter was installed. Now the car has poor acceleration. The 4-cylinder engine acts as if it has lost two of the cylinders. What could have caused this? Where would you start looking for the cause?

circumference of an 8-in. converter is 25.1 in. (63.7 cm); the circumference of a 12-in. converter is 37.7 in. (95.8 cm), about 50% greater. From this, it should be fairly easy to see how a larger-diameter converter can put about 50% more speed and energy into the fluid. A 9-in. converter will have a stall speed that is about 30% faster than a 10-in. converter in the same vehicle. It should be noted that the increased fluid speed and energy requires more power from the engine. A larger converter is tighter and has a higher torque capacity.

The impeller vanes can be angled forward, straight, or backward relative to the direction of converter rotation. ● SEE FIGURE 9–23. A forward or *positive fin angle* produces greater fluid speed and therefore a tighter converter. A rearward or *negative fin angle* increases the stall speed. Changing the impeller fin angle is an easy method for a manufacturer to change converter torque capacity.

Another method of changing converter capacity is the angle of the stator vanes. The greater the curvature, the more the fluid will return to the direction of impeller rotation, and the stall speed and converter looseness will be increased. Straighter vanes produce a tighter converter.

SUMMARY

1. A torque converter hydraulically connects the engine to an automatic transmission and will multiply the engine torque under certain conditions.

2. Torque converters utilize an impeller, turbine, stator, and lockup clutch.

3. Stall and coupling are the extremes of torque converter operation. Stall occurs when the impeller and turbine are operating at different speeds, and coupling occurs when the impellers are turning at nearly the same speed.

4. Torque converter clutches are used to mechanically connect the engine to the transmission. During lockup, torque converter slippage will be eliminated and fuel mileage will improve.

5. Factors that affect torque converter stall are converter diameter, angle of the vanes, and torque of the engine.

1. The two purposes for a torque converter are to serve as an automatic _____ and to multiply the engine's _____.

2. List the four elements of a typical torque converter.

3. The torque converter is bolted to the _____.

4. The torque converter's input member is the _____ and the output member is the _____.

5. The stator is the _____ member of the torque converter and is splined onto the reaction shaft through a _____ clutch.

6. The flow of fluid from the impeller to the turbine is called a _____ flow. The circular flow of fluid leaving the impeller is called _____ flow.

7. The stator _____ the flow from the turbine to the impeller. The effect of this is to increase _____.

8. The coupling phase occurs when the turbine and the impeller are rotating at nearly the _____ speed.

9. The purpose of the torque converter clutch is to eliminate torque converter _____ during the _____ stage of operation.

10. The torque converter clutch is similar to a _____ _____ for a standard transmission.

11. The torque converter clutch is splined onto the _____, and when applied, it is forced against the torque converter _____.

12. The torque converter clutch is released by directing fluid to the _____ of the clutch, and applied by directing fluid to the _____ of the clutch.

13. A torque converter clutch uses _____ springs to smooth out _____ vibrations.

14. Some torque converter clutches use a _____-filled clutch to smooth out torque converter clutch application.

15. Torque converter stall is when the _____ is held stationary and the _____ is spinning.

16. Stall speed is the _____ RPM that an engine can turn while the turbine is _____.

17. Stall testing can be used to check _____ and _____ conditions.

18. Vehicles with small engines typically use a torque converter that has a _____ stall speed, and vehicles with a powerful engine use a torque converter with a _____ stall speed.

19. Four factors that affect torque converter stall speed are:
    a. Engine _____
    b. _____ diameter
    c. Impeller _____ angle
    d. Stator fin _____

1. Student A says that a torque converter is a hydraulic connection between the engine and transmission. Student B says that a torque converter clutch will increase the torque to the transmission. Who is correct?
   a. Student A
   b. Student B
   c. Both Students A and B
   d. Neither Student A nor B

2. The input member of the converter is the _____.
   a. Turbine   c. Impeller
   b. Stator   d. All of these

3. Student A says that the flexplate connects the torque converter to the crankshaft. Student B says that the torque converter is considered part of the transmission. Who is correct?
   a. Student A   c. Both Students A and B
   b. Student B   d. Neither Student A nor B

4. Student A says that fluid motion inside a converter is controlled by the guide ring. Student B says that fluid motion inside a converter is controlled by the stator vanes. Who is correct?
   a. Student A
   b. Student B
   c. Both Students A and B
   d. Neither Student A nor B

5. Fluid flow from the impeller through the turbine and stator is called _____ flow.
   a. Rotary
   b. Impeller
   c. Vortex
   d. Turbine

6. Fluid flow around the circumference of the converter is called _____ flow.
   a. Rotary
   b. Impeller
   c. Vortex
   d. Turbine

7. A strong vortex flow will _____.
   a. Cause the stator clutch to lock
   b. Release the stator clutch
   c. Circulate through the guide ring
   d. All of these

8. During the coupling phase, the _____.
   a. Vortex flow nearly stops
   b. Stator clutch locks
   c. Rotary flow nearly stops
   d. Flow stops

9. A torque converter is more efficient while _____.
   a. Stopped at a stop sign
   b. Accelerating hard
   c. Accelerating under a light throttle
   d. Cruising

10. Student A says that at stall speed the impeller is spinning as fast as the engine can drive it. Student B says that at stall speed the turbine is stationary. Who is correct?
    a. Student A
    b. Student B
    c. Both Students A and B
    d. Neither Student A nor B

11. In most lockup torque converters, lockup occurs when the _____.
    a. Fluid flow in the converter is reversed
    b. Converter switch valve is moved by the lockup solenoid
    c. Turbine speed reaches a certain RPM
    d. Converter speed reaches a certain RPM

12. In a lockup torque converter, the _____.
    a. Clutch plate is splined onto the turbine shaft
    b. Clutch lining transfers power through a mechanical connection during lockup
    c. Fluid is passing through the torque converter
    d. Both a and b

13. Lockup torque converters use a damper assembly to dampen _____.
    a. Noise
    b. Torsional vibration
    c. Lateral force
    d. Spring oscillations

14. Stall testing can be used to find _____.
    a. Problems with the torque converter
    b. Slipping clutches
    c. Slipping bands
    d. All of the above

15. A large-diameter torque converter will _____.
    a. Have a higher stall speed
    b. Have a lower stall speed
    c. Not have an effect on stall speed
    d. All of the above

chapter 10

TRANSMISSION DESCRIPTIONS

OBJECTIVES: **After studying Chapter 10, the reader will be able to:** • Describe some of the transmissions used in domestic vehicles. • Describe some of the transmissions used in the more popular import vehicles. • Explain the operation of a particular transmission. • Identify which transmission is used in a particular vehicle. • Identify a particular transmission.

KEY TERMS: Cruise-O-Matic 235 • Hydramatic 241 • Loadflite 232 • Torqueflite 232 • Turbo Hydra-Matic (THM) 241

10.1 INTRODUCTION

Many different types of transmissions and transaxles have been used in domestic and imported vehicles. It is difficult to describe each one of these with the information provided in a book of this type. We will concentrate only on domestic transmissions and the transmissions installed in the more popular import vehicles.

The transmission technician's job is easier if he or she has a working knowledge of the transmission being diagnosed and/or repaired. It may seem to be a difficult task to learn the many different transmissions, but it is made easier by the fact that many transmissions have similar operating characteristics. We can place the more common transmissions and transaxles into the categories described in Chapter 5. Some of these categories are similar except for the apply devices. Most transmissions used in import vehicles fit into these same categories. Remember that most transmissions and transaxles have the following common characteristics.

- Planetary gear sets achieve the various ratios (Honda, older Saturn, and CVT transaxles are the exceptions).
- Multiple-disc clutches, bands, or one-way clutches control the power flow.
- Hydraulic pressure applies the application devices.
- Most use electronic shift controls.
- Most use a lockup type of torque converter (CVTs with electromagnet clutches are the exception).

In the following sections, we will briefly describe the more common transmission and transaxles. They will be described by manufacturer and cross-referenced by the gear train types described in Chapter 5. The gear train categories are based on the type of gear train and the type of apply devices used.

A particular transmission design may have many small differences. In any single year, there may be many versions of the same transmission depending on the application. The differences may involve the following:

- Number of lined and unlined plates in a clutch pack
- Ratio of the band levers
- Size of the band servos
- Programming of the valve body
- Strength of the spring in an accumulator
- Torque converter stall speed
- Location of the mounting pad bolts
- Shape of the torque converter housing (bell housing)
- Ratio of the drive sprockets and chain
- Exact number of teeth on the gears in the gear sets

Each transmission must be matched to the weight of the vehicle, the strength of the engine, emission and fuel mileage requirements, and sometimes where the vehicle will be sold.

Links to online resources for identifying domestic and import transmissions are provided in Appendix B.

10.1.1 TRANSAXLES
A transaxle is a combination of a transmission, either manual or automatic, and a final drive assembly. The final drive is typically a set of reduction gears and the differential. The differential is made up of two pairs of gears, the differential pinion gears mounted on the differential pinion shaft and the axle or side gears, which are attached to the axles or driveshaft. ● **SEE FIGURE 10–1.** In a front-wheel-drive (FWD) vehicle, the axle shafts are often called *driveshafts* and occasionally called *half-shafts* or *side shafts.* The purpose of the differential is to allow the drive wheels to be driven at different speeds while the vehicle is going around a corner.

There are essentially four types of final drive and differential combinations used in transaxles.

1. The first type uses helical gears and an intermediate/idler gear or shaft to transfer power from the transmission planetary gear assembly to the differential case. ● **SEE FIGURE 10–2.**

FIGURE 10–1 (a) When a vehicle is driving straight, the differential gears rotate as a unit; equal load keeps the pinion gears stationary on the mate shaft. (b) An unequal load causes the pinion gears to rotate on the mate shaft so one axle can turn faster than the other. (*Courtesy of Chrysler Corporation*)

FIGURE 10–2 The 6T70 output carrier and transfer drive gear (not shown) drive the transfer gear and differential through helical gears (a). The differential (b) resembles those used in drive axles.

The helical gears provide the necessary reduction ratio and are relatively efficient, quiet, and inexpensive. Older Chrysler transaxles and the Ford ATX are examples.

2. The second type uses a planetary gear set mounted to the output of the transmission gear set for the final drive reduction gears (see Figure 3–35). The output of the transmission is a sun gear that is also the input for the final drive reduction gears. In this set, the ring gear is splined into the transaxle case so it is always a reaction member and the planet carrier is part of the differential case so it is always the output. The short, right-side driveshaft exits almost directly out of the case, and the longer, left driveshaft runs through the center of the transmission gear set. Examples are the General Motors transaxles and the Ford AX4N, AX4S, and AXOD.

3. The third type uses a planetary gear final drive that is driven by a chain and sprockets from the transmission

FIGURE 10–3 An exploded view from a parts catalog of a Ford CD4E shows a chain (175) to transfer power from the transmission gear set to the final drive and differential. (*Courtesy of Aceomatic Recon*)

section. ● **SEE FIGURE 10–3**. An example of this is the Ford CD4E.

4. Some FWD vehicles use an engine mounted lengthwise in the vehicle so the crankshaft and the transaxle shafts run *longitudinal* (fore and aft) instead of *transverse* or *lateral* (side to side) relative to the vehicle. In these units, the power must make a right-angle turn as it goes from the transmission to the differential. These units use either a spiral bevel or a hypoid gear set that is similar to the gears in the rear axle of a RWD vehicle. The hypoid gear set is the most common. It changes the power flow 90 degrees and provides the gear reduction. Examples of these transaxles are the Acura Legend and Chrysler 42LE. The 42LE uses a chain and sprocket set to transfer power from the transmission output to the transfer shaft, and the transfer shaft becomes the pinion gear of the hypoid final drive. ● **SEE FIGURE 10–4**.

The GM 6T70 compact transaxle uses a helical gear train of the first type, whereas the smaller 6T40 version uses the third type.

Remember that the gear ratio through a transaxle is a product of at least two gear ratios, and in some cases, three gear ratios. In many units, the gear set ratio times the final drive ratio equals the overall ratio. ● **SEE FIGURE 10–5**. In units using a chain and sprockets, multiplying the chain and sprocket ratio times the gear set ratio times the final drive ratio equals the overall ratio. The overall ratio is the actual operating ratio between the engine and the drive wheels. The chain and sprocket ratio can vary between models. This becomes important when transaxles are replaced with a used or remanufactured transaxle. If the overall gear ratio does not match the ratio of the original transaxle, the transmission control module (TCM) will note the difference and may set a diagnostic trouble

FIGURE 10–4 The Chrysler 42LE transaxle uses hypoid final drive gears. Note the transfer chain to connect the transmission gear set to the final drive pinion gear. (*Courtesy of Chrysler Corporation*)

<table>
<tr><td>? </td><td>**FREQUENTLY ASKED QUESTION**</td></tr>
</table>

Were the THM 325, 325-4L, and 425 Models Transmissions or Transaxles?

Another approach to providing FWD was used in the THM 325, THM 325-4L, and THM 425 transmissions installed in the Cadillac Eldorado, Oldsmobile Toronado, and later in the Buick Riviera. They were replaced by the THM 440-T4 (4T60) in the mid-1980s. These transmissions are mounted alongside the engine and use a pair of sprockets and a drive chain to transfer power from the torque converter turbine shaft to the transmission input shaft. ● **SEE FIGURE 10–6.** A final drive gear assembly is bolted to the output of these transmissions, and this unit contains the reduction ring and pinion gears and the differential. Technically, since the final drive gears can be separated from the transmission, these units are not transaxles. This final drive gear set uses a hypoid gear set for the final drive ratio and to turn the power flow 90 degrees.

Chain & Sprocket	Final Drive	Transmission
0.98:1 or 0.91:1	3.85:1 or 4.31:1	1st = 2.89:1, 2nd = 1.57, 3rd = 1:1, 4th = 0.69:1

The overall gear ratio in 1st gear when used with the 2.0 L engine is:
1st gear ratio × chain & sprocket ratio × final drive ratio
2.89 × 0.91 × 4.31 = 11.33:1

The overall gear ratio in 1st gear when used with the 2.5 L engine is:
1st gear ratio × chain & sprocket ratio × final drive ratio
2.89 × 0.98 × 3.85 = 10.9:1

FIGURE 10–5 The overall gear ratio in a transaxle is a product of multiplying the transmission gear ratio by the final drive ratio. This should be multiplied by any transfer gear/chain ratio.

FIGURE 10–6 A THM 3254L transmission is mounted alongside of the engine. The front axle assembly is attached directly to the output shaft (lower left) to drive the front wheels.

<table>
<tr><td>? </td><td>**FREQUENTLY ASKED QUESTION**</td></tr>
</table>

What Is a Dingy or Flat Tow?

Some new transaxles incorporate a *dingy* or *flat tow* feature to lubricate the final drive gears while the vehicle is towed with the wheels on the road. This allows towing behind a motorhome using only a towbar.

code (DTC). Also, the customer might be dissatisfied with the performance, driveability, and fuel economy of the vehicle.

10.1.2 NEW-GENERATION TRANSMISSIONS AND TRANSAXLES Vehicle manufacturers are working to improve vehicle efficiency, performance, and fuel mileage. Transmissions and transaxles are being introduced that are smaller, lighter, and have additional gear ranges, some are nine speeds. The author is trying to keep this chapter current, but the reader must realize that it is not practical to include all transmissions and transaxles.

Transaxle Gear Ratios							
Model	First	Second	Third	Fourth	Fifth	Sixth	Reverse
31TH	2.69	1.55	1				2.1
40TE	2.84	1.57	1	0.69			2.12
41AE/TE, 42LE	2.842	1.575	1	0.69			2.21
62TE	4.11	2.84	2.27	1.57	1	0.68	3.22
F4A33	2.554	1.488	1	0.685			2.17
F4A42	2.842	1.529	1	0.712			2.48
W4A33	2.551	1.488	1	0.685			2.176
Transmission Gear Ratios							
30RH, 32RH, 36RH	2.74	1.54	1				2.22
42RE, 44RE	2.74	1.54	1	0.69			2.21
42RLE	2.84	1.57	1	0.69			2.21
46RE, 47RE, 48RE	2.45	1.45	1	0.69			2.21
45RFE	3.0	1.67/1.5	1	0.75			3.0
545RFE*	3.0	1.67/1.5	1	0.75	0.5/0.6		3.0
68RFE	3.23	1.84	1.41	1	0.82	0.67	4.44
AW4	2.80	1.53	1	0.75			2.39
W5A580	3.59	2.19	1.41	1	0.83		3.0

* These transmissions have two second gear ratios, called second and second prime. Second prime is used as the transition between 4th and 2nd during kickdown.

FIGURE 10–7 The gear ratios for Chrysler transmissions and transaxles.

10.2 CHRYSLER

In 1992, Chrysler adopted an alphanumeric system for identifying and describing its transmissions. The system used for these units is as follows:

1st character: Number of forward speeds

2nd character: Relative torque capacity—0 is the smallest and 10 the highest

3rd character: Wheels driven or transmission position: A = AWD, R = RWD, L = Longitudinal, T = Transverse

4th character: Type of shift control: H = Hydraulic control, E = Electronic control, FE = Fully electronic

Interpreting the code for a Chrysler 45RFE transmission identifies the transmission as a four-speed, relatively high-torque-capacity, rear-wheel-drive transmission that is controlled fully by electronics.

Detailed descriptions of each Chrysler transmission and how it operates is available in the manufacturer's service information, transmission service manuals, and trade publications. The gear ratios of the Chrysler transmissions and transaxles are shown in ● **FIGURE 10–7**.

10.2.1 CHRYSLER REAR-WHEEL-DRIVE TRANSMISSIONS
Several RWD transmissions are currently in production. They can be identified by the transmission code on the vehicle body plate. ● **SEE FIGURE 10–8**. When the

FIGURE 10–8 This body decal identifies the transmission as well as other important features of this vehicle. (*Courtesy of Chrysler Corporation*)

transmission is out of the vehicle, it can be identified by a transmission identification number stamped on the left side of the case, just above the pan gasket surface, or by an identification label attached to the transmission. ● **SEE FIGURE 10–9**. The size, shape, and appearance of the case along with the shape of the pan also help identify a unit. ● **SEE FIGURE 10–10**.

30RH-32RH TRANSMISSIONS. These transmissions are three-speed units that use a type 1 gear train. ● **SEE FIGURE 10–11**. The 30RH was formerly called a TF6 or A904; the 31RH was formerly called a 998; and the 32RH was formerly called a 999.

PARTIAL VIN

SERIAL NUMBER
LOCATION

| 3681057 | W | 4053 | 0250 |

DAILY
PRODUCTION NO.

WARRANTY DATE CODE

TRANSMISSION
ASSEMBLY PART NO.

PLANT CODE LETTER

(a)

23–WAY
CONNECTOR

INPUT
SPEED
SENSOR

OUTPUT
SPEED
SENSOR

IDENTIFICATION
NUMBERS

T1TTJ167710161 099
P52119099AA 45RF AA

(b)

FIGURE 10–9 (a) Older Torqueflite transmissions can be identified by a code stamped in the case. (b) Newer units use a label attached to the case. (*Courtesy of Chrysler Corporation*)

(a)

(b)

FIGURE 10–10 (a) A Chrysler 4WD, 44RE (at the top) and a 2WD, 46RE can be identified by the pan shape and extension housing. (b) Some transmissions can be identified by the shape of the pan gasket. (*Courtesy of Chrysler Corporation*)

FIGURE 10–11 A cutaway view of a 30RH (A940) transmission with a clutch and band application chart. (*Courtesy of Chrysler Corporation*)

ELEMENTS IN USE AT EACH POSITION OF THE SELECTOR LEVER

LEVER POSITION	START SAFETY	PARKING SPRAG	CLUTCHES FRONT	REAR	OVER-RUNNING	BANDS (KICKDOWN) FRONT	(LOW-REV.) REAR
P—PARK	X	X					
R—REVERSE			X				X
N—NEUTRAL	X						
D—DRIVE							
First				X	X		
Second				X		X	
Direct			X	X			
2—SECOND							
First				X	X		
Second				X		X	
1—LOW (First)			X				X

These are similar units with slight internal variations. Electronic controls are used for torque converter clutch operation in models from 1978 on.

36RH-37RH TRANSMISSIONS. The 36RH and 37RH are also three-speed transmissions that use a type 1 gear train. They are larger transmissions than the 30RH-32RH units, and are designed to handle the higher torque loads for larger engines and heavier vehicles. They were formerly called a TF8 or A727. Electronic control for the torque converter clutch began in 1978.

40RH-42RH, 42RE-44RE TRANSMISSIONS. These transmissions are type 5 units that combine a three-speed type 1 transmission (30RH-32RH) with an overdrive gear set positioned at the rear of

the transmission. ● **SEE FIGURE 10–12.** They were previously called the A500. These units are used in pickups, SUVs, vans, and light trucks with 6-cylinder engines. In the 40RH-42RH, the torque converter clutch, 3–4 shift, and 4–3 shift are hydraulically controlled. They are electronically controlled in the 42RE-44RE.

42RLE TRANSMISSION. This transmission is used in 2WD and 4WD vehicles. It is a redesign of the 42LE transaxle. It uses the same type 14 gear set and transmission controls. Because there is no final drive, a redesigned transmission case and output shaft are used.

45RFE TRANSMISSION. The 45RFE transmission is a four-speed transmission that uses three simple planetary gear sets.

FIGURE 10–12 A cutaway view of a 42RH transmission; note that the overdrive unit attaches to the rear of the main transmission section. (*Courtesy of Chrysler Corporation*)

FIGURE 10–13 A cutaway view of a 45RFE transmission showing the three driving clutches, the three reaction clutches, and the complex gear set. (*Courtesy of Chrysler Corporation*)

? FREQUENTLY ASKED QUESTION

What Is a Torqueflite?

In the past, Chrysler Corporation, now Chrysler LLC, has traditionally used the terms **Torqueflite** for passenger car transmissions and **Loadflite** for transmissions intended for pickups, SUVs, and light trucks.

Torqueflites are three-speed, Simpson gear train transmissions of two basic sizes. The A-904 was introduced as a Torqueflite 6 (TF6) in 1960 for use with 6-cylinder engines. The A-727 was introduced in 1962 for use with 8-cylinder engines. The A-727 is called the Torqueflite 8 (TF8). Both transmissions used an aluminum case. A cast-iron-case Torqueflite was used from 1956 to 1961. A two-speed unit called the Powerflite was used from 1954 to 1960. Its operation was similar to the Powerglide transmission produced by General Motors.

The gear sets are called the reaction gear set (at the front of the transmission), reverse gear set (center), and input gear set (at the rear). ● SEE FIGURE 10–13. It uses seven control devices, as shown by the clutch and band chart. ● SEE FIGURE 10–14. With the exception of the freewheel/overrunning clutch, these are all multiplate clutches; there are no bands. Two devices are applied in each gear range, and these are controlled by seven solenoids. These fully electronic units are used in pickups, SUVs, vans, and light trucks.

46RH-47RH, 46RE-47RE-48RE TRANSMISSIONS. These transmissions also use two planetary gear sets like the 40RH-42RH units. They are larger, stronger units—note the higher torque capacity, as indicated by the second character. They also combine a three-speed type 1 transmission (36RH-37RH) with an overdrive unit at the rear. The 46RH and 47RH, formerly called the A518, are used with 8-cylinder engines. Electronic controls are used for the 3–4 and 4–3 shifts and torque converter operation in the RH versions.

Shift Lever Position	Park Sprag	Under Drive	Overdrive	Reverse	2nd	4th	Low-Reverse	Over-running Clutch
CLUTCHES APPLIED								
P–Park	X						X	
R–Reverse				X			X	
N–Neutral							X	
D–Overdrive First		X					X*	X
Second		X			X			
Second Prime		X				X		
Third		X	X					
Fourth			X			X		
Limp–in		X	X					
2–First		X					X*	X
Second		X			X			
Limp–in		X			X			
1–Low		X					X	X

FIGURE 10–14 This clutch chart shows the active control devices for each gear range of a 45RFE transmission.

W5A580/722.6 TRANSMISSION. This five-speed transmission combines a simple planetary gear set with a compound gear set that connects a ring gear of one set with the carrier of the second set. Two overrunning clutches, three multiplate clutches, and three multiplate brakes/reaction clutches control the power flow. This transmission was developed jointly with Mercedes-Benz.

545RRFE TRANSMISSION. The 545RRFE is a five-speed version of the 45RFE. Fifth gear is an overdrive, 0.67:1 ratio.

68RFE TRANSMISSION. This is a redesigned six-speed version of the 48RFE transmission to handle the 650 ft-lb of torque from the 6.7-L diesel engine. It is about 15 lb heavier with a different planetary gear configuration and gear tooth counts. This is a fully electronic transmission that includes manual shift control and trailer towing options.

10.2.2 CHRYSLER TRANSAXLES

Chrysler transaxles can be identified by the transmission code on the vehicle body plate. When the transaxle is out of the vehicle, it can be identified by an identification tag on the case. ● SEE FIGURE 10–15. The size, shape, and appearance of the case and the shape of the pan are also useful when identifying these transaxles.

30TH-31TH TRANSAXLE. The 30TH and 31TH transaxles are three-speed units that use a type 1 gear train. They are used with a transverse-mounted engine. ● SEE FIGURE 10–16. They were formerly called the A404, A413, A414, A470, and A670. The transmission section of these units is very similar to the

FIGURE 10–15 The 41TE transaxle can be identified by an identification label attached to the converter housing and by the shape of the case with the solenoid sound shield, transfer gear cover, and strengthening ribs over the final drive section. (*Courtesy of Chrysler Corporation*)

TF6/A904 transmission. The major exterior difference between these units is the bell housing, which is designed to fit a particular engine. Internally, the final drive ratios may be different.

41TE TRANSAXLE. The 41TE transaxle is a four-speed unit with a transverse engine mounting. It uses a type 14 gear train and was formerly called an A604. ● SEE FIGURE 10–17. This unit uses no bands or one-way clutches. It is a fully electronic transaxle.

FIGURE 10–16 A cutaway view of a 30TH three-speed transaxle. (*Courtesy of Chrysler Corporation*)

ELEMENTS IN USE SHIFT LEVER POSITION	Start Safety	Park Sprag	CLUTCHES				
			Underdrive	Overdrive	Reverse	2/4	Low/Reverse
P — PARK	X	X					X
R — REVERSE					X		X
N — NEUTRAL	X						X
OD — OVERDRIVE First			X				X
Second			X			X	
Direct			X	X			
Overdrive				X		X	
D — DRIVE* First			X				X
Second			X			X	
Direct			X	X			
L — LOW* First			X				X
Second			X			X	
Direct			X	X			
*Vehicle upshift and downshift speeds are increased when in these selector positions.							

FIGURE 10–17 A cutaway view of a 41TE transaxle with a clutch application chart. (*Courtesy of Chrysler Corporation*)

What Is a Ford-O-Matic?

In the past, the Ford Motor Company has traditionally used the terms **Cruise-O-Matic,** *Ford-O-Matic,* and *Merc-O-Matic* for its automatic transmissions. The "C" in C4 and C6 stood for Cruise-O-Matic.

42LE TRANSAXLE. The 42LE transaxle is a four-speed unit similar to a 41TE with a longitudinal-mounted engine (see Figure 10–4). It is a fully electronic unit.

62TE TRANSAXLE. The 62TE is a six-speed transaxle with a transverse-mounted engine. The transmission is very similar to the 41TE with the addition of a compounder gear set on the transfer shaft. The compounder has a 1:1 and 1.45:1 ratio, so the transaxle gear ratios are as follows: first—4.11:1 (2.84 × 1.45), second—2.84:1, third—2.27:1 (1.57 × 1.45), fourth—1.57:1, fifth—1:1, sixth—0.68:1, and reverse—3.2:1 (2.21 × 1.45). The compounder is a simple planetary gear set with two multiplate clutch packs and an overrunning clutch.

10.3 FORD MOTOR COMPANY

Like other vehicle manufacturers, Ford transmissions are manufactured all over the world. Some are from Ford-owned production lines in the United States and France; others are produced by manufacturers in Japan (JATCO and Aisin [AW]) and in Europe (ZF).

Ford Motor Company uses an alphanumeric code and model designation system, as follows:

1st character: Number of forward speeds

2nd character: Transmission features: A = Automatic, C = Vehicle application size, Production year, Chain or Close ratio, D = Drive, E = Electronic, F = FWD, H = Taurus SHO, HD = Heavy duty, L = Lockup, M = Manual, N = Nonsynchronous, O = Overdrive, S = Synchronous, T = Transmission, W = Wide ratio, X = Transaxle

3rd and 4th characters: Torque capacity (maximum input from torque converter): 44 = 440 ft-lb, 55 = 550 ft-lb, 70 = 700 ft-lb

Detailed descriptions of each Ford Motor Company transmission and how it operates are available in the manufacturer's service information, transmission service manuals, and trade publications. The gear ratios for Ford Motor Company transmissions and transaxles are shown in ● **FIGURE 10–18**.

Transaxle Gear Ratios							
Model	**First**	**Second**	**Third**	**Fourth**	**Fifth**	**Sixth**	**Reverse**
4F20E	2.78	1.54	1	0.69			2.27
4F27E	2.8	1.49	1	0.73			2.65
4F50N/AX4N/AX4S/ AXOD	2.77	1.54	1	0.69			2.26
ATX	2.79	1.61	1	0.69			1.97
CD4E	2.89	1.57	1	0.69			2.31
F4E/4EAT	2.8	1.54	1	0.7			2.33
6F35	4.58	2.96	1.91	1.45	1	0.75	2.94
6F50	4.84	2.87	1.84	1.41	1	0.74	2.88
Transmission Gear Ratios							
4R44E/A4LD	2.47	1.47	1	0.75			2.1
4R70W	2.8	1.55	1	0.7			2.32
4R100/E4OD	2.71	1.54	1	0.71			2.18
5R55E	2.47	1.87	1.47	1	0.75		2
5R55N	3.25	2.44	1.55	1	0.75		3.07
5R110/TorqShift	3.09	2.2	1.54	1.09/cold 1/hot	0.71		2.9
6R60/6R80	4.17	2.34	1.52	1.14	0.87	0.69	3.4
C4/C5	2.47	1.47	1				2.11
C6	2.46	1.46	1				2.18

Some transmission models made by other manufacturers have been omitted.

FIGURE 10–18 The gear ratios for Ford Motor Company transmissions and transaxles.

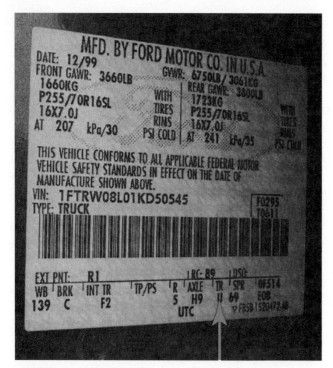

FIGURE 10–19 This body decal identifies the transmission and other important features of this vehicle. The transmission type U (arrow) indicates a 4R70W transmission.

FIGURE 10–20 A 4F50N (AX4N) transaxle can be identified by the tag attached to the top of the case, the stamping on the valve body cover, and the overall shape of the unit.

FIGURE 10–21 Many technicians use the shape of the oil pan gasket and filter to identify a transmission.

10.3.1 FORD MOTOR COMPANY REAR-WHEEL-DRIVE TRANSMISSIONS

Ford transmissions can be identified by the vehicle's label located on the door pillar. ● SEE FIGURE 10–19. When the transmission is out of the vehicle, it can be identified with a service identification tag attached to the case. ● SEE FIGURE 10–20. The size, shape, and appearance along with the shape of its pan can also be used to identify a transmission. ● SEE FIGURE 10–21. Several out of production RWD transmissions will also be described.

4R44E TRANSMISSION. The 4R44E transmission is the updated version of the A4LD introduced in 1986. ● SEE FIGURE 10–22. It is a four-speed that uses a type 6 gear train. This is another dual gear set design that combines an overdrive unit at the front and a three-speed Simpson gear set at the rear. Electronic controls determine the shift strategy. It was used in compact pickups.

5R55E TRANSMISSION. The 5R55E transmission is essentially a stronger version of the 4R44E that uses a different electronic shift strategy to get the five speeds (see Chart 5–8). It is currently used in compact pickups and SUVs.

4R70W TRANSMISSION. The 4R70W transmission is an updated version of the AOD that was introduced in 1980. It is a four-speed that uses a type 12, Ravigneaux gear train. Electronic controls are used to determine the shift strategy. It is used in RWD passenger cars, midsize pickups, and SUVs (see Figure 5–40).

4R100/E4OD TRANSMISSION. The E4OD transmission was introduced in 1990 for use in larger pickups, SUVs, and commercial vehicles. ● SEE FIGURE 10–23. It is a four-speed unit that uses a type 6 gear train. The dual gear set design combines an overdrive unit at the front and a three-speed gear set at the rear. Electronic controls are used to determine the shift strategy.

5R110W TRANSMISSION. This transmission is a five-speed design called the "TorqShift" and is a redesigned 4R100. It was introduced in F-Series trucks and Excursions equipped with the 6.0-L diesel engine. This transmission actually has six speeds available with two different five-speed strategies. When cold, below 5°F (–15°C), it will shift 1–2, 2–3, 3–4, and 4–6 (skipping fifth); when hot, it will shift 1–2, 2–3, 3–5, and 5–6 (skipping fourth). The TorqShift uses a new fluid, Mercon Sp. It is not interchangeable with other Mercon fluids.

6R60, 6R80 TRANSMISSION. This is an electronically controlled six-speed transmission. It features clutch-to-clutch shifts, with

FIGURE 10–22 An exploded view of a 4R44E (A4LD) transmission. (*Courtesy of Aceomatic Recon*)

FIGURE 10–23 A cutaway view of a 4R100 (E40D) transmission. Note the mirror at the bottom showing the valve body.

? **FREQUENTLY ASKED QUESTION**

Were the C3, C4, and C5 Different?

These transmissions were all based on the C4 transmission. ● **SEE FIGURE 10–24.** They are three-speed units that use a type 1 Simpson gear train. They were used in small and midsize passenger cars, pickups, and SUVs.

The C4 was one of the most widely used Ford transmissions. It was used in various configurations from 1964 to 1981. It was upgraded with a centrifugal lockup torque converter and renamed the C5. The C3 was a European-built transmission used in the Pinto, Bobcat, and Capri. These transmissions were used in small and midsize passenger cars, pickups, and SUVs up to 1986.

FIGURE 10–24 An exploded view of a C4 and C5 transmission. (*Courtesy of Aceomatic Recon*)

adaptive shift patterns and timing. It is a type 13 transmission that combines one simple planetary gear set with a Ravigneaux gear set. This is a wide-ratio transmission with a 4.17:1 first gear and a 0.69:1 sixth gear for a 6.04:1 gear ratio spread. The very low first gear provides rapid starts and the two overdrive gears allow economical low engine speed when cruising. This transmission model is similar to the ZF 6HP26.

C6 TRANSMISSION.   The C6 transmission was used between 1966 and 1983. ● **SEE FIGURE 10–25.** It is a three-speed unit using a type 2 Simpson gear train. The C6 was a larger, more refined transmission than the C4 and was used in medium to large-size passenger cars, pickups, SUVs, and commercial vehicles.

JATCO L3N71B.   This transmission was produced by the Japanese Automatic Transmission Company and used in Ford products between 1977 and 1980. It is a three-speed unit that uses a type 2 Simpson gear train, similar to the C6. It was used in small-size passenger cars.

FM, FMX, HX, MX.   These transmissions were also called Ford-O-Matic or Cruise-O-Matic. They were all based on a Borg-Warner

transmission design used between 1951 and 1980. They are three-speed units that use a type 10 Ravigneaux gear train. They were used in vehicles throughout the product line.

TWO SPEED.   This transmission was used between 1960 and 1964. It was a two-speed unit that used a Ravigneaux gear train similar to the type 9. It was used in the Falcon, one of the early compact passenger cars.

10.3.2 FORD MOTOR COMPANY TRANSAXLES   Ford transaxles can be identified by the vehicle's production label located on the driver's side door pillar. When the transaxle is out of the vehicle, it can be identified by a service identification tag attached to the case. The size, shape, and appearance along with the shape of its pan can be used for identification. At this time, all Ford transaxles are used with transverse engine and transaxle mounting.

4F50N/AX4N TRANSAXLE.   The 4F50N was originally named the AX4N. It is an electronically controlled version of the AXOD introduced in 1986 (see Figure 10–20). It is a four-speed unit that

FIGURE 10–25 An exploded view of a C6 transmission. (*Courtesy of Aceomatic Recon*)

uses a variation of a type 15 gear train. ● **SEE FIGURE 10–26**. The low/intermediate band of the AXOD has been replaced with a low/intermediate clutch and low/intermediate one-way clutch to make the AX4N a nonsynchronous gear train. This gives better shift feel with no hesitation between gears. Electronic controls determine the shift strategy. It is currently used in full-size FWD cars.

AX4S TRANSAXLE. This transaxle is another electronically controlled version of the AXOD, but it retains the low/intermediate band, making it a synchronous transmission. ● **SEE FIGURE 10–27**. During the 2–3 shift, the release of the intermediate/low band must be synchronized with the application of the direct clutch. Electronic controls determine the shift strategy. The 3–4 shift also requires synchronization of the friction members. It is currently used in full-size FWD vehicles and vans.

CD4E TRANSAXLE. The CD4E transaxle was introduced in 1995. It is a four-speed unit that uses a type 16 gear train. A centrally located chain and sprocket connects the transmission gear set with the final drive planetary gear set. Electronic controls are used to determine the shift strategy. It is currently used in midsize FWD vehicles (see Figure 10–3).

F4E TRANSAXLE. The F4E is a modern version of the 4EAT transaxle. It is a four-speed unit that uses a type 12 gear train. Electronic controls determine the shift strategy. It is used in compact FWD cars.

4F20E TRANSAXLE. The 4F20E transaxle is built by JATCO. It is used in a joint-venture vehicle, the Mercury Villager van, that is co-produced with Nissan. See Section 10.8 for more information.

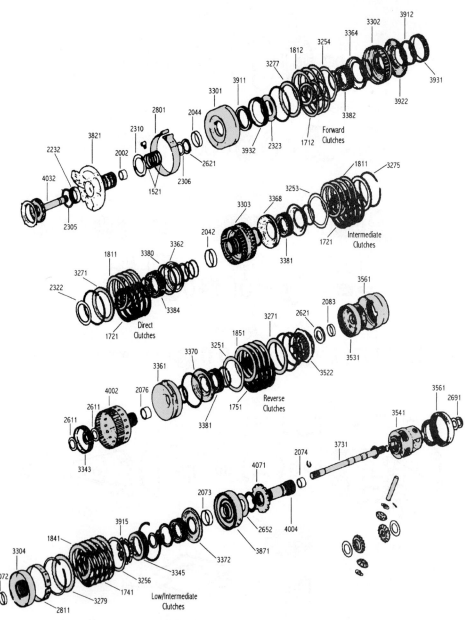

FIGURE 10–26 An exploded view of the 4F50N (AX4N) gear train. (*Courtesy of Aceomatic Recon*)

4F27E TRANSAXLE. The 4F27E is a four-speed transaxle that is used in the Focus. It uses a gear train that is similar to a type 16 gear train. Electronic controls determine the shift strategy.

6F35, 6F50, 6F55 TRANSAXLE. The 6F50 is the Ford version of a very compact, six-speed transaxle that was developed jointly with General Motors. About 40 parts will interchange between the 6F50 and 6T70 transaxles. The gear ratios of these transaxles range from a 4.48:1 first gear to 0.74:1 sixth gear. This gives a gear ratio spread of 6.05. They use a hyper-elliptical torque converter and an offset, chain-driven pump to help shorten the overall length. The gear train uses three simple planetary sets that have the carriers and ring gears interconnected. The transmission module is located inside the transmission, where it has a contact temperature sink in a controlled environment. It has adaptive shift controls, and the driver has the option of tap-up/tap-down shift control.

The 6F35 is a smaller version designed for use with the 2.5-L I-4 and 3.0-L V-6 engines. The 6F55 is a stronger version designed for use with higher-output 3.5-L engines. The 6F35 connects the transmission gear set to a planetary gear final drive using a specially designed silent chain.

ATX TRANSAXLE. The ATX three-speed transaxle was used in compact cars from 1981 to 1997. Power was transmitted through a type 10 Ravigneaux gear train. The ATX was first built using a unique planetary torque converter that split the gear set input between hydraulic and mechanical connections. Later units used conventional and centrifugal lockup converters.

FIGURE 10–27 An exploded view of the Ford AX4S gear train. Note the similarity to the AX4N gear train with the addition of a low sprag and a direct roller clutch. (*Courtesy of Aceomatic Recon*)

Labels visible in figure:

Row 1: 4031, 2305, 2232, 3821, 2002, 2306, 2621, 2310, 1521, 4571, 2801, 2044, 3301, 3911, 3931, 2321 — DRIVEN SPROCKET SUPPORT, OVERDRIVE BAND, LOW SPRAG

Row 2: 3276, 1811, 3252, 3383, 3365, 3302, 2041, 3921, 3912, 3933, 2322, 1711 — FORWARD DRUM, DIRECT ROLLER CLUTCH

Row 3: 3272, 1811, 3382, 3362, 2042, 3303, 3363, 3384, 3252, 1831, 3274, 1721, 1721 — DIRECT AND INTERM HOUSING

Row 4: 2611, 3341, 2611, 4001, 2075, 3361, 3370, 3381, 3251, 1851, 3271, 1751 — INTERM HUB, SUN GEAR, REVERSE CLUTCH

Row 5: 3503, 2081, 2621, 2083, 3531, 3561, 2211, 2071, 3305, 2811 — FRONT PLANET, REAR PLANET, SUN GEAR, LOW INT BAND

10.4 GENERAL MOTORS CORPORATION

Like other manufacturers, General Motors uses transmissions produced in various parts of the world, and supplies other manufacturers with General Motors transmissions. The most notable are Rolls Royce and Jaguar.

General Motors previously identified its transmissions as Turbo Hydra-Matic (THM) followed by an alphanumeric code that described the relative size of the unit. Currently, General Motors uses an alphanumeric model designation system, introduced in the mid-1980s, as follows:

1st character: Number of speeds

2nd character: L = Longitudinal, T = Transverse, M = Manual

3rd character: Relative torque capacity, 10 = smallest

Optional digit: A = AWD, E = Electronic, HD = Heavy duty

Detailed descriptions of each General Motors transmission and how it operates are available in the manufacturer's service information, transmission service manuals, and trade publications. The gear ratios for General Motors transmissions and transaxles are shown in ● **FIGURE 10–28.**

TRANSAXLE GEAR RATIOS							
Model	First	Second	Third	Fourth	Fifth	Sixth	Reverse
3T40	2.84	1.6	1				2.07
4T40	2.96	1.626	1	0.681			2.13
4T60, 4T65E	2.921	1.568	1	0.705			2.38
4T80E	2.96	1.626	1	0.681			2.13
6T70, 6T75	4.48	2.87	1.84	1.41	1	0.74	2.88
AF33-5	4.69	2.94	1.92	1.3	1		3.18
TRANSMISSION GEAR RATIOS							
3L30, 3L80	2.4	1.48	1				2.0
4L30-E	2.4/2.86	1.48/1.62	1	0.723			2.0
4L60E/4L65E	3.059	1.625	1	0.696			2.29
4L80E/4L85E	2.482	1.482	1	0.75			2.08
5L40E/5L50E	3.46	2.21	1.59	1	0.76		3.03
6L45/6L50	4.06	2.37	1.55	1.16	0.85	0.67	3.2
6L80/6L90	4.02	2.36	1.53	1.15	0.85	0.67	3.06
Allison 1000	3.1	1.18	1.41	1	0.71		4.49
Allison 2000	3.5	1.9	1.44	1	0.74		5.09
HM 200	2.74	1.57	1				2.07
HM 200-4R	2.74	1.57	1	0.67			2.07
HM 350	2.52	1.52	1				1.93
HM 400	2.48	1.48	1				2.08

FIGURE 10–28 The gear ratios for General Motors transmissions.

10.4.1 GENERAL MOTORS REAR-WHEEL-DRIVE TRANSMISSIONS

General Motors has produced many different automatic transmissions. Some out-of-production transmissions will also be described in this section. General Motors transmissions can be identified by the identification tag on the vehicle. When the transmission is out of the vehicle, it can be identified by a service identification tag attached to the case. ● SEE FIGURE 10–29. The size, shape, and appearance of the case and the shape of the pan also can be used to identify a unit. ● SEE FIGURE 10–30.

3L30 TRANSMISSION. The 3L30 is a three-speed, relatively low-torque-capacity unit that uses a type 11 Ravigneaux gear train (see Figure 5–30). The 3L30 was formerly called a THM 180 or THM 180C if it had a lockup torque converter. ● SEE FIGURE 10–31. It is used in small RWD SUVs.

4L30-E TRANSMISSION. The 4L30-E is a four-speed dual planetary design that combines a type 11 gear train with an overdrive unit at the front (see Figure 5–42). This combination is similar to types 6, 7, and 8 transmissions, but it uses a Ravigneaux (type 11) gear train. It uses electronic shift controls and is currently used in various RWD vehicles. The Cadillac XLR uses the 5L50E adapted from the 4L30-E and 5L40E.

4L60-E TRANSMISSION. The 4L60-E is a four-speed, electronically controlled transmission that uses a type 13 gear train. It was formerly called a THM 700-R4 or M30. ● SEE FIGURE 10–32. It was also used in the F-cars and Y-cars (Camaro and Corvette) as well as pickups, SUVs, and RWD vans. The low first gear and overdrive fourth gear have made this transmission popular with hot-rodders. The 4L65 is a renamed version of a 4L60E HD.

4L80-E TRANSMISSION. The 4L80-E is a four-speed dual planetary design that combines a three-speed gear train (3L80) with an overdrive unit at the front. ● SEE FIGURE 10–33. The gear train used is similar to a type 4 Simpson gear train. The four-speed combination is similar to types 6, 7, and 8 transmissions, but it uses the different rear unit. The 4L80-E was formerly called the MT1 or THM R2. It uses electronic shift controls and is currently used in pickups, SUVs, and light trucks.

THM 200, THM 200C, THM 325 TRANSMISSIONS. These are three-speed transmissions that use a type 2 Simpson gear train. The THM 200 was used from 1976 to 1987 in compact to midsize cars. Later versions that used a lockup torque converter used the THM 200C designation. This transmission was the first unit built in the United States with stamped steel clutch drums, sintered/powdered iron one-way clutch races, and metric dimensions.

The THM 325 used the same gear train in a manner similar to the THM 425 (see Figure 10–6). It was longitudinal mounted alongside the engine, and was combined with a hypoid final

LEGEND

1 WINDSOR, CANADA
2 CALENDAR YEAR
3 JULIAN DATE
4 MODEL YEAR
5 NO MEANING
6 MODEL
7 SHIFT BUILD
8 CALENDAR YEAR
9 MODEL YEAR
10 MODEL
11 SERIAL NUMBER
12 JULIAN DATE
13 TRANSMISSION ID LOCATION
14 VIN LOCATION

FIGURE 10–29 General Motors transmissions (a) and transaxles (b) can be identified by a label or tag on the case. (*Reprinted with permission of General Motors*)

FIGURE 10–30 The shape of the pan gasket can be used for a general identification of a transmission or transaxle.

FIGURE 10–31 A 3L30 transmission. (*Courtesy of Slauson Transmission Parts, www.slauson.com*)

drive assembly and used in FWD cars. A chain and sprocket assembly coupled the torque converter to the transmission input shaft. With the exception of the pan covering the chain and sprockets, the THM 325 appears identical to the THM 325-4L (see Figure 10–35). The THM 325-4L has a much deeper pan to enclose the overdrive unit.

THM 200-4R, THM 325-4L TRANSMISSIONS. The THM 200-4R is a type 7 four-speed transmission used in a dual-unit design that combined a type 2 gear set with an overdrive planetary at the front (see Figure 5–26). It was used from 1981 to 1990 in smaller and midsize vehicles. ● **SEE FIGURE 10–34.**

FIGURE 10–32 A cutaway view of a 4L60-E transmission showing the internal parts.

FIGURE 10–33 4L80E transmission. (*Courtesy of Slauson Transmission Parts, www.slauson.com*)

FIGURE 10–34 A THM 200-4R transmission. It has the appearance of a stretch THM 200C. (*Courtesy of Slauson Transmission Parts, www.slauson.com*)

The THM 325-4L is the FWD version of the THM 200-4R. ● **SEE FIGURE 10–35**. It is similar to the THM 325 with an overdrive unit located at the torque converter output. In all gears but fourth, the drive chain transfers power at a 1:1 ratio. In fourth gear, power is transferred at an overdrive ratio.

THM 250, THM 250C TRANSMISSIONS. The THM 250 is a three-speed, type 2 Simpson gear train transmission that is a light-duty version of the THM 350 (see Figure 10–36). A band is used for the second gear reaction member, making the THM 250 have a synchronous 2–3 shift. A THM 250 transmission can be identified by the exterior band adjustment. It was used in

the early 1970s in inexpensive vehicles. The THM 250C uses a lockup torque converter.

THM 350, THM 350C, THM 375B TRANSMISSIONS. These are three-speed transmissions that use a type 3 Simpson gear train. ● **SEE FIGURE 10–36**. They have a nonsynchronous 2–3 shift because an intermediate roller clutch is used for second gear (see Figure 4–22). Later versions with a lockup torque converter used the THM 350C designation. The THM 375B was a heavy-duty version with increased clutch pack capacity. At one time, there were more THM 350s on the road than any other automatic transmission.

FIGURE 10–37 A 3L80 (THM 400) transmission. (*Courtesy of Slauson Transmission Parts, www.slauson.com*)

FIGURE 10–35 A THM 325 transmission. A 325-4L will have a larger chain cover (361) to enclose the overdrive gear set. (*Courtesy of Slauson Transmission Parts, www.slauson.com*)

FIGURE 10–36 A THM 350C transmission. The similar THM 250C has a band adjustment screw in the other side (right) of the case. (*Courtesy of Slauson Transmission Parts, www .slauson.com*)

3L80, THM 400, THM 375, THM 425 TRANSMISSIONS. These three-speed transmissions use a similar gear train to the type 4. ● **SEE FIGURE 10–37.** Like the 4L80-E, the Simpson gear train is turned end-for-end. This transmission was used from 1964 to 1990 in larger passenger cars, pickups, vans, and light trucks. The TH-375 was a light-duty version using smaller clutch packs.

The THM 425 version of this transmission was combined with a final drive assembly and used in FWD vehicles (see Figure 10–6). A chain and sprocket assembly was used to couple the torque converter to the transmission input shaft.

TWO-MODE HYBRID TRANSMISSION. This transmission, also called the 2ML70, was developed for full-size hybrid vehicles, SUVs, and pickups in cooperation with Chrysler Corporation, BMW, and Mercedes. It includes two 60-kilowatt, three-phase, 300-volt motors; four multidisc clutches; and three simple planetary gear sets. These produce four fixed gear ratios: first: 3.69:1, second: 1.7:1, third: 1:1, and fourth: 0.74:1 and two variable ratios: EVT Mode 1: infinity to 1.7:1 and EVT Mode 2: 1.7:1 to 0.74:1. A torque-dampener is used in place of a torque converter.

Inside the transmission are two high-voltage, three-phase motor/generators (M/G). M/G 1 is used to move the vehicle forward from a stop and to start the engine; the engine has no starter motor. M/G 2 is used to move the vehicle in reverse, and both motor/generators can become generators during deceleration to help recharge the batteries. This transmission contains an auxiliary, electric fluid pump that provides pressure during operation with the engine off.

6L80E TRANSMISSION. This electronically controlled six-speed transmission features clutch-to-clutch shifts, with adaptive shift patterns and timing. This type 13 transmission combines one simple planetary gear set with a Ravigneaux gear set. This is a wide-ratio transmission with a 4.03:1 first gear and a 0.67:1 sixth gear for a 6.04:1 gear ratio spread. The very low first gear provides rapid starts, and the two overdrive gears allow economical low engine speed when cruising. The transmission module is located inside the transmission; it is attached to the control solenoid assembly for temperature control. It has adaptive shift controls, and the driver has the option of tap-up/tap-down shift control.

6L50E TRANSMISSION. This transmission is a smaller, lighter version of the 6L80E.

PTO Location

Filter

(a)

(b)

FIGURE 10–38 This Allison transmission has an external fluid filter and plates covering the areas where a power take-off (PTO) can be mounted.

ALLISON 1000 AND 2000 TRANSMISSIONS. Allison produces medium- and heavy-duty transmissions used in many trucks, buses, and various types of off-highway vehicles. The 1000 and 2000 series transmissions are used in some General Motors light trucks and pickups. ● SEE FIGURE 10–38. These are five-speed units with an input torque rating of 520 ft-lb (705 N-m) of torque. They have a screw-on fluid filter, much like an engine oil filter, and mounting pads for a power take-off (PTO). The gear ratios are shown in Figure 10–28.

POWERGLIDE. The Powerglide is a two-speed transmission using a Ravigneaux gear train. It was used only by Chevrolet and was produced in two versions: a cast-iron-case unit from 1950 to 1960 and a redesigned, aluminum-case unit from 1960 to 1973 (see Figure 5–33). The TH 300 was used by other divisions from 1964 to 1969 in smaller cars. The lightweight aluminum case and its simplicity make this unit popular for racing applications.

The Powerglide was built into a transaxle that was used in the 1960 and later Corvairs and Pontiac Tempests, making it the first domestic automatic transaxle.

10.4.2 GENERAL MOTORS TRANSAXLES With the exception of the THM 325, THM 325-4L, and THM 425 transmissions used from 1966 to 1985, all FWD transaxles are used with a transverse-mounted engine.

With each of the transaxles, the valve body, which contains the pump, is located in the upper pan at the left end of the transaxle. Most of these units use a variable-displacement vane pump.

Currently, General Motors has five transaxles in production. When the transaxle is out of the vehicle, it can be identified by a service identification tag attached to the case. Like other units, the size, shape, and appearance of the case and the shape of the pan can be used for identification (see Figure 10–29 and 10–30).

3T40 TRANSAXLE. The 3T40 is a three-speed transaxle that uses a type 2 Simpson gear train. The 3T40 was formerly called a THM 125, M34, THM 125C, HM3T40, or MD9 transaxle and

was introduced in 1980 for the X-body car line (Citation). The transmission section is similar to that of a THM 200 transmission with a chain and sprocket assembly connecting the torque converter to the transmission input. ● SEE FIGURE 10–39. It was used with 4-cylinder engines in the J-cars (Cavalier and Sunfire).

4T40-E TRANSAXLE. The 4T40-E is a four-speed transaxle that uses a gear train that is similar to the type 16. The appearance is similar to a 4T60 and 4T65-E (see Figure 10–41). It uses electronic controls for shift timing and quality. It is currently used with 4-cylinder engines in the J-car and N-car lines (Cavalier and Malibu).

4T60-E TRANSAXLE. The 4T60-E is a four-speed transaxle that uses a type 16 gear train. ● SEE FIGURE 10–40. The 4T60-E was formerly called a THM 440 or M13. It is currently used with

FIGURE 10–39 A cutaway view of a 3T40 transaxle showing the internal parts.

RANGE	GEAR	A SOLENOID	B SOLENOID	4TH CLUTCH	REVERSE BAND	2ND CLUTCH	3RD CLUTCH	3RD SPRAG CLUTCH	INPUT CLUTCH	INPUT SPRAG CLUTCH	2-1 BAND	1-2 SUPPORT ROLLER CLUTCH	FRWD BAND
P - N		ON	ON						*	*			
D	1ST	ON	ON						APPLY	HOLD		HOLD	APPLY
	2ND	OFF	ON			APPLY			*	O-RUN		HOLD	APPLY
	3RD	OFF	OFF			APPLY	APPLY	HOLD				O-RUN	APPLY
	4TH	ON	OFF	APPLY		APPLY	*	O-RUN				O-RUN	APPLY
D	3RD	@OFF	@OFF			APPLY	APPLY	HOLD	APPLY	HOLD		O-RUN	APPLY
	2ND	@OFF	@ON			APPLY			*	O-RUN		HOLD	APPLY
	1ST	@ON	@ON						APPLY	HOLD		HOLD	APPLY
2	2ND	@OFF	@ON			APPLY			*	O-RUN	APPLY	HOLD	APPLY
	1ST	@ON	@ON						APPLY	HOLD	APPLY	HOLD	APPLY
1	1ST	@ON	@ON				APPLY	HOLD	APPLY	HOLD	APPLY	HOLD	APPLY
R	REV	ON	ON		APPLY				APPLY	HOLD			

* APPLIED BUT NOT EFFECTIVE

ON = SOLENOID ENERGIZED

OFF = SOLENOID DE-ENERGIZED

@ THE SOLENOID'S STATE FOLLOWS A SHIFT PATTERN WHICH DEPENDS UPON VEHICLE SPEED, THROTTLE POSITION AND SELECTED GEAR RANGE

FIGURE 10–40 A cutaway view of a 4T60-E transaxle showing the control devices.

the smaller V6 engine in the N-car, W-car, and U-body van (Malibu, Grand Prix, and Venture).

4T65-E TRANSAXLE. The 4T65-E is a redesigned version of the 4T60-E and uses the type 16 gear train. Upgrades were made to the case, second gear, and torque converter to improve durability and performance. It uses advanced electronic controls allowing the PCM to control line pressure. It is used in the larger V6 engines in the G-car, H-car, and W-car (Riviera, Le Sabre, and Grand Prix).

4T80-E TRANSAXLE. The 4T80-E is a four-speed unit that uses a gear train that is similar to the type 16. It uses full electronic controls. ● **SEE FIGURE 10–41.** The 4T80-E uses three pumps to move fluid. A primary gerotor pump supplies fluid for the basic needs of the transaxle, and a secondary gerotor pump helps meet demands for fluid pressure during shifts. The third pump is a scavenger, gear-type pump that is used to move fluid from the bottom pan to the side cover. All three pumps are mounted at the valve body and are driven by a driveshaft from the torque converter. The 4T80-E is used with high-torque engines found in the E-car, G-car, and K-cars (Eldorado, Aurora, Seville, Concours, and Deville).

6T30, 6T40, AND 6T50 TRANSAXLES. These are smaller, lighter versions of the 6T70. ● **SEE FIGURE 10–42.** These transaxles use a drive chain to transfer power from the sprocket, attached to the transmission output carrier assembly, to the sprocket on the differential carrier. The differential assembly uses a planetary gear set for the final drive reduction with a variety of ratios between 2.29:1 and 4.11:1.

6T70 AND 75 TRANSAXLES. The 6T70 is the General Motors version of a very compact, six-speed transaxle that was developed jointly with Ford. ● **SEE FIGURE 10–43.** About 40 parts will interchange between the 6T70 and 6F50 transaxles. The gear ratios of these transaxles range from a 4.48:1 first gear to 0.74:1 sixth gear. This gives a gear ratio spread of 6.05. The 6T75 is a high-torque, 300-lb-ft version of the 6T70 (280 lb-ft). It uses a hyper-elliptical torque converter and an offset, chain-driven pump to help shorten the overall length. The gear train uses three simple planetary sets that have the carriers and ring gears interconnected. The transmission module is located inside the transmission, where it has a contact temperature sink in a controlled environment. It has adaptive shift controls, and the driver has the option of tap-up/tap-down shift control.

FWD TWO-MODE TRANSAXLE. A FWD version of the 2ML70, the 2MT70 was to be used in the hybrid version of the 2009 Saturn Vue using a 2.4-L engine.

10.5 SATURN TRANSAXLE

Saturn began as an independent division of General Motors, and these vehicles use a FWD transverse engine and transaxle of their own design. This transaxle is called the TAAT. It is an electronically controlled type 19 nonplanetary gear train, similar to the transaxle used in Hondas (see Figure 5–56). Year 2000 and later Saturn vehicles use General Motors transaxles.

10.6 IMPORT TRANSMISSIONS/ TRANSAXLES

The transmissions and transaxles used in import vehicles are very similar to the domestic units. They use planetary gears (with the exception of the Honda transaxles), multiple-disc clutches, bands, one-way clutches, hydraulic control systems, and lockup torque converters. A detailed description of their operation is normally available in the manufacturer's service manual, transmission service manuals, and trade publications.

In some cases, the import vehicle manufacturer will design and build its own transmissions, much like the domestic manufacturers. In other cases, they use units built by another manufacturer, such as Aisin-Seiki, Aisin-Warner, JATCO, or ZF. These companies are typically subsidiaries of major manufacturers; for example, Toyota owns a large share of both Aisin-Warner and Aisin-Seiki. These two companies build transmissions for Toyota and other Asian, European, and American companies. Companies that have used these transmissions include Chrysler, General Motors, Isuzu, Mitsubishi, Subaru, and Suzuki.

The Japanese Automatic Transmission Company (JATCO) is jointly owned by Mazda and Nissan. JATCO builds transmissions for Asian, American, and European companies such as BMW, Chrysler, Ford, Infinity, Isuzu, Mitsubishi, Nissan, Subaru, and Suzuki. Zahnradfabrik Friedrichshafen (ZF) is a German transmission manufacturer that builds transmissions for many high-end vehicle manufacturers. ● **SEE FIGURE 10–44.** Some companies that have used or are currently using ZF transmissions are Alfa Romeo, Audi, BMW, Chrysler, Citroen, Ford, Jaguar, Peugot, Porsche, Range Rover, Saab, and Volvo. ZF recently introduced an eight-speed transmission, the 8HP, that has the same size and weight as the 6HP. The 8HP uses only five shift elements, and it offers three coupling options: a torque converter with clutch, an electric motor with multiplate clutch pack, or wet-plate clutch pack (see Figure 9–3).

There are too many import transmissions to describe in a book of this type. We will limit the description to the three most popular vehicle manufacturers. The transmissions that are most commonly encountered by technicians are those used in Honda, Nissan, and Toyota vehicles. A brief description of the more common units follows.

10.7 HONDA/ACURA

Honda produces the transmissions used in Honda and Acura vehicles. These units do not use planetary gears like most other automatic transmissions; they use constant-mesh, helical gears like those in a standard transmission. Hydraulically operated

FIGURE 10–41 (a) A cutaway view of a 4T80-E transaxle showing the internal parts and (b) an exploded view of the pump showing the primary pump (200 and 201), secondary pump (205 and 206), and the scavenge pump (223 and 224).

Model	GRS	Max Torque, lb ft (Nm)	Length, in. (mm)	Converter Dia., in (mm)	Weight (wet), lbs. (kg)	Final Drive
6T30	6.0	129 (175)	13.8 (353)	8.6 (220)	157.3 (71.5)	Chain
6T40	6.14	177 (240)	13.8 (353)	9.3 (236)	180.4 (82)	Chain
6T45	6.14	232 (315)	14 ((357)	9.3 (236)	184.8 (84)	Chain
6T70	6.04	280 (380)	14 ((357)	9.9 (246)	224 (101.8)	Gears
6T75	6.04	295 (400)	14 ((357)	9.9 (246)	225 (102.3)	Gears

GRS: Gear Ratio Spread
Chain final drives use planetary gear, final drive reduction

FIGURE 10–42 Five versions of the 6T series transaxles are used in GM vehicles.

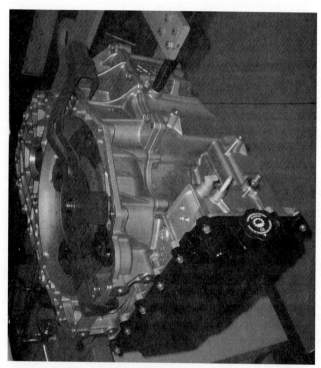

FIGURE 10–43 A 6T70 transaxle is quite compact and well suited for FWD installations.

FIGURE 10–44 The 6HP26 transmission is the first six-speed automatic transmission produced for passenger cars. (*Courtesy of ZF Group North American Operations*)

multiple-disc clutches are used in place of the synchronizer assemblies of a standard transmission.

The early Honda transaxles were two-speed units (1973 to 1980), then three-speed (used from 1981 to 1985), and now four-speed units (since 1983). Honda transaxles are coded to specific vehicles by a small tag on the side of the transmission case. A two-part number is used, with the first part being the transmission model number and the second part being the serial number. The model number should always be used when purchasing parts or locating service information; it can also be used to match a transaxle to a vehicle. ● **SEE FIGURE 10–45.**

10.7.1 HONDA THREE-SPEED TRANSAXLES
Honda three-speed transaxles were used in the 1981 to 1985 Civic and 1979 to 1982 Accord. These units have two parallel shafts: the mainshaft and the countershaft. ● **SEE FIGURE 10–46.** The mainshaft is inline with the crankshaft, and the countershaft provides the output to the final drive and differential. The gears on the mainshaft and countershaft are in constant mesh. Three clutches are used, one for each of the gear ranges. For first gear, the first clutch applies to lock first gear to the mainshaft to drive the first countershaft gear. Second and third gears are very similar, but use gears of different sizes for the higher ratios. All shifts are hydraulic and have to be carefully synchronized. One clutch must be released as the next clutch is applied.

An idler gear is used to obtain reverse. Reverse is achieved by engaging the reverse selector mechanically and applying the reverse clutch.

10.7.2 HONDA FOUR-SPEED TRANSAXLES
A variety of four-speed units have been produced in both transverse and longitudinal models. Their operation is very similar to the three-speed transmissions with an additional pair of gears along with another clutch for fourth gear. A lockup torque converter clutch was used, with the exception of the 1983 Prelude. These units are commonly identified by the number of clutches and shafts used in the unit. For ease of discussion, they will be grouped into two-shaft and three-shaft versions.

TWO-SHAFT VERSIONS. These four-speed transaxles, like the three-speed unit, have the mainshaft inline with the engine crankshaft and a countershaft connected to the final drive and differential. ● **SEE FIGURE 10–47.** The first, second, and fourth clutches are mounted on the mainshaft, and the second clutch is mounted

TRANSAXLE GEAR RATIOS						
Model	First	Second	Third	Fourth	Fifth	Reverse
4-SPEED	2.61	1.55	1.02	0.68		1.91
	2.68	1.54	1.08	0.74		2.0
	2.72	1.52	0.98	0.67		1.95
5-SPEED	2.56	1.55	1.02	0.73	0.52	1.85
	2.65	1.52	1.04	0.74	0.57	2.0
	2.69	1.56	1.02/1.07	0.73/0.69	0.53/0.48	1.89
	2.7	1.57	1.07	0.69	0.48	1.89
	2.7	1.61	1.07	0.77	0.54	1.89

FIGURE 10–45 The gear ratios for the current-model Honda and Acura automatic transaxles.

FIGURE 10–46 This Honda three-speed gear set shows the arrangement of the gears and controlling clutches. (*Courtesy of America Honda Motor Company*)

FIGURE 10–48 A cutaway view of a short-shaft version of a three-shaft, four-speed Honda transaxle that uses five clutches. (*Courtesy of America Honda Motor Company*)

FIGURE 10–47 A cutaway view of a two-shaft, four-speed Honda transaxle. (*Courtesy of America Honda Motor Company*)

on the countershaft. A one-way clutch under first gear is also on the countershaft. This one-way clutch allows first gear to drive the countershaft in first gear. When the transmission shifts into second, third, or fourth gear, the one-way clutch overruns.

THREE-SHAFT VERSIONS. There are two variations of this design: a short shaft and a full shaft.

The short-shaft variation has an additional subshaft with a first-hold clutch for a total of five clutches. ● **SEE FIGURE 10–48.** These provide a means to hold the transmission in manual-low for compression braking. The first-hold clutch is applied only in manual-1.

A second design, short-shaft variation, uses four clutches, and second gear is mounted on the short subshaft. ● **SEE FIGURE 10–49.** This transaxle does not have a manual-1 gear selector position; manual-2 is the lowest manual range available. First gear is mounted on a one-way clutch so it will overrun in all of the higher gears and during deceleration.

The four-shaft variations have three parallel shafts. The mainshaft is the power input from the engine and is inline with the crankshaft. The countershaft is the output to the final drive and differential, and the secondary shaft is parallel to the other

FIGURE 10–49 A cutaway view of a short-shaft version of a three-shaft, four-speed Honda transaxle that used four clutches. (*Courtesy of America Honda Motor Company*)

FIGURE 10–50 A cutaway view of a long-shaft version of a three-shaft, four-speed Honda transaxle that uses four clutches. (*Courtesy of America Honda Motor Company*)

FIGURE 10–51 A longitudinal, two-shaft, four-speed Honda transaxle that uses five clutches. (*Courtesy of America Honda Motor Company*)

FIGURE 10–52 A longitudinal, two-shaft, four-speed Honda transaxle that uses six clutches. (*Courtesy of America Honda Motor Company*)

two shafts. ● **SEE FIGURE 10–50**. The third and fourth clutches and third, fourth, and reverse gears are on the mainshaft. The countershaft has gears for first, second, third, fourth, and reverse along with idler gears and park gear. The secondary shift has the first and second clutches along with first, second, and idler gears. The latest versions of these transaxles use electronic shaft controls to improve shift quality and transaxle durability.

10.7.3 HONDA LONGITUDINAL DESIGNS The longi-
tudinal transaxles are used in the Acura product line. They are two-shaft designs with the mainshaft in line with the engine crankshaft. The countershaft is below the mainshaft and transfers power through the secondary gears to the extension shaft that drives the hypoid ring and pinion final drive gears at the differential. ● **SEE FIGURE 10–51**.

There are two versions of this unit. The five-clutch version has clutches for first, second, third, fourth, and first-hold. The hydraulically operated servo moves the reverse gear into position, similar to the transverse transaxles. The six-clutch version has a clutch for first, second, third, and reverse plus first-hold for manual-1. ● **SEE FIGURE 10–52**.

Model	First	Second	Third	Fourth	Fifth	Reverse
Transaxle Gear Ratios						
RE4F04A, B, V & W	2.785	1.545	1	0.694		2.27
RL4F03A, B & V	2.861	1.562	1	0.697		2.23
RE5F22A	4.657	3.032	1.982	1.341	1.018	5.11
Transmission Gear Ratios						
RE4R01A/ RE4R04A/ RL4R01A	2.785	1.545	1	0.694		NA
RE5R05A	3.827	2.368	1.519	1	0.834	2.61
	3.540	2.264	1.417	1	0.834	
	3.84	2.35	1.53	1	0.834	2.76

FIGURE 10–53 The gear ratios for Nissan transaxles and transmissions.

1. Torque converter clutch piston
2. Torque converter
3. Oil pump
4. Input shaft
5. Brake band
6. Reverse clutch
7. High clutch
8. Front pinion gear
9. Front sun gear
10. Front internal gear
11. Front planetary carrier
12. Rear sun gear
13. Rear pinion gear
14. Rear internal gear
15. Rear planetary carrier
16. Forward clutch
17. Forward one-way clutch
18. Overrun clutch
19. Low one-way clutch
20. Low & reverse brake
21. Parking pawl
22. Parking gear
23. Output shaft

FIGURE 10–54 A schematic view of a Nissan RE4R01A four-speed transmission gear set, torque converter, and apply devices. (*Courtesy of Nissan North America, Inc.*)

10.8 NISSAN

JATCO is the major supplier of Nissan transmissions. Like other manufacturers, Nissan has used several different coding systems. ● **SEE FIGURE 10–53.** The latest system uses a seven-character, alphanumeric system, as follows:

1st letter: E = Electronic TCC, L = Hydraulic TCC, and R = Remote shift

2nd letter: E = Electronic control, L = Hydraulic TCC, and N = Nissan (JATCO trans.)

1st digit: Number of forward speeds

3rd letter: F = Front wheel drive (FWD), R = RWD

2nd and 3rd digits: Transmission style/unit

①	Torque converter	⑨	Front internal gear	⑰	Overrun clutch
②	Oil pump	⑩	Front planetary carrier	⑱	Low one-way clutch
③	Input shaft	⑪	Rear sun gear	⑲	Low & reverse brake
④	Brake band	⑫	Rear pinion gear	⑳	Parking pawl
⑤	Reverse clutch	⑬	Rear internal gear	㉑	Parking gear
⑥	High clutch	⑭	Rear planetary carrier	㉒	Output shaft
⑦	Front sun gear	⑮	Forward clutch	㉓	Idle gear
⑧	Front pinion gear	⑯	Forward one-way clutch	㉔	Output gear

FIGURE 10–55 A schematic view of a Nissan RE4F02 four-speed transaxle gear set, torque converter, and apply devices. (*Courtesy of Nissan North America, Inc.*)

4th/final letter: Series A = First version, B = Second, and so on; can be V = Viscous coupling in the differential

10.8.1 NISSAN RWD TRANSMISSIONS
The JATCO/ Nissan four-speed transmissions use a dual planetary gear train. The SUV Pathfinder and pickups use the smaller RE4R01A. ● **SEE FIGURE 10–54.** 4WD versions are connected to a transfer case, and 2WD versions use a driveshaft for the rear axle. The Infiniti Q45 uses a larger RE4R03A that has four-gear planetary assemblies.

10.8.2 NISSAN FWD TRANSAXLES
The JATCO/Nissan four-speed transaxles also use a dual planetary gear train. ● **SEE FIGURE 10–55.** The major difference is the transaxle output to the final drive gears and differential. The RE4F02, 03A, 03B, and 04A series transaxles are in current production.

10.9 TOYOTA

Toyota has used a variety of transmissions beginning with the two-speed Toyoglide. It was replaced with three- and then four-speed designs. Most of these designs are very similar. Toyota seems to have a large number of different models, because the case might have been changed to suit a particular vehicle model or the hydraulic or electronic shift controls may have been changed. ● **SEE FIGURE 10–56.**

Toyota uses an alphanumeric coding system to identify the various models and configurations, as follows:

1st character: Transmission type: A = Automatic

2nd character: Transmission family

3rd character: Family generation

This system was modified to add another digit plus a suffix. The current system is as follows:

1st character: Transmission type: A = Automatic

2nd character digit: Transmission family

3rd character digit: Number of forward speeds

4th character digit: Family generation

Suffix: D = Overdrive, E = Electronic, F = Four wheel drive/ mechanical transfer case, H = Four wheel drive/electronic transfer case, L = Lock-up converter, I = Intelligence

A typical transmission code of A140E tells us that it is an automatic transmission. It is family number 1. It is a four-speed design that uses electronic controls.

Toyota transmissions can be divided into transverse and longitudinal drive arrangements:

Transverse series (all FWD): A130, A140, A240, and A540

Longitudinal series: A20, A30, A40, A340

10.9.1 TOYOTA RWD TRANSMISSIONS
The A20 and A30 were early Toyota automatic transmissions used in the 1950s and 1960s. The A20 is a two-speed Ravigneaux unit similar to a type 9 gear train. The A30 is a three-speed Ravigneaux gear train, similar to a type 10 gear train. These designs were

TRANSAXLE GEAR RATIOS							
Model	First	Second	Third	Fourth	Fifth	Sixth	Reverse
A131/132	2.81	1.549	1				2.296
A140E/ 240E	2.81	1.549	1	0.706			2.977
A242L/ 245E/241E	3.643	2.008	1.296	0.892			2.977
A244E/246E	4.005	2.208	1.425	0.981			3.272
A350E	2.804	1.978	1.531	1	0.705		2.393
A540E/541E	2.81	1.549	1	0.73			2.296
A650E	3.357	2.18	1.424	1	0.753		3.431
A760H	3.52	2.042	1.4	1	0.716	0.586	3.224
A761E	3.296	1.958	1.348	1	0.725	0.582	2.951
A960E	3.538	2.06	1.404	1	0.713	0.582	3.168
U140E & F	3.938	2.194	1.411	1.019			3.141
U151E & F	4.235	2.36	1.517	1.047	0.756		3.378
U240E/241E	3.943	2.197	1.413	1.02			3.145
U250E	3..93	2.197	1.413	0.975	0.703		3.145
U340E/ 341E/341F	2.847	1.552	1	0.7			2.343
U660E	3.3	1.9	1.42	1	0.713	0.608	4.148
TRANSMISSION GEAR RATIOS							
A43D	2.452	1.452	1	0.688			2.212
A44D	2.826	1.493	1	0.688			2.703
A46DE/46DF	2.452	1.452	1	0.73			2.212
A340E & F	2.804	1.531	1	0.705			2.393
A343F	2.804	1.531	1	0.753			2.393
A440F/A 442F	2.95	1.53	1	0.717			2.678
AB60E	3.333	1.960	1.353	1	0.728	0.588	3.061
A750E & F	3.52	2.042	1.4	1	0.716		3.224

FIGURE 10–56 The gear ratios for Toyota and Lexus transaxles and transmissions.

FIGURE 10–57 A cutaway view of a Toyota A40, three-speed transmission. (*Courtesy of Toyota Motor Sales USA, Inc.*)

followed by the A40 transmission, a three-speed design using a version of the Simpson gear train. This design is similar to a type 3 gear train, but it is unique in that it uses no bands.
● **SEE FIGURE 10–57.** This gear train design is the basis for many Toyota transmissions.

The A40D is a dual planetary gear set, four-speed design that combines the A40 gear train with an overdrive unit.

● **SEE FIGURE 10–58.** This design is similar to the type 8 gear train. The newer version, the A340, is very similar; the clutch arrangement has been changed and modified to simplify the design and increase the torque capacity.
● **SEE FIGURE 10–59.** This transmission is currently used with 6-cylinder engines in pickups and SUVs and with the 8-cylinder engine in Tundra pickups.

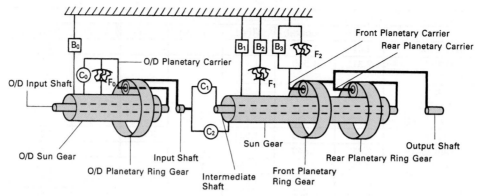

FIGURE 10–58 A schematic view of the gear set and apply devices for a Toyota A40D, four-speed transmission. (*Courtesy of Toyota Motor Sales USA, Inc.*)

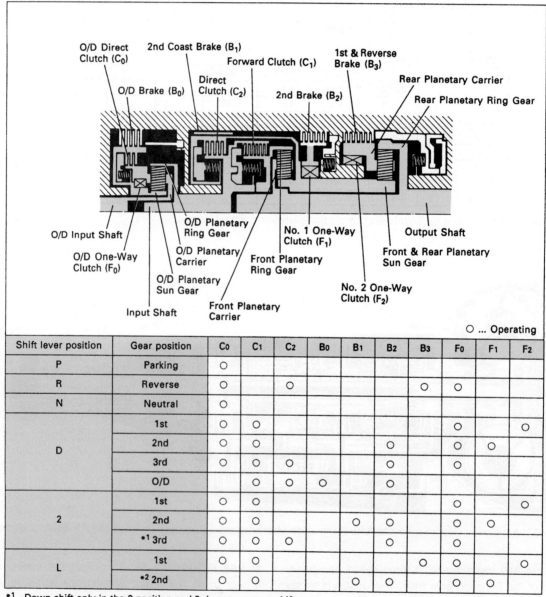

○ ... Operating

Shift lever position	Gear position	C0	C1	C2	B0	B1	B2	B3	F0	F1	F2
P	Parking	○									
R	Reverse	○		○				○	○		
N	Neutral	○									
D	1st	○	○						○		○
D	2nd	○	○				○		○	○	
D	3rd	○	○	○			○		○		
D	O/D		○	○	○		○				
2	1st	○	○						○		○
2	2nd	○	○			○	○		○	○	
2	*1 3rd	○	○	○			○		○		
L	1st	○	○					○	○		○
L	*2 2nd	○	○			○	○		○	○	

*1 Down-shift only in the 2 position and 3rd gear — no up-shift.
*2 Down-shift only in the L position and 2nd gear — no up-shift.

FIGURE 10–59 A cutaway view of a Toyota A340 four-speed transmission gear set with a clutch application chart. (*Courtesy of Toyota Motor Sales USA, Inc.*)

Shift lever position	Gear position	C_1	C_2	B_1	B_2	B_3	F_1	F_2
P	Parking							
R	Reverse		○			○		
N	Neutral							
D	1st	○						○
D	2nd	○			○		○	
D	3rd	○	○		○			
2	1st	○						○
2	2nd	○		○	○		○	
L	1st	○				○		○
L	*2nd	○		○	○		○	

○ .... Operating

*Down shift in L range, 2nd gear only — no up-shift.

FIGURE 10–60 A cutaway view of a Toyota A130 three-speed transaxle with a clutch application chart. (*Courtesy of Toyota Motor Sales USA, Inc.*)

Toyota has introduced a high-torque, five-speed transmission called the A750. It is electronically controlled, has three planetary gear sets (one Ravigneaux and two simple), seven clutches (three driving and four holding), and three one-way clutches. It also uses an ATF warmer and optional ATF cooler to increase transmission performance and fluid life.

Another new electronically controlled six-speed transmission is called the AB60E. It uses a Ravigneaux and two simple planetary gear sets controlled by eight clutches (four driving and four holding) and four one-way clutches. This transmission utilizes advanced electronic controls that include TCC flex lockup control, tow/hauling programming, cooperative powertrain control, artificial shift intelligence, coast downshift, and multimode controls.

10.9.2 TOYOTA FWD TRANSAXLES

The A130 is a three-speed transaxle, Simpson gear train unit that uses no bands. ● **SEE FIGURE 10–60**. Currently, it is being used in the Corolla.

Toyota uses three basic designs for its four-speed transaxles. The first was the A140E series. Introduced in mid-1983, it was the first electronically controlled transmission. It is a dual planetary gear set design, combining the Simpson gear train with an overdrive unit. ● **SEE FIGURE 10–61**. The A540 series

Planetary Gear Unit

O/D Direct Clutch (C₀)

O/D Brake (B₀)

First and Reverse Brake (B₃)

Second Brake (B₂)

Second Coast Brake (B₁)

One-Way Clutch No. 2 (F₂)

Forward Clutch (C₁)

Direct Clutch (C₃)

Counter Drive Gear

O/D One-Way Clutch (F₀)

O/D Planetary Gear

Intermediate Shaft

Rear Planetary Gear

One-Way Clutch No. 1 (F₁)

Front Planetary Gear

Input Shaft

FIGURE 10–61 A cutaway view of a Toyota A140E four-speed transaxle. (*Courtesy of Toyota Motor Sales USA, Inc.*)

transaxles are very similar; they are modified to provide better drivability and increased torque capacity for 6-cylinder engines.

The A240L series is also similar to the A140E units. The overdrive unit was relocated to the countershaft to reduce the overall length of the transaxle and improve durability. ● **SEE FIGURE 10–62**.

Toyota has two new transaxles, the U660E and the U250E. The U250E is an electronically controlled five-speed transaxle. It uses three-simple planetary gear sets that are controlled by seven clutches (four driving and three holding) and two one-way clutches. The U660E is an electronically controlled six-speed transaxle with two planetary gear sets, one Ravigneaux and one simple. Four clutches (two driving and two holding) and one one-way clutch control the power flow through the planetary gear sets. Both the U250E and the U660E have advanced electronic controls that provide TCC flex lockup control, tow/hauling programming, cooperative powertrain control, artificial shift intelligence, coast downshift, and multimode controls.

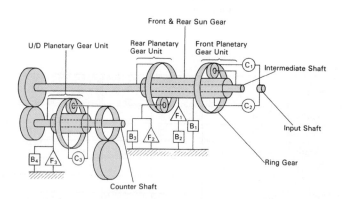

Range (i.e.,) Shift Lever Position	Gear	No. 1 Solenoid Valve	No. 2 Solenoid Valve	C₁	C₂	C₃	B₁	B₂	B₃	B₄	F₁	F₂	F₃
P	Park	ON	OFF							●			
R	Reverse	ON	OFF		●				●	●			
N	Neutral	ON	OFF							●			
D	1st	ON	OFF	●						●		●	●
D	2nd	ON	ON	●				●		●	●		●
D	3rd	OFF	ON	●	●			●		●			●
D	O/D	OFF	OFF	●	●	●		●					
2	1st	ON	OFF	●						●		●	●
2	2nd	ON	ON	●			●	●		●	●		●
2	3rd *	OFF	ON	●	●			●		●			●
L	1st	ON	OFF	●					●	●		●	●
L	2nd *	ON	ON	●			●	●		●	●		●

● : Operating
* : Down-Shift only in the 3rd gear for the 2 range and 2nd gear for the L-range - no up-shift

FIGURE 10–62 A schematic view of a Toyota A244E four-speed transaxle and its clutch application chart. (*Courtesy of Toyota Motor Sales USA, Inc.*)

1. There are many different automatic transmissions. They are easier to understand if the operation of the planetary gears and the application of the clutches and bands are understood.

2. Transaxles combine the transmission and final drive into one unit.

3. Each manufacturer uses specific transmissions and transaxles to meet the requirements of the vehicle in which it is used.

4. Some companies specialize in automatic transmissions and supply many vehicle manufacturers with their products.

5. Most automatic transmissions use planetary gear sets, but some vehicle manufacturers use CVT or constant-mesh transmissions.

REVIEW QUESTIONS

1. In any single year a transmission may have many variations. List eight possible differences between the variations.

2. The purpose of the differential is to allow the drive wheels to turn at _____ _____ speeds while the vehicle is turning a corner.

3. Transaxles that are mounted longitudinally in the vehicle use a _____ or _____ gear set to transfer the power to the drive wheels.

4. Use Chrysler's code to describe the following transmissions.
   a. 37RH _____
   b. 44RE _____
   c. 47RE _____
   d. 42LE _____

5. The Chrysler 44RE transmission is similar to the 32RH, with a(n) _____ unit positioned at the rear of the transmission.

6. The gear ratios for a Ford E40D transmission are:
   1st _____
   2nd _____
   3rd _____
   4th _____
   Rev. _____

   The gear ratios for a Ford CD4E are:
   1st _____
   2nd _____
   3rd _____
   4th _____
   Rev. _____

7. Use Ford's code to describe the following transmissions.
   a. 4R44E _____
   b. 5R55E _____
   c. AX4S _____
   d. AX4N _____

8. The gear ratios for a General Motor's 4L80 transmission are:
   1st _____
   2nd _____
   3rd _____
   4th _____
   5th _____
   Rev. _____

9. Use General Motor's code to describe the following transmissions.
   a. 3L30 _____
   b. 4L80-E _____
   c. 4T65-E _____

10. Name four foreign companies that manufacture automatic transmissions.

CHAPTER QUIZ

1. Student A says that many transmissions have similar operating characteristics. Student B says that all transmissions of a particular type are identical. Who is correct?
   a. Student A
   b. Student B
   c. Both Students A and B
   d. Neither Student A nor B

2. Student A says that transaxles use helical gears for the final drive reduction gears. Student B says that transaxles use hypoid gears for the final drive reduction gears. Who is correct?
   a. Student A
   b. Student B
   c. Both Students A and B
   d. Neither Student A nor B

3. Gear sets that are used in transaxles to turn the power flow 90 degrees are called _____.
   a. Constant mesh
   b. Helical
   c. Hypoid
   d. Hilipoid

4. Student A says that a Chrysler 37RH transmission is a heavy-duty, four-speed transmission. Student B says that the 40RH is a stronger unit than the 37RH transmission. Who is correct?
   a. Student A
   b. Student B
   c. Both Students A and B
   d. Neither Student A nor B

5. Student A says that the Chrysler 30RH and 30TH are the same transmission. Student B says that the 30RH is a rear-wheel-drive transmission and the 30TH is a transaxle. Who is correct?
   a. Student A
   b. Student B
   c. Both Students A and B
   d. Neither Student A nor B

6. Student A says that the General Motors 4L60-E was formerly known as the THM 700-R4. Student B says that the 4L80-E is the smallest transmission made by General Motors. Who is correct?
   a. Student A
   b. Student B
   c. Both Students A and B
   d. Neither Student A nor B

7. Student A says that all automatic transmissions use planetary gears. Student B says that all automatic transmissions use multiple-disc clutches. Who is correct?
   a. Student A
   b. Student B
   c. Both Students A and B
   d. Neither Student A nor B

8. Student A says that import vehicles use automatic transmissions that are nothing like the transmissions used by domestic manufacturers. Student B says that all planetary automatic transmissions are basically similar. Who is correct?
   a. Student A
   b. Student B
   c. Both Students A and B
   d. Neither Student A nor B

9. Student A says that all manufacturers build the automatic transmissions used in their vehicles. Student B says that some manufacturers buy transmissions built by other companies. Who is correct?
   a. Student A
   b. Student B
   c. Both Students A and B
   d. Neither Student A nor B

10. Honda and Saturn use automatic transmissions that have constant-mesh, helical gear trains similar to standard transmissions. In place of synchronizers used in standard transmissions, they use _____.
   a. Planetary gears
   b. Accumulators
   c. Servos
   d. Multiple-disc clutches

11. Honda has built a variety of transmissions. They can be described by the number of _____.
   a. Shafts
   b. Speeds
   c. Clutches
   d. All of the above

12. Student A says that the Nissan RE4R03A is an electronically controlled, rear-wheel-drive, four-speed automatic transmission. Student B says that it is an electronically controlled, transverse, rear-wheel-drive, three-speed automatic transmission. Who is correct?
   a. Student A
   b. Student B
   c. Both Students A and B
   d. Neither Student A nor B

13. Student A says that all current Toyota transmissions use a band for compression braking. Student B says that all current Toyota transmissions do not use bands. Who is correct?
   a. Student A
   b. Student B
   c. Both Students A and B
   d. Neither Student A nor B

14. Toyota's heavy-duty RWD transmission is the _____.
   a. A140E
   b. A40D
   c. A340E
   d. A540E

15. Which Toyota transmission has the overdrive planetary gear set mounted on the countershaft?
   a. A240E
   b. A130
   c. A540E
   d. A140E

chapter 11

TRANSMISSION SERVICE AND MAINTENANCE

OBJECTIVES: **After studying Chapter 11, the reader will be able to:** • Check the fluid level in an automatic transmission. • Check automatic transmission fluid condition. • Change the fluid in an automatic transmission. • Adjust manual shift linkage. • Adjust throttle linkage. • Adjust a band in an automatic transmission. • Complete the ASE tasks related to transmission/transaxle maintenance and adjustment (see Appendix A).

KEY TERMS: Band adjustment 261 • Exchange 272 • Fluid change 265 • Fluid flushing 272 • Hot fluid 261 • Manual linkage 261 • Milky color 265 • Overfill 262 • Pink fluid 265 • Throttle linkage 261 • TV linkage 277 • Underfill 262 • Varnish 265

11.1 INTRODUCTION

Automatic transmissions and transaxles can operate properly for many miles while being totally neglected. Some that fail could have had a longer service life if they had been properly maintained. Several surveys of transmission shops have produced responses that over 80% of transmission failures were the result of neglecting to change the fluid. Newer transmissions require very little maintenance.

Maintaining the correct fluid level and changing the fluid are primary maintenance tasks. Other maintenance checks should be performed occasionally, and problems corrected if necessary; these include:

- **Manual linkage,** to ensure that the manual valve and the internal park mechanism are positioned properly relative to the gear selector
- **Throttle linkage,** to ensure that the throttle or detent valve provides the correct fluid pressures relative to the throttle position
- **Band adjustment,** to ensure the correct band clearance (Note: Adjustable bands are found only on older transmissions.)

11.2 FLUID CHECKS

The operator of a vehicle should check the fluid level in an automatic transmission periodically. A good time is right after every engine oil change. If the level is low, fluid of the correct type should be added. It usually takes 1 pint (0.5 L) to move the fluid

SAFETY TIP

1. Vehicle fires have occurred soon after a transmission service. These fires were probably caused by ATF leaking or spilling onto a hot exhaust system. Other causes could have been a high fluid level, a leaking cooler line, or a plugged transmission vent.
2. Many technicians use this rule of thumb: The fluid is hot if the end of the dipstick is too hot to hold between your fingers.

level from low to the full mark on the dipstick. The fluid should be changed if it looks deteriorated.

Most transmission dipsticks are marked for both cold and **hot fluid** temperatures. ● **SEE FIGURE 11–1.** The most obvious markings are for the hot level, which is the normal operating temperature, about 150°F to 170°F (66°C to 77°C). Some manufacturers use a higher operating range of 180°F to 200°F (82°C to 93°C). Room temperature of about 65°F to 85°F (18°C to 29°C) is considered cold for transmission fluid. When the fluid is cold, use the cold markings on the dipstick. Some transaxles use a thermostatic valve to raise the fluid level in the upper valve body pan as the transaxle warms up. These units have a lower hot level and a higher cold level. The exact procedure for checking the fluid level can be found in the vehicle owner's manual, or occasionally it is printed on the dipstick.

Some transmissions are sealed units without dipsticks. These are commonly called *sealed* or *overflow-type* transmissions. A special fluid-checking procedure is required for these units; always refer to the appropriate service information.

FIGURE 11–1 (a) This dipstick connects the measuring scale to the cover with a flexible cable. (b) The cover shows the fluid type, and the measuring scale indicates to check (c) hot and (d) the fluid-level markings. The vehicle should not be operated if the level is below the "min" or above the "max" marks.

🚗 REAL WORLD FIX

A 1998 Dodge Durango (89,000 miles) transmission slips when taking off and during the 1–2 shift when cold. The fluid level is okay.

Fix

Following advice, the fluid level was checked in neutral, not park, and found to be 1.5 quarts low. Adding the correct amount of fluid fixed this problem.

It is never a good idea to operate a transmission with the fluid level too high (an **overfill**) or too low (an **underfill**). An underfill is below the low, cold level on the dipstick; it is sometimes marked "Do not drive." An underfill condition can allow air to enter the filter and pump intake, which can cause mushy operation, lack of engagement, slipping, or failure of the TCC to lock up and unlock properly.

Overfilling can cause slippage and mushy operation because of the air in the foamy fluid. An overfill can bring the fluid level up to the point where it contacts the spinning gear sets. This in turn causes foaming of the fluid and a loss of the foamy fluid out of the vent or filler pipe. There have been cases of vehicle fires caused by the fluid spilling out of the filler pipe and onto a hot exhaust manifold.

To check transmission fluid, *you should:*

1. Park the vehicle on a level surface, apply the parking brake securely, and place the gear selector in park or neutral as required by the manufacturer. Start the engine, and let the transmission come up to operating temperature.

2. Apply the service brakes firmly, and move the gear selector to each of the operating ranges. Leave the selector in each position long enough for each gear to become completely engaged.

FIGURE 11–2 When checking the fluid level, the engine should be at idle speed, the fluid hot, and the gear selector should be positioned as required by the vehicle manufacturer. Note the fluid level and compare it with dipstick markings. It is also a good practice to note any unusual fluid color or odor.

🔧 TECH TIP

1. If the fluid is fairly new, it appears almost transparent and can be very difficult to read on the dipstick. You can rub the dipstick with ordinary carbon paper, and recheck the fluid level. This will darken the fluid and make it easier to see.

2. It is a good practice to read both sides of the dipstick and believe the lower level. Occasionally, fluid suspended in the filler pipe causes a false high or normal reading. If there is any sign of fluid above the correct range, repeat steps 5 and 6 several times and believe the lowest reading.

---

3. Return the selector lever to park or neutral, depending on the transmission. Leave the engine running at idle speed.

4. Clean any dirt from the dipstick cap, and remove the dipstick. ● **SEE FIGURE 11–2.**

5. Wipe the dipstick clean and return it to the filler pipe, making sure that it is fully seated.

6. Pull the dipstick out again and read the fluid level. Carefully grip the end of the dipstick between your fingers to get an indication of the fluid temperature.
   a. If it feels cold, use the COLD marks.
   b. If it feels warm and you can hold onto it, the correct fluid level will be between the HOT and COLD marks.
   c. If it is too hot to hold onto without burning yourself, use the HOT marks.

7. Replace the dipstick completely into the filler tube. Note that some dipsticks are threaded and must be rotated to lock them in place.

When checking sealed units, a general procedure is to bring the transmission to operating temperature, and then remove the fluid level plug. Fluid will trickle or weep out of the plug if the level is correct. If it runs out, the level is high; if there is no fluid, the level is low.

Some manufacturers require a special procedure or tool in order to check the fluid level of their sealed transmissions, so it is wise to review their fluid-checking procedures. A general procedure follows.

To check sealed transmission fluid level, *you should:*

1. Review the service information for the correct checking procedure.

2. Make sure the vehicle is level.

3. Check the transmission temperature using a contact thermometer, infrared thermometer, or scan tool.

4. Make sure the transmission is at operating temperature range. If specifications are not available, use 120°F to 160°F (49°C to 71°C).

5. Locate and carefully remove the fluid level plug. Note that the level plug can be small, like a pressure check plug, or large, like a conventional plug. The plug can be located in the transmission case or in the bottom or side of the pan. ● SEE FIGURE 11–3.

6. If fluid drips or seeps from the hole, the level is correct. If fluid runs out, the level is too high; allow the excess fluid to drain out. ● SEE FIGURE 11–4. If no fluid comes out, the level is low; add additional fluid of the correct type until the level is correct.

FIGURE 11–3 Fluid level on sealed units (without a dipstick) is checked by removing the level plug, which can be mounted in the bottom or side of the pan or in the case.

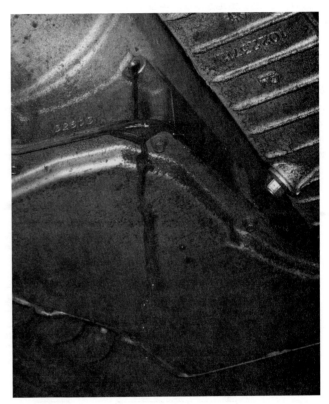

FIGURE 11–4 Fluid running out of the opening tells us that the level was too high, and it is correcting itself. (*Courtesy of Tony Martin*)

7. If necessary, add additional fluid by pumping it into the fill port located at the side of the case or up through the fluid level checking plug opening.

CAUTION: Any fluid that comes out of the fluid level opening will be extremely hot.

11.2.1 TRANSAXLE FINAL DRIVES AND DIFFERENTIALS

Some transaxles separate the final drive assembly from the transmission section and use gear oil for the lubricant. These units may have a separate fluid-checking requirement for the transaxle and final drive. ● **SEE FIGURE 11–5.** The vehicle will still operate with a low final drive lubricant level, but expensive wear and damage can result.

11.2.2 FLUID CONDITION

Fluid condition should always be checked when checking fluid level. A transmission technician will normally smell the fluid and check the color for unusual characteristics. We normally expect the fluid to be a bright reddish color with a smell that is similar to new fluid. It should be noted that some fluids will normally darken and take on a definite odor after a few hundred miles. One manufacturer states that a smokey odor with light brown color is normal. ● **SEE FIGURE 11–6.** Do not confuse this normal occurrence with the signs of fluid breakdown.

FIGURE 11–5 Some transaxle differentials have a plug to allow checking of the fluid level in the final drive section. (*Courtesy of Chrysler Corporation*)

FIGURE 11–6 A useful chart for checking fluid level and condition. (*Reprinted with permission of General Motors*)

(a)

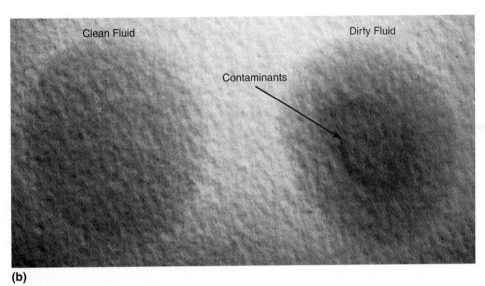

Clean Fluid   Dirty Fluid

Contaminants

(b)

FIGURE 11–7 (a) Fluid condition can be checked by placing a sample on clean, white, absorbent paper. (b) Clean fluid will spread out and leave only a wet stain. Dirty fluid will leave deposits of foreign material.

If the fluid has signs of grit or foreign particles in it or a dirty appearance, it is a good practice to check for solid contaminants. Put a fluid sample onto a clean, white paper towel or blotter. The wetness of the fluid will slowly spread through the paper, leaving a stain. Clean fluid will make a reddish ring. Contaminated fluid will leave specks or deposits of the very fine solid material on the paper as the fluid spreads. ● **SEE FIGURE 11–7**.

Following are indications of fluid breakdown.

- Dark brown or black color indicates dirt or burned friction material.
- A definite burned odor indicates slippage or overheating.
- **Pink fluid** or a **milky color** indicates a coolant leak at the heat exchanger in the radiator.
- A varnishlike odor indicates fluid oxidation and breakdown. This is often accompanied by a gold-brown **varnish** coating on the dipstick.
- Metallic appearance or very fine metal particles indicate wear.
- Foam might indicate a leak in the pump intake system or incorrect fluid level.

11.3 FLUID CHANGES

Most manufacturers recommend fluid changes every 100,000 miles (160,000 km) under normal driving conditions. Some recommend a **fluid change** at 50,000 miles (80,000 km). Fluid change recommendations are usually accompanied with a recommendation that the change interval be shortened to as low as 15,000 miles (24,000 km) when the vehicle is used under severe driving conditions. One vehicle manufacturer recommends replacing CVT fluid every 30,000 miles (48,270 km) or every 2 years under severe conditions. Such severe driving conditions include the following:

- Frequent trailer pulling
- Heavy city traffic, especially in areas where the temperature exceeds 90°F (32°C)
- Very hilly or mountainous conditions
- Commercial use such as taxi or delivery service
- Police or ambulance usage

1. If you suspect the fluid contains water, place a drop from the dipstick on a hot exhaust manifold. The oil will spread and burn off while the water droplets sizzle and move around. One manufacturer recommends that fluid with water contamination should be changed immediately. Then change the fluid two more times, running the engine so all of the old fluid and the water it contains will be mixed with the fluid to be drained.

2. Coolant or water contamination, a strawberry-milkshake-colored fluid, can ruin a transmission in several ways:

   • It can weaken the bond holding the lining to the friction plates.
   • It can cause rust on iron components.
   • It can soften nylon thrust washers.
   • The water can boil, turn to steam, and force fluid out of the dipstick tube, which might cause a fire.

3. Vehicles that use red coolant will not always cause strawberry-milkshake-colored fluid, but a glycol (antifreeze) leak into the fluid can cause clutch lining problems. A fluid test kit for glycol contamination is available for testing this problem.

1. A fluid test kit is available that can provide a record of all the fluids in a vehicle. ● **SEE FIGURE 11–8**.
2. Dirty or contaminated fluid should be changed, the filter should also be changed, and the inside of the pan and transmission case should be checked for contamination, varnish, metallic particles, or other signs of possible transmission problems.
3. When replacing the fluid in a CVT, be sure to use the recommended CVT fluid.

The main factor that determines transmission fluid life is heat or how hot the fluid is during vehicle operation. If the fluid temperature is kept below 175°F (79°C), the fluid should easily last 100,000 miles. At higher temperatures the fluid oxidizes, causing it to break down at a rate of one-half its expected life for every increase of 20°F (11°C). Varnish begins forming at temperatures above 240°F (116°C), and the rubber seals start hardening at temperatures above 260°F (127°C). A chart of transmission fluid life relative to temperature is shown in ● **FIGURE 11–9**.

FIGURE 11–8 A drop of ATF is placed on one of these pads and then compared to the illustrations to determine the condition. (*Courtesy of Robinair, SPX Corporation*)

The 1994 Honda Accord (165,000 miles) transmission whines badly, making the car essentially undriveable. Shifts are normal (except there is no fourth gear), and the fluid level is okay. The vehicle was recently taken to a "quick oil change" shop for an engine oil change, and at the shop's advice, the transmission fluid was also changed.

Fix

Following advice, the technician checked the fluid, and it appeared to be Dexron. He then replaced the transmission with a good used unit, and replaced the fluid in it using the proper Honda transmission fluid. This fixed the problem. The best policy is to always use the fluid recommended by the vehicle manufacturer.

Some transmissions contain very expensive *lifetime fluid* that does not need to be changed. If drained, any solid particles can be allowed to settle, and the clean oil is filtered for reuse.

Fluid temperature is related to the torque converter's operating efficiency. Remember that a converter is not efficient at stall. Mechanical power is going into the converter, but no power is coming out. All mechanical energy is being transformed into heat, which increases the fluid temperature. Heat

Transmission Fluid

Fluid Life (miles)	Temperature (°F)
100,000	175
50,000	195
25,000	215
12,500	235
6,250	255
3,125	275
1,560	295
780	315
390	335
195	355
97	375
48	395

FIGURE 11–9 In many transmissions, the fluid is expected to last 100,000 miles if the fluid temperature can be kept below 175°F (80°C); but the life will be cut in half for every 20°F increase in temperature.

TECH TIP

If the old transmission fluid is extremely dirty, be aware that when the fluid is changed, the new ATF contains a fresh supply of detergents and dispersants, to do the following:

- Loosen varnish and other deposits that have accumulated inside the transmission
- Carry this material throughout the transmission, including valves and solenoids
- Possibly remove varnish that has formed over worn seals and open up a leak

The supply of new friction modifier will increase the "slippery" level of the fluid, which might increase slipping on upshifts.

SAFETY TIP

The material safety data sheets (MSDS) for most transmission fluids indicate that there are few safety hazards when working with new fluid. Some indicate a possible skin reaction. Used fluid, however, goes through an unknown change inside the transmission that might cause it to be more of a hazard. The following is recommended.

- Wear goggles or a face shield to protect your eyes.
- Wear gloves or barrier cream to protect your skin.
- Clean any skin contact with ATF using soap and water.
- Change clothing that has contacted ATF.
- Wash any clothing that has contact with ATF.

If ATF under pressure breaks the skin, medical attention should be sought; consult your doctor.

Fluid Level
Loosen and Remove All Pan Bolts Except for 2 in This Area
Fluid Spill
Loosen 2 Remaining Bolts Slowly
When Pan Has Been Lowered to This Point, Remove 2 Remaining Bolts and Pan

FIGURE 11–10 Since most transmissions do not have drain plugs, the fluid must be spilled in a controlled fashion by lowering the pan at an angle. To do this, all but two bolts are removed. As the last two bolts are loosened, the pan will lower and fluid will spill over the edge.

TECH TIP

1. Most transmissions do not have a drain plug in the oil pan. The fluid is drained by allowing it to spill over the side of the pan as it is removed. The pan is first lowered at an angle to allow the fluid to spill and then removed completely.
   ● **SEE FIGURE 11–10**.
2. Fluid suction pumps are available that can suck the fluid from the transmission. A small plastic hose is inserted down the dipstick tube, and the pump is connected to shop air pressure. Operation of the pump creates the suction. This removes much of the mess of removing a pan full of hot fluid.

is generated whenever the converter is slipping and multiplying torque. A transmission also generates heat because of internal friction: At the bushings, bearings, and gears, additional heat is generated as the pressurized fluid is forced through the

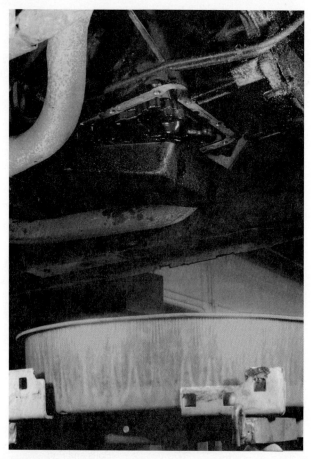

FIGURE 11–11 Fluid is draining from this transmission pan. Note how the pan is hanging from two front bolts.

passages and orifices. The heat generated by friction is fairly small compared with the heat generated by the converter. It can be safely said that the fluid life is shortest in a vehicle that has a lot of torque converter slippage.

The fluid should be changed when it starts to break down, which is best indicated by the fluid appearance and smell. It is wise to change the fluid early, before transmission damage occurs. Dirty fluid may cause the valves to start sticking, which in turn can cause sluggish shifts and slippage and thus more fluid heat, breakdown, contamination, and damage.

11.3.1 FLUID CHANGING, DROPPING THE PAN The
procedure for changing the fluid in a specific vehicle can be found in the manufacturer's service manual or aftermarket service information sources.

To change transmission fluid, *you should:*

1. Raise and securely support the vehicle. This is normally done on a hoist to allow complete access to the transmission pan.

2. Select the best direction for fluid to spill from the pan. Place a large drain pan in this area, and remove all but two of the pan bolts. The remaining two bolts should be at the end away from the drain pan; they will serve as the "hinge" for lowering the pan.

FIGURE 11–12 A gasket splitter is used to break the seal between the pan and transmission case. It is tapped in between the pan and case and then tapped sideways, around the pan.

3. Loosen the two remaining bolts about two turns. ● **SEE FIGURE 11–11**.

4. If the oil pan does not come loose and start dropping on its own, carefully tap on the sides of the pan. The jarring should loosen the pan from the transmission. If the pan is sealed using a form-in-place gasket/sealant, it may be necessary to cut the sealant that tends to glue the pan to the transmission case. ● **SEE FIGURE 11–12**.

5. Loosen the remaining two bolts as needed to get a continuous and controlled spill into the drain pan.

6. When the pan lowers to an angle of about 30 to 45 degrees, support it by hand; remove the remaining two bolts and finish draining the pan.

7. Remove the filter, which is usually attached to the valve body. ● **SEE FIGURE 11–13**. Watch for any small parts that may come loose with the filter.

8. Inspect the pan, filter, and pan magnet for debris and varnish buildup. ● **SEE FIGURE 11–14**. A few metal particles are considered normal. These are the result of wear and transmission break-in. Inspect the inside of the transmission for any visible damage or varnish buildup.

9. Install a new filter using a new gasket or O-ring, and tighten the mounting bolts to the correct torque. If an O-ring is used, it should be lubricated with transmission assembly gel, petroleum jelly, or automatic transmission fluid (ATF) before installation.

10. Clean the oil pan and dry it with compressed air. Check the flanges for dimpling or bends at the pan bolt holes. Repair the damaged flanges as necessary.

11. Install a new gasket on the pan, and install the pan on the transmission. The bolts should be tightened in a back-and-forth, across-the-pan sequence to the correct torque. Overtightening can cause a future leak by

(a)

(b)

FIGURE 11–13 (a) The filter is normally located in the oil pan; note the magnet inside the pan to trap ferrous metals. (b) This filter is held by three screws. *(Courtesy of Chrysler Corporation)*

FIGURE 11–14 This pan magnet has a thin coating of very fine iron particles and the pan is fairly clean. This is normal transmission wear.

FIGURE 11–15 This depth filter has been cut open, and there are only a few small metal particles caught in the fold.

compressing the gasket too tightly and bending the flange.

12. Lower the vehicle, and add the proper amount of fluid. A rule of thumb is 4 quarts.

TECH TIP

1. Some technicians will cut the old filter open to inspect for foreign particles. ● **SEE FIGURE 11–15.** Plastic filters can be quickly broken open by covering them with a shop cloth and striking them on the edge with a hammer. Be cautious of flying plastic parts.
2. Many transmissions are shipped to the vehicle assembly line wet (full of fluid) and a sealing device is used to close the openings for the driveshaft(s) and dipstick tube. When the transmission is installed, the sealing device(s) is pushed into the transmission, where it remains harmlessly inside the pan. ● **SEE FIGURE 11–16.**

TECH TIP

1. Rubber or neoprene seals must be lubricated when they are slid into place. Most greases will cause problems inside a transmission. ATF is always a safe lubricant. Transmission assembly gel and petroleum jelly have more holding or sticking power, and both of these will melt and dissolve harmlessly into the ATF.
2. Some vehicle manufacturers publish fluid specifications for needed changes and transmission overhaul. ● **SEE FIGURE 11–17.** Some technicians measure the amount of fluid that was drained to determine how much fluid is needed.
3. If the flange surface is bent or has dimples, it should be flattened using a hammer and block of wood, vise, or anvil. ● **SEE FIGURE 11–18.** Failure to straighten the pan can result in a fluid leak.
4. The only thing that should be put on a rubber or neoprene gasket is "gasket stick" or assembly lube to hold it in place. Other sealants might affect the gasket or work their way into the hydraulic circuits, where they can cause problems.

FIGURE 11–16 This "popcycle" was found laying in the transmission pan. It was used to plug the dipstick opening while the transmission was shipped to the vehicle assembly line.

Fluid Capacities		
Operation	Quarts	Liters
Bottom Pan removal	7.4	7
Overhaul, Complete	10	9.5
Dry (total) System	13.4	12.7

FIGURE 11–17 This vehicle manufacturer has provided fluid specifications for three transmission service operations.

FIGURE 11–18 The flange area of a pan should be checked for distortion from overtightened bolts. These can be corrected by tapping down the raised areas as shown.

(a) Initial Fill, Engine Off

(b) Engine Idling

(c) Engine Idling

(d) Engine Off

FIGURE 11–19 (a) If the transmission fluid and filter are replaced, the proper amount of fluid will overfill the transmission. (b) The fill procedure should add fluid to a full level and then start the engine. (c) Add additional fluid as needed to bring it to the proper level. (d) Checking the engine with the engine off can show an overfill if the converter drains down.

 REAL WORLD FIX

The 1997 Honda Civic CVT (17,000 miles) came in with a bad shudder. The clutches were rebuilt because they appeared to be burned, but the shudder was still there.

Fix

Following advice, the technician drained the fluid and replaced it with the proper CVT fluid. This fixed the shudder problem.

---

13. Start the engine and check the fluid level as described earlier. Add additional fluid to correct the level if necessary.
● **SEE FIGURE 11–19**.

14. Dispose of the old transmission fluid in an approved manner.

Note that this procedure only changes the fluid in the pan. This is about one-quarter to one-third (1/4 to 1/3) of the fluid in the transmission. The remaining fluid stays in the torque converter, clutches and band servos, accumulators, cooler, and fluid passages.

It is possible to drain the converter by drilling a hole in it and installing a plug when finished. Most technicians do not do this because of the time involved and the possible damage that can occur to the converter. The procedure to drill a converter is

The 2002 Dodge Durango came in with a complaint of delayed engagement into reverse after sitting for awhile. A check in the pan showed metal, evidence of a converter failure, so the transmission was rebuilt. A new solenoid pack and pressure sensor were installed. A Quick Learn was done and the vehicle was driven 60 miles to relearn from harsh N–R and 2–3 shifts. The original problem of reverse shift delay is still there.

Fix

A fellow technician told of a TSB (21-016-05) that describes filters with a faulty check valve. Replacement of the filter cured this problem.

Some technicians have made a transmission fill pump using a Honda remote-reservoir power steering pump that uses hoses for the pump inlet and outlets, a 5/16-in. rubber hose, a drill motor for power, and a small metal tube to fit through the fluid level opening.

The 1993 Mercury Villager van (147,000 miles) will go into neutral under varying conditions. During a test drive it operated normally in all gears until accelerating from a stop; it then went to neutral and after a short period of time, back into gear. The fluid appears and smells good. The transmission electrical connections were checked, and these were good.

Fix

The pan was checked—it was bent upward, apparently blocking flow to the filter. The pan was removed, bent back to the proper shape, and replaced. This repair fixed the problem.

described in Chapter 19. For very dirty transmissions, it is best to (1) change the fluid in the pan as just described, (2) operate the transmission long enough to thoroughly mix the new and old fluid, then (3) change the fluid again.

In cases of very dirty fluid, it is good practice to check for a plugged oil cooler. Debris can plug the cooler, causing severe gear train and bushing wear because of the reduction

FIGURE 11–20 This fluid evacuation system has a small tube that can be inserted into the transmission dipstick tube. A connection to shop air is used to create a vacuum that sucks the fluid into the container. (*Courtesy of ATEC Trans-Tool and Cleaning Systems*)

of lubrication oil flow. The procedure used to check fluid flow through a cooler is described in Section 12.6.2.

Another recommendation for very dirty fluid is to change the fluid, change the filter, and inspect the pan, as just described, and then flush the fluid remaining in the transmission as described in the next section.

11.3.2 FLUID CHANGING, FLUID EVACUATOR Fluid changing by dropping the pan (described in the previous section) is often messy. Fluid spills onto the floor and is absorbed into the concrete, and if not attended to, the fluid can pass through the concrete and into the groundwater. This can create an environmental hazard. Some shops have stopped dropping the pan of an automatic transmission for this reason. Transmission fluid can be changed by sucking the fluid out through the filler tube using an evacuating/extraction tool. ● **SEE FIGURE 11–20.** It should be noted that the pan must be dropped to change the filter and inspect any debris that might be in the pan.

To change transmission fluid using an evacuating tool, perform the following steps.

1. Operate the vehicle to bring the fluid up to operating temperature.

2. Insert the evacuating tool hose into the filler tube until it contacts the transmission pan.

3. Operate the evacuating tool to remove as much of the old fluid as possible.

4. Remove the evacuating tool and dispose of the old fluid in an approved manner.

   Optional Step: Remove the pan for inspection or replacement of the filter.

(a)

(b)

(c)

FIGURE 11–21 (a) This flush machine is designed to pump solvent through the radiator ATF cooler to remove any debris. (b) A set of adapters is available to connect to the lines. (*Courtesy of HECAT Inc.*)

5. Refill the transmission using the correct fluid for the vehicle.

6. Start the engine and check the fluid level as described earlier. Add additional fluid to correct the level if necessary.

11.3.3 FLUID EXCHANGE AND FLUSH UNITS A
complete transmission fluid change can be time consuming. Several different pieces of equipment have been designed to make this operation faster and more efficient.

Fluid flushing typically uses a chemical to dissolve varnish and other deposits. (Transmission cooler flush is described in Section 19.3.2.) **Exchange** usually means taking out the old fluid and replacing it with new fluid of the correct type.

Approved flush solvents are mineral spirits, and technicians using a flushing chemical have a professional responsibility to:

- Obtain, read, and understand the MSDS for that chemical

- Learn how that chemical works and how it should be used

- Determine if that chemical will not harm the system and materials such as gaskets and seals

- Determine how to remove that chemical from the system and properly recycle or dispose of it

If the flush is needed to remove solid debris, there must be enough flow velocity to break the material loose and carry it out of the component. ● **SEE FIGURE 11–21**. Better flush machines will pulsate the flow to increase the cleaning power. In severe cases, such as a plugged cooler, the flush can be set up to pump the solvent into the cooler outlet and remove it from the inlet.

It should be remembered that most vehicle manufacturers specify a filter replacement and pan inspection during the fluid change. At least one flushing machine allows fluid exchange with the pan removed. ● **SEE FIGURE 11–22**.

Fluid exchange machines are usually connected into the transmission cooler lines so that the machine can pump new fluid to the return line as it captures the fluid leaving the transmission. ● **SEE FIGURE 11–23**. Running the engine will pump the old fluid out of the transmission, and a pump in the fluid exchange machine will pump new fluid into the return line. When new, clean fluid starts leaving the transmission, the fluid exchange is complete.

Always follow the manufacturer's instructions when using a fluid exchanger.

To change fluid using a transmission fluid exchange unit, *you should:*

1. Identify the cooler lines so you know which one is the return line.

2. Disconnect the return line from the cooler, and connect the line to the NEW FLUID connector of the machine.

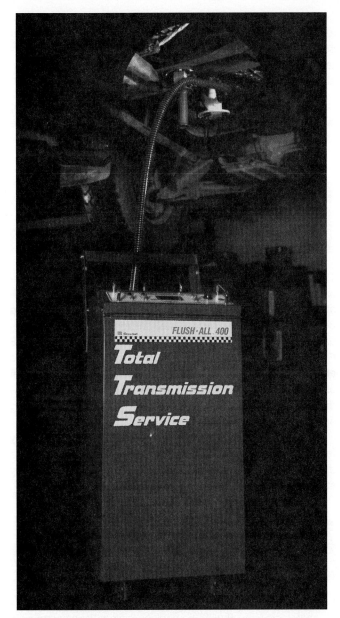

FIGURE 11–22 This transmission fluid exchanger pumps new fluid into the transmission pump intake. It is operated until the old, dirty fluid is forced out. (*Courtesy of Goodall Manufacturing*)

FIGURE 11–23 A fluid exchange unit is normally connected to the cooler return line, and it sends new fluid to the transmission to replace the old fluid being captured from the cooler. (*Courtesy of Goodall Manufacturing*)

TECH TIP

Either line can be used when flushing, but using the return line allows you to check for a plugged cooler. A rule of thumb is that the flow through a cooler should be 3 quarts per minute (1 quart per 20 seconds) or greater.

Connect the USED FLUID connector of the machine to the cooler.

3. Apply the parking brake and shift the transmission into park. Start the engine and observe the fluid flow at the machine. To prevent starving the transmission of fluid, new fluid should leave the machine at the same rate that used fluid enters.

4. When the used fluid has the same appearance as new fluid, stop the engine.

5. Disconnect fluid connections to the machine, and reconnect the cooler return line.

6. Start the engine and check the line connection for leaks.

7. Check the transmission fluid level and adjust as necessary.

8. Dispose of the used transmission fluid in an approved manner.

11.4 HYBRID VEHICLE TRANSMISSION FLUID AND POWERTRAIN COOLING SYSTEM

Transmission fluid service of these vehicles should be performed following the manufacturer's recommendations. One hybrid vehicle with a CVT transmission requires a fluid change every 30,000 miles (48,000 km).

Hybrid vehicle electronic inverters, battery packs, and some transaxles generate a lot of heat, and most of these vehicles have a separate cooling system for such components. ● **SEE FIGURE 11–24.** Most of these systems are liquid cooled, using a coolant recommended by the vehicle manufacturer. Some hybrid vehicles use air-cooled inverters. The motor-generators also generate heat when they are used to propel the vehicle, and nickel-metal hydride (NiMH) batteries are much more efficient when they are cold.

Coolant Reservoir

Coolant Hose

(a)

Coolant Passages

(b)

FIGURE 11–24 (a) The coolant reservoir and hoses are for the electronic coolant system for this hybrid vehicle. (b) This system removes excess heat from the high-voltage inverter and drive motors in the transmission.

❓ FREQUENTLY ASKED QUESTION

Why Doesn't the Inverter, Transaxle System Contain a Thermostat?

Unlike the engine cooling system that keeps the engine at an efficient, hot temperature, the electrical cooling system is designed to keep the electrical components at a cool temperature. Electrical components are more efficient when they are cool.

The electrical cooling system can use the following:

- Separate radiator
- Hoses to connect the component
- 12-volt pump to circulate the coolant
- Expansion tank/reservoir
- Heat exchanger built as part of the inverter or transaxle

Hybrid vehicle manufacturers specify when the coolant should be replaced at the proper intervals. One manufacturer specifies the OEM coolant that is available from the dealer as a

50-50 mix and recommends the first coolant change to occur at 100,000 miles and the following replacements to occur at 50,000-mile intervals. When the coolant is changed, it is important to get all of the air out of the system; components contain air bleeds for this purpose.

CAUTION: When servicing a hybrid vehicle transmission, be careful of any orange-colored electrical wire. Orange indicates this type carries high-voltage current.

11.5 MANUAL LINKAGE CHECKS

The manual linkage is adjustable on most automatic transmissions. This ensures the manual valve is positioned correctly relative to the gear selector. Linkage position should be checked periodically because a misadjusted linkage can cause the manual valve to leak oil pressure into the wrong passage. ● **SEE FIGURE 11–25.** Imagine if a small amount of line pressure were able to leak into the drive passages while in neutral. This might cause a clutch to partially apply and produce a slight creep condition. But even worse, this slippage will produce overheating and eventually burn the clutch out.

A detent is a spring-loaded device that causes the notchy feel and clicking sound as the gear selector is moved. Since the detents act on the transmission's internal linkage, they normally stay correctly aligned with the valve position.

🔧 TECH TIP

A serious problem related to manual linkage adjustment is for the transmission to shift into park without the gear selector entering the locking gate. If the vehicle is left with the engine running, the selector level may slip out of park and the transmission may shift into reverse gear, creating a highly dangerous condition. There have been serious accidents with some fatalities as a result of this happening.

🚗 REAL WORLD FIX

The 1995 Volkswagen Golf (55,000 miles) had the transmission rebuilt. The transmission was installed, but there was no engagement in drive. The car would move in M3 and all shifts were good.

Fix

Following advice, the technician checked the shift linkage adjustment and found the problem, which he cured with a linkage adjustment.

FIGURE 11–25 (a) Proper manual linkage ensures that manual valve position matches correctly with (b) the position of the manual shift lever and shift indicator. You should be able to feel the detents inside the transmission, and they should align with the shift lever position. (*Figure (b) Courtesy of Chrysler Corporation*)

The manual linkage adjustment for a specific vehicle can be found in the manufacturer's service manual or aftermarket service information. Following is a general procedure for linkage adjustment. To check manual linkage adjustment, *you should:*

1. Firmly set the parking brake and leave the engine off.

2. Move the selector lever lock or the selector lever to the unlocked or ungated position to allow moving the selector lever freely through the different ranges. Move the lever through its travel as you feel for the detents inside the transmission.

3. Move the selector level through the ranges, and observe the range pointer as you note the position of the internal detents. You should feel the detent engage as the pointer aligns with the gate for each gear position indicator.

FIGURE 11–26 This neutral safety switch is mounted in the transmission and operated by the manual lever cam. It always stays in proper adjustment. (*Courtesy of Chrysler Corporation*)

FIGURE 11–27 This neutral safety switch is mounted to the outside of the transmission case. If the starter operates with the gear selector in a position other than park or neutral, the switch position should be adjusted. (*Courtesy of Chrysler Corporation*)

4. Move the selector lever to park, and release the lever/lock. The parking pawl should freely engage to lock the transmission, and the lever lock should freely enter the gate and be locked.

5. Check that the starter operates in park and neutral but not in other gear positions.

The neutral start switch in some transmissions is activated by the manual lever quadrant inside the transmission, so it will always be positioned correctly relative to the manual valve. ● **SEE FIGURE 11–26.** Improper starter operation on these vehicles indicates a misadjusted shift linkage. Other transmissions mount the neutral start switch on the outside of the case, or at the shift lever. These switches are adjusted differently; consult the appropriate service information for the proper procedure. ● **SEE FIGURE 11–27.**

FIGURE 11–28 (a) A floor-mounted shift linkage using a cable; (b) a floor-mounted shift linkage using rods; and (c) a column-mounted shift linkage using rods. Each one has a method of adjusting the length for proper gear positioning (circled). (*Courtesy of Chrysler Corporation*)

The range pointer in some vehicles is operated by a cable controlled by a lever on the shift column. On these vehicles, it is possible for the pointer to be out of adjustment relative to the linkage and manual valve. Adjustment of the pointer position is usually a simple matter of changing the pointer or connecting link position.

While checking the adjustment, it is good practice to also watch for any binding or hard movement. This indicates a shift cable that is dirty, rusty, or beginning to fail. Also check for excessive lever side or vertical movement or sloppy motion, which indicates failure of the selector lever bushings.

11.5.1 MANUAL LINKAGE ADJUSTMENT The manual linkage should be adjusted if the starter engagements occur in the wrong position or the transmission detents do not align correctly relative to the gear range pointer. The procedure will vary with vehicle makes and models. Check a service manual for the exact procedure for a particular vehicle. ● **SEE FIGURE 11–28**. The description that follows is general.

To adjust manual shift linkage, *you should:*

1. Shift the gear selector into park, making sure the selector lever is correctly positioned and the lever pawl has completely entered the park gate.

FIGURE 11-29 The manual shift lever is in park. The linkage adjustment is being tightened to lock the adjustment after making sure that the transmission is in park.

Shift Lock Override Button
Shift Lock Plate
Front
Shift Lock Control Switch
Plate Stopper
Shift Lock ECU
Shift Lock Solenoid

FIGURE 11-30 This shift lock mechanism includes a solenoid that can mechanically hold the shift lock plate. Note the shift lock override button that can be used to release the shift lock.

2. Raise and securely support the vehicle on a hoist or jack stand.

3. Locate the manual linkage and the adjustment in the linkage. The adjustment is a slot in the shift rod or cable, a swivel clamp, or a long, threaded portion using a bracket and two nuts. ● SEE FIGURE 11-29. Loosen the clamping nut or bolt.

4. Move the transmission lever to park, making sure that the detent and the parking pawl are completely engaged. Test this by trying to rotate the driveshaft(s); it should be securely locked. Adjust the linkage to the proper length.

5. Tighten the clamping nut or bolt, making sure that the transmission lever and/or the shift rod does not move out of adjustment.

6. Repeat the linkage check described earlier in this section, to ensure correct adjustment.

SHIFT LOCK MECHANISM. The shift interlock mechanism locks the shifter in park position when the ignition key is removed. The brake pedal must be depressed before the shifter can be moved, and the ignition key cannot be removed unless the lever has been shifted into park. These systems operate either electrically or through a mechanical linkage. ● SEE FIGURE 11-30. The

mechanical systems usually have an adjustment to ensure proper positioning. These systems vary so service information for that particular vehicle should be consulted when diagnosing problems or checking adjustments.

A shift interlock can get out of adjustment or fail to release. Vehicle manufacturers have incorporated a fail-safe mechanism so the vehicle can be operated. Located near the shift lever is a small lever or button that can be used to override the shift lock and release the lever. The release is often located under a cover that must be removed for access. This procedure is normally described in the vehicle owner's manual.

11.6 THROTTLE LINKAGE CHECKS

Nonelectronic transmissions may have a throttle rod or cable that connects the engine's throttle linkage to the transmission's throttle valve (TV). This linkage is commonly called a **TV linkage.** The TV linkage controls a valve that produces a rise in TV or line pressure that is matched to the throttle position. ● SEE FIGURE 11-31. This pressure controls the timing and quality of the shifts.

Sticky, binding, or improperly adjusted TV linkage will cause incorrect TV pressure and the following problems.

- Sticky or binding, erratic, irregular shifts
- If high TV pressure, then higher than normal shift points, overly sensitive downshifts, and excessively firm, harsh shifts (cable is too tight)
- If low TV pressure, then lower shift points, late or no downshifts, and soft, mushy shifts (cable is too loose)

On non-fuel-injected vehicles, it should be noted that the TV linkage movement begins at idle speed with the engine at normal operating temperatures. Most manufacturers provide a fail-safe in case the TV linkage breaks or comes loose. The fail-safe will cause very high TV pressure that will cause late and harsh upshifts.

Electronically controlled transmissions can use either a throttle cable or an ECM-controlled solenoid to modify mainline pressure based on engine load.

TV linkage checks are fairly easy and are normally made with the engine off. In some cases, the linkage binds only with

 TECH TIP

On vehicles using carburetors, it is good practice to ensure that the idle speed is correct and the carburetor fast idle cam is off before making a linkage adjustment. Also, the throttle should reach its wide-open throttle (WOT) position before the transmission's throttle valve bottoms in its bore.

Throttle Valve Cable   Cable Bracket

Throttle Body Lever

Accelerator Cable

Speed Control Cable

(a)

Throttle Valve Cable

Torque Shaft Bracket

Cable Return Spring

Throttle Valve Lever

Cable Bracket

(b)

FIGURE 11–31 (a) This TV cable connects the throttle body to (b) the transmission. The adjustment is at the throttle body cable bracket. (*Courtesy of Chrysler Corporation*)

 TECH TIP

A more exact check for proper TV operation can be made using a pressure gauge. With a gauge installed and the engine running, you should be able to see a pressure increase as you move the linkage toward WOT. This procedure is described in Chapter 12.

 REAL WORLD FIX

The 1989 Bronco (74,000 miles) has a harsh 4–3 downshift. On the road test, it was noted that the TCC was not applying. A remanufactured transmission was installed, but this did not fix the problem.

Fix

Following the advice of other technicians, the TV cable was checked and found to be out of adjustment. Adjusting the TV cable fixed this problem.

NOTE: A lot of time and money could have been saved if the proper diagnostic procedure had been followed.

 REAL WORLD FIX

The 1990 Honda Accord (186,000 miles) has an engine flare on hard-throttle 2–3 shifts; light-throttle shifts are okay. The transmission was removed, and the clutches appeared good when inspected. There were no DTCs.

Fix

The technician was advised to adjust the TV cable so throttle pressure would begin increasing as soon as the throttle starts moving. This adjustment fixed this shift flare problem.

the engine running. If symptoms indicate this is happening, some of the checks should be repeated with the engine running.

Check service information for the proper adjustment procedure for a specific vehicle.

To check TV linkage, *you should:*

With the engine off:

1. Make sure that the throttle is closed against the idle stop (idle-speed adjusting screw). Check the cable or rod for any slack or free movement; in most cases, there should be none.

2. Move the throttle to the WOT position and, while doing this, check the cable or rod for free or sloppy movement, binding, or sticking.

The TV linkage should move to the WOT position and release freely and smoothly.

3. With the throttle at WOT, pull on the TV linkage. It should be able to move a very small amount before contacting its stop inside the transmission.

With the engine running:

1. Firmly set the parking brake, and shift the gear selector to neutral.

2. Pull on the end of the TV cable or move the TV rod so it moves through its travel and then release it. During the

linkage movement, check for free or sloppy movement, sticking, or binding. There should be none.

Improper TV operation should be corrected by readjusting, rerouting, repairing, or replacing the linkage.

11.6.1 THROTTLE LINKAGE ADJUSTMENTS

Like the manual shift linkage, TV linkage is adjustable. Always consult the service manual for that particular vehicle when making an adjustment. The descriptions that follow are examples of some of the methods used. All adjustments are made with the engine off and the throttle at normal idle position unless specified otherwise.

To adjust TV linkage, perform the following steps.

"Threaded mounting" adjustment:

1. Measure the cable position as required in the service information. ● **SEE FIGURE 11–32**. Some vehicles require measurements in both idle and WOT positions.

2. If adjustment is required, loosen the adjustment nuts on the cable housing, and move the cable housing to the proper position. Retighten the locking nuts after making the adjustment.

"Sliding swivel" adjustment:

1. Loosen the swivel lock screw; the TV rod should slide in the swivel.

2. Move the TV linkage forward against its internal stop, and retighten the lock screw.

0.5–1.5 mm

Boot

32–43 mm

Measure the distance with the accelerator pedal fully closed and fully depressed

FIGURE 11–32 This throttle linkage is adjusted by turning the two adjusting nuts until the cable stopper ring is the correct distance from the housing end.

"Snap lock" adjustment:

1. Lift the snap lock to the unlocked position; the cable housing should be free to slide in the assembly. ● **SEE FIGURE 11–33**.

2. Rotate the throttle to WOT, and push the snap lock inward to lock.

"Self-adjusting" adjustment:

1. Depress the readjusting tab, and move the slider inward against the base of the adjuster housing and release the tab. ● **SEE FIGURE 11–34**.

2. Rotate the throttle to WOT. As this occurs, the cable slider should move at least three "clicks," or about 1/8 inch.

"Self-adjusting at transaxle" adjustment:

1. Depress the adjuster button, and extend the adjuster to its longest position by pulling on the cable housing.

2. Using the proper special tool, rotate the throttle to the WOT position using a torque of 50 in-lb. ● **SEE FIGURE 11–35**. The adjuster should automatically change to the proper length.

"Gauge" adjustment:

1. Install a 0 to 300 PSI pressure gauge in the proper transmission port (see Figure 12-10).

2. Start the engine and note the gauge pressure.

3. Adjust the linkage as necessary to correct the pressure.

4. Remove the gauge and reinstall the plug.

THROTTLE POSITION SENSOR POSITION ADJUSTMENT. The TV signal on electronically controlled systems originates at the throttle position sensor (TPS) that is mounted on the throttle

---

🔧 **TECH TIP**

Remember that many customers will be dissatisfied with harsh shifts caused by TV linkage that is too short, and the transmission can be ruined if the cable is too long.

STOP ENGINE

PUSH UP TO LOCK

SNAP LOCK

ROTATE THROTTLE LEVER BY HAND TO WIDE OPEN POSITION

PUSH DOWN TO LOCK

FIGURE 11–33 This throttle cable uses a "snap lock" adjuster that is adjusted using the procedure shown. (*Reprinted with permission of General Motors*)

LOCK TAB (UNLOCKED)

SLIDER

STOP ENGINE

DEPRESS LOCK TAP AND MOVE SLIDER IN DIRECTION SHOWN

LOCK TAB (LOCKED)

RELEASE LOCK TAB

ROTATE THROTTLE LEVER BY HAND TO WIDE OPEN POSITION

FIGURE 11–34 This "self-adjusting" TV cable is adjusted using the procedure shown. (*Reprinted with permission of General Motors*)

IN-LB TORQUE WRENCH

IDLER PULLEY

ADJUSTER LOCATED ON TRANSMISSION

FIGURE 11–35 This "self-adjusting" TV cable used with some transaxles is adjusted using the procedure shown. (*Reprinted with permission of General Motors*)

Right Throttle Body

Throttle Position (Sensor)

Intake Manifold

FIGURE 11–36 The throttle position sensor normally has an adjustment so it is positioned correctly on the throttle body. (*Courtesy of Chrysler Corporation*)

body. ● **SEE FIGURE 11–36.** In some cases, the vehicle will run with an improperly adjusted TPS, but the transmission shift quality could be affected. TPS adjustment varies between vehicles; service information should be consulted when checking or making this adjustment. This adjustment could also affect engine operation and vehicle emissions. The TPS cannot be adjusted on some vehicles.

 REAL WORLD FIX

The 1996 Honda Accord (57,000 miles) came in with a shudder at 25 mph when warm. The tires were balanced and rotated, but this did not help. The shudder felt like a torque converter clutch was applying early, so the TCC solenoid was disconnected and the shudder disappeared.

Fix

Following advice, the technician adjusted the TV cable and changed the transmission fluid. The TV cable adjustment fixed this shudder complaint.

11.7 BAND ADJUSTMENTS

At one time, a common transmission maintenance procedure was to readjust the band clearance. Wear of the friction material would increase the clearance to the point where engagement would not be complete and slippage would occur. ● **SEE FIGURE 11–37.** Modern fluids and friction materials have reduced the need for regular band adjustments. Also, the band in many modern transmissions is used only in manual ranges for compression braking. The band is expected to last the life of the transmission. Most new transmissions have no provision for in-car adjustments; any adjustment is made during transmission overhaul.

Proper Clearance =
Short Servo Travel

Excess Clearance =
Excess Servo Travel

FIGURE 11–37 When a band is new, the servo piston travels only a short distance to apply it. As the lining wears, servo piston travel increases; if there is too much wear, the band might not tighten completely.

TECH TIP

When adjusting a band using a threaded adjuster, it is good practice to count the number of turns as the adjuster is turned inward. For example, if the adjuster is turned three complete turns and then backed off two and one-half turns, the difference gives an indication of the amount of lining wear.

TECH TIP

With some transmissions, it is recommended to replace the lock nut with a new one. These transmissions use a rubber sealing ring formed in the nut to prevent a fluid leak.

Some older transmissions have threaded adjusters extending through the case to allow an easy readjustment of the band. Some band adjustments are made inside the transmission and it is necessary to drop the pan to gain access to the adjuster.

It is good practice to check the band adjustments during a fluid change or if there is a shift problem related to a band. Service information should be checked to determine the exact adjustment procedure for each particular vehicle. The following is a general procedure.

To readjust a band, *you should:*

1. Loosen the lock nut on the adjuster screw several turns.
   ● **SEE FIGURE 11–38**.

(a)

(b)

FIGURE 11–38 (a) This band is adjusted by holding the adjuster screw while the lock nut is loosened. (b) Step 2 turns the adjuster screw inward to 72 in-lb (8 N-m) of torque. The special adapter is used if there is tight access. Step 3 is to back off the adjusting screw the proper number of turns and tighten the lock nut to the correct torque. (*Courtesy of Chrysler Corporation*)

2. Tighten the adjuster screw to the specified torque. Special adjuster wrenches with preset torque settings are available for this operation.

3. Mark the adjusting screw position; back it off the specified number of turns. Hold the adjuster screw stationary and retighten the lock nut to the specified torque.

4. Road test the vehicle to check your adjustment. For example, a loose intermediate band (on a Simpson three-speed transmission) can cause a long, drawn-out 1–2 shift; a tight intermediate band will cause a drag in reverse, first, and third.

SUMMARY

1. Automatic transmissions require periodic service and maintenance.

2. Transmission fluid should be regularly checked for correct level and good condition.

3. The transmission fluid should be changed at the required intervals or if the condition indicates the need for a change.

4. The manual shift linkage and the throttle linkage need to be checked and adjusted if necessary.

5. Some transmissions have one or more bands that may need to be adjusted.

1. Servicing and maintaining an automatic transmission includes:
   a. Checking the _____ level
   b. Changing the _____
   c. Cleaning or replacing the _____
   d. Checking and adjusting the _____ and _____ linkages
   e. _____ the bands if required

2. It usually takes _____ _____ to change the fluid level from low to full on the dipstick.

3. Mushy operation, lack of engagement, or slippage can be caused by a transmission that has a fluid level that is too _____.

4. Before checking the fluid level, the vehicle should:
   a. Be on _____ ground
   b. Be in _____
   c. Be at normal operating _____
   d. Have the engine _____

5. All transaxles share fluid between the differential and the transmission. True or False?

6. When checking the fluid level, the _____ and _____ should also be checked.

7. The normal color of automatic transmission fluid is _____.

8. What is indicated by these fluid conditions?
   a. Dark brown color
   b. Burned odor
   c. Pink or milky color
   d. Gold or brown coating on the dipstick
   e. Metallic appearance
   f. Foamy

9. An automatic transmission can be ruined by contaminated _____.

10. Severe driving conditions include:
    a. Frequent _____ pulling
    b. Heavy _____ and _____ traffic
    c. _____ weather conditions
    d. _____ service
    e. _____ or _____ police usage

11. The major factor that affects transmission fluid life is _____.

12. To change fluid in most automatic transmissions, the _____ must be removed.

13. Before installing the clean pan after draining the fluid, check the pan for _____ and _____ sealing surface.

14. The notchy feel and clicking sound when a gear is selected is caused by the spring-loaded _____.

15. To properly adjust the manual linkage, always check the manufacturer's _____ procedures.

16. A sticking, binding, or out-of-adjustment throttle valve cable can cause _____ shifts, _____ shifts, or late, soft, mushy, or no downshifts.

17. An exact check for proper throttle valve operation is made using a _____ gauge.

18. It is always necessary to consult a _____ _____ when making a throttle linkage adjustment.

19. Throttle position sensor adjustment will affect _____ operation, vehicle _____, and transmission _____ quality.

20. Many modern automatic transmissions use a band that does not require adjustment because the band is only used for _____ braking and in _____ ranges.

1. Technician A says that you should check the transmission fluid level with the engine idling in park. Technician B says that if the end of the dipstick is too hot to hold, the fluid can be considered hot. Who is correct?
   a. Technician A
   b. Technician B
   c. Both Technicians A and B
   d. Neither Technician A nor B

2. Technician A says that on most dipsticks, the distance from the bottom of the cross-hatched area to the top is equal to 1 pint of fluid. Technician B says that too much fluid in a transmission can cause poor shifts. Who is correct?
   a. Technician A
   b. Technician B
   c. Both Technicians A and B
   d. Neither Technician A nor B

3. The transmission fluid should be changed if it has _____.
   a. Black or brown coloration
   b. A definite burned smell
   c. Gone the limit of miles recommended by the manufacturer
   d. Any of these

4. Technician A says that too high a fluid level can cause foamy fluid to spill out of the vents or filler pipe. Technician B says that too low a fluid level can cause this same problem. Who is correct?
   a. Technician A
   b. Technician B
   c. Both Technicians A and B
   d. Neither Technician A nor B

5. Technician A says that all ATF is a bright medium-red color. Technician B says that all ATF has the same burnt, oily smell. Who is correct?
   a. Technician A
   b. Technician B
   c. Both Technicians A and B
   d. Neither Technician A nor B

6. A pink transmission fluid color indicates _____.
   a. Normal operation
   b. Too high a level and air in the fluid
   c. Water in the fluid
   d. None of these

7. Technician A says that transmission fluid life is dependent on the transmission's operating temperature. Technician B says that driving conditions that increase fluid temperature, such as trailer towing or delivery-type operations, shorten fluid life. Who is correct?
   a. Technician A
   b. Technician B
   c. Both Technicians A and B
   d. Neither Technician A nor B

8. Technician A says that most transmissions can be drained by removing the drain plug. Technician B says that you should also change the filter when the fluid is changed. Who is correct?
   a. Technician A
   b. Technician B
   c. Both Technicians A and B
   d. Neither Technician A nor B

9. Technician A says that you normally have to start the engine as you refill a transmission with fluid. Technician B says that a torque converter can be refilled with the engine off. Who is correct?
   a. Technician A
   b. Technician B
   c. Both Technicians A and B
   d. Neither Technician A nor B

10. Technician A says that if an engine cranks while the gear position indicator is in drive, the manual shift linkage is out of adjustment. Technician B says that this problem can be caused by a misadjusted neutral safety switch. Who is correct?
    a. Technician A
    b. Technician B
    c. Both Technicians A and B
    d. Neither Technician A nor B

11. You can quickly check the adjustment of the manual shift linkage by _____.
    a. Trying the operation of the starter in the various gear positions
    b. Feeling for the transmission internal detents as you move the gear selector from park to low
    c. Feeling for complete engagement of the lever pawl into the park gate
    d. Any of these

12. Technician A says that a misadjusted manual linkage can cause vehicle creep in neutral. Technician B says that a gear selector can slip out of park if the linkage is not adjusted correctly. Who is correct?
    a. Technician A
    b. Technician B
    c. Both Technicians A and B
    d. Neither Technician A nor B

13. Technician A says that most manual linkages can be easily adjusted by repositioning the adjustable end of the rod or cable. Technician B says that the selector lever should be positioned in reverse while adjusting the linkage. Who is correct?
    a. Technician A
    b. Technician B
    c. Both Technicians A and B
    d. Neither Technician A nor B

14. If the throttle linkage is too short, the transmission will probably _____.
    a. Shift early
    b. Have very late shifts
    c. Have soft, mushy shifts
    d. Both a and b

15. Technician A says that sticky throttle linkage can cause erratic shifts. Technician B says that passing gear engagement is affected by the throttle linkage adjustment. Who is correct?
    a. Technician A
    b. Technician B
    c. Both Technicians A and B
    d. Neither Technician A nor B

16. Technician A says that the bands in modern transmissions can be adjusted using an adjuster screw that extends out at the side of the transmission case. Technician B says that if the intermediate band (three-speed transmission) is too tight, there will be a drag in reverse. Who is correct?
    a. Technician A
    b. Technician B
    c. Both Technicians A and B
    d. Neither Technician A nor B

17. To drain the fluid from the differential of a transaxle, _____.
    a. Remove the transaxle pan
    b. Drain the differential separately from the transmission
    c. Check the service manual for the proper procedure
    d. There is no need to check the differential fluid.

18. The shift lock mechanism is used to prevent the shifter from being moved out of park unless the _____.
    a. Brakes are applied and/or the key is in the ignition
    b. Doors are closed and the key is in the ignition
    c. Seat belts are on and the doors are closed
    d. Doors are closed and the brakes are applied

MECHANICAL PROBLEM SOLVING AND DIAGNOSIS

OBJECTIVES: **After studying Chapter 12, the reader will be able to:** • Perform and analyze the tests that are used to diagnose transmission problems. • Determine the root cause of the transmission's problem. • Recommend the proper repair procedure. • Perform the ASE tasks for general transmission/transaxle diagnosis and the mechanical/hydraulic system.

KEY TERMS: Air test 284 • Electrical system check 284 • Fluid check 284 • Fluid diagram 297 • Fluorescent dye 307 • Hydraulic pressure test 284 • Hydraulic schematic 297 • Known-good 301 • Leak check 284 • Modulator check 284 • NVH (noise, vibration, and harshness) check 284 • Oil pan debris check 284 • Road test 284 • Stall test 284 • TCC (torque converter clutch) test 284 • Technical service bulletins (TSBs) 285 • Vacuum supply/source 299 • Visual inspection 284 • Wet air test 284

12.1 INTRODUCTION

An automatic transmission is a complicated device, and there are many possible reasons for complete or partial failure. When experienced technicians are given a problem, they often go directly to the solution by basing their diagnosis on their experience. If they are not absolutely sure of the cause, they will perform the necessary tests to locate the specific cause of the problem.

A sound knowledge of automatic transmission operation helps greatly when diagnosing transmission failures. An example is a transmission that does not move in drive but starts in manual-1 and then, if shifted back into drive, operates normally. The power flow is the same in drive-1 and manual-1 with one exception. In drive-1, a one-way clutch is the reaction member; in manual-1, the one-way clutch is assisted by a band. In this case, the problem is probably caused by a faulty one-way clutch. Another example is a transmission that moves in drive but does not upshift. Knowledge of this transmission indicates that the intermediate band or clutch is not applying, but why? In this case, there are several possible faults besides the band, for example, no governor pressure, a modulator or throttle valve fault, or a stuck 1–2 shift valve. Additional tests are needed to determine the exact cause of this problem.

The following is a series of tests and checks that can be used to determine the exact cause of automatic transmission problems.

- **Visual inspection.** Involves a quick, preliminary overall check of external factors that affect operation.
- **Fluid check.** Ensures the correct level and condition (described in Chapter 11).

- **Road test.** Gives the technician the opportunity to check the actual operation of the transmission, confirm the original concern, check shift timing and quality under different throttle openings, monitor torque converter clutch operation, and listen for unusual noises and vibrations.
- **Electrical system check.** Ensures that the electronic controls are operating correctly (described in Chapter 13).
- **Torque converter clutch (TCC) test.** Determines if the TCC is operating properly and isolates the cause of the problem.
- **Hydraulic pressure test.** Checks the hydraulic system pressures, which give a good indication of the condition of the pump, pressure control and shift valves, various seals, and gaskets.
- **Modulator check.** Checks the operation of the modulator and vacuum throttle valve system.
- **Stall test.** Loads the apply devices to check for slippage; also checks the torque converter stator one-way clutch.
- **Leak check.** Locates the source of a fluid leak.
- **Oil pan debris check.** The oil pan is inspected to determine if an abnormal amount of debris is present and, if so, the type or nature of that debris.
- **Air test.** Determines if the seals, sealing rings, and gaskets in the hydraulic circuits are operating correctly.
- **Wet air test.** A more precise air test determines the exact location or severity of a leak.
- **Noise, vibration, harshness (NVH) check.** Checks to locate the cause of a noise or vibration.

When diagnosing a transmission problem, a technician will perform only the checks appropriate for the problem.

Diagnostic Test Procedure

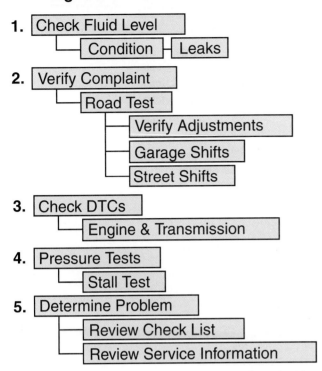

1. Check Fluid Level
  └ Condition ─ Leaks

2. Verify Complaint
  └ Road Test
    ├ Verify Adjustments
    ├ Garage Shifts
    └ Street Shifts

3. Check DTCs
  └ Engine & Transmission

4. Pressure Tests
  └ Stall Test

5. Determine Problem
  ├ Review Check List
  └ Review Service Information

FIGURE 12–1 A general diagnosis procedure flow chart is used to locate automatic transmission problems.

A technician relies on experience to determine which tests are needed, and will perform the checks in the most logical order for the particular problem.

12.2 PROBLEM-SOLVING PROCEDURES

One of the difficulties in describing a diagnostic procedure is caused by the varied types of problems that are encountered. There is no single diagnostic procedure. The process of finding and curing a leak or noise problem is different from the procedure to locate a faulty upshift. With experience, a technician makes the checks or tests that will identify the cause of a particular problem. It is recommended that a sequence similar to that shown in ● **FIGURE 12–1** be followed.

Problem solving should always begin with identifying the problem. This starts with the person who brings the problem to you—the customer. It is important to realize that the customer believes there is something wrong with the vehicle and may not understand automatic transmissions or automotive drivetrains. In most cases, it is helpful to go for a road test with the customer; during the road test, the customer can explain the problem to you or demonstrate what he or she is experiencing. Taking notes while discussing the concern with the customer may prove helpful later in the diagnosis. Some manufacturers recommend that

REAL WORLD FIX

The 1994 BMW 740i (50,000 miles) will not move forward without full throttle or setting the program switch to winter mode. A scan tool check showed a selector signal fault, so the neutral safety switch was replaced. The car operated okay, but it came back in a few days with the original problem. A check showed no electrical fault codes. For some reason, the car moves backwards while idling in neutral. With the control unit disconnected, the transmission operates with a normal neutral.

FIX

A fellow technician provided a TSB describing a similar problem for this transmission. When making the checks described in the TSB, the technician found that a check ball had worn through the transfer plate. Replacing the 0.236-in. ball with a larger, 0.250-in. ball as directed by the TSB fixed this problem.

you follow a check sheet. ● **SEE FIGURE 12–2**. This gives the technician a more professional appearance and prevents skipping important checks.

An experienced technician will check all available diagnostic service information for any **technical service bulletins (TSBs)** for the vehicle. Some vehicles have known problems, and their repair is described in a TSB. These are called *pattern failures*. Diagnostic information is also available on the Internet through various organizations, such as the Automatic Transmission Rebuilders Association (ATRA), Automatic Transmission Service Group (ATSG), and International Automotive Technicians Network (iATN).

12.3 DIAGNOSTIC PROCEDURE

All transmission problem solving should begin with a check of the fluid level and fluid condition. Many problems can be caused by low or high fluid level or poor fluid condition. Fluid level and condition will often give you a clue as to the cause of the problem. Many technicians make it a practice to check the manual shift linkage and the throttle linkage at this time. Linkage checks are not difficult and take little time to complete. Several problems can result if the linkages are not working or are not adjusted correctly.

Poor engine performance can affect transmission operation. It is a good practice to check for recent engine or transmission service. While checking the fluid, look at the engine. Is it idling smoothly? Does it show signs of recent work? Does it

Vehicle _____

Driver _____   Recorder _____

Tach Reader _____   Speedometer Reader _____

1. D Range Upshifts:

	NORMAL	POWER
Quarter Throttle	1-2 _____ mph	1-2 _____ mph
	2-3 _____ mph	2-3 _____ mph
	3-4 _____ mph	3-4 _____ mph
Half Throttle	1-2 _____ mph	1-2 _____ mph
	2-3 _____ mph	2-3 _____ mph
	3-4 _____ mph	3-4 _____ mph

Shift Quality: ☐ Normal   ☐ Excess Shock   ☐ Slippage

2. 2-Range Upshifts:

Quarter Throttle   1-2 _____ mph

Half Throttle   1-2 _____ mph

Shift Quality: ☐ Normal   ☐ Excess Shock   ☐ Slippage

3. 2-Range Engine Braking: ☐ OK   ☐ NG

4. L Range Engine Braking: ☐ OK   ☐ NG

5. D Range Kick-Down:

	OK	NG
OD to 3	_____	_____
OD to 2	_____	_____
3 to 2	_____	_____
2 to 1	_____	_____

6. Manual Down-Shifts:

ECT Transmission—At 35 mph in OD, press OD OFF button; record engine rpm change.   _____ rpm

At 35 mph, shift from D to 2; engine speed increases. _____ rpm

At 25 mph, shift from 2 to 1; engine speed increases. _____ rpm

Comments: _____
_____
_____

FIGURE 12–2 A diagnostic guide/concern checklist leads the technician through a series of systematic checks and provides a place to record the findings. (*Courtesy of Toyota Motor Sales USA, Inc.*)

appear to be well maintained? Are all the sensors, actuators, and controls connected? If the answer is no to any of these questions, make the necessary corrections before proceeding.

The next check varies with the nature of the problem, which can involve over a dozen different areas. The normally encountered problems and the checking procedure are shown in ● **CHART 12–1**.

The diagnostic procedure for electronically controlled transmissions will be slightly different from nonelectronic units. For example, a problem in the electronic controls is indicated if the transmission malfunction indicator light (MIL) is illuminated. The technician should follow a diagnostic routine to solve electrical/electronic faults, as described in Chapter 13. If the transmission MIL is not illuminated, a hydraulic/mechanical system diagnostic routine as described in this chapter should be followed.

 REAL WORLD FIX

The 1988 Ford F150 pickup (300,000 miles) AOD transmission was rebuilt for the second time because there is no reverse. The clutches and bands all appear okay.

FIX

Following advice, the technician checked the reverse sun gear drive shell and found a broken weld. Replacement of the reverse sun gear and drive shell fixed this vehicle. It is a good practice to review the power flow through the gear set when trying to determine the cause of a problem.

PROBLEMS	CHECKS TO PERFORM	DIAGNOSTIC CHECKS
1. Noise	A, G, H, I, L	A. Fluid level and condition
2. Vibration	A, G, O	B. Manual linkage
3. Smell	A, G, N	C. Throttle linkage
4. Leaks	A, N	D. Engine idle speed
5. Blows fluid out of vent or filter	A, J, M, N	E. Electronic controls
6. No forward or reverse gears	A, B, H, J, M	F. Modulator
7. Slips in any gear	A, B, E, H, I, J, K, L, M	G. Road test
8. Slow initial engagement	A, B, C, E, F, J	H. TCC
9. Harsh initial engagement	A, C, D, E, F	I. Band adjustment
10. No upshifts or downshifts	A, C, E, F, H, I, M	J. Hydraulic pressure test
11. Harsh shifts	A, C, E, F, H, I, J	K. Stall test
12. Engine flare during shift	A, C, E, F, H, I, J	L. Oil pan debris
13. Surge while driving	A, E, G, H	M. Air test
14. Converter clutch does not engage	A, E, G, H, J	N. Oil leak test
15. Stalls at stops	A, E, G, H	O. Vibration check
16. Creeps at stops	A, D, H, L	
17. Creeps in neutral	A, B, H	
18. Early, late, or irregular shifts	A, C, E, F, H, J	
19. Skips intermediate gear	A, B, E, H, I	
20. Drags or locks up on shifts	A, B, H	
21. No power, poor accelerations	A, H, K	

CHART 12–1

Diagnostic Check Procedure

12.4 VISUAL INSPECTION

Before beginning any of the complex diagnosis checks, make a quick visual inspection of the vehicle and transmission to avoid overlooking the obvious. These checks should include the following:

- Fluid level and condition
- Fluid leaks
- Engine running condition
- Signs of past repair or tampering
- Motor/transmission mount condition
- Battery condition
- Electrical connections to the transmission
- Vacuum connections to the transmission and engine
- Driveshaft(s), final drive, and differential condition (if the vehicle does not move)

 REAL WORLD FIX

The C4 transmission in the 1982 Mustang was just rebuilt, but it has a long, drawn-out, part-throttle, 2–3 shift. Full-throttle shifts are good. The band adjustments were checked, and they were also okay. The valve body was removed and inspected. No problem was found. The servos were checked, and they were okay.

FIX

Fellow technicians advised checking the modulator. Replacement of the modulator pin with one that was 1/16 in. longer fixed this shift problem.

12.5 ROAD TEST

A road test is used to verify the customer's concern and check the general overall condition of the transmission. The vehicle should be road tested at the start of the diagnosis and after the repair. The first road test helps the technician understand the customer's concern as well as the nature of the problem. The road test after repairs have been completed confirms that the repairs were successful. A road test may involve simply driving the vehicle and mentally reviewing the transmission operation. ● **SEE FIGURE 12–3**. Depending on the problem, a technician may install one or more of the following: a hydraulic pressure gauge to measure line, governor, shift circuit, or cooler line pressure; a tachometer to measure engine speed; a vacuum gauge to indicate engine load; a test light or voltmeter to monitor electrical circuits; an electronic scan tool to monitor engine

or transmission operation; or a special electronic transmission analyzer. ● **SEE FIGURE 12–4**.

Following are items normally checked during a road test:

- Quality of the garage shifts (neutral–drive and neutral–reverse)
- Engagement time for the garage shifts
- Quality of each upshift and downshift at various loads
- Timing of each upshift and downshift at various loads
- Any busyness (hunting) between gear ranges
- Operation of the torque converter and TCC
- Slipping in any gear range
- Binding or tie-up in any gear range
- Noise or vibration in any gear range
- Compression braking during deceleration in drive and manual gear ranges
- Speedometer operation (shows output from VSS)
- Engine operation

There are many shift quality and timing problems that can occur; the common terms used to describe abnormal shifts are described in ● **CHART 12–2**.

A technician will often use a check sheet like the one shown in ● **CHECKLIST 12–1**. This helps to ensure that no important points are skipped during the road test. It is also a good way to record the findings. The checklist becomes a valuable tool when identifying the exact cause of the problem, explaining the nature of the problem to the customer, and in cases of warranty repairs, meeting the requirement for warranty documentation.

On the test drive, the technician will drive the vehicle in a normal manner while evaluating each upshift or downshift by sound and feel. The technician will note the timing and quality of each shift while operating the vehicle in various driving conditions. A tachometer is a helpful tool when checking shift timing and TCC operation. If the vehicle is not equipped with a tachometer, a scan tool can be used. Since the 1980s, important engine and transmission operating information can be obtained

FIGURE 12–3 A road test is performed to verify the customer's concern and provide the technician information that can be used to determine the proper repair. (*Courtesy of Chrysler Corporation*)

FIGURE 12–4 This transmission analyzer allows the technician to check the operation of electronic components. (*Courtesy of Zoom Technology*)

TERM	MEANING
Binding	A very noticeable drag that causes the engine to slow down and labor.
Bump	A sudden, harsh application of a clutch or band.
Chuggle	A bucking or jerking condition, similar to the sensation of clutch chatter or acceleration in too high of a gear with a standard transmission (could be engine related).
Delayed shift	The shift occurs sometime after normally expected. This is also called a "late shift."
Double bump	Two sudden, harsh applications of a clutch or band, also called "double feel."
Dropout	An unexpected shift to neutral or a lower gear, also called "fallout."
Early	The operation occurs before normally expected. An early shift results in a laboring engine, poor acceleration, and sometimes chuggle.
End bump	A shift feel that becomes noticeably firmer as it is completed, also called "end feel" or "slip bump."
Firm shift	A quick, easily felt shift that is not harsh or rough.
Flare	A rapid increase in engine speed usually caused by slippage.
Harsh shift	An unpleasantly firm band or clutch application.
Hunting	A repeated up-and-then-down shifting sequence that produces noticeable repeated engine RPM changes.
Initial feel	The feel of the beginning of the shift.
Late shift	See *Delayed shift.*
Rough	See *Harsh shift.*
Shudder	A more severe form of chuggle.
Slipping	A noticeable loss of power transfer that results in an increase in engine RPM.
Soft shift	A very slow shift that is barely noticeable.
Stacked shifts	An upshift that occurs immediately after another upshift.
Surge	An engine condition that is a very mild form of chuggle.
Tie-up	The result of being in two gears at once. See also *Binding.*

CHART 12-2

Shift Problem Terms

TRANSMISSION PRESSURE CHECKLIST

VACUUM MODULATOR TRANSMISSION

Engine Speed	Vacuum	Park	Neutral	Drive	Manual-1	Manual-2	Reverse
Idle	+15 in. Hg						
1000 RPM	+15 in. Hg						
Idle	0 in. Hg						
1000 RPM	0 in. Hg						

MECHANICAL THROTTLE VALVE TRANSMISSION

Engine Speed	Throttle	Park	Neutral	Drive	Manual-1	Manual-2	Reverse
Idle	Closed						
1000 RPM	Closed						
Idle	WOT						
1000 RPM	WOT						

CHECKLIST 12-1

Checklists allow a technician to quickly record observations for future reference or to show the vehicle owner. The code letter (from the center) is simply placed in the proper square if an improper operation should occur.

TECH TIP

When diagnosing a "vehicle does not move forward problem," it may be possible to cause the transmission to operate by tightening a band all the way so there is no clearance. This should apply the band, and the operation of the transmission working or binding up should give you an idea of what might be causing the problem.

TECH TIP

On some vehicles, the governor weights can be held in the open position by placing a short section of rubber hose under the weights. This should cause the vehicle to make high-gear starts when shifted into drive because the shift valves should be upshifted by the increased governor pressure.

FIGURE 12–5 The DRB (Diagnostic Readout Box) is a scan tool that can communicate with the transmission electronic controls. (*Courtesy of Chrysler Corporation*)

from a scan tool. A scan tool can be used to access and record the data as the vehicle is driven. ● **SEE FIGURE 12–5.** This operation is described in Section 13.3.5.

The technician operates the vehicle at various throttle positions during the road test. Light-, medium-, full-throttle, and through detent or wide-open throttle (WOT) upshifts are made to check shift quality and timing under each of these conditions. The vehicle is also operated under different closed-throttle conditions. The various throttle positions used are defined as follows:

- **Minimum**—the least throttle opening that produces acceleration
- **Light**—when the throttle is about one-fourth open
- **Medium**—when the throttle is about one-half open
- **Heavy**—when the throttle is about three-fourths open
- **Wide-open throttle (WOT)**—fully opened throttle without forcing a downshift
- **Detent**—WOT, which forces a downshift
- **Closed**—a complete release of the throttle, which results in coasting

- **Engine braking**—a closed-throttle manual downshift to produce a condition where engine compression slows the vehicle

Manufacturers publish shift points for their vehicle drivetrain combinations. These are the vehicle speeds at which upshifts and downshifts should occur relative to the different throttle openings. It is easy to check the shift points. Accelerate the vehicle using different throttle openings, and watch the tachometer or listen for the engine speed change that indicates a shift. Note and record the speed for comparison with the specifications. Remember that shift points are related to tire diameter and drive axle ratio. A change in either of these will affect the shift points. If no specifications are available, the approximate shift points are shown in ● **CHART 12–3.**

Observe all speed limits and traffic regulations during a road test to ensure your safety and that of those around you. A road test is not a reason to violate any traffic law or regulation. Experienced technicians use the same test route for every test drive. This route includes all of the necessary driving conditions. Since the route is familiar, any malfunction becomes more obvious.

It is good practice to ensure that park works and will hold the vehicle stationary on a grade in both forward and reverse. While on the road test, stop the vehicle on a hill, shift into park, and carefully release the brake. It should only roll a short distance to completely engage park and then stop securely. Next, you should turn the vehicle around and repeat this test in the opposite direction.

CLOSED THROTTLE	SPEED (MPH)	PART THROTTLE	SPEED (MPH)	WOT	SPEED (MPH)
1–2	5–10	1–2	15–30	1–2	35–45
2–3	15–25	2–3	25–45	2–3	55–65
3–4	30–45	3–4	40–55	3–4	Above 55–65
4–3	30–40	4–3	35–45	4–3	Above 55–65
3–2	10–15	3–2	30–40	4–3	55–65
2–1	5–10	2–1	10–20	2–1	25–40

CHART 12-3

Shift Points

TECH TIP

1. TCC application is felt as a rather mild upshift with less engine speed change than a part-throttle upshift. Depending on the throttle opening, TCC application will cause the engine speed to drop about 50–100 RPM.

2. The recommended TCC test procedure is to operate the transmission in its highest gear and then repeat it at the same speed in the next highest gear range. A greater RPM drop should occur in the higher gear because of the greater load on the converter. The greater load produces more slippage and therefore a greater RPM change during lockup. Converter lockup testing cannot be made on a hoist because of the very small RPM change that occurs when the vehicle has no road load.

3. Poor engine operation has an adverse effect on TCC application. A rough-running or weak engine can cause a chuggle, busy feeling, or jerky TCC application. When the TCC applies, especially at low vehicle speeds, the engine speed can drop below the power band. Any engine malfunction becomes very evident as the engine struggles against the load. Adjust or repair all engine problems before condemning a torque converter.

12.6 TORQUE CONVERTER CLUTCH TESTS

Possible TCC problems are failure to apply, failure to release, hunting or busyness, early application, or harsh application. These problems can be confirmed on a road test by using a scan tool or tachometer to note the engine speed change during clutch application.

When testing a TCC, a light brake pedal apply should cause the converter clutch to release. An increase in engine speed of 50 RPM or more should be noticed as the clutch releases.

REAL WORLD FIX

The 2000 Buick LeSabre (47,000 miles) came in with a misfire DTC and the transmission would not upshift unless the accelerator pedal was lifted. A scan tool shows a DTC for a shorted TCC. The fuses tested good. An exhaust rattle is noticed on the road test.

FIX

Following advice, the technician checked the exhaust system and found a back pressure of 2.5 PSI at idle and 5–6 PSI at half throttle. This indicated a plugged catalytic converter, and replacement of the catalytic converter fixed the shift problem.

REAL WORLD FIX

The 1993 Jeep Cherokee (83,000 km) stalls the engine when shifted into reverse. This occurs after the engine and transmission are warmed up. If the engine does not stall, it bogs down, showing a severe load. When this occurs, the only test port with fluid pressure is the rear servo, and this pressure is normal. There are no DTCs.

FIX

Following advice, the transmission was removed and disassembled. The front pump was found to be severely worn. The customer decided to install a remanufactured transmission.

NOTE: The worn pump allowed a fluid leak into the rear of the converter that applied the clutch.

There are different procedures for troubleshooting each type of TCC. The description that follows will cover the most common electronically controlled systems. There are essentially two areas to check: hydraulic pressure and electrical control circuit; the electrical checks are described in Chapter 13.

FIGURE 12–6 Converter clutch hydraulic operation can be checked by installing a pressure gauge in the transmission-to-cooler line. A change in pressure will be seen as the clutch applies or releases. Note that the gauge can be connected to the most accessible location in the cooler circuit.

FIGURE 12–7 This badly worn turbine shaft caused TCC pressure loss and improper operation. A cut or damaged O-ring would have a similar effect.

TECH TIP

1. When measuring fluid pressures, always use a pressure gauge that has the capability to read higher pressures than you expect. A pressure gauge will be damaged if subjected to higher pressures than it was designed to measure. In other words, a 0–100 PSI (0–690 kPa) pressure gauge does not have the capability of reading pressures over 100 PSI, and it will be ruined if you try.
2. If a pressure gauge is reading near the maximum, stop the engine immediately, and replace it with a gauge of greater capacity.
3. If you miss the pressure change while testing a TCC, lightly tap the brake pedal; this should cause the converter clutch to release and then reapply. The gauge pressure should fluctuate as this occurs.

12.6.1 CONVERTER CLUTCH HYDRAULIC CHECKS

Most torque converter clutches apply when the oil flow through the converter is reversed. If a pressure gauge is installed in the oil cooler line, a slight momentary drop (or, in a few transmissions, a slight increase) in oil pressure can be observed during clutch apply.

To test converter clutch apply pressure, *you should:*

1. Install a 0–100 PSI (0–689 kPa) oil pressure gauge in the transmission-to-cooler feed line at the radiator. ● **SEE FIGURE 12–6.** A tee fitting should be used to prevent blocking the flow to the cooler. Carefully route the pressure gauge hose from under the vehicle, and tape the gauge to the windshield in view of the driver.

CAUTION: Make sure that the hose is not next to a hot exhaust or a location where it can be cut. At least one vehicle was destroyed by fire from transmission fluid spraying on a hot exhaust. This occurred while on a road test with a pressure gauge connected to the transmission.

2. Securely support the vehicle on a hoist or jack stands with the drive wheels raised.
3. Operate the vehicle in drive range until the 2–3 shift occurs and maintains a speed of 45 to 55 mph (72 to 88 km/h) as you watch the pressure gauge. A momentary drop of 5 to 10 PSI (35 to 70 kPa) indicates operation of the TCC control valve.

   TCC Test Results

   If the pressure changed and the converter clutch applied, this is normal operation.

   If the pressure changed and the converter clutch did not apply, there is a problem inside the converter, a worn input shaft, or a cut O-ring on the input shaft. ● **SEE FIGURE 12–7.**

   If the pressure did not change, there is a problem in the converter clutch valve, control solenoid, or solenoid control circuit.

CAUTION: When running a vehicle with the drive wheels off the ground, never exceed 60 mph (96 km/h) on the speedometer. The differential can allow one tire to overspeed to 120 mph (193 km/h). At these speeds, the centrifugal force can cause the wheel cover to fly off or the tire could fly apart.

12.6.2 COOLER CIRCUIT FLOW CHECK
A flow meter has been developed that can be installed into the cooler line. ● **SEE FIGURE 12–8.** This tool is much more accurate than the old test method of disconnecting a cooler line and measuring the time it takes to pump a quart of fluid into a bucket. The flow meter allows measuring cooler flow in different gears as well as on a road test. It can be used to identify the following:

- Restricted cooler
- Worn pump with low capacity
- TCC apply and release
- Worn control valves

To measure cooler line flow, *you should:*

1. Disconnect the cooler line at a convenient location. Connect the flow sensor into the cooler line using adapters as needed.

(a)

(b)

(c)

FIGURE 12–8 (a) A flow meter can be connected into (b) the cooler line and the vehicle's power supply. (c) The vehicle can be road tested and the rate of fluid flow through the cooler line can be read on the display. (*Courtesy of Sonnax*)

2. Connect the display unit to the flow sensor and plug it into the vehicle's power receptacle.

3. Start the vehicle, and observe the cooler line flow rate. ● **SEE FIGURE 12–9.**

4. To check the TCC, drive the vehicle at a moderate speed while observing the flow rate.

This tool can also be used as a quality control check when road-testing a transmission that has been rebuilt. If there is poor cooler flow, the unit will not have good lubrication, and it will probably fail much earlier than would normally be expected.

🔧 **TECH TIP**

The expected flow rate can vary between transmissions and can be determined somewhat by the diameter of the cooler lines; 5/16-inch lines: expect up to 1.8 gallons per minute (gpm); 3/8-inch lines: up to 2.6 gpm; and 1/2-inch lines: up to 6 gpm.

12.7 HYDRAULIC SYSTEM PRESSURE TESTS

The operation of an automatic transmission is dependent on hydraulic pressure. A technician uses a gauge pressure to check the condition of the hydraulic system. Some hydraulic system problems can be cured with the transmission still in the vehicle. For example, it is not a good business practice to remove and replace (R&R) a transaxle if the problem was caused by a loose valve body, faulty governor, or electrical problems.

All transmissions have a pressure test port, and some have more than one. If there is only one port, it will usually be for line pressure. The additional ports provide the apply or release pressure of a particular clutch, servo, governor, or throttle valve pressure. ● **SEE FIGURE 12–10.** Most automatic transmission service manuals include illustrations to identify these test ports.

TIP: The traditional flow check of 1-quart-in-20-seconds corresponds to a flow rate of 0.7 to 0.8 GPM.

FIGURE 12–9 This graph shows the recommended flow through the cooler lines during different operating conditions. Note the flow change during TCC apply and release. (*Courtesy of Sonnax*)

Torque
Converter
Clutch Off

Reverse

Overdrive

Torque Converter
Clutch On

Low/
Reverse

2-4

Underdrive

FIGURE 12–10 The pressure test ports for a 42LE transaxle are used for testing the various hydraulic circuits. (*Courtesy of Chrysler Corporation*)

 TECH TIP

1. A common analog hydraulic pressure gauge is normally dampened, so minor pressure fluctuations are lost. The electrical transducer of an electronic gauge can be connected to a scope, which will allow you to watch small pressure changes and find an important clue as to the cause of a problem.

2. If using a hydraulic pressure gauge, it is recommended that the gauge is 0–300 psi (0–2 kPa) to prevent gauge damage while testing reverse gear pressure.

3. An electronic pressure gauge uses a transducer installed at the test port and a wire to connect the transducer to the gauge. This eliminates the potential danger of a hose being damaged, causing a fluid leak and possible fire. ● **SEE FIGURE 12–11.**

 TECH TIP

1. Always double-check that the fitting has the same threads as the transmission port. They usually have a good match if you can turn the adapter inward several turns using only your fingers.

2. While testing pressure during a road test, watch the gauge pressure before, during, and after a shift. The pressure should drop and then come back; a lower pressure after a shift indicates a leaking fluid circuit.

(a)

No need to have fuel or transmission hoses inside vehicle during a road test.

No makeshift taping of gauges to the windshield.

"Min/Max." pinpoints:
- Fuel restrictions
- Plugged filters
- Weak fuel pumps
- Transmission pressure spikes

Use with OTC's No. 3398 to find clogged/dirty fuel injectors.

Pinpoints worn power steering pumps or racks.

"Delta Zero" monitors fuel pressure drop caused by faulty check valves.

Displays readings in bar for checking European specs.

PSI reading for hydrostatic drives and high pressure hydraulics.

Permits comparison of ABS brake pressures at each wheel.

Finds blocked intake ports and plugged catalytic converters.

Checks transmission cooler efficiency and catalytic converter temperatures.

(b)

FIGURE 12–11 (a) An electronic pressure gauge set includes a pressure transducer(s) to convert pressure to (b) an electronic signal that is displayed on the gauge. Note that the gauge can use four different pressure/transducer inputs. (*Courtesy of SPX/OTC*)

To test the transmission hydraulic pressures, *you should:*

1. Raise and securely support the vehicle on a hoist or jack stand.

2. Locate the pressure ports, remove the plugs, and connect the gauge(s) to the ports. ● **SEE FIGURE 12–12.** Note that most domestic transmission ports use female, 1/8-in. National Pipe Threads (NPT).

3. If the tester is equipped with a vacuum gauge and the transmission uses a vacuum modulator, remove the vacuum hose from the modulator, and connect a tee to the vacuum gauge, vacuum supply line, and modulator.

(a)

(b)

(c)

(d)

FIGURE 12–12 Pressure test kits have adapters to connect to the test ports of various transmissions. Adapter A uses a standard oil pressure gauge; adapter B uses an electronic digital gauge that can also measure temperature. Adapter C uses self-sealing, tapered threads; adapter D uses straight threads that require an O-ring seal. (*Courtesy of Waekon Corporation*)

4. Connect a scan tool or tachometer to the vehicle to monitor engine speed.

5. Route the various lines and wires so they can be read while the vehicle is operated. Be sure to keep them away from the hot exhaust system and rotating parts. Do not run the hydraulic lines or gauge inside the vehicle.

6. Place the gear selector in park, securely apply the brakes, start the engine, and note the readings on the various gauges. Some transmissions will not read line pressure in park; most will. The vacuum gauge should read about 15 to 20 in. Hg, and the tachometer should be reading idle speed.

7. Run the engine at idle speed; shift the gear selector through each of the gear ranges and record the pressure readings. ● **SEE CHECKLIST 12–2.** On vacuum modulator transmissions, vacuum reading should be at least 15 in. Hg.

8. Make sure the brakes are securely applied; increase the engine speed to 1000 RPM and repeat step 7.

9. *On mechanical throttle valve linkage transmissions,* disconnect the transmission TV linkage from the throttle and pull it to the WOT position. Repeat step 7.

10. *On vacuum modulator transmissions,* disconnect the vacuum line and plug the engine end to ensure normal engine operation. Repeat step 7.

12.7.1 INTERPRETING PRESSURE READINGS A

technician compares the pressure readings to specifications to determine if the system is operating correctly.

REAL WORLD FIX

The 1990 Buick (130,000 miles) transmission was rebuilt, but at speeds above 45 mph, it will not downshift. The TV cable is adjusted properly, and the vacuum modulator is getting good engine vacuum. The line pressure is 69 PSI in all gears, with or without the vacuum modulator connected. If the TV cable is pulled toward WOT, the line pressure will quickly jump up to 140 PSI.

FIX

A careful recheck revealed that the modulator was removed to make transmission removal and installation easier. The modulator valve had fallen out, and the modulator was replaced without the valve. Installation of the modulator valve fixed this problem.

The most likely cause for a pressure problem in park or neutral is the pump, intake filter, and pressure regulator because the fluid flow path is usually through the filter, valve body, transmission case, pump assembly, and back through the transmission case to the valve body. These are the circuits that are supplying fluid or are under pressure in that gear range. In park and neutral, the throttle valve, torque converter, and cooler are open to flow but the flow to the rest of the transmission is shut

TRANSMISSION PRESSURE CHECKLIST

MECHANICAL THROTTLE VALUE TRANSMISSION

Engine Speed	Throttle	Park	Neutral	Drive	Manual-1	Manual-2	Reverse
Idle	Closed						
1000 RPM	Closed						
Idle	WOT						
1000 RPM	WOT						

VACUUM MODULATOR TRANSMISSION

Engine Speed	Vacuum	Park	Neutral	Drive	Manual-1	Manual-2	Reverse
Idle	+ 15 in. Hg						
1000 RPM	+ 15 in. Hg						
Idle	0 in. Hg						
1000 RPM	0 in. Hg						

CHECKLIST 12–2

This checklist allows the technician to quickly record pressure readings.

TECH TIP

1. If no specifications are available, the approximate pressures in most transmissions will be as follows:
   - Neutral, park, and drive at idle: 50 to 60 PSI (345 to 414 kPa)
   - Neutral, park, and drive with the TV linkage at wide-open throttle or 0 in. Hg to modulator: 75 to 125 PSI
   - M1 and M2: 50 to 60 PSI; in some transmissions: 100 to 125 PSI
   - Reverse: 150 to 250 PSI
2. If testing the pressures of a transmission with EPC, increase the engine speed to 2000 RPM, observe the pressure gauge, and switch the ignition off. If the pressure increases to normal or above as the engine stops, there is a problem in the EPC circuit.
3. Any transmission that develops normal pressure in reverse is sure to have a good pump and pressure control circuit.
4. Control pressure test results:

   If okay in any range, the pump and pressure regulator pressure control solenoid and circuit are okay.

   If okay in reverse, the pump and pressure regulator valve or pressure control solenoid and circuit are okay.

   If low in all ranges, there is probably a clogged filter, defective pump, or defective pressure regulator valve, or faulty pressure control solenoid or circuit.

   If low in any gear range, there is a problem in that circuit, probably defective seals or sealing rings.

FIGURE 12–13 A properly operating modulator and TV circuit produces line pressure that is inversely proportional to the vacuum modulator. (*Reprinted with permission of General Motors*)

off at the manual valve. High or low pressures in neutral are usually caused by a problem in the throttle valve, torque converter, and cooler circuits.

The throttle valve and modulator circuits are tested by making pressure checks at high and low vacuum to the modulator or normal and full TV linkage movement. If line pressure increases in step 9 (neutral range), the throttle/modulator valve is working. ● **SEE FIGURE 12–13.**

FIGURE 12–14 This A14OE hydraulic diagram shows the fluid path for drive range, second gear. Note the position of the manual valve. Also note the legend (upper right) indicating the color code used to show the circuit pressures. (*Courtesy of Toyota Motor Sales USA, Inc.*)

Clutch and band apply pressures are checked by moving the gear selector to the different gear ranges. For example, normal pressure in every range except drive-3 and reverse indicates leakage in the clutch that is applied for the drive-3 and reverse circuits. This pressure loss can cause slippage in high and reverse. It should be noted that you cannot check all of the servos with the drive wheels stationary. Some technicians take the pressure gauge on a road test or raise the drive wheels to allow upshifts to second, third, and fourth gear.

When a transmission has test ports for individual apply circuits as well as line pressure, the condition of that circuit can be easily determined by comparing its pressure with line pressure. For example, if line pressure is 75 PSI (517 kPa) and third-gear pressure is also 75 PSI, you know that the third-gear circuit, all of the piston seals, and sealing rings are in good condition. If any circuit is more than 10 PSI (69 kPa) lower than line pressure, there is a sealing problem in that gear circuit that must be corrected.

12.7.2 FLUID FLOW DIAGRAMS Manufacturers provide **hydraulic schematics/fluid diagrams** of the fluid passages and valves. ● SEE FIGURE 12–14. They are used to locate the cause of a problem such as low fluid pressure or no upshift. The diagrams are used to trace the fluid flow through a circuit in the same way that you would use a street map to locate the roads between two points.

The symbols (such as for check valves or exhaust ports) vary between manufacturers. ● SEE FIGURE 12–15.

12.7.3 CHECKING GOVERNOR PRESSURE When a nonelectronic transmission fails to upshift and stays in first gear or starts out in third gear, the problem may be caused by

Some students have difficulty the first time they try to interpret a hydraulic schematic. After a little practice, though, they find it is not hard, and the schematic becomes a useful tool. Following are some tips that are helpful when reading schematics.

- When first looking at a diagram, instead of trying to read it all at once, look for the specific circuit needed and only concentrate on it.
- Most manufacturers provide a separate fluid schematic diagram to illustrate the fluid flow path for the different gears. If you need to identify a gear position, look at the position of the manual valve and the shift valves.
- Many fluid diagrams are color-coded, and a legend normally identifies the various colors.
- A circuit is easiest to locate by starting from the servo or clutch and following it backward through the valves going toward the pump.
- Fluid passages often have a different name after they pass through a valve.
- The passages in and out of a valve are normally arranged in the same position as the real passages at the valve.
- The valves are normally shown in their actual position for the gear status of the diagram. For example, in drive-1, the shift valves should be in a downshift position.

	Chrysler	Ford	General Motors
1. Check Valve, Open			
2. Check Valve, Closed			
3. Shuttle Valve, Open			
4. Shuttle Valve, Closed			
5. Orifice			
6. Exhaust Port			
7. Screen			

FIGURE 12–15 Hydraulic symbols used by domestic vehicle manufacturers.

TECH TIP

A rule of thumb is that the governor pressure should be about the same as the speed; governor pressure at 20 mph should be about 20 PSI.

REAL WORLD FIX

The 2004 Dodge Ram 4X4 pickup with a diesel engine and 48RE transmission came in with no second gear. A scan tool showed parameter identification data (PID) but no DTCs. The transmission was recently replaced with a factory rebuilt unit. Disassembly showed a burnt second-gear band and the rest of the transmission like new. The band was replaced, and in an attempt to fix the problem, the valve body was rebuilt and the governor solenoid, sensor, and sealing rings were replaced.

FIX

An analysis of the PIDs showed the transmission PRESENT GEAR PID went from first gear back to second gear, and a check of the hydraulic circuit indicated that a faulty servo or accumulator seal could have caused this. Replacement of these Teflon seals using metal seal rings fixed this problem. A fluid pressure check should have showed this pressure loss.

a stuck governor or shift valve. Some transmissions provide a governor test port. Connect a pressure gauge to this port, raise the drive wheels, run the vehicle in drive, and watch the gauge. A steadily increasing pressure relative to wheel speed indicates a good governor and circuit.

Many transmissions do not have a governor pressure port, but many have a governor cutback of line pressure as the vehicle is moving at 10 to 20 mph. This cutback can be seen on a pressure gauge connected to the line pressure port.

To check governor pressure, *you should:*

1. Raise and support the vehicle.
2. Connect a pressure gauge to the governor pressure port.
3. Disconnect and plug the vacuum line to the modulator.
4. Start the engine, place the gear selector in drive, and slowly accelerate the drive wheels. During acceleration, carefully note the gauge pressures. The pressure should increase at the same rate as vehicle speed.

To check governor cutback pressure, *you should:*

1. Raise and support the vehicle.
2. Connect a pressure gauge to the line pressure port.

FIGURE 12–16 A cotton swab or pipe cleaner is used to wipe the inside of the modulator port or vacuum hose. It should show no sign of ATF.

FIGURE 12–17 Applying a vacuum to the modulator should cause the pin to move inward about 0.25 inch. The modulator should hold the vacuum for at least 30 seconds.

3. Disconnect and plug the vacuum line to the modulator.

4. Connect a vacuum pump to the modulator, and maintain a constant 2-in. Hg vacuum during the test.

5. Start the engine, place the gear selector in drive, and slowly accelerate the drive wheels. During acceleration, carefully note the gauge pressures. At some point above 10 mph (16 km/h), the pressure should decrease.

6. Repeat this check with the gear selector in manual second and with 10-in. Hg vacuum. Pressure cutback should occur at some point above 5 mph (8 km/h).

If line pressure decreases, the governor is working. Governor cutback is also indicated by a pressure increase as the vehicle coasts down through these same speeds.

TECH TIP

1. Some technicians wipe the inside of the vacuum hose with a cotton-tipped swab or pipe cleaner. ● SEE FIGURE 12–16. Any red ATF easily shows up on the white cotton.
2. If the modulator is off the vehicle, a quick way to check the diaphragm is to push the sleeve/plunger all the way inward; it should move smoothly inward against the spring pressure. With the sleeve all the way in, place your finger over the vacuum port and release the plunger/sleeve. The sleeve/plunger should remain inward, and a vacuum should be felt at the port. Release your finger, and the sleeve/plunger should pop out. This is a fast, simple check, but is not as accurate as using a vacuum pump.

12.8 MODULATOR CHECKS

Some transmissions use a vacuum modulator to control shift points and feel. Engine vacuum is used to adjust TV, line, accumulator, or shift valve pressure. Modulator checks should include diaphragm leakage, vacuum supply, sleeve/stem alignment, spring pressure, and on-car operation. The on-car checks are similar to those described in Section 12.7. The modulator should be checked whenever there is a concern about shift timing or quality and when a transmission is overhauled.

12.8.1 MODULATOR DIAPHRAGM LEAKAGE

There are several ways to check the modulator. The easiest is to remove the vacuum hose from the modulator and inspect the inside of the hose for automatic transmission fluid (ATF). Any sign of ATF on the vacuum side of the modulator indicates a faulty modulator diaphragm.

A hand-operated vacuum pump can be used to check the modulator diaphragm. Connect the vacuum pump to the modulator port and apply 20 in. Hg of vacuum. ● SEE FIGURE 12–17. The vacuum should hold and not leak down for at least 30 seconds. This check can be made with the modulator on or off the vehicle. If this test is made with the modulator off the vehicle, the sleeve/plunger should move smoothly inward as the vacuum is applied and smoothly out again as the vacuum is released. A modulator with a leaky diaphragm must be replaced.

12.8.2 MODULATOR VACUUM SUPPLY

A modulator must have a good vacuum supply/source in order to operate correctly. Many technicians check the vacuum source first when they suspect a modulator problem. This is checked by installing a tee and a vacuum gauge at the modulator port. ● SEE FIGURE 12–18. Start the engine, and let it idle in park (parking brake applied). With the engine at operating temperature, the vacuum reading at the modulator should be about 15 to 20 in. Hg. This reading is affected by altitude and engine condition. Higher altitudes produce lower readings; 10 to 15 in. Hg is normal for an elevation of 5,000 ft. Worn or out-of-tune

FIGURE 12–18 A vacuum gauge can be connected into the vacuum modulator line using a tee fitting. A good, strong vacuum signal that varies with throttle opening should be present when the engine is running.

engines also produce weaker vacuum signals. While checking the vacuum, the throttle should be opened and closed quickly while watching the vacuum gauge. The gauge needle should quickly drop as the throttle is opened and then rise as it is closed. A small change in the engine speed or sluggish movement of the vacuum needle as the throttle is operated indicates a restricted or kinked vacuum supply line. Fluctuating vacuum readings indicate an engine problem. A vacuum reading that drops while the engine is at 2000 RPM indicates a plugged exhaust system.

12.8.3 MODULATOR STEM ALIGNMENT

The body of the modulator must be aligned with the stem or else the plunger will bind. The modulator is in a fairly well-protected location, but when a transmission is removed or replaced, there is a possibility of bumping the modulator and bending the stem. The simplest way to check for a bent modulator is to roll it across a bench top and watch for a wobble motion of the stem, which indicates a problem. ● **SEE FIGURE 12–19.** You can expect it to roll in a circle. A bent modulator will produce an easily seen up-and-down wobble.

12.8.4 MODULATOR SPRING PRESSURE

Modulator spring pressure is also called *modulator weight* by some technicians because it is measured by "weighing" the modulator.

FIGURE 12–19 If a modulator is rolled across a bench top, the stem section of a good modulator should not wobble up and down. A wobble motion indicates a bent stem.

FIGURE 12–20 Modulator spring strength is checked by weighing the modulator. Push downward until the stem starts to retract into the modulator sleeve, and note the reading on the scale.

Place the modulator with the stem end down on a 0- to 20-lb graduated scale. ● **SEE FIGURE 12–20.** With some modulators, an extension made from a l/8-in. rod, a small bolt, or an old modulator valve must be used.

Next, simply push downward on the modulator as you watch the extension and the scale. At about 10 to 15 lb of pressure, you should be able to see the extension start to move into the modulator as the spring compresses. This is the minimum

Gauge

FIGURE 12–21 A modulator load check requires a special gauge and a known-good modulator. The two modulators are pushed together, and the gauge is read to determine if the one being tested is faulty.

TECH TIP

1. A modulator with a higher spring pressure produces higher hydraulic pressures at a given vacuum than one with a weaker spring. This in turn produces firmer shifts. A heavier vehicle with a stronger engine generally needs a stronger, heavier modulator, whereas a lighter vehicle or one with a weaker engine needs a weaker, softer, lighter one.
2. Some manufacturers use different sizes of modulators, and the strength of the modulator is affected by its diameter (see Figure 7–28). Remember that a modulator has atmospheric pressure on one side of the diaphragm and the vacuum manifold and the spring on the other. A larger diaphragm makes atmospheric pressure stronger relative to the spring.
3. Some modulators are adjustable. Try turning the adjustment screw after you have weighed the modulator. Turning the screw inward should increase the weight. This causes the modulator-controlled pressures in the transmission to increase and should produce firmer shifts. Turning the screw outward should lower the modulator weight, which should produce softer shifts.
4. With modulators that use a pin between the vacuum diaphragm and the throttle valve, modulator pressure can be adjusted by changing the length of the pin. A longer pin will increase pressures, and a shorter pin will decrease the pressure.

spring pressure, and as you push harder, the extension will move farther inward. At some point if you keep pushing, the spring will be fully compressed, and the inward movement of the extension will stop. This is the maximum spring pressure.

A similar modulator check is called the *load check* or *bellows comparison check*. It compares the strength of a "known-good" modulator with the one you are checking. A **known-good** modulator is one that you know is operating correctly; it must be of the same type and part number as the one you are checking. This check requires a special gauge that can be either purchased or made. The gauge is placed in the stem ends of the two modulators; then the modulators are pushed slowly toward each other. ● **SEE FIGURE 12–21**.

TECH TIP

If the modulators compress at the same rate while they come together, the one you are checking is good. If the modulator being checked compresses easier so that the center of the gauge disappears while it is 1/16 inch or more from the other modulator, the questionable modulator is bad.

12.9 STALL TESTS

Stall tests are used to check the stator one-way clutch and the strength of the apply devices. A band and clutch application chart is used when making a stall test to verify which clutch or band is applied in each gear range. ● **SEE FIGURE 12–22**.

CAUTION: Exercise caution when performing a stall test for several reasons: personal safety, the safety of those around you, and the chance of possible damage to the vehicle and transmission. You will be operating the vehicle with the transmission in gear and the throttle wide open. There is a possibility that the vehicle can get away from you. All four wheels must be on the ground, the brakes must be in good operating condition, and the parking and service brakes must be firmly applied while performing a stall test. Many technicians place blocks at the front and rear tires.

Stall testing the transmission creates high pressure, a lot of heat inside the torque converter, and severe loads to the drivetrain. The period during which the transmission is at stall should be kept as short as possible, never over 5 seconds.

A stall test also places a heavy load on the engine's mounts. It is good practice to have the hood open and keep an eye on the engine while doing a stall test. If the engine appears to lift or rotate too far, stop the test immediately and check the condition of the mounts. ● **SEE FIGURE 12–23**.

Most manufacturers publish stall speed specifications for their engine-transmission combinations. This allows for an easy comparison between your readings and the specifications. If specifications are not available, you can compare the readings between gear ranges; stall speed should be the same in each

TECH TIP

1. It is a good practice to shift into neutral between the checks and run at fast idle for 30 seconds or so to allow a change of fluid inside the converter.
2. Faulty mounts usually cause a heavy clunk or knock when you close the throttle and allow the engine to drop down on the mounts.

Shift Lever Position	Transmission Clutches and Bands					Overdrive Clutches		
	Front Clutch	Front Band	Rear Clutch	Rear Band	Overrun. Clutch	Overdrive Clutch	Direct Clutch	Overrun. Clutch
Reverse	X			X			X	
Drive Range First Second Third Fourth	 X X	 X 	 X X X X		 X 	 X	 X X X 	 X X
2-Range (Manual) (Second)		X	X		X		X	X
1-Range (Manual) (Low)			X	X	X		X	X

FIGURE 12–22 A clutch and band apply chart shows which units are applied during the different gear ranges. For example, with this 42RH/46RH transmission, the rear band and the front clutch are applied in reverse. (*Courtesy of Chrysler Corporation*)

(a)

(b)

FIGURE 12–23 (a) During a stall test, torque reaction tries to lift the left side of a RWD vehicle's engine. (b) It tries to rotate the top of a FWD vehicle's engine toward the rear.

gear. Remember that the brakes of the vehicle hold the transmission output shaft stationary, and the clutches and bands should hold the transmission and the torque converter turbine stationary. Slipping of these parts allows the turbine shaft to rotate and therefore the engine speed to increase. Too high of a stall speed indicates slippage inside the transmission.

FIGURE 12–24 The wheels should be blocked, and both the parking and service brakes should be firmly applied during a stall test. A tachometer is used to measure engine speed, and if needed, a pressure gauge is used to measure system pressure.

To perform a stall test, *you should:*

1. Connect a tachometer to the engine following the directions for the tachometer.

2. Position the vehicle with all four wheels securely on the ground. It is a good practice to place blocks in front and in back of the drive wheels. ● **SEE FIGURE 12–24.**

3. Start the engine and note the tachometer reading.

4. Apply the brakes firmly, move the gear selector to reverse, move the throttle to wide open, and watch the tachometer. The speed should increase to somewhere between 1500 and 3000 RPM. As soon as the speed stops increasing or goes higher than 3500 RPM, quickly note the reading and close the throttle. Record the speed.

5. Shift to neutral, and run the engine at fast idle for 30 to 60 seconds to cool the converter.

1. It is recommended that you mark the upper and lower stall speed limits on the face of your tachometer using a grease pencil or nonpermanent marker. This allows you to quickly note the tachometer reading and determine if the stall speed is good, low, or high.
2. During a stall test, the throttle should not be held open longer than 5 seconds.

TECH TIP

A stall check of a type 2 transmission shows the stall speed is too high only in drive-1. The clutch and band chart indicates that the forward clutch and the one-way clutch are the apply devices for drive-1. The forward clutch must be good because it is also applied in manual-1, and the stall speed is okay in manual-1. Therefore, the high stall speed in drive-1 is caused by a faulty one-way clutch. If the stall speed was too high in both drive-1 and manual-1, the forward clutch would be the cause of the problem.

6. Repeat steps 4 and 5 with the gear selector in drive.
7. Repeat steps 4 and 5 with the gear selector in low.

CAUTION: Direct any bystanders away from the front or back of the vehicle.

12.9.1 INTERPRETING STALL TEST READINGS

If all of the stall speeds were within the specification range, the apply devices for the three gear ranges are all sound and in good shape. The apply devices for some gear(s) cannot be applied with the vehicle at rest so they cannot be stall tested.

If all of the stall speeds were equal but low, the engine is weak, out of tune, or the stator one-way clutch is slipping. Checking engine performance should indicate which is at fault.

If the stall speeds are normal, but the vehicle has normal acceleration and has reduced performance at higher speeds, the stator one-way clutch could be seized in a locked-up condition.

If the stall speed is high in one or two of the gear ranges, one or more of the apply devices is slipping. Consult a clutch and band application chart to determine which apply devices are at fault.

12.10 OIL PAN DEBRIS CHECK

When it has been determined something is wrong with the transmission, the next step is to drain the oil and remove the pan for inspection. The debris in the pan can give a good indication of what is occurring in the transmission.

- A small amount of debris with a blackish oil film is normal. A small amount of metal can be attributed to the wear that occurs during break-in and normal operation.
- An excess of loose, black material is burned lining material from a slipping band or clutch. It usually has a burned smell.
- A heavy golden brown coating is from badly oxidized, old fluid. The lower part of the case and valve body will also have this varnish coating. It usually has a strong odor similar to varnish and indicates that the transmission ran hot.
- An excess of metal is from a gear set, thrust washers, bushings, or the transmission case. Steel and iron are usually from the gears, needle bearings, a spring, or a spring retainer. Aluminum is from the case, a carrier, or a clutch piston. Brass or bronze is from a bushing or thrust washer.
- Any plastic debris (broken or melted) is from a thrust washer, spacer, or clutch spring retainer.

TECH TIP

1. It is a good practice to inspect the pan while the transmission is still in the vehicle. If you wait until it has been removed and placed on a bench, the debris might move around inside the unit. This could cause a misdiagnosis of the problem.
2. Transmissions that use internal input and/or output speed sensors will attract iron or steel particles to the magnetic tip of the sensor. Removing the sensor provides an easy check for iron and steel debris.

12.11 AIR TESTING

Air testing is a valuable diagnostic tool and is also used as a final quality-control check during transmission assembly. Air tests are used to tell if a clutch or band servo operates, if a governor can operate, and if the passages are properly sealed.

CAUTION: You must wear eye protection when making air tests.

FIGURE 12–25 The passages in this Torqueflite transmission are identified so the different components can be air checked. They are exposed when the valve body is removed. (*Courtesy of Chrysler Corporation*)

FIGURE 12–26 A rubber-tipped air gun is commonly used for air checks. Pushing it against the port opening usually makes an airtight seal. It must be removed from the opening to allow air to escape and release the component.

Air tests often are made with the valve body removed. With it removed, the passages to the apply devices are easily accessible. Many manufacturers provide illustrations in their service information that identifies these passages. ● **SEE FIGURE 12–25.**

A rubber-tipped air gun is normally used when making air tests. It is merely pushed against the end of the passage to make a seal. ● **SEE FIGURE 12–26.**

FIGURE 12–27 When the test port is a long slot, part of the slot can be closed off by forcing a shop cloth into the slot.

FIGURE 12–28 A common washer can be used to air test irregularly shaped passages to close oversize or odd-shaped holes.

 TECH TIP

1. If the passage ends in a long slot, a shop cloth can be forced into part of the opening to close it down to a manageable size. ● **SEE FIGURE 12–27.**

2. When air testing through an irregularly spaced hole, a common washer can be placed over the hole, and the air is applied through the washer's hole. ● **SEE FIGURE 12–28.**

3. Some technicians use an air gun that is modified with a piece of tubing for hard-to-reach locations. ● **SEE FIGURE 12–29.** Special test plates are also available to provide air-pressure access to difficult passages. ● **SEE FIGURE 12–30.**

4. Pressures of about 50 PSI (345 kPa) should be used while air checking. Very high pressures (over 90 PSI [621 kPa]) can cause normal seepage to appear as a major leak. Remember that air passes through openings easier than ATF. In some cases, the air pressure should be dropped to 20 PSI (138 kPa).

FIGURE 12–29 The tip of this air gun has been replaced with an adapter and short length of 0.25-inch tubing. The tubing can be bent for difficult-to-reach locations.

Air Pressure Test Plates

2/4 Clutch Retainer Hole

FIGURE 12–30 The two air pressure test plates have been installed to help make the air checks of the LR, UD, REV, and O/D circuits of the 42LE transaxle easier. The 2–4 clutch can be checked without a plate. *(Courtesy of Chrysler Corporation)*

To perform an air test, *you should:*

1. Remove the pan and valve body and identify the fluid passages to be tested.

2. Adjust the air pressure to 30 to 50 PSI. Apply air pressure to the passages one at a time. As you air test the different components, you should get the following results.

   a. **Band servos**—operation of the band with a very small amount of air leakage. Removal of the air gun from the passage should result in band release. Some bands require that air be used to apply the band and a second air nozzle be used to release the band. When the second air nozzle is removed, the band will reapply,

Some clutches have two piston areas—one inner and one outer area. When air is applied to one chamber, it can normally leak into the other and pass out through the other apply port. You can cover this second port with your finger while testing.

It is also possible to air check the whole transmission or an individual circuit by blowing air into the pressure test ports. If checking the whole transmission, insert the rubber tip of the air gun into the "line" test port, set the air pressure to about 90 PSI (621 kPa), and apply air pressure. ● **SEE FIGURE 12–31.**

Depending on the location of the test port in the hydraulic circuit, the airflow can be controlled using the manual valve. In some cases with the transmission on the bench, the pump will rotate, but it can be held stationary by installing the torque converter. With some transmissions, the governor weights can be blocked outward, and the shift valves will operate in an upshift position. This allows pressure checking of each of the gear positions, which you can control by shifting the manual valve. If the transmission has pressure test ports for the different circuits, each of these circuits can be checked by pressurizing each port. Note that this pressure will try to exhaust at the shift valve, but you can often block this flow with your finger. In this case, you might have to drop the air pressure to about 40 PSI (275 kPa). While performing these checks, be sure to listen for escaping air, which indicates leaks.

and when the first air nozzle is removed, spring pressure will release the band.

   b. **Clutches**—a "kachunk" noise indicates the clutch applied. Removal of the air gun should result in the sound of a clutch release. If the air nozzle is kept in place, good clutch seals should hold air pressure for about 5 seconds or more after the air is turned off.

   c. **Governor**—air tests will vary between makes. There are two governor ports to check: One is the feed from the drive circuit and the other is the return from the governor. Check both of them. In some cases, you will get a "click" or "snap" and then a very small leak, a "click" and an open exhaust leak, or a rather heavy "buzz" sound. The exact sound depends on the type of governor, the position of the governor shaft, and whether you blow air into the inlet or outlet passage. The response should change if you plug the second passage with your finger. As you gain experience, you will learn the correct response from the governor for a particular transmission.

FIGURE 12–31 A transmission can be air checked by blowing air into the pressure test ports. In this case, air is being blown into the 2–3 pressure port to check the third-gear circuit. Air leaks can be heard through the filter tube.

 REAL WORLD FIX

The 1994 Chevrolet C-1500 pickup (162,000 miles) makes a 1–3 shift, skipping second gear. The 4L60E transmission was disassembled, and the 2–4 band and input drum were worn out, metal to metal. The transmission was rebuilt using a new band, input drum, shift solenoids, and torque converter. The transmission was reinstalled, but the road test showed the same problem. A scanner showed the 1–2 shift occurring, but the transmission shifts 1–3.

FIX

The 2–4 servo was rechecked and found to be leaking. Replacement of the seals in the 2–4 servo fixed this shift problem. Air checks during assembly could have found this servo problem and prevented the comeback and extra time locating the problem.

 TECH TIP

Teflon rings or seals lubricated with Vaseline or Door-Ease may take more pressure or temperature before normal operation. You can increase the pressure, but you should be prepared for a high-pressure spray of fluid. You must wear eye protection.

12.11.1 WET AIR CHECKS At times, it is difficult to determine excessive leakage during an air test. You hear or feel an air leak, but is it bad enough to condemn a part or cause the problem? Sometimes, you hear the leak, but you cannot determine the exact location. When you need to detect a small leak or determine if valve or bore wear is excessive, you can make a wet air check. This is the same as an air test with a small amount of ATF put into the passage prior to the check. It is recommended to regulate the air pressure to 30 to 50 PSI when making a wet air test. Any leaks show up easily because of the escaping red ATF. With experience you will learn how to tell if the leak is excessive.

To perform a wet air test, *you should:*

1. Put a small amount of ATF into the suspected passage to be checked. A pump assembly or valve body is usually assembled, and all plugs should be installed in the passages.

2. Adjust the air pressure to 30 to 50 PSI, apply air to the passage, and carefully check for escaping air and ATF.
   ● **SEE FIGURE 12–32.** Be careful when removing the air nozzle from the passage, as ATF can blow back. Turn off the air and let the pressure drop before removing the nozzle.

FIGURE 12–32 A wet air test is performed by putting a small amount of ATF into the passage before a low-pressure air test. Fluid leaking from the regulator apply or exhaust passages indicates a worn valve. (*Courtesy of Sonnax*)

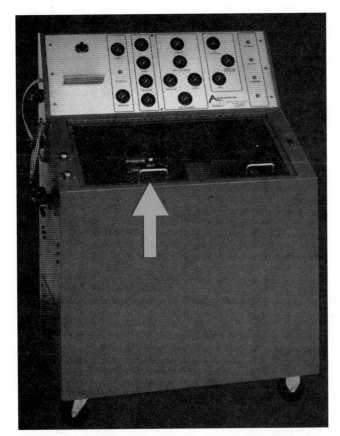

FIGURE 12–33 The valve body under the clear cover (near front) is connected to the diagnostic machine through a series of pressure lines. Fluid under pressure can be directed to the valves, and their operation can be observed on the pressure gauges. (*Courtesy of Zoom Technology*)

Tests Units on Bench

Tests Units in Vehicle

FIGURE 12–34 The Answermatic can be connected to transmissions that are on the bench or in a vehicle. This allows pressure checking the hydraulic circuits using pressurized ATF. (*Courtesy of Zoom Technology*)

12.11.2 ISOLATING VALVE BODY PROBLEMS A hydraulic circuit analyzer is available to test valve body operation, while it is off the transmission. ● **SEE FIGURE 12–33.** The valve body is connected to a series of gauges, and fluid pressure can be sent into the system to simulate the flow from a transmission.

The operator can cause the valve body to perform shifts while watching the pressure change. This unit can also be connected to a transmission that is either on the bench or in a vehicle. This allows pressure testing the transmission using fluid pressure. ● **SEE FIGURE 12–34.** If testing a transmission that is in the vehicle, the technician can operate the transmission using the machine controls.

12.12 OIL LEAK TESTS

There are several tests that can be made to locate the cause of oil leaks. Most leaks originate at the joints or connections between the various parts of the transmission; between the cooler line connections; at the front-torque converter seal, rear extension housing/universal joint seal; or with transaxles, the two CV (constant velocity) joint seals. ● **SEE FIGURE 12–35.**

The cause of a leak can often be found by raising the vehicle on a hoist and making a visual inspection. You can usually follow the red ATF upward and often forward to the source. ● **SEE FIGURE 12–36.** A **fluorescent dye** is available that can be added to the transmission fluid. The black-light causes the dye to glow, making the leak visible. ● **SEE FIGURE 12–37.**

A leak coming from inside the torque converter housing usually indicates a bad front seal, but this can also be caused by a leaking torque converter, faulty pump gasket, or faulty front seal. ● **SEE FIGURE 12–38.** In any case, it is necessary to remove the transmission for a closer inspection and repair.

A. Pump gasket
B. Front seal
C. Pump O-ring
D. Cover gasket
E. Level plug seal
F. CV joint seal
G. Pan gasket
H. Case
I. Cover gasket
J. Vent tubes
K. Shift shaft seal

FIGURE 12–35 Possible leak locations for most transmissions are the pump seal and gasket, output shaft seal(s), pan gasket, manual shift shaft, vent(s), and case porosity. A cover gasket, drain, or fill plug is another possibility.

FIGURE 12–36 A leaking transmission. Note the fluid dripping off the governor cover and the washed area at the rear of the pan. This fluid probably came from above and forward of these points.

 TECH TIP

Some vehicles, including all recent General Motors vehicles, use Dex-Cool antifreeze, and Dex-Cool is dyed orange. Old Dex-Cool antifreeze can appear much like ATF. Be sure of the source for the leak you are trying to locate and fix.

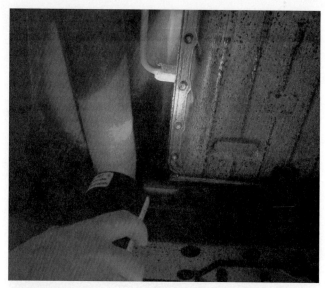

FIGURE 12–37 Fluorescent dye has been added to the transmission fluid. The dye will glow when the blacklight (arrow) shines on it, showing the location of the leak.

FIGURE 12–38 Fluid from a leaking front seal or pump gasket tends to move down the front of the transmission. Fluid leaks from a converter drain plug or bad welds tend to come from the outer surface of the torque converter. A leak from the back of the engine will move across the flexplate. (*Courtesy of Chrysler Corporation*)

12.13 NOISE, VIBRATION, AND HARSHNESS

Noise, vibration, and harshness (NVH) has become the automotive repair trade term for these types of problems. Unpleasant noise and vibration problems can be caused by automatic transmissions. Harshness is defined as an unpleasant motion, above 20 Hz, that can be felt. Harshness is not a major concern for transmission technicians.

The 1989 GMC C1500 pickup (292,000 km) has a fluid leak with an unknown source. The leak is not apparent with the engine running in the shop, but it will leak a quart of ATF after a few miles on the road. Fluid is sprayed all over the vehicle's front suspension.

FIX

Following advice, the technician put the vehicle on a lift and ran it through all of the gears. The leak was coming from some pin holes in the 2–4 servo cover. A new servo cover fixed this leak problem.

TECH TIP

1. The vent of some transmissions is located in the bell housing. A fluid overfill can cause what appears to be a leak in this area.
2. When there is so much fluid that you cannot locate the source of the leak, it is necessary to steam clean the transmission and vehicle underbody. After cleaning the transmission, drive the vehicle briefly to dry things off. Operate the transmission in all gear ranges at high-throttle openings to move the high-pressure oil so the source of the leak can be seen. Then raise the vehicle on a hoist, and using a good, strong light, carefully check the transmission area for the red ATF.
3. If you have located a leak in a general area but cannot find the specific location, thoroughly clean the area and dry it. Next, coat the area using an aerosol-applied foot powder. Most foot powders dry quickly and leave a white, powder coating. Any leak under this coating will show as an obvious red stain. ● **SEE FIGURE 12–39**.
4. To locate those difficult-to-find leaks, it is possible to pressurize the transmission case with air and then locate the escaping air. This requires that you close off the oil filter and vent openings if the transmission is in the vehicle, and the converter, extension housing, and cooler line openings if the unit is out of the vehicle. Caps and plugs can be fabricated for this purpose. ● **SEE FIGURE 12–40**.

NVH problem diagnosis normally begins with a road test, and the technician notes when the noise or vibrations occur. The speed and gear range are varied to note their effect on the problem.

FIGURE 12–39 Foot powder is being spread on the suspected leak area. Next, the transmission will be operated, and the leak should be obvious as a red stain on the white powder.

The 1998 Ford Econoline E350 (91,000 miles) came in with several oil leaks. The easy leaks were repaired using the proper parts, but a small leak in the pump area was still evident.

FIX

The technician added dye to the fluid, and he was then able to locate a cracked pump housing. Replacing the pump assembly fixed this problem.

To make an NVH road test, *you should:*

1. Make sure the vehicle is at normal operating temperature, start the vehicle, and accelerate in drive, using a moderate throttle, to the problem speed or the speed limit. Note any unusual noises or vibrations.
2. Let up on the throttle, and allow the vehicle to decelerate to a stop or a speed below the problem speed.
3. Repeat step 1 using full throttle. Do not exceed the speed limit.
4. Repeat step 2, shifting into neutral to allow the vehicle to coast.
5. Repeat step 1, using different gear ranges or throttle positions to give you a better idea of the origin of the problem.
6. An FWD vehicle can have a driveshaft, CV joint, or differential problem that is sensitive to turns. With these vehicles, it is recommended to repeat these steps while making gradual or sharp turns to cause a speed difference between the driveshafts.

12.13.1 NOISE CHECKS Noise problems are closely related to vibration; they often accompany each other. The

Weld Or Braze

Break Edge

1/16" Min.

1/8"

Seal This End Air Tight

Polish Outside Of Open End For This Distance On Tube

1-3/4"

5"

1.495
1.498

Material: 1-1/2 Inch O.D. Thin Walled Steel Tubing And 1/8 Inch Steel Disc

(a)

Vent Plug Retainer

Retainer

Spring

Converter Hub Seal Cup

Plug – Made From Old Filler Tube

(b)

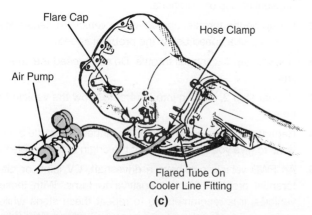

Flare Cap

Hose Clamp

Air Pump

Flared Tube On Cooler Line Fitting

(c)

FIGURE 12–40 When the openings into the transmission are plugged, air can be pumped into the transmission through the cooler return line. Soapy water can now be sprayed onto the transmission, and bubbles will expose the exact location of any leaks. (*Courtesy of Chrysler Corporation*)

sources of most objectionable noises in automatic transmissions can be the transmission mounts, torque converter, flexplate, drive chain and sprockets (in some transmissions), planetary gear set, band application, and transaxle final drive. Noise concerns are usually confirmed on a road test, and it is good practice to have the customer identify the exact noise. Remember that the engine, suspension system, tires, exhaust system, and drive line are also causes of objectionable noises.

The three most common sources of transmission noise are the bearings, gears, and hydraulic system. Bearings, both ball and roller, consist of three parts: the bearing element (rollers or balls with cage), and the inner and outer races. The races can be separate parts or a hardened portion of a shaft, gear, or carrier. Bearing noise, often described as a *whine,* is caused by damage, pits, or scoring that makes the bearing surface rough.

Gear noise is usually the result of a rough gear surface or a worn bearing that allows the gear to change position. Gear noise usually shows up as a whine in a certain gear or multiple gears. Another type of gear noise is a *clack* or *clunk* that occurs when there is a change in power flow; it is the result of excessive clearance in the gear train. Worn differential gears and differential pinion shaft are a major cause of neutral-to-drive or neutral-to-reverse clunk.

Hydraulic noise, often described as a "buzz," is the result of rapid fluid pressure pulsations. With many transmissions, it will occur for a short time period while the fluid is cold and then go away.

When troubleshooting noise problems, it helps to determine how the noise fits into the following categories.

- **Speed relation**—related to engine or vehicle speed
- **Gear range**—related to gear range
- **Pitch/frequency**—low (rumble), medium (growl), or high (squeal)
- **Load sensitive**—heavy throttle, light throttle, or coast
- **Direction**—straight or right or left turn

Hydraulic noise can be seen as a rapidly pulsating pressure gauge needle. Another tip is that the noise will change if the pressure changes. With some transmissions, shifting into or out of reverse will cause a pressure change because of the increased reverse boost, and this will change the noise level or frequency. On transmissions with a throttle rod or cable, move the lever toward full-throttle position, or on units using a vacuum modulator, disconnect the vacuum hose; this should change the TV boost and change the noise level or frequency.

TECH TIP

An NVH diagnostic tool, ChassisEar, consists of a headset and six sensors that can be attached to various locations under the vehicle. The vehicle can be driven on a road test while the technician listens to the six locations. This should help locate the exact source of the noise. ● **SEE FIGURE 12–41.**

REAL WORLD FIX

The 1995 Neon (87,000 miles) has a bad, tinny rattle noise coming from the torque converter area. The noise occurs whenever the engine is running. Visual inspection through the inspection cover area does not show a problem. A cracked flexplate is suspected.

FIX

Removal of the transaxle allowed inspection of the torque converter and flexplate. Visual inspection showed that a balance weight had come loose. Replacement of the torque converter fixed this noise problem.

(a)

(b)

FIGURE 12–41 A ChassisEar has a microphone built into each of the clamps that are connected to various points under the vehicle. During a road test, the technician can switch between them and listen for the problem noise through the headset. (*Courtesy of Steelman*)

To locate the cause of a transmission noise, *you should:*

1. Raise the vehicle so you have access to the transmission mounts. Visually check their condition, and if the mounts appear weak, pry upward on the transmission to check for possible separation of the mounts.

2. Start the engine and shift the transmission through its gear ranges while observing for any mount problems.

3. With the engine running and the gear selector in P or N, listen for the noise problem. Shift into D, and with the brake firmly applied, listen for the noise problem. A torque converter problem is indicated if the noise occurs with the transmission in gear but not in P or N. A pump problem is indicated if the noise occurs in both D and P or N. A faulty input drive chain and sprockets can also cause this problem. ● **SEE CHART 12–4.**

4. With the engine running, shift from N to R while listening for the noise. A hydraulic noise is indicated if the noise

QUIET	NOISY	PROBLEM
In park or neutral	In gear with wheels stopped	Torque converter/input shaft/input drive chain
In park or neutral	In reverse with wheels stopped	Pump
In third gear (1:1 ratio)	In all other gears	Gear set
With wheels stopped	While moving and increases with speed	Final drive or chain drive

Noise Isolation

increases when shifted into R. Shift into D and pull on the TV cable, disconnect the vacuum hose from the modulator or alter the signal to the EPC solenoid to boost line pressure. A hydraulic noise is indicated if the noise increases.

5. Perform a road test and listen for noise changes as the transmission shifts through its gear ranges. A transmission gear set problem is indicated if the noise changes depending on the gear range, especially if it is quiet during the range with a 1:1 ratio.

6. Repeat step 5 and listen for a noise that increases as the vehicle speed increases. A final drive problem is indicated if the noise intensity or frequency increases with vehicle speed. Note that the final drive can include transfer gears or chain drives depending on the transaxle.

Transmission noise problem areas usually fit into the categories shown in ● **CHART 12–5**. The next step is disassembly and careful inspection of the suspected component. The exact cause might be a rough bearing, a loose drive chain, a cracked

NOISE	PROBABLE CAUSE
Chain noise	A whine or growl that increases in frequency and amplitude with vehicle speed. Most noticeable under light acceleration. Input chain noise can be heard in park and neutral.
Final drive	A hum related to vehicle speed. Usually torque sensitive.
Gear noise	A whine or growl related to vehicle speed. Usually torque and gear-range sensitive.
Pump noise	A high-pitched whine that increases in amplitude with engine speed. Most noticeable in park or neutral with cold transmission fluid.

Noise Problems

flexplate, or any number of other defects. Some manufacturers recommend the use of a diagnostic guide to locate the source of noise problems. ● **SEE FIGURE 12–42**.

12.13.2 VIBRATION CHECKS Occasionally a transmission repair or replacement results in a vibration, or a vehicle vibration diagnosis leads to the possibility of the transmission as the cause. Most transmission vibrations are caused by an unbalanced torque converter, an off-center torque converter, or a faulty output shaft–universal joint connection. Misaligned engine or transmission mounts can produce vibrations or noise

DIAGNOSIS GUIDE-ABNORMAL NOISE

INSPECT AND CORRECT THE TRANSAXLE FLUID LEVEL. ROAD TEST TO VERIFY THAT AN ABNORMAL NOISE EXISTS. IDENTIFY THE TYPE OF NOISE, DRIVING RANGES, AND CONDITIONS WHEN THE NOISE OCCURS.

GRINDING NOISE
REMOVE THE TRANSAXLE AND CONVERTER ASSEMBLY; DISASSEMBLE, CLEAN AND INSPECT ALL PARTS; CLEAN THE VALVE BODY, INSTALL ALL NEW SEALS, RINGS, AND GASKETS; REPLACE WORN OR DEFECTIVE PARTS.

GEAR NOISE
CHECK FOR CORRECT LOCATION OF RUBBER ISOLATOR SLEEVE ON SHIFT CABLE (CENTER OF CABLE).

TRANSFER SET
REMOVE THE TRANSAXLE; REPLACE THE OUTPUT AND TRANSFER SHAFT GEARS

PLANETARY SET
REMOVE THE TRANSAXLE; REPLACE PLANETARY SET

DIFFERENTIAL DRIVE SET
REMOVE THE TRANSAXLE; REPLACE TRANSFER SHAFT AND RING GEAR

WHINE OR BUZZ NOISE
LISTEN TO TRANSAXLE AND CONVERTER FOR SOURCE OF NOISE.

KNOCK, CLICK, OR SCRAPE NOISE
REMOVE TORQUE CONVERTER DUST SHIELD AND INSPECT FOR LOOSE OR CRACKED CONVERTER DRIVE PLATE; INSPECT FOR CONTACT OF THE STARTER DRIVE WITH THE STARTER RING GEAR.

TRANSAXLE HAS BUZZ OR WHINE

CONVERTER HAS LOUD BUZZ OR WHINE

REPLACE TORQUE CONVERTER

REMOVE ALL THREE OIL PANS; (SUMP, DIFFERENTIAL, AND GEAR COVER) INSPECT FOR DEBRIS INDICATING WORN OR FAILED PARTS.

NO DEBRIS PRESENT
REMOVE VALVE BODY, DISASSEMBLE, CLEAN AND INSPECT PARTS. REASSEMBLE, INSTALL. CHECK OPERATION AND PRESSURES.

DEBRIS PRESENT
REMOVE TRANSAXLE AND CONVERTER AS AN ASSEMBLY; DISASSEMBLE, CLEAN AND INSPECT ALL PARTS, CLEAN THE VALVE BODY, INSTALL ALL NEW SEALS, RINGS AND GASKETS; REPLACE WORN OR DEFECTIVE PARTS.

REPLACE TORQUE CONVERTER

FIGURE 12–42 This diagnosis guide is designed to help technicians locate the cause of abnormal noises in a 41TE transaxle. (*Courtesy of Chrysler Corporation*)

TECH TIP

1. Driveline clunk usually occurs during garage shifts, neutral–drive, or neutral–reverse. It can often be confirmed by looseness as you shake the universal joint side to side. The cure for this is usually a replacement of the rear extension housing bushing and seal or universal joint.
2. Engine and transmission mounts are usually checked visually by inspecting them for deterioration or breakup of the rubber.

caused by improper U-joint or CV joint clearance. An exhaust system contacting body parts will also produce vibrations that can be felt throughout the vehicle.

Torque converter problems cause an engine-speed-related vibration problem. Output shaft vibration problems are vehicle-speed related. These often are accompanied by driveline clunk.

FWD output shaft problems will usually be most noticeable on turns because of the increased differential and CV joint action.

Engine-speed-related vibrations occur at a particular engine speed range; these vibrations change when the transmission shifts gears. There are several causes, for example, belt-driven accessories such as the fan, alternator, air-conditioning compressor, or internal engine unbalance. Belt-driven problems can be identified by running the engine with the belt removed; if the vibration is gone, you have located the vibration source. Identifying a torque converter problem begins with removing the converter cover and carefully inspecting the torque converter and flexplate. Look for a wobble (called runout) of the converter during engine rotation. Torque converter runout can be caused by the following:

- Improper tightening of the torque-converter-to-flexplate bolts
- A damaged flexplate (● **SEE FIGURE 12–43.**)
- Improper mounting of the torque converter into the crankshaft

If there is no runout, the next thing to do is remove the torque converter and either check its balance or replace it.

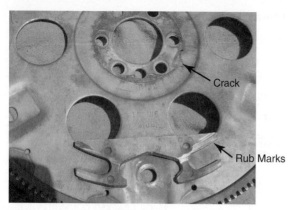

FIGURE 12–43 A cracked flexplate. Note the fine crack near the mounting bolts and the rub marks where the balance weight has been contacting the engine. (*Courtesy of Tony Jewell*)

 TECH TIP

1. A possible cause of torque converter vibration is the use of an aftermarket flexplate; these tend to be thinner than the original equipment and are possibly not flat.
2. One manufacturer recommends this test to find the cause of converter vibration. Raise and support the vehicle; disconnect the converter and slide away from the flexplate; rotate the flexplate and inspect for cracks and missing balance weights; start the engine and observe the vibration.

 REAL WORLD FIX

The 1991 Mazda B2600 4WD pickup (131,000 km) has a vibration at 1300 RPM in neutral. The vibration occurs at the same engine speed while driving. The technician feels it might be a bad harmonic balancer.

FIX

The technician checked the transmission skid plate and saw where the plate was bent and was rubbing on the transfer case. Straightening out the skid plate fixed this vibration problem.

12.14 TROUBLESHOOTING CHARTS

Another important diagnostic tool is the troubleshooting chart or diagnostic guide. ● **SEE FIGURE 12–44.** These charts are published for each transmission and are often found in service manuals. They typically list the more common problems encountered; and then for each problem, list the most probable causes and ways to repair or correct the problem. Often, the causes are listed in descending order, from the most common or easiest to check to the most difficult.

As mentioned earlier, it is a good practice to determine what is wrong with a transmission before disassembly for repairs. This allows time for the necessary checks during disassembly to locate the exact cause of the original problem and helps ensure that you cure all problems the first time repairs are made.

POSSIBLE CAUSE	HARSH ENGAGEMENT FROM NEUTRAL TO D	R	DELAYED ENGAGEMENT FROM NEUTRAL TO D	R	POOR SHIFT QUALITY	SHIFTS ERRATIC	DRIVES IN NEUTRAL	DRAGS OR LOCKS	GRATING, SCRAPING, GROWLING NOISE	KNOCKING NOISE	BUZZING NOISE	BUZZING NOISE DURING SHIFTS ONLY	HARD TO FILL, OIL BLOWS OUT FILLER TUBE	TRANSAXLE OVERHEATS	HARSH UPSHIFT	NO UPSHIFT INTO OVERDRIVE	NO LOCKUP	HARSH DOWNSHIFTS	HIGH SHIFT EFFORTS	HARSH LOCKUP SHIFT
Engine Performance	X	X			X										X			X		
Worn or faulty clutch(es)	X	X	X	X		X	X	X							X	X		X		
—Underdrive clutch	X		X			X	X	X										X		
—Overdrive clutch						X	X	X							X	X				
—Reverse clutch		X		X		X	X													
—2/4 clutch					X	X									X			X		
—Low/reverse clutch	X	X			X	X												X		
Clutch(es) dragging					X															
Insufficient clutch plate clearance					X									X						
Damaged clutch seals			X	X														X		
Worn or damaged accumulator seal ring(s)	X	X	X	X														X		
Faulty cooling system														X						
Engine coolant temp. too low															X	X				
Incorrect gearshift control linkage adjustment			X	X		X	X							X						
Shift linkage damaged																			X	
Chipped or damaged gear teeth									X	X										
Planetary gear sets broken or seized									X	X										
Bearings worn or damaged									X	X										
Driveshaft(s) bushing(s) worn or damaged									X											
Worn or broken reaction shaft support seal rings			X	X	X	X												X		
Worn or damaged input shaft seal rings			X	X													X			
Valve body malfunction or leakage	X	X	X	X	X	X	X			X								X	X	X
Hydraulic pressures too low			X	X	X	X								X	X			X		
Hydraulic pressures too high	X	X													X			X		
Faulty oil pump			X	X	X									X			X			
Oil filter clogged			X	X	X	X					X									
Low fluid level			X	X	X	X				X					X			X	X	
High fluid level													X	X						
Aerated fluid			X	X	X	X				X				X	X			X	X	
Engine idle speed too low			X	X																
Engine idle speed too high	X	X													X			X		
Normal solenoid operation											X									
Solenoid sound cover loose											X									
Sticking lockup piston																				X

FIGURE 12–44 This diagnostic chart is designed to help technicians locate the cause of improper operation of a 41TE transaxle. (*Courtesy of Chrysler Corporation*)

1. Before removing a transmission from a vehicle or disassembling a transmission, the problem should be evaluated to determine the exact fault with the transmission.

2. There are many tests and checks that can be used to determine the exact cause of an automatic transmission problem.

3. A technician should become familiar with how and when to perform the transmission tests to determine the cause of common problems.

4. Experienced technicians determine which tests are needed for a particular problem and will perform the checks in the most logical order.

5. Following a systematic diagnostic approach to a problem quickly leads to the correct repair.

REVIEW QUESTIONS

1. The following is a series of tests and checks that can be used to help determine the exact cause of problems. Fill in the blanks to complete the description of the tests or checks.
   a. A visual inspection is a quick, preliminary overall check of _____ factors that affect operation.
   b. A fluid check is an inspection of the fluid to ensure the correct _____ and _____.
   c. A _____ _____ gives the technician the opportunity to check the actual operation of the transmission.
   d. A torque converter clutch test is used to determine if the _____ is operating properly.
   e. Hydraulic _____ tests are used to check the hydraulic system pressures.
   f. Modulator checks are used to check the operation of the vacuum _____ valve system.
   g. _____ system checks are used to check the proper operation of the electronic controls.
   h. The _____ test loads the clutches and bands to check for slippage and also checks the torque converter stator one-way clutch.
   i. Leak checks are used to locate the source of a _____ leak.
   j. Debris checks determine if an abnormal amount of debris is present in the _____ _____ and, if so, the nature of the debris.
   k. Air tests are made to determine if the seals, _____, and gaskets in the hydraulic circuits are operating correctly.
   l. A more precise air test to locate the exact location or severity of a leak is called a _____ _____ _____.
   m. Checks to locate the cause of a noise, vibration, or harshness are known as _____ checks.

2. Diagnosing a problem with an automatic transmission should always begin by _____ the problem.

3. All transmission diagnosis should begin with a check of the _____ _____ and _____.

4. It is advisable to always _____ drive a vehicle before and after any repairs.

5. Below are the throttle positions that a technician should use while test-driving a vehicle. List the term that fits the description of the driving condition or the throttle position.
   a. The throttle is about three-fourths open.
   b. A complete release of the throttle, which results in coasting.
   c. The least throttle opening that produces acceleration.
   d. WOT, which forces a downshift.
   e. A manual downshift with zero throttle to produce a condition where engine compression slows the vehicle.
   f. The throttle is about one-fourth open.
   g. Fully opened throttle without forcing a downshift.
   h. The throttle is about one-half open.

6. A student is testing a torque converter using a pressure gauge. The pressure changed when the clutch was to apply, but the clutch does not apply. The problem is in the _____ _____.

7. A transmission only has one pressure test port. When checking hydraulic pressure at that port you would be monitoring _____ pressure.

8. A technician is testing line pressure and notices that line pressure reads lower in some of the gear ranges. His or her diagnosis is that there is a _____ problem in the hydraulic circuit for the ranges with low pressure.

9. A good-operating governor is indicated during a governor pressure check by a steadily rising pressure that is relative to _____ _____.

10. If a transmission does not have a governor pressure test port, governor operation can be monitored by watching mainline pressure for a _____ in pressure due to governor _____.

11. When testing a vacuum modulator, the modulator should have _____ in. Hg available to it, and it should be able to hold a vacuum for _____ seconds.

12. A stall test can be used to detect problems with the torque converter _____ _____ and for _____ apply devices.

13. If all of the stall speeds during a stall test are equal but low, the _____ _____ clutch has failed or the _____ is weak. If they are all high, the problem is _____ apply devices.

14. Brass or bronze debris in the transmission oil pan indicates that a _____ or _____ has failed.

15. Air tests are used to check operation of the _____, _____, and/or _____.

16. When doing an air pressure test on an automatic transmission, air pressure used for testing should be set to _____ PSI.

17. To locate those hard-to-find leaks, a _____ light and a special _____ can be used.

18. The acronym NVH is the trade term for _____, _____, and _____.

19. The three most common sources of noise in most automatic transmissions are _____, _____, and the _____ system.

20. A driveline clunk during garage shifts is most likely the _____ _____ bushing or the _____ joint.

CHAPTER QUIZ

1. Technician A says that you should begin by checking the fluid when you are diagnosing a transmission problem. Technician B says to use a pressure gauge to start diagnosing a transmission problem. Who is correct?
   a. Technician A
   b. Technician B
   c. Both Technicians A and B
   d. Neither Technician A nor B

2. Technician A says that when diagnosing an automatic transmission you should do only the diagnostic checks that are necessary to locate the problem. Technician B says that you need to do all of the diagnostic tests to fully evaluate the transmission before starting any repairs. Who is correct?
   a. Technician A
   b. Technician B
   c. Both Technicians A and B
   d. Neither Technician A nor B

3. Technician A says that you should verify the customer concern before making any check of the vehicle. Technician B says that you should check the fluid level and condition before going on a road test. Who is correct?
   a. Technician A
   b. Technician B
   c. Both Technicians A and B
   d. Neither Technician A nor B

4. Technician A says that ATF in a modulator vacuum hose is a sign of a bad modulator. Technician B says that the engine should run differently if you pull the vacuum hose off the modulator. Who is correct?
   a. Technician A
   b. Technician B
   c. Both Technicians A and B
   d. Neither Technician A nor B

5. When making a road test, particular attention should be paid to _____.
   a. The quality of the garage shifts
   b. The timing of the upshifts and downshifts
   c. Any unusual noises that might occur
   d. All of these

6. Technician A says that a minimum-throttle 1–2 upshift should be smooth and soft and occur at about 20 mph. Technician B says that a harsh light-throttle upshift could be caused by a sticky modulator. Who is correct?
   a. Technician A
   b. Technician B
   c. Both Technicians A and B
   d. Neither Technician A nor B

7. Technician A says that both a tachometer and an oil pressure gauge are necessary to diagnose torque converter clutch problems. Technician B says that a tap of the brake pedal causes the converter clutch to release. Who is correct?
   a. Technician A
   b. Technician B
   c. Both Technicians A and B
   d. Neither Technician A nor B

8. If a transmission has a single pressure test port, it will be for _____.
   a. Governor pressure
   b. Modulator pressure
   c. Line pressure
   d. None of these

9. Technician A says that low fluid pressure in all forward ranges could be caused by a faulty pump or plugged filter. Technician B says that fluid pressures should increase when the gear selector is moved to reverse. Who is correct?
   a. Technician A
   b. Technician B
   c. Both Technicians A and B
   d. Neither Technician A nor B

10. When making a stall test, you should _____.
    a. Connect a tachometer to the engine
    b. Completely apply the parking and service brakes
    c. Make sure there is no one in front of or behind the vehicle
    d. Do all of these

11. During a stall test, the stall speed is high in drive-1 but normal in manual-1 and reverse. Technician A says that this indicates a faulty forward clutch. Technician B says that it could be caused by a bad one-way clutch. Who is correct?
    a. Technician A
    b. Technician B
    c. Both Technicians A and B
    d. Neither Technician A nor B

12. A Simpson gear train transmission has a slipping second gear but the fluid pressures are normal. Technician A says that this problem could be caused by a loose intermediate-band adjustment. Technician B says that it is a leaking intermediate servo. Who is correct?
    a. Technician A
    b. Technician B
    c. Both Technicians A and B
    d. Neither Technician A nor B

13. A transmission has no high gear or reverse, but all other gears are normal. Technician A says you could confirm the problem by dropping the pan and valve body to air check the high-reverse clutch. Technician B says that you could make a complete oil pressure check before removing the pan to confirm the problem is in the high/reverse clutch circuit. Who is correct?
    a. Technician A
    b. Technician B
    c. Both Technicians A and B
    d. Neither Technician A nor B

14. When checking the pan contents, _____.
    a. A small amount of metal particles is considered normal
    b. A golden-brown coating is a sign of a needed fluid change
    c. Metal or melted plastic debris indicates a need for a transmission overhaul
    d. All of these

15. Technician A says that you should be able to hear a clutch apply and release when you apply air pressure to test it. Technician B says that an excessive air leak is an indication of bad seals. Who is correct?
    a. Technician A
    b. Technician B
    c. Both Technicians A and B
    d. Neither Technician A nor B

16. Technician A says that you can use foot powder to trace the location of a transmission leak. Technician B says that the actual location of a leak is usually slightly forward of where the fluid is found. Who is correct?
    a. Technician A
    b. Technician B
    c. Both Technicians A and B
    d. Neither Technician A nor B

17. Which of the following is a handy tool for locating transmission leaks?
    a. Foot powder
    b. Blacklight and dye
    c. Air test
    d. All of the above

18. A vehicle vibrates rather violently just before a full-throttle 1–2 or 2–3 shift. Technician A says that this can be caused by a faulty extension housing bushing or universal joint. Technician B says that this can be caused by an engine problem or unbalanced torque converter. Who is correct?
    a. Technician A
    b. Technician B
    c. Both Technicians A and B
    d. Neither Technician A nor B

19. When diagnosing transmission noise problems, it is important to note _____.
    a. When the noise occurs
    b. The frequency or pitch of the noise
    c. If the noise changes with the load on the car
    d. All of these

20. Technician A says that troubleshooting noise-related problems can be done on a road test. Technician B says that noise and vibration problems are not normally a concern of the automatic transmission technician. Who is correct?
    a. Technician A
    b. Technician B
    c. Both Technicians A and B
    d. Neither Technician A nor B

chapter 13

ELECTRONIC TRANSMISSION PROBLEM SOLVING AND DIAGNOSIS

OBJECTIVES: **After studying Chapter 13, the reader will be able to:** • Describe the problems that can occur in electrical circuits. • Test electrical circuits. • Explain what a diagnostic trouble code (DTC) is and how it can be used by the service technician. • Retrieve DTCs. • Perform the ASE tasks related to electronic problem diagnosis and repair.

KEY TERMS: Adaptive function relearn 340 • Analog meter 322 • Clutch volume index (CVI) 344 • Continuity 322 • Diagnostic trouble code (DTC) 332 • Digital meter 322 • Digital multimeter (DMM) 322 • Electromagnetic induction (EMI) 344 • Electronic control module (ECM) 319 • Electrostatic discharge (ESD) 340 • Excessive resistance 320 • Grounded circuit 321 • Hard codes 341 • High resistance 320 • OBD-II 332 • Open circuit 320 • Oscilloscope 333 • Out of limits (OL) 327 • Powertrain control module (PCM) 319 • Radio frequency interference (RFI) 344 • Recalibration 339 • Short circuit 321 • Shrink tube 336 • Signal monitor 343 • Soft codes 341 • Splice 336 • Test light 322 • Transmission control module (TCM) 319 • Voltage drop 320

13.1 ELECTRONIC TRANSMISSION DIAGNOSIS

Electronic shift controls require the transmission technician to learn additional diagnostic and test procedures. When diagnosing an electronic transmission, it must be determined if the cause is faulty electronic controls, a hydraulic system problem, or a mechanical system malfunction. ● **SEE FIGURE 13–1.** Electrical/electronic problems can usually be repaired with the transmission in the vehicle. Mechanical or hydraulic problems usually require transmission removal.

Shift timing and quality are computer controlled in electronic transmissions. The **transmission control module (TCM),** also called an **electronic control module (ECM),** can be an independent control module or a part of another control module such as the **powertrain control module (PCM).** A PCM controls both engine and transmission functions. The transmission control module will be referred to as the TCM for uniformity.

Electrical/electronic service requires an understanding of basic electricity as well as the use of electrical testers and meters.

Transmissions with integrated TCMs (control solenoid valve assembly, Mechatronic, and solenoid body) require scan tool diagnostics because you do not have access to the TCM connections to the various transmission sensors and solenoids.

1. Will the vehicle move forward and backward? → NO → Severe Hydraulic or Mechanical Fault
   ↓ YES
2. Is the vehicle operating in Fail-Safe Mode? → YES → NO
   ↓
3. Is a MIL illuminated or flashing? → YES → NO
   ↓
4. Are there any DTCs? → NO → Check control module and transmission power and ground circuits
   ↓ YES
5. Are they electrical DTCs? → NO → Check hydraulic and mechanical systems
   ↓ YES
6. Repair electrical fault, clear DTCs, and road test vehicle to insure that the fault does not return.

FIGURE 13–1 A diagnostic procedure for an electronically controlled transmission.

The 1992 GMC C3500 pickup (95,000 miles) had a torque converter clutch that was cycling on and off. At 65 mph, the TCC would cycle rapidly. A scan tool check revealed no DTCs, with all scan data normal. The TCM was replaced, but this did not help.

FIX

Following advice, the technician checked the engine distributor and found a bad shaft bushing. This worn bushing caused a variable ignition signal that the TCM interpreted as changing engine load. A new distributor bushing fixed this problem. Vehicles that incorporate electronics may have problems that seem to be unrelated, but they can cause transmission problems.

The 2001 Chevrolet Silverado 2500 HD pickup (55,000 miles) does not shift correctly. A scan tool check shows these DTCs: P0708, transmission range sensor circuit; and P0722, output speed sensor circuit. The shift problems began after the customer removed, recharged, and reinstalled the battery. Following diagnostic procedure, the technician was led to a bad TCM, but replacement of the TCM did not fix the problem.

FIX

Following advice, the technician replaced the black neutral safety switch with a revised, brown switch. After clearing the codes and a test drive, a code check showed that the new switch fixed this problem.

13.2 ELECTRICAL CIRCUIT PROBLEMS

There are three common types of electrical problems: opens, high resistance, and low resistance (short or ground). These problems can occur either continuously or intermittently. Intermittent problems are usually much harder to locate, and are often the result of the vehicle's movement, vibration, or changes in temperature. With the proper equipment and knowledge, most electrical components can be easily diagnosed.

13.2.1 OPEN CIRCUITS An unwanted **open circuit** is an incomplete, broken circuit in which no current can flow.

The 1990 BMW 520i (197,000 km) came in with only second gear, limp-in mode. The customer said the car would operate normally one day and have only second gear the next day. The fluid level is correct and appears in good condition.

FIX

A dealership checked for fault codes and found two: gear position switch and speed sensor. Testing revealed faults in the gear position switch and speed sensor circuits (called Starbucks syndrome). Replacement of these two components fixed the problem. *Starbucks syndrome* is a name given to the results of coffee and food spills onto the center console control switches. Corrosion caused by the spills increases resistance at the wire connections.

The high-voltage circuits in hybrid vehicles must be treated with respect and caution, including every bright orange wire and the HV battery pack. Review Section 1.6.8 before testing or working on the HV electrical components.

A switch is an example of a wanted open circuit. When the switch is closed, current flows and the circuit operates. When the switch is open, no current will flow and the circuit is off. An unwanted open is usually caused by a broken wire, damaged connecter, broken light bulb filament, or a blown fuse or fusible link (caused by an overloaded circuit). An open circuit can occur at any point between the B+ and the ground connections. ● **SEE FIGURE 13–2.** Source voltage will be present up to the point of the open.

13.2.2 HIGH-RESISTANCE CIRCUITS Circuit resistance controls the amount of current flow. An increase in resistance will reduce current flow. **Excessive resistance** is often caused by corroded, loose, or dirty connections. Remember that voltage forces current through the resistance. Ideally, the only resistance in a circuit is the load, which is the electrical component to be operated. Unwanted **high resistance** uses some of the available voltage to force current through the extra resistance. The result is less voltage to move the current through the intended load(s). Unwanted resistance causes an unwanted **voltage drop,** also called a *wasted voltage drop.* Excess circuit resistance can be identified by measuring the voltage drop at various connectors, wires, and components. A high-resistance circuit can be compared with a cooler fluid line that is kinked and restricting the fluid flow.

(a)

(b)

FIGURE 13–2 (a) An open circuit is a break in the circuit that will stop the current flow. (b) Corroded or loose connections will cause high resistance that will reduce the current flow. (*Courtesy of Chrysler Corporation*)

(a)

(b)

FIGURE 13–3 A short circuit is a wire-to-wire connection that can reduce magnetic coil strength or allow current to flow to (a) the wrong circuit or (b) a short-to-ground. (*Figure (b) Courtesy of Chrysler Corporation*)

🚗 REAL WORLD FIX

A 1996 S-10 pickup drops out of fourth gear. It makes a 4–3 shift on its own. There are no diagnostic trouble codes (DTCs).

FIX

On the road test, the technician found intermittent loss of power to the transmission fuse caused by a failing ignition switch. Replacement of the ignition switch fixed the transmission problem.

🚗 REAL WORLD FIX

The 1991 Taurus had a very hard 1–2 shift. The transmission had 2,400 miles on a rebuild and was working properly except for the 1–2 shift.

FIX

A resistance check showed the turbine shaft speed sensor to have a resistance of 0.3 Ω with a specification of 108–146 Ω. This test revealed shorted windings in the sensor coil. Replacement of this faulty sensor repaired this transmission.

13.2.3 SHORTED CIRCUITS A **short circuit** means that the current is taking a shorter path than normal and has by-passed part of the intended circuit. Shorts occur when the insulation breaks down and two bare wires touch or a bare wire touches chassis ground. This gives the current an alternate path back to its source. As a result, the amount of current flow will increase relative to the decrease in circuit resistance.

A short can occur in a coil winding and bypass some of the coils. The effect of the short is a lower coil resistance because of the shortened path, allowing an increase in current flow. The strength of the magnetic field will also be reduced due to the fewer turns in the coil.

A short can also occur between the wires of two separate circuits if their insulation is damaged. A short will allow an unwanted current flow between the circuits. ● **SEE FIGURE 13–3.**

13.2.4 GROUNDED CIRCUITS A **grounded circuit** is a short where a bare wire touches ground. This is commonly called a *short to ground*. The grounded circuit completes a path directly back to battery ground (B–), bypassing the rest of the circuit. Most of the current will follow the path of least resistance. A grounded circuit can have zero resistance, and the current flow will instantly increase to the limit of the fuse, wire, or battery. This usually causes a very rapid burnout, and the resulting smoke and burned wires are often easy to locate. ● **SEE FIGURE 13–4.**

(a)

Short To Ground

Internally Shorted Part
(Often Shows No Sign Of Failure)

(b)

FIGURE 13–4 (a) A ground or short-to-ground circuit occurs when damage to the insulation allows an electrical path to the metal of the vehicle. (b) It can occur at a wire or inside a component. (*Courtesy of Chrysler Corporation*)

(a)

(b)

FIGURE 13–5 (a) A fused jumper wire can be used to bypass portions of a circuit to determine where the problem is located. (b) If the lights come on with the jumper wire installed, the problem is the fuse, switch, or wires to the battery.

13.3 MEASURING ELECTRICAL COMPONENTS

In the past, technicians used a *test light, jumper wire,* and *analog volt-ohmmeter* or *multimeter* (a combination ammeter, ohmmeter, and voltmeter) for troubleshooting automotive electrical problems. Today, the weathertight connectors make the use of a jumper wire very difficult. ● **SEE FIGURE 13–5**. A jumper wire should only be used to check switches and unloaded parts of the circuit. Never use a jumper wire to bypass a load. A **test light** and analog meter should not be used on solid-state circuits because they can cause too much current through the ECM. This current overload can cause erroneous meter readings and possible sensor or ECM damage. The meter must have an internal resistance of 10 megohms (10 million ohms) or greater. LED test

lights and most **digital multimeters (DMMs)** can be safely used on any automotive electrical or electronic circuit.

Test lights are simple, inexpensive, durable, and easy to use. They have one wire that is normally connected to ground, and when the probe contacts B+, the test light lights up. ● **SEE FIGURE 13–6**. Some test lights are self-powered and use an internal battery. Self-powered lights can be used to check **continuity** (a continuous, complete circuit) through a component such as a relay. Most test lights indicate either a pass or fail; they cannot make measurements, so they will not tell us the condition of a circuit or component.

Meters make accurate measurements. There are two types: the **analog meter** (a needle sweeps across a scale) and the **digital meter** (where the actual value is displayed in a series of digits). Analog meters should not be used on electronic circuits because they can cause the circuit to draw too much current, resulting in a damaged circuit. The DMM is more accurate, easier to read, and can be used on all computer circuits. On circuits with changing values, however, the sweep of an analog needle is much faster and

(a)

(a)

(b)

(b)

(c)

FIGURE 13–6 (a) A self-powered test light includes a battery and can be used to check for continuity. (b) A nonpowered test light can be used to determine if (c) a point in a circuit has voltage.

(c)

FIGURE 13–7 (a) Analog and (b) digital multimeters. Do not use analog meters when testing electronic circuits unless instructed to do so. (c) Bar graph and digital display (arrow).

easier to follow than the rapidly changing display of digits. ● **SEE FIGURE 13–7.** For that reason, some digital multimeters include a *bar graph* for a continuous response to value changes. A service manual may direct you to use an analog meter for some tests.

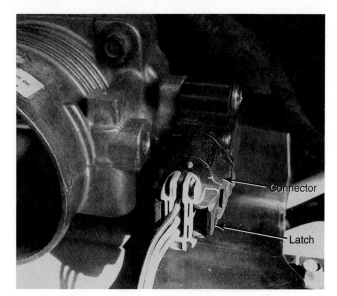

FIGURE 13–8 Many electrical components, including this TPS, use weathertight connectors with latches to keep contacts clean and tight.

TECH TIP

1. Fingernail polish or battery sealant spray can be safely used to seal wire insulation; the coating prevents corrosion and resistance problems caused by water leaking into the connector or component.

2. The common test probes are larger than the small female wire connectors. Forcing the probe into the connector will make it too large to make a good connection with the male wire connector. You can test some female wire connectors using a No. 60, 0.040-in. drill bit; there should be a snug fit between the drill bit and connector. The drill bit chosen should be slightly smaller than the connector pin.

3. When probing female wire connections, T-pins can be used to prevent distorting the connectors. T-pins can be purchased at a sewing or hobby store.

Multimeters have a selector switch that must be set to the desired function before connecting the meter to a circuit. Some meters also have a range switch that is set to the range where the readings are expected to fall. The range selector should always be set above the highest reading expected and then reset downward until readings occur. Many DMMs are *self-ranging* or *auto-ranging*. The technician should always check the range indicator on the display.

Weathertight connectors present a difficult problem when probing for electrical values. ● **SEE FIGURE 13–8**. You can disconnect a connector and probe the ends, but without normal circuit load this can be an inaccurate reading. It is also possible to damage the connector pins. Thin probes are available that allow backprobing a connection by sliding the probe into a connector, through the weathertight seals. Probes that pierce the wire's insulation are also used. Caution should be taken to not damage wire insulation. Some manufacturers suggest that the hole left by the piercing pin should be filled with a sealant when testing is complete.

13.3.1 MEASURING VOLTAGE
A voltmeter is used to measure circuit voltage and voltage drop. Voltage is measured by connecting the negative (–) lead to ground and probing various points along the circuit with the positive (+) lead. ● **SEE FIGURE 13–9**. The meter will display the actual voltage at that point in the circuit. Depending on the circuit and its components, this reading should be B+ (around 12.6 V) or some lesser value. A zero (0) reading indicates an open circuit between the probe and B+. A reading less than B+ indicates a voltage drop and possible problem. If there is full battery voltage to the component and full battery voltage drops across the component, the component is either using all the electrical power or has an open circuit.

REAL WORLD FIX

The 1986 BMW 535i (86,000 miles) came in with a complaint of fourth-gear dropout. This occurs when it is hot with the A/C on. Normal operation returns after the car is shut off for a while.

FIX

The technician checked the A/C evaporator drain and found that it was dripping water onto the transmission hardness connector. Sealing/waterproofing this electrical connector fixed this problem.

REAL WORLD FIX

The 2002 Mazda Tribute AWD (9,000 miles) came in with the AWD MIL intermittently illuminated. Electrical pin checks were made with no problems found. The oil temperature switch and TCM were replaced, but this did not help.

FIX

Following advice, the technician performed the wiggle test, by wiggling the wires while making voltage checks. A faulty terminal crimp was found at one of the connectors into the TCM. Repairing this terminal crimp fixed this problem.

(a)

(b)

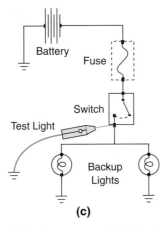

(c)

FIGURE 13–6 (a) A self-powered test light includes a battery and can be used to check for continuity. (b) A nonpowered test light can be used to determine if (c) a point in a circuit has voltage.

(a)

(b)

(c)

FIGURE 13–7 (a) Analog and (b) digital multimeters. Do not use analog meters when testing electronic circuits unless instructed to do so. (c) Bar graph and digital display (arrow).

easier to follow than the rapidly changing display of digits. ● **SEE FIGURE 13–7.** For that reason, some digital multimeters include a *bar graph* for a continuous response to value changes. A service manual may direct you to use an analog meter for some tests.

FIGURE 13–8 Many electrical components, including this TPS, use weathertight connectors with latches to keep contacts clean and tight.

Multimeters have a selector switch that must be set to the desired function before connecting the meter to a circuit. Some meters also have a range switch that is set to the range where the readings are expected to fall. The range selector should always be set above the highest reading expected and then reset downward until readings occur. Many DMMs are *self-ranging* or *auto-ranging.* The technician should always check the range indicator on the display.

Weathertight connectors present a difficult problem when probing for electrical values. ● **SEE FIGURE 13–8.** You can disconnect a connector and probe the ends, but without normal circuit load this can be an inaccurate reading. It is also possible to damage the connector pins. Thin probes are available that allow backprobing a connection by sliding the probe into a connector, through the weathertight seals. Probes that pierce the wire's insulation are also used. Caution should be taken to not damage wire insulation. Some manufacturers suggest that the hole left by the piercing pin should be filled with a sealant when testing is complete.

13.3.1 MEASURING VOLTAGE
A voltmeter is used to measure circuit voltage and voltage drop. Voltage is measured by connecting the negative (–) lead to ground and probing various points along the circuit with the positive (+) lead. ● **SEE FIGURE 13–9.** The meter will display the actual voltage at that point in the circuit. Depending on the circuit and its components, this reading should be B+ (around 12.6 V) or some lesser value. A zero (0) reading indicates an open circuit between the probe and B+. A reading less than B+ indicates a voltage drop and possible problem. If there is full battery voltage to the component and full battery voltage drops across the component, the component is either using all the electrical power or has an open circuit.

REAL WORLD FIX

The 1986 BMW 535i (86,000 miles) came in with a complaint of fourth-gear dropout. This occurs when it is hot with the A/C on. Normal operation returns after the car is shut off for a while.

FIX

The technician checked the A/C evaporator drain and found that it was dripping water onto the transmission hardness connector. Sealing/waterproofing this electrical connector fixed this problem.

REAL WORLD FIX

The 2002 Mazda Tribute AWD (9,000 miles) came in with the AWD MIL intermittently illuminated. Electrical pin checks were made with no problems found. The oil temperature switch and TCM were replaced, but this did not help.

FIX

Following advice, the technician performed the wiggle test, by wiggling the wires while making voltage checks. A faulty terminal crimp was found at one of the connectors into the TCM. Repairing this terminal crimp fixed this problem.

FIGURE 13–9 The positive (+) voltmeter lead is connected to the positive (+) solenoid terminal, and the negative (–) lead is connected to ground. With ground-controlled solenoids, the negative (–) lead is connected to the solenoid TCM terminal.

FIGURE 13–10 Voltage is measured by connecting one voltmeter lead (normally the negative) to ground, and probing the wire connections with the other lead. (*Courtesy of Chrysler Corporation*)

Voltage drop can be measured by connecting the negative lead to the ground side of a component and the positive lead to the B+ side. The reading will be the amount of voltage dropped across that component. Remember that voltage drop only occurs while the circuit is on and under load. *The total voltage drop in a series circuit is equal to the sum of each voltage drop, which is equal to the source voltage.* Ideally, all of the voltage drop should occur across the circuit loads, a light bulb, actuator, or output device. A voltage drop equal to source voltage across the load may be okay, or it may indicate that the load is open. ● **SEE FIGURE 13–10.** If there is source voltage available and the component is not working, the component (load) is open.

In a solenoid circuit, there should be B+ voltage at the solenoid's insulated connection, and there will be a voltage drop equal to B+ across the solenoid. A very small drop across a connection or switch is allowed, but this is usually limited to 0.2 or 0.3 V per connection and a circuit total drop of 0.5 V. Any

drop greater than 0.5 V indicates a high-resistance problem that will cause a circuit to function below normal, and should be corrected. ● **SEE FIGURE 13–11.**

To measure voltage, *you should:*

1. Adjust the voltmeter control to DC volts.
2. Connect the negative, black or –, lead of the voltmeter to a good, clean ground.
3. Determine the point where you want to measure, and touch or connect the positive, red or +, lead to the connector.
4. Read the voltage on the meter.

   To measure voltage drop, *you should:*

1. Select DC volts.

Total B+ side voltage drop is measured by:

2. Connect the positive, red or +, lead of the voltmeter to the positive, or +, battery post.
3. Touch or connect the negative, black or –, lead to the B+ side of the component.
4. Read the voltage drop on the meter.

Total ground side voltage drop is measured by:

5. Connect the positive, red or +, lead of the voltmeter to the ground side of the component.
6. Touch or connect the negative, black or –, lead to the negative, –, battery post.
7. Turn the circuit on.
8. Read the voltage drop on the meter.

NOTE:
$$\frac{1}{1000} \ V = 1 \ mV$$
$$1000 \ V = 1 \ kV$$

1
Select volts AC (V∼),
Volts DC (V⎓) or
300 mV⎓ as desired.

2
Plug the black test probe
into the COM input jack.
Plug the red test probe
into the V input jack.

3
Touch the probe tips
to the circuit across a
load or power source
as shown (in parallel
to the circuit). ⚠

4
View the reading,
being sure to
note the unit of
measurement.

FIGURE 13–11 This meter is connected to measure the voltage drop across the resistor. (*Courtesy of Fluke Corporation; reproduced with permission*)

V (Volts) = C × R
C (Current) = V / R
R (Resistance) = V / C

FIGURE 13–12 This modernized version of Ohm's law memory triangle shows the relationship between volts, current (amps), and resistance.

 TECH TIP

Ohm's law includes a formula that shows the relationship of the three important electrical values. A modernized version of Ohm's law memory triangle is shown in ● **FIGURE 13–12**. If you know two of the values, you can easily calculate the third. This becomes handy if one value, resistance, is hard to measure but two other values, volts and current, can be easily measured.

 REAL WORLD FIX

The 1987 Chevrolet Astro (100,000 miles) has a hunting condition with the TCC going in and out of lockup at 60 mph.

FIX

A voltage check of the wire harness found an open circuit caused by a broken wire between the frame and transmission. Repair of this wire fixed the problem. The hunting condition was probably the result of an intermittent connection at the wire break.

Component voltage drop:

9. Connect the positive, red or +, lead of the voltmeter to the B+ side of the component.

10. Touch or connect the negative, black or –, lead to the ground side of the component.

11. Turn the circuit on.

12. Read the voltage drop on the meter.

13.3.2 MEASURING RESISTANCE
An ohmmeter is used to measure the resistance of electrical components. When the two ohmmeter leads are connected to the ends of a wire or connections of a component, the meter will display the resistance value. Ohmmeters are self-powered by an internal battery. *They must never be connected to a circuit that has power,* because the usually higher voltage from the circuit will damage the ohmmeter. Some meters have a protective fuse that will burn out to save the meter if it is connected incorrectly. Always turn the circuit power off or disconnect the power lead when checking a circuit or component using an ohmmeter. Disconnecting the component from the circuit will also keep the meter from reading other parts of the circuit. When checking components with parallel circuits, remember that the meter does not know which path you wish to measure. It will include all possible paths. To be safe, disconnect one end of the component you are measuring from the circuit. Most DMMs are designed not to affect solid-state components when making resistance measurements.

Many DMMs are self-ranging and give a reading of any resistance value within their ability. ● **SEE FIGURE 13–13.** Analog meters require setting the meter to the desired range (1 K or 1,000 Ω; 10 K or 10,000 Ω; 1 M or 1,000,000 Ω) and recalibrating the meter each time the range is changed. An analog ohmmeter is calibrated by connecting the leads and rotating the calibration knob until the meter reads zero.

An ohmmeter is perfect for checking a component like a solenoid coil when it is off the vehicle. Connect the ohmmeter leads to each end of the coil. If the resistance value matches the specifications, the component does not have a short circuit and has continuity. If the coil includes a diode, reverse the two ohmmeter leads and the resistance should change. Moving one of the leads to the component's mounting point checks for a grounded coil; at this time the reading should be infinite ($\infty \, \Omega$) (see Figure 13–42). A DMM displays **OL (out of limits)** to indicate infinite resistance.

An ohmmeter is also ideal for checking a transmission oil temperature (TOT) sensor, also called a transmission fluid temperature (TFT) sensor. It has a resistance that is inversely proportionate to temperature; if the temperature increases, the resistance will decrease. Measure the resistance at the specified temperatures, and if the resistance matches the specifications, it is good. One commonly used TOT sensor should have a resistance of 20 to 40 KΩ at 32°F to 58°F (0°C to 20°C), 16 to 37 KΩ at 59°F to 104°F (21°C to 40°C), and 5 to 16 KΩ at 105°F to 158°F (41°C to 70°C).

To measure resistance, *you should:*

1. Disconnect at least one lead of the component, and make sure that all electrical power to the component is shut off.

2. Adjust the ohmmeter or DMM to ohms (Ω).

3. Connect the positive, red or +, lead to one side of the component.

4. Touch or connect the negative, black or –, lead to the other side of the component.

5. Read the amount of resistance on the meter.

To check a diode:

6. Measure the resistance of the diode using steps 3 and 4.

7. Reverse the two connections in steps 3 and 4.

8. Read the amount of resistance on the meter. A change in resistance indicates the diode has more resistance in one direction.

13.3.3 MEASURING AMPERAGE
An ammeter measures amperage (current flow). The circuit is opened and the ammeter is connected in series with the circuit. ● **SEE FIGURE 13–14.** Some ammeters use a transformer-type, inductive pickup that is simply placed over or around the wire. ● **SEE FIGURE 13–15.** Most technicians prefer the inductive pickup because it is much easier to connect, and it does not

NOTE:
1,000Ω = 1 kΩ
1,000,000Ω = 1 MΩ

1. Turn off power to the circuit. ⚠

2. Select resistance (Ω).

3. Plug the black test probe into the COM input jack. Plug the red test probe into the Ω input jack.

4. Connect the probe tips across the component or portion of the circuit for which you want to determine resistance.

5. View the reading being sure to note the unit of measurement – ohms (Ω), kilohms (kΩ), or megohms (MΩ).

⚠ Make sure power is off before making resistance measurements.

FIGURE 13–13 A digital multimeter being used to measure resistance. Be sure to turn off or disconnect the electrical power to the circuit when using ohmmeter functions. (*Courtesy of Fluke Corporation; reproduced with permission*)

 TECH TIP

It is possible for the coil of a relay to have a weak internal connection and test showing continuity and correct resistance with an ohmmeter. Ohmmeters measure resistance while the component is disconnected. Circuit load generates heat that in turn increases the resistance. An internal weak connection (resistance) will cause reduced current flow. Many technicians prefer to check circuit resistance using an ammeter. If a circuit has the correct current flow with the correct input voltage, it has the proper resistance, and it is good.

 REAL WORLD FIX

The 1994 GMC pickup (126,000 miles) will not shift. A shift could be forced by grounding the solenoid leads at the transmission. There was 12.6 V at the transmission. The solenoids were removed and tested, and would allow flow when activated. The resistance checked out okay.

FIX

The technician was advised to check the current flow through the solenoids. The 2–3 solenoid would draw 2.5 amps and its specification is 0.75 amp. Replacement of the solenoids fixed this shift problem.

---

change the circuit in any way. If the current readings measured in the circuit are less than specifications, excessive resistance is indicated. If the current readings are higher than specifications, a shorted or grounded circuit is indicated.

A current probe is a handy tester that is used with electronic circuits. ● **SEE FIGURE 13–16**. This tool combined with a scope allows the technician to watch the current flow to a solenoid. ● **FIGURE 13–17** shows the current increasing about

FIGURE 13–14 A digital multimeter is being used to measure current flow. (*Courtesy of Fluke Corporation; reproduced with permission*)

 REAL WORLD FIX

The 1995 Bronco came in with a complaint of "stuck in first gear." When driving the vehicle into the shop, the technician noticed the speedometer and odometer were not working, and a scan tool check showed a 452 code: loss of speedo signal. The fuse for this circuit was blown so the technician checked the wiring diagram for all the circuits that were fed by this fuse. This cluster included the 4WD shift lock, electronic shift control module, airbag module, and compass/outside temperature module. A quick check of the interior showed that the rearview mirror that held the compass had fallen off, and while falling had disconnected the compass.

FIX

Gluing the mirror back in place, reconnecting the compass, and replacing the fuse fixed this transmission shift problem.

FIGURE 13–15 Inductive ammeters can be clipped over a wire to measure the current flow without disturbing the wire connections.

 TECH TIP

Measuring the resistance of a shift solenoid with the solenoid mounted inside the transmission pan can be difficult, but measuring voltage and solenoid current flow can be easy. If the voltage measures 13.9 V and there is a 3-amp current draw, use Ohm's law to find the solenoid resistance: 13.9 ÷ 3 = 4.6 Ω.

FIGURE 13–16 The jaws of the amp probe are around the wire, and the probe is connected to the DMM. The circuit is drawing 2.85 amps, which is read on the volts scale of the DMM.

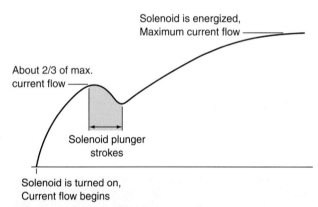

FIGURE 13–17 This graph shows the current flow to a solenoid. The dip near the center shows that the solenoid plunger has actually moved.

TECH TIP

When using an induction ammeter, the readings can be multiplied by forming a loop (if there is enough slack in the wire), and connecting the inductive pickup over the multiple wires. Two wires will double the reading, three wires will triple it, and so on.

six vertical divisions, then dipping a couple of divisions, and then increasing again to the maximum value. The increases are called *ramping*. The dip shows a reduction in the current flow that is caused by the counterelectromotive force that is created when an inductor moves through the solenoids' magnetic lines of force. This is the normal movement of the solenoid plunger.

TECH TIP

1. Current flow is the same at all points through a simple circuit, so current can be measured at a common point of the circuit. A common point and convenient location of measuring current is at the fuse. Remove the transmission fuse and substitute a modified fuse. This is an old, burned-out fuse with a wire attached to each blade of the fuse. ● **SEE FIGURE 13–18**. Connect the ammeter leads to the two fuse connections to read current and operate the transmission using a scan tool. Current flow for each solenoid will be displayed as each solenoid is activated. Use caution if activating low-resistance solenoids such as some PWMs or EPCs with a resistance as low as 2 Ω; these can draw 14 V ÷ 2 Ω = 7 amps.

2. A convenient tool for measuring current is a fuse buddy (see Figure 13–18). It can be inserted into a fuse holder in place of a fuse and the amperage can be read as the vehicle is operated.

The maximum value is the total current flow through the solenoid, and the dip should occur at about two-thirds to three-fourths maximum value. The current probe uses an inductive pickup so it can be clipped over the wire feeding the solenoid. When troubleshooting a problem like a shift failure, the technician can easily connect the current probe, perform a road test, and watch for a solenoid operation. This will help the technician to quickly determine whether the problem is electrical or of a hydraulic or mechanical nature.

To measure amperage/current flow using an inductive pickup, *you should:*

1. Connect the inductive pickup to the DMM, and set the meter to DC amps.

2. Open the inductive pickup jaws, and place them completely around the current-carrying wire.

3. Turn the component on and read the amperage on the meter.

To measure amperage/current flow using the meter leads, *you should:*

1. Select DC amps on the meter control.

2. Disconnect one connector for the circuit being tested at a convenient location.

3. Connect the positive, red or +, lead to the wire or connector that is the most positive or closest to B+.

4. Connect the negative, black or –, lead to the other side (most negative) of the open connection. The ammeter leads should now be in series with the circuit being tested.

5. Turn the component on and read the amperage on the meter.

(a)

(b)

(c)

FIGURE 13–18 (a) A blown fuse has been modified by soldering a short wire to each test point. (b) Replacing a circuit fuse with a modified fuse provides an easy location to check the circuit's current flow. (c) This handy ammeter, called a fuse buddy, can be easily inserted into the fuse box. Note the system fuse has been inserted into the tool to protect the circuit.

13.3.4 MEASURING DUTY CYCLE
Many electronic pressure control (EPC) and torque converter clutch (TCC) solenoids are pulse-width modulated (PWM) and operate with a variable duty cycle. The duty cycle rate at which they operate is used to control transmission line pressure and/or TCC apply pressure. Most digital meters have a duty cycle function and can display both positive (+) and negative (–) pulse readings. Voltage/feed-controlled solenoids use a + pulse, whereas ground-controlled solenoids use a – pulse. If the duty cycle is measured along with

FIGURE 13–19 Measuring solenoid duty cycle is similar to a solenoid voltage check. Note that feed-controlled circuits should be read at + duty cycle while ground-controlled circuits use a – duty cycle.

line pressure, a shift into reverse will produce a change in both duty cycle and line pressure.

The meter reads an upward electrical pulse as a positive pulse. A negative pulse is downward. If the meter is set for the wrong polarity, it will provide an inverse reading. An 80% duty cycle will be displayed instead of an actual 20% signal.

To measure the duty cycle, *you should:*

1. Select the duty cycle function on the meter.
2. Note the meter display to determine if a + or – is displayed, and select the proper polarity to match the solenoid control. ● **SEE FIGURE 13–19**.
3. Connect the negative (–) meter lead to a good ground.
4. Connect the positive (+) meter lead to the solenoid wire.
5. Operate the transmission and read the duty cycle on the meter.

FIGURE 13–20 Two generic scan tools designed to work with most vehicles. (a) The Mastertech uses adapters to connect to the diagnostic connector and an application cartridge to provide data for a particular vehicle. (b) The Genisys scan tool has software cartridges for many vehicles. Note that the screen of (b) shows the engine, transmission input, and transmission output RPM; and (c) shows transmission operating data. *(Figure (a) Courtesy of Vetronix; (b) and (c) Courtesy of OTC)*

13.3.5 SCAN TOOLS

Special tools to scan data from the vehicle computers have been developed by most vehicle manufacturers. Generic scanners are available from aftermarket sources that work on more than one make of vehicle if they have the proper data cartridge. ● **SEE FIGURE 13–20.** These units can be used only on specific circuits for which they have been designed or for which special adapters are available. Scan tools are fairly expensive but can save considerable time when trying to locate a computer circuit electrical fault.

Scan tools are connected to the vehicle's data link connector (DLC). ● **SEE FIGURE 13–21.** They are bidirectional testers that can display the **diagnostic trouble codes (DTCs)**, solenoid off and on signals from the transmission control module (TCM), or scan the various input signals to the TCM. They also allow the technician to request information from the TCM or command the TCM to perform different operations. Scan tools allow the technician to do the following:

- Read DTCs
- Read data from the input devices
- Read TCM signals to the output devices
- Operate the output devices
- Record a snapshot of a problem occurrence showing both the input and output signals
- Clear DTCs
- Recalibrate a TCM

The **OBD-II** DTCs are five-character codes. ● **SEE FIGURE 13–22.** Transmission codes begin with the letter *P*, indicating a powertrain code, followed by four numbers. If the first number is zero, the code was created by SAE; if it is 1,

(a)

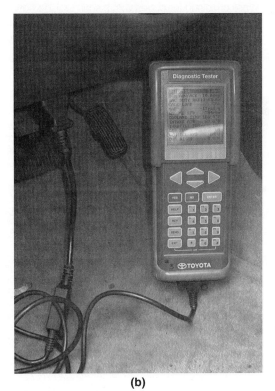

(b)

FIGURE 13–21 (a) This DLC (diagnostic link connector) is under the instrument panel. (b) Connecting a scan tool to the DLC allows it to display and operate vehicle functions.

Example: P0781: 1-2 Shift Malfunction

P0781

Fault (00-99)

B-Body
C-Chassis
P-Powertrain
U-Network

1-Fuel & Air Metering
2-Fuel & Air Metering
3-Ignition System or Misfire
4-Auxiliary Emission Controls
5-Vehicle Speed & Idle Control
6-Computer Output Control
7-Transmission
8-Transmission

0-SAE (Generic)
1-Manufacturer (Specific)

FIGURE 13–22 The first letter of an OBD-II code identifies the function of the fault code area; transmission faults will begin with *P*. The first digit indicates if the DTC is generic or manufacturer specific. The second digit indicates the powertrain system; a 7 or 8 would indicate a transmission fault. The last two digits indicate the fault.

- Gear ratio: calculated value from ISS and OSS speed
- Commanded gear: displays which gear is being commanded by the TCM
- Driver shift request: if a manual gear is selected, it will display the requested gear
- Shift solenoid status: displays whether the circuit has the proper voltage and if that voltage changes properly when solenoid operation is commanded
- Shift time: actual time from TCM shift command to completed gear ratio change
- Pressure switch(es) (TFP): indicates position, high or low, of each pressure switch
- Torque converter solenoid status: displays whether the circuit has the proper voltage and if that voltage changes properly when solenoid operation is commanded
- Throttle position sensor (TPS): displays whether the circuit has the proper voltage and if that voltage changes properly when the throttle is operated
- Engine coolant temperature (ECT): displays the temperature determined by that sensor
- Engine speed: displays engine RPM

Scan tools can only display electrical/electronic signals and can only indicate if a problem occurs in a particular circuit such as a solenoid or speed sensor. Further checks of the affected circuit are required to locate the exact cause of the problem.

13.3.6 OSCILLOSCOPES An **oscilloscope,** or scope, displays a voltage signal over a period of time. This allows the technician to observe the voltage change as an electrical device operates. A scope displays voltage on the vertical scale and time on the horizontal scale. ● **SEE FIGURE 13–23.** Scopes are expensive and more difficult to use than multimeters. They are normally used to find the cause of difficult-to-locate problems that cannot be found using the other types of

the code was created by the vehicle manufacturer. The second number tells what system the problem is in; numbers 7 and 8 indicate the transmission. The last two digits indicate the nature of the problem. The OBD-II DTCs for transmissions are given in Appendix D.

Depending on the ability of the scan tool, the data can include the following information.

- Transmission range switch (TRS)/internal mode switch (IMS) values: measured voltage of each pin from each gear range
- Transmission fluid temperature (TFT) sensor: measured temperature
- Speed sensor (ISS and OSS): measured values from the input and output speed sensors

(a)

781	Hz	FREQUENCY	VIEW
5.12	v	PEAK-PEAK	
56.7	%	DUTY CYCLE v	
640	μα	PULSE WIDTH v	

GENERAL SENSORS

2ms/DIV

BACK ← SEARCH → PRINT

(b)

FIGURE 13–23 (a) The scope is displaying a secondary ignition pattern in which most spark plugs are firing at about 10 kV; one is at 25 kV. (b) A digital-style speed sensor pattern; note the gap indicating a possible problem in the center of the pattern. (*Courtesy of Fluke Corporation; reproduced with permission*)

meters. Some scopes can display more than one electrical signal, and these are called *dual-trace* or *multiple-channel scopes.* Oscilloscopes, like multimeters, can be either analog or digital. Analog scopes allow real-time viewing of the electrical circuit. Digital scopes have the advantage of being able to store the patterns for later viewing.

A scope is ideal for observing electrical events and operations of circuits with changing values, such as the output of a speed sensor or the input to a pulse-modulated solenoid.

TECH TIP

1. Scan tools are limited by the software they contain or in their available software cartridges. Always use the newest available software. Some shops use more than one scan tool because of the limitations of various units.
2. When trying to locate the cause of intermittent problems, an important feature available in some scan tools is the ability to store the electronic events that occur during short time periods. This allows the technician to review these events at a more convenient time.
3. While checking for codes with a scan tool, do not cycle the key off (starting the engine will become a key cycle). Cycling the key may cause the codes to be lost.

TECH TIP

1. Operating voltage at a transmission should be the same as battery voltage (within 0.2 V). If it is lower, check for a voltage drop: Connect the + voltmeter lead to the + battery post and the − lead to the B+ connector at the transmission. The reading should be 0.2 V or less. Next, connect the − voltmeter to the − battery post and the + lead to the ground connection at the transmission. Again, the reading should be 0.2 V or less. Excessive voltage drop indicates a problem in that part of the circuit.
2. A known-good similar component can be measured to find the electrical value.
3. A rule of thumb for a shift solenoid coil is about 20 to 40 Ω of resistance and a current flow of about 0.5 amp. Solenoid resistance values can vary, so the manufacturer's specifications should be used.
4. The green or white corrosion that is found on wire connectors can be cleaned using effervescent denture cleaner and hot water.

13.3.7 INTERPRETING MEASUREMENTS The technician must be familiar with the circuit and its components so he or she knows what to expect while measuring electrical values. Wiring diagrams can be used to follow the current flow through a circuit, much like a road map shows us how to get from one point to another. At one time electrical circuits were quite simple and easy to follow. Powertrain controls have improved greatly, and customers demand more convenience, so today's vehicles have much more complicated circuits. A technician must study the electrical diagram and any additional information that is available on that particular circuit to understand how the circuit operates before trying to diagnose a problem. ● **SEE FIGURE 13–24.**

FIGURE 13-24 This transmission wire diagram shows the wire colors and terminal numbers and how the wires are connected.

FIGURE 13–25 The No. 2 VSS and park–neutral position switch on this transaxle can be replaced rather easily.

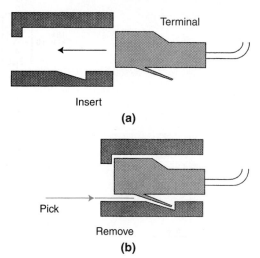

FIGURE 13–26 (a) A terminal is usually pushed into a connector until it locks into place. (b) A pick tool is used to unlock the terminal for removal.

Exact specifications are often not available for automotive circuits. Sometimes the resistance value or current draw for a solenoid coil is given, but not always. When testing with a meter, the technician needs a good understanding of the circuit and what to expect from the meter readings. In most circuits, B+ voltage is available to the switch of an output device (load) except for an allowance for slight voltage drop at the connectors.

13.4 ELECTRICAL/ ELECTRONIC SYSTEM REPAIR

A faulty electrical component such as a switch, relay, blower motor, or clutch is usually repaired by removing and replacing (R&R) it with a new unit. The R&R operation is usually a relatively simple process of disconnecting the wires or connectors, removing the component, installing the new component, and reconnecting the wires and connectors. ● **SEE FIGURE 13–25.**

Occasionally a technician must replace a faulty connector or wire by **splicing** the wire. A few connectors have the wires molded into them, so replacing the connector requires splicing the new connector to each wire. In most cases, however, individual wires can be removed from the connector. These wires have an end terminal that has a locking tang that expands to hold the terminal into the connector. Special terminal disconnecting tools are available. The tool is pushed against the locking tang, and depresses the tang so the terminal can be pulled out of the connector. ● **SEE FIGURE 13–26.**

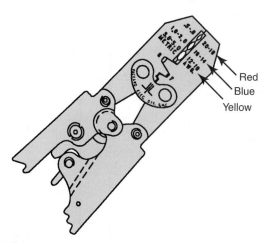

FIGURE 13–27 A wire stripping/crimping tool has an area designed to crimp wire terminals. A cutting area is used to cut insulation and pull it off the wire.

To splice a wire, *you should:*

1. Make sure the new wire is the same gauge size or larger than the original. Strip insulation slightly longer than the splice clip or about 3/8 to 1/2 in. (10 to 13 mm) long. ● **SEE FIGURE 13–27.**

2. Push the two wire ends together so the bare wires overlap inside a splice clip.

3. Use a crimping tool to firmly squeeze the splice clip onto the connection. ● **SEE FIGURE 13–28.** Or, if a splice clip is not being used, twist the connection so the wires are tight. ● **SEE FIGURE 13–29.**

4. Use a soldering gun or iron to heat the wires enough to melt the solder, and apply 60/40 rosin-core solder to the hot wires until the solder flows through the joint. *Do not use acid-core solder.* ● **SEE FIGURE 13–30.**

5. Insulate the splice either by wrapping it with plastic electrical tape or installing a **shrink tube,** a plastic tube that is slid over the splice and heated so it shrinks tightly in place.

FIGURE 13-30 A wire connection is soldered together using rosin-core solder.

FIGURE 13-28 A splice can be made quickly by crimping a wire connector to the two wires.

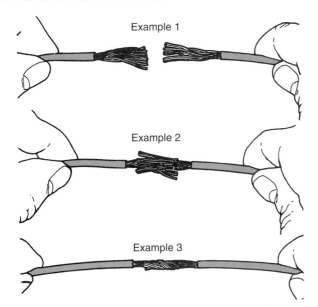

FIGURE 13-29 A wire splice can be made by sliding the bared ends of the wires together, and then twisting them to hold them together. This connection should be soldered for security. (*Courtesy of Chrysler Corporation*)

TECH TIP

The wire stripper can be used as a gauge: The smallest opening that cleanly strips the insulation without nicking or cutting the wire strands is the wire gauge size.

TECH TIP

If using a shrink tube, slide a piece of tube about 1/2 in. longer than the splice over the wire before connecting it in step 2. Slide the tube away from the connection while soldering. After soldering the connection, slide the tube to the proper location. Heat the tube to shrink it, locking it in place.

If using tape, make sure the tape is wrapped tightly, smoothly, and looks neat. ● **SEE FIGURE 13-31.**

TECH TIP

Splicing wires is not recommended by some manufacturers because it might change circuit resistance, or improper insulating might lead to future corrosion problems. The recommended repair is to replace the wire or harness.

REAL WORLD FIX

The Camry transmission was just repaired, but on a road test it shifted 3-2-1-4. This condition can occur if the two shift solenoids have their wire connections reversed. The technician who had previously experienced this problem was sure that he had connected them properly.

FIX

A careful check of the external wire harness showed that the two shift solenoid wires were cut, switched, and spliced back together. Apparently a past technician had crossed the wires and found there was a problem. Rather than dropping the pan and valve body to correctly repair it, the tech swapped the wires for a quick fix.

(a)

(b)

FIGURE 13–31 A repaired wire connection should be insulated by wrapping it tightly with tape or using shrink tubing. The tubing will shrink tightly in place when heated using a hot air gun.

FIGURE 13–32 A signal monitor has three LEDs and wire connections for the transmission harness. On a road test, the LEDs show the electrical signals, and these should occur in the proper order. (*Courtesy of J. S. Popper Inc., www.jspopper.com*)

13.5 ELECTRONIC CONTROL SYSTEM CHECKS

A technician's diagnostic routine will determine if the problem is *inside the transmission* (faulty hydraulic or mechanical operation) or *outside the transmission* (linkage or electrical problems). Systematic diagnosis should locate the problem and/or faulty part(s) that need to be repaired or replaced.

Many technicians begin their diagnosis by making a visual check of the battery and wiring. Green, corroded battery terminals or loose terminals can easily cause improper electrical operation. Modified or altered wire connections also lead to unsuspected problems. This quick inspection gives the technician insight into the vehicle's maintenance and repair history.

The Automatic Transmission Rebuilders Association (ATRA) recommends a three-step procedure for electronic transmission diagnosis.

STEP 1   Check for codes.

STEP 2   Check for signals (electrical signals between the TCM and solenoids).

STEP 3   Force the shifts (mechanically and electrically). A checklist can be followed to record your findings and verify that important checks are not skipped. ● **SEE CHECKLIST IN TASK SHEET 26**.

These steps are easy to follow and are very effective.

The code check identifies an electrical problem recorded in the TCM's memory. You should access and then record the codes. The codes are then cleared, and if they return during the remaining checks, a problem is present. The check for signals is made using a scan tool or simple shop-made signal monitor. ● **SEE FIGURE 13–32**. (Signal monitor use is described in Section 13.5.4.) These tools allow the technician to watch the signals between the TCM and the transmission. The technician can force the shifts mechanically during the road test by shifting into the different gear ranges. The shifts can be forced electrically by providing the proper electrical signal to operate the solenoids. If step 2 or 3 provides proper operation, the problem is in the electronic controls.

A quick way to start isolating the problem area is to road-test the vehicle. The road test gives you the opportunity to verify and experience the problem. Next, remove the fuse that supplies power to the transmission control unit, and conduct a second road test. Without power, the TCM and the electronic controls will shut down, causing the transmission operation to revert to a limp-in mode. In this mode, forward operation in the drive range is limited to a single gear, usually second or fourth. Gear operation is controlled by the manual valve, and there will be no automatic upshifts or downshifts. The transmission's operation will be purely hydraulic and mechanical, so it will start in a higher gear than first, and not upshift. If the second road test has the same problems as the first, you can be sure the problem is not in the electronic controls. It should be noted that a few vehicles will not run if the transmission fuse is removed. Also, some vehicles will turn on the MIL and set a DTC that will need to be cleared after your road test.

FIGURE 13–33 Reprogramming uses a J2534 pass-through device to transfer data/software (downloaded from the Internet) from the laptop PC to the vehicle's TCM.

FIGURE 13–34 This recalibrator device can be connected into the wire connections to the VSS. The internal setting switches can be used to increase or decrease the RPM signal to correct the speedometer readings. (*Courtesy of Autotrans*)

13.5.1 FLASHING/RECALIBRATION

Flashing an ECM, also called *programming, reprogramming,* and *calibrating,* can be done to correct possible software problems. Occasionally there is a concern that a transmission has improper shift points, delayed shifts, or just does not work right, and a thorough diagnosis fails to locate any problems. Many TCMs use an electronically erasable programmable read-only memory (EEPROM) that determines the operating parameters of the TCM. The TCM determines when the transmission upshifts or downshifts, when the TCC applies or releases, and the hydraulic system pressures in some transmissions. This memory function can be changed by connecting a computer interface to the TCM that will erase the old instructions and send new instructions to the vehicle TCM. Flashing will remove adaptive learns. The vehicle dealer will have the equipment needed to perform this operation. Check the service information or TSBs for the need to or possibility for recalibration.

A SAE J2534 compliant module is available that, with a computer (preferably a laptop) and the update program, can reflash all vehicles. ● **SEE FIGURE 13–33.** With some makes of vehicles, this will include all or most of the ECM/PCMs, while other makes limit reflashing to the powertrain modules. A speedometer that is reading incorrectly can be recalibrated in some vehicles.

Recalibration is often necessary when a new TCM is installed. The process must be performed exactly as directed by

TECH TIP

1. Line pressure is software driven, affecting both shift quality and clutch strength. Recalibrating a TCM can change both of these shift characteristics.
2. Some shops obtain used control modules from auto dismantlers to use for diagnosis. This allows them to substitute the TCM and note changes that occur in vehicle operation. If this fixes the problem, they know that the problem should be cured using a new TCM. If using a substitute TCM, be careful that the TCM is the same as that in the vehicle being tested.

TECH TIP

If it becomes necessary to correct electronic speedometer readings when there is no recalibration process built into the vehicle's operating system, an aftermarket device is available. ● **SEE FIGURE 13–34.** It can be spliced into the wiring to the VSS, and the speedometer correction can be programmed through a set of dip switches.

REAL WORLD FIX

The 1995 Chrysler Cirrus (87,000 miles) would go into limp mode intermittently with very erratic scan data (extremely high fluid temperatures and voltages). The control module was replaced with a new OE part. The transmission now worked well, but the speedometer would not work. A second new module was installed with the same results.

FIX

After doing some research, the technician learned that it is necessary to program "pinion factor" into the new module. When this was done, the vehicle worked properly.

REAL WORLD FIX

The battery in the 1999 Mercedes 200E (93,000 km) was replaced. Now the vehicle is locked in limp-in mode. The technician feels the TCM needs to be reset, but does not have the proper tool.

FIX

Following advice, the technician took the vehicle to a Mercedes dealer. Resetting the transmission using the manufacturer's special scan tool fixed this programming problem.

REAL WORLD FIX

The TCC on the 1997 GMC pickup (61,000 km) will not engage. Scan tool data shows TCC duty cycle is 0%, VSS is 95 km/h, brake switch is closed, TPS is 10%, coolant temperature is 90°C, and transmission temperature is 75°C. A comparative test on a similar pickup under the same conditions revealed the same data except the TCC duty cycle was 97% and the TCC was engaged.

FIX

It was found that the PCM was programmed with software for trailer towing. Reprogramming it with the correct software allowed the TCC to apply.

TECH TIP

1. The transmission will readapt shift strategy after repair, and if the shifts are too soft, the change will occur fairly fast. If the shifts are too harsh, however, adaptation is usually very slow going in a softer direction.
2. Many transmissions have a *fast learn* program that uses a scan tool. Fast learn only takes a few minutes as the transmission applies each of the clutches and calculates the clutch volume.

the manufacturer. The TCM can be recalibrated outside of the vehicle in some cases. The TCM in some vehicles has a learn strategy that can compensate for some transmission faults such as low line pressure. These units should be recalibrated after a major repair or overhaul.

ADAPTIVE FUNCTION RELEARN. The TCM of a transmission that uses **adaptive function relearn** will adjust shift control operations to compensate for changes that occur within the transmission as it wears. Worn transmissions tend to have weak, slow shifts because of fluid pressure loss through worn seals. If a worn transmission is repaired, rebuilt, or replaced, the shifts could be harsh until the TCM relearns and readjusts strategy. Repair or replacement of any faulty shift-related component can produce this problem. Unless the technician reprograms or recalibrates the TCM, the customer will notice unacceptable shifts.

TCMs are programmed with default settings; these are the shift values that were used when the vehicle was new. They were changed by the TCM as it learned the new requirements as the transmission wore. Some TCMs can be reset to the original default settings by using a scan tool; others can be reset by disconnecting the TCM from the battery for a short period of time.

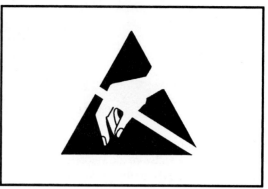

FIGURE 13–35 Extreme care should be used when testing components displaying the electrostatic discharge (ESD) symbol. These components can be damaged by ESD.

TECH TIP

At least one transmission with an integrated TCM will shut down the TCM when the TCM temperature reaches 288°F (142°C). The transmission will go into fail-safe operation until the TCM cools down.

13.5.2 ELECTRONIC CONTROL SYSTEM CAUTIONS

Electrostatic discharge (ESD) is the electrical shock that is felt after sliding across the seat and touching the vehicle's door handle. Sometimes we see small sparks as we take off a shirt made from synthetic fibers. Static electricity is generated when we rub one material across another under the right conditions.

Computer-controlled circuits require care because of possible ESD damage. The shock we feel or the spark that we see is 10,000 V or greater. An ESD voltage as low as 60 V can easily damage solid-state electronic devices. The symbol shown in ● **FIGURE 13–35** is placed on some components and wiring diagrams to indicate components that can be damaged by ESD. Unless you are connected electrically to the vehicle's ground, do not touch that component or its electrical connections. Do not make electrical measurements or checks on these components unless instructed to do so, and always follow directions exactly. If directed to make voltage checks, always connect the negative probe to ground first.

The TCM should never be disconnected while the ignition is on. Also, you should wait for a minimum of 5 seconds before disconnecting a TCM after turning the power off. Some control modules electronically send information to the EEPROM during this time, and interrupting the power flow can cause faults in this information.

Other problems can occur if the battery is disconnected for too long, and these problems can occur in any of the vehicle's electronically controlled circuits. For example, one vehicle requires that the HVAC (heating, ventilation, and air-conditioning) airflow control doors must be recalibrated if the battery is

Diagnostic Trouble Codes

The 42LE transmission control module may report any of the following diagnostic trouble codes:

11	Internal Control Module	27	All Pressure Switch Circuits	47	Solenoid Switch Valve Latched In LR Position	
12	Battery Was Disconnected	28	Check Shifter Signal	48	Torque Management Request	
13	Internal Control Module	29	Throttle Position Signal	50	Output and Input Speed Checks:	Speed Error in Reverse
14	Relay Output Always On	31	OD Hydraulic Pressure Switch			
15	Relay Output Always Off	32	2-4 Hydraulic Pressure Switch	51		Speed Error in 1st
16	Internal Control Module	33	OD/2-4 Hydraulic Pressure Switch	52		Speed Error in 2nd
17	Internal Control Module	36	Fault Immediately After Shift	53		Speed Error in 3rd
18	Engine Speed Sensor	37	Solenoid Switch Valve Latched in CC Position	54		Speed Error in 4th
19	C²D Bus Communication With PCM	38	Torque Converter Clutch	56	Output and Input Speed Checks:	Input Sensor Error
20	Switched Battery	41	LR Solenoid Circuit	57		Output Sensor Error
21	OD Pressure Switch Circuit	42	2-4 Solenoid Circuit	58		Sensor Ground Error
22	2-4 Pressure Switch Circuit	43	OD Solenoid Circuit	60	Low Element Volume:	LR
23	2-4/OD Pressure Switch Circuit	44	UD Solenoid Circuit	61		2-4
24	LR Pressure Switch Circuit	45	Internal Control Module	62		OD
25	LR/OD Pressure Switch Circuit	46	UD Solenoid Circuit			
26	LR/2-4 Pressure Switch Circuit					

FIGURE 13–36 These DTCs are vehicle-model specific. They indicate the nature of the faults for a 42LE transmission. (*Courtesy of Chrysler Corporation*)

TECH TIP

Some technicians have found that they can use a non-CAN scan tool on a CAN vehicle by inputting an earlier-model vehicle. This can disable critical vehicle operating systems. In one case, the scan tool connection disabled the ABS brakes during a road test; the brake pedal was very hard and would not apply.

disconnected. This vehicle will set a trouble code, and the rear wiper switch light will flash to indicate a problem.

CAUTION: Do not touch any of the terminals of a TCM or any part of the circuit board unless you are wearing an ESD safety strap that is properly grounded.

13.5.3 DIAGNOSTIC TROUBLE CODES

Most electronic systems use a control module that can perform a self-diagnosis on the electrical/electronic components, its sensors, and its output circuits each time it starts up. It measures circuit voltage, looking for insufficient resistance caused by shorts or grounds or excessive resistance caused by open or poor connections. If an electrical problem is identified, it will turn on the malfunction indicator light (MIL) or flash the overdrive (O/D) indicator light and set a diagnostic trouble code (DTC). ● **SEE FIGURE 13–36.** The DTC is displayed on a special tester or scan tool, and the code number indicates the electrical component or circuit that is functioning improperly. The DTC does not tell exactly what is wrong, but will indicate a problem such as "Shift Solenoid 1 Circuit Failure," which indicates that the solenoid 1 circuit is open or shorted. Additional testing is required to pinpoint the exact cause of the problem. These tests usually involve measuring voltage or resistance at different points of the circuit. A good service manual or circuit information is essential for the proper test routine.

REAL WORLD FIX

The 1993 Volvo 850 (132,000 miles) has shift problems. A scan tool check shows codes 114, 222, and 313.

FIX

The technician checked the S1 and S2 shift solenoid resistance and found both to be out of specification. Vacuum hose routing was also checked and three were found to be improperly connected. Installing new shift solenoids and connecting the vacuum hoses properly fixed this problem.

REAL WORLD FIX

The 1996 Ford Windstar (50,000 miles) had a remanufactured transaxle installed. It drives and shifts well, but after a few miles the O/D (MIL) light begins flashing. Reading the DTCs shows a P0730 code, incorrect gear ratio.

FIX

The transaxle has the wrong internal ratio. The fix was to install the correct transaxle for this vehicle.

NOTE: This is an extremely difficult problem to avoid. The only way to determine the internal gear ratios is to count the teeth on the sprockets or gear set members. Many remanufactured transmissions are painted, hiding any identification marks, which makes exact identification difficult.

The 1994 Toyota 4Runner (104,000 miles) will not shift into fourth gear most of the time. The shop has limited test equipment. They believe the problem is caused by a faulty overdrive solenoid, but they are not sure which solenoid it is.

FIX

A check of the iATN information network informed the shop to check the engine thermostat. Someone had removed it. Replacement of the thermostat allowed the engine to come up to proper temperature and go into normal operation. This fixed the transmission problem.

Understanding of the proper operation of the transmission is essential to diagnosis. This transmission will not allow overdrive (fourth gear) until normal engine operating temperature is reached. Remember that electronic transmission problems can come from outside the transmission. It is essential to completely understand the system.

(a)

Fault ID:

Code 60 — Low L-R Element Volume
Code 61 — Low 2-4 Element Volume
Code 62 — Low OD Element Volume

(b)

FIGURE 13–37 (a) This DRB II screen shows that no fault codes are stored in the TCM memory; and (b) fault codes are stored. (*Courtesy of Chrysler Corporation*)

The DTC can be either **soft code** (temporary) or **hard code** (semipermanent). A soft code is erased from the control module's memory when the ignition key is turned off. A hard code is erased by performing a special operation, pressing certain control head buttons, removing the fuse for the control module, or by using a scan tool. This process is called *clearing codes.* Some systems can record and display the history of past failures. Self-diagnosis is vehicle-model specific. Carefully follow the directions given by the vehicle manufacturer. If using a scanner, follow the scanner manufacturer's directions.

Not all transmission electrical problems will set a trouble code. Without a trouble code, the technician must check all the circuits, one at a time, using an ohmmeter, voltmeter, test light, or scanner. Checking a circuit requires a wiring diagram as well as a good understanding of the circuit. Understanding the circuit often leads the technician close to the source of the problem. For example, if an electronically controlled transmission operates normally but has no third or fourth gear, a shift control solenoid is probably not allowing the clutches to operate properly. The technician should check both the electrical and hydraulic operation of the fourth-gear shift circuit.

Self-diagnosis is usually entered (started) by manipulating the scan tool or a transmission control switch. The codes resulting from self-diagnosis will be displayed (1) on the instrument panel, (2) on a handheld scanner, or (3) on a voltmeter or test light. The DTC is read as a multidigit or alphanumeric number; some systems display the code by a pattern of pulses from a voltmeter or flashes of a light on the instrument panel. ● **SEE FIGURE 13–37**.

 TECH TIP

Incorrect chain and/or differential ratios can create a DTC. A way of confirming incorrect ratios is to drive the vehicle while streaming data from the scanner. If the TCC lock command reaches 100% and you feel lockup, but the slip ratio is over 50 RPM, you have a transmission with the wrong internal ratio.

When checking electrical circuits, it is wise to remember that the most probable faults are wire connectors or moving mechanical parts. These include all wire connectors, switches, speed sensors, and solenoids. When checking wire connectors, look for loose, corroded, dirty, or bent and misaligned prongs. ● **SEE FIGURE 13–38**.

The least probable cause of failure will be the TCM. It is fairly well protected, and since there are no moving parts, there is nothing to wear out. However, the TCM can be damaged by excessive current flowing through it or a high-voltage spike occurring in one of its circuits. The wrong tester can cause excessive current flow. Testing a circuit using a test light or voltmeter is discussed in Section 13.3. The most common causes for a high-voltage spike are using a solenoid with an

(a)

(C) + 12V Shift Solenoids–Red
(D) PSM–Black
(E) PSM–White
(F) PSM–Blue
(B) Solenoid "B" Ground–Green
(A) Solenoid "A" Ground–Blue
(H) +5 Temp. Sensor–Red
(G) Temp. Sensor Ground–Green
(M) Force Motor–Green
(L) Force Motor–Blue
(K) 12V PWM Solenoid–White
(J) PWM Solenoid Ground–Black

(b)

FIGURE 13–38 A visual inspection of the transmission electrical connector ensures that the terminals are clean and in good shape as well as being completely engaged.

open diode, disconnecting the TCM while the ignition switch is on, and touching the prongs of the TCM with your fingers (ESD). Simple rules to follow while testing and working on electronic-controlled transmissions are as follows:

- Make sure the ignition is off before disconnecting or connecting the TCM.

- Make sure the ignition is off before disconnecting any TCM-related circuits or components.

- Never touch the TCM or electrical components without first connecting yourself to the vehicle's ground.

- Use the proper test equipment.

Following are general descriptions of some test procedures to give you an idea of the diagnostic process. However, you should always follow the procedure described in the service manual for a particular transmission.

After the fault is located and repaired, the codes must be cleared. With soft codes, this is easily done by turning off the key. Hard codes are cleared by performing certain operations with the scan tool, or by removing the control module fuse(s).

After the problems have been repaired and the codes erased, drive the vehicle through the basic road test. Recheck for any DTCs to make sure that all faults have been corrected.

13.5.4 SIGNAL MONITOR
A simple but effective transmission test tool is a shop-made **signal monitor** containing a series of LED lights. By watching the LEDs, you can see when the electrical signal is sent to the solenoids (see Figure 13–32).

TECH TIP

1. A DTC does not always indicate a faulty electrical value. A P0755, shift solenoid B malfunction, will set if the 1–2 shift takes longer than the prescribed period of time. A P0756, shift solenoid B performance or stuck off, will set if fluid pressure does not increase in a circuit at the correct time. A P0758, shift solenoid B electrical, will set if an improper electrical signal passes through that circuit.

2. A scan tool will erase codes without affecting any other electrical circuits. Disconnecting a fuse or the battery could erase all of the electronic memories, including clock settings and radio station presets. The result could be an irate vehicle owner. Removing the control module fuse(s) erases the memory of only that control module, but can also cause other problems. Some electronic transmissions are controlled through the engine control module (ECM). Some of these have adaptive learning for the engine controls. These ECMs adjust certain engine operating functions to particular geographic locations or driving styles. If you pull the fuse on these vehicles, it can take about 100 miles of driving before operating strategies are relearned and switched from a default setting to the owner's location and driving style. During this time the vehicle can run poorly.

3. Repair of a worn or faulty electronically controlled transmission will often result in harsh shifts. The electronic controls have been compensating for excessive clutch clearance or low fluid pressures by increasing the line pressure. The TCM must be recalibrated or the vehicle can be driven, 45 minutes or longer, until the TCM relearns how the repaired transmission operates and shifts. Always check the service information for the proper relearn procedure.

TECH TIP

If it is necessary to disconnect a battery, it is recommended that you first write down the station numbers for the radio presets. After reconnecting the battery, reset the radio stations and the vehicle's clock. Also perform any "relearn" steps for the ECM and the TCM.

The monitor is connected to the solenoid feed wires at the transmission connector and also to either B+ or ground depending on whether the solenoids are computer or internally grounded. When the vehicle is driven on a basic road test, the

The 1990 Plymouth Caravan (152,000 miles) transmission was rebuilt, and it worked well for a while. Now, it will not shift. A check for DTC showed code 24. The DTC was cleared, and the transmission operated properly for 3 weeks, then the problem and code returned.

FIX

A check showed the underdrive clutch volume index (CVI) was high. The transmission was disassembled, and an air check of the underdrive clutch showed a leak. Repair of the clutch seals fixed this problem.

The 1991 Ford Explorer (158,000 miles) shifts in and out of overdrive erratically, and when this occurs, the speedometer shows speed changes, from 140 mph to 0 mph. A scan tool check revealed no DTCs, the VSS output is very erratic, and the park–neutral switch output changes between park and neutral. The VSS and park–neutral switch have been replaced using OEM parts, but this did not help.

FIX

Careful inspection revealed that the number 5 spark plug wire was wrapped around the wiring harness for the park–neutral switch. Rerouting of these wires fixed this problem.

---

monitor LEDs should light up in a pattern that matches the transmission's shift pattern. If the signals differ from the proper pattern, the problem is electronic in nature. If the signals occur, but the transmission does not shift properly, the problem is mechanical, hydraulic, or a bad solenoid and is inside the transmission.

13.5.5 FORCING SHIFTS ELECTRICALLY
Forcing a shift requires disconnecting the transmission electrical connector and connecting a special tool to provide the proper electrical signal to the shift solenoids. Most scan tools have this ability when connected to the DLC. Remember that when the special tool or scan tool forces a shift, it provides either the B+ or ground signal to the shift solenoid. It takes the place of the TCM and, in some cases, provides a redundant or its own ground. Providing power to the solenoids lets you determine if they are working properly. If they are, then the problem is in the wiring, the TCM, or the inputs to the TCM.

13.5.6 CLUTCH VOLUME INDEX
Some vehicles include a code for **clutch volume index (CVI).** This monitors the time needed to fill a clutch as it applies. Each clutch should fill and stroke the clutch in a specified time. This time period usually increases with normal wear.

The TCM determines CVI from the speed differential between the input and output speed sensors. The TCM can determine the actual ratio and how long it takes to complete a shift from the speed differential of the two speed sensors. A high CVI usually indicates a clutch with excessive slippage.

13.5.7 EMI ELECTRONIC PROBLEMS
Electronic circuits can be influenced by **electromagnetic induction (EMI)** and a form of EMI, called **radio frequency interference (RFI).** This is the interaction between ferrous metal objects and the magnetic field around a current-carrying wire. Vehicle manufacturers twist electrical wires together, use shielded coaxial cable, and install metal shielding to protect some circuits from EMI interference.

EMI can cause strange electronic circuit malfunctions and a TCM to set a DTC when there is no real fault. If this is encountered, first check the vehicle for improperly installed aftermarket electronic accessories. These include a cellular telephone, radar detector, remote starter system, radio, or any other non-OEM electrical accessory. Discarded shields or misrouted wires from an improperly performed repair can also cause EMI problems.

13.6 ELECTRONIC COMPONENT AND CIRCUIT CHECKS

After the nature of the problem has been determined, the faulty circuit or components should be checked to locate the exact cause. These are often fairly simple voltage, resistance, or current flow checks. These checks can often be made with the components mounted in their normal position. A *breakout box* or *test box* can be connected into the circuit to allow the technician to check voltage or resistance. ● **SEE FIGURE 13–39.** It is also possible to check internal transmission electrical components at the breakout box. ● **SEE FIGURE 13–40.**

13.6.1 TCM POWER CHECKS
An electronic system cannot function without adequate power or a good ground. The power and ground connections are often overlooked by the technician who is eager to solve a transmission problem. After determining there is a problem in the electronic system, an experienced technician will check B+ voltage at the battery and then at the TCM and transmission power relay if there is one. There should be at least 12.6 V with the engine off and 13.6 to 15 V with the engine running. There should also be a

FIGURE 13–39 This 100-pin breakout box can be connected to a wiring harness to provide convenient points to make electrical checks. *(Courtesy of SPX/O7C)*

(a)

(b)

FIGURE 13–40 (a) External and (b) internal wiring harnesses connect to the transmission electrical components.

TECH TIP

1. When checking a circuit, make sure that all connectors are properly latched. Disassemble the connector and check for loose, bent, or pushed-back pins, cracked connectors, and water intrusion that will cause corrosion.

2. The valve body with integrated TCMs (called control solenoid valve assembly, Mechatronic, and solenoid body) can be removed from the transmission and reconnected to the vehicle using a special harness. A signal generator can be used to input ISS and OSS signals, and if the TCM responds properly, the speed sensor in question must be faulty.

REAL WORLD FIX

The 1995 Lincoln Towncar (160,000 km) was towed in because it would not shift out of park. Pressing the brake does not help. Another problem is that the brake lights are not working.

FIX

The technician checked the brake light circuit and found a broken wire at the switch. Repairing this wire fixed both problems.

minimum voltage drop between the TCM ground (B–) terminal and ground, 0.2 V or less. ● **SEE FIGURE 13–41**.

A relay is a coil of thin wire with an iron core and switch contacts. When current flows through the coil, a magnetic field is produced, and the switch is pulled closed. The amount of resistance in the wire coil can be easily checked using an ohmmeter. First disconnect the solenoid, and then connect one ohmmeter lead to each of the relay electrical coil connectors, read the resistance, and compare the reading to the specifications. ● **SEE FIGURE 13–42**. Solenoids should also be checked for a grounded coil. Relays with a diode should be checked to make sure the diode is good; this is done by reversing the ohmmeter leads at the coil connections. The resistance should be higher in one direction than it is in the other.

BATTERY. An electronic system cannot function properly without a good battery. This should be the first item to check, and there are two battery checks: state of charge and load test. State of charge is measured by simply connecting the two voltmeter leads to the two battery posts. A voltage of 12.6 V indicates a full charge; 12.4 V indicates a charge level

FIGURE 13–41 TCM terminals 16 and 17 receive B+ when the transmission relay is energized. This also sends B+ to the solenoid and pressure switch assembly.

OHMMETER TEST

FIGURE 13–42 Ohmmeter A is connected to check for a grounded circuit: it should read infinite resistance. Ohmmeter B is measuring the resistance of the coil; if the leads are reversed, it will show a different resistance because of the diode.

TECH TIP

1. Wiggling the wire connectors and tapping the TCM sharply with your finger while testing may reveal the cause of an intermittent problem.
2. When diagnosing a problem that has set an MIL and shut down the TCM, and that will shut down the electrical functions, use the following procedure to get circuit values: (1) Clear the codes, (2) connect your test equipment, and (3) turn the key on and measure the electrical values while the TCM is performing its self-check.
3. A TCM is considered a nonserviceable component; a faulty TCM is removed and replaced. However, an experienced technician will check to determine what caused the failure. Checking a TCM follows this procedure: (1) Remove the TCM from the vehicle, (2) give the TCM a gentle shake as you listen for rattles that indicate loose parts, (3) remove the cover, and (4) make a visual inspection for white or green corrosion, black or burned overheated parts, leaky capacitors, and cracked or broken solder joints. A faulty solder joint can usually be resoldered, saving the TCM.

REAL WORLD FIX

The 1995 Buick Skylark (63,000 miles) engine stalls when shifted into reverse. When a scan tool is connected, it momentarily quits reading as the shift is made. With the engine off, the scan tool acts normally.

FIX

Careful inspection showed that the engine harness ground wires had broken, but would make contact. Engine movement during the reverse shift would break the contact and open the circuits. Repair of these wires fixed this problem.

of about 75%. A low battery should be charged before continuing to the next check.

The most accurate battery load test is made using a load tester; this unit applies a discharge load to the battery while observing the battery's drop in voltage. A load test can also be made by using the vehicle's starter to apply the load.

To make a battery load test, *you should:*

If a battery load tester is available:

1. Determine the cold cranking amperes (CCA) rating of the battery. Connect the current and the voltage leads to the battery posts.
2. Adjust the amperage load to one-half that of the battery's CCA rating, and allow the battery to discharge for

REAL WORLD FIX

The 1992 BMW 325 (164,000 miles) stays in first gear unless it is manually shifted into third and then during third gear, shifted back into D for fourth. The circuits were checked using a test light, the solenoids using an ohmmeter, and the sensors using a lab scope. Everything checked out fine. The TCM was replaced with no change.

FIX

A further check of the selector switch using a DMM showed a leakage of 8 V into a circuit that was off and should have had 0 V. This was enough to stop the TCM from operating. Replacement of the gear range selector switch fixed this problem.

REAL WORLD FIX

The 1994 Dodge Intrepid (126,000 miles) transmission does not shift until warmed up. A scan tool check shows a code 66: no ETAX to CCD messages received. The instrument panel gauges do not work until the engine comes up to temperature. These problems are intermittent and the vehicle will work okay for several days.

FIX

The technician inspected all of the grounds plus the ignition switch. One of the ignition switch B+ circuits checked had 0.5 V. A new ignition switch fixed this problem.

15 seconds while watching the voltage. Stop the test if voltage drops below 9.5 V; this indicates that the battery has failed the test.

If a load tester is not available:

1. Disable the vehicle's ignition system so it will not start.
2. Connect the voltmeter leads to the battery posts, and crank the engine for 30 seconds while watching the voltage. Stop the test if voltage drops below 9.5 V; this indicates that the battery has failed the test.

13.6.2 TCC CHECKS The TCM monitors vehicle speed and gear range, engine conditions such as RPM and temperature, as well as brake pedal and cruise control switches to determine apply/lockup and release/unlock. ● **SEE FIGURE 13–43**. When conditions are correct, the TCM will lock up the converter; lockup is cancelled when certain conditions occur.

TCC operation can be checked using a functional test. If it fails, further tests will be needed to find the exact cause.

FIGURE 13–43 The TCM monitors the sensors to determine when the converter clutch should be applied. It also checks for changes in these signals to determine if the clutch should be released.

REAL WORLD FIX

The 1995 Chevrolet S10 (54,000 miles) had no TCC lockup. Use of an electronic tester showed a lockup signal from the TCM, and the TCC will apply from the tester. Voltage checks show proper voltages.

FIX

A check of the ground circuit between the frame and transmission showed a bad connection. Cleaning the connections fixed this problem. The transmission tester provided a redundant ground for the TCC solenoid to operate during the tests. The technician should have made the voltage checks with the tester disconnected.

TECH TIP

If battery testing a late-model vehicle with fuel injection, some technicians prevent starting by pushing the gas pedal all the way to the floor; this should shut off the fuel injectors.

The 1994 Ford Taurus (135,000 miles) came in with a TCC dropout after the vehicle gets to operating temperature. A scan tool check shows DTC 628: TCC circuit slippage. After the code is set, the EPC sets line pressure at 60 PSI and the transmission upshifts and downshifts are harsh from that point. The valve body and EPC solenoid have been replaced twice and the TCM once, but this did not help.

FIX

Following advice, the technician learned that this is the normal strategy programmed for this transmission. When excessive TCC slippage is sensed by the ECM, the fluid pressure will be increased to a certain point, and then the TCM will turn off the TCC and lock line pressure to 60 PSI. This set of symptoms indicates that this transmission has more severe internal problems.

Solenoid Connectors

(a)

Solenoid Connectors

12 V Battery

(b)

To perform a TCC operation test, *you should do the following:*

1. Perform a road test, and drive the vehicle about 40 mph (65 km/h) using a light throttle. Tap the brake lightly, just enough to turn on the stop lights but not enough to start brake application.

2. Observe the tachometer, if the vehicle has one, and feel for a soft, slight downshift indicating TCC release. This should be followed by a soft reapplication of the TCC.

   If you notice the release and reapplication, this is normal operation.

   If nothing happens, this indicates a faulty converter clutch or a stuck converter clutch control valve or a faulty solenoid, internal transmission switch, TCC circuit, or control module.

Some TCC problems will set a DTC, and this code may indicate the nature of the problem. There are several checks that can be made on the circuit, the solenoid, and its diode. These are described in the following section. The TCC hydraulic circuit checks are described in Section 12.6.

13.6.3 SOLENOID CHECKS
A solenoid is a coil of thin wire with an iron plunger. When current flows through the coil, a magnetic field is produced and the plunger moves to the center of the magnetic field. The resistance in the coil can be easily checked using an ohmmeter. A solenoid can be checked either in the transmission or on the bench. Disconnect the solenoid connector and connect one ohmmeter lead to each of the solenoid electrical terminals. Read the resistance, and compare the reading to the specifications. ● **SEE FIGURE 13–44.** Follow this by moving one of the leads to the solenoid body or base to check for a ground circuit. A two-wire solenoid should not have a circuit to the ground, the solenoid mounting point. If the first

FIGURE 13–44 (a) Ohmmeter A is checking for a grounded solenoid coil; the reading should be infinite. Ohmmeter B is measuring the coil resistance; it should be within the specifications for this solenoid. (b) Connecting a solenoid to a 12-V battery should cause it to operate. Make sure the battery is connected using the correct polarity in case the solenoid has an internal diode.

 TECH TIP

1. A quick check for a shift solenoid is to complete the solenoid circuit. Use a jumper wire to the battery for a single-wire solenoid or jumper wire to ground for a two-wire solenoid. A shift solenoid should click, indicating that the coil windings are complete and the plunger is moving. *Do not* use this quick check on a PWN solenoid; the lower internal resistance will allow excessive current flow that can damage the solenoid.

2. A PWM solenoid draws enough current to overheat and burn out if connected directly to a battery. If testing with jumper wires, limit the connection to 1 second, just enough time to hear it click.

3. Many technicians consider solenoids, especially PWM solenoids, to be "wear items" and automatically replace them if the transmission experiences problems after about 70,000 miles. Some PWM solenoids operate at 30 to 50 Hz while the vehicle is in drive.

4. If testing a solenoid using a special tester, use the same voltage and frequency/duty cycle settings that are used in the vehicle.

1. Early solenoid failure can be caused by excessive vehicle electrical system voltage.
2. Solenoid tests can identify if a solenoid is plugged or clear and if it has good coil windings under shop conditions. Most tests cannot duplicate the heat and vibration that occur inside of a transmission, and they will not predict the solenoid's remaining useful life. Some technicians heat the solenoid using a heat gun while making solenoid checks.

(a)

(b)

FIGURE 13–45 You should not be able to blow through this solenoid if it is not activated. If it is connected to a 12-V battery, it should make a "click," and you should be able to blow through it.

reading is within specifications and the second one is infinite or OL (out of limits), the solenoid should operate. A single-wire solenoid will be grounded through the solenoid case, and it should have continuity when one of the ohmmeter leads is connected to the case and the other to the solenoid terminal.

Some solenoids include a diode to eliminate any voltage spikes that might occur as the solenoid is de-energized. As the solenoid is tested, the diode is also checked to see if it allows a flow in one direction but not the other. You can check the diode and the solenoid coil by connecting an ohmmeter lead to each of the terminals. With the solenoid out of the transmission and on the bench, you should connect the positive (+) ohmmeter lead to the positive (+) solenoid lead and the two negative (–) leads together. If checks are made with the solenoid in the transmission, be aware that some transmission circuits include a pressure switch between the solenoid negative terminal and the case connector.

With the ohmmeter connected to the solenoid as just described, the reading should be about 20–40 Ω depending on the temperature. If the reading is less than 20 Ω, the coil or diode is shorted. If the reading is greater than 40 Ω or infinite, there is an open or broken circuit. In either case, the solenoid is faulty.

Next, reverse the meter leads so they are connected positive to negative and negative to positive. The meter reading should now be lower than it was before, usually about 2–15 Ω. If the reading does not change, the diode is open, and the solenoid is faulty.

A solenoid can also be checked by connecting it to a 12-V battery, but take care when making this test. The diode will be destroyed if you connect the solenoid backwards. As the solenoid is connected to the power source, you should be able to feel and hear it "click" as it changes position.

The mechanical operation of a solenoid also should be checked. Since solenoids are basically electromagnets operating in an area that might have some metal debris, they tend to attract metal particles. These can cause sticking or binding of the solenoid plunger or blocking of the fluid passage. Test the solenoid by blowing air through it while energizing and de-energizing the coil. When the solenoid is connected to the power source, you should be able to blow through a normally closed solenoid. The passage should close so airflow will be blocked when it is not energized. Other solenoids are normally

The 1991 Chevrolet Suburban R2500 (154,000 miles) goes into limp-in mode intermittently. Another shop has replaced all of the shift solenoids. A scan tool check shows code 81: shift solenoid B. The solenoid resistance checks are within specifications. The connections to the speed sensors have been checked and they are clean.

FIX

The technician checked solenoid resistances again and found out-of-specification and open circuit readings. A visual inspection of the solenoids showed that the locking tabs of the solenoid connectors were all broken, and solenoid B was almost unplugged. A new internal wire harness fixed this problem.

open; they will test just the opposite. You should be able to blow through a normally open solenoid when it is not energized, but not when it is energized. Specialized testers are available that provide a power source and use air pressure to test solenoid operation. ● **SEE FIGURE 13–45.** Some testers will also test

The 1992 Subaru SVX (115,000 miles) came in with a burned transmission, and the O/D hub was torn off of the output shaft. The transmission was rebuilt, but it came back in a week with a slipping problem on the 2–3 and 3–4 shifts. Disassembly of the transmission showed a burned-up high clutch pack and 2–4 band. The unit was rebuilt again, and a shift kit was installed. A road test shows a good 1–2, mushy 2–3, and slipping 3–4 shifts.

FIX

Following advice, line pressure was checked and found to be low. The line pressure solenoid was rechecked and found to be stuck open, causing the low line pressure. This solenoid had been checked, and it had good electrical values. Replacement of this solenoid fixed this transmission.

A good road test before repairs should have indicated that the original problem was caused by low line pressure so it could have been cured. A good road test after the first rebuild should have caught this uncured problem earlier and saved a lot of time and expense.

(a)

(b)

FIGURE 13–46 A special tester being used to check (a) a solenoid and (b) a pressure switch. The switch should either open or close when air is supplied. The solenoid should allow or block an airflow when activated.

switch operation. Another tester checks solenoid operation using fluid flow.

13.6.4 SWITCH CHECKS

A control switch is checked by removing it from the circuit and checking it with an ohmmeter. The meter leads are connected to the two terminals of the switch. If there is only one terminal, one meter lead is connected to it, and the other lead is connected to the switch body. Some switches are normally open, and the reading should be very high—infinite or OL. Some switches are normally closed, and the reading should be 0 Ω. When the switch is operated, the reading should change to the opposite value. A pressure switch can usually be operated using a specialized tester or air pressure and a rubber-tipped air gun. ● **SEE FIGURE 13–46.**

A mechanically operated switch can also be checked on the vehicle using a voltmeter. Connect the negative meter lead to a good ground or the switch body and the positive lead to the B+ wire entering the switch. Voltage should be available to the switch. Next, move the positive meter lead to the second switch terminal, and operate the switch. As the switch is operated, the output voltage should change from zero to the same as the input voltage or vice versa. If the voltage readings are not close to the same value, there is a voltage drop, and high resistance in the switch is indicated.

Pressure switches can also be checked at the transmission electrical connector.

The transmission range (TR) switch, manual lever position (MLP) switch, or neutral start switch has several circuits and multiple terminals. These switches are checked using an

 TECH TIP

An external switch that has fluid leaking through it has failed and should be replaced.

ohmmeter and service information to determine which terminals should have continuity as the switch is moved through its travel. For example, using the switch connections shown in ● **FIGURE 13–47**, there should be no resistance between three of the terminals and ground in park. There should be infinite resistance between the B/U lamp switch feed terminal

FIGURE 13–47 The five switches inside this MLP switch complete a connection to ground in the various gear positions. (*Courtesy of Chrysler Corporation*)

REAL WORLD FIX

The 1993 Dodge Caravan (58,000 miles) goes into neutral after driving about 20 miles. Road testing with a scan tool connected shows the PRNDL switch going to neutral when this occurs. The gear select switch and the neutral safety switch were replaced, but this did not help. There are no transmission or engine DTCs.

FIX

Following advice, a redundant ground was added between the transmission case and battery ground. The connectors on the gear select switch were also replaced, and one or both of the operations cured this problem.

NOTE: A voltage drop check on the ground circuit would have determined if the redundant ground was needed.

---

and ground in all gear positions except reverse. Some MLP switches will have continuity between various terminals in some gear positions.

13.6.5 SPEED SENSOR CHECKS Two styles of speed sensors are commonly used in automatic transmissions. One style is a switch that opens and closes as a magnet on the transmission output shaft rotates past it. The other style is a unit that generates an alternating voltage signal as a specially designed transmission part rotates next to it.

The switch-type speed sensor normally has a single-wire connector and is tested using an ohmmeter. ● **SEE FIGURE 13–48.** Connect one lead of the ohmmeter to a good ground and the other lead to the switch's connector. Next,

FIGURE 13–48 (a) A single-wire VSS can be checked by connecting one ohmmeter lead to the output terminal and the other lead to ground. Rotating the transmission output shaft should cause the ohmmeter to fluctuate from zero to infinite ohms. (b) A two-wire VSS is checked. Ohmmeter A is measuring the speed sensor coil resistance; it should be within the specifications. Ohmmeter B is checking for a grounded coil; the reading should be infinite. (*Figure (a) Courtesy of Chrysler Corporation*)

? **FREQUENTLY ASKED QUESTION**

What Is the KM No-Reverse Syndrome?

KM transmission designs use a reverse-inhibit feature using two speed sensors: turbine shaft and output shaft. The TCM will not allow a reverse shift if it sees output shaft rotation. The sensors are similar and their connectors are identical so either connector can be connected to either sensor. If they are connected wrong, with the engine running (and the turbine shaft spinning), it will not shift into reverse; but, if the selector is shifted into drive and then into reverse, the TCM will allow a reverse shift. Moving the connectors to the proper speed sensor will fix this problem.

---

rotate the transmission output shaft while watching the ohmmeter. The reading should change from very low (zero to a few ohms) to very high (infinite or OL) as the output shaft rotates.

The voltage-generating unit in a speed sensor normally uses a two-wire connector and is checked using both an ohmmeter

Sensor	Phase of Operation				
	Line Pressure Control	Shift Control	TCC Control	Fail-Safe	Self Diagnosis
VSS	X	X	X	X	X
ISS	X	X	X	X	X
TRS/PNP	X	X	X	X	X
TFT	X		X	X	X
TPS	X	X	X	X	X
Engine rpm	X	X	X		X
TCM Power	X				X

FIGURE 13–49 Switch and sensor operation can affect different phases of transmission operation.

TECH TIP

Access to a VSS is very limited on some vehicles. The VSS can be checked at the TCM, where there may be more room.

TECH TIP

Switches and sensors provide the data that a TCM uses to determine how and when pressure control or shift solenoids operate. ● **SEE FIGURE 13–49.**

REAL WORLD FIX

The 1995 Ford Windstar (109,000 miles) had a harsh shift complaint. A scan tool check showed DTC P0500: VSS missing input. The VSS signal is intermittent, sometimes good and sometimes not there.

FIX

The technician checked the VSS and found the heat shield was missing. When the VSS got hot, the signal would drop out. Replacing the VSS heat shield fixed this problem.

FIGURE 13–50 An ohmmeter being used to check a throttle position sensor. After disconnecting the 5-V reference, a lead is connected to the two TPS terminals. As the throttle is opened, the meter reading should deflect between no resistance and high resistance.

REAL WORLD FIX

The 1996 Ford E-350 van (107,000 miles) downshifts to second gear after reaching 35 to 40 mph; at this same time, the speedometer works erratically, reading up and down. A manual downshift will hold the transmission in that gear.

FIX

The VSS for this vehicle is in the rear axle; when removed for inspection, the sensor had a lot of metal filings stuck to it. Further inspection of the rear axle showed badly worn carrier bearings. The worn bearings allowed the sensor air gap to change, causing an erratic signal.

and a voltmeter. First, disconnect the sensor, and connect the ohmmeter leads to the sensor terminals. There should be a complete circuit through the unit, and the amount of resistance should fall within the range given in the specifications. Excessive or infinite resistance indicates a high resistance or open circuit; too low of a reading indicates a short circuit. The next check is to connect the two leads of a voltmeter to the two sensor connectors, set the meter to AC volts, and then rotate the transmission output shaft. As the shaft rotates, the voltmeter should show a fluctuating AC voltage reading, first + and then – to the same value.

13.6.6 THROTTLE POSITION SENSOR CHECKS A

throttle position sensor (TPS) can be checked using an ohm-meter or voltmeter. Disconnect the TPS electrical connector,

connect the ohmmeter leads to one of the TPS terminals (called ECV signal and ground, in Figure 13–51), and rotate the throttle. ● **SEE FIGURE 13–50.** As the throttle is opened and closed, the ohmmeter reading should change from a low to a high reading, and vice versa.

FIGURE 13–51 A TPS can be checked by connecting a DC voltmeter to the output terminal and ground. The signal should increase as the throttle is opened and stay within specifications.

TECH TIP

Most TPS inputs are 5 V, and the output voltage should vary smoothly between 0.5 V and 4.5 V.

REAL WORLD FIX

The 1990 Taurus runs well except for a 2–3 shift that slides and ends with a hard bump at high-throttle openings. Part-throttle operation is okay. The shift points are good, and the TV adjustment is okay.

FIX

A faulty TPS was found, and its replacement fixed this shift problem.

When using a voltmeter, leave the TPS connector connected. Turn the ignition to the ON position. Connect the negative lead to a good ground, and use the positive lead to probe the input voltage at the connector. ● **SEE FIGURE 13–51.** It should be the specified voltage indicated in the service manual. Next, move the positive voltmeter lead to the TPS output voltage lead, and measure the voltage as you open and close the throttle. The output voltage should increase and decrease smoothly as the throttle is opened and closed.

13.6.7 TEMPERATURE SENSOR CHECKS Temperature sensors are checked by measuring the resistance using an ohmmeter while changing the temperature. The resistance is compared with the specifications for the particular temperature.

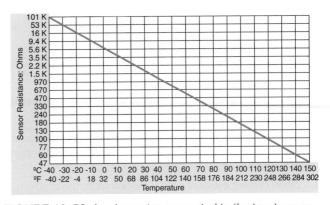

FIGURE 13–52 An ohmmeter connected to the two temperature sensor terminals should show that resistance will vary with the temperature. This sensor should have about 400 Ω at 70°C.

● **SEE FIGURE 13–52.** For accuracy, technicians can immerse the sensor into boiling water during the resistance check; the temperature of boiling water is 212°F (100°C). The resistance should now correspond to the specification for 212°F. A sensor with improper values should be replaced.

13.7 ELECTRONIC REPAIR JOB COMPLETION

Road-test the vehicle after any repair to verify proper operation. This test drive is similar to the diagnostic test drive. You should also check to verify that all of the old DTCs were cleared and no new DTCs were set. Any problems found must be corrected before returning the vehicle to the customer.

1. An understanding of electrical circuits is essential for diagnosing and repairing electronic transmissions.

2. The tools used to diagnose transmission electrical failures include test lights, digital multimeters, scan tools, oscilloscopes, and specially designed testers.

3. When diagnosing an electrically controlled automatic transmission, one of the first steps is to determine if the trouble is mechanical, hydraulic, or electrical.

4. Electrically controlled transmissions store a trouble code if a problem is identified by the PCM.

5. Testing the sensors and actuators involves basic electrical testing that can be done with a multimeter.

REVIEW QUESTIONS

1. The three major types of electrical problems are:
   a. _____
   b. _____
   c. _____

2. Electrical problems can show up as either _____ problems or be _____.

3. When a circuit is open, no _____ will flow.

4. An increase in resistance will cause a _____ in current flow.

5. Excess resistance problems are located by measuring the _____ _____ at the various parts of the circuit.

6. When current bypasses the intended path, the problem is known as a _____.

7. A short where a bare wire touches ground is commonly called a _____ to _____.

8. The most practical meter for testing electrical components is a _____ _____.

9. Voltage drop is the amount of _____ used to move _____ through a load.

10. An _____ would be used to test a component that is out of the circuit.

11. A technician would use a _____ _____ to read the DTCs from an ECM.

12. An _____ would be an ideal tool to observe the operations of a circuit with changing electrical values.

13. When making solder connections, always use _____-core solder.

14. The recommended three-step procedure for checking an electronically controlled transmission is:
    a. _____
    b. _____
    c. _____

15. The most probable causes of electrical problems are _____ _____ and _____ _____ that move.

16. Four simple rules to follow when testing or working on electronically controlled transmissions are:
    a. Make sure that the ignition is _____ before disconnecting or connecting the ECM.
    b. Make sure that the ignition is off before disconnecting or connecting any _____ controlled components.
    c. Never touch the _____ or _____ components without first grounding yourself.
    d. Use the proper _____ equipment.

17. The ECM must have a good _____ source and a good _____ to operate properly.

18. The transmission solenoid must be tested both for _____ and _____ operation.

19. Throttle position sensors are checked for a _____ increase or decrease in meter reading as the throttle is opened and closed.

20. The temperature sensor can be checked by measuring the _____ at a known temperature.

CHAPTER QUIZ

1. Technician A says that a short can occur if the internal wires in a component make contact. Technician B says that a short causes a fuse to open, shutting off the current flow. Who is correct?
   a. Technician A
   b. Technician B
   c. Both A and B
   d. Neither A nor B

2. Technician A says that a check to determine if there is voltage at a component can be made using a voltmeter. Technician B says that a test light is the best way to measure voltage at a component. Who is correct?
   a. Technician A
   b. Technician B
   c. Both A and B
   d. Neither A nor B

3. When checking electronic transmission controls, you should not use an analog voltmeter or ordinary test light because they _____.
   a. Are obsolete
   b. Are slow and clumsy
   c. Draw too much current and can change or damage the circuit
   d. All of these

4. Technician A says that high resistance in a circuit can be located with a voltmeter. Technician B says that excessive resistance can cause a circuit to work improperly. Who is correct?
   a. Technician A
   b. Technician B
   c. Both A and B
   d. Neither A nor B

5. When checking electronic transmission controls, use a digital meter that has at least _____.
   a. 100 Ω of resistance
   b. 10 MΩ of internal resistance
   c. 10 MΩ of external resistance
   d. Any of the above

6. Technician A says that the only difference between an analog meter and a digital meter is the readout. Technician B says that an analog meter could damage an electronic circuit. Who is correct?
   a. Technician A
   b. Technician B
   c. Both A and B
   d. Neither A nor B

7. Technician A says that it is not a good practice to pierce wire insulation during testing. Technician B says that if a wire is pierced during testing, it should be sealed to prevent corrosion problems. Who is correct?
   a. Technician A
   b. Technician B
   c. Both A and B
   d. Neither A nor B

8. Technician A says that a voltmeter is used to check for unwanted resistance in an operational circuit. Technician B says that an ohmmeter is used to check resistance in an operational circuit. Who is correct?
   a. Technician A
   b. Technician B
   c. Both A and B
   d. Neither A nor B

9. Technician A says that a scan tool can be used in place of a voltmeter. Technician B says that a scan tool is used to communicate with the vehicle's ECM. Who is correct?
   a. Technician A
   b. Technician B
   c. Both A and B
   d. Neither A nor B

10. Technician A says that during a road test if the electronic controls are disabled and the problem does not change, the problem is not the electronic controls. Technician B says that the solenoids can be operated by a special tool to check their operation during a road test. Who is correct?
   a. Technician A
   b. Technician B
   c. Both A and B
   d. Neither A nor B

11. Technician A says that all electrical problems will set a code. Technician B says that when the trouble codes are cleared, the problem is repaired. Who is correct?
   a. Technician A
   b. Technician B
   c. Both A and B
   d. Neither A nor B

12. A common problem with electronically controlled transmissions is a bad _____.
   a. Electronic control unit
   b. Throttle position sensor
   c. Vehicle speed sensor
   d. Electrical connection

13. Technician A says that you can ruin an electronic control unit by touching its terminals with your finger. Technician B says that you can ruin a solenoid by connecting it to a battery backward. Who is correct?
   a. Technician A
   b. Technician B
   c. Both A and B
   d. Neither A nor B

14. When testing a pressure switch, it should show a(n) _____.
   a. Open circuit without pressure at the switch
   b. Complete circuit with pressure at the switch
   c. Complete circuit without pressure at the switch
   d. All of the above, depending on the switch

15. Technician A says that the voltage to the ECM is not as important as the voltage to the output solenoid. Technician B says that the ECM must have a good ground connection. Who is correct?
   a. Technician A
   b. Technician B
   c. Both A and B
   d. Neither A nor B

16. Technician A says that torque converter clutch operation can be easily checked on a road test by lightly stepping on the brake pedal and watching the tachometer for a change in speed. Technician B says that the torque converter clutch can be tested using a scan tool to operate the circuit. Who is correct?
   a. Technician A
   b. Technician B
   c. Both A and B
   d. Neither A nor B

17. Technician A says that a solenoid can be tested by checking the current flow. Technician B says that a solenoid can be tested using an ohmmeter. Who is correct?
   a. Technician A
   b. Technician B
   c. Both A and B
   d. Neither A nor B

18. When testing a solenoid with an ohmmeter, reversing the test leads will check the _____.
   a. Transistor
   b. Triode
   c. Diode
   d. Winding

19. Technician A says that all transmission pressure switches are the same. Technician B says that transmission pressure switches can be either normally open or normally closed. Who is correct?
   a. Technician A
   b. Technician B
   c. Both A and B
   d. Neither A nor B

20. When electrical or electronic repairs are completed the vehicle should be _____.
   a. Taken for a complete test drive
   b. Returned to the customer
   c. Held for several days to confirm the repair
   d. All of the above

chapter 14

IN-VEHICLE TRANSMISSION REPAIR

OBJECTIVES: After studying Chapter 14, the reader will be able to: • Describe the repair operations that are performed with the transmission in the vehicle. • Determine the correct procedure for the in-vehicle repairs. • Make in-vehicle repairs in an approved manner. • Repair damaged threads in an aluminum casting. • Perform the ASE tasks related to in-vehicle transmission/transaxle repair.

KEY TERMS: Alignment marks 370 • Bench repair 356 • Heli-Coil 361 • In-vehicle repair 356 • Off-vehicle repair 356 • Remove and replace (R&R) 356 • Seal driver 357 • Stop-off tool 370 • Thread insert 361

14.1 INTRODUCTION

A technician should repair a transmission problem in a thorough manner, but also as quickly and efficiently as possible. Many transmissions require **off-vehicle** or **bench repair;** the transmission must be removed from the vehicle, repaired, and then replaced. **Remove and replace (R&R)** time for a FWD transaxle is about 4 to 10 hours depending on the vehicle. When possible, transmission repairs are made with the unit in the vehicle to save time.

The California Bureau of Automotive Repair (BAR) requires a complete inspection before removal to determine if the problem can be repaired in-vehicle, and the customer must be informed if in-vehicle repairs will resolve the problem.

In-vehicle repairs include those described in Chapter 11, plus other service operations depending on the make and model. The service to be done depends on the access to the component. In most cases, the following are considered in-vehicle repair tasks.

- Oil pan, gasket, filter, and magnet removal, inspection, and replacement
- Manual shift linkage adjustment and seal replacement
- Shift lever assemble and interlock replacement
- TV linkage or cable adjustment and seal replacement
- Vacuum modulator replacement
- Electrical/electronic component and wiring harness inspection, adjustment, repair, and replacement
- Cooler line and fitting replacement or repair
- Neutral start switch replacement
- Valve body removal, repair, and replacement

- Servo piston and cover seal replacement (when accessible)
- Accumulator piston and cover seal replacement (when accessible)
- Speedometer/speed sensor, gear, and seal replacement
- Governor removal, repair, and replacement
- Extension housing seal, bushing, or gasket replacement, RWD
- Parking pawl, shaft, and spring inspection and replacement (when accessible)
- Driveshaft seal replacement, FWD
- Engine and transmission mount alignment and replacement

Some of these tasks will be described in Chapter 18 with other subassembly repair procedures.

Remember that the exact procedure for in-vehicle service operations varies between transmission makes and models. Service information should always be consulted before transmission service. The tasks described in this chapter are normally found under a heading such as "In-Vehicle Service" or "On-Vehicle Service." In this text, they are described in very general terms.

14.2 MANUAL SHIFT LINKAGE, INTERLOCK, AND SEAL

The manual shift linkage attaches to a lever on the outside of the transmission case. A series of rods, levers, or a cable and housing assembly may be used. The cable connects to a shift lever

FIGURE 14–1 A faulty shift cable can be replaced.

(a)	(b)

FIGURE 14–2 (a) Access to the manual control shaft seal is obtained by removing the shift lever and (b) the park–neutral position switch. The seal (arrow) can now be removed and replaced. (*Courtesy of Toyota Motor Sales USA, Inc.*)

using a metal clip or plastic grommet. ● **SEE FIGURE 14–1**. The cable housing is secured to a bracket on the transmission case. The other end of the cable and housing is connected to the gear selector in a similar manner. The removal of a cable is usually done by disconnecting each end of the cable and removing any brackets. As the cable is removed from the vehicle, carefully note the routing so the new cable will be in the same location. Cable replacement is the reverse of the removal procedure and should be followed by an adjustment to ensure correct manual valve positioning.

The shift linkage interlock is the safety mechanism that prevents removal of the ignition key unless the vehicle is shifted into park. It also prevents shifting out of park unless the key is in the ignition and, in some cases, the brakes are applied. Interlocks are vehicle specific, so service information should be consulted before attempting repairs.

A lip seal is used to prevent fluid leaks where the manual selector shaft passes through the transmission case. ● **SEE FIGURE 14–2**. This seal is easier to R&R if the manual selector shaft is removed, but that would require valve body removal in most cases. It is possible to remove this seal using either a slide hammer and self-tapping screw or a sharp chisel. ● **SEE FIGURE 14–3**. Be careful that you do not damage the seal bore. The new seal can be driven into the bore using a **seal driver** or, in some cases, a correctly sized socket can be used as a driving tool. ● **SEE FIGURE 14–4**.

FIGURE 14–3 A seal can be driven out by catching the edge with a sharp chisel. Another removal method is to use a slide hammer that is threaded into the seal's metal cage. Be careful to not damage the seal bore when using either method.

FIGURE 14–4 After the manual lever is removed, the manual shaft seal can be removed and replaced. The new seal should be driven in using a seal driver (B.Vi FM-34) to prevent damage. (*Courtesy of Chrysler Corporation*)

 REAL WORLD FIX

The 1992 Honda Accord (109,000 miles) is very hard to shift from park to reverse and back. The other shifts are okay.

FIX

The technician inspected the shift cable and found corrosion. A new shift cable fixed this problem.

FIGURE 14–5 A cutaway view of a metal-clad seal. Note that the seal must make a static seal with the case and a dynamic seal with the shaft.

FIGURE 14–6 This lip seal has a coating of sealant on its metal backing. Before installing an uncoated seal, a sealant should be applied to this area.

14.3 LIP SEAL REPLACEMENT

A standard metal-backed lip seal must seal against two different surfaces: a dynamic seal with the movable shaft at the inner bore and a static seal where it fits into its bore. ● **SEE FIGURE 14–5.** The static seal is made when the slightly oversize seal backing is driven into the bore. A dry coating on the seal case helps prevent leakage. ● **SEE FIGURE 14–6.** A leak can occur if the bore for the seal is scratched or damaged or if the seal case is bent or distorted. A driver that fits completely against the seal should always be used when installing a seal. ● **SEE FIGURE 14–7.** This ensures that the seal is not damaged, and is driven straight into its bore.

The inner sealing lip is a flexible, elastic compound. It must remain flexible and resilient in order to maintain a fluid-tight seal against the moving shaft. Use care when installing the seal over a shaft or a shaft into a seal. The sharp lip of the seal is easily cut or torn.

(a)

(b)

FIGURE 14–7 (a) A special tool is used to remove the extension housing seal, and (b) a seal driver is used to install the seal. Note how the driver fits the seal so it can be driven straight into the bore with no damage to the sealing surfaces. (*Figure (a) Courtesy of Chrysler Corporation; (b) Courtesy of Toyota Motor Sales USA, Inc.*)

FIGURE 14–8 The sealing lip should be protected when installing a seal over a shaft. A piece of slick paper or plastic can be used to cover the sharp edges on the shaft.

FIGURE 14–9 Removal of this exterior throttle lever, E-clip, and washer allows access to the small seal at the throttle shaft. (*Courtesy of Chrysler Corporation*)

🔧 TECH TIP

1. When installing a seal over a shaft, it is good practice to protect the sealing lip with a seal protector, especially if there are any rough or sharp edges on the shaft. A piece of slick paper wrapped around the shaft will work as a seal protector in many cases. ● **SEE FIGURE 14–8.**
2. The lip of the seal should always be lubricated to prevent wear. Automatic transmission assembly lube, petroleum jelly, or automatic transmission fluid (ATF) can be used for a lubricant.
3. Some seals include a garter spring to increase sealing lip pressure. This garter spring can be dislodged as the seal is driven into position. Filling the recess with assembly lube or petroleum jelly will keep the garter spring in place during installation.

14.4 THROTTLE VALVE LINKAGE AND SEAL

In most transmissions, the throttle valve (TV) cable is a cable and housing assembly, and its replacement is essentially the same as a shift cable. In other transmissions, the TV cable is attached to a lever on a shaft that extends into the transmission, just like the shift lever and shaft. Also like the shift lever, a seal fits over the shaft. ● **SEE FIGURE 14–9.**

The TV cable on some transmissions is attached directly to the case, and it extends into the transmission where it connects to the throttle valve. The transmission end of the cable is disconnected by unbolting the mounting bracket, removing the pan, and disconnecting the cable from the TV linkage. ● **SEE FIGURE 14–10.** The seal can be easily replaced while the bracket and cable are loose.

◆O-Ring

FIGURE 14–10 An O-ring seals the throttle cable where it enters the transmission case. (*Courtesy of Toyota Motor Sales USA, Inc.*)

REAL WORLD FIX

The 1994 Ford Explorer (113,000 miles) transmission uses about 2 quarts of ATF each week, but the shop cannot find a leak.

FIX

The technician removed the vacuum line from the vacuum modulator, and ATF poured out of it. A new vacuum modulator fixed this leak problem.

14.5 VACUUM MODULATOR REMOVAL AND REPLACEMENT

Most vacuum modulators are held in the transmission by a bolt and retaining clamp. Removing the clamp allows the modulator to be pulled out of the transmission case. Some transmissions use a control rod or pin to connect the modulator stem to the valve. ● **SEE FIGURE 14–11.** The control rod and modulator valve can usually be removed once the modulator is removed.

In some older transmissions, the modulators are threaded into the case.

To R&R a vacuum modulator, *you should:*

1. Disconnect the vacuum hose and remove the retaining bolt and clamp.

2. Pull the modulator out of the transmission case.

(a)

(b)

FIGURE 14–11 This modulator is secured using a clamp. (a) Removing the bolt and clamp allows the modulator to be removed. (b) The modulator valve can be removed using a magnet.

3. If necessary, remove the control rod, modulator valve, or both. Note the position of the valve as it is removed. Perform the necessary service and replace them.

4. Install a new seal on the modulator stem, wet the seal with ATF, and push the modulator into the case.

5. Replace the retaining clamp and bolt and tighten the bolt to the correct torque. ● **SEE FIGURE 14–12.**

FIGURE 14–12 When a modulator is replaced, the retaining bolt should be tightened to the correct torque.

FIGURE 14–13 This bolt was too short for the job, and when it was tightened, it pulled the threads out of the aluminum case.

FIGURE 14–14 The thread contact distance (CD) of a bolt should equal about twice the diameter of the threads (D) to prevent thread stripping.

14.6 ALUMINUM THREAD REPAIR

Transmission cases and extension housings are made from relatively soft, cast aluminum. Bolt threads begin to wear after a few uses, and aluminum threads easily pull out if the bolt is overtightened or if too short of a bolt is used. ● **SEE FIGURE 14–13.** The most commonly used thread repair method is to install a special steel coil **thread insert.** Thread inserts are commonly called a **Heli-Coil.** Some thread inserts are solid, like a tube with internal and external threads. These thread inserts provide a stronger and much longer-lasting thread. Another repair method is to form new threads using an epoxy compound. This method is not recommended for threads that will be in contact with ATF.

Thread damage is often caused by the use of a bolt or cap screw that is too long or too short. Too long of a bolt will bottom

FIGURE 14–15 (a) Step 1 in repairing damaged threads is to drill a properly sized hole for the special tap. (b) Step 2 is to use the special tap to cut new threads. (c) Step 3 is to put the thread insert on the installing tool. (d) Step 4 is to screw the insert into the new threads. The final step (not shown) is to break off and remove the insert's installing tang.

 TECH TIP

1. It is a good practice to lightly lubricate bolt threads going into a blind hole with ATF. Bolts going through holes can be dipped into transmission assembly lube. Using the thicker assembly lube in a blind hole could cause a hydrostatic lock and improper tightening or damaged threads.
2. A bolt is usually designed to enter the threaded hole a distance that is about 1.5 to 2 times the bolt diameter. ● **SEE FIGURE 14–14.** In other words, a 1/4-in. (6.35 mm) bolt will have about 2 × 1/4 in., or 1/2 in. (12.7 mm) of thread contact.

in the hole before it is tight, and too short of a bolt will grip fewer threads than needed. Use of a bolt with damaged threads or the wrong threads will produce damaged threads in the casting. Check all bolts before starting them into the threaded hole, and replace any that are questionable.

To install a coil-type thread insert, *you should:*

1. Drill out the worn threads, if necessary, using a drill of the correct size for the special tap. ● **SEE FIGURE 14–15.**
2. Use the special tap to cut new threads slightly longer than the length of the insert.

3. Install the thread insert onto the installing tool, and thread the insert completely into the hole. The end of the last thread should enter into the hole.

4. Break off the installing tang or resize the insert as required by the manufacturer. ● **SEE FIGURE 14–16**.

14.7 ELECTRICAL COMPONENT REMOVAL, REPAIR, AND REPLACEMENT

The testing procedures for electronic components are described in Chapter 13. Most of these components can be replaced in the vehicle. ● **SEE FIGURE 14–17**. With some transaxles, it can be challenging to remove and replace the upper pan where most of the electrical components are located. It might be necessary to lower the engine support cradle. Most of the electrical components are mounted either outside of the case or on the valve body with fairly easy access after the pan is removed. ● **SEE FIGURE 14–18**.

14.8 COOLER LINE AND FITTING REPAIR

A crushed or leaking cooler line must be repaired or replaced. ● **SEE FIGURE 14–19**. A leaky fitting is often fixed by merely tightening it. A cooler line is steel tubing that usually ends at a tube nut that is threaded into an adapter that in turn is

Damaged Threads   Repaired Threads

FIGURE 14–16 The damaged threads (left) have been repaired (right) by installing a thread insert. They are better than new because of the hardness of the insert.

TECH TIP

Joint Venture transaxles with integrated TCMs use the transmission range sensor to position the park pawl operating rod. When the TRS is removed, the park rod can fall out of position if it is moved, and the transaxle must be disassembled to get it back in the correct position.

FIGURE 14–17 Electronic components (both speed sensors, both switches, and the solenoid assembly) can be removed and replaced in-vehicle. (*Courtesy of Chrysler Corporation*)

FIGURE 14–18 Solenoids can be attached to the valve body. (*Courtesy of Toyota Motor Sales USA, Inc.*)

FIGURE 14–19 If replacing the cooler lines, use care to not bend them. The fit in some vehicles is quite precise. (*Courtesy of Chrysler Corporation*)

threaded into the transmission case or radiator cooler. ● **SEE FIGURE 14–20.** The adapter often uses tapered National Pipe Threads (NPTs) to form a seal. Some adapters use straight machine threads that require a gasket or a seal. Many vehicles now use a quick-disconnect-style cooler line fitting. ● **SEE FIGURE 14–21.**

The best repair for a damaged steel cooler line is replacement, but the replacement line has to be the correct length and have the correct bends. Replacing cooler lines can be labor-intensive, so technicians have developed various repair methods for damaged lines. Cooler lines do not wear out, but they do get damaged. Remember to always repair the problem that

(a)

Inverted Flare Fitting   Pipe Thread   Flare Fitting   Pipe Thread

(b)

FIGURE 14–20 (a) The cooler line fittings thread into the case. (b) These fittings normally have a National Pipe Thread (NPT) where they thread into the case and a flare or other style of fitting for the line connection.

Fitting   Release Tool

Cooler Line Flange

FIGURE 14–21 This cooler line fitting uses a push connector. Note the release tool. (*Courtesy of Chrysler Corporation*)

caused the failure. Never use copper tubing for replacement because it has a tendency to fatigue, crack, and break.

14.9 VALVE BODY REMOVAL AND REPLACEMENT

There are many possibilities for valve body problems, and the valve body is removed for repairing these problems. This task is rather messy because removing the valve body opens many fluid passages that will begin draining. Depending on the transmission, you may find check balls, one or more filter screens, a servo piston and spring, or an accumulator assembly above the

 TECH TIP

1. Steel cooler lines have been successfully repaired by cutting out the damaged portion, flaring the cut ends, and using a flare union to rejoin the lines. ● **SEE FIGURE 14–22.** Compression fittings can also be used to join tubing. If a section of the line has been cut away, an additional piece of tubing can be added. Steel tubing should be used; it is available in various sizes and lengths at automotive parts stores. If you make your own flare on the tubing, remember that steel tubing must have a double flare.
2. Another cooler line repair method is to cut out the damaged section and replace it with a rubber hose that is clamped onto the tubing. With this repair method, hydraulic hose or reinforced fuel hose of the correct size is used. The hose must be clamped securely onto the tubing, and it must be located so it will not be cut, burned, or otherwise damaged. It is recommended to keep the length of the rubber hose as short as possible to reduce or prevent damage.
3. If using rubber hose to repair a cooler line, select a hose with a cover to resist oil, ozone, heat, and aging. It should be reinforced with braided cord for increased strength, supporting a working pressure of 250 PSI and be designed to handle transmission oil temperatures up to 257°F (125°C).

 SAFETY TIP

Should this repair fail, it might allow hot ATF to spray on a hot exhaust pipe and cause a fire.

 TECH TIP

When removing and replacing a cooler line, two flare-nut or tube-nut wrenches should be used. ● **SEE FIGURE 14–23.** If a single wrench is used, the tube nut and the adapter often turn together, which causes twisting and damage to the tubing. If the tube nut is tight, a common open-end wrench will tend to round off the corners on the tube nut; a flare-nut wrench has a much better grip that prevents damage to the nut.

(a) (b) (c)

FIGURE 14–22 Cooler line damage can be repaired by removing the damaged section. (a) A piece of steel tubing can be installed using flare or (b) compression unions. (c) A hose can also be used; it is a good practice to make a small ridge at the ends of the metal tube to keep the hose from slipping off the tube.

(a)

(b)

(c)

FIGURE 14–23 (a) Two flare-nut wrenches should be used to (b) loosen a tube nut. (c) Use of a standard open-end wrench can result in a rounded-off tube nut; using a single wrench can result in a twisted line. (*Figure (a) Courtesy of Snap-on Tools*)

FIGURE 14–24 As the valve body is removed, be ready to catch any check balls, filter screens, or accumulator springs.

 TECH TIP

According to some technicians, it is important that a valve body be removed from a transmission at room temperature, especially with aluminum valve bodies. Removal of a hot valve body might produce warpage, which might cause sticky valves.

valve body. Be prepared for these as the valve body is removed so they are not lost or damaged. ● **SEE FIGURE 14–24.**

To remove a valve body, *you should:*

1. Raise and support the vehicle on a hoist so you have access to the transmission pan.

2. Loosen the pan and drain the fluid as described in Chapter 11. Remove the pan and filter. ● **SEE FIGURE 14–25.** Draining the fluid in the transmission is not necessary on transaxles with the valve body mounted inside the upper pan.

3. Disconnect the wires from any switches or solenoids that are attached to the valve body.

(a)

(b)

(c)

FIGURE 14–25 (a) The oil pan and (b) filter are removed from many transmissions to gain access to the valve body. (c) Examine the pan magnet for metal chips and particles. (*Courtesy of Toyota Motor Sales USA, Inc.*)

FIGURE 14–26 As the valve body is removed from many Torqueflite transmissions, the output shaft might need to be rotated so you can pull the park control rod (arrow) past the park pawl.

FIGURE 14–27 Save the old valve body gasket to compare it with the new to ensure that you install the correct gasket.

4. If necessary, remove any modulators and valves or servo covers and piston assemblies that interfere with valve body removal.

5. Remove the valve-body-to-case bolts. Carefully note the size and length of each bolt to make sure you can replace them in the correct location. As the last bolts are removed, carefully lower the valve body, disconnecting any linkages as required. ● **SEE FIGURE 14–26**.

The valve body can be repaired or exchanged as necessary. Valve body service and repair is described in Chapter 18. A separator plate is often used to align the hydraulic passages between the valve body and the case, and a gasket is usually used above and/or below the separator plate. A new gasket(s) should be used when reinstalling the valve body. Always compare the new and old gaskets to ensure the correct replacement. Often several gaskets are provided in the gasket set. They may look identical, but there are slight differences. These extra gaskets are intended for different applications, and a shift timing or quality problem may be the result if the wrong gasket is used. ● **SEE FIGURE 14–27**.

FIGURE 14–28 The No. 1 gasket, transfer plate, and No. 2 gasket, along with any check balls, screens, and springs, must be positioned properly as the valve body is installed. (*Courtesy of Toyota Motor Sales USA, Inc.*)

FIGURE 14–29 Two guide pins are used to ensure alignment of the gaskets, spacer plate, and valve body.

To replace a valve body, *you should:*

1. If used, position a new gasket or any check balls on top of the valve body or separator plate. The check balls can be held in place with assembly lube or petroleum jelly. ● SEE FIGURE 14–28.

2. Carefully position the valve body, making sure to correctly install the manual and TV linkage as necessary. It is recommended that two guide pins or bolts be threaded into the case to hold the transfer plate and gasket(s) in proper alignment. Loosely install a few bolts to hold the valve body in position. ● SEE FIGURE 14–29.

3. Reinstall all of the valve body bolts, making sure the correct lengths and sizes are in the proper position. ● SEE FIGURE 14–30. Remember that the bolts should thread into the case a distance that is about twice the bolt diameter.

4. Evenly tighten the bolts to the correct torque. Normally, you should start at the center bolts and work to the outer bolts using a spiral pattern. ● SEE FIGURE 14–31. Check the manufacturer's recommendation.

FIGURE 14–30 This valve body is secured with bolts of four different lengths; bolts of the correct length must be placed into the proper hole.

FIGURE 14–31 Valve body bolts should be tightened in the correct order. Note that this is a spiraling pattern that goes outward from the center.

 REAL WORLD FIX

The 1996 GMC pickup (132,000 miles) came in with a slipping transmission. A scan tool check showed code 1870, so the valve body was replaced. Now the transmission works okay in all forward ranges, but there is no reverse. There are no new DTCs.

FIX

Following advice, the technician raised the vehicle. With the transmission in neutral, he tried turning the driveshaft, and it would rotate only in one direction. This indicated that the valve body bolts were improperly installed. Placing the bolts in the correct holes fixed this problem.

5. Replace the filter.

6. Check the pan rails for straightness and repair as necessary.

7. Refill the transmission with fluid as described in Chapter 11.

FIGURE 14–32 These four accumulators are held in the case by the valve body.

14.10 SERVO AND ACCUMULATOR PISTON, COVER, AND SEAL SERVICE

A faulty servo piston or cover seal can cause a loss of servo apply pressure and band slippage. A faulty accumulator piston or cover seal can cause poor shift quality. A bad cover seal will leak. The service procedures for servos and accumulators are similar. A leaking servo or accumulator cover can be removed and the seal replaced. With the cover removed, the piston and spring can be easily removed and serviced.

A service manual should be checked before disassembling the servo or accumulator. In some cases, the valve body serves as the cover, so servo or accumulator service becomes an easy operation once the valve body is removed. ● **SEE FIGURE 14–32**. In others, a separate cover is used above the valve body so cover removal is done after the valve body is removed. Some servos are rather complex and have two or more pistons and up to four or five fluid passages and fluid control orifices or check balls. In some cases, a strong return spring is under the piston.

The servo or accumulator cover seal is either a gasket or an O-ring; it is fairly easy to R&R once the cover is removed. The servo or accumulator piston seal is either a metal or rubber ring. Seal ring checks are described in Chapter 17.

REAL WORLD FIX

The 1997 Chevrolet Silverado (52,000 miles) had a P1870 DTC (transmission component slipping), and a lot of brass was found in the pan. The input housing and worn stator bushing were replaced, and new seals were also installed. The vehicle returned after 3,000 miles with the same problem, and disassembling the transmission showed the same problems. The unit was repaired again, but it still had a slippage problem. The PWM and PC solenoids were replaced, but this did not help. The technician was suspicious of the valve body, but could see no problem with it from a visual inspection.

FIX

The technician was advised to recheck the valve body by moving the valves out of the bore far enough to grab them and then trying to move them vertically. The excessive movement showed that the bores in the aluminum valve body were worn. Replacement of the valve body fixed the problem.

Aluminum valves are anodized to harden the surface and reduce wear. The bores in an aluminum valve body are not anodized; they will wear faster than the valves.

FIGURE 14–33 The special tool (arrow) compresses the servo spring and holds the cover inward while the retaining ring is removed. The punch is inserted through a hole to help remove the retaining ring.

 TECH TIP

Depending on the transmission, a special tool is sometimes required to keep the spring compressed so the cover can be removed. ● **SEE FIGURE 14–33.**

 REAL WORLD FIX

The 1998 Ford Taurus (88,000 miles) was towed in because the engine stalls as soon as it is shifted into gear. Disconnecting the transmission electrical power did not help. The technician felt that this was a valve body problem but was not sure if he had access to the valve body on this AXOD transmission.

FIX

Following advice, the technician removed the battery tray, and this allowed removal of the valve body cover. A blown valve body gasket was found, and gasket replacement fixed this problem.

14.11 REMOVE, REPLACE, AND ALIGN POWERTRAIN MOUNTS

Faulty powertrain (engine and transmission) mounts are replaced by lifting the engine and/or transmission slightly to remove the weight, and then removing the mounting bolts. The old mount is then removed and the new mount is installed.

 REAL WORLD FIX

The 1992 Dodge Caravan (115,000 miles) came into the shop in limp-in mode. A scan tool check shows code 22, a 2–4 pressure switch circuit. A bad 2–4 driver in the EATX controller was found, so the EATX controller was replaced. This fixed the electronic problem, but now the van starts in second gear.

FIX

Following advice, the technician checked the valve body and found a badly worn solenoid switching valve. A valve body replacement fixed this vehicle.

 REAL WORLD FIX

The 1994 Volkswagen (135,000 miles) came in for service. This included a fluid change, and the shop was careful to use the correct fluid. The vehicle returned with harsh shifts. A scan tool check revealed no electronic faults.

FIX

Following advice that this transmission is sensitive to contaminants, the technician checked the fluid pressure and found it to be high. The technician removed the EPC solenoid, tested it, and cleaned it to remove contaminants. Cleaning the EPC solenoid fixed this vehicle.

 REAL WORLD FIX

The 2002 Ford Ranger (104,000 km) came in with no second gear. A scan tool check reveals DTC P0733: gear 3 incorrect ratio. The technician thought this fault could be caused by a bad intermediate band, but was unsure of this diagnosis and therefore requested advice.

FIX

Following advice, the pan was dropped, and the valve body gaskets were checked. A faulty gasket was found and replaced, and this fixed the problem. The band adjustment was also checked and found to be slightly out of adjustment.

The mount for an RWD transmission is aligned by the bolts through slotted holes in the mount. Alignment is required so the engine, transmission, and exhaust system do not contact the frame or body. A FWD transaxle must be aligned to the two front driveshafts. The alignment check is accomplished by completely compressing both inboard CV joints, and measuring the distance between the joint and the transaxle. ● **SEE FIGURE 14–34**. The position of the transaxle is then adjusted so that both distances are equal. Adjustment is accomplished by loosening the mounts and sliding the engine and transaxle sideways.

FIGURE 14–34 The enlarged views of the inner CV joints show that the engine and transaxle are misaligned; they should be moved toward the right.

 REAL WORLD FIX

A 2000 F350 Ford pickup (124,700 miles) works well until it backs up. Then it slips in all forward gears. After the vehicle is parked and the transmission cools down, it returns to normal operation until the next operation in reverse. There are no DTCs.

FIX

The technician removed the pan and checked the valve body bolts, and they were loose. After replacing the valve body gaskets and tightening the bolts to the correct torque, the problem was fixed.

 REAL WORLD FIX

The 1999 Ford Taurus (42,000 miles) came in with a flashing MIL (no O/D) and an overdrive that was not working. A scan tool check shows two DTCs: P0761, shift solenoid C performance/stuck; and P0734, incorrect gear ratio 4. The shift solenoids check out fine, and a visual check of the valve body revealed no problems.

FIX

The technician checked the overdrive servo and found a torn piston seal. Replacement of the servo piston fixed this problem.

14.12 EXTENSION HOUSING SEAL AND BUSHING SERVICE

The extension housing seal and bushing can be removed and replaced with the transmission in the vehicle. In some cases the entire extension housing is removed for bearing, seal, governor, speedometer gear, or park mechanism service. A similar procedure is used to R&R the output shaft seal and bushing of a transaxle.

A faulty seal can be removed using a special puller that fits over the output shaft and into the seal. It can also be removed using a slide hammer and self-tapping screw or sharp chisel and hammer. Be careful to not damage the seal bore. A special puller and installation tool is usually required for on-vehicle bushing replacement.

To remove and replace a transmission extension housing seal, *you should:*

1. Raise and support the vehicle on a hoist that allows access to the transmission and driveshaft.

2. Place **alignment marks** on the rear universal joint and rear-axle pinion flange.

3. Disconnect the driveshaft from the rear axle. ● **SEE FIGURE 14–35**. Do not let the driveshaft hang from the transmission; either remove it completely or support it

 REAL WORLD FIX

The 1993 Oldsmobile Ninety-Eight (195,000 km) has a severe driveline clunk. The engine/ transmission mounts along with the upper dog bone mount were replaced. This cured the problem for about a week, but the clunk came back.

FIX

Following advice, the technician checked the cradle mount bushing and found that the two rear bushings had failed. Replacement of these bushings fixed this problem.

 TECH TIP

ATF will begin leaking out of the driveshaft opening. You should either raise the rear of the vehicle enough to stop the flow or place a container to catch the flow. A **stop-off tool** or old U-joint slip yoke can be used to stop the fluid leak. ● **SEE FIGURE 14–36**.

FIGURE 14–35 It is a good practice to place alignment marks on the axle flange and rear U-joint so they can be installed in the same position.

(a)

(b)

FIGURE 14–36 (a) This set of plugs is used to close transmission driveshaft openings. (b) A different set of plugs is used for FWD transaxles. (*Courtesy of ATEC Trans-Tool and Cleaning Systems*)

FIGURE 14–37 This seal is being removed using an old screwdriver. A chisel is a better tool for this. (*Courtesy of Chrysler Corporation*)

FIGURE 14–38 Several styles of pullers are available to remove the rear bushing with the transmission in the vehicle. (*Courtesy of OTC*)

until removal. Check the driveshaft slip yoke for wear at the seal and bushing surfaces.

4. Pull or pry out the rear seal using a suitable tool. ● **SEE FIGURE 14–37**.

5. If necessary, remove the rear bushing using a suitable tool. ● **SEE FIGURE 14–38**.

6. If the bushing is removed, use a suitable tool to drive the new bushing completely into place. ● **SEE FIGURE 14–39**.

7. Use a correctly sized driver to drive the new seal into place. If the replacement seal does not have an outer sealant coating, a film of sealant should be spread around the outer surface of the seal case.

FIGURE 14–39 This tool will hold the bushing so it can be easily driven into place using a hammer. (*Courtesy of OTC*)

FIGURE 14–40 The cavity of this seal has been filled with petroleum jelly to hold the garter spring in position during installation. TransJel™ and petroleum jelly will melt and mix with ATF when the transmission gets hot.

 TECH TIP

When driving a seal into place, it is possible for the seal's garter spring to pop out of position. Some technicians fill the seal cavity with petroleum jelly to help hold the spring in position. ● **SEE FIGURE 14–40**.

8. Lubricate the seal lip and driveshaft slip yoke with ATF. Slide the yoke into place in the transmission. Align your index marks, connect the universal joint to the rear axle flange, and tighten the retaining bolts to the correct torque.

9. Check and correct the transmission fluid if necessary.

The procedure for removing a FWD driveshaft varies with vehicle makes and models. Service information should be consulted for the proper procedure. A generic procedure is described in Section 15.4.2. Once the driveshaft has been removed, seal replacement is essentially a process of removing the old seal and installing the new one.

14.13 EXTENSION HOUSING REMOVAL, RWD TRANSMISSION

The extension housing is removable on most RWD transmissions. Depending on the transmission, extension housing removal allows replacement of the extension housing gasket, seal, and bushing. The governor, speedometer gear, and park mechanism are also accessible for service with the extension housing removed. Parts of the exhaust system may need to be

 REAL WORLD FIX

The 1988 Dodge Caravan (131,000 miles) has a leak at the left axle shaft. The axle can be moved up and down, indicating a worn bearing. The customer could not afford a complete transmission overhaul.

FIX

It was possible to remove the differential by removing the front engine mount and rotating the engine. With the differential removed, the worn carrier bearing was removed and replaced. After adjusting the bearing and installing a new seal, the transaxle was reassembled.

 TECH TIP

A transmission jack is normally used to prevent damage to the transmission pan. If a conventional jack is used, blocks of wood should be placed in a position (under the stronger areas) so the pan will not be dented. Also check the transmission mount at this time.

removed on some vehicles. In the case of the Chrysler 42RH and 46RH transmissions, extension housing removal allows service of the overdrive gear train.

To remove an extension housing, *you should:*

1. Raise the vehicle and remove the driveshaft.

2. Disconnect the speedometer cable/speed sensor connector. If necessary for access, remove the parking brake equalizer and move the cables out of the way.

3. Remove the bolts securing the engine-transmission mount to the transmission support/center cross-member.

4. Place a jack under the transmission pan and lift the transmission just enough to clear the transmission support. ● **SEE FIGURE 14–41**.

5. Remove the transmission support.

6. Place a drip pan under the transmission and lower the transmission just enough to gain access to the upper extension housing bolts.

7. Remove the retaining bolts, the extension housing, and gasket. ● **SEE FIGURE 14–42**. On some transmissions, it is necessary to expand a bearing retainer in order to remove the extension housing.

Extension housing replacement is essentially the reverse of the procedure used to remove it.

To replace an extension housing, *you should:*

1. Clean off all traces of old gasket and sealant from the gasket surfaces.

Item	Torque
A	(35-65 ft lbs.)
B	(10-20 ft lbs.)
C	(200-300 in lbs.)
D	(35-65 ft lbs.)
E	(20-40 ft lbs.)

Bracket

Insulator

4-Wheel Drive

Bracket

Crossmember

Support Bracket

Insulator

Crossmember

2-Wheel Drive

FIGURE 14–41 A transmission jack can be used to support the transmission so the rear transmission mount and cross-member can be removed. (*Courtesy of Chrysler Corporation*)

(a)

(b)

FIGURE 14–42 (a) After the extension housing bolts have been removed, (b) the extension housing can be removed from the transmission.

2. Place the new gasket and extension housing in position. Install the bolts and tighten them to the correct torque. If necessary, petroleum jelly can be used to stick the gasket in position.

3. Raise the transmission, place the transmission support in position, install the bolts, and tighten them to the correct torque.

TECH TIP

When a threaded hole extends through the transmission case, it is recommended that a sealant be placed on the bolt threads.

REAL WORLD FIX

The 1999 Dakota pickup (3,000 miles) will shift into overdrive only once, but not again unless the engine is shut off and restarted. The O/D solenoid was replaced, but this did not help. The wiring checked out fine.

FIX

The technician noted that the scan tool indicated that the transmission was shifting into O/D. The overdrive unit was removed and inspected. A torn inner seal was found and replaced. The transmission now operated normally. The overdrive unit of 42RH and 46RH transmissions is at the rear and can be removed with the transmission in the vehicle.

4. Lower the transmission onto the cross-member as you install the attaching bolts and tighten the bolts to the correct torque. Remove the jack.

5. Reconnect the speedometer cable and the parking brake mechanism if necessary.

6. Reinstall the driveshaft to complete the reassembly.

14.13.1 SPEEDOMETER GEAR REPLACEMENT

Speedometer gear problems show up as a nonoperating speedometer. The cause can be a faulty cable, driven gear, or drive gear. On some transmissions, the speedometer drive gear is a set of teeth cut into the output shaft. On these transmissions, a rough drive gear can sometimes be cured using a three-corner file. Scale on the gear teeth usually can be removed using a wire brush. The other choice is to dismantle the transmission for output shaft replacement. On most transmissions, the drive gear is slid over the output shaft. It can be easily removed and replaced once the extension housing has been removed.

FIGURE 14–43 The speed sensor is driven through a key while a ball is used to drive the speedometer gear; these are positioned between the two retaining rings. Note that a new gasket should be used when the extension housing is replaced. (*Courtesy of Toyota Motor Sales USA, Inc.*)

The speedometer drive gear in some transmissions is held in place by a special clip. To remove the gear, simply push inward on the clip and slide the gear over the clip and down the shaft. ● **SEE FIGURE 14–43**. Other transmissions drive the gear using a steel ball that is halfway into the output shaft and halfway into the gear. To remove the gear, remove the retaining ring and slide the gear off the shaft and drive ball.

Speed sensor diagnosis and repair is described in Chapter 13.

14.13.2 PARK GEAR AND PAWL SERVICE On

some transmissions, the park pawl and spring are mounted in the extension housing, and the park gear is mounted on the output shaft. ● **SEE FIGURE 14–44**. On these units, service such as inspection or replacement of the parking pawl, return spring, or park gear can be done. The operating rod coming from the transmission case can also be checked for correct movement.

14.14 GOVERNOR SERVICE

If the governor is shaft driven, removal of the extension housing allows access to the governor for inspection or disassembly and cleaning. ● **SEE FIGURE 14–45**. Some transmissions use gear-driven governors. These units have a separate cover that

FIGURE 14–44 This park pawl, spring, and shaft are mounted in the extension housing. The park lock rod connects to the manual linkage at the valve body. (*Courtesy of Chrysler Corporation*)

retains the governor in the transmission. ● **SEE FIGURE 14–46**. Removal of this cover allows the governor to be removed.

In-vehicle governor service includes disassembly of the valve and weights to cure sticking, replacement of the assembly, or replacement of the drive gear.

To remove a gear-driven governor, *you should:*

1. Raise and support the vehicle on a hoist.

2. Remove the governor cover attaching bolts or retaining ring and the cover. ● **SEE FIGURE 14–47**. In some cases,

FIGURE 14–45 The governor is mounted onto the governor support/park gear of this Torqueflite transmission. (*Courtesy of Chrysler Corporation*)

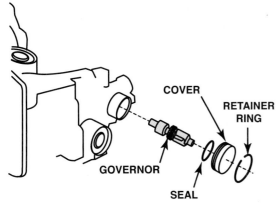

FIGURE 14–46 This gear-driven governor (39) is held in the transmission by its cover (36).

 TECH TIP

1. If there is gear damage, the governor drive and driven gears should be inspected. If there is a problem with low governor pressure, inspect the governor bore in the transmission to make sure it is in good condition. A faulty governor gear will stop governor operation. ● **SEE FIGURE 14–48**. Reaming and installing a bushing in a worn bore is described in Chapter 18.

2. An old connecting rod with a wrist pin hole slightly larger than the governor makes a handy holding fixture. Clamp in a vise and use it to support the governor during service.

(a)

(b)

FIGURE 14–47 (a) After the cover has been removed, (b) this governor can be slid out of its bore.

it is necessary to lower the transmission as described in Section 14.13, steps 1 through 6.

3. Remove the governor. In some cases, it will slide out as the cover is removed; in others, turning the output shaft will move the governor outward.

APPLE-CORED GEAR TOOTH PATTERN

FIGURE 14–48 An apple-cored governor gear can cause erratic or no governor operation. This is usually caused by a rough or damaged drive gear or a governor that is trying to seize in the bore.

FIGURE 14–49 This governor cover is a force-fit. An old C6 servo cover is the right size to use as a driving tool for a THM 350 governor cover.

REAL WORLD FIX

The 1993 Mitsubishi Montero (240,000 miles) starts out in second gear after coming to a stop. It will start in first if you shift to M-1. The governor and valve body were replaced, and the transmission shifted properly for two stops before the second-gear starts began again.

FIX

The technician checked the new governor and found a stuck valve. Inspection also found a faulty oil screen. Replacing the filter screen and cleaning the governor solved this problem.

To replace a gear-driven governor, *you should*:

1. Slide the governor into position in its bore. Some governors use a seal ring at one end; make sure this seal is in good condition before installing.

(a)

Governor Support and Parking Gear

Snap Rings

Snap Ring

Governor Body

Bolts (4)

Lock Straps

(b)

FIGURE 14–50 (a) This speed sensor rotor (90) is held in place by a retaining ring and is driven by a key (91) in the output shaft. (b) Some governors use a pin that passes through the output shaft to connect the weight to the valve. (*Courtesy of Chrysler Corporation*)

2. Install a new gasket or O-ring for the governor cover and place the cover in position. In cases where the cover slides into the transmission and O-ring, wet the O-ring with ATF and carefully tap the cover into place using a brass drift or suitable driver. ● **SEE FIGURE 14–49.**

3. Install the retaining ring or bolts. If bolts are used, tighten them to the correct torque.

4. Check and adjust the fluid level.

14.14.1 GOVERNOR DISASSEMBLY A shaft-driven governor usually consists of the governor body, valve(s), weight(s), support, and sometimes a spring or shaft/pin to connect the weight to the valve. ● **SEE FIGURE 14–50.** Governor service includes operations such as disassembly, cleaning, inspection to ensure the valve(s) and weight(s) move freely, and reassembly. It should be noted that some transmissions use a gasket between the governor body and support. On units where the body fits completely around the output shaft, it is good practice to tighten the body-to-support bolts after the two have been placed onto the output shaft.

A gear-driven governor can also be disassembled for service or replacement of the drive gear. ● **SEE FIGURE 14–51**. Correct movement of the valve can be checked by holding the governor with the gear end upward and squeezing and releasing the weights. ● **SEE FIGURE 14–52**.

To disassemble a gear-driven governor, *you should:*

1. Cut the retaining pins and remove the thrust cap, weights, springs, and valve. ● **SEE FIGURE 14–53**.

2. Support the governor and drive out the gear retaining pin. ● **SEE FIGURE 14–54**.

3. Support the governor using two 7/64-in. (2.7-mm) plates positioned in the exhaust slots and press the gear off the sleeve.

To reassemble a gear-driven governor, *you should:*

1. Support the governor as just described and press the new gear completely into position.

2. Drill a new hole, 1/8 in. (3.17 mm) in diameter, through the new gear and the sleeve. This new hole should be at a right (90-degree) angle to the original hole.

FIGURE 14–51 A typical early General Motors governor that has been disassembled for cleaning or repair.

REAL WORLD FIX

The 1993 Nissan Sentra would not shift out of first gear; reverse was fine. Inspection of the pan shows a black film with no sign of burning or varnish. The TV cable was adjusted properly and seems to operate the valve.

FIX

The technician removed the governor cover and found that the plastic governor gear was stripped. The replacement (OE) governor came with a metal gear. Replacement of the governor fixed this problem.

(a)   (b)

FIGURE 14–52 (a) With the governor weights fully extended, there should be a minimum opening of 0.020 in. at the entry port. (b) With the weights fully inward, there should be a minimum opening of 0.020 in. at the exhaust port.

FIGURE 14–53 The pins are cut so this governor can be disassembled.

FIGURE 14–54 A governor gear can be replaced after driving out the retaining pin. Note the old connecting rod being used as a support fixture.

3. Support the governor and install a new retaining pin. Stake both ends of the retaining pin hole to prevent the pin from coming out.

4. Wash the assembly thoroughly in solvent and air dry.

5. Install the valve, weights, springs, and thrust cap; position new retaining pins in place; and crimp both ends of the pins.

Gear-driven governors that use check balls in place of a spool valve should be carefully inspected for missing check balls, damaged springs, a blocked oil passage, binding weights, or a damaged seal.

SUMMARY

1. Many transmission problems can be repaired without removing the transmission from the vehicle.

2. The pan should be removed and its contents carefully checked before removing a transmission from a vehicle.

3. Components that can be serviced without removing the transmission include linkage adjustment and repair, seal replacement, governor service and replacement, valve body repair, and transmission mounts, to name a few.

4. After making any repair, carefully check your work and road test the vehicle for proper operation.

REVIEW QUESTIONS

1. The replacement of the manual linkage cable or the throttle cable is always followed by a cable _____.

2. Shift linkage _____ is a safety mechanism that prevents a vehicle from being shifted out of park unless the key is in the ignition and the brake is applied.

3. To prevent damage to a seal during installation, a _____ driver should be used.

4. A handy trick to keep a seal spring from coming out on installation is to fill the recess with _____ _____.

5. Thread damage can be caused by using a bolt that is _____ _____ or _____ _____.

6. When removing a cooler line, a _____ wrench must be used.

7. It is important that the _____ of each bolt be noted as a valve body is removed.

8. A special _____ and _____ tool is usually required for on-vehicle bushing replacement.

9. A governor can be serviced by carefully _____, cleaning the parts, and _____.

10. The actual procedures of removal and replacement of various transmission components varies between manufacturers. Always check the _____ manual if in doubt about a service procedure.

1. Technician A says that a faulty governor can be repaired with the transmission in the car. Technician B agrees, but says that gear-driven governors require removal of the extension housing. Who is correct?
   a. Technician A
   b. Technician B
   c. Both Technicians A and B
   d. Neither Technician A nor B

2. Which of these operations cannot usually be done with the transmission in the car?
   a. Valve body removal and replacement
   b. Manual shift linkage seal replacement
   c. Torque converter seal replacement
   d. Vacuum modulator replacement

3. Technician A says that a seal can be pried out of a bore using a sharp chisel. Technician B says that smaller metal-backed seals can often be driven into place using a standard socket. Who is correct?
   a. Technician A
   b. Technician B
   c. Both Technicians A and B
   d. Neither Technician A nor B

4. Technician A says that a metal-backed seal has to seal against two surfaces, the housing bore and shaft. Technician B says that a sealing lip is used to seal the backing to the housing bore. Who is correct?
   a. Technician A
   b. Technician B
   c. Both Technicians A and B
   d. Neither Technician A nor B

5. Technician A says that a new seal will be ruined if the lip is cut during installation. Technician B says that the seal lip should be lubricated with petroleum jelly or ATF before installing. Who is correct?
   a. Technician A
   b. Technician B
   c. Both Technicians A and B
   d. Neither Technician A nor B

6. Technician A says that all throttle/kickdown linkages pass into the case through a metal-backed lip seal. Technician B says that all the cable or rods connect to a lever on the outside of the case. Who is correct?
   a. Technician A
   b. Technician B
   c. Both Technicians A and B
   d. Neither Technician A nor B

7. Technician A says that stripped threads in an aluminum case can be repaired by installing a thread insert. Technician B says that a 1/4-in. bolt should have at least 3/8 in. of thread contact. Who is correct?
   a. Technician A
   b. Technician B
   c. Both Technicians A and B
   d. Neither Technician A nor B

8. Technician A says that the best repair for a kinked, leaky cooler line is to cut out the damaged section and replace it with copper tubing. Technician B says that you should always use two wrenches to loosen a tube nut. Who is correct?
   a. Technician A
   b. Technician B
   c. Both Technicians A and B
   d. Neither Technician A nor B

9. Technician A says that you need to be careful not to lose any of the check balls when you remove a valve body. Technician B says that a transmission must be upside down before removing the valve body. Who is correct?
   a. Technician A
   b. Technician B
   c. Both Technicians A and B
   d. Neither Technician A nor B

10. Some valve bodies have a spring pressure from a _____ that will move them when the bolts are loosened.
    a. Servo or an accumulator
    b. Servo or a relief valve
    c. Shift valves or a servo
    d. Pump relief valve or an accumulator

11. Technician A says that you should carefully place the bolts with the correct length into the proper holes as a valve body is replaced. Technician B says that the valve body bolts should always be carefully torqued. Who is correct?
    a. Technician A
    b. Technician B
    c. Both Technicians A and B
    d. Neither Technician A nor B

12. Technician A says that all servo covers are held in place by a group of three or four bolts. Technician B says that many servos contain a spring that must be kept compressed while the cover is removed. Who is correct?
    a. Technician A
    b. Technician B
    c. Both Technicians A and B
    d. Neither Technician A nor B

13. Which of the following is not a reason for removing an extension housing on a General Motors RWD vehicle?
    a. Speedometer driven-gear replacement
    b. Governor replacement
    c. Park pawl or spring replacement
    d. Extension housing bushing replacement

14. Technician A says that you need to lift the transmission slightly in order to remove the rear mount and extension housing. Technician B says that all transmissions use a paper gasket between the extension housing and case. Who is correct?
    a. Technician A
    b. Technician B
    c. Both Technicians A and B
    d. Neither Technician A nor B

15. Technician A says that a faulty governor gear can keep a transmission from upshifting. Technician B says that it is possible to disassemble a governor so it can be thoroughly cleaned and repaired. Who is correct?
    a. Technician A
    b. Technician B
    c. Both Technicians A and B
    d. Neither Technician A nor B

TRANSMISSION/ TRANSAXLE REMOVAL AND REPLACEMENT

OBJECTIVES: **After studying Chapter 15, the reader will be able to:** • Remove an automatic transmission or transaxle. • Replace/install an automatic transmission or transaxle. • Complete the ASE tasks related to transmission/transaxle removal and replacement.

KEY TERMS: Alignment dowels 382 • Circlip 387 • Engine support 384 • Flywheel turner 381 • Match/index marks 381 • Retaining bracket 383

15.1 INTRODUCTION

A badly worn or damaged transmission is removed from the vehicle for repair, replacement, or a complete overhaul. The repairs can be for specific problems such as a noisy gear set, worn-out band, or leaking front seal. A faulty transmission with considerable mileage, damage, or wear is a candidate for overhaul or replacement.

When choosing between overhaul or replacement, the following should be considered.

- Cost of overhaul (parts and labor)
- Skill of the technician
- Availability of special tools
- Availability of the needed parts
- Cost of the replacement transmission
- Availability of the replacement transmission

Many shops install remanufactured transmissions because they are often less expensive than rebuilding or updating the original transmission.

The California Bureau of Automotive Repair (BAR) regulations require that if a transmission is "exchanged," a descriptive term such as *new, used, rebuilt, remanufactured, reconditioned,* or *overhauled* shall accompany the exchange.

The transmission in a rear-wheel-drive (RWD) vehicle can be removed without removing the engine. In some vehicles, the engine will balance and remain in place on its mounts. In other vehicles, the engine should be supported to prevent damage to the engine or surrounding components. The engine must be supported when the transaxle is removed from a front-wheel-drive (FWD) vehicle (see Figure 15–10). This is especially true if the front cradle is removed.

The torque converter is removed with the transmission. Leaving the converter in the transmission helps prevent a fluid spill

REAL WORLD FIX

The 1997 Dodge Caravan (123,000 miles) transmission was bucking and slipping under a load. A scan tool check revealed no DTCs. A remanufactured transmission was installed, but this did not help. A new transmission controller was installed, but this did not help.

FIX

Following advice, the technician removed the flexplate so it could be thoroughly inspected. The flexplate was checked visually when the transmission was replaced, but this vehicle has a large washer that hides the inner portion. The flexplate appeared fine, but the center was broken, allowing the outer portion to rotate. A new flexplate fixed this problem. The technician recommendation: When replacing the transmission on this vehicle, remove the flexplate so it can be completely inspected.

as the transmission is removed from the engine. The torque converter must be installed into the transmission during replacement to ensure proper alignment with the pump, stator, and input shaft.

15.2 TRANSMISSION REMOVAL

Transmission removal varies between vehicle makes and models. Transmissions and transaxles have slightly different removal procedures. The procedures outlined here are very general and

The 1971 Chevrolet pickup (200,000 miles) had an engine swap; the 400-cu. in. engine was replaced with a 350-cu. in. engine. The vehicle now has a bad vibration at speeds over 2500 RPM. The technician then remembered that the 400-cu. in. engine is externally balanced, and the 350-cu. in. engine is balanced internally.

FIX

Replacement of the flexplate with the proper part solved this problem.

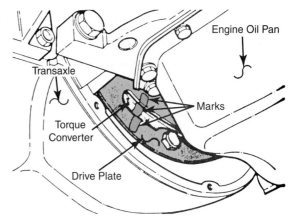

FIGURE 15–2 The converter should be disconnected from the flexplate by removing the flexplate-to-converter bolts. (*Courtesy of Chrysler Corporation*)

FIGURE 15–1 The external wiring harness is disconnected from the transmission speed sensor (A and B) and any other connections. (*Courtesy of Chrysler Corporation*)

FIGURE 15–3 (a) A flywheel turner can be used to turn the flywheel, or (b) hold it while the converter bolts are loosened. (*Courtesy of Snap-on Tools*)

are meant to provide an overview of what is involved. Service information should be consulted to determine the exact procedure for a particular vehicle.

To remove an RWD transmission, *you should:*

1. Open the hood, and disconnect the battery ground cable. Remove the dipstick and throttle valve (TV) linkage if necessary.

2. Raise and support the vehicle on a hoist that allows access to the transmission and driveshaft. Remove the exhaust system as needed to gain access to the transmission and transmission support.

3. Remove the transmission pan and drain the fluid as described in Chapter 11. Be sure to check the pan for debris that would indicate internal problems. Replace the pan and install three or four bolts to hold it in place.

4. Disconnect the electrical connectors. ● **SEE FIGURE 15–1**. The harness on some vehicles is disconnected and removed with the transmission. Disconnect the fluid fill tube if necessary.

5. Remove the torque converter dust cover. Place **match/ index marks** on the converter and flywheel/flexplate/drive plate. Remove the converter-to-flexplate bolts. ● **SEE FIGURE 15–2**. You will need to turn the engine to get access to all of the bolts. The engine can be turned using a **flywheel turner** or a wrench on the vibration damper bolt (at the front of the crankshaft). ● **SEE FIGURE 15–3**. Slide the converter into the transmission as far as possible. It may be necessary to remove the starter on some vehicles.

6. Remove the driveshaft as described in Section 15.4.1.

7. Disconnect the manual shift linkage, TV linkage (if necessary), speed sensor connection or speedometer cable, and fluid cooler lines. ● **SEE FIGURE 15–4**.

8. Support the transmission using a transmission jack. The jack should be positioned so it does not damage the pan. Attach the safety chain around the transmission. Remove the bolts securing the transmission mount to either the transmission or to the cross member.

9. Raise the transmission and remove the center crossmember/transmission support. ● **SEE FIGURE 15–5**.

10. Lower the transmission just enough to gain access to the upper transmission-to-engine bolts and remove these bolts. ● **SEE FIGURE 15–6**. It may be necessary to install an engine support fixture on some vehicles. ● **SEE FIGURE 15–7**.

11. Pull the transmission back far enough to clear the converter housing **alignment dowels** and converter pilot, and to lower the transmission and converter out of the vehicle.

TECH TIP

1. All four fingers/adapters of the jack support pad must make good contact with the transmission. Long or adjustable adapters are available from the jack manufacturers; some technicians have made special adapters for particular transmissions.
2. To stop ATF from leaking out of the lines, compress foam ear plugs and insert them into the cooler lines.

FIGURE 15–4 Position a drain pan and disconnect the cooler lines. Do not bend them any more than needed to remove the transmission. (*Courtesy of Chrysler Corporation*)

FIGURE 15–6 Many transmissions can be lowered enough to remove the upper transmission-to-engine bolt(s).

(a)

(b)

FIGURE 15–5 A transmission jack is positioned under the transmission pan so it can lift the transmission to allow removal of the mount and cross member. (a) A high lift jack is used when the vehicle is on a lift; (b) a low lift jack is used when the vehicle is supported on jack stands. (*Courtesy of OTC*)

FIGURE 15–7 The engine support fixture is supporting the rear of the engine while the transmission and converter are removed. (*Courtesy of Chrysler Corporation*)

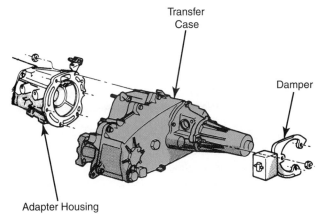

FIGURE 15–8 The transfer case is removed before the transmission is removed from most 4WD vehicles. (*Courtesy of Chrysler Corporation*)

 REAL WORLD FIX

The engine of the 1999 Subaru Forester (123,000 miles) was removed and replaced to repair the head gaskets. When the vehicle was started, the transmission temperature light flashed on and off. A check revealed a code P0748. An inspection showed all the transmission wiring to be correct, with correct internal resistance at the solenoid connectors.

FIX

The technician checked the transmission pan, and discovered that the jack, used under the transmission pan to lift the engine, had bent the pan and damaged a solenoid and connector. Replacement of the damaged solenoid fixed this problem.

 TECH TIP

1. When removing the transmission from a 4WD vehicle, it is often recommended to remove the transfer case before removing the transmission. ● **SEE FIGURE 15–8.**
2. There is a possibility that the converter can slide off its splines and fall as the transmission is being removed. It is heavy and can cause injury or damage if it falls. Some manufacturers recommend installing a converter **retaining bracket.** ● **SEE FIGURE 15–9.** Some technicians run a bungee cord or a piece of mechanics wire to hold it in place.

(a)

(b)

FIGURE 15–9 After disconnecting the torque converter from the flexplate, slide it into the transmission and (a) install a retainer or (b) run a wire or bungee cord across the front of the transmission.

(a)

(b)

FIGURE 15–10 (a) An engine support bar has been installed on this vehicle and adjusted to lift the engine slightly. (b) These fixtures are designed to fit various FWD vehicles. (*Figure (a) Courtesy of ATEC Trans-Tool and Cleaning Systems; (b) Courtesy of Chrysler Corporation*)

15.3 TRANSAXLE REMOVAL

The engine should always be supported when removing a transaxle. Special **engine support** fixtures are available that provide a safe, secure support without damaging the vehicle. These tools are usually placed on the fender flanges and radiator support.

The driveshafts are secured to the transaxle in different ways. Different removal methods are required to remove them, as described in the next section. Some front suspension disassembly is also required; therefore, vehicle service information should be checked to determine what may be required. In some cases, only the right driveshaft will need to be removed. The other can be disconnected from the transaxle as the transaxle is removed from the engine.

To remove a transaxle, *you should:*

1. Open the hood, and disconnect the battery ground cable. Disconnect the cooler lines, shift linkage, TV linkage, speed sensor connector or speedometer cable, and any accessible electrical connectors.

Loosen Hub
Nut (Vehicle
On Floor And
Brakes Applied)

FIGURE 15–11 Before removing an FWD driveshaft, the front hub nut must be removed. It is usually necessary to have the tire on the floor and the brakes applied to loosen it. (*Courtesy of Chrysler Corporation*)

 TECH TIP

Some shops have made support fixtures using a length of pipe or square tubing and a piece of threaded rod. A pair of thick phone books or catalogs can be placed on the fenders to prevent damage.

 TECH TIP

A special tool or a short section of heater hose may be required with some transaxles to hold the differential pinion gears from rotating out of position when both driveshafts are removed.

2. Install an engine support fixture and adjust it to support the engine's weight. ● **SEE FIGURE 15–10.**

3. Remove any accessible transaxle-to-engine bolts.

4. Loosen the front hub nuts. The front wheels should remain on the ground with the parking brake applied, and the transmission should be in park while loosening the lug nuts. ● **SEE FIGURE 15–11.**

5. Raise and support the vehicle so you have access to the transaxle and front suspension.

6. Remove the pan, and drain the fluid as described in Chapter 11. Be sure to check the pan for debris that would indicate internal problems. Replace the pan and install only three or four bolts to hold it in place.

7. Remove the driveshaft(s). ● **SEE FIGURE 15–12.**

(a)

(b)

FIGURE 15–12 (a) A special tool is attached to the slide hammer so that (b) the slide hammer can be used to remove the driveshaft from a transaxle. (*Courtesy of Kent-Moore*)

FIGURE 15–13 A transmission jack has been positioned under the pan to support the transaxle as it is removed. (*Courtesy of Chrysler Corporation*)

8. Remove the torque converter cover/dust shield, place index marks on the converter and flexplate, and remove the converter-to-flexplate bolts. Slide the converter into the transaxle.

9. Disconnect any remaining oil cooler lines, shift linkage, speedometer cable, or electrical connectors. It may be necessary to remove the starter on some vehicles.

10. Place a suitable transmission jack under the transaxle, adjust it to support the transaxle, and attach the safety chain. ● **SEE FIGURE 15–13**.

11. Remove any transaxle support mounts. On some vehicles, it is necessary to remove the engine cradle. ● **SEE FIGURE 15–14**.

12. Remove any remaining transaxle-to-engine bolts.

13. Pull the transaxle away from the engine far enough to clear the engine-to-transaxle alignment dowels and torque converter pilot, and lower the transaxle and converter from the vehicle.

FIGURE 15–14 The lower ball joint (arrow) is disconnected to allow the driveshaft to be removed. Some vehicles require the engine transaxle support/cross member (lower right) to be removed to allow transaxle removal.

TECH TIP

FWD vehicles should not be moved with weight on the front wheels while the driveshafts are removed. Special dollies are available to support the front end so the vehicle can be moved. ● **SEE FIGURE 15–15**.

FIGURE 15–15 A support dollie can be positioned under the front of a FWD vehicle so it can be easily moved while the driveshafts are out. (*Courtesy of The Mighty Mover*)

FIGURE 15–16 An old V-belt can be looped around the exhaust pipe to support the driveshaft. (*Courtesy of Chrysler Corporation*)

FIGURE 15–18 Before removal, make sure there are index marks at the rear U-joint so the shaft can be replaced in its original position. An old screwdriver is being used to scratch a mark onto the U-joint cross. (*Courtesy of Chrysler Corporation*)

(a)

(b)

FIGURE 15–17 (a) An old glove has been slid over this driveshaft to hold the bearing cups in position. (b) Tape can be used for the same purpose.

15.4 DRIVESHAFT REMOVAL AND REPLACEMENT

As a driveshaft is removed, technicians are advised to not allow it to hang from one end, bending a still-connected U-joint or CV joint to its limit. If necessary, support the shaft using mechanic's wire or an old V-belt until both joints can be disconnected. ● **SEE FIGURE 15–16**.

15.4.1 RWD DRIVESHAFT REMOVAL AND REPLACEMENT
Most driveshaft slip joint splines float on the transmission mainshaft rear bushing. When the driveshaft is removed, it will slide out of the transmission, and lubricant will run out of the unsealed opening. To prevent leakage, some technicians raise the vehicle so that the back end is lifted higher than the front. Many technicians use a stop-off tool or an old slip yoke to plug the opening (see Figure 14–36). A plastic bag and rubber band can also be used. When replacing a driveshaft, be sure to put some transmission oil on the slip yoke to lubricate the seal.

 TECH TIP

1. RWD driveshafts with damaged tubes or worn, dry, or tight U-joints and FWD driveshafts with torn boots or worn, dry, or tight CV joints should be repaired before replacement.
2. Many technicians will either wrap tape around the joint or slide a used glove over the U-joint and shaft to hold the bearing cups in place. ● **SEE FIGURE 15–17**.

To remove a RWD driveshaft, you should:

1. Raise and securely support the vehicle so the driveshaft is free to turn.

2. Place index marks at the rear U-joint flange and rear U-joint so the shaft can be replaced in the original position. ● **SEE FIGURE 15–18.**

3. Remove the bolts securing the rear U-joint to the flange, being ready for the two bearing cups to fall off the U-joint cross.

4. Slide the slip yoke out of the transmission, plug the back of the transmission, and remove the driveshaft from the vehicle.

To replace a RWD driveshaft, you should:

1. Most RWD driveshafts are replaced by first sliding the slip yoke into the transmission.

2. Then align the index marks as the rear U-joint is connected to the rear axle companion flange.

3. Tighten the bolts to the correct torque.

4. With the bearing caps held by a U-bolt or strap, make sure that the bearing cups are properly seated inside the locating lugs.

15.4.2 FWD DRIVESHAFT REMOVAL AND REPLACE-MENT

Most FWD driveshafts are held in place at the outer end by the nut securing the outboard CV joint to the front hub. After removing the nut, which is normally very tight, the hub and steering knuckle must be moved outward and off the end of the splined section of the CV joint. This usually requires disassembling part of the suspension system. ● **SEE FIGURE 15–19.** The driveshaft, along with the front hub and bearing, on General

FREQUENTLY ASKED QUESTION

Are All Inboard Joints Retained by a Circlip?

Some inboard joints are bolted to a flange and shaft extending from the differential. Chrysler products from 1981 and earlier retained the CV joint in the differential using a snap ring that must be removed from inside the differential side gear. ● **SEE FIGURE 15–20.**

FREQUENTLY ASKED QUESTION

Why Is a Special Tool Required for Some Differentials?

A problem that can be encountered on some vehicles is that the differential side gears can roll out of position when both CV joints are removed. Normally, the right driveshaft is removed first, then the left shaft is driven out using a special tool, or a 1/4-in. (6.3-mm) rod that is 12 in. (305 mm) long going through the differential. ● **SEE FIGURE 15–21.** This tool, rod, or short hose section is left in the differential to hold the gears in place until one of the driveshafts is replaced.

Motors W series cars (which include the Chevrolet Lumina) can be removed through the steering knuckle; the hub and bearing can then be removed from the outer CV joint if desired.

Inboard joints are usually held into the differential side gears by a **circlip** that usually pops free when enough outward pressure is exerted on it. This style is sometimes called a *plug-in* type of connection.

A FWD vehicle should not be moved while the driveshafts are removed unless the weight is lifted off the front wheels. Damage to the front wheel bearings can result. After the driveshaft is replaced, it may be necessary to check the front end alignment.

The following description is very general. It is recommended that you follow the procedure given in a service manual for the vehicle you are repairing.

To remove an FWD driveshaft, you should:

1. Remove the wheel cover and hub nut locking device, and loosen the front hub nut. ● **SEE FIGURE 15–22.** For nuts that have been staked or bent to lock them in place, merely unscrew the nut. Using an air impact wrench for removal is not recommended.

2. Raise and securely support the vehicle, and remove the front wheel. Finish removing the hub nut. ● **SEE FIGURE 15–23.** If the vehicle has ventilated brake rotors, a pin can be placed into one of the ventilation slots to keep the driveshaft from turning as you remove the nut.

3. Remove the lower ball joint clamp bolt. ● **SEE FIGURE 15–24.** Many manufacturers recommend using a new nut and bolt during reassembly.

4. Pry the lower control arm downward to separate it from the steering knuckle as you pull the steering knuckle outward to separate the front hub from the CV joint. ● **SEE FIGURE 15–25.** It is may be necessary to install a puller to push the CV joint through the hub. ● **SEE FIGURE 15–26.** Never hammer on the end of the CV joint.

   As you separate the hub and CV joint, be careful not to stretch the brake hose. On some vehicles it will be necessary to disconnect the brake caliper and hang it from the strut assembly using a hook or wire. Be ready to support the driveshaft so that it does not drop.

5. The inner CV joint on some vehicles can be removed from the differential with a quick jerk using a prying tool, but do not put excessive force on the transaxle case. An attachment for a slide hammer can be used to jerk the CV joint out of the differential. ● **SEE FIGURE 15–27.** Do not use the driveshaft as a slide hammer.

6. Remove the driveshaft, being careful not to damage the CV joint boots and keeping the shaft horizontal so the plunge joint will not be stressed. ● **SEE FIGURE 15–28.**

To replace an FWD driveshaft, you should: ● **SEE FIGURE 15–29.**

1. Lubricate the seal area on the inboard CV joint. Slide the CV joint completely into the transaxle, being careful not to damage the seal. Test the installation by pulling outward on the CV joint housing; it should not pull free.

(a)

(b)

(c)

(d)

(e)

FIGURE 15–19 The procedure to remove the driveshaft on an FWD vehicle.

FIGURE 15–20 This transaxle has a circlip inside the differential that must be removed before removing the driveshaft. (*Courtesy of Chrysler Corporation*)

FIGURE 15–21 The differential rotator is used to drive the left-side CV joint from this transaxle. It also keeps the differential side gears in alignment. (*Courtesy of OTC*)

FIGURE 15–22 Most hub nuts are very tight, so a long wrench is usually required. The tire must be on the ground and brakes applied to keep it from rotating. (*Courtesy of NEAPCO*)

FIGURE 15–23 With the hub nut loosened and the vehicle raised, the wheel can be removed to allow access to remove the hub nut and other parts. Note the pin to hold the rotor from turning (arrow). (*Courtesy of NEAPCO*)

FIGURE 15–24 On many vehicles, removing the clamp bolt allows the ball joint stud to slide out of the steering knuckle. This allows the steering knuckle to be swung outward far enough for the CV joint splines to slide out of the hub. (*Courtesy of NEAPCO*)

Steering Knuckle

Lower Control Arm

Pry Bar

FIGURE 15–25 A pry bar is being used to force the lower control arm downward far enough to remove the ball joint stud from the steering knuckle. (*Courtesy of Chrysler Corporation*)

(a)

Tool L-4550

(b)

FIGURE 15–27 (a) Most inboard CV joints can be pulled from the transaxle using a slide hammer and special adapter or by prying them out using a pry bar. (b) Some inboard joints are bolted onto a flange at the transaxle. (*Courtesy of Chrysler Corporation*)

(a)   (b)

FIGURE 15–26 (a) This puller is being used to pull the hub outward and off the CV joint splines. (b) The remover is used to push the CV joint through the hub. (*Courtesy of OTC*)

Wear Sleeve

Transaxle Extension

Support Both Joints At Housing

PR2413A

FIGURE 15–28 After the shaft has been disconnected, it should be removed carefully to prevent damaging the CV boots. Support both CV joints and hold the shaft horizontally while carrying it. (*Courtesy of Chrysler Corporation*)

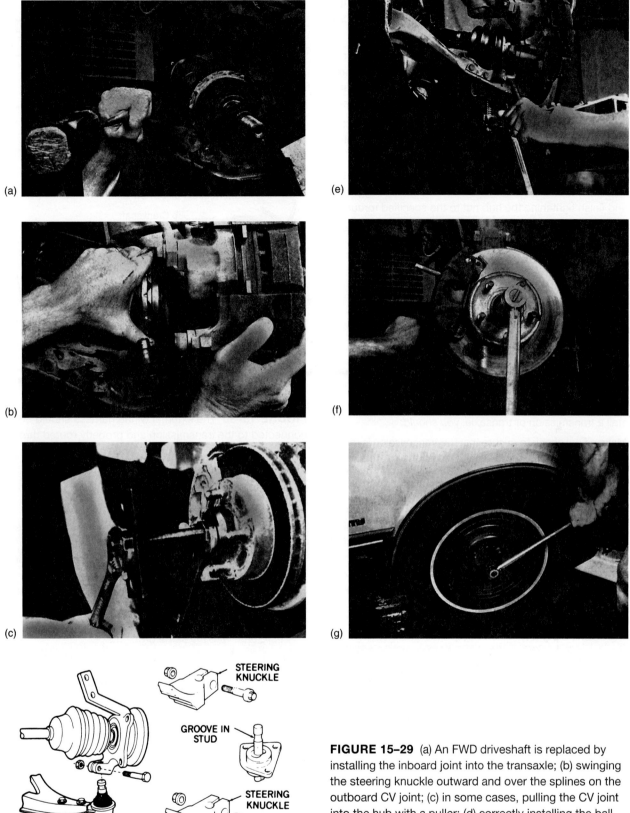

FIGURE 15–29 (a) An FWD driveshaft is replaced by installing the inboard joint into the transaxle; (b) swinging the steering knuckle outward and over the splines on the outboard CV joint; (c) in some cases, pulling the CV joint into the hub with a puller; (d) correctly installing the ball joint stud and retaining bolt; (e) tightening the ball joint retaining bolt; (f) replacing the hub nut; and (g) tightening the nut to the correct torque. (*Figures (a), (b), (c), (e), (f), and (g) Courtesy of NEAPCO; (d) Courtesy of Moog Chassis Parts, a brand of Federal-Mogul Corporation*)

2. Pull the hub and steering knuckle outward as you insert the spline of the outboard CV joint through the hub. Rotate the hub, if necessary, to line up the splines.

3. Thread a new hub nut onto the threads, and tighten the nut just enough to pull the CV joint into place. A special tool is required to pull the CV joint into place on some domestic and imported vehicles; do not use the hub nut for this purpose.

4. Reinstall the lower ball joint using a new bolt where required, and tighten the nut to the correct torque. If the ball joint stud is notched, be sure to align the notch with the clamp hole.

5. Tighten the hub nut to about 50 ft-lb (70 N-m), install the wheel and tire, and lower the vehicle. Set the parking brake, and finish tightening the hub nut to the specified torque.

6. Install the hub nut locking device, raise the vehicle, and check to ensure that the tire rotates freely.

15.5 TRANSMISSION INSTALLATION

Installing a transmission is the reverse of the removal procedure. The last operation in the removal is usually the first step in the installation.

To install a transmission or transaxle, *you should:*

1. Make a final check to ensure that the transmission is ready to be installed, and the wiring harness is in place and all the connectors are clean and properly connected. ● **SEE FIGURE 15–30**.

2. Raise the transmission into position. Watch for wires or hoses that may be damaged as you move the transmission in place. ● **SEE FIGURE 15–31**. Slide the transmission into place against the engine. Something is wrong if it does not go completely into place. Correct this problem before continuing. Never force the transmission up to the engine.

 TECH TIP

1. Before installing the transmission, make sure that the transmission alignment dowels are in place.

2. The proof of correct converter installation is that you should be able to slide the converter forward as it is rotated into alignment with the flexplate. If the converter is jammed in place, it is stacked, and the transmission must be removed so the converter can be aligned and installed correctly. Don't forget to align the converter to the flexplate using the marks you made during removal.

3. As you slide the transmission against the engine, make sure there are no electrical wires, vacuum lines, or other items caught between them. Expensive damage can result.

FIGURE 15–30 The external wiring harness should be connected to the transmission and properly routed through the brackets. (*Courtesy of Chrysler Corporation*)

 REAL WORLD FIX

The 5.7-L engine in the 1995 Suburban was replaced at 85,000 miles with a reputable remanufactured engine. After 7,000 miles, it came back with a knock. Inspection revealed a broken flexplate, which was replaced. It returned again after another 7,000 miles with a knock, and another broken flexplate. A new GM flexplate was installed. Now it has returned a third time with the same problem.

FIX

It was discovered after the transmission was removed that the replacement engine did not come with the alignment dowels, and this omission was overlooked three times. Installation of the alignment dowels and a new flexplate solved this problem.

3. Install the transmission-to-engine bolts and tighten them to the correct torque.

4. Place the transmission supports into position, lower the transmission onto the mounts, and tighten the mounting bolts to the correct torque.

5. Slide the converter forward to align with the flexplate. Install the bolts and tighten them to the correct torque.

Item	Torque
A	27-54 N•m (20-40 ft. lbs.)
B	8-15 N•m (75-130 in. lbs.)
C	3-6 N•m (30-50 in. lbs.)
D	47-88 N•m (35-65 ft. lbs.)

FIGURE 15–31 As the transmission is installed, the converter is aligned and secured to the flexplate; the transmission is aligned and secured to the engine; and all brackets, struts, and other necessary parts will be replaced. (Note that the converter must be installed into the transmission first.) (*Courtesy of Chrysler Corporation*)

 REAL WORLD FIX

The 1992 Explorer (86,000 miles) transmission was just rebuilt, and a rebuilt torque converter was installed. The A4LD transmission worked well on the first test drive, but during a second, early morning drive to check cold operation, the transmission would not upshift. It would only make a whine noise and then quit working. A teardown revealed broken pump gears.

FIX

An ATRA TSB indicated a problem with the A4LD transmission breaking pump gears if the bell housing is warped. Replacement of the bell housing and pump gears fixed this problem.

 TECH TIP

1. Some FWD vehicles will have a vibration problem if the engine is not centered. If no other information is available, compress the inner CV joints and note the amount of clearance to the transaxle case. Move the engine side to side until the clearance is equal before tightening the motor mount bolts.
2. The engine cradle of some FWD vehicles also attaches to the front suspension. Improper installation can adversely affect the wheel alignment. The cradle should be replaced in exactly the same position as it was before removal.

6. Connect the cooler lines and tighten them to the correct torque.
7. Replace the driveshaft(s) and tighten any retaining bolts to the correct torque.
8. Reconnect all linkage and wire connections that were disconnected, making sure they are routed properly. Tighten all retaining bolts to the correct torque.

After installation, the transmission should be filled with the correct amount of ATF and the engine started. If you are unsure of how much ATF is needed, add enough fluid to read slightly high on the dipstick. Adjust the fluid level after starting the engine and operating the transmission in the different gear ranges. Next, complete your transmission overhaul with a road test to ensure proper operation.

The 1988 Volkswagen Jetta (128,000 miles) came in with the transaxle in the trunk to be resealed and installed. After running it, the front seal was leaking so the transaxle was pulled, and a new seal was installed. This did not fix the problem, so another new seal was installed, but the same problem came back.

FIX

The next time the transaxle was removed, the alignment pins were checked; they were missing. Installation of the alignment pins allowed the transaxle to be centered properly and this fixed the problem.

15.6 TRANSAXLE INSTALLATION

Transaxle installation is essentially the same as for a transmission. The major difference is that the transaxle should be centered between the two driveshafts; both of the inner, plunge-type CV joints should have been compressed the same amount (see Section 14.11). Another difference is that the front wheel alignment should be checked on those vehicles that require suspension or cradle removal.

SUMMARY

1. Transmissions are removed to make repairs, for overhaul, or for replacement.

2. The removal and replacement procedures are similar for most transmissions and transaxles.

3. Always check the service information before removing an automatic transmission.

4. Never force the transmission onto the back of the engine during installation.

5. It may be necessary the check the wheel alignment after installing a transaxle.

REVIEW QUESTIONS

1. A special _____ support is used when removing a front-wheel-drive transaxle.

2. A _____ manual should be consulted for the suggested removal and installation procedures for a particular transmission.

3. The first thing removed when removing an RWD transmission from a vehicle is the _____ ground _____.

4. Before unbolting the torque converter, put match marks on the converter and the _____ to aid installation.

5. As the transmission is removed from the vehicle, install a bracket to the _____ _____ to prevent it from sliding out of the transmission.

6. The first thing removed when removing an FWD transmission from a vehicle is the _____ ground _____.

7. To prevent leakage once the driveshaft has been removed from an RWD vehicle, the _____ _____ needs to be plugged.

8. When removing a driveshaft, always put _____ marks on the driveshaft and the differential flange to aid in reassembly.

9. When removing the driveshafts from an FWD vehicle, it is not advisable to let the brake _____ or the _____ hang free.

10. Since the front suspension is removed during removal of an FWD transaxle, it may be necessary to check the _____ of the front end at completion of the job.

11. After the transmission or transaxle is installed in the vehicle, check that the torque converter will rotate freely to ensure that the converter is not _____ into the pump or pump drive and the flexplate.

12. During installation, the transmission should fit easily up against the engine. Never use _____ to connect the transmission to the engine.

13. A _____ converter housing or other serious problem could result if anything is caught between the converter housing and the engine.

14. After the installation of the transmission or transaxle is complete, check the _____ level after shifting the transmission through its gear ranges.

15. After the installation of the transmission or transaxle is complete, the last step is to _____ _____ the vehicle.

1. Technician A says that the torque converter is usually left on the engine when removing a transmission. Technician B says that it is more difficult to remove a transaxle than a transmission. Who is correct?
   a. Technician A
   b. Technician B
   c. Both Technicians A and B
   d. Neither Technician A nor B

2. Technician A says that you should be able to rotate the converter to align the bolt holes with the flexplate after the transmission has been bolted to the engine. Technician B says that a transmission overhaul is not complete until it passes a road test. Who is correct?
   a. Technician A
   b. Technician B
   c. Both Technicians A and B
   d. Neither Technician A nor B

3. Technician A says that the torque converter should be marked for proper installation. Technician B says that the brake hoses are strong enough to support the weight of the calipers. Who is correct?
   a. Technician A
   b. Technician B
   c. Both Technicians A and B
   d. Neither Technician A nor B

4. Technician A says that a special fixture is required to support the engine on FWD cars when the transaxle is removed. Technician B says that it is easier to remove the transaxle than it is to remove an RWD transmission. Who is correct?
   a. Technician A
   b. Technician B
   c. Both Technicians A and B
   d. Neither Technician A nor B

5. Technician A says that it is necessary to shift the transmission through the gears when checking the fluid after installing a transmission. Technician B says that the last thing to connect when installing a transmission is the battery ground cable. Who is correct?
   a. Technician A
   b. Technician B
   c. Both Technicians A and B
   d. Neither Technician A nor B

6. Technician A says that the transmission alignment dowels are not necessary. Technician B says that if the alignment dowels are not installed, a serious vibration or damage could result. Who is correct?
   a. Technician A
   b. Technician B
   c. Both Technicians A and B
   d. Neither Technician A nor B

7. Technician A says that the torque converter should be removed with the transmission. Technician B says that it is easier to leave the torque converter attached to the engine. Who is correct?
   a. Technician A
   b. Technician B
   c. Both Technicians A and B
   d. Neither Technician A nor B

8. Technician A says that when removing the driveshaft on an RWD vehicle, match marks should be made to prevent a vibration after reassembly. Technician B says that the front wheel bearings could be damaged if an FWD vehicle is moved while the driveshafts are removed. Who is correct?
   a. Technician A
   b. Technician B
   c. Both Technicians A and B
   d. Neither Technician A nor B

9. Technician A says that the axle nuts on an FWD car are reusable. Technician B says that the driveshafts on an FWD car are usually removed with a pry bar or special puller. Who is correct?
   a. Technician A
   b. Technician B
   c. Both Technicians A and B
   d. Neither Technician A nor B

10. Technician A says that it is necessary to remove the engine cradle in order to remove the transaxle on some FWD vehicles. Technician B says that it is permissible to let the FWD driveshaft hang down during removal and installation of the transaxle. Who is correct?
    a. Technician A
    b. Technician B
    c. Both Technicians A and B
    d. Neither Technician A nor B

chapter 16

TRANSMISSION OVERHAUL: DISASSEMBLY AND REASSEMBLY

OBJECTIVES: After studying Chapter 16, the reader will be able to: • Describe the automatic transmission overhaul procedures. • Perform the automatic transmission disassembly inspection procedure. • Properly disassemble and reassemble an automatic transmission. • Complete the ASE tasks related to off-vehicle transmission/transaxle repair.

KEY TERMS: Aftermarket 397 • Anticlunk spring 410 • End play 403 • Exchange/used 396 • Hard parts 397 • Overhaul 396 • Rebuild 397 • Remanufactured 396 • Selective 405 • Soft parts 397 • Stacked converter 422 • Teardown 397 • Update 398

16.1 INTRODUCTION

A badly worn or damaged transmission is removed from the vehicle for repair, with essentially four repair choices: (1) Repair or replace the worn/damaged component, (2) **overhaul** the transmission, (3) replace the transmission with an **exchange/used** one, or (4) install a **remanufactured** transmission. An exchange unit is a used unit, usually from a wrecking yard, that is usually sold "as is" or with a very limited guarantee.

When the overhaul is done by a technician working at an automotive repair facility, it will be guaranteed by the shop. If the transmission fails, the shop will be responsible for any needed repairs. As transmissions become more complex and expensive, remanufactured units are gaining in popularity. If these units fail, the remanufacturer is responsible for the repairs. A remanufacturing plant is also better able to update a transmission and make necessary modifications.

16.1.1 OVERHAULED TRANSMISSIONS Most transmission shops are equipped to perform all repairs needed to the vehicle's transmission. Repairing the original transmission ensures that the transmission will be the proper one for the vehicle. The repairs can be for a specific problem such as a noisy gear set, worn band, or leaky front seal. An overhaul implies a **rebuild,** which is generally considered to include the following:

- Transmission teardown or disassembly
- Replacement of all gaskets and seals
- Replacement of all friction materials
- Replacement of worn bushings
- Replacement of the filter and modulator
- Cleaning and inspection of the planetary gears

- Cleaning and inspection of the valve body and all related components
- Cleaning and inspection of the torque converter
- Reassembly with a check of all necessary clearances

Some states have rules and regulations that define what an automatic transmission rebuild or overhaul must include. The California Bureau of Automotive Repair (BAR) states that a rebuilt, remanufactured, reconditioned, or overhauled transmission must include the following:

- Cleaning and inspection of all internal and external parts
- Valve body disassembly, cleaning, and inspection
- Front and intermediate bands that have been replaced with new or relined units
- Replacement of the following parts: lined frictions, internal and external seals, rotating metal sealing rings, gaskets, and organic media filters
- All worn or defective parts repaired or replaced with new, rebuilt, or good parts
- Torque converter inspected or replaced with a new or rebuilt unit

16.1.2 REMANUFACTURED TRANSMISSIONS An alternative to repairing a vehicle's transmission is to install a remanufactured unit. A remanufactured transmission is a unit that has been disassembled, cleaned, inspected, and reassembled using new or like-new parts. It will have any necessary modifications and updates. These units are commonly used by dealerships to repair transmission problems that occur while a vehicle is still under its new-vehicle or extended warranty.

Remanufacturing is done on a production line, with many transmissions of the same model being rebuilt at the same time. The procedure is essentially the same as that described

(a)

(b)

FIGURE 16–1 A remanufacturing assembly line. (a) The valve bodies are moving from left to right as they are being assembled; the computer identifies which parts are to be installed and their location. (b) The transmissions also move along an assembly line; each station has a monitor to show the operation, the parts to be installed, and the special tools to install them. (*Courtesy of Williams Technologies Inc., Div. of Delco Remy International, Inc.*)

in this text, except that each worker does a specific task such as **teardown,** clutch assembly, or valve body assembly. Special tools are at each workstation, so each worker can perform the job in a most efficient manner. As each transmission is assembled, the transmission code moves with the unit so it will be built to the proper specifications. ● **SEE FIGURE 16–1.** Many smaller shops will use remanufactured transmissions when the vehicle's unit is so badly damaged that the cost of the parts comes close to or exceeds the cost of a remanufactured unit. Repairing a transmission in some states means there will be a minimum parts cost to meet the requirements for a **rebuild.** Another reason for choosing a remanufactured unit is that the shop lacks the special tools, service information, or expertise to repair that particular transmission.

16.1.3 TRANSMISSION PARTS
Major transmission components such as the pump, a clutch drum, or a gear set are called **hard parts.** On the other hand, **soft parts** are those normally replaced during an overhaul. These include the gaskets, seals, and friction material.

The parts needed to overhaul a transmission are available from various sources. ● **SEE FIGURE 16–2.** The vehicle manufacturer can supply all parts needed to repair or overhaul a transmission. Soft parts can be purchased from **aftermarket** sources (a supplier other than the vehicle manufacturer). These parts are usually available as individual components or as part of a kit. Kits are available in several forms, and the contents of a kit will vary between suppliers. ● **SEE FIGURE 16–3.**

A kit is more convenient and often less expensive than buying individual parts. A variety of kits are available to fit the needs of the particular job. Some of the kits are as follows:

- **Banner kit**—an overhaul kit plus the friction clutch plates
- **Bearing kit**—all bearings for the transmission

- **Compliance kit**—includes all parts that must be replaced as required for a rebuilt transmission in particular states
- **Deluxe or super kit**—a master kit plus filter, band(s), bushings, modulator, and bonded pistons as required for the transmission
- **Filter kit**—the filter and pan gasket
- **Master kit**—an overhaul kit plus the friction and steel clutch plates
- **Overhaul kit**—all gaskets, O-rings, metal-clad seals, and lip seals
- **Sealing ring kit**—all seals made from Teflon, metal, or other materials
- **Solenoid kit**—shift, PWM, and force motor solenoids, which may include the wiring harness
- **Valve body kit**—additional parts needed for replacing worn valve body parts, including check balls, filters, springs, valves, and other needed parts

New hard parts are generally available only from the manufacturer. Some aftermarket companies specialize in used or rebuilt hard parts.

16.1.4 OVERHAUL PROCEDURE
The overhaul procedure varies between transmissions and transaxles. Each vehicle manufacturer has a recommended repair procedure for its transmissions. Service information should always be followed as you overhaul an automatic transmission. Following a service manual makes the job easier and quicker. It also ensures that important checks and procedures are followed. The repair procedures were developed by experts for that particular transmission. Service information is available in the form

FIGURE 16–2 Aftermarket sources can provide most of the parts needed to repair a transmission as well as supplemental parts and information. (*Courtesy of Slauson Transmission Parts, www.slauson.com*)

	Filter	Rubber Seals	Metal Clad Seals	Seal Rings	Lined Plates	Steel Plates	Bands	Bushings	Gaskets
Rebuilding Kit	x	x	x	x	x	x	x	?	x
Master Overhaul Kit	x	x	x	x	x				x
Gasket And Seal Kit	?	x	?						x

FIGURE 16–3 The soft parts required to rebuild a transmission are available as kits. The contents of a kit will vary with different suppliers.

of printed manuals, CDs, and on the Internet. Service information can be obtained from vehicle manufacturers and aftermarket automotive publishers (Alldata, Chilton's, Identifix, Mitchell, and Motors). Automatic transmission trade organizations such as the Automatic Transmission Rebuilders Association (ATRA) and the Automatic Transmission Service Group (ATSG) provide service information and advice to their members and partners.

The following procedure can be used as a guide for overhauling an automatic transmission.

1. Remove the transmission from the vehicle (see Chapter 15).
2. Remove any heavy deposits of dirt and oil residue.
3. Measure of input shaft end play.
4. Disassemble while making any additional end-play checks.

TECH TIP

1. Many transmissions have gone through a series of improvements after their original introduction. These changes are made to improve the transmission's durability, reliability, and performance. During an overhaul, it is a good practice to **update** the transmission.
2. Remember that the technician who rebuilds a transmission is responsible for the quality of the rebuild. There is no valid excuse for incomplete repairs. As the transmission is assembled, each new or used part should be thoroughly checked to ensure that it will operate correctly.

FIGURE 16–4 These special tools are used when rebuilding a THM 350. (*Courtesy of ATEC Trans-Tool and Cleaning Systems*)

5. Repair subassemblies: pump, valve body, each clutch assembly, each gear set, and the differential in transaxles (described in Chapter 18).

6. Inspect the case, and make any needed repair.

7. Replace worn bushings (described in Chapter 17).

8. Reassemble, including air checks, band adjustments, clearance checks, and end-play adjustments.

9. Inspect the torque converter; replace, rebuild, or service as necessary (described in Chapter 19).

16.2 TRANSMISSION DISASSEMBLY

The disassembly procedure for a transmission varies between makes and models. Special tooling or procedures are often required. ● **SEE FIGURE 16–4.** It is always recommended to consult service information during disassembly. The descriptions given here cover the commonly used procedures and equipment. The disassembly procedure is known as a teardown.

16.2.1 PREDISASSEMBLY CLEANUP
Cleanliness is a must during a transmission overhaul. Many shops steam clean or pressure wash the outside of the transmission as soon as it

FIGURE 16–5 This transmission is being cleaned using a hot, high-pressure washer. A thorough cleaning makes it easier to locate and remove bolts and retaining rings and keeps the work area cleaner.

is removed from the vehicle. ● **SEE FIGURE 16–5.** Precleaning removes all exterior dirt and other debris and helps keep the work area clean. An alternate cleanup method is to use solvent or an engine degreaser with a parts-cleaning brush and scraper.

(a)   (b)

FIGURE 16–6 A transmission-holding fixture (arrows) has been mounted onto this transmission. It will allow the transmission to be rotated to the best working position. The round stem at the left will be slid into a bench fixture.

TECH TIP

1. A clean work area is a must, and intrusion of dirt from outside the transmission can cause a misdiagnosis of the problem. This can result in an incomplete repair. It can also cause plugging of small passages and change precision measurements, leading to an early failure.
2. Some shops use a simple fixture that resembles a three-legged stool; other shops simply use an old transmission case in a rear-side-up position.

Always dispose of hazardous waste following the appropriate disposal procedures and requirements.

After the transmission is disassembled, the individual parts can be cleaned using an approved solvent. For many years technicians used petroleum-based solvent. This solvent type evaporates, releasing harmful hydrocarbons into the atmosphere. These vapors contribute to air-quality problems. The use of cleaning solvent is controlled in areas with serious air-quality problems. In the Los Angeles area, shops are required to use nonpetroleum solvents for parts cleaning. Read the material safety data sheets (MSDS) to learn about any personal health problems and special handling requirements for the cleaning agent being used.

16.2.2 TORQUE CONVERTER REMOVAL The converter is removed from the vehicle with the transmission. It is then removed from the transmission by sliding it out the front of the transmission. Be ready to support its weight because converters are full of fluid and tend to be heavy. Tilt the converter, front downward, as it is removed to reduce the fluid spill. The converter should be either set aside for cleaning and inspection or sent out for rebuilding. Torque converter service is described in Chapter 19. Some transmissions use a turbine shaft O-ring seal, which should be removed at this time.

16.2.3 DISASSEMBLY FIXTURES Automatic transmission disassembly can be fairly messy. Fluid drains out as each hydraulic component is removed or disassembled. Many shops use a teardown bench that has a steel top designed to catch the fluid and drain it into a catch pan. During disassembly, the transmission is placed on the bench and torn down. It is usually placed upside down and rolled over as needed. Some shops use transmission holding fixtures during overhaul. ● **SEE FIGURE 16–6.** Holding fixtures allow the unit to be easily rotated to the best working position, which makes the work faster and easier. When using a holding fixture, a drain pan should be placed under the transmission to catch the dripping fluid.

16.3 PRELIMINARY DISASSEMBLY

The first teardown step is to remove the oil pan, filter, and valve body. Many technicians use the oil pan to store the retaining rings, screws, bolts, and other small parts removed during disassembly. The procedure is to remove the pan, inspect the debris (if it has not been done already), wash the pan in solvent, and air dry it (see Figure 14–25). Next, the filter and gasket are removed and set aside for comparison with the new filter. The valve body is then removed and set aside for cleaning and inspection. ● **SEE FIGURE 16–7.**

FIGURE 16–7 The valve body can be removed after the pan. Some valve bodies have a throttle cable or fluid tubes that need to be disconnected.

TECH TIP

It is recommended to make a simple wiring diagram for electronic transmissions showing the necessary connections needed during assembly.

TECH TIP

1. Many experienced technicians prefer to use hand tools during disassembly. Hand tools enable the technician to feel how tight the bolts were as they are loosened. An air wrench is much faster, but it is very difficult to feel bolt tension. Improperly tightened bolts could have been the cause of the transmission's failure. Using hand tools takes a little longer to complete the repair, but it is an important technique to ensure a thorough, high-quality rebuild.
2. Valve body bolts are often different lengths. Either identify where they belong or leave them in the valve body holes after they are loosened.

Watch for check balls as the valve body is removed, and note their location. Save the valve body gasket (if used) so it can be compared with the replacement gasket. Remove any check balls and screens under the valve body.

Some transmissions use steel tubes to transfer a fluid passage from one location to another. These tubes normally use an O-ring to seal each end and are held in place by a retaining bracket. ● SEE FIGURE 16–8. The tubes will often lift out after the retaining bolt is removed; sometimes it is necessary to pry them out. If a tube does not come loose, check the service information. Some tubes are secured using epoxy and will be damaged if removed.

The valve body of some transmissions can serve as the cover for the accumulator or servo piston(s). Note the position of the piston(s) and spring (if used), and remove them. ● SEE FIGURE 16–9. In other transmissions, a separate cover is used

FIGURE 16–8 Oil tubes/pipes are removed by gently prying upward. Note the block of wood to protect the case. (*Courtesy of Toyota Motor Sales USA, Inc.*)

FIGURE 16–9 (a) This transmission has four accumulators under the valve body. Note the differences in the springs and pistons and remove them. (b) Compressed air can be used to lift the piston out of its bore.

TECH TIP

When prying a tube out of the case, place a piece of wood on the case to prevent damaging the case.

ACCUMULATOR

Accumulator
Plate
Snap Ring

Snap
Ring Pliers

Accumulator
Plate

(a)

(b)

FIGURE 16–10 (a) This accumulator cover retaining ring is being removed using a pair of snap-ring pliers. (b) Retaining rings can be pried out of the groove and bore using a small screwdriver or seal pick (scribe). (*Courtesy of Chrysler Corporation*)

FIGURE 16–11 The punch is passing through a hole in the case to push the retaining ring out of the groove. This allows a seal pick or small screwdriver to pry the retaining ring out.

 REAL WORLD FIX

The 1992 Lincoln Town Car (96,000 miles) had no reverse and the fluid was badly burned. Severe wear became evident during disassembly, so the transmission was rebuilt using many new parts. But when the unit was reinstalled in the car, it had no O/D, delayed reverse engagement, and low pressure (less than 50 PSI). There were no DTCs, and the EPC solenoid checked out okay on the bench. The transmission was torn down and reinspected. No problems were found. The EPC solenoid was replaced, but this did not help.

FIX

Some advice led to a more careful inspection that revealed the 1–2 and 3–4 servo covers had been installed on the wrong bores. The 3–4 cover has a hole in it that caused an internal leak. Replacement of the 1–2 accumulator seals and swapping the covers to the proper place fixed this problem.

 REAL WORLD FIX

The 1992 Plymouth Voyager van (80,000 miles) with an A604 transaxle was rebuilt because the overdrive clutch pack was slipping, and the clutch plates were badly burned. When the unit was reinstalled, it had a ratcheting-type noise, almost a buzz, while operating in forward gears. The proper Chrysler 7176 fluid was used. The solenoid pack was replaced, but this did not help.

FIX

On advice from other technicians, the valve body was removed, and the accumulators were checked. They were installed upside down. Correct positioning of the pistons and springs eliminated the noise problem.

for the accumulator or servo. Each accumulator has its own spring and piston configuration. They may look alike, but there are slight differences. Improper assembly will cause shift timing and quality problems.

Retaining rings are used to hold many parts in the proper position. One style is like a standard snap ring; another looks like a round wire. A handy tool for removing the first style is a thin screwdriver or scribe, which is commonly called a *seal pick.* ● SEE FIGURE 16–10. The second style of ring may have a hole that allows a pin punch to be used to start ring removal. ● SEE FIGURE 16–11. Use caution during servo cover removal because some servos use a strong piston spring. These require a special tool to hold the spring compressed during retainer ring removal and then allow the spring to be safely extended. ● SEE FIGURE 16–12.

On transmissions with gear-driven governors, remove the governor cover and governor.

(a)

(b)

FIGURE 16–12 (a) This accumulator plate/cover is retained by a retaining ring, and the accumulator spring is pushing upward on the cover. (b) With the cover removed, the piston and spring can be removed. (*b is Courtesy of Chrysler Corporation*)

(a)   **(b)**   **(c)**   **(d)**   **(e)**

FIGURE 16–13 The most common styles of retaining rings are (a) external, pin type, (b) internal pin type, (c) plain external, (d) plain internal, and (e) E-clip.

 TECH TIP

Special Notes on Retaining Rings

A retaining ring is commonly used to hold a part in place. It can hold a gear in position on a shaft or a servo cover in a bore. There is a variety of retaining rings; some examples are shown in ● **FIGURE 16–13.** All types come in different sizes as required to fit the shaft or bore diameter.

The two types of retaining rings are external and internal. External rings fit over a shaft and need to be expanded for removal or installation. Internal rings fit into a bore and are contracted or compressed for removal or installation. Many retaining rings can be removed by prying them free with a tool such as a scribe, seal pick, or screwdriver. Snap-ring pliers are often used to remove and install retaining rings; specially designed snap-ring pliers are sometimes required for snap rings that are hard to remove. The correct type and size of snap-ring pliers must be used. ● **SEE FIGURE 16–14.** Once removed, it is recommended that the retaining ring be replaced with a new one.

FIGURE 16–14 Snap-ring pliers for (a) external pin type, (b) internal pin type, and (c–e) three different styles for plain external snap rings. The bottom pliers have jaws that open in a parallel action. (*Courtesy of Snap-On Tools*)

16.3.1 END-PLAY CHECK It is standard practice to measure the input shaft **end play** before removing the pump. End play is the in-and-out movement of the shaft. ● **SEE FIGURE 16–15.** If there is no end play, there will be drag and a possible bind. Too much end play allows misalignment and damage from the excess movement. If the end play is correct, the internal thrust washers are probably in good shape. If the end play is excessive, there is internal wear, which must be corrected during the rebuild.

End play is normally measured using a dial indicator.

To measure input shaft end play, you should:

1. Place the transmission in a vertical position with the input shaft pointing up. Some transmissions require that a

FIGURE 16–15 Input shaft end play is an important check for internal wear in a transmission. Note that a more accurate check is made if the input shaft is vertical. (*Courtesy of Chrysler Corporation*)

FIGURE 16–16 The dial indicator can be attached to the transmission case or pump (top) or to the input shaft (bottom). Moving the input shaft will show the end play on the indicator dial.

special fixture be used to hold the output shaft in during end-play checks.

2. Attach a dial indicator onto the case or front pump, and position the measuring stylus against the end of the input shaft. ● **SEE FIGURE 16–16.** Some units require special tools to lift the turbine shaft and/or to properly position the dial indicator. ● **SEE FIGURE 16–17.**

3. Pull the input shaft upward slightly and then push it inward as far as it will go. Now adjust the indicator to read zero.

FIGURE 16–17 This special tool is used to pull the pump. It can also be attached to the input shaft to allow the shaft to be lifted so end play can be measured.

TECH TIP

To find the average measurement, add the three measurements and divide the result by 3. For example, if the measurements were 0.018, 0.020, and 0.019, add the three measurements (0.057), and divide by 3 for an average measurement of 0.019 in.

TECH TIP

1. The measuring stylus must be parallel to the input shaft. The indicator body should be adjusted to load the stylus about one full needle rotation. ● **SEE FIGURE 16–18.**

2. On some transmissions, the input shaft is not attached and can be easily pulled out of the transmission. On these units, end play is checked by measuring the distance from the end of the stator support to the end of the turbine shaft. End play on some of these units can be measured by prying upward on the gear train.

FIGURE 16–18 (1) A dial indicator should be set up with the indicator stem parallel to the input shaft and the stem is loaded about one revolution of the indicator dial. (2) Move the input shaft completely into the transmission, and (3) rotate the dial to zero the needle. When the input shaft is lifted, the amount of end play can be read on the indicator dial.

TECH TIP

Some transaxles using tapered roller bearings will have no input shaft end play. Transmission end-play specifications will vary and be as little as 0.004 in. (0.102 mm) and as much as 0.91 in. (2.31 mm).

4. On most transmissions, pull up on the input shaft and read the movement on the dial indicator. This is the amount of input shaft end play.

5. Repeat steps 3 and 4 until you get consistent, reliable readings. Then make three more measurements and, if there is a slight difference, average them.

6. Record your reading and compare it to the specification.

Some manufacturers specify gear train end-play checks at the output shaft or other locations. ● **SEE FIGURE 16–19.**

Some transmissions require additional end-play checks. This helps locate excessive wear in specific areas or to determine if the correct selective thrust washers or spacers are being used. For example, a transmission with a center support should have end play on each side of the center support. Manufacturers will specify end-play checks between various components of the gear train. **Selective** washers or snap rings are produced in various sizes. ● **SEE FIGURE 16–20.** This lets the technician select the proper size thrust washer for the best end play or clearance.

FIGURE 16–19 These special tools allow measuring gear train end play so that it can be properly adjusted. (*Courtesy of DaimlerChrysler Corporation*)

SHIM THICKNESS		PART NUMBER
mm	inch	
0.93-1.00	.037-.039	4431662
1.15-1.22	.045-.048	4431663
1.37-1.44	.054-.057	4431664
1.59-1.66	.063-.066	4431665
1.81-1.88	.071-.074	4431666
2.03-2.10	.080-.083	4431667
2.25-2.32	.089-.091	4431668
2.47-2.54	.097-.100	4431669
2.69-2.76	.106-.109	4446670
2.91-2.98	.114-.117	4446671
3.13-3.20	.123-.126	4446672
3.35-3.42	.132-.135	4446601

FIGURE 16–20 This transmission uses 12 different selective thrust plates for the No. 4 position. The proper thrust plate is selected to adjust the input shaft end play. (*Courtesy of Chrysler Corporation*)

Mark

SST

FIGURE 16–21 This special tool is used to measure the servo piston rod stroke as the servo is applied. A different piston rod can be installed if needed. (*Courtesy of Toyota Motor Sales USA, Inc.*)

16.3.2 OTHER PREDISASSEMBLY CHECKS

Depending on the transmission design, other checks should be done before disassembly. An example is the 2–4 band apply pin check for a GM 4L60E. This check requires a special tool that is attached to the transmission case and operated using a torque wrench. This check determines if the intermediate-band apply pin is the correct length for the band. If the check indicates that the apply pin is correct, there is probably not much band wear. If the check indicates the apply pin is too short, either the pin, band, or both will need to be replaced during the overhaul. ● SEE FIGURE 16–21.

16.4 PUMP REMOVAL

The pump assembly is the front cover that holds the gear train inside the case on RWD transmissions. Its removal allows the disassembly of the rest of the internal parts. The pump is held in place by a set of bolts. The close fit between the outer pump diameter and the case plus a rubber sealing ring and/or gasket

Threads For Slide Hammer

FIGURE 16–22 This section of a front pump shows a hole that has internal threads to accept a slide hammer.

makes pump removal a little difficult. Several methods can be used to remove the pump. These include slide hammers, special screw-type pullers, and prying on the gear train. Using slide hammers or prying the gear train is sometimes limited by transmission design.

To pull a pump using slide hammers, you should:

1. Remove the pump-retaining bolts.
2. Check the pump body bolt holes for threads. ● SEE FIGURE 16–22. These threads are one size larger than the pump-retaining bolts. Only two of the holes are threaded and they are on opposite sides of the pump.
3. Thread the slide hammer bolts into the two threaded holes. ● SEE FIGURE 16–23. Adapters are available for different thread sizes.
4. Using the slide hammers along with a lifting action, remove the pump assembly.

One manufacturer makes a special tool that threads into these holes, and turning a center screw/bolt lifts the pump assembly. ● SEE FIGURE 16–24.

To pull a pump using a screw-type puller, you should:

1. Check the end of the input shaft for a check valve that can be damaged by the puller screw. If one is found, a protection device must be positioned between the puller and the end of the shaft. ● SEE FIGURE 16–25.
2. Remove the pump-retaining bolts.
3. Attach the puller to the stator support shaft. Some pullers slide over the unsplined part of the shaft; others clamp onto the shaft.
4. Tighten the puller screw to pull the pump assembly.

To pull a pump by prying, you should:

1. Lay the transmission upside down on the bench.
2. Remove the pump-retaining bolts.
3. Place a large screwdriver between the sun gear input shell and the reaction carrier, and pry the input shell forward to remove the pump.

Transmission Vent

Tool

(a)

Front Clutch

Oil Pump Assembly

(b)

FIGURE 16–23 (a) A pair of slide hammers has been threaded into the pump assembly. (b) After the pump has pulled free, the tools are used to lift the pump out of the transmission. (*Courtesy of Chrysler Corporation*)

SST

FIGURE 16–24 This special service tool is attached to the front pump. Turning the center bolt will push against the input shaft to lift the pump from the transmission.

FIGURE 16–25 An aftermarket tool is connected to the front pump, and turning the center bolt will lift the pump; note the valve protector (arrow) to prevent damage to the check valve at the end of some input shafts.

TECH TIP

Occasionally, a badly worn or burnt transmission will have a seized pump or gear train. These can usually be disassembled by placing two wood blocks on the floor, lifting the transmission several feet, and dropping its front downward, onto the blocks. These units often have internal damage that is beyond repair so there is not much loss if they are damaged during disassembly.

16.4.1 TRANSAXLES USING INPUT CHAIN DRIVE

Some transaxles use a chain and sprockets for gear train input. The main gear train is behind the valve body; case cover, channel plate, or chain cover; and drive chain and sprockets. ● SEE FIGURE 16–26. Removal of these parts provides access to the driven sprocket support, which supports the input end of the gear train.

The drive chain and sprockets are exposed after the valve body and case cover/channel plate assembly have been removed. It is recommended to check for chain wear/link stretch

FIGURE 16–26 Removal of the upper pan/chain cover (361), valve body and pump (419 and 320), and the channel plate (280) allows access to the sprockets (575 and 602) and drive chain (82) along with the other parts of the gear train. (*Courtesy of Slauson Transmission Parts, www.slauson.com*)

FIGURE 16–27 Drive chain and sprocket wear is normally checked by moving the chain inward and outward. Excess movement indicates excessive wear. (*Courtesy of BorgWarner, Morse TEC*)

FIGURE 16–28 The drive chain and the sprockets can be lifted off the case. Note the position of the master link, where the thrust washers are, and how they fit onto the sprockets as you remove them. They must be replaced correctly in this same position.

 TECH TIP

The case cover will probably be stuck on to the case by the gasket. A sideways blow from a soft hammer should break it loose.

 TECH TIP

If the chain is replaced with the master link in the opposite position, it can be noisy. This noise will occur whenever the engine is running, even in park and neutral.

at this time. ● **SEE FIGURE 16–27**. If the chain has stretched, it should be replaced. Locate the chain's master link; it may be a different color. After noting which side is up or down, lift the chain and sprockets from the transaxle. ● **SEE FIGURE 16–28**.

16.5 MAJOR DISASSEMBLY

A service manual should be followed for the disassembly procedure. Some transmissions almost fall apart after the pump is removed; others come apart one piece at a time.

To complete transmission disassembly, you should:

1. To remove a band, carefully note the position of the band struts, loosen the band adjusting screw, and remove the servo cover and piston. Remove the band struts and band. ● **SEE FIGURE 16–29**.

   On transmissions using a clutch mounted next to the pump, remove the clutch friction, steel, and pressure plates. Be sure to note the position of the various clutch plates.

2. Remove the driving clutch assemblies. ● **SEE FIGURE 16–30**.

3. Remove the bolts retaining the extension housing. It may be necessary to remove a snap ring and remove the extension housing. ● **SEE FIGURE 16–31**.

4. Remove the governor and its support on transmissions with shaft-mounted governors. ● **SEE FIGURE 16–32**.

5. The planetary gear train can be slid out of the case as one assembly on some transmissions. ● **SEE FIGURE 16–33**.

FIGURE 16–29 Removal of the band strut frees this band so it can be removed. (*Courtesy of Chrysler Corporation*)

FIGURE 16–32 This governor assembly is being removed from the transfer shaft of this transaxle. (*Courtesy of Chrysler Corporation*)

FIGURE 16–30 This input shaft and clutch hub with planetary gears is lifted out of the case. (*Courtesy of Toyota Motor Sales USA, Inc.*)

(a)

FIGURE 16–31 Removal of the retaining bolts allows the extension housing and overdrive unit to be removed from this 42RH transmission. (*Courtesy of Chrysler Corporation*)

(b)

FIGURE 16–33 (a) The entire gear train of some transmissions is removed as an assembly. (b) The gear train of other transmissions is removed one section at a time.

FIGURE 16–34 Parts 7376, 2341, 9891, and 250 are thrust washers that keep parts properly separated. Parts 9861, 7645, 3956, 7831, 8643, and 3485 are retaining rings that hold components in the proper position. (*Courtesy of Slauson Transmission Parts, www.slauson.com*)

FIGURE 16–35 It is a good practice to place index marks on the driving lugs (arrows) so the direct clutch shell and the low/intermediate ring gear can be assembled in the original position.

On other transmissions, remove the retaining rings to disassemble the gear train; a seal pick or snap-ring pliers are used. Note exactly where each retaining ring is located. As each part of the gear train is removed, note if a thrust washer is used and how it is positioned. ● **SEE FIGURE 16–34.** The condition of each part should be checked as it is removed. Keep a list of the parts that need to be replaced.

🔧 TECH TIP

1. Many transmissions use a drive shell that is connected to a clutch through a set of lugs, and a wear pattern will be established between them. On reassembly, it is important to assemble them in the original position. During disassembly, it is a good practice to place index marks on both parts. ● **SEE FIGURE 16–35.** Some technicians use a permanent felt marker or a small die grinder to make index marks on the parts.
2. A special screwdriver-like tool is available to remove large snap rings. Some technicians modify a large screwdriver, as shown in Figure 16–36, to remove large snap rings.

6. If the transmission uses a center support, remove the retainer, usually a large snap ring, and lift the center support out of the case. The low-reverse clutch assembly in some transmissions is the center support. A special tool may be required to remove the center support. In some cases, lifting the output shaft will push the center support and the rest of the gear train from the case. ● **SEE FIGURE 16–36.**

🔧 TECH TIP

1. Pay attention to one-way clutch assemblies as you remove them. Note the free-wheel and lock-up directions, and record this for use when you assemble the unit.
2. Some center supports use an **anticlunk spring** that loads them in a counterclockwise direction. ● **SEE FIGURE 16–37.** Look for this spring and how it is positioned before removing the center support.

7. On transmissions that use a clutch assembly in the end of the case, remove the retaining ring, pressure plate, and clutch plates. ● **SEE FIGURE 16–38.** Note the position of each of these parts and if a wave or Belleville plate is used. To remove the retaining ring, a spring compressor is required to compress the piston return springs. Remove the retaining ring, return springs, and clutch piston. ● **SEE FIGURE 16–39.** The piston can be removed by blowing air into the apply passage.

➕ SAFETY TIP

When using a spring compressor, compress the springs just enough to allow the snap ring to be removed. Be careful that the compressor is positioned correctly so it will not slip, allowing the springs to fly out. Make sure there is enough travel to allow the springs to extend completely, and watch to ensure that the retainer does not catch on the snap-ring groove during removal. ● **SEE FIGURE 16–40.**

8. As the park gear is removed, the gear and park pawl should be inspected for wear and damage. Also, the pawl return spring should be checked to ensure that the park pawl is moved completely away from the gear when released. ● **SEE FIGURE 16–41.**
9. On RWD transmissions, remove any remaining parts as required by the manufacturer's instructions. On transaxles, remove the final drive gears and differential plus any other remaining parts. ● **SEE FIGURE 16–42.**

Low/Reverse Clutch
Reaction Plate

Screwdriver

Long Tab

Low/Reverse Tapered
Snap Ring
(Tapered Side Up)

Oil Pan
Face

(a)

(b)

SST

(c)

(d)

FIGURE 16–36 (a) Like a center support, this clutch pack is retained by a large retaining ring. (b) A large screwdriver can be modified to hook the retaining ring for quick and easy removal. (c) The special tool is being used to lift the overdrive support assembly. (d) Very large snap-ring pliers are required to remove the internal snap ring in a 6L80E. (*Figure (a) Courtesy of Chrysler Corporation*)

16.6 TRANSMISSION ASSEMBLY

The reassembly procedure for an automatic transmission varies depending on the make and model of the transmission. Service information should be followed to make sure the parts are assembled in the right order and position and that important checks and adjustments are not skipped. ● **SEE FIGURES 16–43 AND 16–44.**

Reassembly begins with a case and subassemblies that are thoroughly clean and reconditioned as necessary. All parts should be thoroughly air dried. Do not dry them with cloth or paper towels, as the lint from the towels can plug filter screens. As the parts are assembled into the case, the bushings and shaft surfaces should be lubricated with transmission assembly lubricant, petroleum jelly, or ATF. ● **SEE FIGURE 16–45.**

Thrust washers are used to separate most of the internal components, and most thrust washers interlock with one of the components next to it. ● **SEE FIGURE 16–46.** It is especially important to hold thrust washers and Torrington bearings in position with either assembly lubricant or petroleum

FIGURE 16–37 The low/reverse support/anticlunk spring (680) is removed with the low/reverse support. (*Reprinted with permission of General Motors*)

(a)

(b)

FIGURE 16–38 (a) The retaining ring locates (b) the clutch pack in the rear of this case.

(a)

(b)

FIGURE 16–39 (a) The special tool is used to compress the clutch piston return springs, so (b) the retaining ring can be removed.

FIGURE 16–40 With the retaining ring removed, slowly release the spring compressor; make sure that the spring retainer does not catch on the snap-ring groove.

jelly. These parts can easily slip out of position. Ordinary grease should not be used for this because it will not mix with ATF, might stay in a lump, and could possibly clog an orifice. Grease can also change the friction characteristics of the transmission fluid.

Transmission reassembly usually follows a procedure that is essentially a reverse of the disassembly—the last part out is the first part installed. A wise technician takes extra steps to ensure that each part will work properly. The following are some examples.

- The gear train should rotate freely unless there is an intended holding member.
- When a holding one-way clutch is installed, the gear train should turn freely in the direction of output shaft rotation but lock up in the opposite direction.

(a)

Lock Pawl

E-Ring

(b)

FIGURE 16–41 (a) Removal of the bracket allows the park rod to be removed. (b) Then the park/lock pawl and shaft can be removed.

(a)

(b)

FIGURE 16–42 (a) After removing the carrier cover, (b) the differential case can be removed from this transaxle.

SST

Front

24 mm (0.94 in.)

FIGURE 16–43 This retaining ring locates the overdrive support assembly; note how the tapered side is positioned toward the front of the case.

 REAL WORLD FIX

The 1993 Taurus transaxle (AXODE) has been overhauled because of a destroyed planetary gear set. A new gear set, clutches, seals, converter, and solenoids were installed and the valve body was cleaned and inspected. Now there is a flare on the 1–2 shift and, occasionally, a harsh 2–1 shift.

FIX

Reinspection of the valve body did not reveal any problems, but rechecking the low/intermediate band pin length showed that it was slightly bent and 0.004 in. too short. Installation of the correct band pin fixed this problem.

Dial Indicator

Special Tool L-4436

Transaxle Stand Special Tool L-4557

Dial Indicator Bracket

Stud

Differential Assembly

Ring Gear

Screwdrivers

FIGURE 16–44 Checking the differential or gear train end play ensures that the thrust washers have the proper clearance. Note that some transmissions require a special tool to lift the gear train. (*Courtesy of Chrysler Corporation*)

FIGURE 16–45 Transmission assembly lubricant or petroleum jelly can be used to lubricate parts and hold them in the proper position.

* Assembled Type Bearing and Race

FIGURE 16–46 Thrust bearings and their races must be assembled correctly.

 TECH TIP

1. A transmission should always be assembled with wet bearings and wet clutches. The bearings should be lubricated with assembly lube, petroleum jelly, or ATF. The clutches should be presoaked in ATF for at least 15 minutes.
2. The lubrication passages should be checked before transmission reassembly. Blow air into the cooler return port; you should be able to hear or feel air escaping from the bushings connected to this port.

 REAL WORLD FIX

The 4T80-E, 1995 Cadillac was rebuilt because of slippage. On a road test, a definite bump was noticed as soon as the accelerator was depressed, and this occurred in all ranges. Fluid pressures were normal.

FIX

On close inspection, with the transmission partially disassembled and the chain cover removed, it was found that the wrong driven sprocket support seal gasket was installed. Installation of the proper gasket fixed the problem.

 REAL WORLD FIX

The 1994 Chevrolet K2500 pickup (134,000 km) transmission was rebuilt because clutch material was found in the pan while diagnosing a shift problem. The 1–2, 2–3 shift solenoids and pressure control solenoid were also replaced. The vehicle came back with the same shift problem. When the pan was removed, clutch material was found.

FIX

Following advice, the technician checked the rear servo and accumulator and found a hairline crack in the accumulator piston. Replacement of the accumulator piston and new clutch plates fixed this vehicle.

- When a driving one-way clutch is installed, power should be able to pass through it in the direction of output shaft rotation but the driven part should be able to overrun.
- Each clutch pack or band should have the correct clearance.

- Each clutch and band should operate properly when air checked.
- Every section of the gear train should have the correct end play.
- All tapered roller bearing sets should be adjusted to the proper preload or end play.
- All bolts are tightened to the correct torque.
- The group of bolts securing some parts should be tightened using the proper order.

FIGURE 16–47 This transaxle uses a hypoid ring and pinion gear set that requires additional adjustment as it is assembled. (*Courtesy of Chrysler Corporation*)

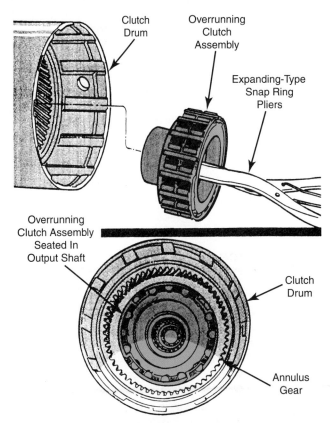

FIGURE 16–48 This overrunning clutch assembly with the inner cam, rollers, and springs should be installed into the clutch drum using a counterclockwise rotating motion. (*Courtesy of Chrysler Corporation*)

On some transaxles, an end-play check should be made as the final drive and differential are installed. On other transmissions the differential and transfer shaft bearings must be adjusted to the correct preload. These operations are described in the appropriate service manual. Transaxles using spiral bevel or hypoid ring and pinion gears require adjustment to ensure proper mesh and bearing preload. An additional adjustment is usually required for the input and output bearings for these two gears. ● SEE FIGURE 16–47.

 TECH TIP

1. As a one-way clutch is assembled, it should be checked to make sure it freewheels in one direction and locks in the other. In most transmissions, a holding one-way clutch freewheels in a clockwise direction (same direction as output shaft rotation in forward gears). ● SEE FIGURE 16–48. A one-way clutch driven by a friction clutch will normally lock up to drive in a clockwise direction. In some transmissions, the freewheel direction of a one-way clutch is hard to remember, but a service manual often shows how to check it.
2. A one-way roller clutch also can be assembled improperly. The accordion spring should preload the rollers in the lock-up direction, and, if possible, place the spring so it will tend to move away from freewheeling race. ● SEE FIGURE 16–49.

 REAL WORLD FIX

The 1997 Chevrolet Tahoe (78,000 miles) transmission was repaired because of a faulty sun gear shell. It worked well for 2 months/2,000 miles, and problems of delayed 2–3 and 3–4 shifts and erratic speedometer operation began suddenly. A check reveals no DTCs.

FIX

Following advice, the technician removed the VSS and checked the sensor drive gear. It was in the wrong location, and it was discovered that the output shaft could be moved back and forth. The transmission was removed and disassembled, and the snap ring that secures the reaction carrier to the output shaft had fallen out of its groove. Reassembly of this transmission using a new snap ring fixed this problem.

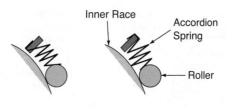

Correct

Incorrect: Spring contact
with inner race can cause
wear and spring breakup

FIGURE 16–49 The Accordion spring in some one-way clutches can be installed in a direction so that it will rub against the inner race. This can cause wear and breaking of the spring.

 TECH TIP

1. If one of the ends of a band is noticeably stronger than the other, the strongest end is usually placed at the anchor.

2. As a gear set is assembled, each part should turn freely without binding (except for one-way clutches in one direction). It is often possible to make the gear set produce each of its gear ratios by turning the input/turbine shaft and holding the correct reaction member. In many cases, you will need to apply one or more clutches with air pressure.

 TECH TIP

1. Remember to install any required preload device, such as an anticlunk spring, in the proper position, as a center support is installed. Usually a clearance or end-play check is required to ensure that the gear train captured by the center support is free to operate and has the proper clearance.

2. A center support with a clutch piston must have a fluid passage between it and the case. This passage is often sealed with a special seal that is installed after the center support is installed. ● **SEE FIGURE 16–50**.

3. A clutch should be stacked with the plates in the proper order and position. There should also be the proper clearance in the clutch stack. ● **SEE FIGURE 16–51**.

4. As a clutch is assembled, it can be air checked by applying air pressure into the apply passage. ● **SEE FIGURE 16–52**. The clutch should apply without excess leakage and release with clearance at the plates.

FIGURE 16–50 (a) After this center support with the rear gear assembly is installed, (b) it must be positioned properly using tool J23093 before the retaining bolt is installed. On some transmissions, a tube seal should be installed as shown to prevent fluid leaks in the center support and its clutch.

16.6.1 PUMP INSTALLATION AND END-PLAY ADJUSTMENT The final assembly point of many gear trains is the pump. A new pump gasket must be used. Many technicians use two guide pins to hold the gasket in place and align

FIGURE 16–51 (a) With the clutch stack correctly installed, the pack clearance can be measured using (b) a feeler gauge or (c) a dial indicator. (d) Applying the clutch with air allows the piston travel/pack clearance to be measured. (*Courtesy of Toyota Motor Sales USA, Inc.*)

 TECH TIP

1. Some clutch assemblies are a little difficult to install because of the close fit of the plates over the hub. Swinging the clutch in a kind of spiral direction will work the plates over the hub. ● **SEE FIGURE 16–53**.
2. Another problem when installing clutches is weight—one forward clutch assembly weighs about 50 lb (110 kg)—and they are not easy to grasp as you lower them into the case. Special tools are available to provide a way to handle these components.
3. You can determine if a clutch is completely installed by measuring its position in the transmission case. ● **SEE FIGURE 16–54**. Another method is to lift the clutch straight up, about 1/4 in. (6 mm), and then drop it. A solid "thunk" indicates the clutch is dropping onto its thrust washer, which is good. If the clutch is dropping onto the edge of a misaligned plate, it makes a quieter, less solid sound.

FIGURE 16–52 After the clutch is completely installed, its operation can be checked by applying compressed air to the fluid passage.

Input Shaft | Front Clutch | Rear Clutch

FIGURE 16–53 These front and rear clutches are installed together. The lugs of the front clutch must engage the notches in the sun gear shell, and the rear clutches must engage the splines on the clutch hub. Swinging the input shaft in a spiral motion can help align the plates. (*Courtesy of Chrysler Corporation*)

FIGURE 16–54 The straightedge is used to check the depth of the parts. If the two surfaces are flush, they are assembled correctly. (*Reprinted with permission of General Motors*)

Seat Oil Pump In Case By Hand

Remove Pilot Studs When Pump Is Seated

FIGURE 16–55 The two pilot studs/guide pins properly align the gasket and pump to the transmission case as the pump is installed. (*Courtesy of Chrysler Corporation*)

the pump as it is installed. ● **SEE FIGURE 16–55.** The internal end play is always checked and adjusted at this time.

Two common methods are used to check end play: an H-shaped gauge or a dial indicator. The H-shaped gauge is simpler and faster. Place the front gasket in position, adjust the gauge to fit the pump mounting surface, and then adjust the gauge rod to touch the thrust surface on the clutch. ● **SEE FIGURE 16–56.** Now turn the gauge over, and place it onto the pump. The clearance between the gauge rod and the thrust surface of the pump is the space you have for the thrust washer plus the clearance for end play.

If the end play is measured using a dial indicator, install the pump using the gasket but without the O-ring. Install and tighten two opposite bolts, and measure the end play as described in

Section 16.3.1. ● **SEE FIGURE 16–57.** Then remove the pump and correct the end play by selecting the correct thrust washers or shims. The selective thrust washer is normally the No. 1 thrust washer, the one next to the pump. ● **SEE FIGURE 16–58.**

	Inch	Millimeter
Measured end play:	0.038	0.97
End-play specification:	0.005 to 0.036	0.13 to 0.91
Excessive play:	0.033 to 0.002	0.84 to 0.06
Existing washer	0.087 to 0.91	2.21 to 2.31
Selected washer	0.113 to 0.118	2.89 to 2.99
Size difference:	+0.026	10.68

(a)

(b)

(c)

FIGURE 16–56 (a) An H-shaped gauge is being used to check end play. It is adjusted to fit the transmission (left) and then moved to check the clearance at the pump (right). (b) A shop-made gauge can be used in the same manner; note the use of an old band to support the gauge at the pump.

The band servos are installed and the band clearance is checked or adjusted after the pump is installed.

In review, the following general rules are used for transmission assembly.

- New or reconditioned replacement components should always be used.
- New rubber seals and new or very good sealing rings should be used.

- Gaskets and metal-clad seals should be replaced.
- All friction elements should be soaked in ATF.
- All clutches and bands should have the correct clearance.
- All one-way clutches should freewheel in the proper direction.
- All support bushings and thrust washers must be in good condition and assembled correctly.

FIGURE 16–57 After the dial indicator is set up, lifting and dropping the input shaft shows the amount of end play. If it is correct, the internal parts have been installed correctly.

Seal Rings — Reaction Shaft Support — Thrust Washer (Fiber)

FIGURE 16–58 In most transmissions, the No. 1 (fiber) washer is selective. The technician selects the proper size to adjust the end play. (*Courtesy of Chrysler Corporation*)

TECH TIP

1. If there is no end play after assembly and the transmission is bound, it is possible that a thrust washer has slipped out of position or a clutch is not completely installed.
2. Most technicians prefer to adjust the end play on the tight side of the specifications. This reduces the thrust movement of the gear train. For example, eight thrust washers between the sizes of 0.076 in. (1.92 mm) and 0.122 in. (3.11 mm) are available, but one that is 0.15 in. (2.94 mm) would provide the least end play that is within specification.

TECH TIP

Some technicians check end play using a feeler gauge equal to the largest specified end play. If it enters easily, there is too much end play, and the next larger thrust washer should be installed.

REAL WORLD FIX

The 1988 BMW had a fluid leak at the front of the transmission that was fixed by replacing the gasket between the bell housing and transmission case. It returned with a leak in the same area.

FIX

It was discovered that the retaining bolts pass through the case. Sealing the threads of the bolts with an anaerobic sealer stopped this leak.

REAL WORLD FIX

The 700-R4 was overhauled, but when driving in D it will not make a 3–4 shift. The seals and pump were replaced during the overhaul. It was torn down again to replace a torn outer forward clutch seal and forward sprag. It now drags in D-4. Fluid pressures were checked, and they meet specifications.

FIX

A later-model pump with the auxiliary valve body was used during the overhaul; installation of a cup plug to close off the unused lube tube opening solved this problem. When replacing parts, always check the replacement part to make sure that it is exactly the same as the original part. The smallest difference can have a major effect on transmission performance.

- All moving parts should be lubricated with ATF or transmission assembly lubricant.
- All end plays should be correctly adjusted.
- All snap rings must be installed completely into their grooves.
- All bolts must be tightened to the correct torque.
- All bolt threads should be lubricated with ATF before installing to reduce thread galling.
- Each hydraulic component should be air checked.
- The gear train should rotate without excessive drag.

Impeller   Oil Pump Outer Gear   Reaction Support Shaft

Flexible Drive Plate   Oil Pump Inner Gear

Torque Converter

Turbine

Engine Crankshaft

Input Shaft

Pump Oil Seal

FIGURE 16–59 A torque converter must fully engage the pump, stator support, and turbine shaft (circles).

TECH TIP

1. After the band servos are installed, many technicians air check the clutch assemblies, servos, and governor, as described in Chapter 12. Each of the components should respond with the correct motion or sound and with a minimum of air leakage. If the air checks produce the correct results, the valve body, filter, and pan can be installed.
2. When assembling a spring-loaded servo cover, hold the cover inward until each bolt has contact with at least five or six threads.
3. When tightening the valve body bolts, use a spiral pattern starting in the center.

16.6.2 TORQUE CONVERTER INSTALLATION
After the transmission is assembled, the torque converter can be installed. The converter should be checked and cleaned, as described in Chapter 19, or a rebuilt unit should be used.

TECH TIP

One manufacturer attaches the torque converter housing to the case using aluminum bolts so they have the same coefficient of expansion as the aluminum housing and case. New bolts must be used when the housing is reattached to the case.

REAL WORLD FIX

The 1999 Chrysler 300M (98,000 miles) came in with a second-gear start, no first-gear problem. The fluid is clean and at the proper level. A check reveals no DTCs, and the shift solenoids all have the proper resistance.

FIX

Removal of the transmission revealed earlier transmission service: Some of the pan bolts were stripped and cross-threaded, and there was an excess amount of RTV sealant used. RTV chunks were inside the solenoid passages. Replacement of the solenoid pack and filter along with a new pan gasket and ATF fixed this problem.

REAL WORLD FIX

The 1998 Saturn (42,000 miles) transmission had overheated and was overhauled because of a torque converter problem. A new valve body was installed during the overhaul. Now there is no reverse, and reinspection does not reveal the cause.

FIX

An air check shows that the reverse servo was moving properly, but the reverse gear was not. The nut securing the assembly was overtightened. Tightening this nut to the correct torque fixed this problem.

The converter must align at three points: at the turbine spline, stator spline, and pump. Most converters use two flats or notches that engage the pump drive gear, and these notches should be positioned to align with the pump drive gear before installation. ● **SEE FIGURE 16–59.**

Ensure that the converter is completely installed into the transmission before installing the transmission into the vehicle.

FIGURE 16–60 The torque converter was rotated and then removed. The pump drive lug (circle) must align with the position of the converter drive tang.

Scale

Straightedge

FIGURE 16–61 This check ensures that the torque converter is installed completely into the transmission. (*Courtesy of Chrysler Corporation*)

 TECH TIP

1. Many technicians pour about 1 quart of ATF into the converter before installation. Remember that the converter must fill before fluid goes to the cooler and back to the transmission lubrication passages.
2. If the drive gears do not line up, there is a **stacked converter** on top of the pump gear. If the transmission is installed with a stacked converter and the engine is started, the pump and possibly the converter hub will be ruined.
3. If a torque converter depth dimension is not available, pump tang engagement can be checked by noting how deep the converter is in the housing, rotating the converter a turn or so, lifting the converter back out, and noting if the pump drive tangs are aligned with the location of the converter hub. ● **SEE FIGURE 16–60**. If they are not aligned, the converter was not completely installed and will need to go deeper into the transmission. Most technicians check for proper converter installation as it is being connected to the flexplate. See Section 15.5.

Some manufacturers provide a dimension for checking converter installation. ● **SEE FIGURE 16–61.**

Shops that specialize in rebuilding transmissions to be sold to other shops may use a transmission test machine, often called a dynamometer, for quality control checks. ● **SEE FIGURE 16–62.** These machines use an engine or large electric motor to drive the transmission while a power absorber provides a load on the driveshaft(s). They quickly provide a realistic and thorough test of the transmission.

FIGURE 16–62 A transmission is installed in this tester. It will be driven at various speeds while loads are applied to the drivetrain. (*Courtesy of Axiline*)

SUMMARY

1. Automatic transmissions are removed from a vehicle for overhaul, repair, or replacement.

2. A transmission overhaul includes inspection of all reusable parts, a check of the clearances, and replacement of all gaskets, seals, friction materials, the filter, and worn bushings.

3. Remanufactured transmissions have been overhauled and updated in a factorylike environment.

4. Transmission parts are classified as hard or soft parts. Hard parts are not commonly replaced. Soft parts are commonly replaced during an overhaul.

5. Although the overhaul procedures for various transmissions are similar, there are differences, and service information should always be consulted when overhauling or servicing an automatic transmission.

REVIEW QUESTIONS

1. The three repair choices for a badly worn or damaged transmission are:
   a. _____
   b. _____
   c. _____

2. _____ parts are replaced during an automatic transmission overhaul.

3. _____ parts include the pump, clutch drums, and gear sets.

4. To learn about possible health problems and special handling requirements, refer to the _____ _____ _____ _____.

5. Excessive end play is a result of _____ wear.

6. Transmission end play is normally measured with a _____ _____.

7. A technician will change a _____ thrust washer or _____ ring to correct transmission end play.

8. Before reassembly, the parts are washed and _____ dried.

9. As a one-way clutch is assembled into the transmission, it should be checked to ensure that it _____ in the right direction.

10. After a clutch pack is assembled, it should be _____ _____ checked to ensure proper operation.

11. Most technicians set the _____ _____ to the tight side of the specifications.

12. During assembly, all of the friction elements should be _____ in ATF.

13. During assembly, all of the hydraulic units should be _____ checked.

14. The torque converter must align at three points. What are they?
    a. _____
    b. _____
    c. _____

15. Damage could result to the pump or torque converter if the _____ _____ is not properly installed.

CHAPTER QUIZ

1. Technician A says that some states have rules and regulations that define what an automatic transmission rebuild or overhaul must include. Technician B says that an alternative to an overhaul is to replace the transmission with a remanufactured transmission. Who is correct?
   a. Technician A
   b. Technician B
   c. Both Technicians A and B
   d. Neither Technician A nor B

2. Technician A says that the torque converter should be left attached to the engine when the transmission is removed from a vehicle. Technician B says that the torque converter should be disconnected from the engine and removed with the transmission. Who is correct?
   a. Technician A
   b. Technician B
   c. Both Technicians A and B
   d. Neither Technician A nor B

3. Technician A says that the transmission must be thoroughly cleaned right after removal. Technician B says that most transmission-holding fixtures allow the technician to move the transmission to the best working position. Who is correct?
   a. Technician A
   b. Technician B
   c. Both Technicians A and B
   d. Neither Technician A nor B

4. Technician A says that some servos and accumulators require special holding tools or spring compressors to hold the internal spring compressed during disassembly. Technician B says that an end-play check should be made before removing the transmission pump. Who is correct?
   a. Technician A
   b. Technician B
   c. Both Technicians A and B
   d. Neither Technician A nor B

5. Technician A says that the old gaskets should be discarded as they are removed from the transmission. Technician B says that the old gaskets should be saved to match with the new gaskets during assembly. Who is correct?
   a. Technician A
   b. Technician B
   c. Both Technicians A and B
   d. Neither Technician A nor B

6. Technician A says that excessive transmission end play is usually caused by a stretched case. Technician B says that loose pump bolts are the major cause of excess end play. Who is correct?
   a. Technician A
   b. Technician B
   c. Both Technicians A and B
   d. Neither Technician A nor B

7. During a transmission rebuild, it is good practice to replace _____.
   a. Rubber sealing rings
   b. Lined clutch plates
   c. Paper and composition gaskets
   d. All of these

8. Technician A says that special slide hammers are used to pull the pump assembly from the case. Technician B says that air pressure in the proper port helps pull the pump. Who is correct?
   a. Technician A
   b. Technician B
   c. Both Technicians A and B
   d. Neither Technician A nor B

9. After the case has been cleaned it should be checked for _____.
   a. Damage, warpage, and cross-leaks at the worm tracks
   b. A worn governor bore
   c. Damaged bolt threads
   d. All of these

10. Technician A says that worn or damaged bushings are repaired by driving them out and replacing them with new bushings. Technician B says that some bushings are removed by cutting threads in them so a puller bolt can be used. Who is correct?
    a. Technician A
    b. Technician B
    c. Both Technicians A and B
    d. Neither Technician A nor B

11. Technician A says that it is good practice to replace all of the friction materials (lined plates, unlined plates, and bands) when rebuilding a transmission. Technician B says that lined friction material must be soaked in ATF before it is installed. Who is correct?
    a. Technician A
    b. Technician B
    c. Both Technicians A and B
    d. Neither Technician A nor B

12. Technician A says that you should ensure the cleanness of all internal parts by wiping them with a clean shop cloth just before installation. Technician B says that petroleum jelly is a good stickum for thrust washers as well as being a good assembly lubricant. Who is correct?
    a. Technician A
    b. Technician B
    c. Both Technicians A and B
    d. Neither Technician A nor B

13. Technician A says that all parts should be thoroughly checked for cleanliness and proper working order during reassembly. Technician B says that some transmissions have several end-play checks that must be done as the transmission is assembled. Who is correct?
    a. Technician A
    b. Technician B
    c. Both Technicians A and B
    d. Neither Technician A nor B

14. Technician A says that transmission end play is normally measured using a dial indicator mounted at the turbine shaft. Technician B says that transmission end play is always corrected at the thrust washer No. 1 next to the pump. Who is correct?
    a. Technician A
    b. Technician B
    c. Both Technicians A and B
    d. Neither Technician A nor B

15. Technician A says that all the clutches and servos should be air checked right after the valve body has been installed. Technician B says that all transmission bolts and especially the valve body bolts should be tightened to the correct torque. Who is correct?
    a. Technician A
    b. Technician B
    c. Both Technicians A and B
    d. Neither Technician A nor B

OBJECTIVES: **After studying Chapter 17, the reader will be able to:** • Properly perform the standard overhaul procedures. • Describe the methods used to clean an automatic transmission and its components. • Inspect, remove, and replace bushings and thrust washers. • Disassemble, inspect, and assemble a clutch assembly. • Remove and replace the various seals used in an automatic transmission. • Complete the ASE tasks related to inspection and replacement of bushings, thrust washers, friction material, and seals.

KEY TERMS: Bearings 427 • Bushings 427 • Cage 432 • Cone 432 • Cup 432 • Door ease 439 • Hook ring 441 • Inner race 432 • Material safety data sheet (MSDS) 426 • Open/plain end ring 441 • Red rag disease 426 • Rollers 432 • Scarf-cut 442 • Selective 433 • Staked 432 • Thrust washers 427 • Torrington 429

17.1 INTRODUCTION

A transmission overhaul is a complete reconditioning that will bring the transmission back to like-new vehicle operation. This requires that worn parts be replaced so the original clearances are restored. An overhaul should include the following:

1. Complete disassembly and cleaning
2. Careful inspection of each part and component
3. Replacement of any worn or damaged hard parts
4. Replacement of any worn or damaged bushings or thrust washers
5. Replacement of all clutch friction plates
6. Replacement of any worn or damaged clutch steel plates
7. Replacement of any worn or damaged bands
8. Replacement of all internal and external seals and gaskets
9. Disassembling, cleaning, and reassembling the valve body
10. Rebuilding or replacing the torque converter
11. Cleaning/flushing the cooler if needed
12. Adjusting all clearances to the manufacturer's specifications

Some states have rules and regulations that define the common terms used to describe automatic transmission repair and what must be done to conform to these definitions. Check with your local governing body for any applicable laws that might apply.

TECH TIP

1. Transmission parts should never be cleaned or dried by wiping them with a shop cloth. More than one transmission has died from **red rag disease.** Lint left on parts wiped by a shop cloth can clog the filter, blocking the fluid flow into the pump. This can cause an early failure of a perfectly good job.
2. Check the **material safety data sheet (MSDS)** label on the cleaning solution container for concerns during usage and for proper disposal methods.

17.2 COMPONENT CLEANING

The internal parts, case, and extension housing are cleaned after disassembly. Some technicians set major components aside to be thoroughly cleaned as they are disassembled and serviced. Cleaning methods that are commonly used are hot spray wash, water solution wash, cold dip, and solvent wash. The parts should be dried using compressed air after washing. Each technician or shop has a preferred method of cleaning. Internal transmission wear or overheating is often caused by poor lubrication, which

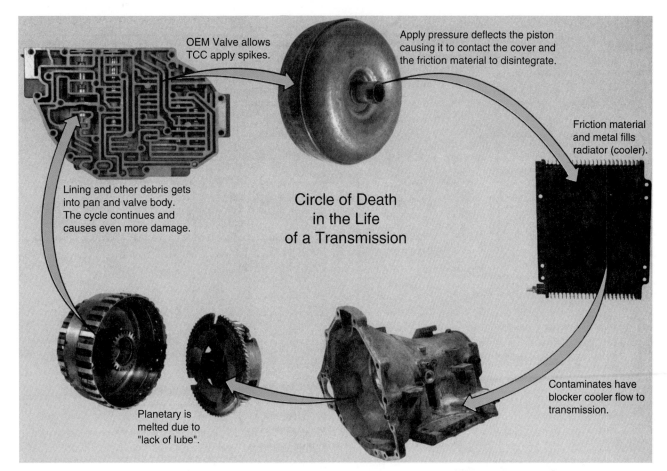

OEM Valve allows TCC apply spikes.

Apply pressure deflects the piston causing it to contact the cover and the friction material to disintegrate.

Friction material and metal fills radiator (cooler).

Lining and other debris gets into pan and valve body. The cycle continues and causes even more damage.

Circle of Death in the Life of a Transmission

Contaminates have blocker cooler flow to transmission.

Planetary is melted due to "lack of lube".

FIGURE 17–1 Expensive transmission failures can be caused by debris in the cooler. (*Courtesy of Sonnax*)

could be the result of a plugged oil cooler in the radiator. ● **SEE FIGURE 17–1.** Flushing a cooler is described in Sections 11.3.3 and 19.3.2.

A hot spray wash cabinet resembles a large dishwasher. ● **SEE FIGURE 17–2.** The parts are placed inside the cabinet, and the washer sprays the parts with a hot-water-based detergent solution as the parts are rotated. It is an effective and quick cleaner. Newer machines are designed to trap the sludge and dirt to make waste disposal easy and inexpensive. The used cleaning solution, sludge, and dirt waste is an identified hazardous waste that is carefully monitored in many areas.

Cold dipping soaks the parts in a strong cleaning agent. There is no special equipment required. The solution used is relatively expensive, and the used cleaning solution must be disposed of as a hazardous material.

Solvent wash is commonly used for small parts. This method of cleaning parts is labor intensive. The parts are brushed as they are dipped or sprayed with a petroleum- or water-based solvent. ● **SEE FIGURE 17–3.** Petroleum solvents are flammable and can cause redness and soreness of the skin. They are also considered pollutants because of the emissions released into the atmosphere and are treated as a hazardous waste when disposed.

 SAFETY TIP

The petroleum solvent–air mixture from drying the parts is highly flammable. Never use cleaning solvent around an open flame, spark, or source of ignition.

The parts should be rinsed with clear water and blown dry to prevent rusting after cleaning with either the spray washer or cold dip. Solvent wash also requires drying with compressed air to remove any residue.

17.3 BUSHING, BEARING, AND THRUST WASHER SERVICE

Bushings and **bearings** are used to support rotating shafts. **Thrust washers** are used to separate rotating parts from each other or from stationary parts. ● **SEE FIGURE 17–4.** Bushings

(a)

(b)

FIGURE 17–2 A spray wash cabinet contains a pump that sprays heated cleaning solution as the parts basket is rotated. (*Courtesy of ATEC Trans-Tool and Cleaning Systems*)

are plain metal bearings that require a flow of ATF lubricant to reduce friction. Bearings have much less friction because they have rolling members, either balls or rollers, as well as a lubricant to reduce friction. Bushing, bearing, or thrust washer

FIGURE 17–3 This parts washer contains a pump that delivers the heated cleaning solution to a cleaning brush and flexible outlet. (*Courtesy of ATEC Trans-Tool and Cleaning Systems*)

FIGURE 17–4 Parts 8657, 730, 677, 5443, 670, 2279, and 655 are thrust washers. The nine replaceable bushings for this transmission are not shown. (*Courtesy of Slauson Transmission Parts, www.slauson.com*)

(a)

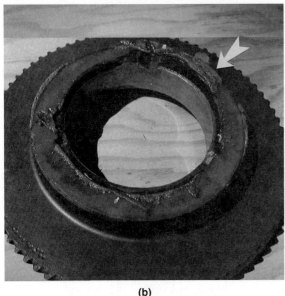

(b)

FIGURE 17–5 (a) The inner and outer bearing journals of this carrier show severe wear. (b) The nylon thrust washer shows that it is deformed and nearly melted. Both failed because of poor lubrication and overheating.

failure causes wear as the hard parts turning at different speeds rub against each other. ● **SEE FIGURE 17–5**.

Thrust washers are plastic, fiber, or bronze- or tin-lined iron. When end-play positioning is critical or thrust loads are very high, a radial needle bearing commonly called a **Torrington** is used. ● **SEE FIGURE 17–6**. This bearing type uses needle bearings to absorb the loads. These bearings must run against a very smooth, hard surface—either the face of a gear or a race. A bushing or thrust washer must have an operating clearance of about 0.003 to 0.005 in. (0.076 to 0.157 mm) to allow a good oil flow across the bearing surface. Torrington bearings and tapered roller bearings are designed to operate with very little clearance; in fact,

(a)   **(b)**   **(c)**

(d)   **(e)**   **(f)**

FIGURE 17–6 A thrust bearing can have a specially shaped race at each side or use the transmission component for the race. The race can be part of the bearing or be separate. Correct installation is essential.

 TECH TIP

Thrust washer condition is judged by the appearance of the washer and the surfaces it runs against. The condition of a Torrington is checked by feeling for rough operation under load.

excessive clearance or end play can cause a pounding that might damage the bearing.

A bushing is a metal sleeve that is lined with a soft bearing material, usually bronze, tin, or both. An experienced technician judges bushing condition by appearance and feel. Any scoring, galling, flaking, excess wear, or rough operation is cause for replacement. ● **SEE FIGURE 17–7**. A bushing is relatively inexpensive, but the damage caused by a worn bushing is very expensive to repair. Most technicians will not gamble on a marginal bushing. If in doubt, replace it. Technicians automatically replace every bushing in certain transmissions, and only some in others. The technician's experience with various transmissions helps to decide which bushings will need replacement. The front (pump) and rear (extension housing) bushings are usually replaced during every transmission rebuild.

17.3.1 BUSHING REMOVAL Several methods can be used to remove a bushing. Always check and note the position of any grooves or oil passages. The size and shape of the bore determines the method of bushing removal and installation. If the bore is straight, the bushing is normally pressed or driven

(a)

(b)

(c)

(d)

FIGURE 17–7 These bushings have failed from (a) embedded debris, (b) abrasion, (c) wiping and overheating, and (d) spin out. (*Courtesy of Sonnax*)

straight out the other end of the bore. ● **SEE FIGURE 17–9**. The driving tool is usually a stepped disk that fits into the bushing bore and has a raised shoulder to press against the end of the bushing. The shoulder should be slightly smaller than the bushing outer diameter to keep it from damaging the bushing bore.

If the bore is stepped so the bushing cannot be pressed through, there are removal tools that can pull the bushing out. These tools are often used with a slide hammer. They can enter the bushing and expand to secure a hold onto the bushing or thread into the bushing. ● **SEE FIGURE 17–10**.

A commonly used method to remove a bushing in a stepped bore is to collapse or cut it. A bushing is collapsed

FIGURE 17–8 A quick and simple check for bushing clearance is to place a strip of paper between the converter hub and bushing. The paper is about 0.003 in. thick, so you should be able to remove it with a slight drag.

FIGURE 17–9 Special tool SP-3629 is being used to drive the bushing out of the clutch housing (top). Note that special tool SP-5511 for the bushing installation has a lip that prevents installing the bushing too deep (bottom). (*Courtesy of Chrysler Corporation*)

(a)   (b)

FIGURE 17–10 (a) A slide hammer with (b) a remover adapter can be used to pull a bushing from its bore. (*Courtesy of ATEC Trans-Tool and Cleaning Systems*) by catching the bushing edge with a bushing cutter or sharp chisel and folding it inward. ● **SEE FIGURE 17–11**. This will be easier if you locate the seam in the bushing and work next to it. Another removal method is to cut a groove in the bushing. This is time-consuming, and there is a possibility of damaging the bearing's bore.

17.3.2 BUSHING INSTALLATION
Replacement bushings are available as individual items or as part of an overhaul set.

TECH TIP

Very small bushings are usually removed by cutting threads in them so a slide hammer can be threaded into the bushing. ● **SEE FIGURE 17–12**. Some output shaft bushings allow standard bolt threads to be cut into them.

TECH TIP

Technicians are very resourceful; they design special tools that may be better than those designed by the vehicle manufacturer. Some technicians remove the THM 350 output shaft bushing using an impact wrench and a C6 band-adjusting screw modified as described in ● **FIGURE 17–13**.

A bushing installer should be used to push the new bushing into its bore to prevent damaging it or the bore. This is often the same tool that was used to remove the bushing. In most cases, the bushing is placed on the tool and pressed or driven

FIGURE 17–12 The special toolset threads into the bushing; turning the nut at the top will pull the bushing out. (*Courtesy of Chrysler Corporation*)

FIGURE 17–13 This band-adjusting screw from a C6 has a cutting groove in the threads, and the nut has been welded into place. With the use of an air wrench, it can cut threads into the bushing at the front of a TH 350 mainshaft; it will bottom in the bore and force the bushing out.

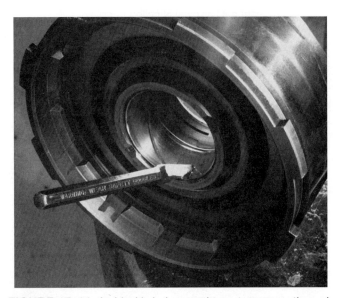

FIGURE 17–11 A chisel is being used to cut a groove through the bushing so it can be collapsed. Be careful to not damage the bushing bore.

(a)

(b)

FIGURE 17–14 Bushing drivers are used to drive bushings into the proper position. (*Courtesy of Chrysler Corporation*)

FIGURE 17–15 Some bushings are locked into position by staking them using a blunt punch. Any raised metal is then scraped off. (*Courtesy of Chrysler Corporation*)

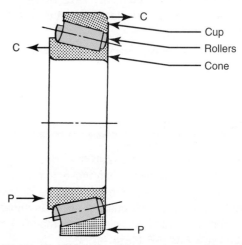

FIGURE 17–16 The cup, rollers, and cone of a tapered roller bearing are machined at an angle as shown. This allows them to resist a thrust in the direction indicated by the P arrows. The bearing is preloaded in this direction; any clearance at the sides of the bearing (C arrows) is called freeplay.

🔧 **TECH TIP**

1. After staking a bushing, you should remove any raised metal with a scraping tool or sharp knife.
2. Some bushings have a hole that must be aligned with an oil passage to permit lubrication of other parts. It is recommended to use a locking compound such as Loctite® to prevent the bushing from rotating in its bore and shutting off the lube flow.

into the bore to the correct depth. ● **SEE FIGURE 17–14.** Some bushing drivers have steps so they "bottom out" and stop at the correct depth. A bushing with a groove or oil passage should be aligned in the original position.

In some cases a bushing is **staked** to lock it in place. Staking is usually done using a punch to bend bushing metal into a recess. ● **SEE FIGURE 17–15.**

17.3.3 TAPERED ROLLER BEARING SERVICE

Some transaxles use tapered roller bearings. ● **SEE FIGURE 17–16.** The bearing consists of the **inner race**, **rollers**, **cage**, and **cup**, which is also called a **cone**. These bearings are checked by visual inspection and by rotating the cleaned and lubricated bearing with a pressure between the bearing and cup. Any scoring or flaking of the cup or roller surfaces or a rough feel is cause for replacement. These bearings are often press-fit onto the shaft, and the cup is press-fit into the bore. Special tools

 REAL WORLD FIX

The 1997 Ford Explorer (69,000 miles) has a delay during the 3–4 shift. Under full throttle, there is a definite engine flare. There are no DTCs, and the fluid pressures are normal in all gears. The transmission was sent to a rebuilder, and no problems were found. Testing on a dyno showed good operation.

FIX

Following advice from experienced technicians, the transmission was disassembled. A very close inspection revealed that a bushing inside of a clutch drum had rotated. This blocked most of the fluid passage, leaving about 10% of the opening. Replacement of this bushing fixed this problem.

(a)

(b)

FIGURE 17–17 Special tools are often required to remove (a) tapered roller bearings and (b) the cups. (*Courtesy of Chrysler Corporation*)

FIGURE 17–18 When roller bearings are to be reused, they should be marked or tagged so they can be put back in the same position with the same races/cups.

are usually required to remove and replace the bearing and its cone. ● **SEE FIGURE 17–17.** If a bearing or its cup are damaged, both should be replaced. If the bearings and cups are to be reused, they should be marked or tagged so a bearing will be installed with the original cup. ● **SEE FIGURE 17–18.**

FIGURE 17–19 This bearing set is adjusted with a selective shim placed under the bearing cup; a thicker shim will reduce the clearance or increase the preload on the bearing. (*Courtesy of Chrysler Corporation*)

FIGURE 17–20 If this bearing set is adjusted correctly, it will take 2.2 inch-pounds (in.-lb) (0.2 N-m) of torque to rotate the differential.

Tapered roller bearings must be adjusted to get the correct end play or preload. This adjustment is normally accomplished by changing **selective** sized shims that can be positioned under the cup. ● **SEE FIGURE 17–19.** A shim of the proper size is selected to provide the correct end play or preload. The procedure for this adjustment varies between manufacturers. ● **SEE FIGURE 17–20.**

17.4 FRICTION MATERIAL SERVICE

There are three opinions concerning replacement of automatic transmission friction material (lined plates, unlined plates, and bands) during an overhaul.

1. Replace all friction material as a standard practice.

2. Replace all lined plates and the unlined plates and bands as needed.

3. Replace only the worn or damaged items.

The second view is the one held by many technicians. As mentioned earlier, some states (e.g., California) require that lined

FIGURE 17–21 The lining is lifted off of this friction plate. It shows rust and corrosion that are evidence of water damage. (*Courtesy of Raybestos*)

FIGURE 17–22 The lining can be easily scraped from the plate; this disc should not be reused.

friction plates be replaced with new parts and the intermediate band be replaced with either a new or relined part if the transmission is being "overhauled" or "rebuilt."

17.4.1 LINED PLATE SERVICE

If lined plates are to be reused, they should be carefully inspected. The requirements for reuse of a lined plate are as follows:

- The lining wear is minimal.
- There must be no breaking up or pock marks in the lining.
- There must be no metal particles embedded in the lining.
- The lining must not come apart when scraped with a coin, fingernail, or knife blade. ● **SEE FIGURE 17–22**.
- The lining must not have a glazed, shiny appearance.
- The lining material must not be severely discolored.
- The plate must be flat.
- The splined area must be flat and even.

17.4.2 STEEL PLATE SERVICE

Unlined steel plates are often reused. They must be carefully inspected before reuse for the following:

- The plate must be flat (except for wave or Belleville plates).
- There must be no sign of surface irregularities.
- The splined area must be flat and even.
- Slightly burned plates must be replaced or reconditioned.

A "good" steel plate is reusable. Other than cleaning, no further preparation is needed. The friction surface of the lined plate has to wear slightly until it matches the surface of the unlined plate. Too rough of a steel plate surface produces severe operation and rapid friction material wear. The ideal surface finish for a used steel plate is a tumbled-finish, smooth, very flat surface like that of a new steel plate. ● **SEE FIGURE 17–23**.

17.4.3 BAND SERVICE

If a band is to be reused, it should be checked to ensure the following:

- The lining material is sound with no breaking up or pock marks.
- The lining material does not come apart when scraped with a thumbnail or knife blade.
- The lining thickness is almost the same as that of a new band.
- The lining material is not badly discolored or does not appear burned.
- There are no metal particles embedded in the friction material.
- The end lugs appear tight and unworn.

If the friction surface on a fabric-lined band has a dark, shiny appearance but is good otherwise, it can be scraped using a knife or bearing scraper to remove the glazed surface. A glazed, paper-lined band should be replaced.

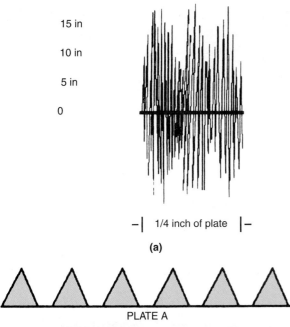

15 in

10 in

5 in

0

−| 1/4 inch of plate |−

(a)

PLATE A

HYPOTHETICAL CONDITION: This type of surface would appear dull, but roughness is the same as Plate B.

PLATE B

HYPOTHETICAL CONDITION: This type of surface would appear shiny, but is no smoother than Plate A.

(b)

FIGURE 17–23 (a) A profilimeter shows the profile of a steel plate; 1 microinch (μin.) equals 0.000001 in. (b) The actual shape of the surface roughness can vary, but both of these plates have the same surface roughness. (*Courtesy of Raybestos*)

FIGURE 17–24 This tool can rotate a basket of steel plates and special media to cause a tumbling action that cleans and retextures the surface. (*Courtesy of ATEC Trans-Tool and Cleaning Systems*)

 TECH TIP

1. A quick way to check the plates for flatness is to stack the plates and look for any gaps between them. Overheated plates tend to warp into either a slightly conical or a "potato chip" shape. Gaps indicate warped, unusable plates. Restack the plates, turning every other one upside down, and recheck for gaps. Any gaps indicate faulty, unusable plates.

2. Some shops use a tumbler to recondition used steel plates. ● **SEE FIGURE 17–24**. This machine rotates a basket of plates along with a ceramic medium and soap; the tumbling action creates the small nicks and dents that produce the correct surface finish. Some sources recommend roughing up a steel plate by sanding or blasting with sand, grit, or glass beads, but these processes are considered too time-consuming. Also, blasting may produce a surface finish that is too rough and severe.

🚗 **REAL WORLD FIX**

The 1994 Explorer (82,000 miles) transmission burned up the frictions in the forward clutch after about 4,000 miles. The clutch drum looked good, and the sealing rings were replaced. The case is flat, and the center support has been replaced. The clutch checks out good using a wet air test.

FIX

Using advice from his peers, the technician installed a manual valve index sleeve (an aftermarket repair item). This part keeps the manual valve properly aligned with the bore.

The drum surface for a band must also be in good condition. The drum surface should be very smooth and flat. ● **SEE FIGURE 17–25**. A rough, badly scored drum should be replaced.

17.4.4 NEW FRICTION MATERIAL PREPARATION

New friction material must never be used in a dry, unlubricated condition. Dry lining acts like an insulator. It easily

FIGURE 17–25 (a, b) Two badly worn drums; both are scored and polished. Note (b) shows burn marks. (c, d) Four faulty bands: two broken bands; (e) the band is burned and flaking lining; (f) the band is worn out; and (g) a servo piston with a broken pin.

Emery Cloth Strip

FIGURE 17–27 If a drum surface is polished, it can be sanded to roughen the surface. If a paper band is used, sand around the drum using 120- or 180-grit emery cloth or sandpaper. If a fabric band is used, sand in a front-to-back direction using 40- to 60-grit sandpaper.

FIGURE 17–26 Stamped steel drums should be checked for dishing. There should be no clearance between the drum and the straightedge.

TECH TIP

1. If the scoring is light and the equipment is available, some technicians true up the drum surface using either an engine lathe or a brake drum lathe. This may require a band with an oversize lining to compensate for the smaller drum diameter.
2. Some transmissions use a drum made from a steel stamping rather than from a forging or a casting. These units should be checked for dishing by laying a straightedge along the drum surface. ● SEE FIGURE 17–26.
3. If the drum surface is smooth but polished, it can be sanded to produce a better finish. If a paper-lined band is used, use 150- to 160-grit sandpaper, and sand in a direction that goes around the drum. ● SEE FIGURE 17–27. If a fabric-lined band is used, use coarser sandpaper (40 to 60 grit) and sand in a front-to-back direction.

overheats and burns from the heat of friction created during the first shift. The lined material should be soaked in ATF for at least 20 minutes before installation; some shops soak the plates overnight.

17.5 INTERNAL SEAL SERVICE

An important part of a transmission overhaul is the correct replacement of the internal seals. These are the rubber and metal seals used on accumulator, servo, and clutch pistons and the rotating metal or Teflon sealing rings used on the pump clutch support, the input shaft, and the governor support. ● SEE FIGURE 17–28. Rubber seals should always be replaced during an overhaul. If the metal or Teflon sealing rings are in good shape, it is possible to reuse them, but this is not recommended.

The piston seals of some transmissions are molded directly onto the piston. ● SEE FIGURE 17–29. The piston must be replaced if the seal is damaged or worn excessively.

17.5.1 FITTING RUBBER SEALS
Always check a seal in the bore where it will operate. In most cases, this takes very little time. An O-ring seal (round or square-cut) is first checked by placing it in the bore by itself. ● SEE FIGURE 17–30. If it is slightly larger or smaller than the bore (3% or less), it will work.

FIGURE 17–28 Four styles of Teflon rings; the uncut, continuous ring requires special tools for installation. The other styles are placed into the groove with overlapping ends positioned properly.

FIGURE 17–30 Each of these accumulator pistons has an O-ring seal that should have a snug fit in the bore. (*Courtesy of Toyota Motor Sales USA, Inc.*)

FIGURE 17–29 The seal is molded onto this servo piston, and the piston should be replaced during a transmission overhaul.

TECH TIP

1. To calculate 3% of the bore, take the diameter, move the decimal point two places to the left, and multiply by 3. For example, a 2 1/4 servo is 2.250 in. Moving the decimal point gives us 0.0225; multiplying by 3 gives us 0.0675 in. The allowable over- or undersize of 3% of 2 1/4 in. is slightly more than 1/16 in.

2. The seals can be checked for size by placing them one at a time in their operating position. Start with the seal that is easiest to remove and replace. Place one seal on the piston, lubricate it with ATF, and work it into the bore. Now stroke the piston, and feel for drag. ● **SEE FIGURE 17–31**. A round O-ring should produce some drag; a square-cut seal is okay if it produces a barely noticeable drag. Now remove the piston, remove the seal, install the next seal, and check its drag.

3. A lip seal is checked the same way. Just like an O-ring seal, it must produce a drag on the way into the drum, but it is okay if it falls outward when turned over. On a piston that uses three lip seals, you should check them each, one at a time.

17.5.2 INSTALLING PISTONS WITH LIP SEALS The clutch piston should be inspected before seal installation. ● **SEE FIGURE 17–32**. A piston that is manufactured from sheet metal stampings should be checked for broken welds or cracks. Also make sure that the check ball moves freely in its cage and seals properly, as described in Chapter 18.

Step #1

Inner Seal Installed

Outer Seal Removed

Step #2

Inner Seal Removed

Installing Outer Seal

Step #3

Outer Seal Installed

Inner Seal Installed

FIGURE 17–31 The inner piston seal is installed, and the piston is slid into the bore to check its fit (step 1). The piston is removed, and the fit of the outer seal is checked (step 2). Then both seals are installed and lubricated, and the piston is installed for the final time (step 3).

During installation, a lip seal often catches the edge of the bore and will roll outward. This will probably cut the seal

FIGURE 17–32 A piston should be checked for any signs of damage, porosity, nicks at the seal groove, and a missing or stuck check ball.

TECH TIP

1. Wax lubricant, often called **door ease,** is commonly used for vehicle door or hood striker plates. Smearing a film of wax lubricant around the seal and at the edge of the bore is often just enough lubricant to allow the seal to slip into the bore. ● **SEE FIGURE 17–33.**
2. Seal installation tools are commercially available or you can make one by rounding the edges of a feeler gauge that is 0.005 to 0.010 in. (0.15 to 0.25 mm) or squeezing a bent, thin piece of piano wire into the end of a small tubing. ● **SEE FIGURE 17–34.** As the piston is being installed, use this tool to coax the seal lip into the bore.
3. Seal guides are available for some clutch units. These are smooth steel bands with a slight funnel or cone shape. ● **SEE FIGURE 17–35.** They are placed in the drum and lubricated. As the piston is being installed, the guides prevent the seal lips from catching on the edge of the bore.

lip and cause a fluid leak. Several procedures can be used to ease installation and produce a reliable clutch: use a wax lubricant, an installing tool, a seal guide, and precompress the seal lip.

A seal should never be installed dry. Both the bore and the seals should be lubricated with ATF, transmission assembly lubricant, petroleum jelly, or wax lubricant.

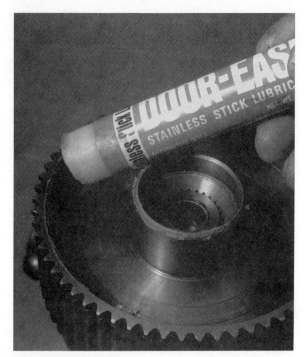

FIGURE 17–33 Piston and seal installation can be made easier if a film of wax lubricant is smeared around the seals and seal area.

(a)

(b)

FIGURE 17–34 (a) When the piston is installed, the seal tends to catch on the upper end of the piston bore (arrow). (b) A shop-made seal installing tool, thin feeler gauge, or a commercial seal installer can coax the seal past this edge.

17.5.3 FITTING SEALING RINGS

A sealing ring has to make a seal on one of its sides and at the outer diameter. Fluid pressure plus the elasticity of the ring pushes the ring outward, where it engages the bore. If the bore is rotating, the sealing ring

(a)   (b)

FIGURE 17–35 Two seal guides can be placed into the clutch drum. With the new seals lubricated, the piston can be installed without seal lip damage.

rotates with the bore. ● **SEE FIGURE 17–38**. Rubbing action should always take place between one side of the sealing ring and the groove. Some sliding action takes place between the ring and the bore. End play allows the bore along with the drum to move forward and backward. Excessive end play causes rapid wear of the sealing ring and possible damage to the ring groove.

FIGURE 17–36 This seal kit is used to squeeze or precompress a seal for easy installation and a lubricant to help the seal slide into place. (*Courtesy of Lubegard*)

FIGURE 17–37 After the clutch is completely assembled, the condition of the seals can be verified by an air check. The dial indicator will give an accurate measurement of the clutch pack clearance. (*Courtesy of Toyota Motor Sales USA, Inc.*)

FIGURE 17–38 A sealing ring is forced outward, away from the fluid pressure. It tends to wear into the sides of the seal grooves.

A metal sealing ring, either **open/plain end** or **hook ring**, should be checked by placing it in its bore. ● **SEE FIGURE 17–39.** There should be a tight and close fit between the outer diameter of the ring and the bore. An undersized or odd-shaped ring should not be used. Open-end metal rings should have a slight gap, about 0.002 to 0.015 in. (0.05 to 0.3 mm), between the ends of the ring to

FIGURE 17–39 A metal sealing ring has been hooked and placed into its bore. It should enter with a slight pressure and make full contact with the bore. There should be a slight gap at the ends of the ring as shown.

TECH TIP

1. If you encounter breakage of metal sealing rings as you install the component over them, check the ring end gap in the component's bore. If the end gap is correct, then fill the ring groove with assembly lube and install the ring so it is centered to the shaft with an equal amount of ring showing all around the shaft. Now, carefully install the component.
2. Be careful when you install the next component over a sealing ring. If the ends stick out, they can get caught and become damaged during installation.

(a)

(b)

FIGURE 17-40 (a) Side clearance of a metal sealing ring is checked by placing the ring into the groove and measuring the clearance using a feeler gauge. (b) While making this check, look for damage to the seal groove.

(a)

(b)

FIGURE 17-41 (a) Compressing a seal ring helps it fit tight in its groove. (b) During installation, make sure the ends interlock properly. (*Courtesy of Chrysler Corporation*)

allow for expansion of the ring metal. Slight nicks or imperfections can be smoothed using sandpaper.

Next, check the ring in the groove. ● **SEE FIGURE 17-40.** A hook- or interlock-type ring should be hooked after installation. There should be a maximum of about 0.003 in. (0.07 mm) of groove wear, and the sides of the groove should be smooth and straight. Small imperfections can be smoothed using a small file. Excessive or tapered wear requires shaft or clutch support replacement.

17.5.4 INSTALLING TEFLON SEALING RINGS Scarf-cut, Teflon sealing rings are easy to install. Merely place them in the groove with the ends lapped in the correct direction. ● **SEE FIGURE 17-41.**

Uncut Teflon rings require two special tools for installation: an installing tool and a resizing tool. To install a Teflon ring, place the installing tool over the shaft; adjust it to the correct depth if necessary; lubricate the ring and the tool; and slide the ring over the tool and into its groove. ● **SEE FIGURE 17-42.** You can expect the ring to stretch during installation. Next,

FIGURE 17-42 This Teflon seal installation set allows you to stretch a seal ring, position it in the groove, and resize the seal so it has the proper fit. (*Courtesy of ATEC Trans-Tool and Cleaning Systems*)

TECH TIP

1. Warming the ring in hot water will soften the material and make installation and resizing easier.
2. It is helpful to leave the seal resizing tool on the seal until you are ready to install the shaft.

lubricate the ring and resizing tool, and work the resizing tool over the ring, being sure the ring enters its groove correctly. The resizing tool should compress the ring to the correct diameter. Once the transmission operates and the ring gets hot, it will take the shape of the bore.

SUMMARY

1. A transmission overhaul includes disassembly, cleaning, replacing worn parts, and reassembling to its original clearances.
2. Transmission parts are cleaned by hand and by automated wash cabinets.
3. Bushings and bearings are carefully checked and replaced as necessary.
4. Clutches are serviced by inspecting and replacing the friction material and seals.
5. Sealing rings must be replaced and the surfaces they seal against must be carefully inspected and serviced as needed.

REVIEW QUESTIONS

1. Shop rags should never be used to clean, dry, or wipe parts because they leave _____ on the parts that could _____ the filter.
2. The commonly used methods for cleaning transmission parts are:
   a. _____
   b. _____
   c. _____
3. The condition of a plastic, fiber, or metal thrust washer is judged by the appearance of the _____ and the _____ it runs against.
4. The front _____ bushing and the rear _____ housing bushing are usually replaced during an overhaul.
5. During installation, a bushing must be _____ with any oil grooves of passages.
6. The _____ plates are usually replaced during a transmission overhaul and the _____ plates are often reused.
7. The bands and friction clutch plates should be soaked in ATF for at least _____ minutes before installation in the transmission.
8. A seal ring should be _____ in its bore before installation.
9. After new seals are installed in a clutch and the clutch is completely assembled, it should be _____ checked for proper operation and leakage.
10. A seal ring seals on its _____ and _____ diameter.

CHAPTER QUIZ

1. During a transmission rebuild, it is good practice to replace _____.
   a. Rubber sealing rings
   b. Lined clutch plates
   c. Paper and composition gaskets
   d. All of these

2. Technician A says that the usual method of cleaning transmission parts is to wash them in solvent and dry them with a shop cloth. Technician B says that spray washers are a fast and effective way of cleaning parts. Who is correct?
   a. Technician A
   b. Technician B
   c. Both Technicians A and B
   d. Neither Technician A nor B

3. Technician A says that worn or damaged bushings are repaired by driving them out and replacing them with new bushings. Technician B says that some bushings are removed by cutting threads in them so a puller bolt can be used. Who is correct?
   a. Technician A
   b. Technician B
   c. Both Technicians A and B
   d. Neither Technician A nor B

4. Technician A says that position of the bushing holes or grooves is not important during installation. Technician B says that all bushings must be stacked after installation. Who is correct?
   a. Technician A
   b. Technician B
   c. Both Technicians A and B
   d. Neither Technician A nor B

5. Technician A says that if a tapered roller bearing cup is worn and needs to be replaced, the rest of the bearing parts also will need to be replaced. Technician B says that if a tapered bearing is to be reused it must be installed in its original position. Who is correct?
   a. Technician A
   b. Technician B
   c. Both Technicians A and B
   d. Neither Technician A nor B

6. Technician A says that it is good practice to replace all friction materials (lined plates, unlined plates, and bands) when rebuilding a transmission. Technician B says that lined friction material must be soaked in ATF before it is installed. Who is correct?
   a. Technician A
   b. Technician B
   c. Both Technicians A and B
   d. Neither Technician A nor B

7. Technician A says that an unlined steel clutch plate can be reused if it is smooth and shiny and only has a little bit of "potato chip" warpage. Technician B says that a lined plate that shows any darkening should not be reused. Who is correct?
   a. Technician A
   b. Technician B
   c. Both Technicians A and B
   d. Neither Technician A nor B

8. Technician A says that seals should always be checked for proper fit before installation. Technician B says that seals should never be installed dry. Who is correct?
   a. Technician A
   b. Technician B
   c. Both Technicians A and B
   d. Neither Technician A nor B

9. Technician A says that excessive end play causes rapid wear of the sealing rings and possibly the sealing ring groove. Technician B says that seal does not rotate in the groove; therefore, the groove could not wear. Who is correct?
   a. Technician A
   b. Technician B
   c. Both Technicians A and B
   d. Neither Technician A nor B

10. Technician A says that Teflon sealing rings require special tools for proper installation. Technician B says that warming a Teflon seal with hot water will help to size the seal. Who is correct?
    a. Technician A
    b. Technician B
    c. Both Technicians A and B
    d. Neither Technician A nor B

chapter 18

SUBASSEMBLY REPAIR

OBJECTIVES: After studying Chapter 18, the reader will be able to: • Disassemble and reassemble automatic transmission subassemblies. • Determine if used subassemblies and their components are usable. • Complete the ASE tasks related to off-vehicle transmission/transaxle repair.

KEY TERMS: Clutch clearance 458 • Cross leak 445 • Drainback hole 448 • Draw file 446 • Free fall 469 • Pump cover alignment 453 • Pump gear alignment 451 • Ream 445 • Sag test 469 • Selective 458 • Spring holder 466 • Subassemblies 445 • Warpage 445 • Worm tracks 445

18.1 SUBASSEMBLY REPAIR

Inspection, service, and repair operations are done to each of the transmission **subassemblies** as part of the transmission overhaul. These subassemblies include the case, pump, clutch assemblies, gear set, valve body, and governor. Subassembly repair ensures that each component is serviceable and will work properly when the transmission is assembled.

Some technicians disassemble the transmission and all of the subassemblies completely. The components are serviced, repaired, and assembled as the transmission is reassembled. Other technicians choose to disassemble the transmission and then service each of the subassemblies separately before starting to reassemble the transmission. The second method is recommended because there will be fewer parts disassembled at one time. This decreases the likelihood of mixing parts, which is easy to do, especially between clutch assemblies, because many parts have a similar appearance. If each subassembly is in good condition and is working properly, the transmission should work properly when completed.

18.2 CASE INSPECTION

Several areas of the case should be checked or serviced after it has been cleaned. These include the bushings, all fluid passages, the valve body **worm tracks** (grooves for the valve

body fluid flow), all bolt threads, the clutch plate lugs, and the governor bore.

Some cases have an output shaft bushing, and it should be checked and replaced if it is worn or scored. Bushing replacement is described in Chapter 17. Occasionally a bushing will seize and spin with the shaft, which can ruin the case. The repair procedure is to **ream** the bore oversize. A bushing with an oversize outside diameter (OD) is then installed to repair the case. ● **SEE FIGURE 18–1.**

Every fluid passage in the case must be clean and open. It is a good practice to blow air into each passage and make sure that it comes out the other end. Next, plug off one end of the passage while air pressure is applied; if you hear air escaping, there is a leak.

Check for **warpage** in the worm track area. Warpage can produce a **cross leak**, which is a leak from one passage to another. A cross leak can cause an unwanted, partial application of a clutch or band that can lead to an early failure. Case warpage is checked by placing a straightedge over the area to be checked and trying to slide a feeler gauge between the case and straightedge.

Most faulty bolt threads are found during disassembly. The telltale sign of failure is when the bolts come out with

TECH TIP

The exact location of a leak can be found by a *wet air test* (Chapter 12) or by placing the case under solvent or water as air is applied to each of the passages.

FIGURE 18–1 This tool is designed to attach to the rear of an E4OD or C6 case. It guides a reamer that will cut the damaged bore to a larger diameter; an oversized bushing is then used to repair the case and a more durable bushing is installed. (*Courtesy of Sonnax*)

🔧 **TECH TIP**

1. Some technicians **draw file** the valve body area using a 16-in., single-cut file as standard practice. To draw file a case, place the case with the worm tracks upward, lay the file flat, grip each end of the file, and draw the file sideways across the case. ● **SEE FIGURE 18–2.** The file should be drawn in both a lengthwise and crosswise direction. The case is flat when a light cut has been made on all of the raised portions of the worm tracks.

2. If a low-mileage transmission has failed because of a burned clutch or band, then check for pressure loss and cross leaks. Check for a cross leak by locating the passages for the two circuits and plug one of the passages with putty and fill it with ATF. ● **SEE FIGURE 18–3.** Fluid leaking from this passage indicates a cross leak, which is probably caused by a crack or porous casting.

FIGURE 18–2 A flat, smooth file is being drawn (moved in the direction of the arrow) across the valve body area of a case to smooth out any dings or warpage.

aluminum on the threads. Damaged threads should be repaired as described in Chapter 14. It is good practice to check all bolt threads visually to make sure they are in good shape. Always replace questionable bolts.

If the transmission has a holding clutch, for example, the low-reverse clutch or intermediate clutch in a THM 350,

check the area of the case where the clutch lugs engage the case. ● **SEE FIGURE 18–4.** A badly worn case should be replaced.

Check the governor bore on cases that have a gear-driven governor. If there is excessive wear in the governor bore, a loss in governor pressure can occur.

(a)

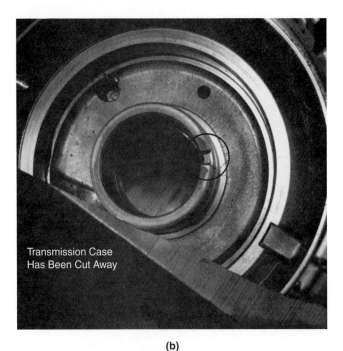

Transmission Case
Has Been Cut Away

(b)

FIGURE 18–3 (a) This worm track (arrow) has been closed off and filled with ATF to check for a suspected leak. (b) The low-reverse clutch failed because of a pressure loss through a crack (circled). It was found by watching ATF leak out of the crack.

TECH TIP

1. The governor bore size can be checked by placing the governor into its bore and filling the passages with ATF. ● **SEE FIGURE 18–5**. The bore should be repaired if the fluid leaks out too quickly (to point A in less than 30 seconds).

2. Minor scores in a governor bore can be cleaned using a small cylinder hone. ● **SEE FIGURE 18–6**. A worn bore can be repaired by installing a special reaming fixture, reaming the bore oversize, and installing a bushing to return the bore to the original size.

3. Some transmissions develop a fluid leak around the shift shaft because of a worn bore. A repair kit has been developed that includes a reamer, reamer guide, repair sleeve, and retaining pins. ● **SEE FIGURE 18–7**. The repair sleeve is installed after the bore is reamed oversize.

4. Some accumulator bores tend to wear because of repeated accumulator piston oscillation. This produces leakage at the accumulator piston and will ruin the case. A repair sleeve can be installed into the accumulator bore, and this sleeve along with a matching piston will allow the case to be reused. ● **SEE FIGURE 18–8**.

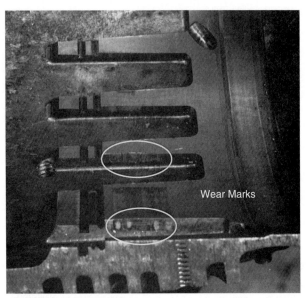

Wear Marks

FIGURE 18–4 This case shows wear in the area where the low-reverse clutch plates contact the lugs. This case is still usable, but excessive wear might hamper proper clutch apply and release.

The final service step for the case service is to install a new seal for the manual shifter and, in some cases, the throttle valve linkage or rear bushing seal. ● **SEE FIGURE 18–9**. These operations are described in Chapter 14. After this is done, the case can be set aside until reassembly.

(a)

Insert Test Tool

Transmission Case Governor Bore

Governor Circuit Test Tool

(b)

Fill Point
Point A

Test Tool

(c)

FIGURE 18–5 (a) Governor bore wear is checked by placing the case on its back; (b) inserting the test tool into the governor bore; (c) filling the passage with ATF; and seeing how long it takes for the fluid to leak down to point A. (*Figure (b) Courtesy of Sonnax*)

18.3 PUMP SERVICE

Service of most pumps consists of the following:

- Disassembly
- Inspection of the pumping members, stator support shaft, front bushing, clutch support surface, and sealing ring grooves

 REAL WORLD FIX

The 1974 Chevrolet Nova (126,000 miles; THM 350) has a late 1–2 shift and no 2–3 shift. Fluid level, TV cable adjustment, and the vacuum modulator are all good. The governor was checked and a bad driven gear was found. The governor gear was replaced, but this did not help.

FIX

Following advice, the technician checked the governor again and the governor bore was found to be bad. A remanufactured transmission fixed this vehicle. The worn governor bore could have been reamed out and repaired.

 TECH TIP

As you remove the pump gears or the rotor and slide, carefully note the front–back positioning. Many gears are marked. If the gears are not marked, use a permanent marking pen to identify the front of each gear.

REAL WORLD FIX

The 1982 Buick (2004R; 137,000 miles) transmission came into the shop with no reverse. Disassembly revealed the problem to be caused by worn sun gear splines. The worn parts were replaced, and the unit was rebuilt using a master kit, new pump, and torque converter. On start-up, the unit had excessively high line pressure.

FIX

The high pressure was caused by the wrong regulator valve for the later-model pump. The old valve (no vent) was installed into a bore that required a vented valve. The vent is a passage so line pressure can act on the end of the valve.

NOTE: This is a hard one, but when replacing a pressure regulator valve or its bore, carefully compare the parts to be sure they are the same.

- Checking of all valves
- Cleaning of all fluid passages, including the **drainback hole**
- Replacement of the front seal
- Reassembly

FIGURE 18–6 A small cylinder hone dipped in ATF can be used to smooth out minor scores in a governor bore. It should be turned by hand. Power tools should not be used.

FIGURE 18–7 An A4LD tends to wear the manual shift linkage bore and leak fluid. The case can be repaired by reaming the bore oversize and installing a repair sleeve. (*Courtesy of Sonnax*)

FIGURE 18–8 A damaged or worn accumulator bore can be repaired by installing a sleeve and a matching piston. (*Courtesy of Sonnax*)

FIGURE 18–9 The manual valve shaft seal is driven into place using a seal driver.

Pump disassembly is fairly easy: Simply remove the bolts that secure the cover onto the body. ● **SEE FIGURE 18–10.**

Experienced technicians check a pump by visual inspection. They carefully check the areas where wear normally occurs. Remember that the pump has a high-pressure area, and this high pressure tries to force the gears outward. A technician will inspect the following areas.

- Sides of the gears or rotors
- Body and cover where the gears run (● **SEE FIGURE 18–11.**)
- Flanks of the gear teeth/rotor lobes for score marks
- Pump bushing

Manufacturers sometimes publish clearance specifications for the pump wear locations. These clearances can be checked using a feeler gauge. ● **SEE FIGURE 18–12.** A worn pump requires replacement with a new or rebuilt unit.

Vane-type pumps are also checked by visual inspection. Besides the inner slide area, be sure to check the pump guide rings, vanes, rotor, pump guide, slide, slide seals, seal support, slide pivot pin, spring, slide sealing ring, and backup

FIGURE 18-10 The pump gears and their cavity are carefully checked for wear and the front seal is normally replaced. (*Courtesy of Chrysler Corporation*)

(a)

(b)

FIGURE 18-11 (a) The rotor and slide of this vane pump are broken, and (b) the pump body is badly scored. This pump must be replaced.

(a)

(b)

(c)

FIGURE 18-12 Clearance checks of the pump gears include (a) end clearance, (b) gear-to-housing clearance, and (c) gear-tooth clearance. (*Courtesy of Chrysler Corporation*)

seal. ● **SEE FIGURE 18-13.** If replacement is necessary, the thickness of the rotor and slide should be measured to ensure the correct replacement parts are installed. ● **SEE FIGURE 18-14.**

With the pump disassembled, it is usually easy to remove and replace the front seal and also the bushing if necessary. It should be noted that some manufacturers recommend replacing the pump assembly if the front bushing is damaged. A seal driver should be used when installing the new front seal. ● **SEE FIGURE 18-15.** If a seal driver is not available, a flat piece of 1/8-in. (3-mm) or thicker metal should be placed over the seal to prevent damage while pressing or driving it into

Pump Cover

Stator Shaft

Vane Ring

Rotor

Vane

Rotor Guide

Vane Ring

Pivot Pin

Pivot Pin
Spring

Slide Seal
Support

Slide
Spring
(Inner)

Slide
Seal

Slide
Spring
(Outer)

O-Ring
Seal

O-Ring

Pump Body

FIGURE 18–13 An exploded view of a vane-type pump. Wear checks include the rotor, vanes, slide, pump body, and pump cover.

place. A damaged stator shaft can usually be pressed out and a new one pressed in while the pump is apart. Upgraded stator support shafts are available for some transmissions. ● **SEE FIGURE 18–16.**

Some pumps include a clutch piston assembly; the piston seals are serviced as described in Chapter 17.

After the pump has been cleaned, thoroughly checked, and the bushings and seal replaced, it can be reassembled. The gears or rotor and slide assembly should be well lubricated and placed in the pump body.

Some pumps require **pump gear alignment** as the gears are installed. This requires a special alignment tool set that

TECH TIP

Metal caged lip seals are not designed to retain pressure. The fluid that is fed to lubricate the front bushing normally drains back into the transmission case through a drainback hole between the bushing and the seal. ● **SEE FIGURE 18–17.** If this hole plugs up, pressure can build up behind the seal and cause the seal to blow out. Make sure the drain passage is open.

REAL WORLD FIX

The 1993 Chevrolet Blazer (87,000 miles) had a front seal leak that was repaired by installing a new seal, but after 1 or 2 weeks, it would begin leaking again. The front pump gasket and O-ring were replaced. The engine crankshaft end play was checked, and it was within specifications. The vehicle returned with the same problem.

FIX

During the next replacement of the seal, the pump bushing was checked and was found to have been spinning in the pump assembly. A new bushing was installed with a new seal, which cured the problem.

REAL WORLD FIX

The 1998 Ford Escort (215,000 miles) was driving at 45 mph when it suddenly neutraled out (no drive or reverse). The technician checked oil pressure and found 0 PSI. A check of the pressure regulator valve shows it to be okay. A check of the pump driveshaft shows it was in good condition, and the shaft seems to engage the torque converter splines.

FIX

Following advice, the technician tried the pump driveshaft in the torque converter again, but this time he pulled the shaft about 1/8 in. out from the front of the drive splines. The splines were stripped in this area. A new torque converter fixed this problem.

FIGURE 18–14 If replacement is needed for (a) the pump rotor, (b) vanes, or (c) slide, they should be measured to determine the proper size.

FIGURE 18–15 A new front seal is being installed using a seal driver (SST).

1. Bushings supplied to allow use in all THM700-R4 and 4L60-E applications

FIGURE 18–16 A replacement stator support shaft for a 4L60 transmission that uses a set screw to prevent rotation of the inner sleeve. (*Courtesy of Sonnax*)

FIGURE 18–17 Fluid flowing through the pump bushing must be allowed to flow to the pan through the drainback passage. If this passage is blocked, a drill bit of the proper size should be used to clean it out.

positions the drive gear properly to the pump housing and front bushing. ● **SEE FIGURE 18–18.** Improper alignment might cause breakage of the gears or housing or damage to the bushing or front seal. In all cases it is good practice to visually center the pump drive gear to the front bushing as the pump is assembled.

On some pumps, the cover has a much smaller diameter than the body. Here, the cover is merely placed in position and the bolts are installed and tightened to the correct torque. Other pump covers and bodies have the same outer diameter. These diameters are only slightly smaller than the bore in the

FIGURE 18–18 These special tools are used to align the pump gears of certain Ford transmissions while the bolts are tightened. (*Courtesy of ATEC Trans-Tool and Cleaning Systems*)

SPECIAL TOOL
J25025-1

(a)

(b)

FIGURE 18–19 (a) Special tool J25025-1 is being used to align the pump body and cover before tightening the bolts. (b) A long screw clamp can be used for this same purpose. (*Figure (a) Reprinted with permission of General Motors*)

 TECH TIP

1. Technicians normally lubricate all moving parts as they are assembled. Normal automotive grease cannot be used because it is thick and might plug a fluid orifice. Special automatic transmission assembly lubricant, petroleum jelly, or ATF is commonly used. These greaselike compounds will melt and be dissolved before the transmission gets to operating temperature.

2. Some technicians lubricate the gears with a heavy coating of transmission assembly lubricant or petroleum jelly to ensure that the pump will prime and start pumping fluid immediately on start-up.

 TECH TIP

1. An alternate aligning method is to place the pump upside down in an empty transmission case before tightening the bolts. ● **SEE FIGURE 18–20**.

2. The torque converter can be used to align the pump gears by placing the pump body on the torque converter hub as the pump is assembled. Torque-tighten the pump cover bolts before removing the pump.

18.4 CLUTCH ASSEMBLY SERVICE

transmission case. The two outer diameters have to be exactly aligned before tightening the bolts. **Pump cover alignment** is accomplished by using the band shown in ● **FIGURE 18–19**. This band is available commercially, or a very large screw-type hose clamp can be used in its place.

At this point, the pump is ready to be reinstalled.

The service procedure for most clutch assemblies is as follows:

- Remove the clutch plates and disassemble the return spring(s) and piston. ● **SEE FIGURE 18–21**.

- Thoroughly clean the parts.

FIGURE 18–20 The pump body and cover can be aligned correctly by placing them into the case upside down while the bolts are tightened.

(a)

(b)

FIGURE 18–22 (a) The large snap ring can usually be removed using a screwdriver or seal pick, and then (b) the pressure plate and clutch plates can be removed.

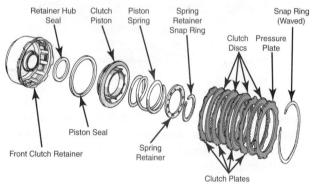

Retainer Hub Seal — Clutch Piston — Piston Spring — Spring Retainer Snap Ring — Clutch Discs — Pressure Plate — Snap Ring (Waved)

Piston Seal

Front Clutch Retainer

Spring Retainer

Clutch Plates

FIGURE 18–21 An exploded view of a clutch assembly; note the clutch stack with four frictions and the strong piston spring. (*Courtesy of Chrysler Corporation*)

- Inspect the drum, piston, and check ball as well as the bushing and seal ring area.
- Install new seals on the piston.
- Install the piston and return spring(s).
- Install the clutch plates.
- Check the clutch clearance.

Clutch plate removal is usually easy. A screwdriver or seal pick is used to work the snap ring out of its groove. The pressure plate and clutch plates are removed next. ● **SEE FIGURE 18–22.** Always note the position of the pressure plate, the number of lined and unlined plates, and if any cushion plates are used and their position.

A spring compressor is usually required to remove the piston return spring(s) and retainer. There is a large variety of spring compressors, and no one unit will work best for all clutches,

  REAL WORLD FIX

The 1995 Impala SS (145,000 miles) transmission was overhauled because of no fourth gear. The 3–4 clutch was badly burned. The case and input drum were replaced because they were badly worn. The transmission now has no low or third gear.

FIX

Disassembling the transmission again revealed that the passage to the forward clutch was plugged with debris. The forward clutch was a used unit, purchased from a dismantler. The input drum had a thorough cleaning. An air check showed proper clutch operation.

A lot of work would have been saved if this used clutch had been disassembled and cleaned during the subassembly repair process.

because some have a bore in the center, a shaft in the center, or are in the case. ● **SEE FIGURE 18–23.** Many shops use bench- or floor-mounted spring compressors because these are usually faster. Be careful when compressing the spring(s), removing the retainer, and allowing the spring(s) to extend.

FIGURE 18–23 (a–c) This variety of clutch spring compressors includes completely portable ones, (d) a bench-mounted style, and (e) a large, foot-operated style. (*Figure (a), left, Courtesy of Chrysler Corporation; (a), right, Courtesy of Kent-Moore; (b) Courtesy of OTC; (d–e) Courtesy of KD Tools*)

TECH TIP

1. Clutch stacks will vary for a given transmission model depending on the application. Note the order of the plates as they are removed. Check them for wear as described in Chapter 17.
2. While the return springs are being removed, be sure to note the number and location of the springs if all of the pockets are not filled with springs. ● **SEE FIGURE 18–24.**

FIGURE 18–24 Some clutch assemblies do not use a spring in each of the pockets. Note how they are arranged in this clutch. (*Courtesy of Chrysler Corporation*)

Some springs store quite a bit of energy (one clutch uses an 800-lb [364-kg] release spring). If they fly loose, they can cause injury. Review the safety note following step 7 of Section 16.5.

Some clutch pistons almost fall out of the bore when the springs and retainer are removed. Other pistons have to be coaxed with air pressure in the clutch apply oil hole or by slamming the clutch drum piston side down onto a block of wood. ● **SEE FIGURE 18–25.** With the piston out, remove the old seals, wash the parts in solvent, and dry them using compressed air.

(a)

(b)

FIGURE 18–25 A piston can be removed by (a) slamming the clutch downward on a block of wood or (b) applying air pressure in the apply port.

FIGURE 18–26 This piston is made from stamped steel parts that can separate. It is tested by inserting a screwdriver and trying to pry the grooves open with a light pressure.

TECH TIP

1. Some clutch pistons are made from stamped steel parts that are pressed and welded together. These parts can shift position, which can cause a seal groove that is too wide or too narrow. Check the groove width; it should be slightly wider than the seal. If you suspect a problem, place a screwdriver into the groove, and try prying it wider. ● **SEE FIGURE 18–26**. If the parts move easily, replace the piston.

2. Some clutch drums are made from stamped steel parts and these can leak at a weld or a crack next to a weld, causing a pressure loss. If you suspect a leaking drum, place the clutch with the bore upward, and fill the piston area with ATF or solvent. If fluid leaks out, you need to replace the drum. Another method is to spray the assembled clutch with a soapy water mix, and air check it using varied low and high pressures.

REAL WORLD FIX

The 1994 Dodge Caravan (143,000 miles) was working fine when the fluid was replaced a few weeks ago. Since the fluid change, it got stuck in snow, and had to be rocked out. Now it moves forward in all shift lever positions, even neutral. The shift linkage was checked and found to be okay.

FIX

When the transmission was disassembled, the front clutch plates were found to have gotten so hot that they welded together. Rebuilding the transmission fixed this problem.

REAL WORLD FIX

A 1991 Acura had a slip in second gear after it warms up. When cold, the transmission operates normal, and when hot, transmission operation is normal except for second gear.

FIX

A very small crack was found next to a weld in the second drum, and this crack opened up when hot and caused a pressure loss. Replacement of the second drum clutch fixed the transmission.

FIGURE 18–27 The check ball should be free to move inside its cage. It should also seal low-pressure airflow in one direction (left) and leak in the other (right).

FIGURE 18–28 This bushing appears usable and the two sealing ring areas (arrows) show normal operation.

 REAL WORLD FIX

The 1993 Pontiac Grand Am (185,000 km) came in with several problems. Dirty fluid and slippage in all forward gears were found, so the transmission was rebuilt. After the repairs, the test drive showed the slippage was still evident. TV adjustment was good, and fluid pressures were close to normal. The transmission was disassembled again, and a burnt input clutch was found (after only 20 km).

FIX

Following advice, the technician checked the forward input clutch housing, and a crack was found around a weld at the center. Replacing the clutch housing fixed this problem.

 TECH TIP

In the heavier cast drums, the ball can be seated by striking the ball using a thin pin punch. This will crush small burrs to make it seat tighter.

 REAL WORLD FIX

The 4T60E transaxle in the 1997 Buick LeSabre was overhauled, but it had only first gear. Forcing a 1–2 shift gets neutral. The fluid pressures were okay, and the governor checked out good.

FIX

The transaxle was disassembled, and the second clutch return spring assembly was found to be installed upside down. A more careful check of the parts as they were disassembled would have prevented the problem.

The clutch check ball should be captured in its cage but still free to rattle when shaken. ● **SEE FIGURE 18–27.** You should be able to move it with either an air blast or a seal pick. If you suspect that you have a leaky check ball, fill the drum with ATF as just described. It should not leak. The check ball assembly can be removed and replaced in stamped steel drums.

The bushing, seal ring bore, and seal ring grooves should be smooth and free from scores and other damage. ● **SEE FIGURE 18–28.** Small imperfections can be removed with a file or by sanding. It should be noted that some turbine shafts have two or more fluid passages. Some passages have a cup plug for fluid flow control. These passages should be clean, open, and not leak into each other.

When the clutch parts check out and are thoroughly clean, perform the following:

- Install the new seals.
- Thoroughly lubricate the seals and bore.
- Carefully install the piston completely into the bore.
- Replace the return springs and retainer.

If three piston seals are used, be sure they all face in the proper direction.

A clutch is assembled by stacking the parts in the correct order. ● **SEE FIGURE 18–29.** Some units use a thick apply plate next to the piston to distribute the apply force onto the plates. The stack is an alternating series of lined and unlined plates followed by a backing/pressure plate. Some units use a wave, Belleville, or selective plate under the backing plate.

FIGURE 18–29 This rear clutch stack has a selective snap ring, top pressure plate, four friction disks, three steel plates, bottom pressure plate, and wave spring to retain the Belleville piston spring. (*Courtesy of Chrysler Corporation*)

TECH TIP

1. Always check to be sure the plates turn freely with the clutch released. ● **SEE FIGURE 18–30.** There should never be a drag between the plates with the clutch vertical. If the clutch is laid flat, you should feel a definite drag between the plates.
2. If clearance specifications are not available, use the rule of thumb that the clearance should be 0.010 in. (0.5 mm) for each lined plate.

When a clutch pack is assembled, the clearance should always be checked and adjusted if necessary. The clearance check ensures that the clutch is assembled correctly and will produce a smooth shift. Depending on the transmission and the particular clutch, different **selective** parts may be used to adjust clutch clearance. The parts that can be of variable (selective) thickness are the piston, pressure plate, snap ring, apply ring, steel plate, and lined plate. Typically, a selective snap ring is used. Most manufacturers publish clearance specifications for some, if not all, of the clutches used in their transmissions.

Feel Drag

Turn Freely

FIGURE 18–30 With the clutch assembled and lying flat, you should feel a definite drag if you try to rotate the plates (left). The plates should rotate easily with the clutch vertical (right).

Clutch clearance, also called piston travel, is normally measured using a feeler gauge placed between the pressure plate and the snap ring. ● **SEE FIGURE 18–31.** If a waved snap

Selective
Snap Ring

Feeler
Gauge

FIGURE 18–31 The clutch pack clearance specification for this clutch is 0.025 to 0.045 in. (0.64 to 1.14 mm). A 0.025-in. feeler gauge should enter as shown, but a 0.045-in. feeler gauge should be very tight or not fit in at all. (*Courtesy of Chrysler Corporation*)

SST

(a)

(b)

FIGURE 18–32 (a) A dial indicator can be set up with the stylus on the piston to measure piston stroke. (b) Applying air to the proper passage should cause the piston to stroke so the travel can be measured.

Use Hook Tool to
Raise One-Clutch
Disc

Dial
Indicator

Dial
Indicator
Tip Tool
6268

Hook Tool

(a)

PART NO.	Thickness
4377150	6.92 mm (.273 in.)
4377149	6.66 mm (.262 in.)
4377148	6.40 mm (.252 in.)
4412268	6.14 mm (.242 in.)
4412267	5.88 mm (.232 in.)
4412266	5.62 mm (.221 in.)
4412265	5.36 mm (.211 in.)

(b)

FIGURE 18–33 (a) This reaction clutch is deep in the case, and the clearance is measured by lifting a clutch plate while watching the dial indicator. (b) Clutch clearance is adjusted by selecting the proper reaction/pressure plate. (*Courtesy of Chrysler Corporation*)

 TECH TIP

1. Clearance can also be measured using a dial indicator. Position the dial indicator as shown (● SEE FIGURE 18–32), and raise and lower the backing plate to measure its vertical travel, which is the clutch clearance. If a wave or Belleville plate is used, the pressure plate should be pushed downward with a light, even pressure so the cushion plate(s) is not distorted.
2. The clearance of a holding clutch can be measured from a point on the transmission case to the clutch pack. ● SEE FIGURE 18–33. In others, the clutch has to be assembled temporarily before installation in order to measure the stack height. ● SEE FIGURE 18–34.
3. Measuring clutch clearance seems to be a lot of trouble to some, but it is well worth the time if it saves a comeback for a burned-out clutch or poor shift quality.

FIGURE 18–34 This clutch pack is assembled and the height is measured. The height should be within the specified dimensions.

FIGURE 18–35 (a, b) Clutch clearance can be reduced by adding an extra unlined plate, or (c) lined plate. If two lined plates are next to each other as in (c), clearance can be increased by shaving the lining off one or both adjacent sides of the two lined plates.

 TECH TIP

1. Many technicians prefer to build a clutch toward the lower end of the clearance to reduce piston travel; this usually produces crisper shift quality. For example, if a 4R70W forward clutch (five plates) has 0.099 in. (2.51 mm) of clearance and a 0.075-in. (1.9-mm) retaining ring, to reduce the clearance to the 0.050- to 0.094-in. (1.27- to 2.38-mm) specification, a snap ring that is either 0.086 to 0.092 in. or 0.102 to 0.106 in. (2.23 to 2.34 mm or 2.59 to 2.69 mm) can be used. The larger snap ring (assume it is 0.104 in.) would be preferred because it would reduce the clearance by about 0.029 in. (0.104 − 0.075 = 0.029 in.) (2.64 − 1.9 = 0.74 mm) to a clearance of about 0.070 in. (0.099 − 0.029 = 0.070 in.) (1.78 mm). The snap ring that is 0.088 to 0.92 in. reduces the clearance by about 0.015 in. (0.38 mm) to about 0.084 in. (2.13 mm)—acceptable but not as good as 0.070 in.

2. If the selective parts do not correct the clearance or are not available, clutch clearance can be reduced by using extra-thick steel plates or adding an extra unlined steel or lined friction plate. ● **SEE FIGURE 18–35.** If an additional friction plate is too thick, one or both of the adjacent friction linings can be scraped off using a knife or gasket scraper.

 REAL WORLD FIX

A 604 transmission from a 1992 Chrysler (72,000 miles) was being rebuilt, and new clutches were being installed. These clutches use five frictions and five steels. The 2–4 clutch pack went together okay, but the low-reverse pack does not have enough clearance, even with the thinnest reaction plate.

FIX

It was discovered that the technician was trying to use 2–4 frictions that are 0.085 in. in place of the thinner low-reverse frictions that are 0.075 in. The low-reverse clutch had the proper clearance when the correct frictions were used.

ring is used, position the feeler gauge in the widest area under a wave portion.

Clutch clearance is adjusted by changing the selective component.

The clutch is ready for installation at this point.

18.4.1 ONE-WAY CLUTCH SERVICE
One-way clutches are visually inspected during transmission disassembly and reassembly (see Section 16.6). The commonly encountered problems are severe wear from poor lubrication or metal fragments from a failed part; wear or scoring of the race(s), rollers, or sprags; and a sprag(s) that flips over. One-way clutches should always be lubricated using assembly grease, petroleum jelly, or ATF during assembly. After assembly, they should be tested to ensure that they rotate freely in the proper direction and lock up in the opposite direction.

(a)

(b)

FIGURE 18–36 (a) Air pressure is applied to the shaft clutch apply port to apply and air test the clutch piston. The amount of piston stroke and clutch pack clearance are measured using a dial indicator. (b) The special service tool (SST) allows the dial indicator to reach the piston. (*Figure (b) Courtesy of Toyota Motor Sales USA, Inc.*)

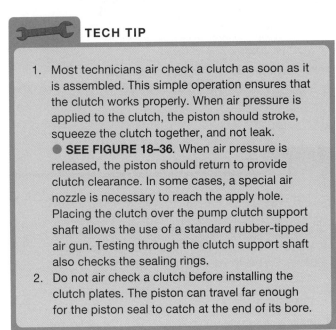

🔧 **TECH TIP**

1. Most technicians air check a clutch as soon as it is assembled. This simple operation ensures that the clutch works properly. When air pressure is applied to the clutch, the piston should stroke, squeeze the clutch together, and not leak.
   ● **SEE FIGURE 18–36.** When air pressure is released, the piston should return to provide clutch clearance. In some cases, a special air nozzle is necessary to reach the apply hole. Placing the clutch over the pump clutch support shaft allows the use of a standard rubber-tipped air gun. Testing through the clutch support shaft also checks the sealing rings.

2. Do not air check a clutch before installing the clutch plates. The piston can travel far enough for the piston seal to catch at the end of its bore.

18.5 GEAR SET SERVICE

Servicing gear sets is primarily a visual inspection of the various gears and a side play and rotation check of the planet gears. In some cases there is also an end-play check of the assembled gear train to ensure the thrust washers are not worn excessively.
● **SEE FIGURE 18–37.**

Output Shaft

Rear Annulus Gear

Feeler Gauge

FIGURE 18–37 This gear set should have 0.005 to 0.048 in. (0.12 to 1.22 mm) of end play. A 0.005-in. feeler gauge should enter as shown, but a 0.049-in. gauge should not. (*Courtesy of Chrysler Corporation*)

In many transmissions, the gear set comes out one part at a time. A technician always inspects each part as it is removed. After cleanup, the parts are carefully inspected again. Parts to rebuild a planetary are available from aftermarket sources. ● **SEE FIGURE 18–38.**

All ring and sun gears should be checked for chipped or broken teeth and worn or stripped drive splines.

Pinion Pin
lube holes reduce planetary burn-up

"Bat Wing" Thrust Washer
solid bronze, eliminates washer spin and rapid wear

Pinion Thrust Washer
thru-hardened steel helps eliminate needle rollers thrust wear

Helical Pinion Gear
case hardened alloy steel

Needle Rollers
closely toleranced to be used specifically with patching pins and gears

FIGURE 18–38 This kit includes the parts needed to rebuild a 4L60 planetary assembly. (*Courtesy of Sonnax*)

 REAL WORLD FIX

The 1996 GMC Vandura G3500 (142,000 miles) came in with a shift problem. A scan tool check showed code 87, solenoid stuck off. Clutch material was found in the pan, so the transmission was overhauled. The vehicle came back after a day with the same problem. The solenoid, fuse, and harness all checked out okay.

FIX

Following advice, the technician disassembled the 4L80E transmission and checked for a leak at the center support. A faulty seal was found, and replacing the center support seal fixed this problem.

 REAL WORLD FIX

The 1991 Ford Explorer (156,000 miles) transmission was rebuilt. But a road test showed it has a very harsh engagement after the vehicle starts out from a stop. It seems to slam into first gear. The governor was replaced, but this did not help. The valve body was disassembled and rechecked, with no problem found.

FIX

After studying the clutch apply charts, the technician determined that the problem had to be the overrun clutch. An inspection showed that this clutch was bad, and replacing the overrun clutch fixed this problem.

● **SEE FIGURE 18–39.** The thrust surfaces at the sides of the gears and any support bushings or bushing surfaces should be checked for scores, wear, or other damage. ● **SEE FIGURE 18–40.** Drive shells should be checked for stripped splines, damaged lugs, or cracks. ● **SEE FIGURE 18–41.**

When checking a carrier, the pinion gears must be undamaged and turn freely. Check for worn or missing pinion thrust bushings. If they appear sloppy, measure the pinion gear end play and/or side clearance. ● **SEE FIGURE 18–42.** Some manufacturers provide pinion gear side clearance specifications,

(a)

(b)

(c)

(d)

(e)

FIGURE 18–39 (a–d) Planetary gear train damage shows up as wear, or (e) cracks and breakage.

but if no specifications are available, use the rule of thumb of 0.005 to 0.025 in. (0.167 to 0.635 mm). In some cases, the pinion gear assembly can be removed from the carrier to replace the bearings, gear, or thrust washers. The needle bearings commonly used can make this a tedious task. Shims are available to tighten the side clearance on some carriers.

The 2001 Ford Escape (96,000 miles) came in with no drive; it would move forward in manual first or second. There were no DTCs. The transmission was removed, sent to a rebuilder, and reinstalled. A cracked pressure plate and worn friction plates were replaced, but the transmission had the same problem—no drive. The valve body and gaskets were checked and the shift solenoids were replaced, but this did not fix the problem.

FIX

Following advice, the transmission was disassembled, and a bad one-way clutch was found. Replacement of the one-way clutch fixed this transmission.

TECH TIP

1. If the electronics are disconnected and a CD4E transmission (and most others) will not move forward in drive, there is a large probability that the one-way clutch is at fault.
2. The low one-way clutch/sprag used in Honda and Acura transmission models used with V-6 engines between 2000 and 2009 tends to fail the inner race. This can show up as "Failure to move forward after driving a short distance and coasting to a stop," but will move in manual-2 or low. Checking the clutch rotation by feel is not an adequate check; the low one-way clutch should be disassembled, and if the inner race appears damaged, it should be replaced.

18.6 VALVE BODY SERVICE

Despite its complexity, the valve body is one of the more reliable parts in a transmission, probably because the valves are so well lubricated. In a way, valves do little, as they move only slightly and only once in a while. Most valve body service operations consist of disassembly, cleaning, checking for free movement, reassembly, and in a few transmissions, adjusting the pressure regulator valve. ● **SEE FIGURE 18–43.** Valves

(b)

(a)

(c)

FIGURE 18–40 These three gear train components show severe wear and scoring in the thrust surfaces.

(a)

(b)

FIGURE 18–41 These sun gear drive shells show (a) stripped splines and (b) broken, dislodged splines.

← Excess Clearance

FIGURE 18–42 This planet pinion gear has too much side clearance; it should be repaired or the carrier should be replaced.

 TECH TIP

1. Mark the pinion gears before removing the pinion shafts. The gear set can become noisy if you install a pinion gear upside down.
2. If gear set replacement is necessary, make sure the new gear set has the same gear ratio. The TCM in electronic transmissions compares input and output speed. If they are not correct, it will illuminate the MIL and set an incorrect gear ratio code.

 REAL WORLD FIX

The E4OD in the 1996 Ford F350 (152,000 miles) was rebuilt because of a delayed/no-reverse problem. There were a lot of metal particles throughout the transmission. The transmission was rebuilt, and the torque converter was replaced. After replacing the transmission, there was no drive; it did not move in drive or manual-1. Line pressure was good, and there were no DTCs.

FIX

Following advice, the transmission was disassembled to check the low sprag. It had been installed upside down; reinstalling the low sprag in the proper position solved this problem.

 REAL WORLD FIX

The 1990 Nissan Maxima (125,000 miles) transmission had no reverse. It was rebuilt, and the clutch plates, band, seals, and solenoid valve assembly were replaced. All the clutches were air checked for proper operation. The transmission was reinstalled, but the original problem is still there. The technician thought that the TCM was the cause of this problem.

FIX

Following advice, the technician checked the fluid pressures, and they were good in drive and reverse. The transmission was then disassembled, and a thorough check found that a sun gear had sheared cleanly from its shaft. Replacing this shaft and reassembly of the transmission fixed this problem.

(a)

(b)

FIGURE 18–43 (a) An exploded and (b) cutaway view of the valve body from a four-speed transaxle. Note the various valve groups and how they are retained in their bore.

FIGURE 18–44 A sheet of stiff paper has been folded to create this simple valve holder. Note that a valve group can be placed in order and also labeled.

TECH TIP

Most technicians complete a valve body repair as quickly as possible; the longer it takes, the easier it is to forget which spring goes where or how it fits on a particular valve. In many cases, the service manual is only an aid. Each transmission model and version is slightly different. These differences are often in the valve body and are often just a spring change. Remember that when taking a valve body apart, you become the expert in how that particular unit goes back together.

TECH TIP

1. Some technicians make a valve organizer by folding a piece of cardboard into an accordion shape. ● **SEE FIGURE 18–44**.
2. Some technicians make a **spring holder.** ● **SEE FIGURE 18–45**. This unit is shop-made from two electrical box covers and a group of small, 2-in.-long machine screws. Each screw location on the holder is numbered. As a valve and spring are removed, the spring is placed on a screw and the number is written next to the spring in the manual illustration. This does two things: It helps locate a certain spring and helps teach the technician the name of the spring and valve. As each spring comes out, a mental or written note should be made of how it fits the valve, how many coils it has, and its color.

REAL WORLD FIX

The 1995 BMW (110,000 miles) had no reverse, and it would not move backward in neutral with the engine running. The transmission had been repaired a year earlier because of a burned clutch. The internal seals were replaced, but this did not help.

FIX

Following advice from experienced technicians, the valve body was removed and inspected. A small piece (about 3 mm × 5 mm) of foreign material (probably gasket) was found to be blocking movement of one of the valves. Removal of this object fixed this problem.

(a)

(b)

FIGURE 18–45 This simple shop-made tool is a valve body spring holder. It is made from two electrical box covers, a 1/4 in. × 2-1/2 in. stove bolt and nut, and 16, 8 × 2 in. machine screws and nuts. As a valve is removed, the spring is placed over a numbered peg, and the number is written on a picture of the valve body.

Upper Housing

1-2 Shift Control Valve And Spring

2-3 Shift Valve And Spring

Cover

Throttle Pressure Springs And Plug

Plug Sleeve

Line Pressure Plug

Pressure Plug Cover

1-2 Shift Valve And Spring

FIGURE 18–46 These valves are retained by two cover plates; with the covers removed, the valves should slide out of their bores. (*Courtesy of Chrysler Corporation*)

in a governor and pump assembly are serviced in the same manner.

The biggest problem during valve body repair is getting it back together with everything in the right order and location.

Several methods are used to retain the valve(s) in a bore. Many units use a cover plate that holds one or more valves. ● **SEE FIGURE 18–46.** Removal of the retaining screws allows removal of the plate, valve(s), and spring(s). Many

FIGURE 18–47 These valves are held in the valve body by a plug and a pin or retainer. (*Courtesy of Toyota Motor Sales USA, Inc.*)

valves use a plug or sleeve at the end of each bore. The plug/sleeve is retained with a keeper, which can be a pin, plate, or key. ● **SEE FIGURE 18–47.** The keeper cannot come out while the valve body is in place on the transmission, and the valve's spring pressure keeps it in place while the valve body is removed. Pushing the plug/sleeve slightly inward allows the keeper to be pulled out easily, and then the plug/sleeve, valve(s), and spring(s) will come out.

An unworn aluminum valve in an unworn valve body might not free fall if it is tested wet; sticking should be tested by feeling the effort required to slide the valve in its bore.

(a) #49 DRILL BIT

GROUND TO TAPER

ALLEN WRENCH (b)

GROUND TO TAPER

FIGURE 18–48 (a) A drill bit or (b) Allen wrench can be modified so that it enters a roll pin, and then is rotated to lift the pin out.

FIGURE 18–49 If the valve body is moved to vertical position, steel valves should slide freely from the bore. Be prepared to catch the valves when making this check.

 TECH TIP

1. Some valve bodies use a coiled spring pin (roll pin) to hold the valve plug/sleeve in place. ● **SEE FIGURE 18–48**. In some cases, this coiled pin can be pulled out by gripping it with a pair of pliers. In other cases, you will need to make an extractor tool. Grind the flats of a small (about 3/32 in. [3 mm]) Allen wrench or the end of a No. 49 drill bit so it tapers to a point, as shown in Figure 18–48. Tap this pointed end into the coiled pin; rotate the pin in a direction that wraps the pin tighter; and as the pin rotates, lift it out of the bore.

2. Most technicians place a lint-free shop cloth(s) or a carpet scrap under the valve body while disassembling it. The cloth helps keep the check balls, screws, and pins from rolling away and might prevent a nick or dent in a valve if one happens to drop.

3. The reasons for disassembling a valve body are to clean it thoroughly and ensure that all valves are working freely and not sticking. The **free fall** test is a standard check for a sticking valve. Hold the valve body so the bore is vertical. In this position, a steel valve should fall freely from one end of the bore to the other; it should at least fall through the area of normal valve movement. ● **SEE FIGURE 18–49**. Any valve that does not fall freely is sticking, which can be a fault of the valve, the bore, or both.

 TECH TIP

1. Aluminum valves and valve bodies should be checked for wear. Position the valve so you have something to hold onto, but as deep in the bore as possible. Some valves can be inserted into the bore backward for this check. Next, try to move the valve vertically, and note the amount of movement. Vertical movement should be very small. Compare the amount of movement to a new or known-good valve body.

   A wet air test can also be used to check for wear. Valve body wear can also be checked using a vacuum test; more information for this test can be found at www.sonnax.com/tech_info.php.

2. Fluid can leak out the end of the bore, past the plug. If a round, aluminum plug is used, it can be enlarged by using a tubing cutter to score a groove around the plug. This displaces and raises metal and should create a tighter fit.

3. Short valves that are located between fluid pressure and a spring tend to tip in the valve bore. This can cause ridges in the bore that can cause the valve to jam; check these using a **sag test**. ● **SEE FIGURE 18–50**.

(a)

Ridges

(b)

(c)

FIGURE 18–50 (a) A valve sag test; the valve is inserted backwards into the bore so the inner land is in the area where it normally runs. The valve should not sag off-center. (b) This aluminum valve body has been cut to show the ridges that indicate bore wear. (c) Some valve bodies can be saved by reaming the bore oversize and installing an oversize valve. *(Courtesy of Sonnax)*

Carefully inspect the valve and valve body for varnish, a light brown or golden brown coating. It can be cleaned off with carburetor/automatic choke cleaner. ● **SEE FIGURE 18–51.** Soak the valves, springs, and valve body for 5 to 15 minutes, rinse them in hot water, and then dip the valves and springs in ATF and dry the valve body using compressed air.

If a valve is smooth but still sticks in the bore, carefully examine the bore for debris or nicks that might cause raised metal. Small metal particles tend to become embedded in the bores of aluminum valve bodies.

REAL WORLD FIX

The 2000 Ford Mustang (61,000 miles) came in with a complaint of stalling when shifted to drive after the transmission warmed up. A scan tool check showed no unusual activity of the shift or TCC solenoids. The TCC solenoid seemed sticky so it was replaced along with the MLPS, but this did not help.

FIX

The valve body was checked, and several of the aluminum valves were severely scored and worn. Valve body replacement fixed this problem.

TECH TIP

If a valve is still sticky, inspect it for nicks or dents. The raised metal can be removed using a fine-grit knife-sharpening stone. Lay the valve on the stone and carefully rotate it until all traces of raised metal are gone. ● **SEE FIGURE 18–52.** Be careful not to make a flat or groove on the valve or round off the corners of a land.

FIGURE 18–51 This valve body is being washed and air dried in a parts washer. It will be cleaned again when the two major parts are separated.

Oil Stone

FIGURE 18–52 Place the valve on the wet sharpening stone and rotate the valve. Slight imperfections and burrs can be removed without rounding off the sharp edges. Do not do this with aluminum valves.

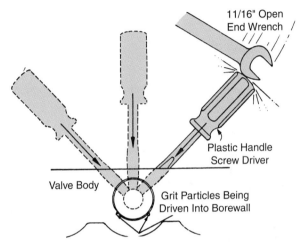

11/16" Open End Wrench

Plastic Handle Screw Driver

Valve Body

Grit Particles Being Driven Into Borewall

FIGURE 18–53 Sometimes a valve in an aluminum valve body will stick in its bore because of grit embedded in the bore wall. This valve can often be freed by gently striking the valve as shown.

FIGURE 18–54 A scored valve body bore can be cleaned by inserting a small roll of crocus cloth into the bore and rotating it in a direction to unroll it. Be very careful to not remove any metal and cause an oversize bore when cleaning the bore of an aluminum valve body.

TECH TIP

1. One cure is to drive the metal completely into the aluminum. ● **SEE FIGURE 18–53**. A few sharp taps on the valve is often all that is necessary.
2. If tapping does not free up the valve, clean the bore using crocus cloth or a lapping compound. Crocus cloth is a very-fine-grit abrasive cloth. Wrap a section into a tube or roll it with the grit outward, slide this tube into the valve bore, and then rotate it in a direction that tries to unwrap the tube. ● **SEE FIGURE 18–54**. After turning the crocus cloth tube several revolutions, clean the bore and retry the valve fit.
3. Some technicians make a lapping compound by mixing household scouring powder and ATF to make a thin paste. This paste is spread onto the valve and in the bore, and then the valve is stroked and rotated in the bore. ● **SEE FIGURE 18–55**. The valve and bore are then cleaned in solvent and dried using compressed air before retrying the valve fit again. Do not use lapping compound on an aluminum valve or bore.

REAL WORLD FIX

The 1996 Ford Taurus (107,000 miles) had an illuminated MIL with no drivability problems. All underhood items checked good. A scan tool check showed code P0761, shift solenoid C circuit stuck in OFF position. Voltage and resistance checks of the solenoid and wiring harness showed no problem. Line pressure was within specifications.

FIX

Following advice, the technician checked the forward clutch control valve and found a broken retainer clip. This caused the spring to bind the control valve, causing it to stick. A new retaining clip fixed this vehicle.

A valve that has excessive movement, such as a pressure regulator valve, can wear into the bore and cause excess leakage. Leakage can be checked using a wet air test. ● **SEE FIGURE 18–56**. Sometimes the leaking valve can be replaced with an upgraded valve.

(a)

(b)

FIGURE 18–55 (a) A wire handle has been attached to an old valve so it can be used to lap a governor bore. (b) A mixture of scouring powder and ATF is used for the lapping compound.

FIGURE 18–56 This boost valve can be checked by putting a small amount of ATF into the EPC boost and D2, low passages, and applying low-pressure air to the same passages. More than minimal leakage through the cutback and other passages indicate a worn boost valve or boost sleeve. (*Courtesy of Sonnax*)

After all the valves, springs, and valve body are cleaned and the valves move freely in their bores, the valve body can be reassembled. The springs should be checked to make sure they are not damaged and do not have distorted coils. Each valve should be dipped in ATF before installation. The reassembly procedure is generally the reverse of the disassembly procedure. As each valve is installed, make sure that it moves freely in its bore. Ensure that all check balls and filter screens are replaced in the proper locations. ● **SEE FIGURE 18–57.** Be sure to tighten each retainer screw to the correct torque. ● **SEE FIGURE 18–58.**

FIGURE 18-57 This valve body contains one large and six small check balls. (*Courtesy of Chrysler Corporation*)

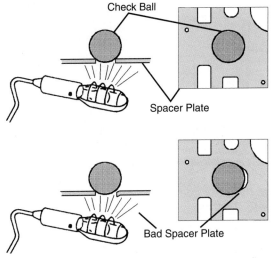

FIGURE 18-59 A check ball should seal off light from coming through the spacer plate. A problem is indicated if light shines through an opening alongside of the check ball.

FIGURE 18-58 The valve body bolts should be tightened in order, starting from the center and working in an outward spiral.

 TECH TIP

A kit has been developed to repair some valve bores; this kit contains a drill jig (reamer guide), reamer replacement valve, and spring (see Figure 18-50). The reamer is used to restore the bore to be round, straight, and to the correct size for the new valve.

 REAL WORLD FIX

The 1990 Ford Aerostar (130,000 miles) was towed in because the engine died when shifted into drive or reverse. On a test drive, the vehicle operated normally. The fluid level was okay, and there were no DTCs.

FIX

The technician found a TSB that describes this problem and gives a recommended repair. It required removing the valve body, separator plate, overdrive solenoid, retainer, and plug. A stuck shuttle valve was found. Cleaning this valve and bore along with replacing the other parts fixed this problem. New gaskets and O-rings were used during the reassembly.

 TECH TIP

If a faulty check ball–transfer plate seat is suspected, place the ball on its seat and hold a flashlight behind the transfer plate. Light shining between the ball and transfer plate indicates a problem. ● SEE FIGURE 18-59.

The pressure regulator valve spring is adjustable in some Chrysler Corporation transmissions. ● SEE FIGURE 18-60. The adjustment can be checked using a small ruler and, if necessary, adjusted using an Allen wrench.

The valve body should now be ready to be installed.

Wrench

1-5/16 Inch

FIGURE 18–60 The pressure regulator spring of this valve body should be adjusted to 1-5/16 in. to get the proper line pressure. (*Courtesy of Chrysler Corporation*)

 REAL WORLD FIX

The transmission in the Mercury Grand Marquis taxi (255,000 km) was rebuilt because of a delayed engagement problem. The transmission was replaced, and the vehicle left operating okay. It came back after a few months with a lockup shudder and other symptoms indicating a hydraulic pressure control problem. Scan tool checks did not show any DTCs or electronic control problems.

FIX

Following advice, the technician checked the O-ring on the EPC solenoid, and it was found to be damaged. It was probably damaged during solenoid installation. Replacement of this O-ring fixed the problem.

18.7 SOLENOIDS AND SWITCHES

Some sources recommend replacing all switches and solenoids to eliminate a possible cause of future problems. A pulse-width solenoid or pressure control solenoid is in almost constant motion while the transmission is operating; these units wear out. Any external switch that leaks fluid should be replaced. Switches and solenoids should be cleaned and checked for proper operation, as described in Chapter 13.

18.8 DIFFERENTIAL SERVICE

Transaxle differentials should be checked to make sure that the differential gears, thrust washers, and the differential pinion shaft are in good condition. ● **SEE FIGURE 18–61.** A differential can usually be disassembled by removing the lock pin and driving the differential pinion shaft out. This allows removal of the gears and thrust washers. ● **SEE FIGURE 18–62.** The gears should be inspected for chipped or broken teeth and scoring on the bearing surfaces. The thrust washers and differential pinion shaft should be checked for wear and scoring.

Some differentials are combined with a planet carrier that includes a set of planet pinions along with the differential. Like those inside the transmission, these pinion gears must turn freely on their shafts and not have excessive end play. The thrust washers and needle bearings can be replaced. Replacement of the needle bearings can be made easier by applying a thick film of transmission assembly lubricant to stick them in place during assembly.

 REAL WORLD FIX

The 1996 Audi A6 (106,000 miles) came in with a no-drive and no-reverse condition. Fluid pressure was good. A scan tool check showed three codes: 0652, range control incorrect signal; 00753, wheel speed sensor or electrical connection; and 00526, brake light switch incorrect signal. The transmission was disassembled and everything looked okay. The input-shaft-to-torque-converter splines were inspected and were found to be good.

FIX

Following advice, the technician disassembled and checked the center differential of this AWD transmission. He found it to be badly burnt and worn. Replacing the center differential fixed this problem.

 TECH TIP

If differential clearance is excessive, replace the thrust washers. In many cases, the new thrust washers will correct the clearance.

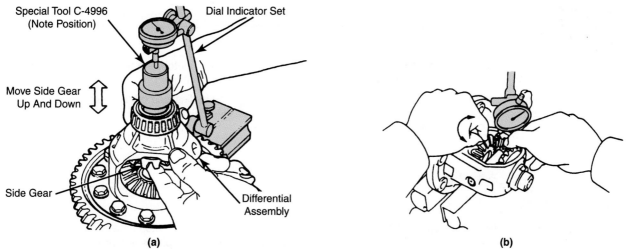

FIGURE 18–61 (a) Differential side gear end play can be checked using a dial indicator and special tool. (b) Another check for the same purpose is to measure the side gear backlash. (*Figure (a) Courtesy of Chrysler Corporation*)

FIGURE 18–62 Removing the pinion shaft allows the differential pinion and side gears with their thrust washers to be removed from the differential case. (*Courtesy of Toyota Motor Sales USA, Inc.*)

SUMMARY

1. Inspection, service, and repair are done to each transmission subassembly during the transmission overhaul.

2. The pump is disassembled and inspected. The bushings and seals are replaced before reassembly.

3. When rebuilding a clutch, the fiction plates, piston seals, and bushings are replaced.

4. The valve body is disassembled, cleaned, inspected, and carefully reassembled.

REVIEW QUESTIONS

1. The areas of the case that should be inspected are:
   a. _____
   b. _____
   c. _____
   d. _____
   e. _____
   f. _____

2. The pump should be inspected for _____ marks and damage to the gears and housing.

3. When assembling a pump, it might be necessary to _____ the pump halves before torquing the pump body bolts.

4. Like a gear pump, a vane-type pump should be _____ inspected.

5. When disassembling a clutch assembly, note the location of any _____ plates and the _____ and order of the clutch friction and steel plates.

6. Transmission gear sets are inspected for _____ to the gears and pinion gear _____.

7. Valve body repair consists mainly of disassembly, _____, and reassembly.

8. When cleaning a valve body, all of the parts must be kept in _____.

9. Any external switch that is leaking should be _____.

10. If differential clearance is excessive, replace the _____ washers.

CHAPTER QUIZ

1. Technician A says that a cross leak can cause damage to the clutches or bands. Technician B says that damage that would cause a cross leak can be checked using a feeler gauge and a straightedge. Who is correct?
   a. Technician A
   b. Technician B
   c. Both Technicians A and B
   d. Neither Technician A nor B

2. Technician A says that aluminum on the thread of a bolt indicates that the threads in the case are damaged. Technician B says that all bolts should be checked for damage before they are reused. Who is correct?
   a. Technician A
   b. Technician B
   c. Both Technicians A and B
   d. Neither Technician A nor B

3. Technician A says that a pump can be checked with a visual check or by measuring the clearances. Technician B says that worn pump bushing will result in a leaking pump seal. Who is correct?
   a. Technician A
   b. Technician B
   c. Both Technicians A and B
   d. Neither Technician A nor B

4. Technician A says that it is good practice to replace all of the friction materials (lined plates, unlined plates, and bands) when rebuilding a transmission. Technician B says that lined friction material must be soaked in ATF before it is installed. Who is correct?
   a. Technician A
   b. Technician B
   c. Both Technicians A and B
   d. Neither Technician A nor B

5. Technician A says that the location and number of springs in the clutch pack should be noted and that the same number of springs must be placed in the same location during reassembly. Technician B says that a clutch piston can be removed with air pressure or by tapping the clutch housing on a piece of wood. Who is correct?
   a. Technician A
   b. Technician B
   c. Both Technicians A and B
   d. Neither Technician A nor B

6. Technician A says that the check ball in the clutch piston should rattle when shaken. Technician B says that it is okay if the check ball has a small fluid leak. Who is correct?
   a. Technician A
   b. Technician B
   c. Both Technicians A and B
   d. Neither Technician A nor B

7. Clearance in a multiple-disc clutch is adjusted using any of these selective parts, except _____.
   a. Clutch pressure plates
   b. Clutch housings
   c. Pressure plate snap rings
   d. Steel plates

8. Technician A says that the gear set is visually inspected for wear or damage to the gear teeth. Technician B says that the planet pinion gear end play should be checked using a feeler gauge. Who is correct?
   a. Technician A
   b. Technician B
   c. Both Technicians A and B
   d. Neither Technician A nor B

9. Technician A says that the valve and springs must be kept in order during valve body service. Technician B says that the valve body springs should be checked for damaged or distorted coils. Who is correct?
   a. Technician A
   b. Technician B
   c. Both Technicians A and B
   d. Neither Technician A nor B

10. Technician A says that during an overhaul of a transaxle, the differential should be disassembled and inspected. Technician B says that the differential is not a part of the automatic transaxle. Who is correct?
    a. Technician A
    b. Technician B
    c. Both Technicians A and B
    d. Neither Technician A nor B

TORQUE CONVERTER SERVICE

OBJECTIVES: **After studying Chapter 19, the reader will be able to:** • Diagnose torque converter and torque converter clutch problems. • Explain the conditions when a torque converter should be reused or rebuilt. • Describe the procedure used to rebuild a torque converter. • Complete the ASE tasks related to torque converter inspection.

KEY TERMS: External leakage 479 • Internal interference 479 • Lock-up clutch operation 479 • Stator one-way clutch operation 479 • Turbine end play 479 • Visual condition 479

19.1 INTRODUCTION

A torque converter is considered to be part of the transmission. It should be serviced or replaced when a transmission is overhauled. A torque converter is always replaced with a new or rebuilt unit if it has an internal failure. Most shops do not rebuild torque converters. There are companies that specialize in torque converter overhaul.

A torque converter does not usually wear out and require replacement. Torque converters tend to collect the metal, dirt, and other debris that enters with the fluid. It is impossible to thoroughly check a torque converter without cutting it open. The internal shape and the centrifugal force inside a torque converter can pack dirt and debris around the outer diameter. Foreign material can also lodge in the clutch lining of a lock-up torque converter. ● **SEE FIGURE 19–1.** It is extremely difficult to remove this material without opening the torque converter. A *reconditioned* or *overhauled* torque converter has been cut open, cleaned, inspected, and assembled using new or like-new parts.

Many transmission rebuilders are concerned that removing the torque converter during an overhaul and repositioning it may loosen any internal debris. If the torque converter is not serviced, this debris can leave the torque converter and return to the lubrication passages of the transmission. It may start the wear process in the transmission as soon as the engine is started after the transmission overhaul. The debris might also plug the cooler, causing future problems.

Many shops flush and check the torque converter during every transmission overhaul. Other shops install a rebuilt torque converter as standard practice. High-mileage transmissions, ones that show a lot of metal wear, and units with lock-up

FIGURE 19–1 This cutaway view shows where debris and foreign material will tend to collect inside of the outer rim of a torque converter. (*Courtesy of Chrysler Corporation*)

torque converters are candidates for replacement. Installing a rebuilt torque converter is more expensive than servicing the existing one. Cleaning and reinstalling a good torque converter is an adequate and safe repair in cases when the transmission is relatively clean.

(a)

(b)

FIGURE 19–2 Converter inspection begins with visual checks to ensure that the pilot, drive lugs, starter ring gear (if used), hub, and pump drive tangs are in good condition.

19.2 TORQUE CONVERTER CHECKS

The torque converter should be checked to make sure it is in usable condition when the transmission is removed. These checks include the **visual condition, stator one-way clutch operation, turbine end play, internal interference, lock-up clutch operation,** and **external leakage.** A torque converter that passes inspection is reusable. One that fails one or more of the checks should be replaced with a new or rebuilt unit. A torque converter that has turned blue from overheating has failed internally and should be replaced.

19.2.1 VISUAL CHECKS The first checks performed are visual. A technician often performs a visual inspection as the torque converter is removed from the transmission. Visual inspection includes the following:

1. The outside (especially at the welds) for wetness, which might indicate a leak
2. The drive lugs or studs for physical damage (**SEE FIGURE 19–2.**)
3. The pilot for damage
4. The hub for signs of seal or bushing area wear
5. The pump drive tangs or lugs for wear or damage
6. The starter ring gear, if used, for wear or damage (**SEE FIGURE 19–3.**)

A torque converter with excessive damage to the hub, pump drive lugs, or converter drive lugs should be repaired or replaced.

REAL WORLD FIX

The 1992 Oldsmobile Achieva (162,000 miles) had the transmission rebuilt almost a year ago. Now there is a complaint of a lack of power, and it has been this way since the rebuild. All adjustments are correct, the engine has good vacuum, and a scan tool check shows no trouble codes. A stall check shows a stall speed of 1560 RPM.

FIX

The stall speed for this vehicle should be 2760 RPM, so it was determined that the wrong torque converter was installed during the earlier rebuild. Replacement with the correct torque converter solved this problem.

REAL WORLD FIX

The 1991 Acura (85,000 miles) runs good in park and neutral, but the engine dies as soon as it is shifted into gear. Tests reveal no problems outside of the transmission.

FIX

When the transmission was removed, the torque converter was found to be blue from overheating and seized up internally. It had also sent metal particles throughout the transmission. Rebuilding the transmission along with a replacement torque converter was required to fix this problem.

19.2.2 STATOR ONE-WAY CLUTCH CHECK

There are several ways to check a stator one-way clutch. The stator clutch must lock in one direction and slip or freewheel in the other.

REAL WORLD FIX

The 1991 Nissan Pathfinder (133,000 miles) will not move in any gear. An inspection of the pan revealed some metal particles and dirty fluid. Engine speed does increase when shifted into gear, which is a normal response.

FIX

The transmission was removed, and following advice from experienced technicians, the torque converter splines were checked. They were stripped, and replacement of the torque converter fixed this problem. The shift solenoid pack was also replaced as a precautionary measure.

TECH TIP

1. A small imperfection on the torque converter hub can be cleaned and smoothed using crocus cloth. Roughness or damage that can be felt by running a fingernail or coin across the hub can wear the new front seal.
2. Stripped or damaged female threads in the drive lugs can often be repaired by installing a thread insert, as described in Chapter 14.

To check a one-way clutch, you should:

1. Place the converter flat on a bench top.
2. Reach into the hub so one finger contacts the splines. ● SEE FIGURE 19–4.
3. Rotate the splines in a clockwise direction. If you cannot rotate them, the clutch is probably locked.
4. Try to rotate the splines counterclockwise. If you can rotate them, the clutch is slipping. A slipping one-way clutch will cause a vehicle to have a power loss and poor acceleration. A locked one-way clutch will hurt fuel economy because of fluid drag at speeds below TCC lock-up.

A commercial stator-holding tool may be used to check a one-way clutch. This tool can be inserted into a groove in the thrust washer on some stators to keep it and the stator from rotating. Next, a special one-way clutch-tool is inserted into the stator splines, and a torque wrench is used to apply torque to the tool and one-way clutch inner race. The one-way clutch should turn freely in a clockwise direction, and it should lock and hold at least 10 ft-lb (14 N-m) of torque in a counterclockwise direction. Do not apply any more torque than this because the special tool can break.

A torque converter with a faulty one-way clutch must be replaced or rebuilt.

TECH TIP

Grip the stator splines using long, thin, flat-jaw snap-ring pliers in order to rotate the stator. ● SEE FIGURE 19–5. The added leverage of the pliers allows you to turn the splines in both directions; but in one direction (clockwise), only the inner race revolves. In the other direction, the entire stator and clutch rotate. The difference can be felt, especially if you turn it rapidly.

FIGURE 19–3 A bad starter ring gear can be changed by cutting the welds using a hack saw or grinder and driving the old gear off. The new gear must be secured by welding following the procedure recommended by the manufacturer. (*Courtesy of Chrysler Corporation*)

Brass Drift

Wood Blocks

Welds (6)

FIGURE 19–4 A stator clutch can be checked by reaching into the hub so your finger contacts the splines. You should be able to rotate the splines in one direction but not the other.

FIGURE 19–5 A stator clutch can be checked by gripping the splines using snap-ring pliers. Rotate the splines quickly; in only one direction, you should feel the weight of the stator.

FIGURE 19–6 The major wear points inside a torque converter are these thrust surfaces. Internal end play increases as these surfaces wear.

19.2.3 END-PLAY CHECK

Thrust washers at the stator and turbine control internal end play. ● **SEE FIGURE 19–6.** End play is normally measured using a dial indicator. Two styles of dial indicator fixtures are commonly used to measure end play. One fixture uses an expandable stem that fits into the turbine splines and is expanded to lock into the splines. ● **SEE FIGURE 19–7.** The dial indicator is positioned and adjusted so the measuring stylus is against the fixture and the dial reads zero. The fixture and turbine are lifted as far as they will go. The travel (end play) is read on the dial indicator.

Another fixture for checking end play is designed so the torque converter sits on top of it. ● **SEE FIGURE 19–8.** The measuring stem is moved upward to contact the turbine splines, and the dial indicator is adjusted to zero. Then the turbine is lifted as far as possible. The end play is read on the dial indicator.

FIGURE 19–7 The special tool is locked into the turbine. Moving the tool handle up and down allows the end play to be read on the dial indicator.

FIGURE 19–8 The torque converter is placed onto the end-play fixture. After setting the dial indicator to zero (0), the handle is moved downward to lift the turbine and read the end play. (*Courtesy of TCRS Inc.*)

 REAL WORLD FIX

The 1986 Chevrolet Caprice (2004R transmission; 80,000 miles) makes a grinding/whining noise as soon as the engine is started, and the noise gets louder when shifted into drive or reverse. The noise goes away at speeds above 30 mph. The fluid is clean and at the correct level.

FIX

When the transmission was removed, and the torque converter was removed from the transmission, stripped splines were found on the stator support shaft. A used transmission was installed.

FIGURE 19–9 A quick end-play check can be made by gripping the turbine or stator splines and trying to move the turbine or stator in and out.

TECH TIP

Turbine or stator clutch end play can be checked by gripping the splines with a pair of snap-ring pliers or your fingers. ● **SEE FIGURE 19–9.** You can feel the end play as the turbine or stator is lifted and then lowered. With experience, you can judge the approximate amount of end play.

Some manufacturers publish torque converter end-play specifications. If no specifications are available, use the rule of thumb that 0.030 in. (0.76 mm) is normal and 0.050 in. (1.27 mm) is the maximum end play allowable. A torque converter with excess end play (more than 0.050 in.) should be rebuilt or replaced.

19.2.4 INTERNAL INTERFERENCE CHECKS The
thrust washers inside a torque converter can wear to the point where the impeller, turbine, or stator can rub against each other. The normal wear pattern caused by the dynamic fluid pressure moves the turbine toward the front of the torque converter and the stator toward the rear. Torque converter interference should be checked twice, once with the turbine and stator toward the front and again with them toward the rear.

To check a converter for internal interference, you should:

1. Set the torque converter on a bench with the hub up. Gravity will move the turbine and stator toward the front of the torque converter.

2. Insert the transmission pump stator support into the torque converter so the support splines engage the stator clutch splines.

3. Insert the transmission input shaft into the torque converter so its splines enter the turbine splines. ● **SEE FIGURE 19–10.**

FIGURE 19–10 An internal interference check. The pump body with (a) stator support and (b) clutch with turbine shaft have been installed and are rotated to feel and listen for internal contact. The assembly is then turned upside down and the checks are repeated. Internal contact in either position indicates a faulty converter.

4. Rotate the pump and input shaft in both clockwise and counterclockwise directions, one at a time and together. If there is any sign of contact or rubbing, either a rubbing or grating sound or rough feel, the torque converter needs to be replaced.

5. Turn the whole assembly over so the turbine and stator move toward the rear of the torque converter.

6. Repeat step 4. Again, any sign of internal contact indicates a torque converter that should be rebuilt or replaced.

19.2.5 TORQUE CONVERTER CLUTCH CHECKS The
clutch of a lock-up torque converter can fail in several ways: The friction lining can break up or wear out, the pressure plate seals can leak, or the damper assembly can fail. The damper assembly and lining material cannot be checked on the bench. The only way to check them is on a road test or to cut the torque converter open. Lining breakup often shows up as a plugged oil cooler or lining material in the cooler line. Occasionally, a fragment of a broken damper spring can be found in the cooler line. These are definite signs of a faulty lock-up torque converter.

Two styles of testers are available for checking torque converter clutches. One type uses adapters that replace the turbine shaft and allow a vacuum to be exerted on the front side of the clutch plate assembly. If this chamber can hold a vacuum, the center seal and the clutch lining (which forms the outer seal) are good. The second tester style uses adapters that attach to the turbine, which uses air pressure to apply the clutch. ● **SEE FIGURE 19–11.** With the clutch applied, torque is exerted to try to turn the turbine. A good torque converter clutch locks the turbine and prevents it from turning.

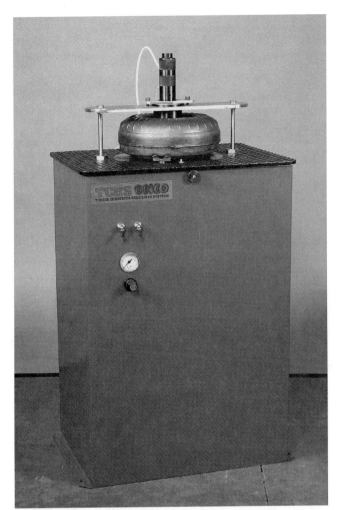

FIGURE 19–11 A torque converter lock-up dyno. It tests the TCC to make sure that it will lock up properly. (*Courtesy of TCRS Inc.*)

 TECH TIP

Some vehicles require a TCC with graphite lining. Because this type of lining can conduct electricity, you can check a converter to ensure that it has this lining type. Slide an input shaft into the turbine just far enough to contact the turbine and clutch plate. Now connect an ohmmeter to the turbine shaft and the outside of the torque converter. A continuity reading shows graphite clutch lining. No continuity shows standard lining.

 REAL WORLD FIX

The 1993 Toyota Camry (117,000 miles) had the transmission rebuilt because of a worn gear set. All of the soft parts, gear set, and torque converter were replaced. The transmission operation was normal for about 25 miles, and then it stopped working. A scan tool check showed no trouble codes. The filter was found to be plugged with clutch material, but all of the transmission clutches appeared good when inspected. It was noted that the replacement torque converter required different bolts than the original.

FIX

Following advice, the technician checked the front of the torque converter and found six dimples. The installer used six slightly long mounting bolts that dented the front of the converter. Replacement of the torque converter using the proper bolts fixed this problem.

 REAL WORLD FIX

The 1991 Suburban (126,000 miles) torque converter goes into lock-up in second gear, and then it intermittently releases and reapplies. A scan tool shows the circuit switching. The TCC will release when the brake pedal is tapped as designed. The TCC solenoid, TOT sensor, 3–4 pressure switch, and ECM were replaced, but this did not help.

FIX

Following advice, the technician checked the transmission external wire harness and found the insulation had rubbed through, allowing the TCC wire to make an intermittent ground connection. Repairing the wire fixed the problem. This TCC circuit is controlled by an internal governor switch that provides a ground.

Checks of the electronic TCC circuits are described in Chapter 13.

19.2.6 LEAK CHECKS A torque converter can leak at the welds, fittings, or plugs. Leaking fluid will show up at the bottom of the torque converter housing and can be mistaken for a front seal leak. The difference is the location of wetness on the torque converter.

The torque converter must be pressurized to test for a leak. A special tool with an expandable plug that fits into the hub and a device to keep the plug in place is used. The plug is equipped with an air chuck to allow pressure to be added.
● **SEE FIGURE 19–12.**

The following description of the procedure to check a torque converter is very general. Always follow the exact procedure for the equipment you are using.

(a)

(b)

FIGURE 19–12 (a) This torque converter leak-test fixture has adapters to fit hubs of different diameters. (b) A different tester is shown with a converter installed. (*Figure (a) Courtesy of Kent-Moore*)

FIGURE 19–13 A leak-test fixture has been placed on the torque converter. It will be inflated with air pressure, and then soapy water will be sprayed on it to identify any leaks.

FIGURE 19–14 Pinhole leaks in a converter can be sealed using a punch and hammer. A series of punch marks around the hole should displace metal to close off the hole.

To check a torque converter for leaks, you should:

1. Drain as much fluid out of the torque converter as possible.

2. Select the correct size plug/adapter for the torque converter hub.

3. Place the torque converter and adapter into the holding fixture. ● **SEE FIGURE 19–13**.

4. Tighten the adapter as required, and apply an air pressure of 30 to 40 PSI (207 to 275 kPa).

5. Spray a soapy water solution on the areas where you suspect a leak. Foamy bubbles indicate a leak. Some types of test equipment allow the pressurized unit to be immersed in a tank of water. Air bubbles will show the location of any leaks.

6. When finished, completely release the air pressure before removing the test tool.

 SAFETY TIP

Be sure the assembly is mounted so the adapter cannot be blown out of the hub when it is pressurized.

 TECH TIP

Very small pinhole leaks can be sealed by peening the hole closed. This is done using a punch and hammer and striking the area immediately around the hole. ● **SEE FIGURE 19–14**. The malleable iron material of the torque converter or weld is forced over into the hole. Larger holes are sealed by welding, which can cause an unbalanced torque converter, or by installing a new or rebuilt torque converter.

19.3 TORQUE CONVERTER CLEANING

Torque converters are very difficult to clean because of their internal shape. Most shops use rebuilt torque converters to ensure a completely clean unit without any concerns of internal wear or damage. Trying to clean a torque converter by running solvent or cleaners into it does no good. In fact, it may even be harmful if all the solvent is not removed. A torque converter cleaner is an effective but expensive piece of equipment. It pumps cleaning solvent under pressure through the torque converter in a reverse direction, and at the same time, the device rotates the turbine in order to create a fluid flow that loosens the debris so it can be flushed out. The cleaning operation usually runs until the solvent leaving the torque converter runs clear, about 5 to 15 minutes.

After cleaning, the internal end play should be rechecked. Occasionally, end play increases as varnish or debris is removed.

Exactly how much of the packed dirt and metal debris is removed from a really dirty torque converter can be questioned. Any remaining debris can damage the transmission. Many technicians prefer to rebuild a dirty torque converter. This will ensure complete cleaning and a thorough inspection of the internal components so all worn or faulty parts can be replaced.

19.3.1 DRILLING A TORQUE CONVERTER
It is possible to drill a torque converter to provide a drain opening. This requires installing a plug to seal the opening. Drilling a torque converter is not generally recommended.

Normally the plug used to fill the hole is a special closed-end pop rivet or a 1/8-in. National Pipe Thread (NPT) plug. The pop rivet is the lightest and quickest to install, but the pipe plug is the most secure.

 TECH TIP

1. The solvent must be removed completely from inside the torque converter. If the torque converter has a drain plug, this is fairly easy. If there is no drain, drain as much solvent as possible out through the hub. Pour 2 quarts (1.9 L) of clean ATF into the hub, and agitate the torque converter to mix the ATF and the solvent. Then drain as much of the ATF-solvent mixture out through the hub as possible. The small amount of solvent remaining will probably not cause a problem.

2. If a pipe plug is used to plug a drain hole, a recessed-head type is recommended because it weighs less and there is a lower possibility of disturbing the balance of the torque converter. If balance is a problem, install two plugs placed exactly opposite each other.

Drain Hole Location

FIGURE 19–15 A hole can be drilled into the torque converter so that it can be drained. This hole should be tapped to accept a small pipe plug.

 TECH TIP

1. When drilling a torque converter, it is important not to drill into any of the internal components. Drill only deep enough to penetrate the cover and, preferably, into the impeller area. ● SEE FIGURE 19–15. With lock-up torque converters, it is important not to drill into the clutch friction area. The hole size is usually 1/8 in. (3.5 mm) if a pop rivet is to be used or 11/32 in. (8.7 mm) if a 1/8-in. pipe plug is to be used. Before drilling, place a depth stop or a piece of tape on the drill bit so you can drill to a maximum depth of 1/4 in. (6.3 mm). This is deep enough to penetrate the outer cover.

2. If you are using a pipe plug, apply grease to the flutes of a 1/8-in. NPT tap to catch the metal chips, and cut threads in the hole. While tapping, make sure not to run the tap into any internal parts. Also periodically back the tap up to break the chips and cut clean threads. Then apply sealing tape or sealant to the threads of the pipe plug and tighten it to 8 ft-lb (10.8 N-m) of torque.

After the torque converter has drained, simply remove any burrs from the outside of the hole if you are using a pop rivet. Then apply a small amount of sealant on the rivet; place the rivet into the hole; and use the pop rivet tool to expand the rivet and lock it in place.

After installing a plug, it is good practice to pressure test the converter before installing the torque converter in a transmission.

19.3.2 COOLER CLEANING

A dirty transmission cooler can reduce the fluid flow or release abrasive debris into the fluid that is being sent to the lubrication passages. This debris can usually be removed by pumping a solvent like mineral spirits through the cooler in a reverse-flow direction, sometimes called *reverse flushing*. The flushing unit should be able to move at least 1 gallon of solvent through the cooler in 1 minute; some units have a pulsating flow to help break the debris loose. ● SEE FIGURE 19–16. The cooler is fairly compact so cleaning it is usually a quick and fairly easy job.

Technicians using a flushing chemical have a professional responsibility to:

- Obtain, read, and understand the MSDS for that chemical.

- Learn how that chemical works and how it should be used.

- Determine if that chemical will do no harm to the system and materials such as gaskets and seals.

- Determine how to remove that chemical from the system and how to properly recycle or dispose of it.

When the flush is completed, the solvent should be removed from the cooler by blowing clean, dry air through the system, and the solvent should be recycled or disposed of properly. The air should be blown through the system for a few minutes to evaporate the remaining solvent.

Cleaning a cooler is normally done by pumping solvent backward through the cooler lines and cooler (called *reverse flushing*). The cleaner or fluid pump is connected to the transmission end of the lubrication cooler return line. The transmission end of the cooler feed line is opened to return the solvent to the cleaner or to a catch bucket. ● SEE FIGURE 19–17. Fluid is then pumped through the circuit until it runs outs clear. Some cleaners produce a pulsating solvent flow intended to loosen and remove packed debris. Other units heat the cleaning solution to help remove any wax deposits.

FIGURE 19–16 This cooler line flusher pumps solvent through the cooler lines and cooler. (*Courtesy of HECAT, Inc.*)

FIGURE 19–17 A cooler flusher is connected to the cooler lines so a cleaning agent can be forced in the reverse direction through the cooler unit until it is clean.

 REAL WORLD FIX

The 1995 Dodge D250 truck (120,000 miles) has delayed engagements after sitting for a long time. It works fine after that. A drain-down problem is suspected.

FIX

A Dodge TSB recommended replacement of the cooler line. The replacement line included a check valve to control drainback. Replacing the cooler line fixed the problem.

 TECH TIP

A cooler that has been flushed can be checked by blowing a large volume of clean, dry air into one of the ports while clean cloth is held over the other port. If the cooler was really cleaned, there will be no debris, oil, or solvent caught on the cloth.

TECH TIP

If torque converter drainback is suspected, run the vehicle until it is at normal operating temperature, and drive the vehicle through several full-shift cycles. Check and adjust the fluid level if it is low, and shut off the engine. Allow the vehicle to sit for 30 to 60 minutes, then recheck the fluid level and mark it on the dipstick. Allow the vehicle to sit for 24 hours and then recheck the fluid level. If the level has risen by 1 in. (25.4 mm) or more, converter drainback has occurred.

TECH TIP

Flush kits consisting of an aerosol can of flushing solution with adapters to connect to the cooler are available. ● **SEE FIGURE 19–18.** These are popular with many smaller shops that do not have flushing equipment.

REAL WORLD FIX

The 1997 Dodge 1500 Ram pickup (36,000 miles) was repaired after an accident. It had an erratic shift problem, and an inspection of the pan showed a lot of metal, so a remanufactured transmission was installed. After a short test drive, the transmission became noisy with a metallic-type noise.

FIX

The technician learned that this vehicle has a check valve in one of the cooler lines. A thorough cleaning of this clogged valve allowed proper lubrication to the transmission and fixed the noise problem.

REAL WORLD FIX

The 1993 Camry (75,000 miles) drives okay, but it loses all gears when it gets hot. The transmission was disassembled, and a badly worn gear set was found. The gear set, thrust washers, O-rings, worn frictions, and torque converter were replaced, and the valve body and solenoids were cleaned and inspected. The transmission was reinstalled, but the same problem remained.

FIX

The technician retraced the fluid flow and decided to replace the filter and clean the cooler. These repairs fixed the problem.

FIGURE 19–18 A cooler can be back-flushed using an aerosol flushing kit. (*Courtesy of Life Automotive Products Inc.*)

19.4 TORQUE CONVERTER REBUILDING

A torque converter is rebuilt by cutting it open, cleaning and inspecting the parts, replacing any worn or damaged parts, and welding it back together. Expensive specialized equipment is required to rebuild a torque converter. The equipment operator should have some machining and metalworking skills. These requirements limit torque converter rebuilding to companies that specialize in torque converter rebuilding or the larger transmission shops.

A transmission shop may prefer to rebuild its own torque converters to ensure the proper one for the vehicle. Remember that a transmission model can use torque converters with different stall speeds. Installing the wrong torque converter can cause drastic changes in vehicle performance. At least eight different torque converters are used with one of the common transaxles. They look about the same and fit any of the flex-plates and transaxles. They are easily interchanged, but the result is improper vehicle operation.

A rebuilt torque converter of poor quality can ruin an otherwise perfect transmission overhaul. Some shops have found that it takes about 20 to 30 minutes to rebuild a torque converter—not much more than the time spent to check, clean, and flush or locate an exchange unit.

When a torque converter is rebuilt, all damaged or worn parts are either repaired or replaced as necessary. Rebuilding a torque converter consists of the following operations.

- Inspect the exterior for damage.
- Cut the torque converter open on a specially equipped lathe.

(a)

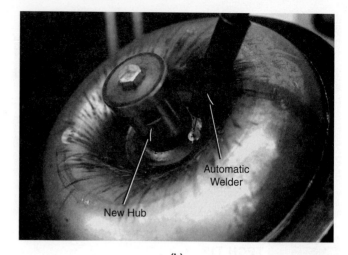

New Hub

Automatic Welder

(b)

FIGURE 19–19 (a) This worn converter hub has been removed to allow replacement. (b) A new hub has been installed and welded in place using a special welder.

- Inspect the interior components for wear or damage.
- Thoroughly clean the interior parts.
- Disassemble and inspect the stator one-way clutch.
- Replace all worn or damaged parts.
- Prelubricate the internal bearing surfaces.
- Adjust the internal end play.
- Carefully reassemble and weld the two sections together.
- Leak check all welds.
- Balance the assembly.

19.4.1 DISASSEMBLING A TORQUE CONVERTER

Since a torque converter is welded together, the weld must be cut to open it. The torque converter is mounted in a metal-cutting lathe for the cutting operation. To ensure that it is mounted true, the torque converter is centered to the lathe using an adapter that matches the crankshaft pilot and is bolted to a face plate at the drive lugs. Duplicating the mounting points should give true, wobble-free rotation for accurate machining.

When the lathe is started, runout of the hub can be observed. Excessive hub runout causes wear at the front pump, bushing, and seal and an added strain on the flex plate. It is corrected by careful alignment during reassembly of the torque converter housings. A faulty hub will be removed and replaced at this time. ● SEE FIGURE 19–19. The hub weld is cut using a hardened steel alloy cutter bit to remove the weld metal. The new replacement hub is welded in place using an automatic wire welder.

The torque converter housing weld is cut using a hardened carbide cutter bit. A skilled operator will remove just enough of the weld to allow separating the two parts, the front "bowl" from the rear impeller. ● SEE FIGURE 19–20. This makes reassembly of the torque converter easier and leaves enough metal for future rebuilding.

(a)

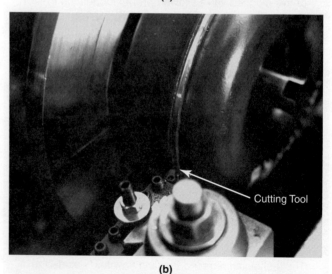

Cutting Tool

(b)

FIGURE 19–20 (a) To rebuild a converter, first cut it open on a machine lathe. (b) A carbide tool is used to cut the weld so the converter can be split apart.

The transmission in the 1997 Ranger was overhauled because of a broken low and reverse sprag. The overhaul included a master kit, rebuilt torque converter, EPC solenoid, and No. 2 shift solenoid, along with a shift kit. The vehicle came back with a DTC P1743 (TCC solenoid open or shorted) and P1744 (TCC slip/engagement problem). The TCC solenoid and internal harness were replaced. This cured the P1743 DTC. The vehicle still loses TCC operation when it gets hot (about 10 miles), resets DTC P1744, and EPC goes to zero duty cycle.

FIX

Further tests revealed a pressure leak in the TCC apply circuit. The torque converter rebuilder was contacted, and another rebuilt torque converter was installed. The new torque converter fixed this problem.

FIGURE 19–21 After being cut open, the usable components are placed in a spray washer for thorough cleaning.

19.4.2 CLEANING

A hot spray washer is used to clean the disassembled torque converter parts. ● **SEE FIGURE 19–21.** Some of the parts are cleaned several times as they go through different repair procedures. For example, the front bowl and rear impeller must have the packed-in debris removed, be deburred from the lathe cut, and have the edges beveled slightly to ease reassembly. They are rewashed after these operations to ensure complete cleanliness.

19.4.3 SUBASSEMBLY REPAIR

With the torque converter disassembled, the following items are checked and repaired as necessary.

- Torque converter hub: removed and replaced
- Starter ring gear: removed and replaced (● **SEE FIGURE 19–22.**)
- Crankshaft pilot: welded to build up material and machined back to original size
- Drive lugs/studs: removed and replaced
- Turbine drive hub: removed and replaced
- Thrust washers: removed, lubricated, and replaced or upgraded to Torrington bearings
- Support bushings: removed and replaced
- Impeller fins: spot welded to lock in place
- Stator clutch: disassembled, inspected, lubricated, and reassembled
- Stator clutch outer race: pinned to lock into the stator
- Clutch lining: relined (● **SEE FIGURE 19–23.**)
- Damper springs or assemblies: removed and replaced

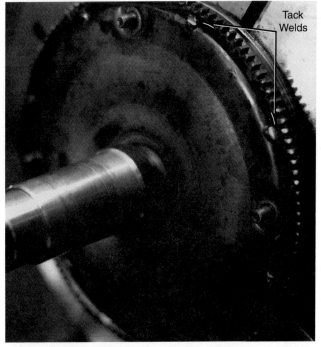

FIGURE 19–22 A new starter ring gear has been installed and tack welded. After ensuring that it is straight, it will be welded securely.

With the exception of the stator one-way clutch, which is always disassembled and inspected, these operations are done on an as-needed basis.

19.4.4 TORQUE CONVERTER REASSEMBLY

Torque converter reassembly requires the following operations.

FIGURE 19–23 This torque converter piston bonder is used to bond new lining onto a torque converter clutch piston. (*Courtesy of TCRS Inc.*)

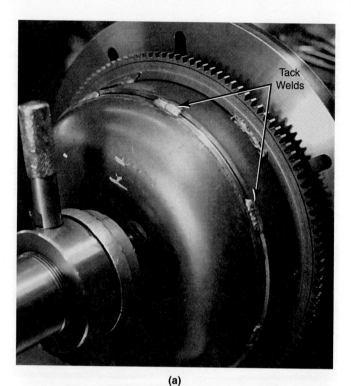

(a)

(b)

FIGURE 19–25 This converter is assembled, and the two housings are tack welded together (left). Checks made at this time ensure that the hub is centered and true with the front of the converter (right).

FIGURE 19–24 This fixture is used to ensure that the converter will have the correct overall length after assembly. Shims are added internally to correct end play if necessary.

- Check the height of the stacked components to ensure that the assembled unit is not too long or too short.
  - ● SEE FIGURE 19–24.
- Check and adjust the internal clearance to ensure there is correct end play. Adjustment is done by changing or shimming the thrust washers.

- Make sure the bowl and impeller housings are correctly aligned so there is a minimum of hub runout, and tack weld them securely into position. ● SEE FIGURE 19–25.
- Weld the housing in an automatic wire welder to provide a continuous, leak-free weld. ● SEE FIGURE 19–26.

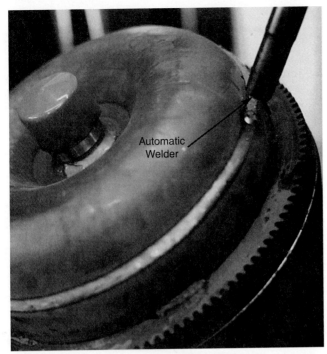

FIGURE 19–26 The assembled converter is welded together on an automatic welder.

FIGURE 19–28 This converter is balanced using a special balancer. Small weights will be spot welded onto it to correct any unbalance.

FIGURE 19–27 This converter is pressure tested for leaks in this special fixture. Soap will be sprayed on it, and bubbles will show any leaks.

19.4.5 POSTASSEMBLY CHECKS After the torque converter has been welded back together, it is pressure checked for no leaks. ● **SEE FIGURE 19–27.** This operation is similar to that described in an earlier section. Small leaks can often be repaired by peening the hole closed using a punch and hammer. Larger leaks require rewelding.

The final torque converter rebuilding operation is to balance the assembled unit. ● **SEE FIGURE 19–28.** This compensates for changes in the amount of weld metal and the possible repositioning of the two housing sections. During the balancing operation, the turbine and stator must be locked in a centered position to prevent them from affecting the overall balance. Balancing a torque converter is made more difficult by the three units that can revolve together as one unit or as three separate units.

1. When a transmission is rebuilt, the torque converter is serviced, rebuilt, or replaced.

2. If a torque converter is to be reused, the technician should visually inspect it and test it for leaks, check the one-way clutch operation, and measure internal end play.

3. Torque converters are rebuilt by disassembling them. They are then inspected, cleaned, parts replaced as necessary, adjusted, and reassembled.

REVIEW QUESTIONS

1. Torque converters should be checked for:
   a. _____
   b. _____
   c. _____
   d. _____
   e. _____
   f. _____

2. The six areas of a torque converter that are visually checked are:
   a. Housing for _____
   b. Drive lugs or _____ for damage
   c. Pilot for damage or _____
   d. Hub for signs of seal or _____ wear
   e. _____ drive tangs or lugs for wear or damage
   f. Starter _____ gear for wear or damage

3. If the stator one-way clutch can be easily turned in both directions, it is said to be _____.

4. A customer concern about poor fuel economy or higher-than-normal engine speed could be the result of a _____ stator clutch.

5. As a rule of thumb, the torque converter should have no more than _____ end play.

6. A check for a leaking torque converter is to _____ it and spray it with soapy water.

7. Transmission coolers are flushed out by forcing _____ through the cooler in a reverse direction.

8. Torque converters are welded together and must be _____ to be rebuilt.

CHAPTER QUIZ

1. Technician A says that a dirty torque converter can ruin a transmission rebuild. Technician B says that most used torque converters are worn out. Who is correct?
   a. Technician A
   b. Technician B
   c. Both Technicians A and B
   d. Neither Technician A nor B

2. Visual checks to be made on a torque converter include condition of the _____.
   a. Drive lugs or studs
   b. Hub and pump drive tangs
   c. Pilot
   d. All of these

3. Technician A says that it should not be possible to turn the stator splines in either direction with one's finger. Technician B says that normally these splines can be turned both ways by gripping them with a pair of snap-ring pliers. Who is correct?
   a. Technician A
   b. Technician B
   c. Both Technicians A and B
   d. Neither Technician A nor B

4. Technician A says that a torque converter with a bad stator one-way clutch should be replaced with a new torque converter. Technician B says a torque converter can be rebuilt and the one-way clutch repaired. Who is correct?
   a. Technician A
   b. Technician B
   c. Both Technicians A and B
   d. Neither Technician A nor B

5. Technician A says that excessive end play in a torque converter is caused by a worn-out stator. Technician B says that torque converter end play can be accurately checked with a pair of snap-ring pliers. Who is correct?
   a. Technician A
   b. Technician B
   c. Both Technicians A and B
   d. Neither Technician A nor B

6. Technician A says that a good rule of thumb for the maximum allowable amount of torque converter end play is 0.050 in. Technician B says that any torque converter with less than 0.040 in. of end play should be replaced or rebuilt. Who is correct?
   a. Technician A
   b. Technician B
   c. Both Technicians A and B
   d. Neither Technician A nor B

7. Technician A says that a stator support and a turbine shaft are needed in order to check a torque converter for internal interference. Technician B says that this is a simple check in which one merely rotates parts in the torque converter while listening and feeling for internal rubbing. Who is correct?
   a. Technician A
   b. Technician B
   c. Both Technicians A and B
   d. Neither Technician A nor B

8. Technician A says that if the torque converter clutch lining breaks up, it probably plugs the cooler. Technician B says that a failed torque converter clutch can cause too little internal end play. Who is correct?
   a. Technician A
   b. Technician B
   c. Both Technicians A and B
   d. Neither Technician A nor B

9. Technician A says that during a leak check the torque converter is filled with oil to a pressure of about 80 PSI. Technician B says that a very small leak at a torque converter weld can be stopped using a hammer and punch. Who is correct?
   a. Technician A
   b. Technician B
   c. Both Technicians A and B
   d. Neither Technician A nor B

10. When a transmission is rebuilt, the torque converter should be _____.
    a. Balanced
    b. Painted
    c. Cleaned
    d. All of these

11. Technician A says that a torque converter can be drained adequately by merely turning it so the hub is downward over a container. Technician B says that one can clean a torque converter quite well by running a solvent hose into it and turning on the parts washer. Who is correct?
    a. Technician A
    b. Technician B
    c. Both Technicians A and B
    d. Neither Technician A nor B

12. Technician A says that after a torque converter is flushed with solvent, it should be filled with ATF and then as much of the ATF/solvent mix as possible should be drained. Technician B says that it is possible to completely drain the torque converter by drilling a hole in it. Who is correct?
    a. Technician A
    b. Technician B
    c. Both Technicians A and B
    d. Neither Technician A nor B

13. During a rebuild, a torque converter _____.
    a. Is taken apart and cleaned
    b. Has the stator clutch disassembled and checked
    c. Is adjusted to the correct internal end play
    d. All of these

14. Technician A says that special equipment is required to rebuild a torque converter. Technician B says that the only sure way to get all of the dirt and debris out of a torque converter is to rebuild it. Who is correct?
    a. Technician A
    b. Technician B
    c. Both Technicians A and B
    d. Neither Technician A nor B

chapter 20

AUTOMATIC TRANSMISSION MODIFICATIONS

OBJECTIVES: **After studying Chapter 20, the reader will be able to:** • Describe the modifications that can be made to improve the reliability or change the operating characteristics of an automatic transmission.

20.1 INTRODUCTION

There are several reasons for modifying an automatic transmission. Most involve matching the transmission to the driver's or vehicle's driving characteristics or operating conditions. Most transmission modifications are intended to improve shift quality and are relatively mild and inexpensive. Other changes, such as those done to produce an all-out race transmission, can be very involved and expensive.

Many transmission repair shops routinely perform minor modifications. When considering transmission modifications, remember that any transmission work that does not follow a manufacturer's recommendations affects the operating characteristics, transmission life, and perhaps safety. The manufacturer's warranty may be voided if modifications are made. The technician making the changes is responsible for any adverse results.

When planning transmission modifications, first consider the different stages or levels of modifications, as follows:

1. Street usage: changes to improve shift quality
2. Street usage: alter TCC application
3. Street usage: changes to improve fuel economy
4. Street usage: changes to improve strength and longevity
5. Street strip: changes to improve vehicle acceleration rate
6. Racing: numerous changes strictly for racing purposes

Most transmissions are designed and programmed to suit the average new-car buyer. At one time, a major design criteria was to produce a transmission in which the shifts were very smooth, to the point where they could not be felt. ● **SEE FIGURE 20–1.** All shifts have a certain amount of slippage, and the slippage can produce wear and heat. It is possible to change the shift characteristics of many transmissions to the other extreme, a shift that jerks the vehicle and produces tire chirp.

We will discuss several types of modifications. Some are inexpensive, such as plug-in electronic modules, a shift kit, increasing the size of a transfer plate orifice, or removing a spring

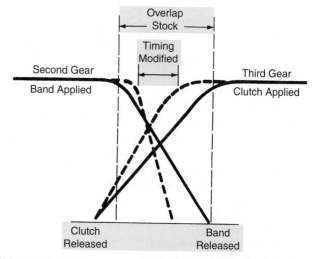

FIGURE 20–1 The overlap period is relatively long with stock shift programming. It is usually reduced to a minimum when transmissions are modified.

from an accumulator. Other changes are expensive, such as a special-purpose gear set or a highly modified torque converter.
● **CHART 20–1** lists various modifications and the ones often used for the modification stages. Each modification will be discussed in more detail.

Most of the stage 5 modifications require specially made, nonproduction parts that are only used on competition units. Although they might provide a benefit for street use, they are usually not worth the cost. Some of the parts for modifying a transmission are available from the new-car dealership or the original equipment manufacturer (OEM). These components are designed for transmissions used with the largest engines or the heaviest or sportiest vehicles. They are designed to handle more torque or provide firmer, tighter operating characteristics. These parts should be used when the transmission requires a warranty. Aftermarket suppliers that service the transmission repair industry are a good source for shift kits, heavy-duty components, and high-performance friction materials. Some

Stage	A	B	C	D	E	F	G	H	I	J	K	L	M	N	O	P
1	X	X		X												
2	X	X														
3	X	X	X	X	X	X	X	?		?						
4	X	X	X	X	X	X	?			X						
5	?	?	X	X	X	X	X	?	X	X	X	X	?	X	?	X

CHART 20-1

Modifications to Produce Operating Characteristics

A: shift kit
B: plug-in electronic module
C: increase clutch pack size
D: improve friction material quality
E: added fluid/deep pan
F: added cooling
G: improve lube flow
H: low-ratio gear set

I: lightweight drums
J: high-strength components
K: heavy-duty sprag races
L: low-drag components
M: low-volume oil pump
N: special valve body
O: internal transmission brake
P: converter stall speed change

Symbol: ?—might be made depending on exact usage and other variables.

suppliers pride themselves in providing parts that cure many transmission weaknesses. All-out racing components are available from companies that specialize in high-performance transmissions and are available through most speed shop catalogs and over the Internet.

Transmission modifications are often developed through a trial-and-error operation. The changes made often depend on the transmission design and are determined after studying its operation, hydraulic circuit, and physical construction. Most technicians use a kit that has already been developed and tested by the supplier

In order of difficulty, the easiest transmission systems to modify are:

1. Electronic control system
2. Hydraulic control system
3. Torque converter
4. Friction material
5. Gear set

20.1.1 SHIFT QUALITY

It is a good idea to determine what a "good shift" is before getting too deep into improving shifts. Most of us realize that too soft of a shift has a lot of slippage that can cause an engine flare and also create wear and heat. Some believe a good shift should be felt by a definite "bump" as the shift occurs, but is this really good? The bump might be a tie-up—being in two gears at one time and thus trying to tear up the transmission.

The two major elements of a good shift are length and firmness. Shift length (duration) is the time period it takes for the shift to occur. Remember that several things *must* occur during a shift. A clutch, band, or one-way clutch must release, another clutch or band must apply, and the engine speed must change (usually drop) to the RPM required for the next gear. A review of Section 7.7.1 describes this process. Also remember that if one

TECH TIP

1. As you tear down a transmission that you think shifts too softly, inspect the friction material. Overheated friction material can easily be spotted by the discolored and warped plates. Is it really overheated from shifting too softly?
2. Some people equate a good shift with a strong bump, but if you watch the front of the hood during a WOT shift, you can sometimes see it drop sharply and then lift again. If the front of a vehicle drops, the transmission is binding up, trying to stop the vehicle—a very bad thing, indeed.

member applies faster, the other member must release faster to prevent a tie-up. The two apply devices must be coordinated or synchronized. A firm shift is felt by the steady pressure at the back of the seat as the vehicle accelerates or a slight lifting of the front of the vehicle during the shift.

20.2 SHIFT IMPROVER KITS

Shift improver kits are the most popular transmission modification. Kits for some transmissions are available from aftermarket transmission part suppliers. Some transmission shops install a shift kit as a standard practice when rebuilding certain transmissions. This is done to increase the life of the rebuild and to make a noticeable firmness in the shift quality, thus increasing

FIGURE 20–2 Shift improver kits vary from minor ones that firm up the shifts to major ones that involve significant internal changes. (*Courtesy of Superior Transmission Parts*)

FIGURE 20–3 The small holes in this separator plate are fluid orifices. Checking where the fluid passage goes from an orifice will identify the purpose for that orifice.

 TECH TIP

Assume there is an orifice with a diameter of 0.180 in., and we want to increase its size (area) by 10%.

The area of a 0.180-in. hole is 0.180 ÷ 2 = 0.090 (radius),

**0.090 × 0.090 = 0.008 (radius squared), and
0.008 × 3.1416 = 0.025 in² (hole area).**

We need to make the area of the hole 0.0025 in² larger (0.025 × 0.10 = 0.0025) (area increase) for a total of 0.0275 in² (0.025 + 0.0025) if we want to increase it by 10%. To determine the diameter of a hole that has an area of 0.0275 in², we work through the formula backward:

**0.0275 ÷ 3.1416 = 0.00875 (radius squared),
and the square root of this is 0.0936 (radius).**

Multiplying this by 2 gives us a hole diameter of 0.187 in.

Increasing an orifice diameter from 0.180 to 0.187 in. should increase the flow rate about 10%. Although it appears rather complicated, a simple pocket calculator makes the mathematics rather easy.

customer satisfaction. The contents of a shift kit vary depending on the transmission and the supplier. It can be a drill bit and direction sheet for increasing an orifice size, a replacement transfer plate, a valve body spring, a spacer block for an accumulator, an orifice plug, or any combination of these. ● **SEE FIGURE 20–2.** Some shift kits are designed to provide changes in stages from the barely noticeable to rather firm shifts.

20.2.1 ORIFICE CHANGES

The size of an orifice in the feed passage is used as a major control for the quality of a shift. The speed and/or quality of that shift can be easily altered by changing the size of the orifice. The orifice is normally located in the transfer plate, a part that can be easily replaced. ● **SEE FIGURE 20–3.** As described earlier, the speed at which a clutch or band servo strokes to take up a clearance and apply the clutch or band is directly related to the size of the servo piston and the fluid flow rate to the piston. An orifice reduces the flow rate and therefore increases the time for the piston stroke. Simply put, if we were to increase the area of the orifice by 10%, we would increase the flow rate by 10% and reduce the time by 10%. This will speed up the shift and reduce slippage.

Remember that we are referring to the area of the orifice, not the diameter. The area of an orifice is the product of:

$$A = \pi r^2 \text{ or } A = 0.785 d^2$$

where

π(pi) = 3.1416

r = radius, one-half the hole diameter

d = hole diameter

(a)

(b)

FIGURE 20–4 If a transfer plate orifice has been drilled to a larger diameter, the edges of the hole should be chamfered slightly to remove any possible burrs.

FIGURE 20–5 (a) If an orifice needs to be made smaller, it can be filled with solder and redrilled to the proper size; the chamfers ensure that the solder plug does not get pushed out of the hole. (b) Another way of doing this is to peen the hole partially closed before redrilling it to the proper size.

TECH TIP

1. When drilling an orifice, finish the hole so there are no burrs or rough edges. These can create fluid turbulence that reduces the flow. Normally the hole is drilled using a sharp drill bit to the desired size, and then a larger drill or a scraper is used to debur or chamfer each end of the hole. ● **SEE FIGURE 20–4.**

2. If a hole is too large, the diameter can be reduced by soldering the hole closed or plugging it with a soft rivet and then drilling it to the desired size. ● **SEE FIGURE 20–5.** It is good practice to counterbore each end of the hole before soldering it to give the solder a good mechanical bond. Another method of reducing the diameter of an orifice in a transfer plate is to peen the metal around the hole to displace metal toward the hole. After peening, the orifice should be drilled to the desired diameter.

3. The flow through a round passage in the case or a shaft can be closed by driving a cup plug (slightly oversize) into the passage. ● **SEE FIGURE 20–6.** The cup plug is then drilled to provide the desired orifice.

FIGURE 20–6 A small cup plug can be driven into a passage to close it off. It can be drilled to the proper size to provide an orifice.

20.2.2 ACCUMULATOR CHANGES

An accumulator is a relatively easy device to alter. In some cases, it is mounted at the outside of the case to allow quick and easy access. The most common change made with accumulators is to block their motion. If the piston cannot stroke, it will not take fluid away from the clutch or band operation and the application will be faster and firmer. Like modifying orifice size in a transfer plate, blocking an accumulator is fairly easy to change back if it does not produce the desired results.

TECH TIP

In a few cases, an accumulator can be blocked by turning the piston upside down relative to the bore and guide rod. Another way to block one is to cut a piece of tubing to a length slightly shorter than the accumulator piston stroke. ● **SEE FIGURE 20–7.** The tubing diameter should be smaller than the piston diameter so it fits against a strong portion of the piston.

Front Servo

Accumulator

(a)

Tubing

(b)

FIGURE 20–7 (a) The action of some accumulators can be eliminated by cutting a piece of thin wall tubing to the right length and (b) installing it to block movement. Note that the spring has been removed.

FIGURE 20–8 A plug-in electronic device can be used to change the shift and TCC characteristics of electronically controlled transmissions. (*Courtesy of Autotrans*)

20.2.3 PROGRAMMING CHANGES, ELECTRONIC-CONTROLLED TRANSMISSIONS

Electronic transmission controls can be easily modified by plugging a module between the case connector and the wiring harness. ● **SEE FIGURE 20–8.** In most cases, the electrical harness is disconnected at the transmission end, and the module is connected between the harness and the transmission. Some modules include adjustments so the operation can be tailored to suit the driver's wishes.

FIGURE 20–9 This E-Place set contains an electronic transmission controller, TPS, VSS, and the wiring harness to connect to the vehicle and transmission. It allows the installation of an electronic-controlled transmission into a nonelectronic-transmission vehicle. (*Courtesy of Autotrans*)

TECH TIP

If you want to swap an electronic transmission into a vehicle not having electronic controls, an electronic transmission control unit is available. ● **SEE FIGURE 20–9.** This is a system that includes a TPS and wiring harnesses as well as adjustments that allow the tailoring of shift points and shift feel.

20.2.4 PROGRAMMING CHANGES, NONELECTRONIC-CONTROLLED TRANSMISSIONS

Depending on the intended operation, the following modifications can be made to the hydraulic circuits to reprogram the automatic operation.

- Modulator or modulator rod length to change shift quality and timing
- Shift valve spring to change shift points
- Governor weights or springs to change shift points
- Line pressure to apply more pressure on the friction material
- Removal of center seal from clutches using three seals to increase clutch apply force
- Removal of certain check balls to allow increased fluid flow

Shift quality can be changed by modifying the modulator. Many transmission shops install a firmer modulator (one with a high spring pressure or a smaller diaphragm area) or use a longer modulator pin to obtain firmer upshifts. ● **SEE FIGURE 20–10.** A softer modulator or shorter pin is used for softer, smoother shifts. Adjustable modulators can be adjusted to make minor changes in shift quality. In addition to these changes, there are

FIGURE 20–10 Line pressure can be increased using a longer modulator pin, turning the modulator adjusting screw inward, or using a modulator with stronger spring pressure.

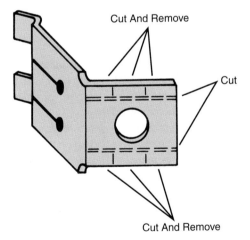

FIGURE 20–11 Cutting material off the secondary weights reduces the centrifugal force of the weights and reduces governor pressure. The result will be later upshifts.

different kits available; one kit is driver adjusted and another technician adjusted. They vary the vacuum signal to the modulator to produce the desired shift quality.

Many shift kits contain one or more replacement shift valve springs. The strength of these springs is altered from stock

TECH TIP

1. You can see how a modulator change affects the operation if you road test a vehicle after installing a vacuum gauge and fluid pressure gauge, as described in Chapter 12. Before making any modifications, make a moderate-to-high-throttle acceleration from a stop to high-gear shift and note the shift quality. This will be the baseline for the next tests. Lower the vacuum available to the modulator, note the effect on the vacuum and line pressure gauges, and repeat the baseline test. Depending on the amount of vacuum, a definite change in shift quality should be noticed. It should be noted that reducing the vacuum signal will not affect full-throttle shifts because the vacuum is zero during wide-open throttle.

2. Shift timing for all shifts is altered by changing the governor weights or springs. Some manufacturers have a selection of governor weights available. Drilling a hole or cutting away some of the metal in the weights reduces the effect of centrifugal force. This produces lower governor pressure and higher-speed upshifts. ● **SEE FIGURE 20–11.** Adding additional metal onto the governor weights produces earlier and higher governor pressure and lower-speed shifts. Changing the springs has a similar effect. Stronger springs produce later, higher-speed shifts, and weaker springs produce earlier, lower-speed shifts.

3. It is difficult to locate a spring of a particular diameter, length, and strength. A good, complete spring selection is not commonly available. The strength effect of a spring can be increased by stretching it slightly or by placing a shim under one end of it. If tinkering with springs, remember that all straight-wound springs have a constant rate of compression. Even though valve body springs are relatively small, they follow the normal rules for springs. Spring rate refers to the rate of compression relative to the load. This means that if it takes 1 ounce (28.4 g) of pressure to compress the spring 1/4 in. (6.35 mm), it will take 2 ounces (56.8 g) of force to compress it 1/2 in. (12.7 mm), and 3 ounces (85.2 g) of force to compress it 3/4 in. (19 mm). Shimming or stretching a spring causes it to enter further into its rate increase and to do so sooner. If a spring can be shortened by squeezing it, it enters the rate slower and is weaker. The actual strength of a spring is determined by the diameter of the wire, the coil diameter, and number of coils. The thicker the spring's wire, the stronger the spring.

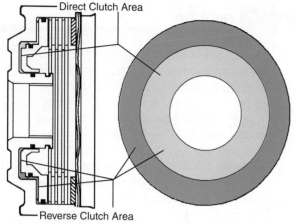

Direct Clutch Area

Reverse Clutch Area

FIGURE 20–12 This direct clutch has two fluid chambers separated by the center piston seal. The inner chamber is used in third gear, and both chambers are used in reverse.

Horsepower Absorption
(HP/SQ-IN @ 180 psi, 220 deg F)

3.25 HP.SQ-IN

2.5 HP/SQ-IN

1.5 HP/SQ-IN

Stop time .45 sec for all tests

■ BPS ■ Kevlar ▨ Stock

FIGURE 20–13 Special-purpose clutch plates designed for racing have a higher static coefficient of friction that produces firmer shifts that can absorb more torque. (*Courtesy of Raybestos*)

to produce different shift timing for that particular upshift or downshift.

Many people raise line pressure when reprogramming a transmission by shimming the pressure regulator spring. This produces firmer and stronger shifts, but it also increases the horsepower loss in the transmission and produces more heat in the fluid. A knowledgeable transmission tuner uses other methods that are described in this chapter to produce stronger and firmer shifts. Line pressure increase is used as the last resort. Some tuners can reduce line pressure, and make other changes, to produce the desired result. Reducing line pressure improves transmission efficiency.

Some transmissions use outer, center, and inner seals in the direct clutch pistons and some forward clutch pistons. ● **SEE FIGURE 20–12**. The center seal divides the piston chamber into two separate chambers. These chambers can be filled separately, progressively, or simultaneously. They are normally used to produce smoother neutral–first and neutral–reverse shifts while producing a strong direct clutch in reverse. When building a high-performance transmission, the center seal can be removed to increase the piston area and produce a stronger forward clutch application. If this modification is done on street-driven vehicles, the 2–3 shift will be considered harsh. Removing the center seal from the direct clutch also produces a severe leak into the reverse passages in third gear. This requires significant altering of the fluid passages.

20.3 CLUTCH PACKS

Clutch pack modifications are used to improve the torque-carrying capacity and the longevity of the transmission. Changes include using the best friction material available, increasing the number of clutch plates, and drilling the hub and drum for improved fluid flow in and out of the clutch plate area.

Friction material quality is important in any transmission. High torque loads or extended transmission life demands using the best material available. This is often a top-quality OEM material with new steel plates. Some shops grit-blast the steel plates. This usually produces a firmer shift, but the rougher plate friction surface causes reduced life expectancy of the clutch lining.

If the transmission is to be used for racing, special-purpose racing clutch plates should be used. These plates use friction material that is designed to absorb the increased torque. ● **SEE FIGURE 20–13**. They also will work better under the higher-heat conditions found in racing transmissions. These friction plates, along with the microfinished steel plates to be used with them, are made to higher standards to ensure proper operation.

20.3.1 INCREASING PACK SIZE
Adding one more friction and a steel plate to a four-plate clutch increases the torque capacity by 25%. The longevity or number of shifts that the clutch can make also increases 25%.

Most manufacturers produce different clutch assemblies with various numbers of plates depending on the engine torque and body weight of the vehicle. The differences that determine the number of plates are usually the piston thickness, pressure plate thickness, drum depth, and hub length. ● **SEE FIGURE 20–14**. In some transmissions, the entire clutch pack assembly must be replaced in order to increase the clutch pack size.

Increasing the pack size can cause other problems. Each pair of plates has a slight drag while released; we can expect a six-plate clutch to have one-sixth more drag than a five-plate clutch. This parasitic drag reduces transmission efficiency and increases heat. Another problem is caused by the thinner plates that are often used. A thinner plate does not have as much heat-sink ability; if it absorbs the same amount of heat as a normal thick plate, it will become hotter. If it gets too hot, it can warp and produce still more heat, possibly causing a loss in the static coefficient of friction.

Piston Thickness — Pressure Plate Thickness

Useable Drum Depth

(a)

Position for new snap ring groove
Snap Ring
Pressure Plate
Friction Plate
Steel Plate
Piston

(b)

FIGURE 20–14 (a) In many cases, the number of plates that are used in a clutch is determined by the thickness of the pressure plate or piston; in some cases, changing one of these allows another friction and steel plate to be added. (b) In some clutches, the drum can be modified to move the snapring groove so another friction and steel plate can be added.

Friction Plate Thickness

Steel Plate Thickness

FIGURE 20–15 Measuring the thickness of a lined and unlined clutch plate and adding a clearance of 0.010 in. determines the space required to add an additional plate.

20.3.2 DRILLING A HUB OR DRUM
Drilling the clutch hub and drum increases the shift speed and clutch longevity. When a clutch is released, fluid must enter between the clutch plates to reduce lining heat, friction, and wear. When a clutch

(a)

(b)

FIGURE 20–16 (a) The clutch pack with eight friction plates is designed to replace an AOD six-plate pack. (b) The clutch pack with nine frictions replaces the stock six friction, 3–4 clutch pack of a 4L60/TH 700. (*Courtesy of Alto Products Corp.*)

TECH TIP

1. The thickness of the piston from some four-plate clutch assemblies is the thickness of a three-plate clutch piston minus the thickness of one friction plate, one steel plate, and a clearance of about 0.010 in. (0.25 mm). ● **SEE FIGURE 20–15.** Using the four-plate piston in a three-plate clutch usually allows enough room for an additional friction and steel plate. When doing this, you should always compare the length of the clutch hubs to ensure that the added plate is positioned correctly on the hub. In some transmissions, a clutch with more plates has a longer hub.

2. Some clutches vary the position of the clutch plate retaining snap-ring groove in the drum depending on the number of plates used. The drum can be replaced using one for the desired clutch pack, or a new groove can be machined into the drum to allow more plates to be installed.

3. One aftermarket manufacturer markets thinner clutch plates so more of them will fit into the clutch drum. ● **SEE FIGURE 20–16.** Some sources do not recommend these plates because they have a reduced heat-sink ability. This causes them to run hotter with possible warpage, drag, and overheating problems.

4. The clutch for a road or endurance racing transmission needs a little more clearance than a stock unit. About 0.013 to 0.016 in. per plate is recommended.

applies, this fluid must leave. ● **SEE FIGURE 20–17**. The clutch hubs in many transmissions have holes drilled in them to allow the fluid to escape. ● **SEE FIGURE 20–18**.

FIGURE 20–17 When a clutch applies, fluid must leave the area between the plates. Usually it flows out the end of the clutch assembly. It can flow outward if the drum is drilled.

Direct Clutch Hub Fluid Holes

FIGURE 20–18 This THM 700 clutch hub was drilled during manufacture to provide a fluid flow into the clutch area.

FIGURE 20–19 When drilling a clutch hub, cut a strip of paper to the width and circumference of the hub. Divide the circumference into fourths and then into smaller sections as desired (twelfths are shown). Wrap the paper around the hub, transfer the hole locations, drill 1/8-in.-diameter holes, debur the holes, and clean off any metal chips.

FIGURE 20–20 When drilling a clutch drum, lay out and drill the holes using the same procedure as a hub. After drilling the holes, chamfer the outer edges to remove the sharp edges.

TECH TIP

1. Use 8 to 12 holes of about 1/8 in. (3.17 mm) in diameter if drilling a hub. The holes should be spaced equally around the hub so that pairs of holes are directly opposite. ● SEE FIGURE 20–19. The hole pattern should be staggered so oil is directed to all of the clutch plates. After the holes have been drilled, remove any burrs from the drilling. Carefully spaced holes of equal size should not disrupt the balance of the hub.

2. A series of holes can be drilled through the band friction surface of the drum to reduce band release time. Drill 8 to 12 equally spaced 1/8-in.-diameter holes through the drum. Again, the holes should be staggered across the friction area. The holes should align with grooves for the clutch plate splines. ● SEE FIGURE 20–20. The sharp edges of these holes tend to cause band wear. It is good practice to chamfer their outer edge using a 3/16-in. (4.76-mm) or 1/4-in. (6.35-mm) drill bit.

Floater spring
between lugs of
steel plates

FIGURE 20–21 These thin floater springs (arrow) are placed between the outer edges of the steel plates. When the clutch is released, they will help separate the plates to reduce drag and friction.

Many three-speed Simpson gear train transmissions have a band fitted around the direct clutch drum. This band must release as the clutch is applied. Clutch apply and band release time can be reduced slightly by routing the fluid from between the clutch plates to the area under the band.

20.3.3 FLOATER SPRINGS
Floater springs reduce clutch drag. These are thin, wavy springs that fit between the outer edges of the steel plates. ● **SEE FIGURE 20–21**. These springs separate the steels from the friction plates to reduce drag when the clutch is released.

20.3.4 BAND CHANGES
Changes to increase the strength of a band are limited to drilling holes in the drum surface as just described and using the replacement parts available from the OEM manufacturer or specialty aftermarket supplier. Different band levers are available for some transmissions that increase the apply force on the band. Some transmissions use servo pistons of different sizes. Replacing the servo assembly with one of a larger diameter will increase the band apply force and reduce apply speed, but this speed increase can result in timing problems. The band should also be one with the best-quality friction material available.

20.4 IMPROVING LUBRICATION

A transmission's life can be severely reduced if the fluid becomes too hot or too dirty. This applies to all transmissions and especially those used for heavier-than-normal operation, such as RV, trailer towing, off-road, street-strip, or competition operation. Anything that increases fluid temperature will tend to reduce a transmission's life and performance.

Extra-deep oil pans are available from several aftermarket sources. These pans hold 1 to 4 more quarts of fluid than the stock pan. ● **SEE FIGURE 20–22**. The increased fluid provides a larger heat sink, which reduces the rate of heat buildup. The increased surface area, which allows more air contact, provides

FIGURE 20–22 This extra-capacity pan, which holds about two additional quarts of ATF, is finned to provide extra cooling ability. (*Courtesy of A-1 Automatic Transmissions*)

FIGURE 20–23 A supplementary oil cooler can be installed to provide additional cooling capacity. (*Courtesy of A-1 Automatic Transmissions*)

added cooling. Some deep pans are made from cast aluminum with fins to increase the amount of metal-to-air ratio even more. Some deep pans have air tubes passing through the sump area to provide increased oil-to-air surface area. Most deep pans have an extension to place the filter lower, near the bottom of the pan, to ensure fluid pickup under all operating conditions. A drawback with a deep pan is reduced ground clearance, which might allow the pan to hit road obstructions.

Supplementary transmission coolers are available from many aftermarket sources. These come in kits to make installation easy. ● **SEE FIGURE 20–23**. Coolers are available in different sizes to suit the cooling needs of different applications. Larger vehicles or heavier loads generate more transmission heat and require more cooling. Cooler setups for street-driven vehicles commonly use rubber hoses with slip-on connections secured by hose clamps. Remember that there is a potential fire hazard should a hose rupture and spray ATF onto a hot exhaust. The coolers for racing/competition vehicles normally use more positive, threaded connections. The coolers using threaded connections also use larger lines to ensure adequate oil flow.

Remote filters can be added to the cooler line if increased longevity is a concern. ● **SEE FIGURE 20–24**. Filters are available in different sizes. Some are rather small, inline devices; others use a standard, spin-on filter cartridge. Filters provide

FIGURE 20–24 A filter can be added into the cooler line to remove any contaminants that might clog the cooler. (*Courtesy of A-1 Automatic Transmissions*)

FIGURE 20–25 Low-ratio gear sets for THM 400, C6, and Torqueflite. They provide a low-gear ratio that is about 11% lower and a 6% lower second-gear ratio than stock. (*Courtesy of A-1 Automatic Transmissions*)

 TECH TIP

1. If installing a remote filter, check to see if it contains a bypass valve. If not, this filter can become plugged as it removes debris from the fluid, and thus restrict the fluid flow through the transmission lubrication passages. Be sure to change filters at the recommended intervals.
2. Many racers use synthetic ATF because of the increased ability to withstand high-heat conditions.
3. A modification to ensure lube circuit flow is to grind a portion of land 2 (or whichever land separates torque converter feed pressure from line pressure) from the pressure regulator valve or drill a small feed hole (0.060 in. [1.5 mm]) in the passage wall between torque converter feed and line or supply pressure. This change might drop line pressure in some gear ranges slightly, but it ensures a converter and lubrication flow at all times.

 TECH TIP

1. When building a transmission for racing, it is good practice to trace out the cooler-lubrication circuit and study the fluid path. Restrictions can often be reduced by drilling the passages to a larger diameter and removing any sharp corners that might restrict fluid flow. Lubrication flow can be increased significantly in some transmissions. Always use discretion when removing metal from a transmission.
2. Some all-out racing transmissions, like many race engines, are converted to dry sump lubrication systems. The fluid is pulled from the transmission pan by a scavenger pump and stored in a special reservoir, and the transmission pump intake pulls from this reservoir. This system allows all the air and foam to separate from the fluid in the reservoir and allows additional fluid storage.

positive cleaning of the fluid returning to the transmission as lubrication oil.

The valve body or pressure regulator can be modified to provide increased fluid flow into the torque converter, cooler, and lubrication circuit. Remember that the pressure regulator valve in some transmissions will shut off flow to this circuit when line pressure falls below the pressure regulator setting.

An abundant quantity of lubrication oil is required for competition transmissions. Some types of competition transmissions require operation in first and second gear at extremely high

engine RPM. Under these severe operating conditions, the gear set and the released apply devices must have an adequate fluid flow to reduce friction and remove heat. Some transmissions have rather complicated and restrictive lubrication passages. They require extensive work to achieve adequate lubrication.

20.5 GEAR TRAIN CHANGES

Replacement planetary gear sets are available from several aftermarket sources—some cater to racing, others to heavy-duty and recreational vehicle (RV) usage. Heavy-duty/RV emphasis is to increase strength and reduce drag to improve longevity and fuel mileage. Some of these gear sets are made from stronger materials and use improved bearings. ● **SEE FIGURE 20–25.**

The torque capacity of some transmissions can be increased by using upgraded parts from the vehicle manufacturer.

1. A possible disadvantage with the lower gear ratio is that the engine RPM in first gear increases by 10%, and the top speed is reduced by 10%. There is also a greater RPM drop during the shift to the next higher gear. Another disadvantage is the high cost of the gear set.
2. Remember that electronic-controlled transmissions monitor the input and output shaft speeds to check for slipping. A ratio change can set a DTC and illuminate the MIL.

For example, a THM 400 can use many of the gear train parts, clutch parts, and other parts from the much stronger 4L80 E.

Lower gear ratios are desirable for certain applications. Several aftermarket sources provide low-ratio gear sets for some popular transmission models. Special-purpose components are relatively expensive. They provide additional torque and pulling power in first and second gears. For example, the replacement gear set for a THM 400 lowers the first-gear ratio from 2.48:1 to 2.75:1. If it is used in a vehicle with a 4:1 rear-axle ratio, the overall ratio is reduced from a stock ratio of 2.48 $\times$ 4, or 9.92:1, to the lower ratio of 2.75 $\times$ 4, or 11:1. The modified ratio is over 10% lower so it should increase the torque and pulling power by more than 10%.

Low-ratio gear sets are designed primarily for competition vehicles. They are also popular for use in trailer towing, off-road, and recreational vehicles that need more pulling power.

Another way to achieve a gear ratio change with RWD vehicles is the addition of an overdrive gear set, which provides one overdrive gear ratio. The most common sets are units placed behind the transmission. These require a shorter driveshaft plus mounting brackets to support the unit and absorb any torque reactions. Overdrive units are available that adapt to the extension housing area of some of the more popular transmissions. This installation, like the addition of a low-ratio gear set, usually requires complete transmission teardown and rebuilding.

20.6 COMPETITION TRANSMISSIONS: STRENGTHENING AND LIGHTENING CHANGES

When there is an increase in the engine's horsepower, in the tire size, or in the vehicle's load, some stock automatic transmission parts will fail. They are not designed to handle the added torque requirements. Several extra-duty or high-performance parts are available from aftermarket sources

to cure the weaknesses in the more popular transmissions. Examples of these parts are:

- The outer sprag race for a THM 350: Special sprag races are over three times as strong as the stock unit.
- The intermediate sprag for a THM 400: Special sprags more than double the strength of the stock unit.
- The Powerglide high clutch hub: The special unit is significantly stronger and more reliable than the stock unit.
- Input shafts for some transmissions are made from stronger steel alloys than the original ones.

Some companies market special parts that allow the use of needle or roller bearings to support the rotating parts and Torrington bearings to replace the plastic or metal thrust washers. These reduce the friction loss and some of the heat that is generated in the transmission. An alternative to the expensive special bearings is to use wider-than-stock replacement bushings or two stock bushings (right next to each other) when possible. Increasing the bushing support area often reduces the amount of wobble and misalignment that a part can produce when spinning at high speed.

Lightweight clutch drums, hubs, and planetary gear set parts are also available for some transmissions. Some clutch drums are rather heavy. The high-reverse clutch of a three-speed Simpson gear train spins about 2-1/2 times faster than the engine in first gear. During a hard acceleration, it takes a significant amount of power to bring this heavy drum up to speed. Bringing the drum to a stop in second gear puts a heavy load on the band. Lightweight components reduce the inertial load, allowing these parts to change speed easier. These lightweight units are made from high-strength aluminum or steel alloys and are rather expensive. They offer the optimum performance in racing situations that demand rapid acceleration. Some lightweight gear set components are drilled with rather large holes to further reduce weight.

20.7 MANUAL SHIFT VALVE BODIES

Manual shift valve bodies eliminate automatic upshifts and downshifts. The shifter has a gear position for each gear, and the driver manually selects the gear range. Most manual shift valve bodies are designed for drag racing and use a reverse shift pattern. The gear positions will be in the order: park, reverse, neutral, first, second, and third. Manual shift valve bodies are also designed for pulling (tractor or truck), off-road, and rally racing vehicles.

Most manual shift valve bodies look like stock valve bodies on the outside. The internal fluid passages and valves have been significantly changed. They are designed so the shifts occur instantly with no lag.

Some drag-racing valve bodies have an internal transmission brake. These units use an electric solenoid that opens passages to shift the transmission into both first and reverse at the same time. ● **SEE FIGURE 20–26**. When the solenoid is deactivated by a driver-controlled switch, the transmission

FIGURE 20–26 A THM 350 valve body with a solenoid valve and tubing added for a transmission brake. (*Courtesy of A-1 Automatic Transmissions*)

| 8"
"Competition-XS81" | 10"
"Super Launcher" | 11"
"Launcher" | 12"
"Plus Torque/MPG" | 13"
"Plus Torque/MPG" |

FIGURE 20–27 These five converters are built especially for five different purposes. Note the different diameters that help determine the stall speeds. (*Courtesy of A-1 Automatic Transmissions*)

is instantly in first gear only, and the vehicle is free to accelerate. The purpose of this is to produce a rapid response so the vehicle will "launch" instantly, much like a vehicle using a clutch and standard transmission. If used excessively with the converter at full stall, a transmission brake will significantly shorten the life of the converter.

20.8 HIGH-STALL CONVERTERS

Remember that stall speed is the maximum speed that an engine can run against a stalled, stationary transmission input shaft and torque converter turbine. Stall speed is determined by the engine's strength and tightness or looseness of the converter. A high-stall converter is one that allows the engine to reach a higher-than-normal stall speed. When the engine is accelerated against a stationary transmission input shaft, the RPM will flash up to a certain RPM, and this speed will usually drop slightly to the actual stall speed. As described in Chapter 9, the stall speed is primarily controlled by the following factors.

- **Converter diameter.** The smaller the converter, the higher the stall speed. There is about 30% difference in speed per inch in torque converter diameter.

- **Impeller vane angle.** Negative vane angle produces a higher stall speed.

- **Stator vane angle.** The greater the angle, the higher the stall speed and the greater the torque multiplication ratio.

- **Impeller-to-turbine vane clearance.** The greater the clearance, the higher the stall speed and the lower the converter efficiency.

High-stall converters are commonly used in drag racing and truck- or tractor-pulling vehicles. On these vehicles, it is important that the engine be allowed to quickly reach the best RPM for producing maximum power. For example, a typical 305 (5-L) engine that is built for racing produces about 90 horsepower (hp) at 2000 RPM and about 350 hp at 4500 RPM. Acceleration from a dead stop with a stock (about 2000 RPM stall speed) converter begins with an engine turning 2000 RPM and producing 90 hp. A higher-stall-speed converter allows the engine speed at stall to be higher, and the vehicle's acceleration begins with an engine that is producing more power. At coupling speeds, there is very little difference in the performances between the two converters.

Efficiency and torque multiplication ratios are also very important torque converter considerations, as these two factors help determine the amount of power leaving the converter. ● **SEE FIGURE 20–27.**

Most high-performance torque converter manufacturers market a variety of converters. They range from loose, very-high-stall competition converters at one extreme and tight, high-torque, improved-gas-mileage units at the other. ● **SEE FIGURE 20–28.** Tight converters are popular with RVs and trailer-towing vehicles as well as vehicles where low-end pulling power and fuel mileage are important. These

(a)

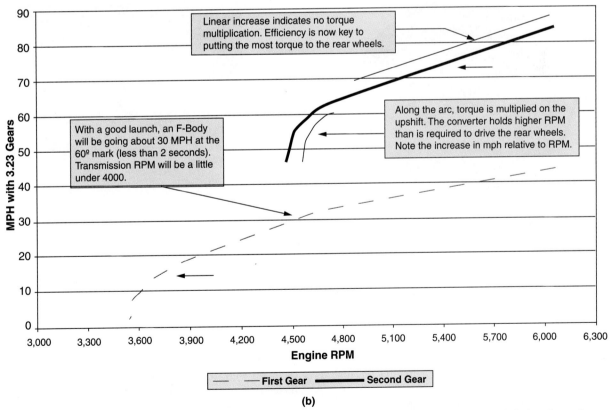

(b)

FIGURE 20–28 Graph (a) shows the stall torque ratios of two special-purpose torque converters. The full-throttle performance of one of them is shown in graph (b). (*Courtesy of Yank Converters*)

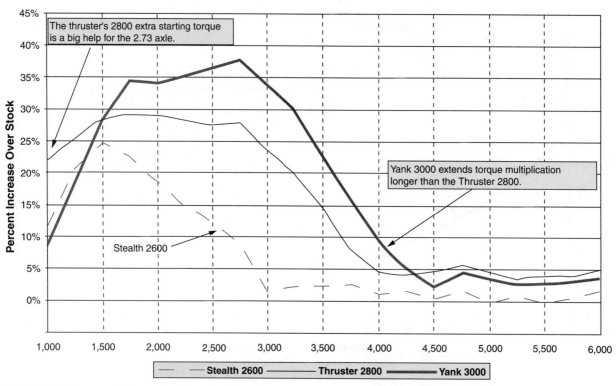

FIGURE 20–29 This graph shows the torque increase over a stock torque converter that is available from special-purpose converters. (*Courtesy of Yank Converters*)

(a)   (b)

FIGURE 20–30 These competition converters have additional reinforced mounting points. (*Courtesy of A-1 Automatic Transmissions*)

converters have a lower-than-stock stall speed and often have a greater torque multiplication ratio. If purchasing a special converter, it is recommended to provide the converter manufacturer with the engine torque curve, vehicle weight, final drive gear ratio, tire size, vehicle center of gravity, and the elevation and climate where the vehicle will operate. This information allows the supplier to deliver a unit that will match any special needs.

Heavy-duty torque converters are built to be stronger with reduced internal drag. Some of the internal modifications

are brazed fins, a steel turbine hub, a high-strength cover, heavy-duty clutch lining, and improved thrust bearings. ● **SEE FIGURE 20–29.**

All-out competition converters are usually precision re-manufactured stock converters. They may have the fins welded or brazed in place for improved strength, stock thrust washers replaced with Torrington bearings, steel turbine splines, and heavy-duty stator clutches installed for improved durability. In some cases the drive lugs are reinforced for added strength. ● **SEE FIGURE 20–30.**

FIGURE 20–31 This coupler attaches directly to the flexplate and is used to drive the transmission pump and input shaft. (*Courtesy of A-1 Automatic Transmissions*)

20.8.1 DIRECT COUPLERS Automatic transmissions are used without torque converters for some applications. Direct couplers are used in boats and in some circle-track racing cars. The transmission input shaft and hydraulic pump are driven by a shaft connected directly to the crankshaft or flywheel. ● **SEE FIGURE 20–31.** This allows the length, weight of the transmission, and the rotating mass to be reduced significantly. The transmission becomes essentially an in-and-out box with two or three forward-gear ratios plus reverse.

20.9 CONCLUSION

It has been the intent of the author to introduce you to the aspects, possibilities, and some of the excitement of automatic transmission tuning. It is impossible to cover every aspect needed to fully develop a transmission for all of the various vehicles (racing and production) in a book of this type. More than a few knowledgeable manufacturers of specialized transmission components can provide information concerning transmission modifications for those who want to carry this further.

Some transmission tuning, such as shift kit installation and torque converter swapping, is done in the average transmission shop to cure minor transmission problems and improve customer satisfaction. The more specialized work involved in producing a custom racing transmission is done by specialists. It is considered too time-consuming and raises problems of warranty for the average shop if something goes wrong. This type of work is usually left to the highly specialized shop, race car builder, or highly knowledgeable hobbyist.

Performance-oriented automotive magazines occasionally have articles describing automatic transmission performance modifications. Past issues of these magazines can be found in many libraries. Ask the librarian for help in locating such articles. The Internet will also produce useful information on this subject as well as general transmission repairs.

SUMMARY

1. An automatic transmission may be modified for many reasons, such as to improve shift feel, increase road performance, or for all-out racing.

2. The most common transmission modification is installing a shift kit. The kit may by installed by the vehicle owner or a transmission repair shop to improve shift timing and/or quality.

3. More extensive modifications include changing the gear train, increasing the clutch plates, and replacing the valve body.

4. The torque converter can be replaced with a higher-stall unit that will better match the torque output of the engine.

5. Technical articles should be reviewed before making any modifications to ensure the desired results.

Automotive technicians have the opportunity to voluntarily take the National Institute for Automotive Service Excellence (ASE) certification tests to become ASE-certified automotive technicians. Certification verifies technicians' technical knowledge to themselves, to their employers, and to their customers.

ASE certification requires that you pass one or more certification tests and have at least 2 years of automotive repair work experience. School training can be used to substitute for part of the work experience requirement, and you may take the certification test(s) before completing the work or school requirement. After taking the certification tests, you will receive the score report, and then when the experience requirement is completed, you will receive the ASE certification.

There are nine automotive service tests, and one is the Automatic Transmission/Transaxle (A2). The A2 test has 50 questions that are taken from the following content areas.

SPECIFICATIONS FOR AUTOMATIC TRANSMISSION/ TRANSAXLE (A2) TEST

CONTENT AREA	QUESTIONS
A. General Transmission/Transaxle Diagnosis	25
1. Mechanical/Hydraulic Systems (11)	
2. Electronic Systems (14)	
B. In-Vehicle Transmission/Transaxle Maintenance and Repair	12
C. Off-Vehicle Transmission/Transaxle Repair	13
1. Removal and Installation (4)	
2. Disassembly and Assembly (5)	
3. Friction and Reaction Units (4)	

If you intend to take the A2 test and feel a need to study for it, each of the content areas is divided into groups of tasks. These are the jobs that a drivetrain technician should be able to perform. A copy of *The Official ASE Preparation Guide to ASE Automobile Technician Tests* is available from ASE. This guide includes the current task list and sample test questions with an explanation of how the proper response should be selected.

Further help in test-taking skills can be obtained from these sources/websites:

ASE telephone: 1-877-ASE-TECH

ASE website: www.ase.com

ASE Test Preparation: www.asetestprep.com

Prentice Hall ASE Test Preparation Series: http://autotech .prenhall.com or call 1-800-526-0485

AUTOMATIC TRANSMISSION/ TRANSAXLE TEST TASK LIST

A. **General Transmission/Transaxle Diagnosis**
1. **Mechanical/Hydraulic Systems**
   - Road test the vehicle to verify mechanical/hydraulic system problems based on driver's concern; determine necessary action.
   - Diagnose noise, vibration, harshness, and shift quality problems; determine necessary action.
   - Diagnose fluid usage, type, level, and condition problems; determine necessary action.
   - Perform pressure tests; determine necessary action.
   - Perform stall tests; determine necessary action.
   - Perform torque converter clutch (lock-up converter) mechanical/hydraulic system tests; determine necessary action.
2. **Electronic Systems**
   - Road test the vehicle to verify electronic system problems based on driver's concern; determine necessary action.
   - Perform pressure tests on transmissions equipped with electronic pressure control; determine necessary action.
   - Perform torque converter clutch (lock-up) electronic system tests; determine necessary action.
   - Diagnose electronic transmission control systems using appropriate test equipment and service information (shop manuals, technical service bulletins, schematics, etc.); determine necessary action.
   - Verify proper operation of charging systems; check battery, connections, vehicle power, and grounds.

- Differentiate between engine performance, or other vehicle systems, and transmission/transaxle-related problems; determine necessary action.
- Diagnose shift quality concerns resulting from problems in the electronic transmission control system; determine necessary action.

(The content areas and task list are provided courtesy of the National Institute for Automotive Service Excellence.)

B. **In-Vehicle Transmission/Transaxle Maintenance and Adjustment**
    1. Inspect, adjust, and replace manual valve shift linkage, transmission range sensor/switch, and park/neutral position switch (inhibitor/neutral safety switch).
    2. Inspect, adjust, and replace cables or linkages for throttle valve (TV), kickdown, and accelerator pedal.
    3. Inspect and replace external seals and gaskets.
    4. Inspect and replace driveshaft yoke, drive axle joints, bushings, and seals.
    5. Check condition of engine cooling system; inspect transmission lines, and fittings.
    6. Inspect valve body mating surfaces, bores, valves, springs, sleeves, retainers, brackets, check balls, screens, spacers, and gaskets; replace as necessary.
    7. Check and adjust valve body bolt torque.
    8. Inspect accumulator and servo bores, piston, seals, pins/pin bores, spring, and retainers; repair or replace as necessary; adjust bands.
    9. Inspect, test, adjust, repair, or replace electrical/electronic components and circuits including computers, solenoids, sensors, relays, fuses, terminals, connectors, switches, and harnesses.
    10. Inspect, replace, and align powertrain mounts.
    11. Replace fluid and filter(s); verify proper fluid level and type.

C. **Off-Vehicle Transmission/Transaxle Repair**
    1. **Removal Installation**
        - Remove and replace transmission/transaxle; inspect engine core plugs, rear crankshaft seal, transmission dowel pins, dowel pin holes, and mating surfaces.
        - Inspect converter flex (drive) plate, converter attaching bolts, converter pilot, converter pump drive surfaces, converter end play, and crankshaft pilot bore.
        - Inspect, test, flush, or replace transmission oil cooler.
    2. **Disassembly and Assembly**
        - Disassemble, clean, and inspect transmission case, subassemblies, mating surfaces, and thread condition.
        - Inspect, measure, and replace oil pump components.
        - Check bearing preload; determine needed service.
        - Check end play, inspect, measure, and replace thrust washers and bearings as needed.
        - Inspect and replace shafts.
        - Inspect oil delivery circuit, including seal rings, ring grooves, sealing surface areas, feed pipes, orifices, and encapsulated check valves (balls).
        - Inspect and replace bushings.
        - Inspect and measure planetary gear assembly; replace parts as necessary.
        - Inspect case bores, passages, bushings, vents, mating surfaces, thread condition, and dowel pins; repair or replace as necessary.
        - Inspect and replace transaxle drive chains, sprockets, gears, bearings, and bushings.
        - Inspect, measure, repair, adjust, or replace transaxle final drive components.
        - Assemble after repair.
    3. **Friction and Reaction Units**
        - Inspect hydraulic clutch assembly; replace parts as necessary.
        - Measure and adjust clutch pack clearance.
        - Air test the operation of clutch and servo assemblies.
        - Inspect one-way clutch assemblies; replace parts as necessary.
        - Inspect bands and drums (housings and cylinders); replace and/or adjust as necessary.

(The content areas and task list are provided courtesy of the National Institute for Automotive Service Excellence.)

There are many different automatic transmission models used in modern vehicles. Small booklets/guides are available to help identify them. These guides list the transmissions by vehicle make. The guides shown are available from:

Axiom: www.axiom.com, www.transtar1.com

Transtec: www.transtec.com

Toledo Trans-Kit: www.parker.com

Whatever It Takes: www.wittrans.com

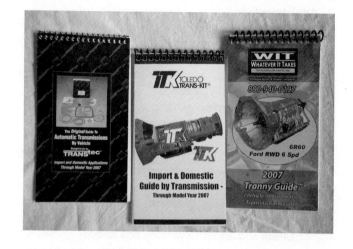

Following is a listing of the transmission diagnostic trouble codes (DTCs) as defined by the SAE. These universal codes can be used to locate the cause of a malfunctioning electronic-controlled transmission. A transmission DTC will appear as **P07XX** or **P08XX.** The *P* indicates powertrain. The 0 indicates a generic code; a 1 would indicate a manufacturer-specific code. The 7 or 8 indicates a transmission, and the last two digits indicate the problem area. Remember that other areas such as engine controls can affect transmission operation.

P0700	Transmission Control System Malfunction
P0701	Transmission Control System Range/Performance
P0702	Transmission Control System Electrical
P0703	Brake (Torque Converter) Switch Circuit Malfunction
P0704	Clutch Switch Input Circuit Problem
P0705	Transmission Range Sensor Circuit Malfunction (PRNDL Input)
P0706	Transmission Range Sensor Circuit Range or Performance
P0707	Transmission Range Sensor Circuit Low Input
P0708	Transmission Range Sensor Circuit High Input
P0709	Transmission Range Sensor Circuit Intermittent
P0710	Transmission Fluid Temperature Sensor Circuit Malfunction
P0711	Transmission Fluid Temperature Sensor Circuit Range or Performance
P0712	Transmission Fluid Temperature Sensor Circuit Low Input
P0713	Transmission Fluid Temperature Sensor Circuit High Input
P0714	Transmission Fluid Temperature Sensor Circuit Intermittent
P0715	Input or Turbine Speed Sensor Circuit Malfunction
P0716	Input or Turbine Speed Sensor Circuit Range or Performance
P0717	Input or Turbine Speed Sensor Circuit No Signal
P0718	Input or Turbine Speed Sensor Circuit Intermittent
P0719	Torque Converter or Brake Switch B Circuit Low
P0720	Output Speed Sensor Circuit Malfunction
P0721	Output Speed Sensor Circuit Range or Performance
P0722	Output Speed Sensor Circuit No Signal
P0723	Output Speed Sensor Circuit Intermittent
P0724	Torque Converter or Brake Switch B Circuit High
P0725	Engine Speed Input Circuit Malfunction

P0726	Engine Speed Input Circuit Range or Performance
P0727	Engine Speed Input Circuit No Signal
P0728	Engine Speed Input Circuit Intermittent
P0730	Incorrect Gear Ratio
P0731	Gear 1 Incorrect Ratio
P0732	Gear 2 Incorrect Ratio
P0733	Gear 3 Incorrect Ratio
P0734	Gear 4 Incorrect Ratio
P0735	Gear 5 Incorrect Ratio
P0736	Reverse Incorrect Ratio
P0740	Torque Converter Clutch System Malfunction
P0741	Torque Converter Clutch System Performance or Stuck Off
P0742	Torque Converter Clutch System Performance or Stuck On
P0743	Torque Converter Clutch System Electrical
P0744	Torque Converter Clutch System Intermittent
P0745	Pressure Control Solenoid Malfunction
P0746	Pressure Control Solenoid Performance or Stuck Off
P0747	Pressure Control Solenoid Stuck On
P0748	Pressure Control Solenoid Electrical
P0749	Pressure Control Solenoid Intermittent
P0750	Shift Solenoid A Malfunction
P0751	Shift Solenoid A Performance or Stuck Off
P0752	Shift Solenoid A Stuck On
P0753	Shift Solenoid A Electrical
P0755	Shift Solenoid B Malfunction
P0756	Shift Solenoid B Performance or Stuck Off
P0757	Shift Solenoid B Stuck On
P0758	Shift Solenoid B Electrical
P0759	Shift Solenoid B Intermittent
P0760	Shift Solenoid C Malfunction

P0761	Shift Solenoid C Performance or Stuck Off
P0762	Shift Solenoid C Stuck On
P0763	Shift Solenoid C Electrical
P0764	Shift Solenoid C Intermittent
P0765	Shift Solenoid D Malfunction
P0766	Shift Solenoid D Performance or Stuck Off
P0767	Shift Solenoid D Stuck On
P0768	Shift Solenoid D Electrical
P0769	Shift Solenoid D Intermittent
P0770	Shift Solenoid E Malfunction
P0771	Shift Solenoid E Performance or Stuck Off
P0772	Shift Solenoid E Stuck On
P0773	Shift Solenoid E Electrical
P0774	Shift Solenoid E Intermittent
P0780	Shift Malfunction

P0781	1–2 Shift Malfunction
P0782	2–3 Shift Malfunction
P0783	3–4 Shift Malfunction
P0784	4–5 Shift Malfunction
P0785	Shift/Timing Solenoid Malfunction
P0786	Shift/Timing Solenoid Range or Performance
P0787	Shift/Timing Solenoid Low
P0788	Shift/Timing Solenoid High
P0789	Shift/Timing Solenoid Intermittent
P0790	Normal/Performance Switch Circuit Malfunction
P0801	Reverse Inhibit Control Circuit Malfunction
P0803	1–4 Upshift (Skip Shift) Solenoid Control Circuit Malfunction
P0804	1–4 Upshift (Skip Shift) Lamp Control Circuit Malfunction

Automotive terms have been standardized by the Society of Automotive Engineers (SAE) directive J1930. The following is a list of J1930 terms and acronyms related to automatic transmissions.

TERM	ACRONYM
Automatic transaxle/transmission	A/T
Battery positive voltage	B+
Crankshaft position sensor	CKP sensor
Data link connector	DLC
Diagnostic test mode	DTM
Diagnostic trouble code	DTC
Electrically erasable programmable read-only memory	EEPROM
Engine coolant temperature	ECT
Engine coolant temperature sensor	ECT sensor
Engine speed sensor	RPM
Erasable programmable read-only memory	EPROM
Flash electrically erasable programmable read-only memory	FEEPROM
Flash erasable programmable read-only memory	FEPROM
Fourth gear	4GR
Keep alive random access memory	Keep alive RAM
Malfunction indicator lamp	MIL
Mass airflow sensor	MAF sensor
Park/neutral position switch	PNP switch
Powertrain control module	PCM
Programmable read-only memory	PROM
Random access memory	RAM
Read-only memory	ROM
Scan tool	ST
Service reminder indicator	SRI
Third gear	3GR
Throttle position sensor	TPS or TP sensor
Torque converter clutch	TCC
Torque converter clutch relay	TCC relay
Torque converter clutch solenoid	TCC solenoid
Transmission control module	TCM
Transmission range	TR
Transmission range sensor	TR sensor

TERM	ACRONYM
Transmission range switch	TR switch
Vehicle speed sensor	VSS
Wide-open throttle	WOT
Wide-open throttle switch	WOT switch

Following are other acronyms, not standardized by J1930, that are commonly used.

ACRONYM	TERM
ISS	Input speed sensor
OSS	Output speed sensor
PRNDL	Park/reverse/neutral/drive/low
PWM	Pulse-width modulated
TCIL	Transmission control indicator lamp
TCS	Transmission control switch
TFT	Transmission fluid temperature
TOT	Transmission oil temperature
TRD	Transmission range drive
TRL	Transmission range low
TROD	Transmission range overdrive
TRR	Transmission range reverse
TSS	Transmission speed sensor

ENGLISH-METRIC-ENGLISH CONVERSION TABLE

MULTIPLY	BY	TO GET/MULTIPLY	BY	TO GET
LENGTH				
inch (")	25.4	millimeter (mm)	0.3939	inch
mile	1.609	kilometer	0.621	mile
AREA				
inch²	645.2	millimeter²	0.0015	inch²
PRESSURE				
PSI	6.895	kilopascals (kPa)	0.145	PSI
PSI	0.06895	bar	14.5	PSI
PSI	0.006895	megapascal (kPa)	14.5	PSI
VOLUME				
inch³	16,387	millimeter³	0.00006	inch³
inch³	6.45	centimeter³	0.061	inch³
inch³	0.016	liter	61.024	inch³
pint	0.473	liter	0.528	pint
quart	0.946	liter	1.057	quart
gallon	3.785	liter	0.264	gallon
WEIGHT				
ounce	28.35	gram (g)	0.035	ounce
pound	0.453	kilogram (kg)	2.205	pound
TORQUE				
inch-pound	0.113	Newton-meter (N-m)	8.851	inch-pound
foot-pound	1.356	Newton-meter	0.738	foot-pound
VELOCITY				
miles/hour	1.609	kilometer/hour	0.6214	miles/hour

TEMPERATURE

(degree Fahrenheit − 32) × 0.556 = degree Celsius

(degree Celsius × 1.8) + 32 = degree Fahrenheit

Training standards have been developed by the National Automotive Technicians Education Foundation (NATEF) for automatic transmission repair. *Automatic Transmissions/Transaxles* includes information for each of the NATEF tasks. The following identifies each of the NATEF tasks, their priority, and where the related information can be found in the text and worktext/NATEF Correlated Task Sheets. A check list for task completion can be found in the NATEF Correlated Task Sheets Appendix 2.

NATEF TASKS: AREA II. AUTOMATIC TRANSMISSION AND TRANSAXLE

The tasks are given a completion priority: 95% of Priority 1 (P-1) tasks must be completed, 80% of P-2 tasks must be completed, and 50% of P-3 tasks must be completed.

II. AUTOMATIC TRANSMISSION AND TRANSAXLE		SECTION
A. GENERAL TRANSMISSION AND TRANSAXLE DIAGNOSIS		
1. Complete work order to include customer information, vehicle identifying information, customer concern, related service history, cause, and correction.	P-1	12.1–12.3
2. Identify and interpret transmission/transaxle concern; differentiate between engine performance and transmission/transaxle concerns; determine necessary action.	P-1	12.1, 12.4
3. Research applicable vehicle and service information, such as transmission/transaxle system operation, fluid type, vehicle service history, service precautions, and technical service bulletins.	P-1	6.12, 16.1
4. Locate and interpret vehicle and major component identification numbers.	P-1	10.1, 10.9
5. Diagnose fluid loss and condition concerns; check fluid level in transmissions with and without dipstick; determine necessary action.	P-1	11.2
6. Perform pressure tests (including transmissions/transaxles equipped with electronic pressure control); determine necessary action.	P-1	12.7
7. Perform stall test; determine necessary action.	P-3	12.9
8. Perform lock-up converter system tests; determine necessary action.	P-3	7.3
9. Diagnose noise and vibration concerns; determine necessary action.	P-2	12.8
10. Diagnose transmission/transaxle gear reduction/multiplication concerns using driving, driven, and held member (power flow) principles.	P-1	12.13
11. Diagnose pressure concerns in a transmission using hydraulic principles (Pascal's law).	P-2	6.2, 12.7
12. Diagnose electronic transmission/transaxle control systems using appropriate test equipment and service information.	P-1	9.1–9.6
B. IN-VEHICLE TRANSMISSION/TRANSAXLE MAINTENANCE AND REPAIR		
1. Inspect, adjust, and replace manual valve shift linkage, transmission range sensor/switch, and park/neutral position switch.	P-2	11.4, 11.5
2. Inspect and replace external seals, gaskets, and bushings.	P-2	14.3, 14.4, 18.2

3.	Inspect, test, adjust, repair, or replace electrical/electronic components and circuits, including computers, solenoids, sensors, relays, terminals, connectors, switches, and harnesses.	P-1	13.5–13.6
4.	Diagnose electronic transmission control systems using a scan tool; determine necessary action.	P-1	14.11
5.	Inspect, replace, and align powertrain mounts.	P-2	14.12, 15.5, 15.6
6.	Service transmission; perform visual inspection; replace fluid and filters.	P-1	11.2, 11.3, 12.4

II. AUTOMATIC TRANSMISSION AND TRANSAXLE

C. OFF-VEHICLE TRANSMISSION AND TRANSAXLE REPAIR

1.	Remove and reinstall transmission/transaxle and torque converter; inspect engine core plugs, rear crankshaft seal, dowel pins, dowel pin holes, and mating surfaces.	P-1	15.2, 15.5
2.	Disassemble, clean, and inspect transmission/transaxle.	P-1	16.2–16.5, 17.2–17.5, 18.6
3.	Inspect, measure, clean, and replace valve body (includes surfaces, bores, springs, valves, sleeves, retainers, brackets, check valves/balls, screens, spacers, and gaskets).	P-2	14.9, 18.6
4.	Inspect servo and accumulator bores, pistons, seals, pins, springs, and retainers; determine necessary action.	P2	14.10, 17.4
5.	Assemble transmission/transaxle.	P-1	16.6, 18.3, 18.4
6.	Inspect, leak test, and flush or replace transmission/transaxle oil cooler, lines, and fittings.	P-1	14.8, 19.3
7.	Inspect converter flex (drive) plate, converter attaching bolts, converter pilot, converter pump drive surfaces, converter end play, and crankshaft pilot bore.	P-2	19.2
8.	Install and seat torque converter to engage drive/splines.	P-1	16.6.2
9.	Inspect, measure, and reseal oil pump assembly and components.	P-1	16.6.1, 18.3
10.	Measure transmission/transaxle end play or preload; determine necessary action.	P-1	16.3.1, 16.6.1
11.	Inspect, measure, and replace thrust washers and bearings.	P-2	17.2
12.	Inspect oil delivery circuits, including seal rings, ring grooves, and sealing surface areas, feed pipes, orifices, and check valves/balls.	P-2	17.4
13.	Inspect bushings; determine necessary action.	P-2	17.2
14.	Inspect and measure planetary gear assembly components; determine necessary action.	P-2	18.5
15.	Inspect case bores, passages, bushings, vents, and mating surfaces; determine necessary action.	P-2	18.2
16.	Inspect transaxle drive, link chains, sprockets, gears, bearings, and bushings; perform necessary action.	P-2	16.4.1
17.	Inspect, measure, repair, adjust, or replace transaxle final drive components.	P-2	18.8
18.	Inspect clutch drum, piston, check balls, springs, retainers, seals, and friction and pressure plates; determine necessary action.	P-2	17.3–17.4
19.	Measure clutch pack clearance; determine necessary action.	P-1	18.4
20.	Air test operation of clutch and servo assemblies.	P-1	12.11
21.	Inspect roller and sprag clutch, races, rollers, sprags, springs, cages, and retainers; determine necessary action.	P-1	16.6
22.	Inspect bands and drums; determine necessary action.	P-2	16.6, 17.3.3
23.	Describe the operational characteristics of a continuously variable transmission (CVT).	P-3	3.13
24.	Describe the operational characteristics of a hybrid vehicle drivetrain.	P-3	3.14

CHAPTER 4

PROBLEM SOLVING 4–1

Case 1: The problem is in the clutch or band that is applied during the 1–2 shift. It is either severely worn or there is low fluid pressure.

Case 2: Check the clutch and band application chart to see what is applied during reverse.

PROBLEM SOLVING 4–2

Case 1: The band is not releasing fast enough, and this could be caused by a sticking servo.

Case 2: The one-way clutch used in drive-1 is slipping.

CHAPTER 5

PROBLEM SOLVING 5–1

Case 1: Yes, the intermediate band.

Case 2: The intermediate clutch and/or the intermediate one-way clutch is bad.

PROBLEM SOLVING 5–2

Case 1: Yes, the intermediate band.

Case 2: The one-way clutch used in drive-1 is slipping.

PROBLEM SOLVING 5–3

Case 1: Yes, the intermediate clutch and/or the intermediate one-way clutch could be slipping.

Case 2: Wear or tooth damage in the planetary gear set—not a driving or reaction member.

PROBLEM SOLVING 5–4

Case 1: Yes, the 2–4 clutch.

Case 2: The 2–4 clutch is not applying.

PROBLEM SOLVING 5–5

The second driving and/or driven gears are damaged and will probably need to be replaced.

CHAPTER 6

PROBLEM SOLVING 6–1

Case 1: This could be a low fluid level, so this is the first check.

Case 2: This could be caused by quite a few things; start by checking the fluid level.

PROBLEM SOLVING 6–2

Case 1: No, not a worn band. Yes, it could be a stuck shift valve. No, a worn third-gear clutch would show as neutral.

Case 2: There is excess fluid pressure; check the throttle valve or throttle position sensor.

PROBLEM SOLVING 6–3

Case 1: Probably not; check the throttle valve or throttle position sensor.

Case 2: This could be a bad throttle valve adjustment.

CHAPTER 7

PROBLEM SOLVING 7–1

Case 1: This could be low fluid pressure; start with a check of the throttle linkage and fluid pressure.

Case 2: Ensure that the transmission fluid cooler and fluid lines are not plugged.

PROBLEM SOLVING 7–2

Case 1: The apply device for second gear is slipping; it could be caused by low fluid pressure or low throttle pressure.

Case 2: The throttle valve could be out of adjustment; check the TV adjustment and the fluid pressure.

PROBLEM SOLVING 7–3

Case 1: This could be a sticking governor valve.

Case 2: If the second gear apply device does not apply, this could be a stuck shift valve (check to see if the valves are series or parallel fed) or a faulty apply device. Check the fluid pressure.

PROBLEM SOLVING 7–4

Case 1: The 1–2 shift valve is stuck in an upshift position.

Case 2: Yes; look at the hydraulic diagram.

CHAPTER 8
PROBLEM SOLVING 8–1

Case 1: There is a short circuit in the backup lights. Measure the current flow at the fuse.

Case 2: Yes, measure the voltage at the TCC solenoid.

PROBLEM SOLVING 8–2

Case 1: Yes, it could be one of the three; check for DTCs.

Case 2: The VSS signal is interrupted; check for DTCs.

CHAPTER 9
PROBLEM SOLVING 9–1

Case 1: Yes, it could be one of the three; touch the brake pedal to release the TCC, and note if the reapply has the same shudder.

Case 2: This could be the wrong converter; check the converter number and its application.

ENGLISH GLOSSARY

Accelerate   To increase speed.

Accumulator   A device used to dampen fluid apply pressure so as to cushion or soften a shift.

Additives   Chemicals added to automatic transmission fluid (ATF) to improve the operating characteristics.

Aerated fluid   Fluid of a foamy nature that has been whipped to the point that it contains air bubbles.

Aftermarket   Referring to repair parts produced by companies other than OEM.

Alignment dowels   Metal pins that are located on the back of the engine block to ensure proper alignment of the transmission.

Alignment marks   Marks that are placed on parts as they are removed so they can be replaced in the same position; also called *index marks* or *match marks*.

Annulus gear   Ring gear, internal gear.

Apply device   Hydraulically operated clutches and bands and mechanical one-way clutches that drive or hold planetary gear set members.

Atmospheric pressure   Pressure of the atmosphere around us; generally considered to be 14.7 PSI at sea level.

Automatic transmission   A transmission that changes forward-gear ratios automatically.

Automatic transmission fluid (ATF)   The oil used in automatic transmissions.

Balanced valve   A valve that is in a balanced position between two opposing forces.

Ballooning   The undesirable expansion of a component, such as a torque converter, because of excessive internal pressure.

Band   A lined metal strap that wraps around a drum; used to stop or hold the drum stationary.

Bearing   Nonfriction bearings that use balls or rollers as rolling elements to reduce friction.

Belleville spring   A conical steel ring that gives a spring action because of its resistance to forces that try to flatten it.

Bevel gear   A gear with teeth that are cut at an angle so it can transmit power between shafts that are not parallel.

Bump   A harsh shift condition produced by a sudden and forceful application of a clutch or band.

Bushing   A simple soft metal bearing surface that must use lubricants to reduce friction.

Case   The rigid housing for a transmission.

Centrifugal force   The force on a revolving object that tries to push it away from the center of revolution.

Chuggle   A bucking or jerking condition usually most noticeable during acceleration and when the torque converter clutch is engaged. Chuggle is often engine related.

Clutch   A device that controls the power transfer between two points. It can allow or stop the transfer.

Clutch clearance   The amount of air gap at the clutch plates, available also as piston travel, when a clutch is released.

Clutch-to-clutch   A transmission that shifts by releasing one clutch as it applies another clutch to change the power flow.

Coastdown   A complete release of the throttle so the moving vehicle slows down; sometimes called *zero-throttle coastdown.*

Coefficient of friction   A reference to the amount of friction between two surfaces.

Continuously variable transmission (CVT)   A transmission that uses two variable-width pulleys and a belt to change ratios from the lowest to the highest in a continuous, stepless manner instead of a group of fixed ratios.

Coupling phase   A condition where the torque converter turbine speed is almost equal to that of the impeller.

Damper   A device that reduces torsional vibrations between the engine and transmissions.

Decelerate   Reduce speed.

Delayed   When a shift occurs later than expected; also called *late* or *extended.*

Detent   A spring-loaded device used to position the manual valve correctly.

Detent (throttle position)   A movement of the throttle to the maximum. *See* Wide-open throttle.

Differential   A gear arrangement that allows the drive wheels to be driven at different speeds.

Direct drive   A 1:1 gear ratio.

Double bump   Two sudden and forceful clutch or band applications.

Driver shift request   An electronic signal indicating that the driver has moved the shift control to change gears.

DTC   Abbreviation for *diagnostic trouble code*

Dual clutch transmission   A transmission that uses one clutch to drive the even-numbered gears and a second clutch to drive the odd-numbered gears. It can deliver power in a continuous manner with no lag between gear changes.

Dynamic friction   The relative amount of friction between two surfaces that are at different speeds. *See* Static friction.

Early   When a shift occurs before the correct speed is reached and causes a lugging or laboring of the engine.

End bump   A condition that produces a firmer feel at the end of a shift. Also called *end feel* or *slip bump.*

End play   The amount of movement a gear set or shaft has in a direction that is parallel to the input shaft.

Energy   The ability to do work.

Engine braking   A condition where engine compression is used to slow the vehicle down.

Exhaust   The release of fluid pressure back to the sump.

Final drive   The last set of reduction gears before the power flows to the differential and drive axles.

Firm   A noticeable quick application of a clutch or band that is considered normal.

Flare   A condition that produces an increase in engine RPM with a loss of torque during a shift; also called *slipping.*

Flexplate   The thin drive plate that connects the torque converter to the crankshaft of the engine.

Fluid coupling   A device that transfers power through the fluid.

Flywheel The rotating metal mass attached to the crankshaft that helps even out power surges.

Flywheel turner A special tool that is used to rotate the flywheel as the converter is unbolted.

Force A push or pull measured in units of weights, usually pounds.

Force motor *See* Pressure control solenoid.

Friction The resistance to motion between two bodies in contact with each other.

Friction modifier An additive that changes the lubricity of a fluid.

Fulcrum The pivot/supporting point for a lever.

Garage shift A shift from neutral to drive or reverse.

Gear ratio The relationship between two gears determined by dividing the number of teeth on the driving gear by the number of teeth on the driven gear and expressed as a ratio to 1.

Gear reduction A condition in which the driving gear is smaller than the driven gear. This produces a torque increase.

Governor A hydraulic device that provides hydraulic pressure that is relative to road speed.

Harsh A noticeable and unpleasant application of a clutch or band; also called *rough*.

Heavy throttle An acceleration with the throttle opened more than three-fourths of the pedal travel.

Helical gear A gear that has the teeth cut at an angle.

Hertz A unit of measurement of frequency; abbreviated as Hz. One Hz is one cycle per second.

Hook ring A seal ring with the ends that hook together.

Hunting A series of repeating upshifts and downshifts that cause noticeable engine RPM changes; also called *busyness*.

Hydraulics The transfer of power through fluids under pressure.

Hydrodynamics The action of transferring power through fluids in motion.

Hydrostatic The action of transferring power through fluids under pressure.

Hypoid gear A special form of a bevel gear that has the teeth cut in a curvature and that positions the gear on nonintersecting planes; commonly used in rear-wheel-drive (RWD) final drives.

Idler gear A gear positioned between two other gears in the gear that is used to reverse the direction of rotation.

Impeller The input member of the torque converter; also called *converter pump*.

Inertia The physical property that a body at rest remains at rest and a body in motion remains in motion and travels in a straight line.

Initial feel A distinct feel that is firmer at the start of a shift than at the end.

Internal gear A gear with the teeth pointing inward toward the center of the gear; also called an *annulus* or *ring gear*.

Kickdown A downshift when the driver pushes the accelerator pedal all the way down.

Land The large-diameter portion of a spool valve.

Late: A shift that occurs above the desired speed that causes over-reving of the engine.

LePelletier gear train An automatic transmission gear train that combines a simple planetary with a Ravigneaux gear set to produce six or more gear ratios.

Light throttle An acceleration with the throttle opened less than half of the pedal travel.

Lockup torque converter *See* Torque converter clutch.

Malfunction indicator lamp (MIL) An instrument panel amber warning light that flashes to indicate a problem.

Manual valve The valve operated by the gear selector that directs pressure to the apply devices needed to put a transmission in gear.

Mechanical diode A one-way clutch that uses a set of spring-loaded struts for a lighter but stronger clutch action.

Medium throttle An acceleration with the throttle opened about half of the pedal travel.

Micron A unit of measurement equal to one millionth of a meter.

Minimum throttle The smallest throttle opening that can accelerate a vehicle and produce an upshift.

Modulator A vacuum device that senses engine load and causes a hydraulic valve to change pressure relative to that load.

MSDS Abbreviation for *material safety data sheets*.

Multiple-disc clutch A clutch that uses more than one friction disc.

Needle bearing A very thin roller bearing.

Nonsynchronous transmission A transmission using one-way clutches that allow an upshift that requires only the application of the next driving or reaction member.

NVH Abbreviation for *noise, vibration, and harshness*.

OEM Abbreviation for *original equipment manufacturer*; the company that produces the specific vehicle.

Oil cooler A radiator-like component that reduces the fluid temperature.

Oil filter The part that removes dirt and debris from oil that is circulated through it.

One-way clutch An overrunning clutch that locks in one direction and overruns or freewheels in the other.

Open/plain end ring A seal ring with the ends cut at a right angle.

Orifice A restricted opening in a fluid passage designed to reduce fluid pressure while fluid is flowing.

O-ring A sealing ring made from rubberlike material.

Overdrive A gear arrangement that causes the output shaft to turn faster than the input shaft.

Parking gear A transmission lock that prevents the output shaft from turning.

Passing gear A forced downshift to the next lower gear.

Pawl A locking device that fits into a gear tooth to hold the gear stationary.

Pinion gear A small gear that meshes with a larger gear.

Piston The moveable portion of a hydraulic cylinder or servo.

Planetary gear set A gear set that contains a sun gear, ring gear, and a carrier with planet pinion gear to produce one or more gear ratios.

Planet carrier The part of a planetary gear set that contains the planetary pinion gears.

Planet pinions The gears of a planetary gear set that mesh with both the sun and ring gears.

Power The rate at which work is done.

Pressure A force per unit area; generally measured in pounds per square inch (PSI) or units of atmospheric pressure (bars or kilopascals).

Pressure balanced release A clutch design that uses fluid pressure to help release the clutch.

Pressure control solenoid A computer-controlled solenoid that maintains the proper pressure in the hydraulic system of an electronically controlled automatic transmission. Also called a *variable force solenoid* or *force motor*.

Pressure regulator valve The valve that maintains the proper pressure in the hydraulic system.

Pulse-width modulation (PWM) Operation of a device by an on–off digital signal that is controlled by the time signal so that the device is turned on and off.

Pump A device that transfers fluid from one point to another.

Ratio The relative value between two things.

Reaction member The portion of the planetary gear set that is held stationary in order to produce a reduction or overdrive.

Ream A machining operation that makes a hole larger and more precise.

Rebuilt *See* Remanufactured.

Remanufactured A term used to describe a component that is disassembled, cleaned, inspected, and reassembled using new or reconditioned parts.

Remove and replace (R&R) A common repair operation where the old part is removed and replaced with a new or reconditioned part.

Reservoir A tank or pan where fluid is stored.

Resistance The opposition to current flow measured in ohms.

Retaining bracket A bracket that is used to hold a part(s) in place.

Ring gear The outer gear of a planetary gear set; also called an *internal gear*.

Roller clutch A one-way clutch that uses a series of rollers positioned in a special cam for the locking elements.

Rotary flow The fluid motion inside a torque converter in the same direction as the impeller and turbine.

RPM Speed expressed in *revolutions per minute*.

RTV Abbreviation for *room temperature vulcanization*.

Sag test A check to see how far a valve sags/droops, which is an indication of valve or bore wear.

Scan tool An electronic test device that can communicate with the vehicle's control module and determine operational data.

Scarf cut A seal ring with the ends cut at an angle.

Seal driver A tool designed to fit a seal so it can be driven into place without damage.

Servo A hydraulic device that changes fluid pressure into mechanical motion or force.

Shift feel A clutch or band application or release that is usually described, for example, as firm or soft.

Shim A thin metal spacer.

Shudder An easily noticed jerking sensation that is a more severe form of chuggle.

Slipping A loss in torque with a noticeable increase in engine RPM.

Soft A slow and almost unnoticeable clutch or band apply.

Solenoid An electromagnet actuator that uses a movable core.

Spline A groove(s) or slot(s) cut into a shaft or bore that is used to connect a matching spline.

Sprag The locking element in a one-way sprag clutch.

Spur gear A gear with straight-cut teeth.

Stall A condition where the engine is running but the transmission input shaft is not rotating.

Stall speed The maximum engine RPM that can be achieved with an automatic transmission in gear, with the brakes applied and the accelerator wide open.

Static friction The relative amount of friction between two stationary surfaces or two surfaces that are turning at the same speed. *See* Dynamic friction.

Stator A component in the torque converter that is used to change the direction of fluid motion.

Subassemblies The major transmission components.

Sump The fluid storage point or reservoir; usually the transmission pan.

Sun gear The gear in the center of a planetary gear set.

Surge A barely noticeable engine feel that is similar to chuggle.

Synchronous transmission During an upshift, the timing of the new driving or reaction member must be timed or synchronized with the release of a driving or reaction member.

Thrust washers Bearings that separate rotating parts that turn against each other.

Tie-up A condition where two opposing clutches or bands are attempting to apply at the wrong time. This tends to slow down the engine or vehicle. Also called *fight*.

Torque Turning or twisting effort; usually measured in foot-pounds or Newton-meters.

Torque converter A fluid coupling that transfers power from the engine to the transmission and can produce a torque increase.

Torque converter clutch The clutch inside the torque converter that locks the turbine to the impeller to prevent any slippage; also called a *lockup torque converter*.

Transaxle A transmission that is combined with the final drive assembly; normally used in front-wheel-drive (FWD) vehicles.

Transmission A device in the powertrain that provides different forward-gear ratios as well as neutral and reverse.

Turbine The output member of a torque converter.

Vacuum A negative pressure (below atmospheric); measured in inches of mercury (in. Hg).

Valley The area of a spool valve between the lands.

Valve A hydraulic device that controls fluid flow.

Variable force solenoid *See* Pressure control solenoid.

Viscosity The resistance to flow in a fluid.

Vortex flow A recirculating fluid flow in the converter that is outward in the impeller and inward in the turbine.

Warpage A fault that occurs when mating surfaces become less flat.

Wide-open throttle (WOT) Full travel of the pedal to produce maximum power from the engine and full travel of the throttle or detent valve in the transmission.

Work The result of force that changes speed or direction of motion.

SPANISH GLOSSARY

Acelere   el incremento O acelera

Acumulador   Un dispositivo solió humedecer fluido aplica presión a fin de cojín o suaviza un desplazamiento.

Aditivos   Los productos químicos agrandaron cambio automático elocuente (ATF) para mejorar las características en operación.

Aireado fluido   El fluido de una naturaleza espumosa que ha sido llevada a toda prisa al punto que contiene aire burbujea.

Aftermarket   En lo referente a piezas de repuesto producidas por compañías aparte de fabricante de equipo original.

Las clavijas de alineación   Los alfileres de metal que están ubicados en la parte trasera del bloque del motor para garantizar alineación correcta de la transmisión.

Las marcas de alineación   Las marcas que están puestas en partes tal como están cambiaron de dirección así es que pueden ser rplaced en lo mismo posiciona, también llamado índice y las marcas del fósforo.

Annulus engrane   El engranaje del anillo, engranaje de dientes interiores.

Aplique dispositivo   Hidráulicamente los embragues del motor accionados y las bandas y los mecánicos embragues del motor de una sola vía que conduce o sujeta a los integrantes planetarios del gearset.

Presión atmosférica   La presión de la atmósfera alrededor de nosotros; generalmente considerados para ser 14.7 libra por pulgada cuadrada a nivel del mar.

Cambio automático   Una transmisión que cambia proporciones del engranaje delantero automáticamente.

El fluido del cambio automático (ATF)   El aceite usado en cambios automáticos.

Simétrica válvula   Una válvula que está en una posición simétrica entre dos fuerzas opositoras.

Soplándose   La expansión indeseable de un componente, como un convertidor de torsión, por la presión interna excesiva.

La banda   Un forrado fleje de metal que se pliega alrededor de un tambor; usado para detenerse o sujetar el tambor estacionario.

Rumbo   Los rumbos de poco fricción que usan bolas o los rodillos como rodar elementos para reducir fricción.

Belleville brinque   Un anillo acerado cónico que da una acción primaveral por su resistencia para las fuerzas que intentan aplanarlo.

Engranaje cónico   Un engranaje dentado que está cortado en ángulo así es que puede transmitir poder entre ejes que no son paralelos.

El golpe   Una condición de desplazamiento ruda producida por una aplicación repentina y enérgica de un embrague del motor o una banda.

Buje   Una superficie suave simple de rumbo de metal que debe usar lubricantes para hacer más pequeña fricción.

Case   La vivienda rígida para una transmisión.

Fuerza centrífuga   La fuerza en un objeto giratorio que intenta apartarlo a la fuerza del centro de revolución.

Chuggle   Un salto de carnero o avanzar a brincos acondiciona usualmente más notable durante la aceleración y cuándo el embrague del motor del convertidor de torsión es engarzado. Chuggle es a menudo motor relacionado.

Embrague del motor   Un dispositivo que controla el traslado de poder entre dos puntos. Puede permitir o puede detener el traslado.

La liquidacion de mercaderías del embrague del motor   La cantidad de intervalo de aire en el embrague del motor chapa, disponible también el viaje del pistón, cuando un embrague del motor es soltado.

El embrague del motor al embrague del motor   Una transmisión que cambia de posición por liberatorio embrague del motor como aplica otro embrague del motor para cambiar el flujo de poder.

Coastdown   Una edición completa del obturador así es que el vehículo en movimiento baja la velocidad; *el coastdown del obturador* a veces *cero* llamado.

Coeficiente de fricción   Una referencia hasta un total de la fricción entre dos superficies.

La transmisión continuamente variable, CVT   Una transmisión que usa dos poleas de anchura variable y un cinturón para cambiar proporciones de lo más bajo para lo más alto en una manera continua, stepless en lugar de un grupo de proporciones fijas.

Asociando fase   Una condición donde la velocidad de la turbina del convertidor de torsión es casi igual para eso del impeller.

Más húmedo   Un dispositivo que reduce vibraciones de torsión entre el motor y transmisiones.

Desacelere   Reduzca velocidad.

Retardado   Cuando un desplazamiento ocurre más tarde que esperado. También llamado *retrasado* o *extendido*.

Detent   Un dispositivo cargado por resorte solió posicionar la válvula manual correctamente.

Detent (la posición del obturador)   Un movimiento del obturador para el máximo. *Vea* obturador Totalmente Abierto.

El diferencial   Una disposición del engranaje que deja las ruedas motrices ser conducidas en las velocidades diferentes.

Accionamiento directo   Una proporción del engranaje del 1:1.

Duplique golpe   Dos las aplicaciones repentinas y de embrague del motor enérgico o de la banda.

DTC   La abreviación para código diagnóstico de problema.

La petición de desplazamiento del conductor   Una señal electrónica que el conductor ha movido el control de desplazamiento para cambiar la engrana.

La transmisión dual del embrague del motor   Una transmisión que usa un embrague del motor para conducir los engranajes incluso numerados y un segundo embrague del motor para conducir los engranajes de números extraño. Puede dar poder en una manera continua sin atraso entre los cambios de marcha.

Dinámica fricción   La cantidad relativa de fricción entre dos superficies que están en velocidades diferentes. *Vea* fricción Estática.

Temprano   Cuando un desplazamiento ocurre antes de que la velocidad correcta sea alcanzada y cause uno halando a tirones o trabajando del motor.

El golpe de fin   Una condición que produce una percepción más firme al final de un desplazamiento. También *la percepción* llamada *de fin* o *el resbalón avanza a brincos.*

Juego longitudinal   La cantidad de movimiento un gearset o un eje tiene en una dirección que es paralelo para el eje de aporte.

Energía   La habilidad para hacer trabajo.

El motor frenando Una condición donde la compresión del motor se usa para desacelerar el vehículo.

Expele La edición de presión elocuente de regreso al pozo negro.

Final empuje El último set de engranajes desmultiplicadores antes del poder fluye para el diferencial y los árboles de empuje.

La firma Una aplicación rápida notable de un embrague del motor o una banda que es considerada normal.

Llamarada Una condición que produce un incremento en rpm del motor con una pérdida de par de torsión durante un desplazamiento. También el llamado *deslizamiento*.

Flexplate El plato delgado de empuje que conecta el convertidor de torsión para el cigüeñal del motor.

El acoplador fluido Un dispositivo que transfiere poder a través del fluido.

Volante La masa rotativa de metal atribuyó para el cigüeñal que ayuda incluso fuera de las subidas de tensión.

El tornero del volante Una herramienta especial que se usa para rotar el volante como el convertidor es de la que se descorrió el cerrojo.

La fuerza Un empujón o un tirón medido en unidades de pesos, usualmente late.

El motor de fuerza *Vea* Presión controlar solenoide.

Fricción La resistencia a la moción entre dos cuerpos en el contacto entre sí.

El modificador de fricción Un aditivo que cambia la lubricidad de un fluido.

Punto de apoyo El giratorio punto de apoyo para una palanca.

El desplazamiento del garaje Un grupo de trabajadores del turno de neutral para conducir o poner al revés.

La proporción del engranaje La relación entre dos engranajes determinados dividiendo el número de dientes en el engranaje controlante por el número de dientes en el engranaje conducido y expresado como una proporción para uno.

La reducción del engranaje Una condición en la cual el engranaje controlante es más pequeño que el engranaje conducido. Esto produce un incremento de par de torsión.

Gobernador Un dispositivo hidráulico que provee presión hidráulica que es relativo para la velocidad de la vía.

Rudo Una aplicación notable y desagradable de un embrague del motor o una banda. También el llamado *grosero*.

El obturador pesado Una aceleración con el obturador abierto más que tres cuartos del viaje de los pies.

El engranaje helicoidal Un engranaje que tiene los dientes hizo un corte en ángulo.

Hertz Una unidad de medida de frecuencia; abreviado como hertz. Un hertz es un ciclo por segundo.

El anillo del gancho Una sortija de sello con los fines que se engarzan juntos.

Cacería Una serie de repetitivo cambia a una marcha superior y cambia a una marcha inferior esa causa los cambios notables del rpm del motor. También lo llamado *ocupado*.

Hidráulica El traslado de poder a través de fluidos a presión.

Hidrodinámica La acción de transferir poder a través de fluidos en marcha.

Hidrostático La acción de transferir poder a través de fluidos bajo presión.

Hypoid engrane Un formulario especial de un engranaje cónico que tiene los dientes intervino en una curvatura y eso posiciona el engranaje en poco intersectar aviones; comúnmente aprovechado de adentro erige empuje de la rueda (RWD) recorridos finales.

El engranaje del holgazán Un engranaje posicionado entre dos otros engranajes en el engranaje que se usa para poner al revés la dirección de rotación.

Impeller El miembro de aporte del convertidor de torsión, también llamó a la *bomba del convertidor*.

Inercia La propiedad física que un cuerpo en restos de descanso en reposo y un cuerpo en marcha permanece en marcha y recorre en línea recta.

La percepción inicial Una percepción bien definida que es más firme en el principio de un desplazamiento que al final.

Engranaje de dientes interiores Un engranaje con los dientes señalando hacia dentro hacia el centro del engranaje, también llamado unos annulus o un anillo engranan.

Kickdown Uno cambia a una marcha inferior cuando el conductor empuja el pedal acelerador hasta abajo.

Aterrice La porción de diámetro grande de una válvula del carrete.

Tarde Un desplazamiento que ocurre arriba de la velocidad deseada que le causa overreving del motor.

LePelletier engrane tren Un tren automático del engranaje de transmisión que combina uno simple planetario con un Ravigneaux Gearset para producir seis o más proporciones del engranaje.

Ilumine obturador Una aceleración con el obturador abierto menos de la mitad de viaje de los pies.

El convertidor de torsión de la prisión *Vea* embrague del motor del Convertidor de Torsión.

La lámpara del indicador de funcionamiento defectuoso (MIL) Una lámpara indicadora de ámbar del panel de instrumentos que brilla intermitentemente para indicar un problema.

La válvula manual La válvula funcionó por el selector del engranaje que dirige presión para lo aplique que los dispositivos necesitaron para poner una transmisión en engranaje.

Mecánico diodo Un embrague del motor de una sola vía que usa un set de puntales cargados por resorte para un encendedor pero acción más fuerte del embrague del motor.

El obturador mediano Una aceleración con el obturador abierto cerca de la mitad de el viaje de los pies.

Micrón Una unidad de medida igual para una millonésima parte de un metro.

El obturador mínimo El obturador más pequeño abriéndose eso puede acelerar un vehículo y producto uno cambie a una marcha superior.

Modulador Un dispositivo de vacío que siente carga del motor y le causa una válvula hidráulica para cambiar presión referente a esa carga.

MSDS La abreviación para hojas materiales de datos de seguridad.

El embrague del motor del disco múltiple Un embrague del motor que usa más que un disco de fricción.

Cojinete de agujas Un rodín muy delgado.

La transmisión Nonsynchronous Una transmisión usando embragues del motor de una sola vía que le permiten uno cambia a una marcha superior eso requiere sólo la aplicación de la siguiente conducción o el miembro de reacción.

NVH La abreviación para el ruido, la vibración, y la dureza.

Fabricante de equipo original Fabricante de equipo original, la compañía que produjo el vehículo.

El enfriador de aceite Un componente como de radiador que reduce la fiebre elocuente.

Filtro de aceite La parte que remueve suciedad y basura de aceite que se circuló a través de eso.

El embrague del motor de una sola vía Un embrague del motor que invade que traba en una dirección e invade o vive despreocupadamente en el otro.

El anillo de fin del claro /llanura Una sortija de sello con los fines hizo un corte en un ángulo recto.

Orificio Una abertura restringida en un pasaje fluido diseñado para reducir presión elocuente mientras el fluido está fluyendo.

O-ring Un anillo sellador hecho de material del rubberlike.

Superdirecta Una disposición del engranaje que le causa el eje de salida para volver más rápido que el eje de aporte.

Estacionando engranaje Un cerrojo de transmisión que previene el eje de salida de dar vuelta.

Pasando engranaje Uno forzado cambia a una marcha inferior para el siguiente engranaje más bajo.

Trinquete Un dispositivo trabador que cabe dentro de un diente del engranaje para sujetar el engranaje estacionario.

El engranaje del piñón Un engranaje pequeño que engrana con un engranaje más grande.

Pistón La porción movible de un cilindro hidráulico o servo.

El trasportador planetario La parte de un gearset planetario que contiene el piñón planetario engrana.

Los piñones planetarios Los engranajes de un gearset planetario que engranan con ambos el sol y los engranajes del anillo.

El gearset planetario Un gearset que contiene un engranaje del engranaje planetario, del anillo, y un trasportador con piñón planetario se orientan hacia producto un o más proporciones del engranaje.

Poder La tasa en la cual el trabajo se hace.

La presión Una fuerza por área de la unidad; generalmente medido en libras por pulgada cuadrada (la libra por pulgada cuadrada) o unidades de presión atmosférica (los bares o kilopascals).

La presión balanceó edición Un diseño del embrague del motor que usa presión elocuente para ayudar a soltar el embrague.

Ejerza presión sobre solenoide de control Un solenoide controlado por computadora que mantiene la presión correcta en el sistema hidráulico de un cambio automático electrónicamente controlado. También llamado un *solenoide de fuerza de variable* o *un motor de fuerza.*

La válvula del regulador de presión La válvula que mantiene la presión correcta en el sistema hidráulico.

La modulación de anchura de pulso (PWM) La operación de un dispositivo por uno en señal digital/feriada que es controlada por la señal horaria a fin de que el dispositivo está encendido y feriado.

Bomba Un dispositivo que transfiere fluido de un punto para otro.

Proporción El valor relativo entre dos cosas.

El miembro de reacción La porción del gearset planetario que está sujeto estacionario para producir una reducción o la superdirecta.

La resma Una operación de mecanizado que hace un hueco más grande y más preciso.

Reconstruido *Vea* Reconfeccionado.

Remanufactured Una cláusula solió describir un componente que se desmantela, limpió, pasó revista, y reensambló utilizadoras partes nuevas o reacondicionadas.

Cambie de dirección y reemplace (R y R) Una operación de reparación del comon donde los viejos dividen es eliminada y reemplazada con una parte nueva o reacondicionada.

Estanque Un tanque o una cacerola donde el fluido se guarda.

Resistencia Los opositores para el flujo actual midieron en los ohmes.

Reteniendo corchete Un corchete que se usa para sujetar una parte (s) en lugar.

El embrague del motor del rodillo Un embrague del motor de una sola vía que destina una serie de rodillos posicionados en una leva especial para los elementos trabadores.

El flujo Rotario La moción elocuente dentro de un convertidor de torsión en la misma dirección como el impeller y la turbina.

RPM La velocidad expresada en las revoluciones por minuto.

El engranaje del anillo El engranaje exterior de un gearset planetario. También llamado un *engranaje de dientes interiores.*

RTV La abreviación para la vulcanización de temperatura ambiente.

La prueba de pandeo Un cheque a ver hasta dónde unos sags/droops de la válvula que es una indicación del desgaste de válvula o del aburrido.

La herramienta de tomografía Un dispositivo experimental electrónico que puede comunicarse con el módulo de control del vehículo y puede determinar datos operacionales.

La bufanda cortada Una sortija de sello con los fines hace un corte en ángulo.

El conductor del sello Una herramienta diseñada para equipar un sello así es que puede ser metido en el lugar sin daño.

Servo Un dispositivo hidráulico que convierte presión elocuente en moción mecánica o fuerza.

Desvíe percepción Una aplicación del embrague del motor o de la banda o la edición que está usualmente descrita, por ejemplo, como firma o suave.

El calce Un espaciador delgado de metal.

El estremecimiento Una sensación fácilmente advertida que sacude con fuerza que es una forma más inclemente de chuggle.

Deslizamiento Una pérdida en el par de torsión con un incremento notable en rpm del motor.

Suave Una agarre lento y casi imperceptible o banda tiene aplicación.

Solenoide Un accionador del electromagneto que usa un corazón móvil.

La tira Un surco (s) o una ranura (s) hace un corte en un eje o se aburre eso se usa para conectar una tira que hace juego.

El calce El elemento trabador en un embrague del motor del calce de una sola vía.

Engranaje cilíndrico Un engranaje con dientes directamente cortados.

Puesto Una condición donde el motor está manejando excepto el eje de aporte de transmisión es no rotar.

La velocidad del puesto El máximo rpm del motor que puede ser logrado con un cambio automático engranado, con los frenos aplicados y el acelerador sin obstrucción a la vista.

La fricción estática La cantidad relativa de fricción entre dos superficies estacionarias o dos superficies que están dando vuelta en la misma velocidad. *Vea* fricción Dinámica.

Estator Un componente en el convertidor de torsión que se usa para cambiar la dirección de moción elocuente.

Subassemblies Los componentes principales de transmisión.

Pozo negro El punto fluido de almacenamiento o el estanque; usualmente la cacerola de transmisión.

Engranaje planetario El engranaje en el centro de un gearset planetario.

Oleada Una percepción del motor apenas notable que es similar al chuggle.

Síncrona transmisión Durante uno cambie a una marcha superior, la oportunidad del momento de la nueva conducción o el miembro de reacción debe ser cronometrado o sincronizado con la edición de una conducción o miembro de reacción.

Empuje máquinas de lavar Los rumbos que separan rotar partes que se vuelven en contra de uno a otro.

La Relación Una condición donde dos embragues del motor opositores o bandas musicales están tratando de aplicar a destiempo. Esto tiende a desacelerar el motor o el vehículo. También la llamada *pelea*.

Par de torsión Dando vuelta o tergiversando esfuerzo; usualmente medido en las libras pie o Newton-Meter.

Convertidor de torsión Un fluido asociando eso transfiere poder del motor a la transmisión y puede producir un incremento de par de torsión.

El embrague del motor del convertidor de torsión El embrague del motor dentro del convertidor de torsión que cierra la turbina para el impeller para prevenir cualquier slippage. También llamado un *convertidor de torsión de la prisión*.

Transaxle Una transmisión que es combinada con la asamblea final de empuje; normalmente usado en vehículos de la tracción delantera.

Transmisión Un dispositivo en el tren de poder que provee el diferente el delantero el de engranaje el de proporción así como también el neutral y reverso.

Turbina El miembro de salida de un convertidor de torsión.

Vacío Una presión negativa (debajo atmosférico); medido de adentro avanza lentamente de mercurio (adentro. El mercurio).

Valle El área de una válvula del carrete entre las tierras.

Válvula Un dispositivo hidráulico que controla flujo elocuente.

El solenoide variable de fuerza *Vea* Presión controlar solenoide.

Viscosidad La resistencia a fluir en un fluido.

El flujo del vórtice Un flujo elocuente recirculante en el convertidor que está hacia afuera en el impeller y hacia dentro en la turbina.

Warpage Una falla que ocurre cuando superficies copulativas conviértase en menos reventón.

El obturador totalmente abierto (WOT) Abatane viaje del pedal para producir máximo poder del motor y el viaje completo del obturador o la válvula detent en la transmisión.

El trabajo El resultado de fuerza que cambia velocidad o la dirección de desplazamiento.

INDEX